THE EMERGING CONSTITUTION

THE EMERGING
CONSTITUTION

★

By REXFORD G. TUGWELL

HARPER'S MAGAZINE PRESS

Published in Association with Harper & Row, New York

"Harper's" is the registered trademark of Harper & Row, Publishers, Inc.

FIRST EDITION

Designed by Sidney Feinberg

Library of Congress Cataloging in Publication Data

Tugwell, Rexford Guy, 1891-
  The emerging Constitution.
  Includes bibliographical references.
  1. United States—Constitutional history.
I. Title.
JK39.T84   342'.73'029   73-6316
ISBN 0-06-128225-1

CONTENTS

PREFATORY NOTE

The chapters of this book were written as papers to be discussed at the Center for the Study of Democratic Institutions. This was a continuing project and was contributed to not only by the Senior Fellows of the Center but by many Visiting Fellows during several years. After discussion the papers were revised and gradually assumed their present form.

The papers were the background for a succession of constitutional models. These served to focus and to make more precise the constitutional changes believed to be necessary after nearly two hundred years. There were frequent modifications of the model, and the number of revisions grew to forty. Still more are in prospect to meet the criteria of the papers.

None of these models is presented here because none has satisfied all the conditions of a democratic constitution. Further study and discussion should result in improvements, and gradually, it is hoped, one will emerge that may be useful to those who are called on in the future to consider amendment not merely of specific provisions but of the whole.

Whatever changes may result from further discussions, it is believed that the theory and structure have by now reached sufficient stability to warrant publication. The problems have gradually disclosed themselves as exploration has proceeded, and their solution, if not satisfactory, is at least forecast by realistic statement of their elements.

There will certainly be more ingenious devices, new perceptions of relationship, new protections for liberty, and new allocations of duty. The fitting of a constitutional scheme to characteristic values and preferences has guided the work throughout, and although it has sometimes seemed almost impossible to create an integrated whole, that has been the attempt. Whatever else emerges ought to require additions or modifications rather than complete reworking.

This is said with due respect for time and its inevitable effects. One emerging conclusion has been that coming generations ought not to be precluded from making their own basic law. This offering is for now and for the immediate—not the far—future.

R.G.T.

INTRODUCTION

Concerning Constitutions

It could be denied that a nation needs a constitution, but if the decision is that it should have one, some questions are inevitable. What should that constitution be expected to do, or could it be done in some alternate way? The argument would not be conclusive, but it would be more convincing than the argument that none is needed because none has existed. There are nations with, and nations without, constitutions.

It is more interesting to observe what such a charter does—what all existing ones do. They establish a government, make a more or less complete statement of purposes (a preamble) and a brief but specific indication of its structure; they provide an indication of powers and their distribution among officials, together with a statement of rights given to and duties expected of citizens. So a constitution is not only a profession of intention by its people but also a guide for the governing and the governed. This last, in a country with pluralistic inclinations, may well be as important as any other characteristic.

Evidently few nations—and always the ones with advanced economic and sophisticated social systems—feel capable of maintaining a satisfactory, organized existence without a written charter. Most nations have such a document even when it is easily abrogated by coups of various kinds. There is, of course, the much admired British exception. But even the British— proud as they are of going on quite well without one (with perhaps an inference that it is only inferior peoples who do need them)—constantly and confidently use the word "constitution." In fact, their *principles* are referred to as often as and in the same sense that Americans refer to theirs.

The British instance is often said to be especially relevant because so many institutions in the United States are inherited from the British, and it is often suggested that it would be well to follow their example in this as well as other matters. The difficulty is that transatlantic affairs have evolved in a quite different way. The United Kingdom has remained a relatively small and homogeneous nation with universally understood traditions needing minimal enforcement. Influxes of people from different cultures have been limited, and it has to be recalled that even when there was an empire, British subjects were not admitted to the circle of home citizens. When immigrants came to America they did indeed become part of us.

Because, in the United States, growth has been of a more extensive and heterogeneous nature, the British example has less relevance than it might have had a century ago. The United States is so many times its original size, and it has taken in so many immigrants from other cultures, that it may well be the least homogeneous big area in all history.

Another element in American development makes an enormous difference. By a combination of circumstances, levels of affluence have risen beyond those of any other people, and this has given the nation an involuntary position of power in the world that most Americans resent and would ignore if they could. They nevertheless are always finding themselves involved in affairs beyond their shores. Also, this affluence has precipitated the necessity of adjustments completely foreign to human experience; the management of wealth and its civilized use present problems more difficult than could have been anticipated.

In Britain, recent evolution of institutions has taken place without convulsive argument; yet it has to be admitted that many desirable adjustments have come more quickly there than here. This instance, however, is another unique British characteristic. Others have found it necessary to have a formal agreement about governmental powers and about the rights and duties of groups and individuals. This in part is because people profoundly feel that governments need restraining, as well as because some citizens prefer not to recognize their duties or to respect the rights of others. Standards must be established and constantly enforced if the sort of relations are to be maintained that originally were agreed upon when close attention was being given to their definition, and when a consensus was being reached and embodied in a constitution.

The demand for constitutions arises from essentially protective impulses; and it is true that most of them are more attentive to restraints than to the necessary functions of a modern state or to the duties of a loyal citizenry.

It is noticeable that in countries where coups d'état have occurred the first serious problem confronting a dictator, after some relaxation of military rule, is the demand for a constitution. It almost always happens and almost always has to be satisfied in some way. It was the reason why King John was forced to accept Magna Charta in 1215, and sovereigns ever since have been limited in some way—even democratic sovereigns whose institutions escape the intended limitations of their charter.

Popular governments once attained, often by revolution but sometimes by evolution, are not supposed to be dictatorial; usually they have been established to escape some sort of oppression. Still, they can be so shaped or so managed that they are unfair to certain interests or groups, often a minority in numbers. The framers in 1787, belonging to such a minority, had the problem of keeping the majority of their day within bounds. They were more afraid of unruly masses than they had once been of royalty. Revolutionary (and post-Revolutionary) "mobs" were very disrespectful to their betters and not much interested in the protection of property. This fear is reflected in the original Constitution—something often pointed out. Indeed, the tenderness of the framers for property rights so annoyed those who were more interested in liberty that before the document could be ratified as written it had to be supplemented with specific mention of the inviolable liberties. So the Bill of Rights was added as the first ten amendments.

2

A serious difficulty with any agreement embodied in a document and widely accepted, as the Constitution of 1787 eventually came to be, is that its provisions eventually tend to become scriptural and that those who have an advantage under its provisions, and so have an interest in its perpetuation, are able to organize active protection for its provisions. Proposals for change have immense defenses to penetrate. Because this charter is thus massively founded it may easily if gradually become obsolete as economic and social changes occur.

The American instance of obsolescence is a serious one, strangely ignored in constitutional commentaries even by students of public law. As we shall see, a theory had to be invented to justify a frozen charter in a changing society.

The fact is, however, that after the Constitution became effective and the government it provided for was established, nearly every characteristic of the society the framers knew proceeded to disappear within two generations. Defenders of the Constitution are inclined to forget that the new America would soon have been unrecognizable to late eighteenth-century statesmen. Their work had been done before the industrial revolution, before westward migration began, and before transportation and communication had really begun to make the nation one. The framework of government and its directives were congealed in the glaciation of a stable rural civilization even while that civilization was dissolving into complex rearrangements with an urban cast.

Another difficulty, equally serious, was that the institutions of the democracy that evolved in the United States during the nineteenth century assumed the existence of an enlightened and self-disciplined citizenry, not just the dominant elite the framers had in mind. Enlightenment, however, such as was assumed to exist, could only be the product of universal education; self-discipline could exist only when there were generally accepted rules of conduct. As Americans have discovered, a system of education is not quickly established, even in a wealthy counrty; and a settling down to homogeneity is still longer in coming, even when most citizens have access to the appurtenances of civilization.

If we look ahead far enough it may be allowable to guess that the eventual end of American endeavors will be such a society, capable of dispensing with the governing rules; in it a constitution affecting both individuals and government would be superfluous. While active change is going on, however, with continued irritations from its differential effects, a governing agreement is evidently considered to be useful, even essential, as a guide and standard.

If it is accepted, for the moment, that a constitution is needed, it obviously ought to be relevant to contemporary circumstances; otherwise, it can hardly occupy the position intended for it. Take that of 1787; it has not been, in any essential, accommodated to modern conditions. It is hardly an exaggeration to say that—despite much expressed reverence—it is, taken literally, no longer the containing instrument for *existing* government and no longer a sufficient definition of citizens' rights and duties. Some considerable number of its clauses are so obsolete that they no longer are heeded and could be eliminated without their absence being noticed. Others have taken on entirely unexpected meanings by Court interpretation.

How this happened is not at all obscure. The nation in 1787 was new and was surrounded by powerful and unfriendly neighbors; it was strung along the Atlantic seaboard; and the frontier, a few miles inland, was intermittently besieged. What was first set up was a meager establishment in a frontier land, reflecting the situation of a people with many reasons for being fearful of attack, and many reasons too for suppressing the forces of disunity within the nation itself.

We do not often enough recall the desperate circumstances of 1787. The post-Revolutionary government had all but disappeared in the few years of its existence. The separate states were imposing barriers against one another as though they were indeed sovereign; they refused to support the central government with taxed funds; the aggressions of Britain, France, and Spain were an imminent danger, and there were no defense forces. The frontiers were almost everywhere open and undefended, and the cities of the seaboard were primitive and disorderly. It was obvious that the nation, achieved in the enthusiasm of revolution, had all but disintegrated. Unless union could be more firmly established and reinforced by central (federal) institutions, the United States would disappear. What the revolution had achieved was rapidly being lost. The empires, it seemed, might soon meet and divide the tempting territories.

Looking back over the social and economic changes of the intervening decades and viewing the uses made of the constitution, one can understand its obsolescence easily enough. It is easy also to explain why a modern elite would like to keep the undertaking in its present deep freeze. It is, however, another thing to ask agreement on the part of everyone else.

Asking whether a constitution is ever needed—that is to say, whether such a statement has abstract virtues—is a question of less interest than asking whether one is needed in the particular situation of the United States today. It was certainly needed in 1787; is it needed now? Avoiding for the moment complex questions about the nature of a useful constitution, we can ask whether, assuming unfreezing and consequent adaptation to modern conditions, one is needed at all.

To ask this is really to ask whether the United States, after nearly two hundred years, has reached a situation—as the result of educational effort and a maturing process—roughly like that of the British. To argue that it has is to argue that tradition and understanding are now so advanced in our country that both government and citizenry are ready to be bound by them. Is this so unreal that it can be dismissed?

We may go somewhat further with this argument. It is certainly not necessary to point out that the United States, in its contemporary phase, is not like so many other nations emerging from recent dictatorship. It is not under the pressure of actual or potential poverty; it does have an advanced technique of organization; and by now it has behind it a relatively long experience with its chosen institutions. These are elementary facts known to all; and when so simply stated, conclusive—so conclusive that today it may well be thought possible to dispense with a binding agreement such as was needed for a frontier society that no longer exists.

The argument against doing so would necessarily rest on the assumption that the present majority, affluent as it is, and sophisticated in the productive arts, still does not have such wisdom and restraint in public affairs that no guiding compact is needed; or that it does not have the kind of government needed to hold the Union together and to control its members. Recall that the first end sought *was* union, that the second was the establishment of an administration competent to govern, and that the third was the imposing of restraints on authority for the protection of the states and of individual citizens!

Could the present majority be trusted—without constitutional restraints —to keep the Union secure, to ensure the competence of government, and to guard the rights of states and the liberties of citizens?

3

As to the Union, it would seem to be secure enough, although it has to be said that this was not the result of the compact of 1787. The Constitution in this respect had a fatal flaw. It attempted simultaneously to achieve union and to make the states sovereign. These were totally incompatible ends, and the tensions set up by the attempt to reach both had finally to be resolved in a civil war.

The war did not abolish the states; it only settled in the negative their claim of the right to secede. Their defenders remained unwilling collaborators even in defeat; they soon came back into the federal establishment; and to a degree they succeeded, as legislators and officials, in continuing the compromise arrangements they had tried to turn into the hard line of the secessionists.

The war did furnish the conditions for an evolution toward more integrated union, however, and that evolution went on relentlessly against such resistance as occasionally flared up. Whatever area of authority the federal government preempted, the states had to surrender; but in many of them it was done reluctantly.

Looking back over the post-Civil War period, it can do no harm to recall, even for the instructed, some of the cultural and technical changes. For instance, even the victors (the northern states) did not actually want the absolute integration of perfect union. Evidently they had almost as much feeling for states' rights as did the southerners. Their new armies had been raised by governors of the states, and for the most part they had volunteered and had fought as the First Ohio, the Ninth Wisconsin, or the Sixth New York—not as the Fifth or Eighth Infantry of the United States. When the army was disbanded its soldiers returned to states very little impaired in function because of the conflict. Brevet generals became governors, and amateur soldiers formed the Grand Army of the Republic. This organization was the most potent political force in the nation for the next generation. Its posts were as local as its regiments had been. The states were still very much in being; their decline was slow.

If what had been won, and what was kept, was the principle that secession was inadmissible, the states did not seem to mean much less to their citizens, although the Union, sealed in blood, became something even more precious. The southern theories of state sovereignty and of interposition were never again successfully maintained. They were occasionally appealed to by their own orators, but they were mostly addressed to a local audience.

The effect of victory for union, then, was not to abolish states' rights immediately, but to furnish a departure point and a fairly steady support for certain institutional changes during the next hundred years. There was, nevertheless, a relentless erosion of the federal principle.

Technological influences had much to do with the redefinition of federalism. As trading areas grew wider, and as businesses drew for capital, customers, and markets on a multistate public, central regulation had to follow. Only a government as wide-reaching as the new economic organizations could maintain a relationship with them. That relationship might be of any sort, but it could not be anything at all unless it had an interstate reach.

In the gradual, and not always happy, process of accommodation that followed, the states steadily lost sovereignty but gained duties. This is another way of saying that what the states were expected to accomplish increased in complexity and seriousness, if not in scope. No state could control a railroad or the sugar or oil trusts; but it could devote itself to local government, to its police powers, to education, and to welfare. It took a long time for these last to escape from state control; it began to happen finally because the states could not carry the financial burden.

The welfare measures of the New Deal, coming relatively late and after long agitation, nearly all devolved on state administrative organizations—Social Security, as an example. And later, as assistance of this sort expanded, the states seemed to have a kind of renaissance. It was, however, not in the direction of independence or of wider responsibilities; the states became mostly centers, however indispensable, of administrations whose larger center was in Washington.

There were peculiar complications about this readjustment. During the later decades of the nineteenth century, it became convenient for business leaders to support states' rights; state officials were much easier to suborn. The Republican party, usually dominated by business interests, became a party more of states' rights than of Union, although it was as the protector of union that it had for years kept itself in power. Democrats, reform- and welfare-minded, gradually, in contrast, became Unionists because only the central government could carry out desired reforms or furnish the funds for welfare. This party reversal was bound to last only as long as business leaders failed to recognize, or could not find accommodation with, the larger power in Washington. They gradually did find it, and their discovery alienated them from the Republican party; they found the Democrats more useful, at least for the time being, because they were a majority. There was a suspicion, after 1964, that so little remained for Republicanism that it might disappear—as Whiggism had done in the 1850s.

The Democrats' claim to usefulness rested largely on a modified relation between states and nation; the nation was paramount; the states were provincial administrative units, suffused with sentiment but not left with much power. Only a fragment of the unreconstructed South continued to fly the secessionist flag and to argue that the Constitution could be interpreted to suit its governing class.

The Union, a hundred years after the Civil War, had become the Union that the war had been fought to establish; however, as late as 1960 the Republican presidential candidate was hinting that the Democratic party was a treasonous one, a theme that had won so many victories in the past. But Nixon was the last aspirant who would dare make such an appeal. It had a furious backlash. He himself in later campaigns avoided any such attribution.

4

Does the undoubted security of the Union, or the advanced organization of industry and finance, make it possible or desirable to dispense with a written constitution? There are still the *second* and *third* constitutional purposes to be examined. With reference to the *second*: Is the government firmly enough established? And the *third*: Can the majority, through the representation provided, now be trusted to decide matters with wisdom and restraint? That is, today, can that majority be trusted to exercise wisdom in structuring and in operations; would it be restrained in its relations with groups and individuals without being bound by a constitution, but only by the commonly understood principles, say, of a preamble? Or would the majority be likely, if not restrained, to let the government disintegrate and allow areas of essential liberties to be invaded?

It can easily be seen why the answer to such questions would frequently be that the majority *cannot* be trusted—or, to put it another way, that the democracy is not yet mature enough to trust itself without the directives and prohibitions of a constitution, even an attenuated one.

It is true that many of the restraints provided by the Constitution have already been redefined by the Supreme Court. This has been the result of a theory—the theory of the "living" constitution. It is said to "live" when new interpretations are made; it "awakens" when the Court recognizes new needs; novel meanings of old terms are put forward as "what the framers would have said" if they had been doing their work today.

Some embarrassing specific questions can be asked about the "living" theory, ones its defenders do not like to answer. Does the Constitution "awaken," for instance, when the president dispenses with treatymaking and invents the Executive Agreement, or when he carries on wars without asking the Congress to declare them? Or, instead of an awakening, is this a smothering? Does the Constitution "live" when the Congress, intending to subdue and dominate the executive, passes a Tenure of Office Act, when it delegates powers to regulatory bodies, or when it uses investigative procedures to create a kind of inquisition? Or are these merely signs of chronic hostility?

These, and many other undertakings of the executive and legislative branches, are entirely extraconstitutional. Some have persisted; others, after some use, have been abandoned. Strict construction would have forced an appeal to the amending process rather than attempts to impose new and sometimes bizarre interpretations of old clauses. Would this not have been a better way for the Constitution to awaken?

But, of course, the real meaning of "living" becomes apparent only in the Court's assumed right of "interpretation," and its fullest stretch is seen when the Court makes itself the arbiter of powers for the other branches as well as for itself.

The Supreme Court does undertake, and quite often, to substitute itself for the electorate whence the president and the Congress get their independent powers; it "extends" the meaning of due process, interstate commerce, the right of petition, and many other clauses. It invents a "rule of reason" to govern permissible departures; it applies an old common-law rule, unknown to the Constitution, that certain businesses may be regulated because they may be "affected with a public interest"; and it holds that a logical extrapolation of the one-man, one-vote rule applies to the election of even the upper houses of state legislatures.

The situation seems to be this: everyone agrees that changes must be made from time to time, and because they are hard to make in any other way, the Supreme Court is a convenient agency for doing it. Whether or not, in carrying out this function, the Court goes too far or not far enough seems to depend on interested judgments. If the critic is an atheist he wants a strict interpretation of the clause in the First Amendment enjoining the Congress from making any "law respecting the establishment of religion or prohibiting the free exercise thereof. . . ." If he is a member of one of the church hierarchies he wants this to mean that religious establishments may not be taxed or perhaps that parochial schools may be subsidized.

Similarly, if he wants big business suppressed or regulated, he sees no obstacle in the due-process clause of the Fourteenth Amendment; but if he is a lawyer for a corporate enterprise he may urge passionately that *any* regulation, and certainly any that is "unreasonable," is a taking of property, *due* process being a very narrow and difficult process indeed. No one bothers to recall that corporations were dragged into coverage by a tour de force of extension. They had to be called "persons."

Because these are changing concepts and their meaning must somehow be defined, even after the Congress and the president have had their say, it has been quite generally agreed—with some conspicuous dissents—that the Court shall have the last say. On the whole there has been remarkable submission to the Court's interpretations, even though some of them have verged on sheer invention, having only a fictional relation to any constitutional clause.

This devotion to pragmatism is usually clouded with immemorial principle of some sort; actually, it represents response to an irresistible need.

5

What would have happened in these respects during the last hundred years if there had been no constitution? For one thing, the Congress, not the Court, would have had to decide all these matters; it would have compiled gradually a body of law covering all disputed processes. That is what the British constitution is—a body of parliamentary acts. But the Congress has notoriously ignored principle and has responded only to insistent demands. No Congress can commit its successor Congresses, and there have been some remarkable reversals. In spite of the Constitution there have been astonishing forays into the executive and judicial realms by the legislative branch in almost every generation, and there has been remarkably impulsive and unwise legislation. Evidently a thorough reform of congressional habit would be necessary in a nonconstitutional regime.

Of course, there might well be a different sort of legislature, for the Congress originated in a constitution it now frequently ignores. Nevertheless it may be supposed that if popular sovereignty still prevailed there would be a representative body of some sort, and it probably would not behave too differently from the one now existing.

It may be a fair assumption that if there were no constitution and no Court to interpret it, the executive would soon become an adjunct of whatever legislature existed. The resulting situation in this respect would be somewhat the same, again, as exists in Britain. But the resulting body of law would be a mélange of partisan, perhaps contradictory acts, a conglomeration that would hardly serve a genuinely constitutional purpose. Such a Congress as the United States has had, and probably would have in any circumstances, would be led into occasional excesses, and the majority would almost certainly become oppressive. The president would become first an agent of the Congress, then its leader, and finally its dictator—just as the British prime minister is. Of course he would be answerable to party discipline; he would in fact be chosen in party meetings, not in presidential elections giving him the independent status he now has.

If this is at all a reasonable anticipation, it is not an attractive one.

6

As to competence: to speculate about this is to do just that—speculate! There are, however, some fairly obvious reasons for thinking that competence might be considerably less if there were no constitution.

It always has to be recalled that departures from the undertakings of 1787 have been important; they have affected all the branches. The Constitution in this sense has "lived," sometimes in a very spirited way. It might be argued that the government would at least be no worse, and might be better, if there were no constitution or if departures from it had been impossible. This argument would be more tenable if most of the strange growths had not taken place in the areas of silence, those places where nothing is said about what may or may not be done. The nonconstitutional extensions might have been regularized—if that seemed desirable—by amendments correcting the original avoidances or inadvertent omissions.

An illustration of this is the position occupied by the president as leader of the majority party. This is a very powerful and demanding addition to his anticipated duties. Every president since Washington has used it to strengthen his adversary relationship with the Congress and has become in consequence the official looked to by the electorate for the furthering of legislation. At the same time, politics has required that he keep his leadership by any means he could command. One of the most useful of these means was discovered to be patronage. Patronage, however, is a doubtful reliance. Before being awarded, it is a powerful weapon; afterward, it turns upon its awarder. A jobholder is loyal to his sponsor, not to his appointer. The president, presently, may find himself more managed than manager.

In a nonconstitutional government, still adhering to popular sovereignty, the majority must somehow prevail, and if it prevailed, as in Britain, through its representatives, it would then dominate the executive branch, both politically and administratively. The departments of the United States government now have a political cast through the appointment of their officials by the elected president; but the president after all is responsible for their performance. If the president lost such independence as he has now, even though it is diminished by his political duties, the responsibility for performance would be entirely transferred to the party—and this might well be disastrous. Congressional interferences under present circumstances are a serious hindrance, tending as they do to undermine the loyalty of bureaucrats to their directing head and transferring it to their congressional sponsors. It might be very much worse if this process should be uncontrolled except by legislators who find it quite easy indeed to retire into anonymity when things go wrong and the responsible authors of policy are sought.

This is certainly the wrong sort of check to presidential power; it may now be excessive, but it is known that it is his. In his executive posture he ought to control and be responsible for control. A constitution ought to direct that this should happen. That the present one does not direct effectively is a defect, not a virtue. The existing Constitution does, of course, say something about this. It says, in fact, that "he shall take care that the laws are faithfully executed," and this has always been, for presidents, something of a protection from aggressions. Congressional subversions are at least not legitimate, and he may resist them with some constitutional backing.

On the other hand, presidents have without doubt chosen to neglect their administrative duties in favor of others. This is not necessarily a criticism. They have had to. But it is a neglect that might become worse if there were no constitution. As chief of state of the most powerful of nations, with all the responsibilities of power to be carried, the president must always give first thought to the nation's security and its relations with other nations. If this relegates domestic administration to second place, that is inevitable.

A more specific distribution of powers in a constitution would recognize this problem, but if left to the majority, functioning through representatives, patronage might be greatly extended through the institutions a majority would favor; it is not likely that administration would improve. A constitutional distribution would be better than one done by any sort of Congress.

Still this is certainly all speculation. A different set of institutions would result from the accumulation of legislative acts; how different they would be it is hard to say. The present Constitution, for instance, although departed from in important respects, still does exercise some control. It ensures that there are three branches with separate but interdependent powers, the checks still operate in a modified way, and the allocation of powers is at least recognizably that intended by the framers.

The impression seems justified that the process of constitutionmaking is quite a different one from that of legislation. Constitutions are created in earnest conclaves whose members are impressed with the seriousness of their task. The nature of that task demands assignment to it of learned and experienced individuals; there ensues a dialogue among them, and to it there must be brought the full resources of scholarship and wisdom possessed by a generation. What is most important, there finally must be an instrument that the whole nation will recognize as an expression of its intentions, and as furnishing a means for their realization. Some sort of referendum would be inevitable, and referral would be to the people—not to the state legislatures.

Legislation, in contrast, is the action of a representative body largely controlled by political leaders answerable (presumably) to local constituencies, or sometimes to "special interests." It acts to solve problems, usually under pressure, and is deviled by the harassments of lobbyists. What issues therefrom is law, but of an entirely different genre from that embodied in a constitution.

7

What then about protection of the states in their traditional roles? What about the liberties of citizens? Would a majority unrestrained by a constitution maintain the states and at least protect the citizens from governmental tyranny?

Again, these questions must be separated. The rights once possessed by the states have been eroded not so much by the aggressions of a political majority as by sheer circumstances. These have been so harsh that the states themselves have on occasion pleaded for less of the sort of liberty that assumes they will always be on their own. Their responsibilities are heavy; they need federal funds. True, their political leaders—most of them—would like to have this assistance without having to observe constricting rules about its uses; but because the giver may always make conditions, and because the federal government is that giver, the states have gradually recognized the inevitable. They have become not givers of an apportioned sovereignty, as was intended by the framers, but sharers in a larger one they receive instead of giving. They indulge themselves in what verbal face-saving they can without too deeply offending Washington, but they are usually careful not to go too far. A certain number of rather comic rebels appear from time to time—mostly in the old South—who are noisy, but more bizarre than important; even they seldom reject the benefits flowing from Washington.

For purposes other than that of administration and local government, it has to be said that the states have not been able to protect their autonomy. What has been happening in the gradual adjustment is experimentation with functions best done by a smaller organization than the federal administrative machines. There have been numerous trials and failures, some successes. The process is not yet completed, and may never be. It has been complicated by several concurrent happenings—by the growth of cities, for instance. Their monstrous expansion has embarrassed the states. There are cities where the population is as large as, or larger than, the rest of their parent states, and subordination has become irksome and clumsy. This has happened too while the states were themselves becoming mostly subordinate agencies in a federal pattern, and mostly carrying out national policies. There is a good deal of holdover state sentiment as against both federal and city aggrandizement, but it should not be taken for other than what it is. Guardianship of the states by the constitution has failed; there is no doubt of that.

Have the liberties of citizens, then, been more successfully sustained? The answer to this is quite different. The Bill of Rights has had a renaissance. This, indeed, is what lawyers mostly refer to when they speak of "awakening." But there has also been a stirring among the constitutional clauses affecting the distribution of powers. The principle that no absolute authority should be lodged anywhere is still honored, but there is the anomalous exception of the Supreme Court. The powers of the president and of the Congress are limited; so, in consequence, are those of their subordinates; and the limitations, when not self-imposed by traditional canons of restraint, are made very explicit by the third branch. This may be thought to exceed the powers of the judiciary, assuming it to be co-ordinate with the other branches. However, in recent years the judicial branch has not always been constrained to respect these limits, and there has been no check such as might have come from president or Congress standing on their constitutional directives.

One reason for the emboldenment of the justices is that their protection of individual liberties has met with such general approval in their own profession. There is far less interest in the original meaning of the Constitution than in the results to be had by assuming that modern meanings are allowable. The Court has legislated with what can only be described as abandon in recent decades, and generally has been defended by the contention that *some* agency had to do what it has done. If the legislature refused to do its duty, that duty, carried out by the Court, was at least accomplished.

Whatever may be thought of these judicial excursions, they were under-taken because Congress was laggard in undertaking them. The civil rights directives of Amendments Fourteen and Fifteen, defining the victory of the Civil War, went without legislative implementation for a hundred years. Both had concluding clauses saying that the Congress "shall have power to enforce, by appropriate legislation, the provisions . . ." of the amendments. The Congress, with the southerners back in their seats, chose to ignore what was intended (actually the language was not mandatory, but only permissive). Little was done to protect minority rights until economic and political oppressions became intolerable. Yet the Congress, dominated by committee chairmen from the safe districts, could not be brought to act. When cases could be brought, the Court enforced—it really did enforce with federal marshals—its preferred interpretation of those amendments.

If this is evidence, it would seem to show that representative majorities will not—even in the United States, and with directives from the Con-stitution clearly stated—protect the liberties of the citizen. But here it should be recalled that if it were not for those constitutional directives, the Court could not have acted either. What revolutionary pressures might have built up, except for the Bill of Rights and the Fourteenth and Fifteenth Amendments, is easily possible to imagine. Pressures have been serious enough as things are, but they might be infinitely worse if the legislative majority had been relied upon to act. This would *seem* to be a point favoring the existence of a constitution, even if it is roughly handled by those who use it.

8

This brings the discussion to an old dilemma. It was well illustrated by the ordeal of the Dred Scott case and the intransigence of Chief Justice Taney.[1] The important issue in this case, for our purpose here, is whether enlargement or extension is permissible, or whether the Court ought to accept the Constitution as written and obviously meant—whether it *lives* or simply *is*. Obviously, there can be variations in understanding by the most earnest searchers; but interpretations by the Court have gone far beyond the search for meanings; and the tendency is to go further. Original intentions have been ignored entirely in favor of ones more consonant with contemporary views or, at least, the views of the Court's majority. This is the awakening so generally praised.

Is there any obligation on the part of the Court to discover what the framers had in mind? Or if they think they understand the framers' intent, to apply it as constitutional doctrine? Or was Taney right to insist, in effect, that if the framers were not to be followed, there must be new framers? That is to say, the way to change the Constitution was not to allow his Court to do it, but to follow the procedure provided when the original was ratified? There was a way to amend; it had not been taken or even suggested. Taney, it would seem, did not make a whimsical interpretation; indeed it was a quite reasonable one. Yet ever since, Taney has borne the guilt of having precipitated civil war: because he insisted that the Constitution meant what it said and the Court might not depart from it.

Other justices have allowed themselves a certain inconsistency in this. When convenient, they have suddenly become literal, as the late Justice Black did in several instances. On other occasions, they—or some of them —feel no such compulsion. Justice Douglas, reading freedom of movement into the First Amendment, was being anything but literal.

No doubt Taney's personal preference concerning slavery ran with his Dred Scott opinion. Still, it leaves the issue of literalness just where it was. Saying that there might not have been a civil war if he had been more "flexible"—and this in the Dred Scott case meant ignoring the framers' intention—is an argument used ever since for judicial supremacy. But it has to be recognized that if the justices may rewrite the Constitution whenever it appears that inconvenience, or even disaster, may follow a faithful interpretation, then dependence on the processes provided is

1. *Dred Scott* v. *Sandford,* 19 How. 393 (1857).

abandoned. It raises, indeed, the question whether another amendment procedure is not called for. But it is a doubtful justification for departure from the solemn undertaking represented by the Constitution—even under the covering rubric of "awakening."

Another argument for the "living" theory is that the Congress will not do what needs to be done. There are still many reasons for both these situations, and, of course, they are real. But on the other hand, it can hardly be contended that either of the two theories is irreparable, since amendment is possible, and even the amending clause can be amended. Then, too, the Congress can be made to respect the popular will as the framers supposed that it would. If it falls into a state that precludes this, it can be reorganized—if necessary, again, by amendment. Neither of these difficulties can be approached by amendment, it appears, as easily as getting five justices to say that the Constitution means what it does not say it means; but still it may be that the process is in the long run safer for a democracy—if it really intends to remain a democracy.

This does not resolve a paradox we dislike to acknowledge, that we want a constitution for the justices to maneuver with, while at the same time we do not want one they cannot rewrite whenever it seems necessary. That the latter position is an option for *no* constitution must seem clear enough to anyone not pleased with the variable moods of the Supreme Court; others will no doubt continue to evade the fairly obvious fact that the Constitution in important respects has been superseded. Lawyers seem to want a constitution for the rest of us to respect, but in addition they want one they can extend or *awaken* whenever the Court can be persuaded that the country will be better off because of some decision of its majority.

9

Another thought with some bearing on the question whether a constitution is actually needed in modern circumstances is that if one did not exist the Supreme Court would not exist either—at least not in its present refulgence. It should be clearly kept in mind what is so often slurred over: that what the Court is depended on to do now in awakening, interpreting, or enlarging its clauses would, in the absence of a constitution, be done, if it was done at all, by the Congress—or *a* Congress. That is to say, an elected majority of representatives, not an appointed majority of justices, would establish rights and duties as well as the forms and expected actions of government, and there would be no appeal.

There is a recent literature, produced by practitioners and professors of public law, that gives the Supreme Court credit for "expanding liberties" in the United States. A typical one of these, by Milton Konvitz, traces the recent civil rights explosion to the Jehovah's Witnesses cases (among them *Cantwell* v. *Connecticut*, 310 U.S. 296 [1940]): "These . . . cases, by giving the Supreme Court repeated opportunities to vindicate the rights of a small, weak and unpopular minority . . . placed the Court at the center of the American system of government as the protector of fundamental freedoms."[2]

Perhaps the opening paragraph of an article in the *New Republic* may be cited:

To read the recent Supreme Court opinions of William Brennan is to see affirmed and advanced the basic freedoms of American society. To lawyers at least, they are soul-stirring, like old-fashioned Fourth of July parades or an Inaugural Address; *Dombrowski, Jacobellis, NAACP* v. *Button, New York Times* v. *Sullivan,* and others have significantly widened the area in which citizens can express their political beliefs. "Brennan is proud of the First Amendment," a friend of the Court mused the other day; "he thinks he invented it."[3]

And it is quite true that the Court has occupied that center. The most "living"—and most controversial—opinions for some time had to do with the rights of blacks, but academic freedom and that of association and assembly were also extended, and censorship was redefined by the Warren Court. The right to travel, conscientious objection to military service, and a stricter definition of permissible police methods in handling suspected criminals soon followed.

What is interesting here is that all of this is the expansion of clauses that can be interpreted as the Court has interpreted them only because the "living" theory has been followed and has been supposed to mean that growth should be in the direction preferred by the justices.

Evidently this theory is now established. Konvitz, like others, contemplated it with lyrical approval; it is apparent, he said, that the Court's decisions "cannot take a dogmatic, canonical, final form. Its work is never done, and never can be; for every day it must face historical tasks." Since 1966 many opinions have changed, of course, and perhaps it is not relevant to subject this theory to democratic measurement. This is not a consideration that seems to affect liberal approval of the Warren Court. On the other hand, there are questions that in fairness may be asked.

It was always evident that not much further along the road being followed by the Warren Court there was a point beyond which a democracy could not pass and still remain a democracy. If these advances toward the expansion of freedoms had not been extrapolated from the Bill of Rights, and the Congress perforce had to accept responsibility for them, they might

2. Milton R. Konvitz, *Expanding Liberties: Freedom's Gains in Postwar America* (New York: The Viking Press, 1966). Cf. the discussions in C. Herman Pritchett, *The American Constitution* (New York: McGraw-Hill, 1959).

3. Arthur Kopkind, *"Brennan v. Tigar,"* New Republic, 155, 8 (Aug. 27, 1966).

have emerged, if ever they were to emerge, from popular demand. As it is, the elected branches have followed along, reluctantly in some instances, but still with substantial majorities. The Roosevelt appointees remained one jump ahead; but only a short one. Is that where the decision belongs?

The liberal who views the Court's leadership with such approval should be asked to acknowledge that he is opting for determination of these matters without waiting for the elected branches to act. There is even reason to believe that the liberal does not care whether the elected branches act at all. Particular rights may seem important enough for them to abandon the principle of representative government. But here the paradox cannot be concealed; the liberal is also opting—although he sometimes seems not to know it—*for* a constitution. This is because something that does not exist cannot be enlarged upon, or interpreted, or made to awaken. But confusion becomes worse and worse. The enlargement, the "livingness," soon becomes absurd. When meanings are added which previously were not considered, then the justices not only are making their own constitution but also are pretending that this imaginary constitution was originated by the framers, when obviously it was not.

Those who approve this sort of thing would appear to be saying simultaneously that they want a constitution for the justices to interpret, and that they do not want one whose meanings cannot be made to be what the justices prefer. This is very close to saying that the Constitution is both wanted and not wanted.

It is certainly true that in any good constitution a judicial role in decisionmaking for the nations should be recognized; this takes the argument into a more positive field. It assumes that there has been amendment; that the judiciary has been told what its place is to be, what kind of decisions it may make, and within what limits. It has also, it is assumed, been told what its relations are with the other branches; if there is interdependence, then the Court will be as interdependent as the others and therefore should not assume to interpret its own powers.

This last would be difficult to arrange; perhaps it would prove to be the most difficult phase in the drafting of any new constitutional model. There can never be quiescence, never be complete anticipation of future issues, and so there cannot be a closed possibility of interpretation or even of variation in response to changed conditions. The difference from the present situation would be—among other things—that the Court would be *charged* with this duty, and charged also to carry it out in certain ways. Its interpretations would be legitimized.

In all this there is somewhere the answer to our question about the protection of constitutional rights. They have been protected; they have even been enlarged. Only a theorist, perhaps, would object to the way it was accomplished. But theorists have to look beyond immediate results to additional—and perhaps more important—ones. If rights can be enlarged, it should be recalled, they can also be diminished. This would seem to be an argument for a more carefully drafted constitution—but still for a constitution.

10

Finally, a reminder may be in order that consideration of the need for *a* constitution is not to be confused with a defense of the Constitution of 1787 (as amended), however admirable its results have been, or for any other new version that may be suggested.

The argument must center, as has been suggested, on the desirability of an instrument for definition, limitation, and guidance. It must have been adopted in circumstances very different from those surrounding a legislative act; that is to say, not to meet an exigency of the moment. Its statement of duties and rights would need to be time-tested ones running deep into general acceptance so that would-be violators would be convicted of sin and recognize the justness of punishment, and upholders would have a sense of devotion to principle. The government it provided should be planned to meet the needs of a sophisticated society.

This is not a description of the existing Constitution. Because it has, in essentials, not been amended and has fallen, in certain respects, into irrelevance; because it has been warped by the aggressions of the branches; and because it has been extended in such ways that its original organic nature has been broken up, the Constitution cannot be taken as the prototype meant by those who would argue that some such instrument as was originally intended is necessary.

11

A good many years after it had happened, but while it could still be seen to be happening, de Tocqueville said in his simple but acute way: "The American Revolution broke, and the doctrine of sovereignty of the people came out of the townships and took possession of the states."

Did the earlier constitutions, and did the federal one, emerge from the process the traveling Frenchman thought he observed? At any rate, the sovereignty of the people becomes less clearly identifiable as the resulting institutions spread over wider jurisdictions. The town meetings were democratic in the original sense, but neither colonial legislatures nor those of the states were exactly the same thing. The people, except symbolically, were not there; they had sent others as representatives. This was inevitable, but it was not the pure democracy of colloquy.

In regard to sovereignty, a profound change began when representation had to be accepted. In the end it would result in a general government whose powers had overwhelmed those of the people who had allowed it to be devised. The Constitution of 1787 was one of the early results of this reversal; and the Bill of Rights was a convulsive reassertion of original authority. By that time the reassertion for the most part could be satisfied only by making it plain what the new sovereign could not do to the old one. The Bill was entirely negative; it may be significant that it was added on but not built in.

The framers, at least the Madisons among them, would argue that the additions were not necessary and that the rights were already there; but a dissatisfied skepticism simmered among the people and kept on simmering. It still does.

This discontent, in psychological terms, is the expression, in the governmental area, of an unwillingness to be disciplined, characteristic of Americans. Through the generations they have had the greatest difficulty in bringing themselves to a civilized acceptance of rules whenever the rules have been inconvenient, or whenever their impulses were strong enough to break through all limitations.

Restraints on individuals are peculiar in that they do not come from the people but are created by officials; they have been told by the Constitution to operate a set of institutions in most difficult circumstances. No one wants these institutions to infringe on his liberty, and infringement becomes almost intolerable when one is asked to pay for the operation through taxes.

Only rights, not restraints, are usually nominated in the constitutions, state and federal; it is simply said that there shall be laws accomplishing certain purposes; then follows a terrific struggle to shape the laws so that the purposes do not affect any interest strong enough to escape. The result is very plainly a corruption of the intention. It is often argued that the monstrous lobbying that goes on in Washington is justified as a representation of affected interests, that it is democratic. Legislation becomes a contest of interests, and the strongest wins. But this is not the people or the people's interests.

12

The best reason for having a constitution is that it may create and maintain institutions that confirm the sovereignty and express the intentions of the people. The Constitution of 1787 might have done that, or might have come closer to doing it, if such damaging compromises had not been made—the ones Franklin spoke of in his last address.

There is nothing wrong with government by an elite if it represents the people's sovereignty and shares their purposes. What a good government should do is to act as the instrument of people in their most conscientious and neighborly mood. Sinners know when they sin; lawbreakers know about the laws they break; and neither, speaking generally, want rules that allow just anyone to sin or to break laws. They want ones their cleverness allows them to evade.

It will be said that this is a sublimation of popular sovereignty. But is it not true that this is the general attitude? Every sensible person knows that his discontent with rules is a reaction against processes he cannot reverse; that rules are necessary to the civilization he is proud to share; and that in good conscience he can really ask for no exemptions.

People are people; they are proud, unruly, individual, selfish—all that sort of thing. But they are also gregarious, neighborly, peaceable, and proud of being democrats.

They know perfectly well that the one set of impulses cannot be the basis for permanent social arrangements, and that the other set must be. They also know that when tolerance, reason, and learning have created a government that represents, with some faithfulness, their civilized relationships and rules, it should be recognized and retained. No one and no minority, not even a majority in high emotion, should be allowed the instruments of subversion. The process of amendment ought to be one carried out in solemn dedication to the national interest.

It is not to be taken lightly that Americans regard their Constitution as a symbol of their better selves. It may very well be that it does not come anywhere near their ideal. It is, however, what they have. It causes them, they believe, to behave better than they would if they did not have it. It represents protection from the unruliness in themselves and in others. It is a compromise, of course, between rules and liberties; but the inherent liberties in the Constitution are as important as the rules.

13

Obviously, as has been implied, the argument for *a* constitution is not an argument for *any* constitution. Like any human contrivance, such undertakings among a people can be more or less admirable. The best constitution, it may be said again, would be one that confirmed people in their good intentions and discouraged them in their unruly ones; that established an effective government rather than an ineffective one; that opened the way to more rather than less popular participation; and that provided for adjustment or accommodation to changing circumstances.

The framers of the Constitution of 1787 did not reach the highest standard in all these respects. The compromises were damaging; perhaps in such an effort they always would be. For even the most serious and dedicated company gathered to create such an instrument would have among its number those who have more limited concepts, and would prefer commitment to ideas and purposes of another sort. At Philadelphia, there were those who were opposed to union and meant to protect states' rights, those who insisted on the perpetuation of slavery, those who looked forward to a restricted rather than a wide participation in government, cherishing, as they did, a deep distrust of all equalitarian ideas.

It will be recalled that Hamilton, after making his plea for limited monarchy, withdrew for a long period, and that afterward Washington wrote to him in New York, saying that although he was sticking it out in Philadelphia, he too was fearful of complete failure because so many men "of local views" would not concede the powers a genuine nation must possess. Neither Hamilton nor Washington now would be judged to have been right about all the disputed issues, but they were right about the essential ones. And those in the company who were most wrong were those men of local views so disparaged by Washington.

It is interesting to speculate about the scene and the process if by some circumstance the United States citizens today were to undertake a reenactment of the Philadelphia effort.

The place without doubt would be the Capital; the commissioners would be legalists, political leaders, and "distinguished citizens." They would meet in more comfortable circumstances than those of the eighteenth-century Philadelphia summer. Since the nation is much larger, there might be more of them; and since it has a social admixture it did not have in those early days, the sources of its ideas would be wider.

There would be many other contrasts, yet the similarities would be more notable than the differences.

There would be hearings, investigations, studies, and finally discussions leading to recommendations. These would result in masses of complaints, criticisms, defenses, and expressions of attitude; the extremes of these would be, on the conservative side, that the old Constitution is sacred and untouchable; on the radical side, that there should be an entirely new constitution providing for a one-party state with virtual dictatorship of a new elite.

The reasonable center might acknowledge the necessity for improved representation and for better execution, and might even accept the warnings of heightened danger from emergency brought on by rapid technological changes and a continuing power struggle on the borders of the great imperiums; it might accept the conclusion that the presidency has lost the capability to "execute the laws," and that the president's responsibility as chief of state is as much as one individual could carry without having to assume numerous other duties. And so on.

Many other disputable issues can be guessed at; there would be need for tiresome dialogue before nonessentials were put aside and the genuinely national needs centered on. Not until then would the great issues be debated, but if the new framers were genuinely in the American tradition, such a time would come.

It would be hazardous to suggest what the controlling considerations would be. But it may be that an interesting discovery reported by recent inquirers shows what might very well come to dominate the thoughts of the company.

Ours is a nation that has its internal troubles. These come partly from our bewildering technology, rapid growth, and differential access to the products of our economic success. Also, they come partly from rapid growth and an extraordinary mixture of races and cultures. Those who came here first were inclined not to welcome those who arrived later; and those who came still later were resentful of those who followed them; but a most insistent prejudice among the majority of early white Christians persisted against two special groups—the Jews and the blacks. It can be guessed that the process of assimilation for these groups is only slower and more difficult than it has been for, say, the Eastern Europeans or the Spanish-speaking Americans; but, for the time being, it has generated in both Jews and blacks a feeling of not being wanted, of insecurity, of alienation.

In recent years there has been an opportunity for both to migrate—the Jews to Israel and the blacks to the emerging nations of black Africa. Very few actually have migrated, but some attempt has been made to find out what the experience has been like for them. The clear conclusion is that it has not been what they had anticipated. If they felt isolated in America, they have felt more so in their new environments. An extraordinary number discovered that they were, after all, Americans. Something in the culture, the tradition, the agreements, the living together, the institutions, could not be escaped.[4]

Blacks, who have lived in this land longer than most of those with whiter skins, have a right to feel themselves Americans; but it is a right many of them do not accept as truly theirs until they try to live elsewhere. Only then do they recall that they helped to make America what it is; they feel a commitment to its future, and not to the future of another nation. It often seems to be the same with migrants among the Jews who have gone to Israel. In the United States they often kept themselves somewhat apart; they were inclined to feel themselves Jews before they were Americans; in Israel they discovered that, after all, they had become Americans—helped to make America, shared its hopes, and were at home with its institutions.

If this conclusion is at all true, it furnishes a sort of background to our history. The Constitution may have defects; it may have become obsolete and tortured out of original meanings; but it permitted the distinctiveness of the American identity to extend even to those who have had most diffi-

4. The investigation cited here was made by Harold L. Isaacs and appeared in two issues of *The New Yorker*, August 27 and September 2, 1966.

culty in absorption. Thus, it has had enormous value, something not easy to assess, but the kind of quality that any reassessment of constitutionality ought to look for and try to re-create.

A company of the modern elite, purged of self-interestedness and holding to this sense of identity as the framers held to union, might go on from that point to implement the already discovered ideas with the means for their preservation.

The experience undergone by Jews and blacks, whose effort to find a closer national identity elsewhere ended only with the discovery that they already had one they could not escape, ought not to be used as proof that the Constitution of 1787 was perfect; all the cited effects did not flow from the Constitution. Some of them did, however, and this was because the framers penetrated sometimes, and in some of the emerging clauses, to an essential, a universal human need.

Constitutionmakers have not always succeeded in this way, but some have.

14

It very well may be that the United States has already opted for *no* constitution. That is to say, it may have been agreed that no serious change will be undertaken—a decision amounting to abandonment as the process of "interpretation" goes on, and as extraconstitutional institutions proliferate.

If this is so, it will be seen whether a people who believe themselves to be democratic will go on believing themselves democrats as their institutions drift further into another pattern; or whether, perhaps, they will accept the institutions they have evolved as the reasonable outcome of their historical progress, not worrying about their being democratic or undemocratic.

Even those who refuse to worry about this, however, must worry about the competence of the newly devised institutions to meet the needs of the present. It is generally recognized that emergency has become an ever-present potentiality; that vast and increasingly vaster powers are being concentrated in a president who is not physically or mentally different from the first president nearly two centuries ago; that both legislative and judiciary are very much changed; that striking alterations have been made in the Constitution, not by consciously undertaken revision but by other processes; and that certainly the economic and social systems have been transformed since the existing Constitution was devised. No one denies these facts. Why is it then that no one proposes revision?

It seems almost frivolous to suggest that the answer to this question is what it appears to be: everyone thinks revision impossible. If it is no sufficient solution to any of the problems created by obsolescence to say that amendment is difficult, that still is the answer usually given to anyone who seems excited about the situation.

It is possible to suggest that there is satisfaction with Court opinions among lawyers, that politicians are professionally so involved with their own activities that they regard their competitions as all-important, and that citizens are not likely to go beyond carping when the behavior of their officials is displeasing.

All this, however, is no guarantee that obsolescence unattended to will not result in disaster. And it is no explanation at all of the unwillingness of political scientists to meet a responsibility peculiarly theirs.

Discussions of new patterns such as those being discussed at the Center for the Study of Democratic Institutions were commenced with a full realization of these difficulties and resistances. Those engaging in the discussions had no illusions about the likelihood of a new convention or of complete revision. They did have some legitimate hope, however, that lawyers, politicians, and citizens might be convinced that the situation is serious enough for action looking toward amendment.

An additional usefulness of such models is that they move the discussion from vague arguments about desirable changes to specific ones; that is, what those changes would look like when translated into propositions.

A further claim would be that modelmaking is an experimental or tentative way of finding out whether it is actually possible to find a charter that (1) protects the great fundamentals and (2) provides for adjustment to constant change. If such an instrument is inherently unattainable, this may be one way of finding that out.

PART ONE

THE REASONING
(Or Part of It)

CHAPTER 1

GENERAL CRITERIA
FOR CONSTITUTIONMAKING

A Weighted Compromise

There is a persistent impression that the American Constitution was the product of a conclave whose delegates were detached from ordinary interests, learned in politico-legal theories, and intent on providing a charter for the nation's guidance into and through a far future.[1]

This elevated conclusion is no more than partly sustained by a dispassionate examination of Madison's record of the proceedings. The statesmen were not all Washingtons, Morrises, Franklins, or Wilsons.[2] A consider-

---

1. Professor Henry Steele Commager made such a characteristic statement in reviewing *Miracle at Philadelphia* by Catherine Drinker Bowen (in *Book Week*, Nov. 27, 1966). It was, he said, one of the puzzles of history that "a people of some three million . . . scattered over an immense territory on a distant frontier and wholly lacking in those institutions which had traditionally produced statesmen and jurisprudents, produced in a single generation Franklin and Washington, Jefferson and Hamilton, Wilson and Dickinson, John Adams and Sam Adams, Tom Paine and Judge Wythe and John Marshall. . . . That is better than we have been able to do since." It was better too, he said, than any other nation had done. Europeans were supercilious about American colonists; but they had no such galaxy of statesmen.

2. Even Wilson, who was the most learned, was deeply involved in speculation, and presently would be forced to evade his creditors and complain that he was being hunted "like a wild beast." On the Pennsylvania court and in the Congress he had already been accused of "special pleading." Robert Morris, who was Washington's host during the Convention, was already bankrupt and would end his days in debtors' prison. There were others whose human weaknesses were already known. It is ridiculous to picture them as impeccably detached and the possessors of superior moral qualities. They were a company of upper-class statesmen, many of whom were concerned with saving the nation from threatened collapse. But they were convivial and pleasure-loving, conscious of their positions; and they enjoyed being in the country's largest city for the summer even though it was an exceptionally hot one and there was a torment of insects and a pervasive smell of excrement in the narrow streets of the riverside neighborhoods where they lodged.

able number were more taken up by trading and maneuvering than by study of political theory, meditation on fundamentals, or statesmanlike work in committees. Some, it is necessary to say, had no thought whatever of discovering and reducing to constitutional clauses the wisdom of the ages, or of devising practical institutions of government; even if some sort of union had to be accepted, they meant to prevent changes adverse to their own agreeable situations, and nothing much more.[3] To an extent, they succeeded. Their effect on the Constitution was seriously adverse.

Another thesis, that the design of government was intended to protect the privileged class—or, at least, that this intention prevailed in the summer's controversies—has a certain validity. It is, however, a simplification that hides the complex motives of that company, and especially the bargaining that went on for the protection of local and regional advantages. These were so persistent that Washington at one time wrote to Hamilton in New York that men of local views seemed likely to bring the convention to an end without result. It was because he had been so discouraged, perhaps, that he later spoke of the result as a "miracle."

There was, however, a driving motive that went some way to neutralize all the maneuvering and holding back. It was the always present knowledge that disunion was actually at a final and dangerous stage. This uneasiness, complicated with suspicions and distrusts, haunted the delegates throughout their deliberations.[4]

Similar mixed motives and emotions have characterized constitutional development ever since. The conflicts have sometimes seemed to reach, or be about to reach, some sort of resolution; but much more often an uneasy compromise has resulted; and when this has happened the pulling and hauling for final settlement, or even for advantage, has tended to go on and on. Continuous tensions have become so usual as hardly to be considered abnormal; very often they have been excused as necessary and even desirable; and an acute listener can hear habitual compromise spoken of as a virtue. It works its way into procedures and even influences the shape of institutions.

By a curious sort of protective urge, compromise is elaborately defended as an admirable characteristic. What apparently happens is that minds

3. Their terms of reference from the Continental Congress, meeting at the same time in New York, called for a revision of the Articles of Confederation, not the writing of a new constitution; this last was a word not heard until almost at the end of their meeting. But they had other commissions from their state legislatures, where worry about the future was apparently more acute than it was in New York. It was in these charges that union was so prominently mentioned, although there was no clear conception of what it meant for the states.

4. Hamilton (in *The Federalist,* No. 15) was moved to remind his fellow citizens of this: "We may indeed, with propriety be said to have reached almost the last stage of national humiliation. There is scarcely anything that can wound the pride or degrade the character of an independent nation that we do not experience."

weighing fears against advantages cannot reach a determination; either that, or, when some minds are made up, others are still uncertain or, worse still, have come to an opposite conclusion. Neither can convince the other, and they inevitably create and perpetuate institutions with uncertain direction and badly defined intentions. Since we have become affluent and powerful it is reasoned that even our defects must have had a part in our progress.

Contemporary comments display opposing theories concerning a guiding rule for economic life, to take a large issue; or about freedom to limit the numbers of children, to take a smaller one. Everyone knows that there are opposite views of the right to bear arms by citizens, and the disposal of property as its owner may desire. There are dozens of others; they sometimes disappear, but often there are lingering dissents.

Is education worth the taxes needed to pay for the apparatus demanded by educators? Is the resort to violence so common, so serious, and are criminals so mobile, that a national police force is needed? Does private enterprise require rules for the protection of workers and consumers? Have the losses from work stoppage made imposed settlements necessary? Is the disposal of waste by industries a matter for civil decision even if it is costly enough to jeopardize profits? These are a few of many disputed issues.

Such questions tend also to become more refined and complicated. How much or how little? How far? How serious? How threatening? When is the conduct of an individual or an association so unseemly as to require restraint? How much restraint? May workers strike in disputes not only with private but also with public employers? Health, security, education, enterprise, liberty: these practical everyday concerns demand attention, but there is sharp disagreement about the policies they require.

Such policies may never be satisfactorily defined, but the compromises they compel are ones we have to accept with whatever residue of dissatisfaction we must bear. They reach upward through social arrangements, becoming more and more frustrating; at bottom they remain the same. Guards for households become armies for nations; faint public interest in property escalates to severe restriction of its uses in an urban environment; elementary education for frontier life is transformed into a mastery of techniques for sophisticated productive activities—and then it is discovered that only a few are capable, and a damaged image of equality results. We dislike the restrictions and fear their extension; we evade the burdens; we resent the overturn of accepted beliefs; but the necessity cannot be denied. Change is inevitable; and if it is, it makes accommodation necessary.

This weighing of fears against advantages, of dissent against conformance, was never better illustrated, probably, and certainly not in a more consequential proceeding, than that at Philadelphia in 1787; and, it might be added, in the subsequent evolution of the institutions created there. Fierce differences showed themselves among the delegates; the struggle for differing solutions several times almost broke up the meeting. The most important center of contention was, of course, the formation of a union from separate and reluctant states. Since some delegates had come with active fears concerning the loss of sovereignty, and some with a determination to eliminate the states, if necessary to create a union, the compromises, after deliberation, were of the kind reached by differing advocates only when they have tested one another's strength and concluded that a bargain must be made on terms less than they may have put forward in the beginning, the reduction being what they regarded as the maximum sacrifice they could accept.

Even if all this is well enough known—relying on Madison's recording —there are some lessons from it that seem to have been missed or neglected. Some further recalling can do no harm.

Pressures do often force such a result as was reached in Philadelphia, especially when the forecast of loss from not agreeing is worse than the sacrifice involved in compromise. In 1787, even for the most determined states' righters, there were actual and immediate risks in separatism. If the life of the young nation was threatened, the lives of the states were more seriously threatened. Only recently independence had been judged precious enough to have been fought for in a treasonous rebellion. The conflict had divided colonial society and had been won only when unyielding loyalists were outmatched and forced into exile, and after invading armies had been defeated. It would be a curious ending of such an ordeal to have the new nation disappear because some citizens bargained so hard to keep local prerogatives or to make the citizens of other states pay its expenses that both were reconquered. Even then, however, those who were most reluctant would not accept that a set of regrettable institutions was better than to fall again into the colonial status so lately escaped. Or perhaps people like Henry, Randolph, Mason, and others simply would not face reality. Not much can be told from the sophistical arguments they used.

The bargaining that took place behind the formal façade of the meetings makes the situation of the adversaries at the time of the signing in September of 1787 difficult to assess; there is no way of knowing what each gave up or how reluctantly, or at what point those who withdrew had had more than they could take.

Moreover, much the same observation can be made of bargaining that resulted in constitutional change in many subsequent generations. There is no real reason to suppose that the framers thought themselves infallible; how could they in such an atmosphere of dispute? Nor did many think of their result as something permanent; it would do for the contemporary circumstances; but it was not a guide for the ages. Later generations, fearing to reopen controversial issues, have invented a mystique of permanence; but does anyone imagine, actually, that practical men like Washington,

Franklin, Gouverneur Morris, and Hamilton thought they had reached an infallible standard—especially since none of them had got anything like what he wanted? [5]

There is also another difficulty: compromise may have a weight of one kind or another, not recognized at the time, but important in determining the development of the institution accepted after negotiation. Unexpected results may become more and more marked as the weighting has its effect in time. Looking back, it is sometimes almost impossible to judge what each party to the agreement thought had been sacrificed and what gained. Too much has usually happened since the bargain was struck.

It is a commonplace that bargainers are sometimes stupid about understanding that whatever has to be given up had better be given up before concessions become more costly than they might have been when negotiations began. It is all very well to plot the shifting of burdens to others, as some of the delegates at Philadelphia were doing, but it has to be admitted that political processes are constantly demeaned by efforts to shape policies calculated to achieve position or obtain an advantage for an individual, an interest (group, corporate, industry, association), a region, a city, or a class.

The results, however, cannot be presumed to be favorable even to those who thought they had got the best of the bargain. Very often everyone loses, the successful with the unsuccessful. The hard negotiators overreach, are stubborn, and find themselves involved, eventually, in the penalty exacted of the whole group. This rule grows more general as society becomes more complex until finally the penalty is severe. For instance, depressions in an industrial society are largely the result of policies shaped by dominant businessmen for their own advantage; businessmen inevitably suffer along with others when depressions occur. Their success in having things the way they want them (high prices, low wages) deprives them of customers. Thus disaster for the whole involves every one of its members. It is an imperative of civilized society that such consequences must be foreseen and the practical rule of fair sharing accepted.

The Philadelphia negotiators believed they had reached an arrangement in federalism that satisfied the conditions of fairness to representatives of both the small and the large states by dividing responsibilities and costs, and sharing powers. The signers, at least, thought it would stop the quarreling. One legislative house whose representation was according to population, and another whose representation was equal for all states regardless of size,

5. There were a few who seem to have had such ideas; Wilson, for instance, said one day that they should consider that they were "providing a Constitution for future generations." But when Madison said that the plan now being digested would "decide forever the fate of Republican government" he was certainly not claiming infallibility. He was concerned with the general opinion that republics were unstable. This one had to last, but not necessarily unchanged.

seemed a reasonable result. It ensured survival for all and extinction for none. Besides it provided an upper house to add an element of further deliberation and so would modify the impulsiveness so much dreaded by many of the delegates.

This agreement depended somewhat on the adoption of a clause providing for federal taxation. This by-passed the states and reached individuals, something reluctantly conceded by the states' righters, although it was agreed as part of the bargain that taxes should be uniform, and so would draw revenues from the larger states most heavily. The House of Representatives, with the most members from those states, was given the power to originate revenue bills. Control of the taxing power would limit the spending. This was another check to ambitious nationalism.

It is rather harsh to say that the bargain in this matter was concluded not because it was a foresighted view of the public interest but because it offered the most that either contesting group could get, but that does seem to have been the feeling on either side. Of course, in the background was the situation all found themselves in because the Articles of Confederation, without such arrangement, had been a complete failure. The confederated states had then been trusted to support the central government without compulsion, but the fear of contributing more than neighbor states had before long resulted in some making short payments and others approaching the same miserliness. The most selfish had finally found themselves in the same danger as the least selfish. The securities of nationhood and the facilities for common existence gradually vanished; and when virtually no government remained, only hungry enemies all around the nation's indefinite boundaries were pleased. The most determined states' righters were thoroughly frightened by the recurrent raids of these invaders, and what they heard of imperial aggressors poised on every border brought the most reluctant to a recognition of approaching disaster.

The more recalcitrant states yielded what they had to on this issue, but it was certainly to escape danger rather than to establish a strong central government, which they still hoped they had avoided.

Many incidental effects of this bargain appeared as time went on, one of the most important resulting from a slight weighting in the agreement not recognized at the time. A trend had been started toward a federal power much more vital than was anticipated even by those who thought they had prevailed. A government that reached to citizens through its taxing power and one whose president was chosen by them directly was one that would eventually assume the powers necessary to its functioning.

The Senate insisted on by the smaller states also developed in an unexpected way. Its members, being elected by state legislatures, were chosen by local machines already long in existence; and the machines were supported by economic interests, a connection that was soon shaped into powerful, often corrupt, alliances. The organization that became the Albany Regency was typical of these, although perhaps in an exaggerated way. Van Buren, who rose to power in New York through this local cabal, learned its national uses from Jackson, who, in turn, had learned from Jefferson. These early machines were ruthless, and had effective characteristics that all later ones would imitate. Their potentialities were allowed full scope by the constitutional compromise. Later, Fillmore, then Cleveland, were boosted to the presidency by Albany politicians—Fillmore by Thurlow Weed, and Cleveland by Daniel Manning—and neither had any initial interest in the nation. Much later, Theodore Roosevelt similarly owed his vice-presidency to Boss Platt. The worsening had gone on and on. Many future national decisions were to be made in deals among state bosses.

Jefferson and Jackson had brought their influence to bear in the lower house, arranging presidential nominations through caucuses, and getting their legislative supporters elected by the use of patronage and favoritism. But Van Buren—with Jackson's contrivance—developed a machine that disoriented the Senate as well. The nominating convention was dominated by state bosses from that time on.

The flaw in the original compromise was by then widening into a systematic undermining of original purpose. Senators, representing states, not people and not the nation, were answerable to the bosses who controlled the machines. From Van Buren's time until the Constitutional Amendment of 1912, the number of senators who put their interest in the nation first were very few indeed, and those who did were freed from local control by some peculiar circumstance. It was the boss who was the usual source of power. Legislators who are famous in our history for their forensic brilliance and supposed statesmanship cannot really be allowed their reputations. Webster took pay for services to outsiders; by later standards, Clay could have been impeached; Douglas worked for policies that would increase the value of his landholdings and those of his friends; and Calhoun put the southern interest above that of his country. It was a regular thing.

The compromise of 1787 was allowed to go on spreading its consequences for 125 years before amendment provided for the direct election of senators. By that time, the Senate had become a notorious rich-man's club, entangled with what were delicately called "special" interests. Laws were contrived in the offices of corporate lawyers, and senators made the legislative arrangements, involving the House committeemen when necessary. Finally the scandal became intolerable even for a careless democracy. The compromise destroyed itself.

There were framers who all along had wanted a stronger central government than was finally agreed on, but a larger number were opposed. Some—like Patrick Henry—"smelled a rat," and did not attend at all because they feared that what might happen would somehow diminish

Virginia sovereignty. Others were reluctant for much the same reason; they feared that federal power would grow, and they wanted no responsibility for it. Altogether, seventy-four delegates were supposed to come and fifty-five turned up at some stage; only thirty-nine signed; the rest either simply disappeared or refused to accept the final result. So it was only a few more than half who feared dissolution of the Union more than the sacrifice of local interest.

It seems remarkable that only six signers of the Declaration of 1776 were signers also of the resolution adopting the Constitution. It is true that Jefferson, John Adams, and Tom Paine were in Europe; but Sam Adams, John Hancock, and Richard Henry Lee were conspicuously missing. The most influential dissenters were not present.

From the fact that Henry and Randolph withdrew as Virginians and that Madison and Washington were the most active nationalists, it can be seen that even within the Virginia delegation, where the nationalists' plan originated, there were those who refused to compromise with one another. Some had quarrels even with themselves. That Washington had moments of uneasiness we know from his troubled letters, and Madison was not nearly so satisfied (nor were Hamilton or Jay) as might be gathered from *The Federalist Papers*. Those papers were pleas for the acceptance of the best bargain the nationalists had been able to make. Still, all three authors estimated correctly that time would make the bargain better because circumstances would favor the course they had advocated. Both the supporters of union and those who feared it proved to be right about the strong central government they foresaw. The results were not by any means what either would have approved, but the nationalists had the better of it year after year as events unfolded. Some delegates who signed would probably have approved secession in the circumstances of 1860; there were hidden dangers in the compromise that they did not see. When they awoke to what was happening, the states' righters were willing to divide the nation to recover for part of it what had been lost in the Philadelphia bargaining.

The Loss in Compromise

The hopes and fears of the framers, in spite of the contrasts between the society of their time and that of ours, were not essentially different from those of later years. The passage of time has not changed very much the *kind* of decisions to be made, nor has anything changed the yearning to escape costs and other disadvantages. The same is true of efforts to shape national policies in ways favorable to individuals, interests, or regions. But there have remained a few, as there were in 1787, concerned that the compromises impossible to avoid shall have small weights that may be enlarged to further the national interest.

Since the agreement of 1787 very soon escaped its first formulation—

because it had to—and began to "live," and because there was no practical arrangement for renewed constitutional consideration, it has remained, in fixed form, at the center of extremely complex and often bitter conflicts. And although it may be regarded as a mere commonplace to say that the contentions of the present are very much like those of the past—something like repeating the cliché that human nature does not change—on reflection it will be seen that, like human nature, some of the contentions *ought* to have changed even though they have not done so. Also it will be seen that unlike human nature they *might* have changed.

What emerged from Philadelphia would evolve into a victory, long after they were gone, for those who hoped they had started an evolution toward nationalism—an increase of federal power. But since there had been compromise, something was gained as well by those of opposite views; and what was gained was terribly enfeebling. The increase of national power and responsibility was accompanied by a persistent decline in the proclivity to shape policies in the national interest.

This is a rather awful conclusion, and one that needs some substantiation. Also enlargement of power with a concurrent decline of wisdom in governance yields a frightening picture, rather like that of a mindless giant threshing about with monstrous irresponsibility, a danger to itself and to others. This is an exaggerated statement of the situation, no doubt, but much of the exaggeration is substantiated by recounting the occasions when the giant has narrowly escaped the consequences of its own recklessness by having at the right moment a dedicated, courageous, and nation-minded leader—almost always a president—or has somehow been tranquilized and has lazily let things drift until, luckily, circumstances brought about a favorable conclusion. On several occasions calamity has been escaped by what can only be described as sheer good fortune.

Polk was present to extend our domain to the Pacific; Monroe and Adams saved Latin America from colonization; Lincoln had the resolve to oppose the drift toward disunion; F. D. Roosevelt checked the Great Depression and persuaded the nation that totalitarianism had to be destroyed; and Nixon withdrew from an undeclared war that was sapping our resources. In another genre Roosevelt established collective bargaining and social security, Truman and Marshall saved Europe from disintegration, and Johnson moved the rights of ethnic groups closer to realization. These were acts of leadership not really deserved by a careless electorate.

As for the good fortune, we can recall the vast prairies and the Pacific littoral. The plains at first were a wilderness of blowing grass to be crossed by migrants to the rich transmountain valleys. They turned out to be the one reliable source of food not only for America but also for more unfortunate countries. Other riches were fortuitously granted: oil under the earth and the sea, minerals and timber lands sufficient for national needs.

As for issues that settled themselves: the Blacks might have been resettled in Africa; our brief period of imperialism might have been enlarged instead of dying; industrial enterprise might have been atomized according to the Brandeis formula; the tariff and money issues so prominent in public discussion for many years might not have resolved themselves in reasonable ways; and a basic tolerance might not have overcome, at several junctures, the disruptive extremism of superpatriots on the one hand or Communists on the other. These are a few of many possible illustrations.

In the pretechnological world, drift into tolerable solutions was not so dangerous, or at least was less dangerous, than making the wrong choice. Penalties were not exacted quickly, and when they did come were not so serious that muddling through to recuperation was impossible. In this way not only were economic depressions survived, production increased to support a growing population, and social conflicts damped down, but also wars were got through somehow. Lesser follies such as soil exhaustion, unplanned urban growth, and pollution of air, water, and food supplies were endured and in the end were not terminal; they could be corrected even if by costly belated measures. None of these, however, was as innocuous as those would have it who make a virtue of temporizing; and it has always to be considered what remarkable progress could have been made if national decisions had been wiser. The time is approaching when recovery from near-disasters may not be possible; then survival will be jeopardized by further allowances of power to mindless forces. Avoidances will exact the penalties inherent in chance.

There are those to whom it seems a wonderful circumstance that the Constitution has been made to grow in the way it has. Others hold the opinion that it has not grown nearly enough; they say that institutions and processes modified by extraconstitutional evolution, with bargains reached in largely irrelevant political engagements, never entirely legitimate, have *not* brought the nation close to its two-hundredth year matured as it should be in foresight and with the appropriate institutional equipment for avoiding future disasters—not to speak of failures to reach desired ends. Powers have not been quite balanced; their distribution has never been properly reconsidered.

These others—nationally minded and with concern for the future— say that nothing less will do than rebirth in a concerted effort similar to the constitutional convention. Unfortunately, it still has to be asked how further compromises, reached by newly chosen delegates, would result; for it is all too likely that those delegated to create the new institutions would be traders in the fashion of their ancestors. However trite it is to say so, fears still overcome the impulse to secure the future.[6]

6. When J. F. Kennedy was making notes for his *Profiles in Courage* (New York: Harper & Row, 1956), he made the following observations (quoted in *A Thousand Days* by A. M. Schlesinger, Jr. [Boston: Houghton Mifflin Company, 1965]): "Politics

There is some reason for modifying the forecast. The citizens of the present may not have reached an advanced state of reasonableness, but some lessons have been learned by some people—those having to do with the consequences of violence, neglect, waste, and ugliness, for instance; and there seems to be a general recognition that governance of the whole is permanently necessary. If this is so, public agencies may be made more effective instruments. If the framers in 1787 had a small nation to preserve, valued by many because it would protect local interests, there is now a society possessing a rich continent needing to be organized for social purposes; and the first principle of such an effort must be integration.

We Americans ought not to fool ourselves; a main source of our troubles is a constitution that does not provide for integration. To put it more moderately, constitutional processes could have helped to avoid the worst of our present troubles; and until they are used, the troubles will continue. They will yield neither to legislation reached in the way provided nor to presidential importunities, nor to directives of the Court. They will yield only to a new constitution as similar ones did in 1787.

This should not be taken as a wholesale condemnation; given the conditions of its adoption, the Constitution embodied some remarkably durable principles as well as others not so durable. The useful ones we ought to identify and consider for enlargement; the others we ought to discard; the complaint here is that we are unaccountably reluctant to do either.

One of the interesting observations to be made about the Constitution, however—and one with lessons for later drafting endeavors—is that the principles meant to be followed were not clearly and carefully embodied in the institutions. This was especially true when the framers were dealing with a new principle that affected an old institution.[7]

Several of these dilemmas were never really resolved. One with really serious consequences was the conflict between the balancing of powers and the prejudice in favor of legislatures (or against the executive).

Part of the difficulty here was that execution was never distinctly seen as something other than a minor duty of the chief of state. To administer

---

is a jungle—torn between doing the right thing and staying in office—between the local interest and the national interest—between the private good of the politician and the general good."

Kennedy was then a senator and suffering through a long ordeal of illness. For the first time, evidently, he was considering survival in the jungle he spoke of—and doing something for the public good while still holding political position. He finished by speaking of courage and remarking how universally it was admired. "The greenest garlands," he said, "were for those who possess it."

Reviewing our political history he found a few—only a few—and wrote a book about them.

7. The words "old" and "new" here need some apology. They are rather venturesomely used to characterize the specific problems of 1787.

the laws was to order operations from a presidential study. An office with a staff larger than a secretary or two was beyond the framers' conception. The secretary of the treasury would have one; the secretary of state would need amanuenses for correspondence with other foreign offices; but the president was visualized as sending them instructions in handwritten notes; at least it looks that way; and that was what Washington actually did.

The difference between the chief of state who represented his country to other nations and the executive who arranged the operations of his government in accord with these representations was only dimly seen, and the spread of those operations into the concerns of daily life was not seen at all. Perhaps it was not wanted; this, indeed, seems probable, since private and public affairs were so loosely related in that society.

This was one difficulty. Another, emerging from faulty forecasts of this nature, and complicated by a still-lingering assumption that legislatures were the heart and soul of democracy, and therefore of government, made the principle of balance one that really had no chance of operating as was contemplated. It was meant to prevent the centering of an uncontrolled authority anywhere in government. As it was formulated, it favored the legislature enough to make authority anywhere else doubtful. If any such tendency should develop, the Congress had ready means for its repulsion.

The other branches, however, were given no such devices to be used on the Congress if it assumed arbitrary powers. The concession here, after discussion, was that the Congress should not choose the executive as was first proposed, but that it might control him by its monopoly of the purse and by choosing to pass or not pass laws.

That the comparative weakness of the presidency was actually intended is shown by the directive to "give the Congress information of the state of the union." The key word here is *union*, and the most reasonable interpretation of the passage is that it referred to the original term of reference governing the delegates about creating "a more perfect union." The president was to watch over the states in their relations with each other and give warning of dangerous divisiveness. It had reference also, very likely, to dangers from outside which then were so prevalent. If, however, there was any intended reference to internal affairs of other kinds it was not made manifest in any of the president's specific powers. Even the power of nominating "officers of the United States" was emasculated by the following provision when it came to "others" than "ambassadors, other public ministers and consuls, and judges of the Supreme Court": ". . . but the Congress may by law vest appointment of such inferior officers, as they think proper, in the President alone, in the Courts of law, or in the heads of departments."

Take it all together, the powers to be balanced were not actually equated; the principle of balance was one that was not allowed to have its way with the adopted institutions. What happened subsequently was what had to happen. The president did become an executive (as he had so carelessly been denominated), but he also became a political leader and the initiator of policy. This was inevitable; but these were duties the Constitution had not provided for; and the powers of the Congress were such that the president could carry them out only by finding ways to compel congressional consent—by mustering popular support for himself, by bringing congressmen within party disciplines, or by chivying a majority by diverse methods into support of his policies—indignities we prefer not to emphasize.

This tremendous and unheard-of responsibility for national leadership, made difficult by the terms of his constitutional situation, made of the American president a far more powerful and significant figure than had ever before existed in political annals (if the absolute monarchs and dictators are excepted). His uniqueness consisted in not being constitutionally absolute but in having to maintain ascendancy despite every possible handicap.

The balance of powers was a principle recognized by the framers, but so imperfectly used that the complicated struggles it caused between two branches, sometimes disastrous, became a continuing characteristic. These, at various times of crisis, were further complicated by thrusting into the struggle the third branch asserting implied powers of decision. Altogether the principle of balance was unsuccessful, partly because it was not consistently followed, partly because the branches it affected were not sharply visualized. More likely the principal cause was a lingering preference for legislative processes. Whatever the reason, it stands as a warning to future constitutionmakers. If principles are to be followed, it must be understood what their consequences will be. If they are not understood, the necessities of operation will have their way, and the constitution meant to be an ordering of political life will soon be shattered. If it has by then become a symbol of nationhood, its ruins will have historic honor but very little operational significance.

A Pluralist Economy

Opposed processes of erosion and of accretion have been at work all these years, but have often been undetected until they have gone further than would have been thought tolerable considering their sometimes serious consequences. Some guiding ideas from the eighteenth century have helped in resisting, but some even of these have disappeared or are hardly visible anymore.

Let us see: there is still a fierce attachment to rights generally conceived as original and beyond the reach of anyone or any government. We are still pluralistic, since these rights belong to individuals—even though certain monstrous organizations are permitted to wear masks of individuality. We still have the conviction that no authority should be allowed to get above itself and that certainly none should become arbitrary. We have been known to make it a point of honor not to respect such pretension even when we concede its formal legitimacy. Especially our ancestors' notion that the tendency of power to become absolute can be checked by setting one pretender to it against another, and letting them contend for advantage, has continued to be an accepted device. This is considered to be a necessary, or at least a useful, corollary of pluralism, a way of limiting the consequences of a struggle it is desired to perpetuate. But there have never been any adequate institutions to embody the theory.

Then too, many of us are contrivance-minded, after the fashion of Benjamin Franklin. Also we tend to measure our social arrangements by results, although there are exceptions to this. There have been many names for it; there are technical ones—pragmatism, instrumentalism, experimentalism, for instance. But whether named or not, it is recognized everywhere (sometimes disparagingly) that Yankees are hard characters to deal with. They are, it is said, crude but practical. This necessarily involves a resistance to ideologies that is the despair of exasperated purveyors of isms.

Let us at least consider these: the disposition to bargain for advantage, holding to rights considered inherent, independence, suspicion of authority, and a propensity for contrivance. Let us see, then, what their influence was on the framers and what it has been on constitutional changes through the years.

It seems, even at first look, that some conclusions are justified: bargaining for advantage resulted in a political apparatus for the purpose whose effect was not foreseen; that effect was to prolong the states' resistance to national supremacy and in the end to precipitate a disastrous confrontation. The propensity for contrivance was linked with independence and self-sufficiency and was largely responsible for the individualistic cast of the Bill of Rights; and holding so tightly to these (and related) rights made the nation derelict or late in developing institutions suited to a more neighborly situation.

The accumulation of advantages from these arrangements in constitutional law made so many citizens reluctant to change that no amending convention was ever held. Such a convention would have had to be convened by pressures on the Congress, and neither grievance nor foresight was ever sufficient for this purpose. Besides, ways were found to proceed without actual amendments. In much easier procedures, the clauses of the original document were reinterpreted, expanded, or, often, simply ignored

—as in the invention of the regulatory agencies—and affairs could take their course. It was an uncertain course, but it was made to do.

The difficulty with this has been pointed out. It left the nation with an obsolete statement of principle, referred to when convenient by those in positions of power or expounded in convenient ways. There remained, it has to be said, only a standard of reference whose meaning was subject to change and could never be counted on by the ordinary citizen. Nor could it be counted on by the officials who sought guidance in its clauses; this offered a temptation to assume that what was wanted needed no justification but its convenience.

So much for the Constitution. But it did not end there; continuing suspicion of authority allowed laissez-faire to thrive beyond its time and allowable scope; and the propensity to contrive produced an affluence we did not use to advantage because we held to individualism and independence in theory although we created a system of social and economic complexes requiring integration and organic management.

If these generalizations are accepted, they describe a curious and un-anticipated outcome. It is not certain, for instance, how much of our affluence is owed to the individualism that now threatens to choke its own further growth. Also our most precious principles are showing a tendency to interpenetrate and nullify one another. There is difficulty in considering them separately; yet disentanglement is necessary. Some ingenious devices for weaving them together have to be understood. The attempt to accomplish several contradictory purposes at once has worked tolerably when the purposes could be reconciled; but slight advantage for one or the other usually remained; and in the end this resulted, as it did in the instance of Union and states' rights, in the preponderance of one.

Federalism is an illustration on the grand scale; it was considered to be one of the most remarkable of political inventions and has been much admired and imitated.[8] This is strange in view of the clear consequence that looms so large in our history, but that it is still regarded as a remarkable contrivance there is ample evidence.

Most other contrivances had no such fatal consequences as this. There were, however, other attempts to achieve two contradictory ends by a simple device thought by the advocates of each to be something they could manipulate, and if what followed was not fatal it was certainly unfortunate.

8. This admiration stresses different results, depending on the admirer. Vukan Kuic (in a paper published by the Center for the study of Democratic Institutions) recalls that the framers thought a republican constitution ought, in theory, to provide "a republican remedy for the known diseases of popular government." But, he says, the federal principle is more general than is implied in such a statement. Federalism is actually a species of political democracy in which the political subdivision is the equivalent of the citizen in a democratic state. So the states should be autonomous if we are to have a democracy, just as citizens are autonomous in the states.

Economic organization is an example of this. Freedom to compete has been under pressure from the obvious need of general direction for well over a hundred years. We have ended by allowing private management to usurp the field. It wears the mask of competition, but the mask becomes less and less credible. Its beginning is easily enough traced to Philadelphia. It would be unreasonable to blame the framers for not having foreseen developments that had not yet begun or were just barely visible. The mercantile system provoked the Revolution, or went some way toward provoking it; and the new nation felt itself well rid of it. There was no intention of substituting another system for it; what had been fought for was simply freedom. Men wanted to do as they liked. Why not? No one objected.

It may be recalled that by 1787 *The Wealth of Nations* was in circulation (it had been published in the year the Declaration had been signed) and free enterprise was very likely an accepted theory, but there was no talk of such matters. A late eighteenth-century American would have been as outraged by any limitation on his producing, or his selling and buying, as he would if told he might not build a house, use a gun, or raise livestock. When it was suggested at the Convention that the states might attempt to obstruct commerce, the so-called supremacy clause was quickly added to the proposed draft. This made it certain that no state could favor one economic interest over another. Much the same impulse caused the specification that taxes must always be uniform. The slaveholders were active in this argument. They were afraid the slave trade might be discriminated against. But the effect reached commerce of all kinds. Any tax, when laid, must be the same for all.

There was an obvious commercial interest in the sound-money clauses. The states were forbidden to coin or print money or to legitimize the payment of debt in anything but gold or silver. They had been known to cheapen money so that debts would be easier to pay. Because some of them, also, had made bankruptcy easy, it was agreed—almost without discussion—to include a provision that no law could be passed by the states that would impair the obligations of contract. The recollection of Shays's Rebellion was active in all the framers' minds; and if it had not been, they had Elbridge Gerry to remind them.

It is curious that this prohibition was not made to apply also to acts of the Congress, but this may have been because it was thought that such restrictions would result only from competition among the states. At any rate the intention was to make trade freer by specifying necessary rules, something that might have been a precedent for other provisions concerning commerce.

On the whole, however, the finished document had very few allusions to commercial matters other than these, and none at all that suggest a systematic theory. Clearly this was because no regulation was thought necessary. It was an area for free functioning. If almost any framer had been asked, he might have explained that the pursuit of profit is the generator that causes progress and that competition disciplines producers and protects consumers. It was enough to provide that debts must be paid in honest currency and that government might not favor one competitor over another. This was not a matter of contention as so much else was; everyone was agreed.

If this kind of economic order was only assumed and was not recognized in the Constitution, it was nevertheless actual. So much so that within its loose system something very like sporadic civil war became almost endemic within a generation or two. When farmers on the frontier found themselves overextended and unable to pay back what they had borrowed from eastern bankers, they demanded that the Congress legitimize cheaper dollars, just as they had once demanded similar action from the state legislatures. Anticipation of this demand had been the reason for prohibiting state coinage; but since the Congress had not been forbidden to do what the state legislatures were prohibited from doing, a recurrent struggle, sometimes involving violence, went on in Washington as long as a frontier existed and agricultural surpluses rolled into processing centers to overwhelm limited markets. Low prices and high debts led to populism, then to the Farmer-Labor movement, and were more than half the support of Progressivism. They even fueled much of Wilson's New Freedom, and remained to haunt F. D. Roosevelt. The Populist strain in Lyndon Johnson's policies was obvious, and it did not end with him.

If the framers can hardly be blamed for not having made provision for developments beyond their economic horizon, still they might have anticipated that *some* changes would occur. They were amply warned by Mason and others. The frontier revolt that erupted in the 1820s and helped Jackson to unseat the second Adams had been in preparation for some time. And the demands of the Appalachian frontiersmen were only a beginning; more insistent ones from the prairie farmers (the Populists) would presently appear.

It could be contended—and was—throughout the next century and far into another that laissez-faire had been positively intended instead of negatively assumed. It was convenient; since businessmen, financiers, and speculators were free, they could operate in the developing system as they liked. If this involved war among themselves, as it did, they could combine to suppress competition from the weaker brethren, and, becoming monopolists through holding trusts, exploit the entire community. Smithian theory would no longer serve to justify a let-alone policy, and economists were soon advocating the strangely contradictory one of *enforcing* free competition. They clung to "classical" economics, but their assumptions were further and further from the realities of economic life.

Since all of us have become more and more caught up in the industrial machine, conforming to its requirements and accepting its effect on our civilization, its importance does not need to be argued. What does need to be argued is the question whether we shall continue to be passive. No individual by himself can assert any control; he cannot even resist with any effect. It is only through and by his political organization that he can exert a really countervailing power.

The industrial complex is responsible for so many of the good things in life that it may seem ungrateful to enter a dissent to the self-government it has so long enjoyed. It is, however, not too difficult to show that with integration and planning, its productivity might have been enormously larger and certainly more benign. It is only necessary to suggest the social costs just now beginning to be counted, and the wastes inherent in competition, to support this conclusion.

Surely we have reached a time when mindlessness in so important an area of human endeavor need not be regarded as a virtue. We have the capability of foresight and control. It ought to be used. If this was beyond the view of the framers it is not beyond ours. And our Constitution ought to reflect it.

Conflicts Not Contemplated

There was another civil conflict that tormented the entire country for at least as long as those between the farmers and their creditors, and between small and big businessmen. This was the struggle of workers for the equality they understood to be their inheritance. If there was any one virtue in American society more praised than any other, it was this; yet it was honored more often than practiced. Equality as a practical matter always evolved toward advantages for some; and those who were favored became more and more defensive, just as those who were disadvantaged became more and more aggressive.

It must be admitted that nowhere in the Constitution is there a hint of anticipation that such a struggle might occur and might need to be contained. The Bill of Rights? That was mostly intended to prevent the invasion by government of traditional freedoms. The aggressions of other individuals, or of such monstrosities as corporations, were nowhere mentioned. The First Amendment admonished the Congress in some detail to make no law infringing rights; and the eighteen specifications for congressional powers in Article I had to do with national facilities, their establishment and maintenance. There was no mention of corporate organization or its place in the economy, and no mention, even, of enterprise carried on by individuals. There was plenty of it in 1787, but there was no need to mention it.

When the time came, no constitutional provision prevented employers from exploiting their workers or from assembling armies and deploying them to suppress protests. It was an unmarked area for the courts; and the judges chose—ironically, it now seems—to rely on the Fourteenth Amendment, after that amendment was ratified, until loud and threatening voices were heard. Vox populi did finally reach judicial ears, but for a century employers were more free and more equal than their employees. Employers had property to be protected; the workers had no call on due process.

When the formative instruments of the new nation were being shaped— successively the Declaration, the Continental Congress, and the Federal Government—Britain was emerging reluctantly from mercantilism. The colonies, it was considered, were worth developing and being brought within the imperial circle of protection because they were profitable to the homeland. Their commerce was rightfully monopolized by British companies. The colonists did not see it that way, and it was largely to escape monopoly and exploitation that the rebellion occurred. It is interesting in view of this that in Philadelphia the framers should have agreed without difficulty on a clause "regulating commerce with foreign nations and among the several states." Clearly, however, this was meant merely to prevent the states from imposing regulations against one another. Another provision of Article II prohibited any preference for the ports of one state over others. There could be federal tariffs on imports but none on exports, and tariffs had to be uniform; but no state might, without the consent of the Congress, impose any duties, or, if it did, the yield must go to the federal treasury; and anyway, any such law would be "subject to the revision and control of the Congress."

In this new nation, commerce, internal and external, was not to be interfered with by the states. There would be a common coinage; some facilities would be provided—such as post offices and post roads; the useful arts would be encouraged; there would be protection (a militia and a navy); and a judiciary would ensure justice.

It was not thought necessary to make any of this explicit. An individual might use such talents as he had for getting ahead. Everything was arranged so that he would have a clear field and no favors. There were taxes to worry about, but those were no heavier for one than for another; taxes were to be "uniform." And they would pay for a minimal government establishment. Not much else was necessary.

If this was a suitable arrangement at the beginning of the nineteenth century, it certainly ceased to be so during its course; the industrial revolution, including mines, factories, and all the rest, developed very rapidly; so did cities; so did agriculture beyond the Mississippi. Undeterred by the loose provisions of the Constitution, employers and workers went to war, investors were periodically mulcted, and customers were treated as a convenience to be exploited without hindrance. The industrial system was no system at all; it was war without rules. And if it was bad for the workers, it was just as hard for farmers who had to take what processors were willing to allow them and to pay what the bankers, the railroads, and the storage companies wanted to charge.

The long-continued outrages perpetrated by uncontrolled business were not the result—like the differences about states' rights—of compromise; they were the result of an honored principle. It was, if it may be put that way, a principle gone wrong, or, perhaps, misapplied. For what the framers meant to ensure was freedom, freedom of the citizen from interference by authority, especially the new authority of central government. There had been too much of this in colonial times; so a comprehensive recital of things government might not do was considered sufficient for the Constitution. The section defining legislative duties was most explicit about limitations on governmental powers. These are the most definitive and exhortative passages in the whole document.

Even this was not enough; the distrust of government was not altogether allayed by these strictures; and the arguments in *The Federalist* were not wholly convincing; there arose, when ratification came to be acted on, a demand for further assurances that individuals in their usual occupations and activities would not be interfered with; the assurances were given and were embodied in the amendments of 1789.

Nor was this all or nearly all. Governmental powers had been divided by the architecture decided on. Checked and channeled as these were, arbitrary authority had nowhere to lodge. Laws of certain sorts could not be made at all; but such as could be made were complete only when two legislative houses and the president concurred; and presently, by agreed extension, when the Supreme Court also approved. The Constitution was a charter of freedom—for enterprisers no less than for other citizens.

In circumstances hardened in succeeding decades, and with no interferences, workers in expanding industries who asserted rights had to confront employers who also had rights; and these were held to be prior and privileged. The right of assembly, for instance, did not extend to the assembly of strikers at factory gates. That threatened property, and the militia could be called out to suppress the threat; as the courts defined the Constitution, strikers' gatherings were insurrections. And all that long list of legislative powers in Article II contained nothing of use to citizens caught in the vast impersonal industrial machine. Their needs could not be extrapolated as rights. It did them no good to be citizens of a nation that could collect taxes, maintain armed forces, and regulate commerce. Fair prices, decent conditions of work, security in sickness and old age—nothing of this sort could be read into the Constitution; and a business-minded Congress would certainly not clear the way for further amendment.

There are some names in our history that call up scenes and emotions as vivid as those of the Civil War. Shiloh, Chancellorsville, Antietam, and Vicksburg are no more evocative than Homestead, Laurence, Pullman, Centralia, and Gastonia. What happened in those places were incidents in a civil war too. They were not battles that ranged region against region, and so there were no mustered armies and no sweeping national fervor. They were mean, sporadic, miserable conflicts, breaking into violence when men could bear the conditions of their work no longer and could no longer endure the sufferings of their families. Their only real weapon was the strike. This stopped production and caused losses to owners. But often there were substitutes who could be hired; and there were police (and the militia, if necessary) to keep workers from becoming violent, to protect the facilities they threatened, or, worse, to prevent interference with strike-breakers.

It was a struggle that went on intensifying as industrialism spread. It came to almost a full stop, however, in the thirties of the twentieth century, when collective bargaining was finally made legal—found finally to be within the permissiveness of the Constitution. Injunctions against strikes were prohibited to judges. Unions became respectable, and order began to be imposed on a still-pluralistic industry. Workers suddenly had counter-vailing powers.

But then it was discovered that another problem could arise within the Constitution's limitations. Employers and their organized employees, settling their own differences by contract, could agree to exploit consumers. There was no way to prevent them from sharing between them the profits from increased productivity to the exclusion of others in the community. The small number of employers, and those workers who were unionized, had no more mercy on consumers than employers had once had on workers. A new civil conflict was in progress as the century entered its seventh decade.

The farmers had done better—or, perhaps, in another sense, worse. More than two-thirds had vanished from their farms, driven away first by long-continued exploitation and then by the superior efficiency of large-scale operations. They were bought out and migrated to the cities, where they joined the growing pool of unskilled labor. Their long fight from Populist days to the New Deal was won finally in the Congress; farming was entitled, the lawmakers decided, to parity with industry. The trouble was that the new prosperity was conferred only on those few who knew how to run farms as factories were run. The troops who had suffered in the conflict got none of the benefits. They had taken refuge in the slums.

Where was the Constitution while these wars were being prepared, being fought, and finally, being somehow settled? The answer is that none of its provisions was relevant. It was appealed to, used for the advantage of one or another; but in none of the savage confrontations did its rule have a truly constitutional effect. It is not meant to say that the framers ought to be taxed with responsibility for events they cannot have foreseen; but actually they might have left more doors open; and where were those who ought to have been later framers? There was, after all, an amending clause.

One of the most important terms of reference for constitution revisers in the future will certainly be a legalized economic order. The assumed system is so infused with hypocrisy and so scaled to unreality that the whole of economic life has become a legal wonderland.

If it is intended that we should preserve the principle of pluralism, allow the contriving propensity to function, yet avoid conflict between workers and management and see that consumers are protected, a wholly new constitutional effort is needed. None of these has any guidance from the charter of 1787.

Pseudoconstitutionalism Will Not Do

If the nation needs a constitution it is to secure the great purposes of the people; and this cannot be done by perpetuating an instrument of convenience to be abused, expanded, interpreted (and reinterpreted) in processes not legitimately those of original constitutionmaking. When it is thus misused, it becomes—or continues to be—a mass of evasions, avoidances, anomalies, and even silences on crucial issues. It cannot constitute a system of government suitable to the circumstances of a society drastically different from the one that existed during its preparation. A charter created by accretion, by custom, and by unauthorized inferences will never become the materialized instrument of conscience, foresight, and wisdom. It will always be a thing of shreds and patches.

In the attempt to maintain the sovereignty of the states and also give the federal government sufficient powers, and in the choice between free competition and economic management, there are illustrations of avoidances that finally demanded insistently to be resolved. In both instances, a long and uneasy history, with recurring crises of more or less consequence, was undergone. In each instance, moreover, the indeterminate situation was taken advantage of—in the federal-state conflict, by politicians; in business, by speculators and financiers. The nation not only endured demagogues who appealed for a nostalgic return to simplicity as distances diminished and made return less and less possible, but had also to suffer the operations of piratical adventurers in the centers of finance and industrial management.

This exchange of concessions illustrates the folly of indecision when historical situations demand certainty; and each uncertainty, of course, has its own traceable train of consequences. Much of American social history consists of successive unfortunate incidents in one or the other progression.

It is hard to explain why the myth of states' rights persisted long beyond the time when such rights really existed, but perhaps it was because of identification with, or at least a supposed relation to, the familiar constellation of virtues: independence, self-reliance, liberty, individualism, initiative, inventiveness. It is hard to see why a state with a budget larger than that of the nation no more than a generation ago should successfully be pictured as a beleaguered bastion of individualism or as a defender of local interests suffering the attacks of a monstrous bureaucracy in Washington. Yet effusions on this theme are an everyday occurrence in the Congress, or, anyway, are prepared for *The Congressional Record,* designed for home consumption. Naturally they are even more often heard in state capitals, frequently by those that draw most heavily on federal aids and whose politicians have most to gain from loose supervision. Candidates are always winning governorships with no more solid material than variations on this theme.

Such specious appeals must be presumed to please constituents. The supreme effrontery of the congressman or governor who complains about federal tyranny while he is doing his best to see that more generous funds are allocated to his district or state has become so expected as to be a sort of ritual. Everyone—constituents included—knows that only federal resources can reach and solve many problems that beset the complex world. Yet the fulminations against Washington continue, and continue also to be good for votes.

Still, it seems to be thought, there is a good possibility of satisfactory resolution. The contenders can be brought together if judicial rule is imposed. Peace will then return to old battlefields. The contenders will become cooperators if the Court, recognizing reality, brings the Constitution up to date.

This possibility is ardently urged by a school of lawyers. In this strain Professor A. S. Miller [9] has in effect congratulated the Supreme Court for the discovery that "law . . . cannot run contrary to the main impulses and beliefs of society." There was, he thought, a "series of landmark decisions, recognizing the unifying forces of American society." The beginning of this could be distinguished in the 1930s, when a series of opinions "gave final constitutional approval to the outlines of cooperative federalism."[10] What was said of the Court's "discovery" is quite true—all too true. To reach it, Chief Justice Hughes had to ignore two opinions handed down shortly

9. The three quotations from Professor Miller that follow are excerpts from "Private Governments and the Constitution," a Center for the Study of Democratic Institutions paper, 1959.

10. Beginning with *National Labor Relations Board* v. *Jones and Laughlin Corp.,* 301 U.S. 1 (1937).

before.[11] The sequence of years—1935, 1936, and 1937—will be noted.

These were not unanimous decisions, a point significant only because it reduces the number of individuals to whom first resistance to change, then giving way to it, is owed. The argument here does not depend on it, but "turning points" in social history do seem more appropriate times for constitutional reexamination than for "discovery" by a majority in a court of nine. Since this may, and often does, come down to five, with the other four dissenting, it emphasizes the unsuitability of reliance on such an uncertain legalization. It also makes rather inappropriate the word "final" for describing decisions of the Court. They are hardly ever that.[12]

It is not meant, here, to suggest that the assertion of judicial supremacy and the continued practice of judging the constitutionality of legislative and executive action is the only source of pseudoconstitutional law. Law, with somewhat less claim to legitimacy, is made all the time by others, many others, not only in government, but outside it—in corporate offices, by unions, trade associations, and farmers' organizations, for example. Lacking the guidance of true constitutional rule, everyone and every agency crosses the limits of traditional authority; and unless and until somehow checked, these initiatives govern conduct; and by no means are all the checks administered by the Court, although those are considered more respectable and worthy.

It is unsettling to consider how often the executive branch has proceeded as best it could against a barrage of congressional appeals to nostalgia, constantly accused of sinning against tradition, yet, of course, expected to do what must be done—and what a majority of the Congress, when it comes right down to it, accepts and will implement with appropriations.

It is almost as unsettling to consider how long a similar hypocrisy has been the rule in the governance of industry. There is a constant chatter in corporate boardrooms and in the pronouncements of business leaders about "competition" and in governmental circles about protecting "small" business (there is even a Small Business Administration). The limit was perhaps reached when the Full Employment Act of 1946, which was as near to a planning measure as prejudice would allow, was prefaced by an elaborate preamble describing what was to follow as, of all things, a measure to encourage "free enterprise."

It has been a long time since there has been any expectation that discovery and initiative in important matters will originate from competitive endeavors. Invention emerges, rather, from research, making

11. *Schechter Poultry Corp.* v. *United States,* 295 U.S. 495 (1935); and *Carter* v. *Carter Coal Co.,* 298 U.S. 238 (1936).

12. C. Herman Pritchett, in *The American Constitution* (New York: McGraw-Hill, 1959), speaking of this same "discovery," said of the chief justice and the former decisions that he "said as little about them as possible."

sophisticated use of vast accumulations of knowledge. These are available only to an elite; they are used in the laboratories and libraries of universities or other research institutions where groups of scholars and experimenters are assembled and work together.

Yet the myth of independence and individualism persists, mostly nowadays as a political appeal, but it often furnishes assurance to unthinking citizens. These words are regarded with cynical tolerance by intellectuals; but they still have an appeal to the electorate, and they will until a more realistic appraisal has made its way into people's minds.

It would be a mistake to conclude that such patently hypocritical exhibitions do not represent something persistent and characteristic. They do. Initiative, originality, the propensity to contrive—these were as much responsible for the conquering of the continent, and for the later productivity of the industrial system, as the richness of resources so often credited with American progress. Perhaps American success was owed in considerable part to what animal and plant breeders call hybrid vigor. At any rate, the encouragement and protection of initiative is an unmistakable propensity. It rejects the smothering of rule and system and looks constantly for ways to renew the sources of its life. It is not strange if the Alger hero is still regarded as the prototype of the successful businessman.

It is a curiosity of industrial development that the products of such extraordinary vigor should have turned at a stage in their success to the suppression of its further manifestations. Large-scale industry, achieving efficiency, characteristically uses its power to eliminate competitors. If they do not disappear in fair competition, conspiracy and subterfuge are resorted to. Corporate bodies do this so that they need no longer be progressive but can maintain themselves by exploiting their consumers. They seek to profit not from further gains in efficiency but by the suppression of potential rivals who *are* making such gains.

This habit is not new; it became so oppressive almost at once when merger and expansion began after the Civil War that by the 1880s there was a fierce reaction. But instead of recognizing that large-scale enterprise might be adapted to good use, the political attack on it was oriented to suppression. "Trusts" were to be broken up. The policy was one of forcing industries back to their takeoff point, and keeping them poised there permanently. There was general resistance to identifying efficiency with growth in scale. Rugged individualism, theretofore a fact of American life, became a fetish. The reality disappeared as the myth spread.

When the Constitution was being written, free men on free soil and in small independent shops did make up the economic system; and there were few facilities—not even dependable mail or well-organized transport. But there was no questioning, no suggested alternative; it just was. Since nearly all the people lived in situations requiring them to be self-sufficient, they hardly did more than feed and clothe themselves, the whole family cooperating. Today one worker in agriculture provides food and fiber for some forty in other occupations; and as toolmaking, butchering, and baking have undergone similar transformations, output per man hour has increased a hundredfold or even a thousandfold; moreover, it continues to double in incredibly short periods. In the United States per-man-hour productivity even in the 1970s was at least double that of the British, the Germans, and the Scandinavians, and was several times that of Russia.

Economic progress depends on this vigor and this organization of the initiative it supplies. Since adjustment has been made to it, present society could not exist without it; and obviously, in spite of a continual looking backward, there is no intention of returning to the economy of the last century. No matter how the politicians talk, the dominant trend is toward further use of laboratories, computers, sophisticated administration, teams of workers, and mechanized factories. It is expected that these will open new opportunities, especially if measures are taken to keep exploiters and monopolists away from the processes they find so rich a source of wealth. Trouble will doubtless continue with simplistic demagogues who blunder about in the complexities of modern technique with obfuscating remedies for their frustrations; but their lot can be made a good deal harder, and further progress will be conditioned on making it harder.

The Constitution, it is sad to say, has not helped but has hindered in both the progressions spoken of here; nor does it furnish any line of direction; and this leaves all such matters to legislators and courts. Neither has shown much interest in, or respect for, vigor and productivity—although plenty has been shown for property, however possessed, and for profits, however won. Neither has understood that the problem is to find scope for the gifted individual within the new system; and to respect efficiency in a world committed—despite the legislators' and judges' best efforts to prevent it—to integrated activity.

It is a problem not suited to the talents of politicians or lawyers, as such. It might be easier for detached, analytical, and patriotic statesmen, able to see what must be preserved and what must be abandoned, in addition to understanding how it must be done. But in any case solutions ought long ago to have been undertaken in the same way that the problems of disunion, insecurity, and the preservation of rights were met by the framers.

Of them it cannot be said that they failed. It is hard to see how they could have done very much better without being able to see beyond their horizon. They did in fact provide a tolerable governance for theirs and a succeeding generation. No more could be expected. The fault in our constitutional history is that the framers' document was taken as permanent even though the world was being transformed; this, naturally, gave those in a position to do so support for shaping meanings as they liked. They made the Constitution live; and if living consisted in protecting their privileges, attaining their ends, disciplining those of whom they disapproved, they were able to have it their way.

The result has been to choke progress and waste a people's natural vigor.

Economics and a "Living" Constitution

For the support of this "living" Constitution its advocates and apologists have depended a good deal on the politicians' expert evocation of fears: of Wall Street and money barons, heartless monopolists, economic royalists— any enterprise so large as to escape individual, commonsense control, any-thing, as Brandeis said simply, that was big. Fears often have been elaborately masked as denunciations; but they were fears, nevertheless, of the large, the strange, the complex, the new. This seems incongruous in a people so proud of their initiative and self-reliance. Evidently some explanation is in order.

The first—and one of the strangest—remarks to be made about it is that the delays, lasting until the thirties, in accommodating public policy to industrial integration were not approved unanimously by industrial leaders. True, the trustmakers were responsible in a way; they had presumed that the habit of noninterference implicit in the free enterprise so generally approved would allow them to extend without resistance into the whole area of business operations. They expected to grow big unnoticed, especially if they kept on talking about competition; and they hoped to establish virtual private governments with no more than a minimum of rules (dictated by themselves) about fairness in mutual dealings. This would relegate the government once more to about the same position it had occupied in the beginning. Economic affairs would go on in a sphere of liberty with the public looking on but not interfering. Interference would threaten freedom, so they claimed.

There were, however, a few more thoughtful big businessmen (industrialists, not financiers) who had concluded that this was a utopian conception quite beyond any possibility of realization; and presently they developed doubts, or some of them did, even about its desirability. They understood that the welfare of so sophisticated a society would have to be accepted as a responsibility by those who made its policies and administered its management. In this respect they would have the same debts and duties any government would have, and this might be costly; it would involve fairness to competitors, higher wages, and standards of quality they were not used to maintaining. Competitors could not be undercut; workers would have to be listened to; customers' demands would have to be met.

There would be entirely new rules, and the resulting responsibilities would be tremendous.

This sort of thing had not been necessary in the short run. For several generations businessmen had pretty successfully appropriated the gains of progress and evaded or sloughed off the losses. For instance, when hard times were brought on by speculators, creditors, and mismanagers, they lost profits for a time; but the heavy losses, the kind that wrench men's souls and bring into question the need for such privation, were borne by farmers and workers, together with their families. The farmers might lose their land; the workers might be—they often were—reduced to the agonies of cold, hunger, and homelessness.

There was a growing realization that this was avoidable, that increasing productivity made higher levels of sharing possible. Besides, the new technology had its own irresistible logic. A high-energy system, turning out an ever-increasing volume of goods, had to have customers. Otherwise it would simply choke up and stop.

When customers for mass-produced goods were looked for, it was obvious that many of them were workers who bought goods with the wages they received for making the same goods. It was easy to reason from this to the conclusion that high wages sustained continuous activity. Once this feedback principle was thoroughly understood by a better-educated generation of executives, the workers' war was, in effect, won.

This was good for the workers, but there was some distance yet to go. There were others to be considered who were outside this relationship. Something had to be done about them, not only because their case was heartrending but also because it made sense to bring them into the economic circle. To provide a sharing income for the disabled, the orphaned, the unemployed, and the aged was to create a sure market for goods, just as higher prices for farmers made good customers.

The new industrial elite, however, was not ready to surrender its control. It kept its hold on legislatures and bureaucracies by claiming an identity of interest with a wide spectrum of the electorate. There were several commitments to policy believed good for business, and there was an instrument for effecting them. This was the Republican party. It succeeded in attributing "the full dinner pail" to protective tariffs, and later improved on this by promising "a chicken in every pot," and finally "two cars in every garage" if protection was combined with what was still called "free competition"—meaning, of course, freedom for business from governmental interference. Successive victories for these policies could not have been won as they were if many workers had not believed what they were told by their employers. Similarly, the farmers' votes were kept by representing the tariff as providing a market at high prices for the crops they raised. How this could be, when agricultural products were not imported anyway, was always a mystery to realists; but the fact was that a majority of the farmers' votes could be counted on to support protection. The farmers, together with small businessmen who admired big businessmen, workers who were grateful to be employed, and other citizens who accepted the warning that Democrats were dangerous, made up a safe Republican majority.

The party controlled the federal government continuously from the Civil War until the onset of depression in the thirties. (The Democratic intrusions of Cleveland and Wilson merely proved the rule. They happened because the Republicans presumed too much on rank-and-file loyalty and generated temporary revolt. Both Cleveland and Wilson were minority presidents; and after them, Republican rule was resumed under big-business auspices.)

Fear and its insecurities were important in the continued Republican hold on its majority. Workers dreaded the low wages and unemployment that they were told would follow Democratic election victories; farmers believed that if tariffs were lowered, corn, cotton, pork, and beef would pour across unprotected borders into American markets from foreign sources; others took fright at the expenditures always being thought up by Democratic candidates; the balanced annual budget became the most powerful of all political appeals when patriotism faded out forty years after the Civil War. It still had potency in the 1930s when depression had the nation in its tight-fisted grip. F. D. Roosevelt was aware of this; and even when he was violating the rule, he talked largely of a return to balance in the immediate future.

The industrialists, who had become aware that their policies were self-defeating, saw, when the depression persisted, that it might turn into a great exposure. Some even saw that there had to be a change from reliance on scaring the electorate to that of a credible promise of better living for all. They saw, too, that this involved integration. The public interest included their own interest; this was the lesson of the depression. It was with the assistance of a few such leaders that a complex device, given impetus by the failure of the old policies, was made into law which might have developed into what was needed—the preservation of initiative with rules for its guidance that would amount to an imposing of responsibilities. It was billed as a "recovery" measure, but this was too bad; it had been meant to be one that brought countering powers into operation and, at the point of focus, recognized the necessity for overall decisionmaking by government. Businessmen seemed about to admit that there had to be planning and policymaking that comprehended all economic activities. Not recovery but stability was the aim.

Unfortunately even the original promoters of this theory became disillusioned with the operations of the particular organization established to operate the stabilizing device—the National Recovery Administration. It reached too far, and in operation it was tormented by capricious administration; but, much worse, it attempted to right wrongs that were irrelevant to its central purpose. Labor sympathizers, such as Frances Perkins (then secretary of labor) and her satellites, demanded that there should be included in the act provisions to satisfy the long-delayed demands of reformers. Immediately these caused irritations and contentions that made businessmen wish their integrational ideal had never been thought of.

Title 7A of the Industrial Recovery Act later became the Wagner Labor Act and began a useful life of its own. It should always have been separate. Included in the recovery act, it so confused the proceedings of the administration that urgently necessary attention was not given to integration. Even the president seemed sometimes to be so elated over the elimination of such remaining abuses as child labor that he would approve any code, however deficient or unwise in other respects, if it accomplished this.

Some of the agreements he approved had barely hidden provisions for fixing prices and allocating markets; this alienated the Progressives who had staked their political careers on opposition to monopoly. The NRA hearing rooms had become sounding places for John L. Lewis and others of his sort, and the inevitable reaction had occurred. Even its inventors deserted it, and NRA was discredited. In the end it was these extraneous activities—some of them abuses—that brought NRA to such a state of general confusion that Roosevelt was glad to have it declared unconstitutional by a Supreme Court led by Brandeis.

One reason for the Court's rejection was that the administration was exceeding the powers provided in the Constitution. It was reaching into the states and regulating intrastate commerce. This was so patently an excuse for following prejudice, and had such repercussions, that within a year it was reversed. One justice (Roberts) changed his mind, or saw the light, or recognized the absurdity of the position. And since about that time the Rooseveltians were going back to the policy dictated by Brandeis, no attempt was made to revive it. The antitrust division of the Department of Justice was expanded. Thurman Arnold was put in charge, and a vigorous breaking-up campaign was begun. But this phase ended abruptly when war came on and expanded production became essential to national security.

It is interesting to note that the Schechter decision[13] followed the initiative of one justice supported by another with whom he had seldom agreed on any other issue. It seems about as incongruous as anything in our legal history that Justices Brandeis and Sutherland should have acted together to strike down an act sponsored by President Roosevelt. Both justices longed for the conditions of a past they recalled in different ways. The corporation lawyers on the Court of that time meant to limit governmental regulation of

13. *Schechter Poultry Corp.* v. *United States, 295 U.S. 495 (1935).*

business; Sutherland was one of them. Brandeis had something different in mind. He meant to smash the system of big business he had seen developing during his lifetime despite his persistent efforts. He had come to attribute all injustices to bigness. He saw that competition no longer forced businessmen to behave; but that, he chose to think, was because competition was not "enforced." The NRA legitimized big businesses he felt ought to be broken up and returned to their preintegration components. He was outraged; he rarely concealed in public the bitterness he expressed freely in private, and that reached the president's ear.

It was these reactions, not only among the justices but elsewhere, that caused the abandonment of all integrative efforts. For Roosevelt, although he spoke angrily at first, made no suggestion for reconstituting the planning and countering of powers intended by the originators of NRA. It was not because he assented to the constitutional theory of the Court that he abandoned the effort; theirs, he said, was a "horse and buggy" attitude. Like most lawyers, he thought the Constitution ought to "live"—that is to say, it ought to be so interpreted that it met modern demands. To get a Court more agreeable to this idea he presently tried a "packing" maneuver. He lost; not because the *living* theory was objected to, but rather because his opponents wanted the Court, not the president, to take the lead in showing what "living" meant.

Not long afterward one emotional lawyer was heard to remark, "Thank God, some power exists to check such presidents as Roosevelt." He seemed amazed to have the question asked: "Should that checking power really be entrusted to five men who have not been chosen as nominees by a party or elected by the people—and when four equally wise men dissent?" In his regard, the Court majority was sovereign.

In all the public furor attending the events of those "turning point" years, no loud suggestion was heard that the Constitution itself ought to be revised, only that different "interpretations" should be made. These mostly concerned the clause of Article I giving the Congress power to "regulate commerce . . . among the several states," supplemented by the Fourteenth Amendment's prohibition against the deprivation of property without "due process." The latter was operative on the states; the former was a congressional directive limiting its regulative powers to commerce that was interstate. Roosevelt pointed out that this made regulation by either state or nation almost impossible. The Carter Coal case was got around by Justice Sutherland, who disclosed, according to one student of public law, "a judicial dreamworld . . . where there was no difference between one ton of coal and a million tons. A production crisis in every part of the country simultaneously could never add up to a national problem with which Congress could deal."[14]

14. Pritchett, *op. cit.*, p. 244. The case referred to was *Carter* v. *Carter Coal Co.*, 298 U.S. 238 (1936).

What does this last mean? Obviously that the Court ought to stop dreaming and recognize realities. But there is no suggestion in this, any more than there is elsewhere, that the Constitution ought to be reconsidered and rewritten. Political scientists are mostly in agreement with the lawyers. The *Court* ought to get itself up to date, but the Constitution must be let alone; it ought to "live" but not be rewritten or even seriously amended. It is sometimes suggested that the justices ought to confine themselves to a more constricted and more clearly defined ambient; but the suggestion is not made very often, and when it is no one seems to be listening.

If it is anomalous that a nation whose economic activities are relied upon for that nation's strength, and for the well-being of its people, should have a Constitution written before the industrial build-up (and never revised), then there is a conspiracy not to recognize the anomaly. Nearly every phase of economic life is at present governed by extrapolated or improvised rules, not yet questioned seriously. Most of these rules are made by what can only be described as private governments. These are reachable by public authority, but until reached they are autonomous. If these private governments are unconstitutional they apparently do not know it.

The first concern of any movement to revise the Constitution would certainly be to settle some of these unexamined questions. What are economic enterprises supposed to accomplish? What are the proper places in society for such enterprises? What ought to be their relations to each other? What do they owe their workers and their consumers? Then there are even larger questions about sources of capital and its management, as well as others about responsibility for the social costs of operation. And, above all, do such elaborate plans for private expansion fit the national purpose?

The vast constitutional area indicated here even at present is not exactly a blank; there is a welter of tangential—and often conflicting—rules mostly derived from these sources: (1) the police power of the states, (2) the interstate commerce clause, (3) the due process clause of the Fourteenth Amendment, and (4) a phrase in the Preamble referring to the "general welfare." None of these directly concerns industrial or financial organization.

If there is one criterion more important than any other for a constitution it is that it shall comprehend and regulate the economic activities of the people it governs. If the Constitution of the United States does not do this, it seems reasonable enough to suggest that it should.

Individualism and Organization

It is often said that there is so marked a difference in spirit between the Declaration of Independence in 1776 and the Constitution of 1787 that the same kind of individuals could hardly have devised both; either that or there must have been a radical change in circumstances. Both were true; they were mostly different people if not quite a new generation, and the circumstances were very different indeed. What was needed in 1787 was quite different from the rebellion proclaimed in 1776.

Consider the second paragraph of the Declaration: it asserted the principle agreed on then that all men were "created equal," and that they were "endowed by their creator with certain inalienable rights." But those rights were of distinctly secondary interest to the framers of the Constitution. That is to say, the rights were assumed to have been won. Now it was necessary to think of security and continuance for the nation. There was a radical difference in purpose. What had come to be of first interest by 1787 was the making of an effective government, not the elimination of an old one. The nation had tried too long to live on revolutionary ideas. Revolutionists had proved to be better at overthrowing government than at creating or improving one.

The three general rights enumerated in the Declaration were "life, liberty, and the pursuit of happiness."[15] The government provided for the colonies by the British had violated these rights. This justified the demand for a new regime "laying its foundations on such principles, and organizing its powers in such form, as to them shall seem most likely to effect their safety and happiness."

To life, liberty, and happiness (property), *safety* was thus added; and presently it was reiterated that there was a duty to "provide new guards for their future security." Thus, the Declaration.

By 1787 the government provided for the new nation by a generation of revolutionists had failed miserably; it was evidently judged that a better one could not be provided if the Declaration was taken as guide. That, indeed, had been the earlier mistake. No powers had been surrendered to the Congress provided in the Articles of Confederation, not even that of taxation. It had been a single house consisting of delegates appointed by state legislatures; these delegates remained subject to instruction; they were, in effect, ambassadors; and a group of ambassadors could have no plenary powers.

Consequently the Confederation had no effective executive; it had no judiciary, either, except for dealing with interstate disputes. Congressional authority clearly did not derive from the people, except indirectly, by way

15. This "pursuit of happiness" phrase was invented by Jefferson to substitute for the word "property"—so usual in earlier documents. It was a time when anyone could have property and anyone who did not was a shiftless indigent who certainly should not be given any rights. No one has satisfactorily explained Jefferson's phrase, but Catherine Drinker Bowen made a try in *Miracle at Philadelphia* (Boston: Little, Brown and Company, 1966): "To pursue happiness signified that a man could rise in the world according to his abilities and his industry." And—who knows?—this may have been what Jefferson did mean. He was a man who rose—acquiring, as he did so, 10,000 acres and 200 slaves.

of the state legislatures. Funds for operation could be allocated and requested but not collected; commerce could not be regulated; and although treaties with other nations could be made, the states need not honor them. To make futility complete, there were these provisions: the delegates remained in the pay of their states; the adoption of any measure required a two-thirds vote; and any amendment of the Articles had to have unanimous consent. The Confederation was, indeed, described as a "league of friendship" entered into by *sovereign* states; and this was accurate. It could hardly be called a government. Such was the beginning of the Americans' effort to see that their "inalienable rights," their happiness, and their safety were established.

Assuming that throughout the years since then the essential purpose has not changed, and that life, liberty, happiness, and security have all along been first among the ends in view, it is interesting to examine these as criteria for various subsequent additions, extensions, and revisions by interpretation.

The concern of the Convention's conveners is obvious from their correspondence. There was a desperate situation. Mistakes had been made in 1779 that if not immediately corrected would result in the partition of the nation among contending foreign empires. In the effort to meet the criteria of the Declaration, the authors of the Articles had succeeded only in lodging power in centers whose opposition to one another guaranteed paralysis. The states were quite unable to establish security, and as a result, liberty and happiness were giving way to constriction and insecurity. Inalienable rights were not self-sustaining. Left to themselves they simply vanished.

The primary defect was all too evident; it was the lack of centrality; and federal sovereignty had to be the first consideration.[16] What was indispensable was a direct relationship between the people and the central government. There must be a legislature and a chief of state for the whole. A nation without such organs had no focus and no authority. As this last problem was discussed it became more and more obvious that the executive would have to be independently chosen and so have his own source of power. This departed from a proposal that he should be chosen by the legislature as was at first generally expected.

In the Declaration, and in the writing and adoption of the Articles, what had been uppermost in contemporary statesmen's minds was the sovereignty of the people who had those God-given rights that were so eloquently proclaimed. It had been demonstrated that without organization this was an empty promise. The revolutionists had really not attended to

16. It probably is not necessary to note that the meaning of "federal" was reversed within a few years. What once meant confederation or alliance, with some organs of defense, came very soon to mean "national" or "central." The Federalists as a party were made up of those who at the Convention were called "nationalists."

this. Their government was being defeated by divisiveness, and their rights lost for lack of discipline. There should have been an arrangement for concentrating a power that was now dispersed.

The problem of the framers was to effect a transition from the sovereignty of state legislatures to its materialization in better-articulated national institutions. Everything was complicated by the sensitivity and suspicion of the revolutionists who still regarded their victory as having won authority for the legislatures of the states. It had not, after all, been so long since the Articles had been approved. There was a widespread feeling that the states were the genuine lodging places of the people's sovereignty. It was an empty land—thirteen small worlds. There was no transport to speak of among them; there was a meager exchange of intelligence, and ordinary folk, having expelled the British, had little interest in distant cousins—Massachusetts for Virginia, New Jersey for Georgia. The citizens of each seldom saw anyone but their neighbors; even their state capitals were usually days away by horseback. That was remote enough, but a national capital would be still more remote. The trouble with this isolation and self-sufficiency was that there were still dangers from old enemies, and each state by itself was too weak to resist.

In these circumstances the task of the framers was both impossible and essential; when they assembled in Philadelphia to make the effort, they had to devise a government for a people who, as a practical matter, had not been able to make good their independence. Their first attempt had not proved viable in a hostile and complex world. But others among them were not convinced of the necessity and came mostly to prevent what they feared was the intention of the nationalists.

The Constitution shows throughout how hard the unionists tried against not only the hostility of politicians with power to lose but also against those who were more devoted to liberty—as they interpreted it—than to making the nation secure. They would see it die rather than modify their resistance to authority. When the conditions of safety were spelled out and the delegates were forced to face their problem, the purer among the libertarians simply defected and either left or went back to conducting the familiar irresponsible guerrilla warfare. They did not so much deny that the Constitution offered the institutions necessary to the aims they professed as refuse to acknowledge that dangers were rising all about them. They did ask what the security was that seemed so precious to their colleagues. It was, they felt, protection for life but not for liberty and not for the pursuit of happiness. They even preferred, in the familiar words of one of them, death. Patrick Henry has had successors in every generation. Americans have usually respected them, and even found it impossible not to be rather proud of them as a continuing tribe; but if they had had their way the Confederation would have broken up and its states would have been occupied by predatory enemies. There had to be union; it was the price of nationhood, of independence.

The problem at Philadelphia was to channel popular sovereignty into gathered strength, allowing it to come through and embody itself in agencies of administration. When it was done most of those who had prevailed did not regard the result as perfect, not even very close to perfect; but it must have been expected by others than Mason—who said so—that as defects appeared they would be corrected. Almost at once the contentious period of ratification prevented them from saying so; they had to exaggerate. Later, the practical impossibility of amendment stifled such initiatives before they began. The amending clause reflects a controlling fear of democracy.

This was not the only evidence that they distrusted the people. The indirectness of presidential and senatorial election procedures were other results of suspicion; so was the provision (in Article I) that qualifications for voting should be those "requisite for electors of the most numerous branch of the state legislature." Since at that time property and other qualifications excluded all but a small percentage of white male adults, sovereignty was indeed restricted; realistically, it could hardly be called "popular" at all. That provision would be modified eventually in two ways: by the Jeffersonian and Jacksonian widenings of state qualifications, and by later amendments providing against discriminations. Finally, blacks (in 1870) and even women (in 1920) were admitted to the privilege of voting, and exclusions by the use of poll taxes, literacy tests, and other devices were overcome. But the signers were no believers in popular wisdom. They would have been outraged by the admission to the voting privilege of all who were eighteen or over.

Going through the first gate of a two-thirds majority in a Congress chosen by a restricted electorate, and then running the gauntlet of later legislative approval in three-quarters of the states, was so difficult that passage was possible only in circumstances of emergency and only in matters not touching the interests of federal or state legislators. Revisions, when they were made (infrequently), were not gained by any appeal to reason but only when there was emotional reaction to civic disturbance—not a good way to reach constitutional conclusions. On the contrary it is so bad a way that amendments, the first spate of them excepted, have sometimes been injurious or unwise rather than beneficial (Articles XI, XVIII, XXII).

The survival of rights so forthrightly set out in the Declaration were to be the obligation of those who would be given the responsibility of the Constitution. These were the better people, the limited numbers who could vote, their representatives in the Congress, and the carefully chosen president. Besides, there were the extraordinary precautions against concentrations of arbitrary power.

There was to be a central government, commissioned to look out for defense and to see that commerce was not interrupted at state borders. For this it could tax and spend. But the whole business was to be controlled very closely by the elite. They were trustees who were to see that what had not been done by the Confederation would now be done by a more effective organization.

The Declaration had been an incitement to revolution; the Constitution was an effort to consolidate the gains of the revolution and make them safe from popular caprice. If they seem inconsistent it is because there were different aims.

Modern constitutionmakers would not have these problems. Universal suffrage is no longer limited to those who own property, and the electorate has expanded. These changes have overcome even the difficulties of amendment and are evidences of a new attitude. The first consideration would not now be to circumvent an unruly electorate. What would be the first concern would be a system of representation that not only honored but made effective the sovereignty proclaimed in the Declaration. In fact, the principles of the Declaration would not be considered safer directives than they were by the thirty-nine signers in September, 1787.

It is hardly necessary to point out that the insistence in several of the ratifying conventions that a bill of rights ought to be appended was a revolutionary sentiment surviving into a new age. Not that the framers were opposed to rights; they considered that the checks and balances, preventing the establishment of any supreme authority, were sufficient. It was not the new people who had labored and brought themselves into consonance with the later circumstances who demanded a renewed statement of rights. It was the backwoods delegates, together with the unreconstructed revolutionists, who made the unexpected demand. Their indignation very nearly defeated ratification in Virginia and Massachusetts, and it was only the willingness of the surprised defenders to append such a statement that saved the day. It was not necessary, they felt, especially since the states had such constitutional safeguards; but they had no objection.

So the Declaration came into the Constitution belatedly, by way of amendments introduced by Madison at the first session of the Congress.

Constitutional, and Other, Law

Continued existence is said to demonstrate virtue, and, of course, virtue is by definition admirable. Survival is often said, also, to show that what has survived wells up from deep springs that flow persistently, regardless of attempts to dry them up. But it might also be argued that virtues are relative—that is, those praiseworthy in one situation may well be disastrous in another, and persistence may simply show unwillingness to change.

Pioneers did need to increase if they were to possess the earth; but when it was possessed, unchecked multiplication threatened to become overwhelming. Or, another instance, independence, either for individuals or, say, for nations, may lead to dangerous confrontations, something as true of contending individualists in society as of nations under compulsion, in the nuclear age, to live in peace or suffer the constant danger of destruction.

It must not be concluded too easily that new attempts at constitutional construction ought to preserve even what formerly seemed most precious. What has survived many crises, come through many bargaining sessions, and may even have been fought for and have produced national heroes may have become anachronistic, so much so that it stands in the way of progress. It may require for its further protection an expense or disadvantage disproportionate to the gain.

Many illustrations of this can be found. One that comes to mind is the persistent defense of the family farm in a time of technological change. Many an agricultural measure in this country has frankly favored small farmers, sometimes at enormous cost; and the steady decline of their number because of inefficiency in spite of being thus favored is a fact most reluctantly accepted. It was a pioneer survival and was supposed to embody the virtues of the struggle with nature that subdued the forests and plains. A sturdy peasantry was held to be the firmest bulwark of society. Such pronouncements, with variations, can still be heard, and measures for their implementation are still on the books.

The defense of states' rights in inappropriate circumstances and the endless repetition of the rubric that "competition is the life of trade" are other examples. They lodge in people's minds and seem impervious to the battering of fact or the avalanche of innovations. They are often defended by the very individuals who are busily engaged in their destruction.

This kind of stubborn ambivalence is quite characteristic of our time and place. Our minds are encysted with reactionary nodules, and these are often protected by the most devious arguments—when any argument at all is made. The family farm is not open to question; to a businessman, competition is a closed conception. Similarly, many conservationists have a protected area in their minds called "wilderness" that yields to no discussion.

Rich areas of illustration are opened again and again by the mention of words that describe our most closely guarded rights: liberty, independence, equality, initiative, ownership—and others of this traditional sort. All of these have been transformed by circumstance and have lost their one-time meaning. Liberty—what is it today? It is not the ability to cross a busy street at will, to hunt or fish out of season, to build a house, to raise children, to keep domestic animals, to buy or sell property. The most ordinary of everyday occupations is conditioned by rules, resented perhaps, and often violated, but enforced by such agencies as are agreed to be reasonably necessary—and everyone is under penalty to assist in their support. They have been accepted even by those who most resent compliance.

It is empty rhetoric that spouts about freedoms without saying what their limitations are, and when they may be exercised. On the other hand, defining them is so important that it ought to be thoughtfully provided for. Purposes ought to be set and areas established with the most careful consideration of circumstances. To be civilized is to make and to accept such rules.

With the best intentions, creative individuals find themselves resisting the agencies of enforcement. They resent restriction and may even go to law. Some of them get exceptions, but most have to conform. It is important that their conformance should be to reasonable rules; and reasonable rules are derived from agreements of a solemn and considered sort, not ones carelessly adopted, outgrown, or punitive.

The grievance of an individual subject to a discipline he regards as capricious, partial, or unreasonable is a justifiable one, and he ought not to be satisfied to have it so. He lives, and he knows he lives, in a constriction that free men have never accepted. He will struggle against such governance, and he should. What he is entitled to is legitimacy, and this means rules he has either participated in adopting or has agreed to see adopted as part of a civilization whose rules are necessary to its existence.

It would be exaggerated to contend that this legitimacy is to be found only in constitutional specification. This would require a voluminous document dated no longer ago than yesterday. It is, however, equally absurd to contend that it may be found in a document of a few pages put together a hundred years or more in the past. Legitimacy may be achieved, without either absurdity, by the careful relating of rules to the actual environment, not to imaginary circumstances derived either from tradition or from a fanciful image of reality; and by representatives who are properly chosen. Men do not come to such determinations easily or quickly, and they do not come to them as inferences or tangentials in the settlement of disputes. But they ought to come to them often.

It has to be said, also, that such determinations are not satisfactorily formulated in the processes of legislation. Legislation has to do mostly with what seems best to be done in some exigency; what emerges is practically always a compromise among conflicting regional, group, or economic interests. Very often it has more to do with some such irrelevant consideration as a legislator's political fortunes than with a solution for the difficulty. Moreover, the legislative process permits bargaining. Most important measures, by the time they are approved, have been amended many times, and such changes are concessions calculated either to gain adherents or to conciliate affected interests. Then, too, amendment is a lobbyist's favorite way of softening undesirable provisions. When a law emerges from this process it is a badly battered survival of the original intention. Its proposers have had to take what they could get. It may serve tolerably or it may not. But it is something less than a solution for the problem it was meant to solve.

The differentiation of constitutional formation from the process of legislation, of adjudication, or of rulemaking is so marked that persistent confusion among them seems unaccountable. The generally repeated saying that politics is the art of compromise is true enough of legislation; and because it is, the gradual formation by accretion of a constitutional structure by legislative acts can result in nothing but a monstrosity without relation to the great purposes of a people.

What is meant here is illustrated by the gradual building up of this nation's regulatory system by legislation and administrative rulemaking without constitutional guidance. It turns out to be less a system than a series of discrete measures provided to direct the behavior of recalcitrant industries. As regulatory agencies were set up, one after another, because of obvious necessity, they were fought for and against, not only during a legislative history that may have lasted through several sessions but also prior to that in long agitations for reform. Inevitably there was resistance from the industry involved and pressure from others who may have been tangentially affected.

Any one of these agencies might serve as an example. But we are far enough now from the events preceding the Federal Reserve Act to appraise at their ludicrous worth the bankers' propaganda as well as the reformers' claims during the first year of Wilson's administration when the whole country was agitated over his proposal for a decentralized system. The bankers maintained that it was a close approach to communism. Its proponents claimed for it the bridling of the "money power." The exchanges during the House and Senate hearings were emotional and heated. Hundreds of amendments were offered, and many were accepted at various stages. This was in 1913–14. The system, as we know, made the banks more profitable than ever. And as for the reformers' claims, the new system did not prevent the depression of 1929 and after; and it did not prevent the failure or near-failure of most of the banks. There had to be much more drastic reforms, again viewed with alarm by financiers. Even these, during the Roosevelt administration, were subjected to the familiar pulling and hauling and, when passed, still were not satisfactory.

How different all this is from the establishment of constitutional rule! Banking is an industry to be regulated. So are many others: insurance, transportation, and communication facilities are obvious; but less obvious ones affecting health, safety, or welfare have to be regulated too, each in a different way. Since there is no standard, the rules imposed undergo the ordeal described for all legislation. They emerge suited to their purpose only as well as is permitted by the bargaining power of the resisting industry as opposed to the drive of proponents. Pharmaceuticals, automobiles, food processing, moneylending—these have recently been so offensive as to come into regulative question. Some have escaped regulation entirely; some have avoided serious interference; none of the devices has emerged as it was proposed. What is lacking is a constitutional rule that industries must serve the public equally and honestly.

Perhaps constitutional construction is not included in what is usually meant by politics, although it would seem to belong there. In any case compromise is not appropriate to its nature, and enormous damage can be done by assuming that it is. A constitution, far from being a conglomeration of compromises, ought to be a compendium of integrated conceptions solidly set in national purpose. It should establish a general rule for every industry and for every citizen.

We have seen how easy it is to show that hurtful consequences of the Convention in 1787 came from its compromises. Whenever there was consideration of desirable agencies, apart from frightened wariness lest local or individual interests be adversely affected, the result, in the sense of proving to be useful for a long time, was admirable. Such an agency was the presidency, and such another was the judiciary. The framers could not guarantee that some future president would not exceed his powers, or that the Supreme Court would not find it easier to legislate than to adjudicate. No arrangement is perversion-proof. The temptation to reach and grab is strongest when circumstances change and there is no revision of the constitutional guide. What began with Washington's resistance to French revolutionary penetration resulted finally in his appropriation of the power to control foreign policy. All this happened as the result of fairly simple language allowing the president to make treaties and nominate officers of the foreign service (with senatorial advice and consent). So it is true that neither the presidency nor the Court went on being what was contemplated by the framers. But there was a reason for this other than that they were conceived in compromise and fitted to the desires of the most self-seeking delegates.

The most justifiable complaint about the presidency is that there has never been any reconsideration comparable with the original colloquies; and the same observation is true of the Court's position in the whole composition of government. Judicial supremacy grew out of a hardly argued agreement that there must be interpretation when differences arose. It was assumed, obviously, that these differences would be narrow, not that they would involve the adaptation of the Constitution to such altered circumstances as resulted from conquering a continent and undergoing an industrial revolution. It was foreseen that there would be future changes; but there also should have been provision for other constitutional conventions.

On the whole the president and the Supreme Court were inevitable and wonderfully ingenious institutions. They were arrived at by consideration; and if there had been a reconstitutionalization every twenty years, say, their admirable qualities would have been preserved, but a resurveying would have given them renewed usefulness.

In contrast, there were the devices arrived at by bargaining among delegates who did not realize, or who refused to recognize, why they were meeting. There was never much agreement on the terms of union. What was finally done about this emerged from controversy rather than dialogue; the delegates dickered rather than sought a solution. And naturally no one was satisfied.

The discussion about this federal arrangement took up some two-thirds of the summer, and out of it emerged the Congress with its list of permissive powers; and, as well, the federal system that provoked the endless struggle over the division of powers.

It is usually argued that if agreement had not been reached by the middle of July, after weeks of wrangling, the Convention would have broken up. It may be so. On the other hand, if Washington had thundered a little at the states' righters, they might just possibly have yielded. We shall never know. What we do know is the high price paid for that one compromise. And we can conclude that the price would always be high. Perhaps even Washington's intervention would not have persuaded delegates bound by instructions. If nothing could persuade them, it might have been better for the delegates to have dispersed and for another meeting to have taken place after further pressure from circumstances.

What is certain is that constitutions and constitutional law are unique. A constitution cannot properly be created by *representatives,* as the word is usually meant, because representatives at worst are under instruction and at best are tied to those they represent. They are thus unable to undertake dialogue whose purpose is to discover the wisest instruments for men's purposes. Only a body chosen for this sole duty and purged of other interests can be trusted to create a supreme law. The members of this body are representatives, too, but in a quite different sense, since they will owe their duty to the whole body politic, not to any part of it. They would effect an escape from the additive theory and would embrace the holistic one made inevitable by the technical advances of civilization.

The Argument for Periodic Revision

From the time Jefferson was commissioned to draft the Declaration, and the rights were named that men were entitled to simply because they were men, there was no question about the recognition of such rights. They were considered to have been created when men were created; they were an endowment. But sentences in the Declaration, just following, concerning government have sometimes seemed best forgotten; for they said that when any government became destructive of these ends, the people had another overriding right—they might abolish the government and institute a new one:

That, to secure these rights, governments are instituted among men, deriving their just powers from the consent of the governed; that, whenever any form of government becomes destructive of these ends, it is the right of the people to alter or to abolish it, and to institute a new government. . . .

The constitutionmakers originally paid little enough attention to natural rights; but the one, of all others, that was most strikingly ignored was this last. They did perhaps assume, as is often said in defense, that they had found the formula for securing the blessings of liberty for posterity. But this does not appear from the record. A reasonable interpretation is that the amending clause was an afterthought. They were tired; the heat was wearing; after four months their own affairs needed attention. They did not pay attention, as they should, to the fact that, short of violence, such conclaves as their own were the only means for establishing new governments. And it did not occur to them that a renewed and revised government is actually a new one. It need not be achieved by violence if reason is institutionalized.

It seems not to have occurred to those who adopted the Bill of Rights, either, that the value of the ones they designated might be changed by circumstances—that they were best thought of not as inherent and immutable but, like most else, relative. We see now that freedom of speech was one thing in the Philadelphia of their day and quite another, as Justice Holmes remarked many years later, for an individual who might be moved to shout "fire" in a crowded theater. It was one thing too in a political discussion and another when national security might be involved. And the associated right of the press to be free had to be strained so that protection could be extended to the uses of media undreamed of in 1787. Radio and television were beyond the imagination even of a Franklin.[17]

Because constitutional revision not only was not made easy but, on the contrary, was made extraordinarily difficult, such stretching and adapting had to be done or, at least, has been done, by trial and error, with the

17. An honest effort on both sides to agree about the disclosure of information by newsmen in crises affecting national security has always left both dissatisfied. A particularly serious attempt during the Kennedy presidency is recounted by Pierre Salinger in *With Kennedy* (Garden City, N.Y.: Doubleday & Company, 1966). Newsmen stood on the First Amendment. Nothing in the Constitution said they had a duty to consider national security, and they were not disposed to accept presidential rules modifying the flat permissiveness of the amendment.

As in so much else, rights were conferred but duties were not mentioned. Kennedy was disposed to remind them that duties were an obligation even if not mentioned in the Constitution, and that they had become more so under nuclear pressure.

Court, when it got around to it, finally determining limits and making definitions.

This is more important than it is usually represented to be by eager defenders of "evolution." For the agreements of a dedicated and instructed conclave, it substitutes conclusions reached—perhaps incidentally—by those not chosen for such a purpose, who, because of this, tread warily among the "political thickets" of their own years. This has gone on so long that what exists now is a huge compendium of mostly narrow and evasive rulings by the Court and a mass of makeshift rules waiting for decision in adversary proceedings. These are properly called pseudoconstitutional, and they have all the deficiencies of such agreements. They are impermanent, since they are subject to challenge; and they do not originate in the public mind or have the authority of the sovereign.

The Court is not to be blamed for this; it is only the arbiter in such cases as come before it. Other constitutionmakers in our society are always busily at work. It goes without saying that they are quite unfitted, for one or another reason, for such determinations. This unfitness is well enough recognized. It gives matters needing constitutional rule an uncertainty that there is no good reason for being allowed to continue.[18]

The need for revision is so frequent and so pressing that many ways have had to be found for evading the literal governance of the old clauses. Judicial supremacy is one, but there are others. The areas of silence, for instance, are filled with seizures, and these go on existing until challenged. The economic system is an example of unforeseen activity that has an improvised governance continually in controversy.

This category of the unforeseen is as large as space and time, and materializations within it are numerous. To name a few, there is poverty, something government was not responsible for in the eighteenth century; there is the conservation of irreplaceable resources, a matter of little former interest; there is education, something of concern to eighteenth-century parents but certainly no responsibility of the nation; and there are many

18. For instance, freedom of the press is to a much greater extent determined by initiatives of news purveyors than by the Courts. Newspapers and other media occupy more advanced positions all the time and only occasionally are checked in a suit brought by an outraged victim. The Sheppard case is an illustration of this. The newspapers found the murder trial a convenient sensation and badgered judge and jury into a conviction. Sheppard spent years in jail before his case was taken to the Supreme Court. Then it was determined that his right to a fair trial had been jeopardized by the newspapers' interpretation of their right to freedom. (*Sheppard* v. *Maxwell,* 384 U.S. 333 [1966].)

In all the years since the Constitution was written there had been no clarifying amendments of either the First or the Sixth Amendment. It was suddenly realized that the Sixth, for instance, says nothing about a 'fair" trial, only about a "speedy and public" one. There was general agreement that trials ought to be fair, but there was no constitutional foundation for saying that they must be. If the agreement was general, as it did seem to be, why should there not be an amendment saying so and delegating to the Court the duty of definition?

others, such as planning for the future in a world whose most noticeable characteristic is continual change.

None of these has any constitutional rule. But even more curious, neither has the whole realm of politics. This omission of the framers is the strangest of all. It is owed, of course, to their distrust of democracy. They spoke often of equality, but that was more an echo of revolutionary enthusiasm than a principle to be applied in making a government. They meant the better people—like themselves—to be established in power. As for posterity, it would be produced by the potency of the first families. This, to say the least, was a curious interpretation of the word.

The framers do really have to be faulted for narrowness, for lack of foresight, and for restricting power to a propertied elite. The reservation about this is that all questions having to do with the future and its uncertainties were made the responsibility of legislatures when the initiation of amendment was delegated to the Congress and to the houses of the states. This was only one manifestation of a prevailing respect for legislatures. There was another concession: responsibility conferred on legislatures pleased delegates from the smaller states; and it was not too dangerous with the several prohibitions against state action, and as long as the electorate was restricted.

The arrangement adopted, it will be recalled, was that the Congress might initiate amendment (by a two-thirds majority of both houses); or, on application of the "legislatures of two-thirds of the several states," must call a convention "for proposing amendments." These would then have to be ratified by legislatures or conventions in three-fourths of the states. This last choice was to be made by the Congress.

Whether the framers foresaw that the second procedure was unrealistic we do not know, but the fact is that it has never been used. They ought at least to have seen that the Congress they were creating would be unlikely to initiate any change certain to affect itself. This reluctance to accept any reform has gradually hardened into systematic protectiveness. Criticism of legislative procedures has been continuous, and legislators have become the butt of innumerable sardonic observations; yet every thrust still is ignored, and ridicule is suffered without reaction. The Congress has been quick to authorize examination of the executive branch and has agreed to a dozen reorganization plans, but no serious examination of itself from outside has ever been allowed. It is apparent by now that none can be counted on except in a general reexamination of the whole Constitution.

It may be guessed that such an occasion will arise from general disillusionment; very likely it will have followed after a long period of criticism and agitation, and will be authorized not by the first but by the second—never yet used—procedure. But the preliminaries will be earthshaking, and the cries of the fearful will be pitiable.

Not the identification of specific changes to come, but recognition that changes are inevitable, is the justification for occasional revision. There is the further justification that legitimacy is to be found only in this way. Moreover, revision is the transfusion that maintains a constitution's vigor. Lacking this, it becomes anemic and eventually lifeless; its relation to society becomes one of tradition only, and thus mostly historical. Undoubtedly it is important that an honored document should be available for exhibit; it is tragic if the existence of that document prevents, or helps to prevent, the continuous reexamination that justified its prestige. Since the Constitution is the central source of legitimacy, its relevancy ought to be guarded with appropriate care.

It is not too much to say that the amendment provisions of the original Constitution, since they made substantive change so difficult, are responsible for its obsolescence and so for extraconstitutional developments that have no anchoring in the bedrock of national sense. This might not have been so serious if compromise had not already resulted in a Senate that was a house of ambassadors from the states instead of being one devoted to national, rather than state, interests. Upper houses in other governments had always had that function, but when our Senate was created the nation was left without any agency in the central complex whose duty was to the whole and not to a part—a state or a district—with the exception being the president. And he had no stated duty to suggest amendment; in fact, he was allowed no part in the amending process.

Of course, prior even to this, the delegates had unanimously decided on a lower house made up of representatives from districts. They were not, and are not, expected to give the nation priority. Their home precincts are their first care. And their last care would be—and has been—the reformation of the Constitution's provisions.

It is not too much to say that the first concern of an enlightened citizenry ought to be the health of its constitution, and that this can best be maintained by periodic reexamination. In a society as mobile and complex as ours, the Constitution ought never to be more than one generation old. A way to ensure that this might be one provision in a first rewriting—to be copied in others with, if necessary, variations in the intervals—is for a permanent constitutional study commission, to be enlarged as the time approaches for adoption. Then the Constitution would never be older than those who were active in its creation.

This would not eliminate the need for judicial interpretation. It would, however, give the courts live directives without meanings wrung from them that were never intended by the framers. Best of all, the courts would no longer need to legislate as has become a modern habit. This is not an easy prescription for new framers. For one thing, it involves a nice determination of the line between permissiveness and limitation. Too much of the one would allow degeneration into legislative procedures; too much of the other would prevent reasonable interpretation. This is, however, so important in the nation's life that a constant search for relevant renewal ought to be institutionalized.

Along with a continuing commission for the purpose, with stated periods for consideration of its proposals, a general dialogue about great principles to be embodied in the Constitution ought to be maintained through political processes. A people governed by a constitution ought to understand it and ought to be its main support. Even the Ten Commandments could benefit from revision, and constitutions serve somewhat the same purpose. But they are honored only if they command respect, and respect is rooted in relevance.

CHAPTER 2

CRITERIA FURTHER CONSIDERED

Necessary Negotiation

The point has been made that too often political processes are assumed to have common or, at least, similar standards, rules, and even procedures, and that this assumption is responsible for regarding compromises as inevitable resorts for the revising of constitutions. Constitutions are equated with party platforms, legislative acts, and pronouncements of the Court. It is here suggested that this similarity does not actually exist. Political life is more various than this would imply. And particularly, there is a contrast of first importance among the several activities involved in creating and operating governmental institutions.

There is, first of all, constitutionmaking; then the election of representatives and the appointment of officials; then legislation, followed by administration; and finally, adjudication when interpretation is needed. Each has its own nature and its appropriate procedures, but to describe all in the same terms is to make certain that none will be understood for what it is. Also, the ways of creating and administering each are quite different.

The compromises so lightly spoken of as characteristic of politics describe more accurately the procedures of legislation. Laws are put together in bargaining sessions where adversaries each give something to end their quarrels, and what emerges is a tolerable directive to later administrators. But if it does not serve well it may be changed at any time. Laws are often amended after some experience in application. This takes the curse off whatever compromise has been made.

The Court's opinions correct legislation. The justices say, after due consideration, that laws are or are not in accord with the Constitution as they see it. There is not always initial agreement, but there is room for persuasion. When a justice finds that impossible he may dissent, but the opinion of the majority constitutes decisional law. For the moment that defines the Constitution's meaning.

Administrative law extends legislative acts, filling in the rules of practice. They too are subject to correction by a court or by the legislature. There may be important compromises under pressure from regulated interests, and there may be others for the sake of practicality. In fact there must always be this flexibility. It is necessary to the operations of a regulating agency, and it does offer the possibility of modifying inept legislation.

The categories mentioned here are not always sharply defined. Judges and administrators sometimes legislate, legislatures are tempted to invade the executive, and so on. These tend to become habit, so that separation is a principle not always followed in practice. Disputed ground is often fought over as power is reached for, and there is no final victory for any operating agency of government. The only definite sources of reference are to be found in the Constitution. True, that charter may allow for, may even arrange for, a certain flexibility in the distribution of duties. But a constitution that has been made in full recognition of what constitutionality *is* will mark the limits of such struggles. It will say how choosing must take place, how laws shall be made, set the standards for administration, and mark out the limits of judicial interpretation. It will, as far as possible, reduce the occasions for conflict between the branches; and its silences will not be such that they can be filled out by any suddenly aggressive branch.

These were faults, chargeable to inexperience, of the original Constitution—the areas of contest, and the ambiguities—but they would not have had serious consequences if provision had been made for corrective revision when experience had shown what ought to be done. It very soon became apparent that the branches as they were first outlined were not entirely suited to their assigned functions; moreover, there were others the framers had not thought of. When the next generation took over it shaped institutions to suit itself, but since this was done outside the Constitution there was no proper guidance. Subsequent amendment has not notably narrowed borders or filled in silences.

If there is no constitution to order and dominate governmental processes, they will be in constant confusion, and often in conflict; duties and powers will have no certain limit; no individual will know what he may and may not do; and no organization, public or private, will have a secure place in the social scheme. Or, if the constitution has been made by those who have not recognized the nature of the task and the norms it must establish, storms of controversy will soon begin to center on the resulting document; compromises will begin to show their weighted tendencies; and, in the end, civil strife will have to accomplish what the constitutionmakers or later revisionists ought to have done.

These generalizations, it is contended, are amply substantiated by the history of American institutions. Compromise crept in and left issues to be settled by further compromise. That is what "living" means. It can be concluded that bargaining will always be injurious to constitutions, just as it was to that of 1787. These guiding charters have to rest on national sense, reached after prolonged consideration but formulated finally as an act of gathered and accepted wisdom by those appointed for the duty. This is as true of amendment as it is of origination—indeed, there is, or should be, no difference.

Obviously there is more to be said about this. The sense of generality spoken of here does not imply unanimity or even acceptance by all those who will be affected. There will always be those who are disappointed because their interests, as they believe, are not properly recognized; and they will be subject to a discipline they resent; but it will be a discipline incident to integrated institutions and must, because of this, be best for the most. Individualism of the rugged sort is an inevitable victim of growth and expansion. But what is not rugged, but creative, need not be sacrificed. It may indeed be made more secure in a society whose aggressors are kept in check and whose citizens are encouraged to be creative.

Constitutionmakers in a proper process are representatives entrusted with a supreme purpose. Since they have their credentials from the whole —not any separate part—of the nation, they are charged with a duty so different from that of any other political body that no similarity can be used as a standard to gauge their usefulness.

Brought together in conclave, with terms of reference emphasizing integration and wholeness, as well as the familiar defenses of equality, justice, and security, their indicated purpose is not to damp down sharply differing opinions but to reach agreements that satisfy the conditions of continuing existence for the nation and its people, including an existence that is satisfactory.

A good deal of ground has been covered here without acknowledging that compromise is a word with several meanings. One of these at least may be ruled out. When an individual's integrity is questioned it is said to be compromised. The same is true of principle; when it is compromised it has fallen into disrepute.

Quite another meaning is employed here. This is the process of coming to a conclusion after argument. It is important to distinguish between giving way or prevailing in a dialogue because of persuasion, and yielding the substance of an interest intensely believed in. The first is not actually compromise, although it is sometimes called that. It might better be called conversion, acknowledgment, acceptance, or some other term to describe what happens when an individual listens, studies, considers, and concludes that he was wrong and that another was right.

Compromise that holds the seeds of trouble emerges from quite a different situation. It happens when an individual, not persuaded at all, and believing compromise in such an instance to be a mistake, nevertheless gives way. It may have been done in the interest of peace—to lessen controversy—or it may have been done to gain an end considered to be more important than the sacrifice and not attainable otherwise. Or, again, it may result from such other pressures as threats of withdrawal and consequent disunion, from sheer tiredness, from a basic indifference, from uncertainty, or even from modesty.

Thinking of this term in connection with the work of the framers, it can be seen how difficult it would have been to establish the central government exactly as advocated by the nationalists, and to have done it in one uncomfortable Philadelphia summer. Some states' righters did withdraw, and enough more might well have withdrawn to have made any conclusion likely to have been ratified quite impossible. The delegates were under instruction and were closely watched by the politicians back home. As it was, those who did leave—for instance, Yates and Lansing of New York—and others who had been more or less active in the discussions and then refused to sign made an embarrassing situation. Mason, Gerry, and Randolph, for instance, could not be convinced, although they had taken part in the discussions. They very nearly prevented adoption.

The thirty-nine of the fifty-five original delegates who did sign were entitled to say that they had reached the only conclusion possible in the circumstances. These circumstances, if listed, would include the hard position of the states' righters, who, even if persuaded, could not have agreed to more centralization and would have had to defect as others had done. Even if some delegate gifted with foresight had said to the company that a civil war would result from the ambivalence inherent in the federalism of the Constitution, and even if he had been believed, a stronger government could hardly have gained approval; and, if approved, certainly could not have been ratified. This is the accepted interpretation that excuses compromise.

A particular pattern of federalism was thus projected into history to be fought over for the best part of two centuries. It is usual to praise the delegates for agreeing on it, the reason for the praise being that it survived. That it has been a recurrent source of irritated contention, rising to one climax of conflict after another, is suppressed in most appraisals.

A contrast, referred to earlier, is relevant here and may be worth repeating. It shows how different are the results of taking the sense of a meeting and of forcing agreement by those who are not convinced. It has been noted that the presidency was arrived at in this way. After long consideration it was concluded that it had better not owe its powers to election by the legislature. Discussion about this national symbol went on intermittently almost until adjournment, and it was a cool and reasonable exchange. There was an early proposal for an executive council of three, coming from Randolph and approved by Madison; Gerry thought this would be like "a general with three heads," and, almost at once, a single head was agreed on—not, it will be noticed, because a conclusion was all-important and dissenters gave way, but because everyone had become convinced that it would be best.

There followed debate in various later sessions about the manner of choosing the president: should he be chosen by the Congress or by some special electoral body? It was generally felt that there were good reasons for keeping him independent from any other branch of government; but everyone was afraid of direct popular election, and several schemes were proposed for indirect choice. These finally resulted in the electoral college device.

In the course of these discussions there were several different proposals; there was a real interchange; everyone listened when others spoke; the result was agreement, not compromise. This is in complete contrast with the contention that produced federalism and failed to define its limits.

The electoral college was created in another way. It resulted from fear of democracy, not from trust in it; but since, in later years, democracy developed rather than declined, the college was adapted to the change until it approached peaceful abolition.

These are not perfect illustrations of compromise on the one hand and consensus on the other, but they illustrate well enough the preferred process in constitutionmaking. There was for federalism a confrontation and a bargain that both sides were unhappily bound by from then on. For the presidency and the college dialogues resulted in the most reasonable of the proposed solutions. It can at least be inferred that compromise leaves the bargainers unconvinced, having given way only because of pressure, and that devices or rules agreed to by the use of invention, consideration, and acceptance leave no such bitterness to be resolved in the future. If, someday, change is seen to be needed, no emotional confrontations will take place.

Except for angered politicians, in and out of the Congress, there have never been serious suggestions that the presidency was a mistake; and such dissensions as there have been went not to the institution but to the uses made of it by incumbents. The directives for these might, indeed, have been revised in a new constitutional convention. But this is not to advocate abolition such as may be in the future for federalism.

The point has already been labored; but it may be recalled that even the belligerent Elbridge Gerry, when the federalism struggle had gone on for weeks, complained that instead of coming to Philadelphia as "a band of brothers . . . we seem to have brought with us the spirit of political negotiators." In the matter of the presidency, however, even though it took sixty ballots to decide on the manner of his selection, there was no "spirit of negotiation," political or otherwise. There was an honest attempt to find the right solution.

In Another Convention

It is not the survival of institutions or customs that ought to impress future constitutionmakers, persuading them that change would be mistaken. True, the lodgment in tradition of received rights, duties, rules, relations, limits of activity—all this sort of thing—does indicate something of a general will; but hardly any even of these are definable for circumstances likely to arise more than two decades in the future.

It is fine to recognize the independence and initiative that lead to progress; it is equally fine to keep open the way to mutual understanding and neighborliness. But which of these has quite the meaning it once had? Eighteenth-century man could be independent in many ways that would be intolerable in the urban environment of the late twentieth century. This does not mean that the deep impulse to become a self-governing adult needs to be, or ought to be, stifled. It does mean, however, that behavior has to be limited and channeled.

If hunting and fishing are regulated, if the use of property is restricted, and if a public interest is asserted in the bargains of everyday life, there are also enlarged and more varied opportunities in a more sophisticated environment. Independence, interpreted literally, is not indispensable to creativity. Men nowadays make use of predecessors' discoveries, each contributing what he can of talent or inventiveness; they seldom work alone.

Social behavior is circumscribed in many ways; yet the freedoms of the Bill of Rights have never been formally redefined; and their reinterpretation has been so casual and incidental that they no longer have the generally understood meaning they once had. This has been referred to in other connections, but it does have a recurrent importance.

The First Amendment, for instance, forbids the Congress to abridge "the right of the people peaceably to assemble." After all these years does this mean what it seems to mean? The Supreme Court's justices were recently very sharp with one another because of a difference about this. Five of them, Justice Black speaking, said that the state "has power to preserve the property under its control for the use to which it is lawfully dedicated." He was denying that "people who want to propagandize have a constitutional right to do so whenever and wherever they please." This, said Justice Douglas, dissenting, sets into the record "a great and wonderful police-state doctrine."

At about the same time the Court refused to review a Maryland court's decision denying public funds to educational institutions with a religious cast. The funds in question, however, were appropriated by the state; did the same ruling apply to federal grants? The question of church-state relations raised here refers again to two lines in the First Amendment. They were ambiguous; they have never been made clearer by amendment; and no one knows what they may be held to mean when next a case is considered. One United States senator (Ervin of North Carolina) was plaintive about this. Federal grants had been going to church schools under a 1965 Aid to Education Act. Were they unconstitutional? "I thought sure they'd set the matter at rest," the senator said. "This leaves the Congress in Constitutional darkness." Some day, perhaps, when a case is properly brought and the justices choose to entertain it, they may make a clear decision. Meanwhile the senator has a justified complaint that might be generalized to include ambiguity about other rights and prohibitions.

An individual might well be forgiven for concluding that there are only things that he may *not* do in the bewildering tangle of rules and regulations. His situation generates a natural resentment. He feels helpless. His participation in decisions is remote. Dictates about what he may and may not do issue from mysterious bureaucratic offices whose denizens seem indifferent or hostile. He knows there are rights defined in his Constitution that ought to support his instinct to survive as an individual; but what has become of them? The limitations hedging him in are supposed to be in conformance with constitutional definitions; but who says so to him, personally? All he knows is that if he tries to exercise his rights as he understands them, he is likely to find himself in some sort of trouble.

When his situation is made worse by this suspicion, he may not lose his instinct for independence, but there is apt to develop about it a chronic resentment that approaches rejection. He feels that the regulations governing his activities are capricious or even partial, and regaining his freedom is a more and more remote possibility because of continued rulemaking that he has no part in. A Constitution was drawn up a long time ago, and important people have learned how to evade or to interpret it in their own interest. For him its clauses are understood to be something different from what they seem to say. They have been worked on.

Have the wise and trustworthy men of his own generation ever met to consider his situation? They have not. His situation results from a fuddled scramble among applicants to the courts for favorable interpretation, or among bargainers who assume advantages until in time they become customary. Even then there is uncertainty, since whatever has been traded away is what at the moment could be sacrificed by whoever let it go without too much hurt to himself—not a stable agreement.

This is the way freedoms are too often limited in legislative processes and in administrative rulemaking. Since the Court is apt to recognize accepted custom, definitions often rest on "practical considerations," and practicality is always temporary.

Constitutionmaking is in almost complete contrast with this when it is undertaken separately and on its own account in forthright fashion. Legislative, administrative, or judicial additions to the Constitution, being the product of bargaining or arrangement among those with some interest to protect, do not satisfy the surviving instinct in men to be free and to have equal justice—to have those rights said by the Declaration to be theirs because they were endowed with them by their Creator. Life, liberty, and the pursuit of happiness! Fine words: but what, nowadays, do they mean?

It is not their mere survival that is essential; it is their respectful use in modern circumstances.

So it is principles that ought to prevail; and a constitution should be a compendium of them recently worked over. How is it that compromise is agreed to be a political inevitability, and yet that the framers are mostly praised because they were men of principle? Is it because they were men of different principle? No, we must remind ourselves again that their terms of reference were to provide for "a more perfect union." It is because fear and suspicion did often lead to bargaining; it is because some were anxious to shift the costs to others; it is because some belonged to cliques whose purpose was the circumvention of union in whatever degree it threatened themselves and their supporters at home that we inherit confusion.

Looking further, it may be suggested that many were (1) lawyers and (2) legislators, and that both occupations require dealings.[1] They saw no difference, it seems, between getting the best bargain possible for a client, getting the best law possible in a legislature, and getting consent to the provisions of a constitution.

It would have been different if they had followed more closely the procedures used by judges in multijudge courts. For in their customary dialogues these jurists may not end by agreeing with their colleagues, but the majority is allowed to prevail.

The Supreme Court set up (by the Judiciary Act of 1789) as part of the new government began operating at once in just this way. Each member considered each cause. Pleadings brought into consideration all available facts, precedents, and considerations of consequence. Dialogue followed with all this material available. Those who were moved to do so, or those who were appointed to put into words what dialogue had shown to be agreed, formulated a conclusion. That is how it was still done nearly two centuries later.

This begins to suggest a way of making a constitution—with certain differences. The causes to be considered are not the same—not by any means—and framers are not, and ought not to be, eminent only in the law. The causes, in fact, are indicated by the circumstances of civilization;

---

1. Of the fifty-five, thirty-four were lawyers, and six were judges of various jurisdictions.

they are thus broader and more difficult than most cases considered by the courts. And the framers ought to be found among the wise persons of their generation with the instinct for justice, with a bent for the appropriate devices of existence, and with a knowledge of governmental possibilities.

Such a convention, however chosen (a problem not here considered), with proper terms of reference, and with majority rule, constituted anew in each generation, producing consecutive versions of a constitution, might furnish a secure and integrated foundation for social life that would compel the support of all reasonable people. There would be confidence in its wisdom. Not everyone would agree that the clauses as written were perfect, but everyone must agree that due consideration had produced them and that they had indisputable legitimacy. It is this confidence that is lacking in present-day procedures. Moreover, it is an extremely serious matter that the Constitution is remade only when a case falls into the purview of the justices. They do not say, "The Constitution ought to be changed." They say, when they have to decide, *what it means*. They are always a court, never a convention. In a sense, the Court is an extension of the legislature, since it is bound to the legislature's acts and since these are suffused with compromise. But its procedures are dialectical and so do offer a pattern of reasoned agreement.

What might happen at a future convention, it may be guessed, would be in some ways similar to what happened at the one in 1787. That is to say, principles originating in historic sources would be in the delegates' minds. Hopefully, however, there would be differences. There would be, shall we say, more Madisons and Wilsons and fewer Ellsworths, Lansings, or Patersons. Another Washington may be too much to hope for; but it would certainly be possible to find men of detachment, learning, and patriotic passion who would devote themselves to civilized dialogue and, after due consideration, come to agreement. Suggestions for a more effective government would be settled on; the making of policy would be provided for, and men's rights and duties would be redefined.

The rights and duties would be different, but not of another order—that is to say, they would belong to the same constellation as those of an earlier day. Recall that those earlier ones centered in men's desire for independence, liberty, security, and—with an understood license for contrivance for carrying on trade—free enterprise. As things have developed, independence has merged into interdependence, freedom is being modified to emphasize the demand of others for equal and concurrent freedom, contrivance is becoming more sophisticated after generations of adding one invention to another until a system has resulted, and free enterprise is now contained and limited in the public interest, or, if it is not, there is a growing realization that it must be.

There is ample reason for reconstituting the rules for living together.

The tasks of government are not the same, relations among men are not so irresponsible, and their activities are carried out in organizations. Since government now must perform a hundred duties men did for themselves when the Constitution was written, it must be shored up to carry that burden as well as others. Since the common way of life has become urban, freedom to speak, to assemble, to move, and to trade can be assured only if there are limitations. In order to ensure liberty, restraints must be imposed on those who would deny it to others. Since a condition of decent existence has become a high level of education, health, and assured income not dreamed of formerly, these new conceptions must be of a kind to assure the rights and privileges appropriate to the life of our time.

It is not necessary to tell those in authority now that they may never quarter soldiers in any house without the consent of the owner, or that because a militia is necessary to the security of a free people, the right to bear arms shall not be infringed; and twenty dollars is hardly a realistic minimum to mark the dividing line for trials by jury. There is much unnecessary confusion because each state must "give full faith and credit to the public acts, records, and judicial proceedings of every other state." These are simple anachronisms, but they ought to help us see that the charter we live under is, in many of its provisions, an uncertain guide.

On the other hand, the rights to be treated equally and to have equal justice, if we still value them, might be defined in modern terms; the rights of children and of the aged regarding care they cannot provide for themselves might be made more specific; and the rights of workers, competitors, and consumers caught in the system of large-scale industry might be defined more realistically.

All this is not because men have changed or because their desires have changed, but precisely because they have not changed, and their Constitution no longer gives them adequate protection. Besides, their desires have become attainable—or many of them have—whereas once they were not.

There is one thing, however, that is very much changed. In order to achieve the old original purposes it is no longer sufficient merely to extend the list of prohibitions—to say what people may not do to each other or what restraints government must observe. It is necessary to be positive rather than negative. It is not enough to say that a man's house shall be inviolable; he must be assured that he will have a house. It is not enough to assume that businesses may be carried on without interference; it must be insisted that they have a social function and are not to be operated for profit alone; the continuance of a pluralistic economy must, indeed, be conditioned by a willingness to accept direction. Borrowing money, coinage, the promotion of useful arts, the maintenance of security forces—these and many other duties of government are so changed in nature that the provisions of the original Constitution are no longer much more respected than the prohibition against the quartering of soldiers in private homes.

Setting type by hand, harvesting grain with scythes, hunting for food, and traveling by horse-drawn coach—all these belong to the years of constitutionmaking. A government shaped in that environment and remaining unchanged would be helpless in our age; and, of course, ours has been adapted in many ways to the new demands upon it, even though most of the adaptations have been outside the constitutional process. The document itself is rapidly coming to resemble the scythe, the spinning wheel, the steam locomotive, and the wood-fired kitchen stove. The kitchen stove was meant to prepare food; food still has to be prepared, but not by burning wood. The original document of the Constitution, now in a preservative gas, is regarded wonderingly by millions of Washington visitors. It properly belongs under glass in the archives building to display the courage and wisdom of the framers. But it does not belong in the halls of justice to be strained and tortured to fit the problems of a changed civilization.

Those who maintain that the Constitution—being the product of timeless wisdom, and being based on natural principles—needs no reconsideration would not consider it subversive to make technical advances in communication, transportation, and the provision of daily necessities. Only the Constitution must be protected from those who would make it contemporary.

There is really no more reason for describing rights, natural though they may be, in Gouverneur Morris's phrases, than there is for identifying a modern locomotive in terms describing the puffing steamer of the 1870s on the B & O. Neither is suited to present needs, even though the purposes are the same. The old steamer has disappeared, but the old Constitution still exists; moreover, it has become more and more sacred. Every year it seems more outrageous to suggest that it needs to be reconsidered in any part, much less as a whole.

This leads to suggesting that there is one overriding criterion not yet mentioned. This is the duty of framers to achieve consonance with their environment. The governing charter of a nation is at best a small cluster of rules and institutions; nevertheless it ought to reflect the responsible involvement of man with the world he lives in. Nature may seem for a time to be passive and permissive, but we know well enough that it is not so. We have come a long way by harnessing her forces and exploiting her resources. But it has been done too often in ways that will exact penalties. As her forces have been uncovered and put to use, warnings of danger have been ignored. Consider, for instance, the danger of resource exhaustion. Many resources are irreplaceable, and they are often used prodigally; many others are replaceable but only in a costly and protracted process. So we use precious metals and fuels, destroy forests, and allow the soil to erode.

Much of this is chargeable to our preference for pluralism again; one person or organization does the exploiting; the repair of damage is left to the community. Then there are the by-products of progress—pollution of air and water, urban decay, and all the other results of carelessness or simple greed. Some of this, again, is the result of ignorance, but not much anymore. It is easier to forgive the pioneer farmers who cut down the eastern forests to make farmland, or those who broke the plains to the plow, than it is to forgive their present-day counterparts who offend in the same way but with full knowledge of the damage being done. There are rights and duties here not contemplated in the original Constitution. They ought to be acknowledged in a revised one.

Consonance with nature is the most serious lack of our growing charter. Natural rights were in the framers' minds, but not natural duties. The obligation to learn nature's imperatives and to obey them had no recognition. For the putative framers of a new constitution this should be the first of all considerations.

What is currently being taken or wasted from nature's store is variously estimated at from five to ten times what is being restored for future availability. That this cannot go on is hardly arguable, and of course the takers and wasters do not argue. They have to be prevented from going on in the same way. It should be a constitutional as well as a natural imperative.

In considering how much is now known about these matters that was not known in 1787, it becomes very strange indeed that this knowledge has not worked its way into the Constitution. Because it is not there, but is applied only in extraconstitutional regulation, it is always half-hearted and ineffective. Legislators cannot say to lobbyists that what predators want they cannot have because the Constitution will not permit it. So unwittingly, or under pressure, they give way. The public lands are overgrazed; the water tables are lowered; the minerals are used up; the forests are cut —and all the other resources similarly are given away.

This is not all. There are people whose lives are arranged to suit speculators and landlords. The human wastage from this cause is perhaps the most serious of all.

The duty of a new conclave, if there should be one, would be to establish such a consonance with nature that utilization of her resources should not make the earth poorer for those who are to come.

Definitions and Directives

It is often claimed, with obvious pride, that the original structure of our government has survived; but the truth is that almost none of it has survived intact. There is still a federal system, and in the central government there are three main branches with separate and independent powers. These branches are still independent, but we have seen that each of them has been transformed in ways that would have amazed the framers. It is true that the framers would also have been amazed by the transformations in our society and the consequent responsibilities thrust upon government. If they were assembling now for a constitutional convention, they would undoubtedly shape a more appropriate system; they would have to; and even if it preserved some of the characteristics of the one they did shape in 1787, they would be almost unrecognizable.

The sovereignty of the people and its expression through representative institutions would certainly survive. So, probably, would the combination of independence and interdependence among the branches which the framers sought to establish in 1787. This has turned out to be not so resistant to time and aggressive interests as was originally hoped; however, it remains a way of preventing encroachments on the liberties of citizens; and that is an intention we still honor.

It is this separation of powers that our ancestor system—the British—has lacked since the Commons made itself supreme. Hardly any American would like to see the House of Representatives given such a position; that is to say, hardly any would care to give up altogether the separate but interdependent branches. Each has demonstrated its own utility; and even though each, as the result of reaching for powers not mentioned in the Constitution, or ones that are ill defined, has assumed powers beyond its warrant, that does not, in our view, necessitate the abandonment of any.

But what about the first responsibility of the Convention, the perfection of the Union? It will be recalled that this admonition was first among the delegates' instructions. The expiring Continental Congress had withered until the life of the new nation was jeopardized. Its bureaucracy had dwindled to a few clerks, mostly under the direction of a discouraged John Jay, who went on trying to persuade foreign nations that the United States was something more than a name, but who knew that he was not succeeding. He warned that the wolves were gathering to pull down the dying prey, and he made the warning as emphatic as he could.

Everyone knew this was so. A closer union was actually the condition of survival. If the politicians in Massachusetts, New York, and the rest of the states wanted to be left alone to face the world, they had just about achieved it, but actually they did not want the nation to die; they merely wanted to buy their partnership cheaply.[2] They wanted independence and at the same time to have it paid for by others. As Washington, Hamilton, and others—including Jay—had been telling them for years, they were

2. At the height of the controversy preceding the Great Compromise in July, 1787, Madison, replying to Ellsworth of Connecticut, asked if the gentleman had forgotten that his state had declined to pay her share during the war. Had she not *positively refused?* (Madison's italics.) He went on, "Has she paid, for the last two years, any money into the continental treasury? And does this look like government or the observance of a solemn pact?"

risking their own and the nation's existence by trying to please reluctant taxpayers and, at the same time, pretending to be guarding their interests. But when the delegates came to Philadelphia they were well aware that the politicians in the states they had come from had not reformed in this respect. They were still hoping to get the union they talked about at no sacrifice of their own powers and prerogatives, and at cut rates.

As we have seen, there are many clauses in the Constitution whose wording was distorted in this discouraging effort. The hazy commitment to nationalism was compounded by the avoidance of clarity when giving way was unavoidable. Much was left to the shaping of Washington and his associates when the new government should begin to operate. With Washington's immense prestige he could assume the unpleasant task of imposing a discipline the delegates were afraid to define.

It was recognized, tangentially, that there might be a bureaucracy to carry on the government's business, but aside from telling the president that he should "take care that the laws be faithfully executed," there was no provision for specific agencies or for the establishment of any. And the only reference to his duties as chief of state was a subordinate clause saying that he should "receive ambassadors and other public ministers," presumably as the government's representative. When the Convention had finished, the presidency really remained to be created, and sufficient authority for it was not to be found in the document submitted for ratification.

Consequently, Washington's situation, as the first president, was embarrassing. It had been carefully not stated that, in taking care to see that the laws were faithfully executed, he might engage or dismiss subordinates. He could not dispose of them as he liked either, because all the important appointments had to be positively approved by the Senate. These provisions meant that he would have to ask for permission even to organize the executive office. He could receive foreign ambassadors, but since treaties had to have agreement by two-thirds of the senators, he could deal with them only tentatively about mutual problems. If the security of the nation were to be threatened from outside, he could not take action as commander in chief until the Congress had given formal permission and until it had appropriated any funds he might need.

A study of the Constitution might lead to the conclusion that perfecting the Union was not meant to be accomplished by the president. What is known about the debates, however, indicates that in actuality Washington was expected to do what he had not been armed to do; he evidently understood it this way because he proceeded to try. He set up an establishment that can be described only as regal, paying for most of it himself. He dealt with foreign nations threatening the frontiers, and he suppressed internal insurrection. Altogether he created a *chiefship of state*, but he had immense trouble with the limitations. He found that he could not count on the acceptance of his leadership by the Congress; nor could he persuade senators to consider his actions in advance. And when John Jay, the first chief justice of the United States (a locution that Washington felt meant what it implied), told him on the first possible occasion that the Court could act only when cases came to it for decision, Washington was left without the counsel he so much desired.

If union was forwarded by the new presidency, it was rather in spite of the Constitution than because of it.

Nor did any of the other branches contribute to this stated purpose of the meeting. The Congress consisted of the two familiar houses; but the representatives owed their election to districts, and so to local interests; and the Senate represented state legislatures, and so state interests. When, on occasion, the Congress was required to consider national interests, there was reluctance because of suspicions back home that, as constituents, the voters were not having first consideration; besides, the state of the Union had nowhere been said to be congressmen's business; it was the president's, and if he wanted anything done about it he could make recommendations they might consider when convenient.

The fact is that the legislative responsibility for the nation was very slight, and that of the president was mostly implied; but it was he who did assume the leadership in national affairs; and it has continued to be so.

As for the judiciary, Jay's immediate reaction shows how repugnant any general responsibility was to the justices. Courts were places of resort for litigants. That position, said Jay, the Court meant to keep on occupying; and, friendly as he was to Washington, it must be understood that judges were judges, that they had traditional duties, and that these did not include giving advisory opinions to the president or anyone else.

If, then, these principal institutions established by the Constitution did not meet frankly and clearly the essential reason for attempting to shape a constitution in the first place, and if they did not represent a forthright acceptance of the charge in their terms of reference—that is to say, if the delegates, or a majority of them, dealt, traded, and finally shrank from what everyone knew had to be done—how is it that the resultant document has survived substantially intact for nearly two centuries? How is it that its place in the American regard has grown in importance until it has become the central symbol of national existence? How can presidents who, on taking office, with no intention of doing it—perhaps may even have campaigned earnestly for changes affecting it—swear to "preserve, protect, and defend" the Constitution?

It is, of course, all symbolic and is understood as such. The Constitution is not what it seems to be, or what it says it is; it is something very different, made so by:

1. A few amendments (although most of them do not affect structure, or many of them, substance).

2. Interpretation or extrapolation, not examined for literal identity with the document, but simply assumed to be agreeable.

3. Extensions caused by necessity, some not provided for but not forbidden, some fought over by the branches relying on election by the people or by appointment for life.

4. Some changes—the most important—imposed by the Court. It would not give Washington advice when Jay was chief justice; but when John Marshall succeeded, it began to give directions, and not only to the president but to the Congress and to all individuals and interests it wanted to reach.

How curious it is that, when pressed, none of us can tell exactly what most of the Constitution's clauses mean now, or what they will mean tomorrow. Yet, that it is held in high regard shows the need we have for it—and shows, as well, it might be argued, the benefits we might have from clearer definition of the meanings now so uncertain.

This need is not admitted by those who support judicial supremacy. The justices, it is contended, adequately interpret the Constitution "in the light of its applicability to present problems." Resisters contend that this is an inadmissible claim. The Constitution was not meant to be expanded, they say; it was meant to govern; and if it could not govern, an amending process was provided. One was provided even for the process itself if it proved too obstructive.

It is certainly true that the Supreme Court has immensely expanded its powers. Perhaps this was inevitable; yet exigencies have repeatedly arisen and have been so serious, on occasion, that action simply had to be taken without regard to its rule of direction for the other branches. It is perhaps ironical that the first and still most often-quoted strict constructionist, Thomas Jefferson, was the most notable contributor to what became in time a Rule of Necessity. This comprehended the use of powers not conferred by the Constitution, justified by the presidential assessment of a clear and present danger or an important advantage to the nation. The variety of occasions for its use, and the various controversies caused when it was used, illustrate, as well as anything, probably, the impossibility of framing any document that will cover any and every exigency in a future that may be distant and is certainly more or less—usually more—unknown.

What Jefferson said in his apologetic explanation for the Louisiana Purchase deserves to be quoted:

The Constitution has made no provision for our holding foreign territory, still less for incorporating foreign nations into our Union. The Executive, in seizing the fugitive occurrence which so much advances the good of their country, have done an act beyond the Constitution. The Legislature, in casting behind them physical subtleties, and risking themselves like faithful servants, must ratify and pay for it, and throw themselves on their country for doing for them, unauthorized, what we know they would have done for themselves, had they been in a situation to do it.

This example is only one of many. Nearly all presidents have been confronted with more or less serious decisions of a similar sort—that is to say, ones that required them to act in ways not expressly authorized.

When Lincoln, for instance, resorted to implied powers he was rebuked by Chief Justice Taney in an indignant outburst. But, as usually the case, what had been done, stood, and in fact, the result could not be argued against, in popular opinion; and Lincoln is, like other presidents, more praised than blamed. He too wrote about it afterward in a private letter. Was it better, he asked, to have preserved one clause of the Constitution than to have sacrificed all the rest in order to preserve it? That was what the Court of that time would have had him do.

The same doctrine has been resorted to often, and by a variety of presidents, including those we regard as the most heroic; and action has only once been stopped. It is obvious that the procedure ought to be constitutionalized in some form. The problem is not met by being subjected to the determination of the Court for reasons easily understood; they can intervene only late, and when an appropriate pleading can be devised. By then the crisis is usually past.

Students in schools of law or in political science who undertake courses in constitutional law find that what they are asked to study is a succession of Supreme Court opinions. What can be read in the original document is not what the Constitution really is in these later times; what it is is what has been extrapolated by the Court from the skimpy clauses defining the judicial branch. It ought to be better done another time.

As for the Congress, it too has become something other than was originally intended. What it was meant to be was a deliberative body (or bodies). Representing the people or the states, and counseling together, Congress would come, after consideration, to the good of the whole by acting for the good of the parts.

The House of Representatives was thought of as the heart of the government. Its exclusive power would be the precious one belonging to the people—to lay taxes; that is, to require participation in common activities, at least by paying for them, if not in any other way. Everything else of a legislative nature was apportioned to "the Congress," and this allowed the Senate to participate. But the House, like the Court, built on its express directions a structure of formidable proportions. It was assumed that the power to tax included that of spending, so appropriation bills presently began to originate in the House. This made the Senate a distinctly secondary body. But it also had an enormous effect on the executive. If the House could refuse to pay for any of the executive proposals, the president would only be embarrassed by suggesting them. When, for instance, agencies had to be set up to "faithfully execute the laws," they were established in bills passed by the Congress and originating in the House.

During its entire history the country has never been permitted to have an executive establishment competent for the duties it has had to undertake. It is almost within the memory of those living that labor and commerce joined interior and agriculture in the president's establishment; health, education, and welfare have only recently been put together as a department in an unwieldy mélange; urban affairs is still inchoate and would not have been authorized at all if it had not carried the humiliating prefix of *housing*. Transportation was organized late; communications may have been thought of but has not yet been pushed out for critical consideration.

There were at least two decades of active agitation, preceded by other decades of growing criticism and demand, before either a civil service agency or a budget office was accepted by a stubbornly hostile Congress. As yet this same hostility, in an implacable form, has prevented the most modest approach to planning for the future. It has to be said of both the civil service and the budget office that although the Congress was forced by attacks on it from all sides to concede the acts setting up these agencies, its subsequent behavior toward them betrayed its recalcitrance and its intention to give way only in form, not in reality.

The civil service was reluctantly authorized only after a succession of presidents had complained bitterly about the rapacity of office seekers seconded by their congressmen. Lincoln was besieged during the worst days of crisis in 1861; even guards borrowed from the army could not keep order among the hordes. These incidents occurred whenever there was a change of administration, and became positively chaotic when the change involved a taking over by an alternative party.

As for the budget, congressmen had no intention of allowing bureaucrats controlled by the president to say how annual appropriations should be allocated. They meant to keep this power intact. The president might send them an elaborate budget, calculated to serve the general interest, but they would not honor it. Each item represented an interest, and a congressman could use that interest. He could favor his constituents generally, or he could favor those among them who in turn favored him. That this served to keep congressmen in office (campaign contributions) and in positions of prestige or affluence (connections with law or consulting firms) they did not like to have emphasized, but it was obvious. If it operated against the national interest or, at least, not for it, that was unfortunate; but politicians must think first of survival.

The Constitution obviously permits this partiality, but the permission is owed mostly to the framers' inability to see into the future. They had no conception of the nation's growth potential or of the responsibilities this growth would thrust upon the government. If someone had suggested to them that presently the government they were framing would become by far the biggest and most varied organization in the world, as well as the most intimate influence in the lives of all its citizens, they would have been appalled. They would certainly have dismissed the prophecy as too fantastic for a moment's consideration.

If this is really so in strict truth, the new meanings discovered by the Congress as a whole and its members individually can be comprehended in a quite different way than if the viewpoint accepted is that the framers were all-wise and prescient, and the result of their summer's effort was adequate for all time to come.

The Congress was expected to be a small and intimate body of like-minded men who would make laws governing the affairs of the farms, villages, and small cities they knew about, and keeping free the commerce of the time. It has expanded to an unwieldy number, making it necessary to invent an inner-circle control over most of its functions; and this control has been concentrated by the rule of seniority in those members who come from "safe" constituencies. This has put a few members in the position of wielding immense power with practical anonymity and with a minuscule sense of responsibility. If a clause in a law or a budget arrangement, surreptitiously inserted, causes inefficiency, embarrassment, or even disaster, it is impossible to say what legislator is to be blamed.

Responsibility has all but disappeared in the evolution of congressional institutions; and it must be admitted that when the framers adopted section 8 of Article I, they made this inevitable. The Congress should have the power, it was said, to do a variety of things; and when it is recalled that a previous section (5) had said that each house should be the judge of the elections, returns, and qualifications of its own members, that it should determine the rules of its proceedings, and should be exempt from prosecutions for anything said, it is clear that the corruptions made possible by national growth were inherent in the original charter. There were powers to affect many interests, and the holders of those powers were anonymous.

But the Congress has lost what the framers meant it to have—deliberation. Of course, laws of importance almost never originated in either house. Initiative, in this respect, passed at once to the president; and the Congress was reduced to the niggling bargains incident to the passage or defeat of presidential proposals. Dialogue disappeared.

Nor has the Congress exercised with wisdom and responsibility the process of investigation. This is an implied procedure, depending for any validity it may have on its relevance to a legislative purpose. The theory is that laws cannot be formulated and considered without knowledge, and that this knowledge comes from privileged journeys (many of them called "junkets" by sardonic critics) or from staff investigations and the questioning of witnesses. What excursions into irrelevancies have followed is well enough known. No one can define for an investigative committee what legislative purpose is, and there are concealed in the words frequent attacks on organizations or individuals which committeemen may desire to discredit.

Because it is hard to say, with any preciseness, what the framers intended for the presidency, to go on and say what has been lost and what has been gained is correspondingly difficult. It can be said with some certainty, however, that the ability to execute the laws with any efficiency has been lost, and that political and legislative influence has been gained. What has been lost, the presidency was charged to do; what it has gained did not exist, and was not anticipated. It is more questionable to assert, as many writers do, that the management of foreign policy was originally intended to be a presidential responsibility. Section 2.2 of Article II reads in part: "He shall have the power . . . to make treaties . . . and he shall nominate . . . and shall appoint ambassadors, other public ministers and consuls." But these powers were to be exercised only with the two-thirds consent of the Senate. It was, in fact, to be more than consent; it was to be with the Senate's advice. Whatever was meant, when he could get no advice Washington began to assume that it was a primary presidential responsibility; and his successors have followed his example. There seemed to be no other course open. The senators might have to consent, but it was unthinkable that they—or any of them—should take the lead in representing the nation's interests. The secretary of state became, under Washington's direction, a presidential agent; and no president has ever allowed occupants of the office to become subordinates of the Senate.

Still, the presidential authority is limited by several constitutional checks. Although the president is the designated commander in chief of the armed forces, only the Congress can declare war. Presidents have shown that they can make this limitation inoperable by so committing the forces at their disposal that a formal declaration has little further effect, but often there is loud objection, and the presidential initiative is always in question.

The Congress has the authority to define offenses against the law of nations; besides, there is always the latent power to refuse appropriations for any action needing them. Then there is the whole field of international trade. The Congress in 1934 did concede to the executive the power to negotiate reciprocal trade agreements, but the authority was limited to two years. After that there began a series of exhausting struggles every two years over the issue.

Occasionally, also, the Congress complicates matters by adopting a resolution or even passing a law, such as, for instance, the Japanese exclusion act in 1924 that was protested by both President Harding and Secretary of State Hughes. On the other hand, the executive has expanded the use of "executive agreements," many of them almost indistinguishable from treaties. Some have been important: for instance, those made at

Yalta and Potsdam. There have always been contentions, since agreements began to be used, that they were not, like treaties, "the laws of the land." In this, as in other matters, the Supreme Court has intervened; it upheld the agreements by President Roosevelt with Soviet Russia.[3] It is obvious that the Court intends in this matter, as in others, to maintain a position of final determination.

The president's authority has without doubt grown with the years. It has been more and more apparent that it must. As international rivalries, backed by threats of force, have created more emergency situations, the executive, as the only ready and quick-responding agency, has had to be conceded more leeway. It still has to be said, however, that it is far from complete; also, that it lies in the shadow of Court interpretation. Practically the whole of the presidential expansion in this field might be nullified at any time by an adverse opinion. It is not clearly constitutional—at least not much of it is—and when a situation of this sort exists, it is possible that the Court may reexamine it at any time.

Concerning the presidential directive to execute the laws, the framers may well be criticized for not distinguishing between executive and chief of state, and for not recognizing that in failing to do this, one duty was certain to jeopardize the other. Of course, they may well be criticized, also, for not foreseeing the role of the president as political leader; and for failing, consequently, to see that this might jeopardize both the stated duties of execution and the president's acting as symbolic head.

The inevitable did happen; and in gaining political and legislative leadership, and in becoming more and more resplendent as the chief of state, the president became a neglectful administrator. It has been a tragic circumstance that besides having to devote himself to politics, to foreign relations, and to being chief of state, the president has had to preside over the overwhelming expansion of domestic undertakings. The execution mentioned in the Constitution so casually, in a subordinate clause, has now put upon a single man the responsibility for an infinitude of duties. It was bound to fail as a way of conducting government—and it has.

The multifariousness of the presidential duty has been made more difficult by the changing nature of his qualifications. Only one president since Washington has been chosen because he was known to possess superior administrative abilities; that, of course, was Hoover, and although he was indeed an effective administrator, he was destined to be rated as a presidential failure. Presidents are not judged in this way but rather on their abilities as politicians, legislative leaders, and chiefs of state. It is no wonder that administrative duties are the ones they neglect when a choice has to be made.

3. *United States* v. *Belmont,* 301 U.S. 324 (1937).

President, Congress, and Court—none is clearly defined by the existing Constitution, and so none has been legitimized as it actually exists. The first duty of revisionists would be the correcting of these deficiencies.

Matters of Procedure, Form, and Style

Too much attention may have been given in this chapter to the Convention in Philadelphia and not enough to other and similar experiences. The excuse, if one is needed, is that the gathering there was entirely in the American grain and therefore has a certain historic relevance. Dickinson, Wilson, and Gouverneur Morris were very like a succession of jurists both before and after their time. Gerry was like other crabbed but alert New Englanders. Randolph, Mason, and Lee were recognizably Virginian, and even Gunning Bedford and Luther Martin, inclined to verbosity and inconsistency, seem like familiar characters.

The delegates often referred to the classics and occasionally paraded their knowledge of Coke and Blackstone as well as Locke and Montesquieu. But they were not merely imitating; their references were literary. Actually, they were pragmatic. If they thought too much of their home-based interests and too little of national ones, this had always been an American fault and would continue to be.

Taken all together, there probably is no experience anywhere so revealing, so full of lessons, both good and bad. If apology is needed for relying so much on the precedents established in Philadelphia, this is it.

At the very beginning, when a quorum had assembled, decisions were made that we can still regard as important. Two of the most valuable were the covenant of secrecy made among them and the rule that every motion should be voted on but could at any time be called up for reconsideration. There were others, such as discussion without limit of time in Committee of the Whole. The drawback to this group was the lack of a detailed record. Only Madison's diligence in taking notes makes it at all possible to follow the development of ideas, the changes of opinion, and the hardening and softening of agreement during the dialogue. There were other note takers, but none of them had Madison's ability to condense and none was so indefatigable.[4]

Even Madison's notes, however, were unauthorized. There was an official secretary, William Jackson, but what his *Journal* amounted to was, as John Quincy Adams said years later, "no better than daily minutes from which the regular journal ought to have been, but never was, made out." This meant that there was not much more than a record of yeas and nays.[5]

4. They are gathered in *The Records of the Federal Convention of 1787,* ed. by Max Farrand (New Haven, Conn.: Yale University Press, 1937).

5. *Ibid.,* I, xii.

Historians ever since have been understandably annoyed about this lack, but it may have been owed to something more than Jackson's incompetence.[6] The delegates had taken a resolve to discuss the matters before them wholly in private. It was honored to a most unusual degree.

It is notorious that nothing is kept secret when legislators are present. There are always whispered leaks to be exploited by the press even when no more than a small committee meets in executive session. But in Philadelphia, curious as everyone on the outside was, the disputes and agreements of the Convention were kept very close. Even when the delegates wrote home to their friends among the politicians they were discreet. Why this was no one has been able to say. Perhaps they felt the awesome responsibility; perhaps they had been warned by a stern Washington who presided. Whatever the reason, in this and in other procedures, their behavior was in sharp contrast with that customary among legislators. They were more intent on producing an acceptable result than on making personal records.

To this there were a few exceptions. Bedford was a notorious demagogue who not only bored the company through heated hours but publicly gave broad hints of his opinions; the same was true of some defectors, such as Yates and Lansing, who were known to have left because of the nationalist trend they saw developing. But the debates and even the conclusions were kept in remarkable privacy.

The conception had been that only with such protection would the delegates speak freely, and only if they had not taken public positions would they be able to change their minds. There was much free speaking, and minds were changed. The rule that made this possible would seem to have been an important one. Posturing was infrequent, and those who were inclined that way relaxed as the company became familiar.

This did not free the delegates from instructions or from their commitments. The states' righters were especially bound in this way, and when they found the nationalists firm, as a matter of principle, there came about the month-long stand-off that very nearly ended in dissolution. The Great Compromise offered, finally, a way out; but the escape was so narrow and the consequences of compromise so serious in later years that the experience offers a clear lesson. It is this: in constitutionmaking, if those who participate have had prior instruction, they cannot listen to reason. Delegates may have attitudes and may put them forward emphatically; they may even give way without being wholly persuaded, as did Madison, Washington, and Hamilton; but none of these repudiated the result. All of them argued loyally for ratification, and this could not have happened if they had been bound by instructions.

The other procedural matter of some utility was the agreement to find

6. Jackson was chosen over Franklin's grandson, William Temple Franklin. He had been a major in the army and probably had been favored by Washington for this reason, but he was incompetent and was ignored by Madison.

the sense of the meeting by voting, but not to regard any vote as final. On matters having to do with their new invention—the presidency—there were, on some issues, as many as a dozen votes; and much of this voting disclosed a majority on one day that had been a minority a day or a week earlier. This changing of sides very easily shows the result of secrecy and lack of commitment. The delegates were in the process of making up their minds, and even though the minds were firm ones, they could be changed.

Randolph wanted a plural presidency, and Madison agreed, but both ultimately were convinced that a single head would be better because of the obvious difficulty, pointed out by others, that decisive action was impossible if several individuals had first to agree. And no one suggested anything other than a single head as an alternative, although Madison, in earlier papers, had spoken of a *primus inter pares*. There was, in fact, very little discussion; why, it is not known. Madison's suggestion still remains to be explored as a possible solution for a problem that becomes more serious every year.

Franklin tried his best to persuade his colleagues that a single house would be best for the Congress. This was the scheme followed in Pennsylvania, and Franklin thought it much superior to two houses pulling against each other. His famous illustration of the two-headed snake did not persuade the others. Then the Great Compromise intervened, and his cause was lost. That in this deal the Senate was to represent the states made it impossible to think of it as a delaying and consultative house, as would have been more sensible.

For the most part, despite the sharp differences, some petulance, and a number of defections, commitment to secrecy held; and the free reconsideration brought about agreement even when there were reservations. Without these procedural rules the Constitution could not have been produced. It may be concluded that it would always be so.

There comes a time, as collective deliberations go on, when a small group or even a single individual will be designated to put into draft form the agreements reached in the discussions. In the Convention at Philadelphia this occurred on July 26. This was after eight weeks of almost daily meetings of six or seven hours and innumerable informal conferences. It was ten days after the Great Compromise had been agreed on and after the executive had taken shape. More recently there had been a prolonged, and sometimes heated, controversy about the admission of new states, now resolved.[7] Slavery had been equally, or even more, difficult. Washington, Madison, and others who were against slavery in principle were aware that

7. The territories to the west, now rapidly filling up with migrants, were claimed by the original states, or some of them—Massachusetts, Virginia, New York, and Georgia being the largest claimants. They were reluctant to see new states erected from them. It was feared that they would become rivals likely to overwhelm their older relations. Also they would be poor at first, and being on the frontier they would demand protection which they themselves could not furnish.

abolition was not possible; an abolition clause would prevent ratification in Georgia, the Carolinas, and perhaps Virginia. So compromise had produced the result we know of.

These were the most controversial questions; but there had been others such as the government of three parts, not so difficult in principle, but much argued about when it came to the source and extent of the powers each was to have; such, also, as the right of suffrage, the veto power of the executive, and the establishment and jurisdiction of a supreme court. In each case there were many minor issues, and when they turned up in discussion they often caused disputations and required time for resolution.

Madison's notes say simply that the proceedings of the last few days were handed over to the "Come. of Detail." Then the convention adjourned until August 6. These proceedings consisted of the much-amended Resolves adopted in principle. The committee[8] was to report a preliminary draft based on these generalities. It could then be considered how the whole was to be submitted for ratification.

The committee duly reported; then there began the final sessions running on into the third week of September. All commentators note that about this time the heat, the humidity, and the consequent discomfort were all but unbearable. Nevertheless this was the time when the final form of the document was decided on after long days of earnest argument and some sharp disagreements.

Since Randolph was a member of the committee, considerable interest attaches to notes made by him about the task of producing a résumé. These notes were discovered and published many years later.[9] His preliminary observations have such point for any similar venture that they deserve inclusion in any statement of criteria.

In the draft of a fundamental constitution, two things deserve attention:

1. To insert essential principles only, lest the operations of government should be clogged by rendering those provisions permanent and unalterable which ought to be accommodated to time and events.

2. To use simple and precise language and general propositions, according to the example of the constitutions of the several states (for the construction of a constitution necessarily differs from that of law).

It will be seen that the first of the communications written to Randolph by himself had to do with form and that the second had to do with style. They were excellent admonitions, and in the drafting of the report they were faithfully followed. The summer, however, had been a crowded one.

---

8. Randolph of Virginia, Wilson of Pennsylvania, Gorham of Massachusetts, Ellsworth of Connecticut, and Rutledge of South Carolina.

9. Reference to the notes and to their history is to be found in Farrand, *op. cit.*, II, 137.

Many of the issues had been discussed and some no more than half resolved in spite of lengthy speeches pro and con and the free reconsideration. It was an unwieldy mass of material to organize. What emerged was a document divided into articles and sections—as the Constitution would be when it was finished.

There were many familiar models to be used as reference. Articles and covenants had been drafted over and over as statements of principle in the years when the colonies were becoming independent. There were also state constitutions, and as long ago as 1754 Franklin had written a *Plan of Union*. Something similar had been produced by others as well. Then, of course, there were the Articles of Confederation.

It was a time of constitutionmaking, not only in America but also in Europe; that is to say, there was much interest abroad in the process. Americans, however, were the first to make models for actual use.

What was produced by the Committee was a revision and expansion of the Virginia Resolves, quite naturally, since Randolph had been involved in drafting these. After the discussions of the past weeks there were now twenty-three propositions. They were printed overnight; on August 6 they were distributed, whereupon there was adjournment so that they might be studied. There followed five more weeks of debate, much more concentrated now on the essentials. For this concentration the Committee on Detail could be thanked. Its work was most helpful.

In that later debate many of the old questions were gone over again and votes of reconsideration taken. The differences were still acute about many matters, and as the meeting approached its end there were more defections. Among these, surprisingly, was Randolph. He found himself unable to agree with the majority that nine states would suffice for ratification. He, and several others, thought this exceeded by altogether too much their terms of reference. He proposed, because of this, that the draft constitution be submitted to state conventions, that they should offer amendments or objections, and that afterward another convention should be held to produce a final document. When this was rejected, Randolph announced that he would not sign, and he was joined by Mason and Gerry.

For this reason it was not Randolph but Gouverneur Morris who was the Constitution's final draftsman. Morris was only one of a Committee on Style; the others were chairman William Samuel Johnson, Hamilton, Madison, and Rufus King. Johnson, president of King's College in New York, had during the summer accumulated respect for his learning and diligence—if not for imagination. Madison and Hamilton have come down to us with greater reputation than Morris; but nevertheless it was to him that the task of doing the actual writing was delegated.

Whether consciously or not, he followed Randolph's rule, and the Resolves were again the guide. Morris reduced these products of the

Committee on Detail to six; as to style, he was even more economical and hortatory. Mason and Gerry, for instance, now showed signs of the reluctance that finally resulted in their not signing. Others had defected and were already agitating back home against the anticipated constitution.

All of this would very likely happen in any group with a similar duty if it was made up of delegates who were representatives of localities. This is, therefore, one of the lessons of most use for the future. Framers ought to owe their duty to the nation for whom the constitution is intended and to no other principal. This will obviate compromises, deliberate evasions, and defection of the disgruntled. It will not, of course, enable the delegates to improve their foresight. For this there is only one remedy: the provision for stated revisions no further apart than foresight may reasonably be expected to run.

What emerged for final consideration at Philadelphia in September, 1787, was the charter with which the nation has lived ever since. During that time, faults as well as virtues have shown themselves. Future framers can see that if later conventions had been held some future difficulties of interpretation would have been cleared up. As it was, the "inserting of essential principles only" resulted in language so laconic that it could be interpreted in alternate ways. This brevity allowed the branches to develop doctrines of implication and claim what often proved to be conflicting powers.

All this haziness of formulation cannot be charged to Morris and his committee. Much of it resulted from failure of the delegates to foresee what might happen when the government began to operate, and at least some resulted from deliberate evasions. In its last phase the convention was haunted by the possibility that ratification might be refused. Fears of this kind were voiced again and again and by some of those prominent in the discussions.

Until Randolph, for the Committee on Detail, codified the apparent agreements reached in the first five weeks of the Convention, what had been accomplished was confused, and most minds were not really made up. When the delegates were faced with his clear and succinct formulation they had something definite to center on. Some appear to have been shocked when they saw how far they had gone toward centralization, some found that parts of the proposed structure were inconsistent with others, and some realized that the compromise between the large and small states was not likely to be satisfactory. Still, these were decisions hardly anyone wanted to reopen; and the remaining weeks—until September 16—were mostly kept within the subjects already opened.

Not all, however. Randolph said too much power had been given to the Congress; and this, added to his objection that ratification ought to be unanimous, reinforced his suggestion for submitting the draft to state conventions and holding another general convention at a future time to consider their advice. Such embarrassments, it may be guessed, would always be a hazard of similar efforts. The question whether Randolph and Mason would be followed by others was, however, in this instance quickly settled. The delegates voted against Randolph's proposition. Madison's notes say that "all the states answered 'no.' "

It is unlikely that unanimity on all matters will prevail in any serious undertaking. But the Philadelphia experience shows that on most matters, reason can be relied on if the conferees are free to decide. Delegates who came with no notion of agreeing to a national government with powers to tax, to control commerce, to conduct foreign relations, and to preempt the privilege of making "the supreme law of the land" moved from one position to another—each more advanced toward nationalism—until they found themselves committed. It frightened many of them, but when they reviewed the collective reasoning they undertook to stand firm.

Those who would not agree were—except for Randolph and Mason— not the most respected members. The subsequent decision of all the states (except abstaining Rhode Island) to ratify, however bitterly fought against by such local politicians as Clinton in New York, vindicated the judgments of the thirty-nine signers. They continued to think that no better could have been done; not that they would not have liked to have things other- wise in some respects, and not that they did not have misgivings. They may have expected the weaknesses to be corrected at a later meeting, but for the present they were satisfied.

After Randolph's outline made everything plain, and Morris's draft made it final, even the compromises were there for all to see. There was at least no evasion. Not everything had been anticipated; some powers were poorly defined; but no one wanted to go on arguing.

There is one final lesson: an argument in such a meeting should go on until it is finished—not until everyone becomes exhausted, but until everyone is settled in his mind.

Gouverneur Morris, writing the final draft of the Constitution, had a much easier task than that of Randolph five weeks earlier. Most decisions had been taken, even though they consisted of resolves that were often general and sometimes ambiguous. Morris was expected to make every- thing terse and exact. He met the expectation of terseness, but only by leaving out much that should have been retained; his exactness, however, left even more to be desired. This was especially true of the presidency. The longest clause in Article II was devoted to selection—the electoral college, a device that proved to be unworkable. The shortest—actually not a clause at all but only a subordinate statement at the end of a section— said that the president should take care that the laws be faithfully executed.

It is incredible that these few words still serve to define the president's duties. But they have never been revised or expanded. The section including them followed discursive clauses not only about election but about qualifications, the method of impeachment if he should misbehave, his compensation, and his oath of office.

The truth is that, as a job of drafting, the presidential clauses could hardly have been worse, but the clauses concerning the Court were even more terse—and even more ambiguous. One thing, however, was made quite clear: the area of the Court's jurisdiction could be fixed by the Congress, and the establishment of inferior courts was to be "by law." This made the judicial branch definitely inferior to the legislature. It might have been thought that since so many delegates were judges, or at least lawyers, they would have been more specific about this than anything else. They were, however, conscious of a prejudice against them, holding over from the Revolution, and being sensitive men, they did not insist on prerogatives for the judicial branch. This allowed Marshall, after some years, to assert that if judicial supremacy was not mentioned in the Constitution that was because it was too well understood to need specification.

This experience of final drafting after long discussions, many reconsiderations of disputed points, and numerous compromises does suggest warnings. In trying to be brief, Morris and his committee left open many unresolved questions. Everyone was depleted after the summer in Philadelphia, September being the worst month of all. Moreover, the room used by the Convention belonged to the legislature of Pennsylvania, and its stated meeting was overdue. It can only be concluded that, industrious as the remaining delegates had been, they were, at the end, disposed to accept what the prestigious Committee on Style put before them. The clauses defining the main branches, at least, ought to have been reexamined and redrafted after an interval of reflection. There was, however, no disposition to reassemble, the physical difficulty being what it was. Travel before next spring would have been out of the question for many of the delegates. And anyway, they had reached either agreement or compromise on issues that most of them would not like to see reopened. What had been accomplished was not so firmly established in their minds that they were convinced of its rightness. How would the faults be corrected? We do not know.

It had been one way to make a constitution, but the difficulties—physical, cultural, and mental—had been enormous. As the president of the University of Chicago once said of his institution, it was not a good one, merely the best there was. So with the Constitution; it was far from perfect, but it was the best that, under the circumstances, could have been written.

From that experience it ought at least to have been learned that in constitutionmaking, time should be given, circumstances should be favorable, and delegates should be both reasonable and free from instruction.

General Structural Criteria

The state of tension among the branches has sometimes been described as a virtue; it is said to be responsible—at least in part—for the durability of the structure. It has done this, it is argued, by allowing each branch to find its proper place in recurrent conflicts. More than this, it has kept any of the branches from accumulating excessive authority—just as the framers hoped. Justice Brandeis was one of those who firmly believed this last claim:

The doctrine of the separation of powers was adopted by the Convention of 1787 not to promote efficiency but to preclude the exercise of arbitrary power. The purpose was not to avoid friction, but, by means of the inevitable friction incident to the distribution of the governmental powers among the three departments, to save the people from autocracy.[10]

In spite of this pronouncement, however, it cannot be allowed that the framers accomplished quite so much. The conflicts have taken place in very extensive unassigned borderlands, and in these areas continual struggle has often failed to establish any but temporary and uncertain interludes of peace. Actually, disputes are never really settled. They could not be except by amendment.

The consequent waste of time and effort has been immense and has increased with the years. Frequently, amid the conflict the end in view has been entirely lost. The Congress has by now, as one of its traditional aims, visceral opposition to the president and a strengthening assertion of its own prerogatives. Nothing so infuriates its leaders as to be called "rubber stamps"; and the president, for his part, has developed—as one of the most active sections of his staff—a lobbying organization whose function is to persuade huffy senators and representatives that they ought to permit the passage of legislation proposed by the president. The means of persuasion are well enough known. They consist of favors, patronage, promises, and the bizarre kind of blackmail so often practiced in politics. If this particular conflict precludes the establishment of arbitrary power, it also keeps a good deal of business from being done.

Reduction of the areas where these struggles take place is easily possible by structural change together with reassignment of duties. The Congress can be differently selected and differently organized; and it can be recognized that scrutiny of the budget, line by line, is not a proper legislative function but amounts, actually, to interference with the executive. The controlling of executive appointments and functions is not the duty of legislators. A change of this sort, brought about by amendment, would eliminate enormous waste and would center attention on the public business rather than internecine conflicts.

10. *Myers* v. *United States*, 272 U.S. 52 (1926), 293.

Then, too, there are the familiar differences about federal and state jurisdictions. Redefinition of these is now more possible than in the past, and would heal one of the oldest breaches in the government system. The residual position of the states may always have been doubtful because of the last phrase in the Tenth Amendment—*"and to the people."* There has been, however, very little reference to the people during subsequent years. States have preempted all the attention. It is long past time for these ambiguities to be eliminated.

There is, of course, the supremacy clause in the present Constitution, but this has not prevented the states from resisting federal "encroachments." This clause seems clear enough in itself, but taken together with powers reserved to the states, it has often been held to mean what it does not say.[11]

It has never been assumed that any or all of these governmental powers, so long fought over among officials, were the only ones in our pluralistic society. Powers have always been exercised quite outside of government, and some of them seriously affect the public interest. There has been some control, when necessary, by the regulatory agencies (sometimes referred to as "semijudicial" and sometimes as "independent"); and since more effective controls are needed, these might well be comprehended in a newly established branch. In such an organization the responsibilities of all these agencies could have more uniform definition and a central direction they have never had in the past.

Clear distribution of responsibilities and the addition of other needed branches would at least reduce conflicts and obstructions. The interdependence among them, if reapportioned, might make them more cooperative and less combative; and at the same time might make certain the centering of attention on public affairs and the adequate regulation of private business. The president would be the initiator (as he is now, but under severe handicaps); and an administrative branch for domestic affairs might relieve him of numerous heavy duties he is not able to perform, and might provide these departments and agencies with much-needed administrative direction.

A distinction of some importance is lacking in the present Constitution. What is necessary to be done by the government ought to be defined, but a convinced pluralistic society has many ways of satisfying its demands. Government is only one of these. The others are usually profitmaking enterprises, but the pursuit of profit needs control. Shareholders can be greedy.

There are other anomalies. The framers could not have guessed that taxation would be used as a stabilizing device for the economy. But since

11. "This Constitution, and the laws of the United States which shall be made in pursuance thereof; and all treaties made . . . under the authority of the United States, shall be the supreme law of the land; and the judges in every state shall be bound thereby, anything in the constitution or laws of any state to the contrary notwithstanding." Article VI, section 2.

stabilization is a welfare objective, and since welfare was mentioned in the preamble, taxes have been used in this novel way without objection, relying only on a few undefined words for authorization. It would be interesting to guess what might have been meant by "welfare" in 1787, but it could not have included relief for the unemployed or, for example, assisting in the development of foreign nations. This is something of a warning about making objectives too narrow even when there is a general desire to reach them.

The Congress might be instructed to promote welfare, security, equality, and freedom, perhaps more explicitly than in a preamble, since such introductions are mere statements of intent. And it might be told that it *may* accomplish these results by capturing the profits of progress for distribution to those disadvantaged by that progress, but it should not be told that it *must* do this or how. The matter is too complicated. Progress needs encouragement rather than discouragement. Ways of reaching stability also should be permissive—such, as for instance, management of the flow and price of credit and of fiscal policies.

The liberties and the immunities mentioned in the Bill of Rights are negative prohibitions in contrast with the positive intentions mentioned in the Preamble. It is proper, for instance, to say that no law shall encourage an establishment of religion and that none shall abridge freedom of speech or of the press, and so on. What was intended was that in these matters the government should keep out entirely. But in the case of welfare, it would mean nothing to say that no law should impair it; welfare can often be reached and kept only through government action that the Congress should be instructed, not only empowered, to take. But again, it should not be told *what kind* of welfare or *how much,* and not what methods to use. Welfare may be enhanced by devices not yet conceived, and definitions of it may well change.

The making of three lists—*don'ts, permissions,* and *musts*—and their inclusion in a draft document might be guided by this kind of distinction. For instance, after conferring on the Congress the lawmaking power, it might be said that the laws it makes shall have the purpose of ensuring peace and security for the nation and well-being and happiness for its citizens. Further it might be said that no law should impair a list of liberties and freedoms. In another area, it might be said that laws should require private associations of individuals to behave in such ways as will promote the general welfare.

If it is true that much of what needs to be done is *prevented* by the Constitution, that achievement (progress, accommodation, adjustment, modernization, efficiency) is hampered or blocked because (1) the Constitution does not prescribe duties for the various agencies of government or (2) because those prescribed are not carried out effectively, then structural

change is desirable. Such revisions should focus on (1) a listing of assignments and (2) a reassignment of powers calculated to make them effective.

If contemporary immunities need to be only those within view in 1787,
the existing constitutional provisions are sufficient, although, as we have
seen even in this, both freedoms and duties are much altered in character.
If new duties are to be prescribed, rather than merely authorized, they will
mostly be those arising from the characteristics, the possibilities, and the
effects of expansion, growth, and technological change. Both the citizen and
his government will be affected, and there should be an earnest effort to
get advantages without strait-jacketing—that is, to encourage and not to
hamper, recognizing that individuals are varied, and that their initiative must
not be stifled, this last being a problem the Philadelphians were altogether
spared.

The government could be more recognizably an extension of the citizen
himself than it has become in the complexities of growth. It could be made
easier for the citizen to participate in his own degree. He might be involved
more actively in choosing representatives, feeling, consequently, the delegation of his authority as a citizen to be credible. Because differences of
opinion exist, however, majorities must prevail. Loyalty in a democracy
amounts largely to consent as its processes go on. Even if a citizen may
think or talk as he likes, protected by an immunity, he is under obligation to
accept the decisions he has delegated to his representatives. Loyalty, however, will never be yielded without reservation if there is no confidence in
political processes, and confidence will depend on the integrity of those
processes.

Integrity of this sort is reached only when special interests are unable
to invade the areas of principle essential to the democratic idea. Principles
need structural embodiment; but if there be no favor, there will be no
suspicion and no disaffection. A concurrence in a constitution between
immunities and delegations is required. For instance, the definition of liberty
should not allow a citizen or an association to escape duties or necessary
regulation in the public interest established by elected representatives. They
have been delegated to do precisely this.

As for amendment, if it is left to the decision of legislatures, demands
for change will almost never be successful. Legislatures, like other branches
of government, will consult their own preferences. Amendment should be
the result of deliberation; there should be stated times for reconsideration;
and revisions should somehow represent the general will of those to be
affected by them. Because of this the document should include only such
rights as are general and can be foreseen to be essential during the period
until the next revision. The agencies established for government should be
calculated to gain only those ends that are, as Justice Douglas has said,
worthy of being established in granite. This is not because they ought to
be made permanent but because they will tend to be made so by those who

prosper with them, and so will outlive their usefulness. They ought to be few and general.

Duties the government might be directed to assume can be listed tentatively:

1. Maintaining the strength and integrity of the nation, including protection of the environment.
2. The furthering of well-being, increasing productivity, making sure that goods and facilities are fairly shared once they have been produced, and rewarding those who do the producing.
3. Cooperating with other nations: in attaining peace or in approaching it; in helping others to reach the level of well-being enjoyed at home, and in establishing international agencies for such purposes.
4. Making sure that the provision for welfare reaches all those who can benefit from it. This involves not only securities (against the insurable hazards of life, such as ill health, disability, and old age, and against the misfortunes of orphanage and unemployment), but also urban and rural improvement, facilities for recreation, and the encouragement of creative activities. Flexibility in choosing and administering the agencies for these purposes will be essential.
5. Regulating such activities outside the sphere of government as are nevertheless affected with a public interest. Individuals and associations of individuals have a duty beyond that of their own prosperity. But regulation should be limited to the public interest; it should protect initiative and creativity; but it should control enterprises intended to make profits at the expense of the public. It should not be prejudiced against the large or favor the small, but each should be held to the same standards.
6. Making sure of progress and stability, if necessary by acquiring and operating industries or facilities unsuited to private ownership and operation.
7. Making long-range plans and in some degree requiring performance in their carrying out.
8. Arranging itself so that democracy functions through representation and delegation in ways that engage wide participation and command general support.
9. Requiring from its citizens the performance of essential public duties, and compliance with majority decisions.
10. Improving capabilities, particularly through education, but also by helping to enlarge and improve the information necessary to democratic decisionmaking.

In order to meet these demands and requirements restructuring might be conceived on somewhat the following pattern:

1. *A Political Agency* (perhaps a branch): To organize and carry on

political activity by any group commanding a certain percentage of the total vote. It should be paid for with public funds; it should have an appropriate organization; it should see that policies are discussed among its members; it should elaborate a platform or general plan; it should hold regular meetings or conventions; it should have the responsibility for nominating the party tickets and for supporting the party program.

2. *A Presidency:* Nominated by a party, elected by a national constituency, and recognized as the source of leadership and initiative. There might be vice-presidents elected with the president, but all should be under the president's direction.

3. *A Legislature:* The legislature, as the lawmaking body, might have two houses—one directly elected by the people (but partly "at large"), and one so constituted that its whole attention might be given to national interests.

4. *A Judiciary:* A *system* of courts is suggested; at its head would be a supreme court with the duty of constituting and regulating the other courts and acting on appeals from their decisions; it would also determine jurisdictions and direct the assignment of cases. The chief justice would be elected for a long but definite term, and would generally direct the whole system.

   The "other" courts, it is suggested, might include a constitutional court to judge whether laws and executive behavior accord with the Constitution (its duties might include advisory opinions); a people's court to act on appeals in adversary proceedings involving individuals and associations of individuals; a court of administrative appeals to judge the rights of individuals and associations or corporations affected by administrative regulations (the ombudsman function).

5. *A Regulatory Agency* (perhaps a branch): To make general rules for, and to supervise, the activities of governmental agencies designated to regulate private and semipublic businesses, industries, associations, or corporations. This body would have the additional duty of chartering all corporate bodies and seeing to it that they comply with charter terms.

6. *An Assessing Agency* (perhaps also a branch): Having the duty of foreseeing national needs and equating them with emerging resources. It would make annual budgets at the end of its ten- or twelve-year effort to foresee and assess forthcoming needs and resources.

The restructuring of the court system is suggested for several reasons. The first of these is that judicial review needs to be regularized—that is, the bringing of laws and actions into accord with the Constitution. This involves setting the judiciary above the legislature, but it would seem unavoidable unless the Constitution is to be so detailed and specific as to defeat the purpose of having a constitution.

The undemocratic nature of the Court may be somewhat modified by having the chief justice nominated and elected as the president is, and for a term, after which he—and certain other justices—might become members of the Nation's House.

The reorganization of the legislative branch, it is suggested, ought to provide for one house with a duty only to the nation as a whole, something lacking at present. This house would assume some of the appointive powers now assigned to the president, thus lessening the pressure on him from those demanding patronage. But its most important duty would be to review, and perhaps delay, legislation passed by the other house. It might also be entrusted with certain great decisions concerning the use of emergency powers. Its members ought to be the most trusted elders of the nation, removed from most immediate pressures and possessors of undoubted wisdom and loyalty. In addition to its other functions it might be required to establish a permanent commission to suggest constitutional amendments, thus remedying one of the most serious deficiencies of the present Constitution.

Furthermore this house might be entrusted with the postauditing of executive actions, now partly carried out by a comptroller general responsible to the Congress who behaves in ways reflecting this single loyalty. The function might be widened to one of genuine oversight, calling attention to wider and deeper issues than any body in the government is now charged with doing—such as warning of undue proliferations and, similarly, of neglects needing to be remedied.

The suggestion for a separate political branch is meant to return, in such degree as is possible in a modern state, to the gaining of consent, perhaps even the origination of policy by citizens. Each party, having an organization in the capital and in the states, on a permanent basis, would be responsible for continuous discussion of national issues. A system of meetings, it is conceived, would develop leaders and organize opinion so that as elections approached, policies would have been considered not only in local but in state conventions. Platforms at present are haphazardly prepared. They are developed by informal committees of those most powerful in the party, and will not necessarily represent the views of party members.

The returning of policymaking to the democratic process might in this way be attempted and might possibly be achieved.

Without going further with this reconsideration of means, it may be concluded that the tripartite theory of the framers is no longer valid. The three branches need to have added to them at least the four suggested—political, executive, planning, and regulatory. And what there is of further usefulness in the "checks and balances" among the branches needs consideration. It may be that *unchecked* authority ought not to be lodged anywhere, but this ought not to go so far as to preclude leadership. The president, as chief legislator, is essential.

The general shape of a new government is indicated in these observations. It would be a government of more branches intended to legitimize emerging functions; it would provide for the provoking of discussion and for carrying out majority preferences; it would contain and regulate the pluralistic economic system; it would establish a chief of state freed of many other burdens; it would confine the House of Representatives to passing laws and would provide for their examination by a second deliberative body; it would provide for continuous constitutional study and periodic amendment, and also for a judiciary to bring laws into accord with its precepts. And it would clarify the increasingly confused relations between the states and the nation.

If all of this were to be done, and if the directives and prohibitions concerning rights and duties were redefined, a new generation might be able to claim that it had matched the achievement of the original framers.

It is to be hoped that, like the group who produced the Virginia resolutions, there will be others who will produce models calculated to focus discussion of the new constitution so clearly needed.

Acceptance

If there were no other experience to go on, the furor about ratification in 1787–88 ought to be warning enough that some other procedure ought to be found. The country was deeply disturbed by an agitation that centered on none of the real problems and developed a fury over the unreal ones.

Most of those who took the lead in dissenting were states' righters, local politicians who saw the new government as a threat to their prerogatives. The first such engagement was in Pennsylvania; but it was got through rapidly. The more formidable oppositions were organized in Virginia, Massachusetts, and New York.

The Virginia agitator who was the most extreme was Patrick Henry. He tried his best to excite a Kentucky delegation (Kentucky was a western outpost of the state) with the threat that the Mississippi would be closed to them by federal control of commerce. He ranted against the first words of the Preamble. "Who authorizes," he demanded, "gentlemen to speak the language of We, the people, instead of We, the states?" He went on to ask whither the genius of America had gone, and shouted that "chains of consolidation" were about to convert the country into an empire. The balances spoken of by the Constitution's defenders, he said, were specious; they were "imaginary, rope-dancing, chain-rattling, ridiculous . . . contrivances."

There were others who contended that federal courts would "swallow up and destroy" the state courts. There also appeared the familiar argument that the country was too large and too various for one government. Congressmen from New England would never understand the needs of the South. Others still contended that requisitions on the states, instead of direct taxation, would be sufficient.

The holders of these opinions were some of the most prominent citizens. Among them were two future presidents, Monroe and Tyler, and the father of another, Benjamin Harrison. There was one future chief justice, Marshall. There were also Mason and the Lees (Henry and Light-Horse Harry) and a number of old revolutionary heroes.

One day Patrick Henry spoke uninterruptedly for seven hours. When Washington heard of the proceedings he was discouraged. He had not been suggested as a candidate for the Convention and was at home in Mount Vernon, but he kept in touch through Madison and others. Madison was no match for Henry in an oratorical contest, nor was Wythe, the scholarly lawyer who had been Jefferson's teacher; but it was Wythe who, when he judged the time to be propitious, moved for adoption of the ratifying resolution. This was on June 25, nearly ten months after the signing. The vote was 89 to 79. This was more in the nature of a capitulation than an agreement, and it was certain that the long and heated period of dissension had left an unhappy aftermath.

Somewhat the same sort of struggle took place in Massachusetts and New York. In Pennsylvania, after a sitting of five weeks, the vote had been 46 to 23; but in Massachusetts there were 187 yeas to 168 nays. There Daniel Shays's old followers rallied the farming West against the mercantile East; and when the vote went against them, they were still sullen and resentful.

The struggle in Poughkeepsie was still going on when Virginia ratified. Governor Clinton had been made president of the Convention. He was ably supported by Yates and Lansing, who had left the Philadelphia meeting before it was well started. Supporters, however, included such names as Jay, Duane, Roosevelt, DeWitt, and Hamilton. Hamilton was never more eloquent and energetic, but the cause seemed to be lost until the news came from Virginia. The vote, when it came, was 30 to 27.

The smaller states were not so impressed with their own importance, and all but Rhode Island (where no notice at all was taken of any of the constitutional proceedings) ratified without such serious dissent. There was much dissatisfaction because of the lack of a bill of rights, a complaint answered by Madison and others who pointed out that such declarations existed in most of the state constitutions, and these could be added later by amendment.

This long year of agitation and animosity was, of course, the aftermath of confrontation in the Convention. It was a victory for the federalists (nationalists were now being called that). But it had serious consequences. If Jefferson had been at home, he would have joined Monroe, Harrison, and Marshall against Madison and Wythe. And when he became president, he won by being an antinationalist (called, then, Democratic-Republican). And his view of the Constitution he had sworn to support and defend had been made known as soon as he had read it. He became the most powerful of the early strict constructionists, the reputed instigator of the subversive Kentucky Resolutions.

Not to labor the lesson from this experience, so much more traumatic than later Americans are disposed to admit, it does seem to indicate that the procedure was badly conceived. The alternate would appear to be a more careful preparation of the constitutional drafts through continuing study by unexceptionable assignees. If the framers were known to be both disinterested and wise, ratification might well be by a reverse process. The people, voting at large, might have a veto rather than a vote, based on the theory that they had already agreed to what would be produced and would reject it only if it proved altogether unsuitable.

This would obviate or, at least, reduce the opposition of the self-interested, the "men of local views," and the hopeful demagogues.

CHAPTER 3

PARTS AND THE WHOLE

A Federal Arrangement Is Difficult

The advocate of federalism has a difficulty inherent in his subject. This, of course, is duality. When authority is divided, proprietors of both allocated powers feel themselves challenged to enlarge their shares, and this issue will always be a favorite of politicians. The possibility of creating a cause is attractive because it so easily takes on the characteristics of a crusade. However earnestly the original arrangers may have tried to establish a stable situation, dissatisfaction is apt to gnaw at unhappy minorities. Parties form around them or are held together by their attraction. Only the most disinterested and prescient original arrangement can prevent this sort of division and continuing acrimony. It has never yet happened.

The controversy originates in conflicting purposes among those who framed the agreement. In so many instances—and certainly in that of the United States Constitution—some among the framers have not really tried for stability. In Philadelphia a strong contingent was more interested in protecting local advantages or power groups than in strengthening the Union. In such circumstances a perfect distribution is unlikely to result from the proceedings. Bargaining will leave a remaining advantage for unionists or for those distrustful of union, and however slight it may be, the temptation to enlarge it will be irresistible. Also, the resistance of the losers will be strong. From almost imperceptible beginnings such a difference can become the cause of violence. In the United States one such agreement resulted, after seventy-three years of continuous bickering, in civil war.

This sort of quarrel engages the most dangerous emotions, not only those of prestige or gain but of patriotism; and decisions involving loyalty to state, province, or country tear at men's souls. Americans recall Patrick

Henry and the Lees of Virginia who went so far as to insinuate during the ratification convention in 1788 that Washington had betrayed his homeland for an oppressive Union. Further along in our constitutional history, Jackson, wrenched out of his old states' right commitment, found that he had to threaten the use of force to suppress a rising separatism; the Union had by then—because he was president—become the object of his concern. His forthright commitment served to stifle disloyal activity for nearly a generation.

The Calhoun dinner was in April, 1830, and in the 1850s presidents were no longer Jacksons; they were conciliators who sought to appease the secessionists who were more and more insistent that the federal compact allowed the states to leave the Union or refuse obedience to its laws. Buchanan, the last of these presidents, was so weak a unionist that, after infiltrating the government, the southern states felt capable of challenging the North.

The war settled the issue of separatism, but it did not settle that of divided authority; that was still an untouched principle of the Constitution. The states' righters went on campaigning to hold the central government within stiffly contracted limits. Strict construction remained a cause almost as often appealed to in the 1900s as it had been in the 1800s. The issue, strangely, was not touched by the postwar amendments proposed and ratified by the victors. It remained to be fought over in political wars in nearly every succeeding national election. "Encroachments" by the central government were always an issue for the *outs* who wanted to oust the party in power. These were more usually Democrats, who were traditionally southern and agrarian in the years before the Great Depression. Besides, the Republicans controlled the government most of that time—and so were the *ins*. Strict constructionists continued to insist that the "powers not delegated to the United States by the Constitution, nor prohibited by it to the states" were, without any flexibility, reserved respectively to the states. This, of course, would give the states enlarging responsibilities as the nation expanded and became more affluent.

The words just quoted are from the Tenth Amendment of the ten that make up the Bill of Rights. The other nine are devoted to individual immunities from governmental control. This last one is meant to protect the states as well as individuals; however, four words at the end have a different implication. These are ". . . or to the people." It has never been certain what was meant by this addendum, or how it may be interpreted. If it is set over against the so-called supremacy clause that seems to establish the primacy of the Union, the ambivalence inherent in federalism is made apparent. That clause says that the "Constitution and the laws of the United States which shall be made in pursuance thereof . . . shall be the supreme law of the land." The doubtful words here are "in pursuance thereof."

It was this doubt that gave the loose constructionists their basis for argument. It was very hard to say that a law approved by the Congress was *not* necessary to the carrying out of some enumerated power; it was almost as hard to distinguish between very necessary and lesser degrees of exigence. The question whether some law was essential moved the issue into the only forum able to settle specific controversies—the Court. But it could move there only if it was admitted that the Court too had an implied power, the serious one of saying whether congressional acts complied with the terms of the Constitution. The alternative to this was, of course, clarifying amendment. This, however, had been made so difficult, especially in issues affecting the Congress, that it was not a practicable remedy. Judicial judgment was allowed by default. Everyone could see that some authority had to decide; and since the judges were willing, it was allowed that they should take the responsibility.

The strict constructionists were undoubtedly correct in contending that the original sovereignty of the people had been conferred on the states, and that only so much of it was yielded to the central government as was specified in Article I where the powers of the Congress were enumerated. This was the core covenant between the nationalists and the states' righters at Philadelphia. Everything else done there centered in their agreement. Whether the bargaining was done in good faith on both sides does not matter; it was agreed to. What is important is that neither side was satisfied with it, and when they had to implement it, neither felt compelled to honor it. There had been ample discussion, but the protagonists still had not changed the conceptions they had held when they arrived. The compromise document was indeed signed and submitted for ratification; but since it was signed by only thirty-nine of the fifty-five who, at some time, participated (another nineteen never even appeared), it was by no means a consensus document. It is significant that of the New Yorkers, only Hamilton signed; such noted Virginians as Mason and Randolph refused—they had participated in the debate up to the last day but would not join in the signing.

Even when the Constitution had become effective, these dissenters from the bargain, together with those who accepted what had been done so long as the central government held to its assignment, but only so long, continued to oppose vehemently any expansion of central powers. The issue served to establish an opposition party—the Democratic-Republicans—and after only twelve years it elected a president.

The Constitution had made no provision for further consideration of such an issue. There had always been parties within the states with differences about local issues, but it had been conceived that the central government would be above all that. The representatives in the lower house would reflect sentiment in their districts, and the senators would do the same for statewide constituencies; but the president (and vice-president), chosen by a carefully devised electoral college, having the stature and prestige of national leadership, would be far removed from such considerations. The president would preside; he would not participate in electoral decisions.

The effort of the framers to make the presidency immune to what they called "faction" did not last very long. Jefferson, at the head of the states' righters, had resigned from Washington's cabinet to conduct a campaign opposing the nationalists (now called federalists). He could not defeat John Adams in 1796, but he managed it in 1800. He was a master of the political tactics so feared by the nationalists. Since he used his gifts in the interest of strict construction, it was expected by his followers that once he possessed the presidential power, he would keep the central government well within the bounds of literal constitutional writ.

It was by a tour de force in the desperation of Federalist defeat that the judiciary held the line by imposing on the Constitution the doctrine of implied powers. The judiciary, Marshall said, must, in all reason, have been intended to be the Constitution's interpreter. And in 1819, relying on the Tenth Amendment, he concluded that the states had "no power . . . to retard, burden, or in any manner control, the operations of constitutional laws" necessary to the implementation of the Constitution.[1] It will be seen that Marshall's limiting word "constitutional" was quite as ambivalent as "necessary" in the amendment itself. It was more and more obvious that someone or some agency must say whether in a specific instance what the Congress had done was constitutional as well as necessary; otherwise the Congress in effect would be all-powerful. For this, again, the only alternative was amendment. The Court, by seizing the interpretive power, made amendment unnecessary. This relieved a pressure that might have become intolerable if the Congress had insisted that anything it did must be constitutional.

Marshall did not deny that the federal government was limited; it was "acknowledged by all," he said, "to be one of enumerated powers." This, however, was not a very meaningful concession. The principle might be universally admitted, but the extent of the powers actually granted was continually arising and would continue to arise as long as our system existed. If it lodged in the Court the duty of determining "the extent" of the granted powers, the justices, in spite of some serious handicaps—such as the possibility of being overruled by the Congress's power to determine their jurisdiction, and their inability to make any decisions except in actions not originated by themselves—continued to think themselves appointed to accept such responsibility.

It may be suspected from these American experiences, and from the judgment of Marshall and his colleagues, that this reveals the nature of the federal system, that there shall be an agreed allocation, but that the agreement shall always be subject to interpretation—judicial interpretation.

1. *McCulloch* v. *Maryland*, 4 Wheat. 316 (1819).

What made good Marshall's conclusion that the uncertainty of "extent" justified expansion not of state but of central powers was the development of a particular kind of civilization to be controlled and contained by public authority. A country that expanded, that increased in population, and that created an industrial system simply overflowed state boundaries and became unitary. The appeals to constitutional limits, and to local sentiments, were so patently out of harmony with the actualities of growth that they could not be allowed to prevail.

Was Marshall's pronouncement final? Can federalism never find a successful constitutional embodiment? And is federalism necessary anyway; or is it a principle belonging to a simpler past, never expected to return?[2]

The answers to these questions are to be found in redefinition, in periodic redistribution, and in a narrowed grant for interpretation. At least, such answers will be argued here.

But, as a Temporary Expedient, Not Impossible

The division of powers between the states and the general government adopted by the American framers is not the only possible one. That arrived at in Philadelphia was, in fact, the result of bargaining more than of principle. It was not even determined by a view of the future, but rather in a compact resulting from protracted bargaining between a group of nationalists and one of states' righters.

During the discussions there was never any serious dissent to the states' claims of autonomy. The Union was a convenience (actually it had become a necessity) for warding off aggression on the borders and reducing dissension within them. The British, for instance, had not drawn back from their outposts required by the peace treaty; the French were in an expansionist phase; and the Spanish were refusing to recognize the southern borders. The internal dissensions, arising as they did partly over the competition among the states to escape paying for the common facilities established by the Congress and partly over the tendency of each to obstruct the commerce of the others, made some sort of general rule necessary. It seemed more desirable to those states with good harbors and many merchants than to those whose incoming goods used the ports of their neighbors and were taxed by them, but there was a general recognition of the need for regulation.

2. Federalism as used here had better be defined at this point. It is taken to mean a union of originally sovereign states whose representatives have delegated to a central government specified powers (as in Switzerland or the United States). It does *not* mean a central government that has delegated or left certain powers to its constituent units (U.S.S.R.); and it does *not* mean a unitary government with administrative provinces or departments (France); and, of course, it does not mean an absolute monarchy or a dictatorship with similar administrative regions.

A group coming together for such purposes would naturally proceed from the assumption that the states, being sovereign, were to make such concessions to a general government as would establish a common defense and regulate commerce among them; but there was no intention of conceding further powers. For this limited purpose, the original Articles of Confederation, it was supposed—and was stated in the resolution of the Congress authorizing the meeting—would be rather simply amended. As the discussions advanced, however, it began to be apparent that a common defense—and the establishment of some common facilities—involved a certain source of revenue. To make it secure, and to provide for equitable sharing in the obligation, the old system of requisitions would not do; that had consisted merely in notification to the states of needed contributions; they could respond or not as they chose; and all too often they did not choose, sometimes when it was merely inconvenient. But if authority to tax would have to be conferred, only a rule of uniformity would make it acceptable; and this involved going beyond amendment of the Articles. It involved a wholly new jurisdiction for the central government.

The delegates from the smaller states—such as Connecticut, New Jersey, and Delaware—felt that the larger and richer ones ought to do the paying, since they had more to protect; and even with a uniform rule, they would not trust the allocation and collection of revenues to a government dominated by the larger states. For more than a month the Convention was unable to get over this difficulty. The fears of the smaller states caused the original Virginia Resolves offered by Randolph to be countered by another set offered by Paterson of New Jersey. These would have amended the Articles of Confederation as the Congress had directed to be done, "so as to render the federal constitution adequate to the exigencies of government and the preservation of the Union." It would have acknowledged the sovereignty of the states; it would have narrowed the enumeration of conceded powers and limited their application. The institutions to be created would have been a single legislative chamber with equal representation from all states, large and small, and a plural executive. The states, finally, would retain a veto over congressional acts.

When this plan appeared, it instantly polarized the company. It now appeared that the issue was not only one between the small states and the large, but more importantly between local politicians and national-minded statesmen. Immediately Paterson found allies in the New York and Massachusetts delegations, where there were long-seated political machines whose leaders had been suspicious from the start. Lansing of New York was vociferous. The Virginia Plan, he said, was one the delegates had no power to discuss; in a violent tirade he denounced the nationalists' proposal and supported that of Paterson. "It sustains the sovereignty of the states," he said; "and that of Mr. Randolph destroys it." He continued, saying that if it had been suspected that a consolidation of the states and the formation of a national government was to have been proposed, delegates from New York would never have been sent.

Lansing's sentiments were also those of a formidable number of other delegates, among them his colleague Yates of New York, Luther Martin of Maryland, Gerry of Massachusetts, Sherman and Ellsworth of Connecticut, and Mason of Virginia. The issue was now clarified. The alternatives were before the Convention, and a group of delegates were ranged on each side, with a few open to persuasion in the middle. What emerged after the acrimonious debates of the following month was a compromise. It was agreed that there would be two legislative bodies, one with members directly elected from districts, the other from the states but giving all the states equal representation. This Congress would have powers limited to those enumerated and without freedom to compass any others. In these respects the states' righters prevailed. The nationalists, however, got their way about majority rule (the New Jersey plan would have allowed a minority to veto any proposal, and allowed the states to veto congressional acts). They got their way too about a single nationally chosen executive who could be removed by an impeachment proceeding but not, as Paterson proposed, on demand of a majority of the states.

The nationalists had finally won only a limited general government; the states remained in possession of the residual powers. Nevertheless the more determined states' righters were unappeased; they wanted especially a veto against even these enumerated powers. Some of them left and did not return. New York, for the rest of the summer, was represented only by Hamilton, who, for opposing reasons, felt that the outlook for a strong government was dim. Some others left as well, for various reasons; but all the defections—such as that of Wythe—weakened the national cause.

The lesson offered by this experience is that almost any apportionment of powers arrived at by contention and, finally, compromise among delegates who still remain unconvinced will result in continued dissension. After ratification, the acrimony between the American nationalists and states' righters continued unabated and even intensified. The states' righters insisted on strict construction of the clauses defining congressional powers; and the nationalists invented the implication theory to allow the enlargement of governmental operations if the Congress should make such attempts.

To have escaped this long and costly quarrel, several conditions would have had to be met. It would have been necessary to have had the Constitution drawn not by representatives of local political groups but by men of acknowledged stature, trusted by at least a majority of citizens and owing no allegiance except to the nation. Such disinterest, coupled with wisdom, is admittedly rare; but it does exist. Among the delegates to the Philadelphia meeting there were, besides Washington and Franklin, Morris, Wilson, and Dickinson; but there were also Yates and Lansing; Gunning Bedford, the demagogue from Delaware; Elbridge Gerry, the petulant man from Massachusetts who was haunted by the memory of Shays's Rebellion; and several minor Patersons who had come with the sole idea of preventing the formulation of an effective government.

Some even of the nationalists felt that it was possible to divide sovereignty by compromise, not really recognizing that such a feat is successful only as an allocation to a subordinate jurisdiction, with revision possible as circumstances demand. The Philadelphia Constitution made the allotment from the wrong principal to the wrong subordinate. The states remained sovereign in everything the future held. The interests of the thirteen conflicted, and the conflicts would be energetically pursued. They had political parties whose favorite target would be a central government attempting to enforce national rule, and this would commit them to the narrowest possible interpretation of federal powers.

If Hamilton's speech (on June 18) had been listened to, things might have turned out differently. By then both the Virginia and the New Jersey plans were before the Convention but the differences had not yet caused hard feelings. What Hamilton proposed was a national government with a legislative branch of two houses, a lower one elected by the people for three years, and an upper one (a Senate) chosen for life; also, a single executive chosen for life by electors and having an absolute veto. State governors would be appointed by the national government. This, it will be seen, was a reversal; original powers ran from the people to a national government, and then to the states, not from the people to the states and then to the nation. He wanted, he said, a general and national government, completely sovereign.

Such a system has been painfully evolving during the subsequent years and predictably may be completed at somewhere about the two-hundredth anniversary of the original compromise Constitution.

Hamilton did not expect to be asked, and was not asked, for details. The delegates allowed him to speak, and then went on with their argument about the apportionment of powers. Hamilton went home to New York and took no further part in the proceedings. But he was loyal; he came back to sign. He thought the result better than the Articles of Confederation, and he defended it eloquently in *The Federalist*. But it had in it the seeds of dissension, and he was more apprehensive than his argument for the defense showed.

It may be too much to expect any constitution to anticipate the future rather than to reflect the past. But that constructed at Philadelphia was exaggerated in this respect. It reflected no intimation, such as Hamilton clearly had, that the whole was to be knitted together by technology, and

that the parts would have their meaning as subordinates in that whole—
whether or not political arrangements reflected such an organic reality.

Nevertheless it had reflected this meaning at the beginning; and Washington found that he could enlarge a presidency outlined only for purposes
of national leadership in the simple circumstances of his time. It remained,
after he had gone, for John Adams to use the instrument in ways so
offensive to the opposition party that he was displaced and Jefferson was
elected to give the office shape. Strangely enough, and somewhat to his own
consternation, Jefferson found himself enlarging it; but the enlargement that
really counted was that made possible by the doctrine of implied powers.
This reinforced the federal powers, but did not make the states' righters
like it. And the differences from this cause deepened all during the half-
century after Adams.[3]

It Must Be Organic

Any organic theory must have a view first of the gestalt and then of
the contributing members. It makes no sense to consider that any part
should dictate to the whole, dominate its actions, or withhold its cooperation—unless, that is, the preferred theory is an additive or separatist
one.

It was not at all clear to most of the delegates at Philadelphia that
the nation was to be one whole with integration as an inevitable characteristic. The colonies had fought separately in the past for a measure of
independence. It was true that by 1776 they had created a Congress, and
that during the Revolutionary War there had been a commander in chief of
the armies; but local affiliations were still strong, and the Congress had
few powers. The colonies (states) contributed volunteers and funds but
only as they themselves decided. Congressional quotas and requisitions
were very often not honored at all—or only partially. Connecticut, for instance, was generous with men but not with money. The separation continued. While the Convention was meeting at Philadelphia conversations
were going on between New York politicians and Canada, looking to some
sort of affiliation; this was a measure of the separatism in that state; and
only Hamilton, among the New York delegates, was finally a signer. The
ties were weak; loyalties were local; the concern for national unity among
many citizens was a matter of practical necessity more than of sentiment.

The "government of enumerated powers" provided in the Constitution
was a grant from the states; it amounted to permission from the parts for
the whole to function. The nationalists were conscious of this, and it was
the reason they insisted that ratification was to be by state conventions;

---

3. Criteria for constitutionmaking merely mentioned here were explored in Chapters 1 and 2.

this would show that their work had been accepted by the people in a new act of consent. The people, not the states, were the source, and ratification was permission for the national government to begin operations. Madison was quite clear about this and on numerous occasions reminded his colleagues, who were inclined to doubt the people's competence, that the states' legislators were inherently unable to authorize the changes about to be proposed. They were creatures of their own state constitutions, and they had no authority to participate in establishing a new government. The argument about this went on intermittently all summer, complicated by the distrust so many delegates felt for conventions that might be dominated by "mobs" as well as the fear that local politicians, anticipating displacement, would use every art known to them to oppose an increase in central powers. And if ratification should fail, the summer's work would have been futile.

In the end the proposal went to specially elected delegates to state conventions, not to state legislatures, and not to a general referendum. The prevailing apprehension was, however, recognized by providing that it should become effective when nine ratifications had been completed. This was a tour de force, much criticized; even Hamilton thought it wrong for nine states to institute a new government with authority in thirteen. Very late in the proceedings there was a formidable movement for a second national convention to consider objections certain to be made when meetings to consider the draft were held in the states. Since it was obvious that delegates to such a renewed convention would come with numerous proposals for amendment, this meant starting all over again. This the majority could not face. Besides, the situation was sufficiently exigent so that years ought not to be spent in further discussion.

All of this points to the real trouble at Philadelphia: that many of the delegates neither represented the nation nor felt any such loyalty as would override what they felt for their states. Some of them did not even represent their states actually, but factions within their states, and such representation was certainly not by election of the people. These delegates knew well enough that they did not have to have the authority needed for such a radical departure as the draft was becoming. What they could do safely, and what they did, was to oppose and obstruct throughout the proceedings; and since they were politicians, they were effective. Very likely they had an approving public opinion to count on, just as later congressmen have had when appealing to local rather than general interests. National sentiment did, of course, become a deep patriotic feeling in time, but very little support could be mustered for national interests in 1787; and not, indeed, until threats from outside excited everyone and dedicated leaders appeared.

If it now seems incredible that at least one-third of the delegates were there to see that what was done did not adversely affect the interests of their local factions, nevertheless it is true. That any charter for a general government could have been put together in such circumstances does seem, as Washington said it was, "a miracle." But also the immense difficulties overcome ought not to obscure the energy it required to overcome them—or the compromises that had to be accepted. There were bargainings, dealings, and, generally, continuous efforts to conciliate "men of local views." The result was such agreements as were thought necessary to ensure a majority of signers and eventual acceptance in the states.

Since what emerged from this process was later ratified in people's conventions, it has been interpreted as creating an organic whole; the people, it has been said, *were* the whole. This was an argument used by the authors of *The Federalist* in their polemic in favor of ratification. Those authors—who were among the nationally minded statesmen of their day—were not at all satisfied with what the state conventions were being asked to approve. They were able to argue honestly that it was an improvement on the Articles of Confederation—it could hardly have been worse—and as they thought it over, it may have seemed that it might be adapted to the nation's needs; perhaps, but probably not; all three were legal realists.

Still it must be remembered that these needs were demanding only in very simple matters, as they would be viewed later. They were, essentially, only a few: defense, prevention of interruptions to trade, a secure source of revenue for the goverment, and an executive. It was about these last that there were the most serious differences. The states' righters still contended that contributions ought to be voluntary, and no one had any clear idea of the duties to be performed by the newly invented president. He was left an anomalous figure without any considerable authority. Even Washington, as he began, could not see how he could do what was obviously needed.

The developments so soon to show themselves were, however, not yet apparent. Expansion into the West, it is true, was imminent, and there was concern about the territories claimed by the seaboard states. Many of the most prominent delegates had large investments in the reaches beyond the known frontiers. Washington's were the most extensive, but Robert Morris and Wilson were involved to the extent of later bankruptcy. But there was no movement in the Convention to protect these interests. Those involved were all nationalists, and a strong nation with secure borders would help to make good their investments; but nothing specific was proposed.

Apart from this, even immediate changes were not anticipated and so not discussed. If the delegates could have looked ahead a few decades to the tying together of then remote communities by roads, canals, a postal service, and a widely circulating press, they might at least have considered the bonds of union so essential to nationhood. They would have seen to it that the nation, not the states, possessed the residual powers and the authority to dispose them.

What they created was a system of enumerated powers. The meaning of this is that the states remained free, and its having been found that, unless bound, they would not cooperate in common concerns, they agreed to concede certain of their powers to a general administration. They were logical about this, or the majority was. It was beyond their competence to surrender any part of their autonomy if it had been conceded to them conditionally by the people; but they could do it if the people consented. This was Madison's view, and his logic prevailed; it was because of this that ratification was not asked of the state legislatures but of specially elected conventions. This made the new government legitimate in theory. Its power to act was conveyed from the original source—the people; this was the same legitimacy as that claimed by the state governments.

This cured the dichotomy of two governments derived from the people, with overlapping or conflicting directives. But there was a flaw in the logic. Only ratification was a people's act. It was quite forgotten that the Constitution provided for concessions to the general government *by the states* of authority they had formerly had. One government, it was conceived, had a general grant; the other only those delegated to it not by the people but taken from the states. This is what was meant by "enumerated powers." If the states held all but a few conceded powers, given for convenience, they, being closer to the people, and being older in that relationship, might repel inroads with perfect right. If expansion resulted from the exigencies of national growth, the general government was still held to its specific list of duties; but the states were not. Anything added belonged to them.

It can be seen from this where the great error was made at Philadelphia; or, perhaps it should be said, how immense the failure of anticipation was. If the holder of general powers had been the central government, and the designee of residual ones the states, it could be argued that the Constitution made the nation one whole.

Everything that has happened since 1789 has certainly reinforced the need for recognizing the gestalt as superior to its organs. But it was not done at Philadelphia.

Anomalies and Obstructions

Speaking still of the United States, technology has by now demonstrated a virtually complete indifference to political boundaries. These are often a nuisance, but they have hardly ever slowed technological advance. This is particularly true of the states of the Union, but not so true of the United States, since it stretches from sea to sea and includes many natural zones.

Government for a technological age, it seems, must be at least nation-wide, and state authority not only has become insufficient but is likely to be obstructive. The federal government has had continual difficulty, as transportation, communication, and other service industries have developed, in imposing its regulations as against those of the states. A railroad crossing New Jersey to carry goods and passengers between New York and Philadelphia could be controlled (and taxed) by New Jersey even though its trains were mostly running to Pennsylvania or other distant places. Most states had, and still have, public utility commissions duplicating those of the federal government. For a considerable period states taxed the operations of "foreign" corporations more heavily than those based at home; some still do. National merchandisers have been handicapped in this way. Even today telephone and power companies are answerable to state utility commissions.

Tax systems in various states maintain different rates and thus create a thriving commerce in smuggled goods. Special divisions of Maryland and Virginia police are maintained to prevent liquor from being "imported" from the District of Columbia; and New York (as well as other states) has special police to suppress a massive influx of tobacco products from the Carolinas, where they are not taxed. One truckload of cigarettes can yield a profit of thousands of dollars to bootleggers. It is a traffic that supports many criminals in affluence.

It is possible to go on at length listing strange situations of this sort. There has never been an arrangement to prevent duplicating taxes or other regulations. As a result, liquor is heavily taxed by both states and the nation. Worse than this, in the case of liquor, taxes are imposed on retail sales prices made up largely of federal taxes, thus multiplying the cost to consumers; and, of even more importance, the same rule applies to other commodities such as gasoline.

For the explanation of these and many other irritating inconveniences, the nonorganic nature of the Constitution is to be blamed. But this, it is argued by those who oppose constitutional revision, is so considerably modified by the "living" theory that any serious anomaly will be cured, in time, by appeals to the Supreme Court. This theory has been explored in former chapters; it is sufficient to say here that its source is the power claimed by the Court of adapting the Constitution to practical circumstances. The obvious difficulty about this is that interpretations with such purposes in view depend on the reasoning of a majority of nine judges or, as unkindly critics say, on their prejudices or, even worse, on their interests. Lawyers, become judges, it is said, are still corporate, criminal, or civil rights specialists.

This is not an easy criticism to meet; but the difficulty of amendment is so serious and the prestige of the Court is so formidable, that the theory has become almost universally accepted. As Pritchett has remarked, the judges do not go so far as to turn the President's four-year term into one of five years; but the meaning of such clauses as that giving the Congress authority to regulate commerce among the states is believed to be legitimately given different interpretations as the judges choose.[4]

This theory again rests on Marshall's statement that the Constitution was "intended to endure for ages to come. . . ." He reasoned from this that it must be adapted to "the various crises of human affairs." By whom? By the Court, of course.

This last was a sensible enough conclusion from the premise of permanence. But it is altogether improbable that the framers thought of the Constitution in this way, since all of them, in different ways, were dissatisfied with it and would have changed it if they had not felt forced to compromise.

This dissatisfaction grew until Marshall relieved the pressures by inventing the theory of flexibility.[5] No one, any longer, looks to the Constitution itself for definitions or rights or governmental powers; he searches through Court opinions, seeking the last and, therefore, the presently authoritative interpretation. It is not necessary to say that this has become a complicated and uncertain matter so that, on fine issues or on new ones, it is necessary to initiate and carry through several expensive proceedings in lower courts, hoping finally for consideration by the Supreme Court itself.

It is in proceedings of this sort that enterprises carried on in more than one state have had to discover whether their operations were subject to regulation by state or federal authority; sometimes they have had to repeat the proceedings to find out whether the courts, after some time, still held the same opinion. That the Constitution "lives" means, simply, that it may change, and its changes are changes of mind by judges. True, the judges are serious and responsible men; but they often differ among themselves, showing that even superior minds can come to opposite conclusions. There are such things as unanimous decisions; but many are reached by majorities with their "brothers" more or less politely dissenting. It is hard to give such pronouncements oracular dignity; it is nevertheless earnestly attempted.

Why have such important matters as the nature of federalism had to evolve in such an uncertain process? Perhaps it is because amendment is so difficult. Still, if the situation of those who initiated the proceedings leading up to the meeting in Philadelphia is considered, it will be seen that there were serious difficulties. It was no more likely in 1785 that an entirely new government would be fashioned in 1787 than it has been in any recent year that a thorough revision would be undertaken two years hence. And, in fact, although there was much dissatisfaction among merchants

4. C. Herman Pritchett, *The American Constitution* (New York: McGraw-Hill, 1959), p. 47.

5. *McCulloch* v. *Maryland,* 4 Wheat. 316 (1819).

and traders about interferences with commerce, and apprehension concerning the intentions of predatory powers, there was no immediate crisis. And at least two-thirds of the delegates to the Convention had no intention whatever of instituting a new government.

Technology and the enterprises created by its use have by now created a more exigent crisis than that of 1787. The result of deliberations then was to give the national government restricted powers. The focus of similar deliberations now would be the need for enlarging those powers. And it may be guessed that the result would be as surprising as that of 1787.

The delegates then were charged to revise the Articles of Confederation. They, in effect, discarded the Articles for a new Constitution. They arrived at this drastic decision after months of deliberation, in closed and extraordinarily secretive exchanges. Enough of them were convinced by the few original nationalists that such a tour de force was necessary. There were many defections along the way. Nationalism became a rumor before the meeting began, and this was why some states' righters stayed away and others came for the purpose of preventing a nationalist report.

The ratification proceedings were troubled ones in several states. They were very nearly riotous in Virginia, New York, and Massachusetts. And the votes were very close. It might be the same in a modern version of the proceedings if the same rules operated. But, of course, they need not. The selection of delegates, and the method of ratification, particularly, might well be different. The redefining of state-federal relations, certain to be a central purpose, ought to have precluded the sending to Philadelphia of delegates committed to states' rights. They were certain to force compromises, and these might be—as they were—crippling ones. If the delegates had been chosen not by the state political machines dominant in the legislatures but by some other method, perhaps conventions similar to the ratifying ones, the result might have been to have saved the nation continuous controversy, now approaching two centuries in length and including a civil war.

The excuse to be made for the separatists is that technology had not yet established its imperatives. The devotion to nationalism of Washington, Madison, Wilson, Morris, and others was largely derived from the need for securing independence, not for facilitating intercourse and development. There was already a need to stop interferences with commerce; this, indeed, was the excuse for the meeting; but what was more important was wide realization that congressional futility under the Articles was weakening the nation. What had been gained by the sacrifices of the revolution could be lost to great powers who might isolate and win away the states, one by one. These were not dangers of a sort to arouse again the spirit of mutual help and resistance to oppression, but they were there in the background; and if commercial obstructions were the excuse for the meeting, the more foresighted of the statesmen did realize that if something was not done, the new nation would disintegrate. If it did, no state would be capable of resisting attack from without.

This is not the issue now. What was secondary in 1787 is now primary. The admonition to perfect the Union, so imperfectly carried out in the Philadelphia meeting, still waits to be carried out in another, not so that the nation will be made more secure, but so that it can go forward.

This is a positive, not a negative, purpose. But among the developments owed to such union as had been achieved is an enlarged awareness of this need. The modern American is not a more intelligent individual than his ancestors, but he has an education they did not have; he has, besides, many sources of information and is therefore able to conceive the future as well as to understand the lessons of the past.

A new move for revision of the Constitution would not proceed from an apprehension of danger, although it might have support from interests discommoded by remaining state interferences with commerce; it would have to proceed from general realization that the Constitution has been outgrown and that the general interest requires one suited to the present.

The Technological Imperative

It would be difficult to say at what time, precisely, the United States began to become a de facto if not a de jure organized whole. Beginning with seemingly insignificant events, it gradually developed more and more significant ones until it was indisputably a Union.

It had seemed to such nationalists as John Jay, even before 1789, that "the prosperity of the people of America depended on their continuing firmly united"; but he was disconcerted by politicians who sought "safety and happiness in a division of the states into distinct confederacies." Arguing this matter in *The Federalist* (No. 2) Jay wrote several eloquent paragraphs that were anticipatory. If it seems to us now that the country then had miserably inadequate communications, slow transportation, and a primitive press, it seemed to Jay that even then the nation was by nature united. It had often given him pleasure, he said, "to observe that independent America was not composed of detached and distant territories, but that one connected, fertile, wide-spreading country was the portion of our western sons of liberty." He continued:

Providence has in a peculiar manner blessed it with a variety of soils and productions, and watered it with innumerable streams, for the delight and accommodations of its inhabitants. A succession of navigable waters forms a kind of chain round its borders, as if to bind it together; while the most noble rivers in the world . . . present them with highways.

This country and its people, he went on, seemed to be made for each other, and it appeared "as if it was a design of Providence that an inheritance so proper and convenient . . . should never be split into a number of unsocial, jealous, and alien sovereignties."

Jay was contemplating the seaboard country, the domain of the original states. The vast regions beyond the mountains were not so comfortably contained by waters or laced with navigable streams. But on a larger scale a twentieth-century commentator might have said much the same thing of bordering oceans and mightier rivers. Union in later circumstances was as logical as it had been in those spoken of by Jay, perhaps even more so. Instant communication and rapid travel had given it oneness.

In the early years of the nineteenth century the Appalachians, so long a barrier to westward expansion, were already being penetrated. Some legendary heroes belong to this Daniel Boone period. It was not very long, however, before the transmountain country produced a president; and presently there were others from the new prairie states—Ohio, Indiana, and Illinois. These had been far and unknown reaches of country when the Constitution was written. Their boundaries were largely unmarked and their exploration was just beginning. Their settlement, hardly begun thirty years later, was within fifty years made certain by a massive migration.

The occupation of the West was, however, recognized as inevitable all along—so much so that the most prominent of the framers were land-poor from investments in huge tracts of property they had never seen. And from the first, the policy of bringing them into communication with the old East was a settled one. Many families sent their younger sons and daughters out there to live at first in sod huts or in tiny hamlets. It was they who broke the land to the plow and established a transmountain empire. The migrants inched into the short-grass country, finding it so inhospitable that some gave up and returned. But more stayed and others came, finding, presently, that for part of the way there were well-worn trails, and much better knowledge of ways to survive. The first generation never prospered—pioneering was a hard and lonely ordeal—but later ones did, and in an incredibly short time there were towns and cities to rival those of the East.

Then there was the challenge of the Rockies and the Sierras, with the promise of California, if a way could be found to get there. The Rockies were crossed by wagon trains enduring hardships and encountering adventures that still furnish the stuff of endless heroic tales. When this migration began to be better organized in such jumping-off places as Wichita and Independence, and the Santa Fe, Oregon, and California trails were mapped, there soon followed the beginnings of communications systems. For a few years there was a pony express from midcontinent to the coast over mountain and desert. Mails now were delivered in weeks instead of months. The risky crossing of Panama went out of use as a passage, and rounding the Horn in sailing ships was nearing an end.

The pony express gave way to the rails, and after 1880 crossing the continent in wagons was no longer needful. New developments now began to come swiftly. There was an era of railroad building, and railroads brought the telegraph. Presently there were roads and telephones, and toward the end of the century oil and the internal-combustion engine began to displace horse transportation and even to threaten the railroads. Electricity came into use, and newspapers could circulate more widely. Also politicians could reach larger audiences, and wider issues could be discussed.

In the eighties there was already a reaction against the capitalists who had built and who controlled the railroads. The farmers of the plains resented the rates charged for shipping their products to Chicago and Kansas City. The Populists, as a party, gave the eastern investors and financiers a real scare. They had a hero too—Bryan. And he very nearly upset the long-lasting Republican monopoly by capturing the Democratic nomination in 1896 and ignoring the custom that kept candidates in retreat during campaigns. He traveled up and down and across the country by rail, reaching many city and small-town audiences with his remarkable oratory.

But Bryan did not have what his successor candidates would have in the 1920s—the radio; then in the 1940s—television. Besides these, swifter and swifter airplanes allowed candidates to visit every one of the states. Bryan's opponent, McKinley, had stayed at home, relying on the Republican faithful. His front-porch campaign called for the organization of pilgrimages to his seat in Ohio. They came daily—farmers, church congregations, labor unions, neighborhood clubs from the cities, and in long trains of Pullman cars. McKinley spoke to them in kindly and dignified style as they crowded together on the lawn of his home, and they went away feeling themselves privileged.

It was not the first really national campaign, of course, but transportation facilities were first used then to good effect in a presidential contest. McKinley won, not because he stayed at home, but because he appealed to a wider electorate than Bryan, whose constituency was the narrower one of the agricultural West and South. The lesson was well learned; there was never another candidate who confined himself to a sectional electorate. All the voters could be reached, and most of them were. This tended to blur party differences, but it did prevent serious ideological line-ups, and it began to unite the nation politically as it was already being united economically. There were differences, but there now was a way of making democratic decisions.

As to this, grain was still raised in the prairie states and cotton in the South, and these made powerful interests the politicians had to recognize.

There was still a concentration of manufacturing in Chicago, Detroit, and on the eastern seaboard, and the financial center remained in New York. But dispersal and technical changes had begun that would turn farms into factories, take factories into the fields, and transform the nature of urban life. The megalopolis of the Northeast would be matched by one on the Great Lakes, another in California, and still another in the Southwest. Because the nation was one it did not so much matter where production facilities were located.

In the eighties the first school of administration, the Wharton School of Finance and Commerce, began to operate at the University of Pennsylvania. During the next three decades one appeared at every important university. Improvement in managing large enterprises was concurrent with the enlargement of the enterprises themselves and the proliferation of facilitating industries—transportation, communications, banking, insurance, accountancy, and the like. By growth and by merger, enterprises such as the primary ones of steel and other metals, oil and its derivatives, food, pharmaceuticals, and automobiles spread throughout the states. The railroads adopted diesel locomotives and were freed of water stops, and at the same time they began to lose their passengers to a tremendous surge in motorcars and roadbuilding. Americans took to wheels and moved about over distances in hours that would have taken days in 1900, and weeks in 1800.

The old limitations to movement were already breaking down when the airplane began its swift development. From machines of canvas and wires to ones of steel, aluminum, and even taconite, and from propellers to jets, was a transformation compassed within a few years. It was concurrent with the radio-television development. By 1960 it was possible for citizens everywhere to know what citizens knew everywhere else and at the same time; and if they needed or wanted to move from where they were to any other location in the country it could be done in hours. Both time and space had been syncopated until simultaneity was obviously approaching. Dialing for himself, any telephone subscriber could call any other over a national network. The telegraph, so lately a marvel to rural regions, almost disappeared; and every day thousands of passengers flew across thousands of miles in air-conditioned comfort.

It is useful to remind ourselves of these rapid changes and the transformation of national life caused by them. One consequence, for instance, of this conquest of time and space was that by 1960 Washington was nearer to Sacramento by some hours than it had been to the midcontinent state capitals of Springfield or Indianapolis in 1950; another was that an executive in New York, Chicago, Houston, or San Francisco controlled nationwide enterprises more easily by computer, teletype, and improved organization than his predecessor had been able to control an organization confined within a county—or certainly a state. And political boundaries had become completely irrelevant. Railways and highways were now national systems; large industries had their sources of supply, their markets, and their manufacturing plants in widely separated locations. And government had to expand if it was not to lose all relevance to reality.

The bureaucracy in Washington, in spite of politicians who continued to long for simpler times, was enlarged by thousands every year, coming to public work from educations in administration, law, government, economics, and other useful techniques.

There had been a startled awakening when the paralyzing crisis of depression occurred in the thirties. It overwhelmed a business system grown complacent with easy prosperity. There was another awakening when the second Roosevelt mobilized a corps of educated officials to assess the damage and rebuild the system instead of waiting out the hard times and trusting to the ancient rule of patronage for manning the agencies for relief, recovery, and reform. The educational growth of two generations then had its effect for the first time. The politicians did not realize it, but their own trade was marked for a similar transformation. In a few years both houses of the Congress would have a growing number of former professors among their members. There had always been lawyers, but now there were economists, political scientists, and graduates in public administration. Governmental customs were in for a change; patronage would give way to respect for competence, seniority to proved performance, and logrolling to studied lawmaking. The giving way would be painful, noisy, and slow, but it was inevitable.

The expert bureaucracies and the educated legislators would extend the rule of the federal government inexorably over the whole nation. They had the facilities, the resources, and the abilities. All other centers would sink into secondary importance. The programs for regulation of industry—including agriculture—ignored the states. Welfare became a common demand; education had to be for objectives irrelevant to locality. There were only trivial differences and small concerns that were different in Oregon and the Carolinas. The fashions of New York were indistinguishable from those of Seattle. Local dialects disappeared. What was left of different cultures was conserved with nostalgic earnestness as something about to be lost and consequently precious.

Crossing twenty states in hours, or several in a day's drive, travelers spent nights in hostelries identical with the ones they had recently left. Hotel and motel chains had units running into the hundreds and stretching from coast to coast. These establishments had the same carpets on their floors, the same sheets on their beds, and the same food in their restaurants. Moreover, the travelers saw the same news programs on identical television sets in every room. The news centered in the nation's capital, it was current, it was dispensed by familiar voices, and it was the same everywhere.

The nation was indeed far more unified than any single state had been when the Constitution was written. It had not been made so by that Constitution; indeed it had all happened in spite of the compromise that had recognized the primary residual authority of the states and had yielded the nation only those powers necessary to security and the suppression of interstate competition, and that had institutionalized the equality of Delaware and Pennsylvania, New Jersey and New York, New Hampshire and Massachusetts.

Coming into the new age had been made possible by "interpretations." It was the work of judges, not of statesmen; and if further changes were made it would have to be the judges who made them. They had successfully interdicted any other sort. For a democracy it was a curious delegation to a particular and narrow elite. Because such a "judgeocracy" was strangely out of character for America, it was still more curious that no suggestion was made for amendment of the Constitution that allowed it. But there was none. And since the courts had handicaps, and since what they were doing was allowed by nothing more legitimate than custom and prestige, the structure of government, in spite of universal education and technological transformation, became more and more anachronistic as the states fell into the lethargy of obsolescence. There would come an awakening, but it could not be said when.

Unionism in Theory and Practice

The confederate republic described by Montesquieu in his *Spirit of the Laws* was something of a model for the authors of *The Federalist* when they were urging ratification, just as it had been for the scholarly Madison working for years in his Montpelier study or conferring with Randolph and Wythe to organize the Virginia Resolves. The French theorist had been quoted in many of the legal discussions of the preceding years. Adams and Wilson were familiar with his works. Like most influential theorists, however, he could be quoted with some effect by both sides of the nationalist–states' rights controversy. The states' rights advocates had thought him a useful authority for their case; it was true enough that he had recommended small, almost miniature principalities; but, said Hamilton, in *The Federalist* (No. 9), this, for America, would argue only for a reduction in size of the larger states; it would not militate against their being all comprehended in one confederacy. Indeed a confederacy was the preferred expedient for "extending the sphere of popular government."

He went on to quote a passage that does still seem to comprehend the theory of federalism:

This form of government is a convention by which several smaller *states* agree to become members of a larger *one* which they intend to form. It is a kind of assemblage of societies that constitute a new one, capable of increasing, by means of new associations, till they arrive at such a degree of power as to be able to provide for the security of the united body.

Hamilton enlarged on this passage as applied to the American instance:

The proposed Constitution, so far as implying an abolition of the State governments, makes them constituent parts of the national sovereignty, by allowing them a direct representation in the Senate, and leaves in their possession certain exclusive and very important portions of the sovereign power.

In view of Hamilton's position both before and after this statement, it is apparent that the approval this seems to imply was purely for practical purposes and did not express his real belief. Because he did want the Constitution to be ratified, he was bound to argue for it as it stood; but he was a thorough nationalist, so much a one that he would gladly have seen the states extinguished as possessors of exclusive powers. He had said as much in his one extended speech to the Convention. That, however, had been unacceptable to the others. He was willing to begin with what had been agreed on.

As might have been expected from the inherent difficulties, the discussion preceding ratification continued after it. When Jefferson became president it seemed that nationalism had been defeated permanently and that the states would be able to limit strictly the central power. But this overlooked another passage—the modest-appearing clauses that established a judiciary whose power extended "to all cases, in law and equity, arising under this Constitution." This, together with the clause saying that the Congress might make all laws "necessary and proper for carrying into execution all the powers vested in the government . . . or any department or officer thereof," gave the judiciary an indefinitely expansible opportunity for reversing Jefferson and sustaining Hamilton.

The later remark of Dicey that federalism meant legalism—the predominance of the judiciary—was an entirely justified generalization.[6] The developments in theory after the government began to operate were to be found in Court opinions. This is where the arguments ended. The first of these decisions was reached in *McCulloch* v. *Maryland*.[7] This case con-

6. Albert V. Dicey, *Introduction to the Study of the Law of the Constitution,* 9th ed. (New York: St. Martin's Press, 1939), pp. 171–80.

7. 4 Wheat. 316 (1819). *Gibbons* v. *Ogden,* 9 Wheat. 1 (1824) five years later made the contributing argument more subtle and confused by distinguishing between interstate and intrastate trade. The phrase "among the several states," Marshall said, did not comprehend commerce which is "completely internal." But "completely" was as ambiguous as "among." There followed a succession of opinions in varied proceedings leading to wider and wider national control until by the middle of the twentieth century what was left to the states had almost vanished. It was a long controversy, largely settled by the hard facts of technological evolution, finally recognized by the Court. There was, however, a wider issue involved than the control of commerce. This was, in effect, the continued existence of the states as originally sovereign.

cerned the competence of the United States to charter a bank and the right of a state to tax the bank's operations if it chose.

Question about this particular issue had begun when Washington, wondering whether he ought to sign a bill establishing the Bank of the United States, asked for an opinion in writing—as he was entitled to do by the Constitution—of Hamilton, Jefferson, and Randolph. Randolph was ambiguous and so not helpful; Jefferson was adverse; Hamilton was strongly favorable. Certainly the chartering of such an institution was not one of the enumerated powers. On the other hand it might be a necessary extension of the power to regulate commerce, but especially that permission granted the government to do what was needed to implement its enumerated powers.

In 1819, twenty years later, Chief Justice Marshall accepted Hamilton's view and, indeed, relied heavily on his argument. This was that, in all reason, there must be implied powers if duties assigned to the federal government were to be exercised at all. It was in this connection that he accepted responsibility for deciding what was, and what was not, necessary to federal functions. He relied on Article I, section 10, of the Constitution, and argued that the word "necessary," not having been prefixed by the limiting word "absolutely" (as had been suggested but rejected in the debates), was left to be interpreted by the Court. It was used, like others, "in various senses; and, in its construction, the subject, the context, the intention of the person using them," were all to be taken into consideration.

Since he was about to say in an immediately following passage that the Constitution was "intended to endure for ages to come, and consequently had to be adapted to the various crises of human affairs," he was not only holding that the states had "no power, by taxation or otherwise, to retard, impede, burden, or in any manner to control the operation of the constitutional laws enacted by the Congress to carry into execution the powers vested in the general government," but was also absolving the sovereign people from any duty to revise the Constitution. The judges would take care of that, remaking it as seemed expedient, just as he was doing in the present case.

This was a serious setback for the states' righters; but it did not end their efforts to recover the authority lost to the central government. From *McCulloch* v. *Maryland* (1819) until South Carolina led the way into outright rebellion in 1860, the controversy went on, coming recurrently to the surface and infusing national political contests with ugly threats of secession.

The anger that moved the southern states to attack the Union had been long preparing. As can be seen now, it was inevitable in the settlement between the opposing theorists at the Constitutional Convention. As it was left then, further developments might go either way. But even though the government established at that time was one of specified powers and one whose creation had been authorized by the states, much could be made, as has been suggested, of ratification by people's conventions rather than state legislatures.

The nationalists, however, had gone softly. For fifty years they carefully avoided abrasiveness when they could. During most of this time, also, they were out of power, a minority party. It was the secessionists who were persistently aggressive. They demanded recognition of their position and would be satisfied with nothing less than complete surrender. They had been encouraged by successive Democratic victories in presidential contests. Buchanan, the last of this line, was a kind of caricature in this style, a "northern man with southern views" (in political parlance, a "doughface"). The growing hysteria in the South, acerbated by the slavery issue, established the romantic notion in southern leaders' minds that the North could be defeated by force when political means failed. When their foolish splitting of the Democratic party—which, if united, constituted a majority—allowed the Unionists' candidate to win in 1860, their fury escaped all bounds, and, as men have so often done, they resorted to an armed conflict they could not win.

The Civil War was a war about federalism; and Appomattox put an end to the illusion that the parts could dictate to the whole. But even that conflict, with all its internecine horrors, could not bring an end to the states' righters' demands. Within a decade they were back at the old arguments. Their representatives had returned to the Congress, they had judges in the federal courts, and they were demanding autonomy in large matters and small. Presently, besides, they discovered a new ally, a powerful one. Big business, swollen by war profits and grown tremendous by the proliferation of facilitating techniques, developed leaders who were irritated by the intervention in their affairs of federal agencies. Within twenty years of the war's end, the first of the federal antitrust acts was passed, and more, obviously, were to come. Big businesses, like the secessionists, had an unreal view of their position; they sought the advantages of technology but refused to acknowledge the obligations it imposed on them. Their empires could not be separate and autocratic; they were parts of a whole whose health comprehended their own. But about this their obtuseness was stubborn. Even though their resistance to the acceptance of decent standards did stop short of civil war, many incidents in their resistance had the stigmata associated with outright conflict. After these lengthening decades, there are still issues remaining unsettled in this weary progression toward the inevitable.

The most corrupt period in American history followed the Civil War; and of all loose public institutions, the state governments were the most notorious. Since their legislators could be bought more cheaply than federal congressmen, and were not so closely watched, business spent its available money where it would get the most favorable results. But something was necessary besides the corruption of the states; it had to be made certain that regulation was an exclusive function of the states and forbidden to the federal government. There thus began a renaissance of localism boosted by business. It was concurred in by the courts for some time, in fact for two generations. Then, however, the judiciary began to reverse itself and revert to the principles announced in *McCulloch* v. *Maryland.*

The significance of Dicey's pronouncement that a federal government was a judicial one could be seen in all this. For several generations now the doctrine of judicial supremacy has not been successfully challenged. Roosevelt tried and failed. But when Truman was rebuked in the steel case he submitted supinely in spite of the fact that he had been vigorously supported by the chief justice in a stinging dissent.[8] This, however, served only to establish the judiciary in full primacy; it did not touch the central issue of federalism. That came later. Proceeding from the position of security it had attained, the Court presently began to legislate, and when necessary invented constitutional principles. Because the Court was more disposed to interpret approvingly the First, Fourth, Fifth, and Sixth Amendments, this was accepted by the legal fraternity, and especially its liberal members, with joyful praise. The Court was doing what the Congress ought to have done long ago.

That Courts are not appropriate constitution framers was a protest these paeans of praise for the results of the enterprise tended to drown. Civil rights neglected by the Congress were discovered by the judges; they also erected a one-man, one-vote principle that enabled them to decree the apportionment of the states' upper houses; and their expansion of the First Amendment was beyond any imagining a few years earlier. These decisions, and others, coming one after another, opened a new phase in the argument about states' rights.[9] What the framers had not done—or the legislature, or the president—the judges had. Federalism had failed, at least in the 1787 version; it could be guessed that it would never be revived with the same aggressiveness. Its political appeal was by no means

---

8. *Youngstown Sheet & Tube Co.* v. *Sawyer,* 343 U.S. 579 (1952).

9. One of the most interesting inventions (whose conclusions all liberals must approve) occurred in 1967 in the case of *Harvey Keyishian et al., appellants,* v. *Board of Regents of the State of New York, et al.* Among other statements, Justice Brennan offered the following (he was joined by four others; there were four dissents): "Our nation is deeply committed to safeguarding academic freedom, which is of transcendent value to all of us. . . . That freedom is therefore a special concern of the First Amendment which does not tolerate laws that cast a pall of orthodoxy over the classroom."

This free and original reading of the First Amendment is a representative illustration of how buoyantly the Constitution may expand with the nourishment of the Court—or, anyway, a majority of its members.

extinguished, but there would thereafter be an air of unreality in appeals to the principle as it was originally understood. Unless it was rejuvenated under original authority it would not revive.

In a deeper sense of course it was not the judges who were doing federalism to death, it was the technology that had made it absurd—too absurd for serious acceptance as a working principle.

This evolution took place over a relatively long period. It is sometimes forgotten that the government of the United States is the oldest continuous one in existence. The British Empire—not the United Kingdom —has in the same time risen and fallen, its falling evidenced in the replacement of empire by commonwealth. This attenuated remaining association was a sort of federalism, but of so weak a sort that it had only consultative functions. It lacked the essential features of government. And unlike the American Union, its members were compelled neither to remain within nor in any way to support its central government.

Other federal schemes have been or are being tried in the numerous new nations formed as the old empires of the French and the Dutch, as well as the British, have broken up. Independence generates such strong sentiments, and offers such attractive opportunities for politicians, that there is no other way short of conquest to create a nation. The world would be reduced to thousands of minuscule nations if federalism had not been invented. And even when small units have come together in confederacies for sheer viability, they have shown a persistent tendency to break up under the hammering of ambitious and usually incompetent demagogues. Since the great powers no longer permit conquest on the Napoleonic scale, voluntary union is the only recourse, and larger units do somehow tend to be formed and hold together. However, in underdeveloped countries it is characteristically under the compulsion of military dictators.

What can happen under the influence of localism can be seen in Africa, where numerous nations have been set up, been given such blessing as the United Nations can confer, and been promised immunity from outside interference. For them to become powers of any consequence, or perhaps even to go on existing, there must be wholesale confederation. In such instances the unfortunate experience of the United States will undoubtedly be repeated. The central government will not be given powers commensurate with its responsibilities; if it tries to expand its powers, it will have to suppress separatist movements. Such governments will be subjected to dictatorships, and the way back to republicanism and a representative form of government will be agonizing and slow.

Unlike the primitive communities, Switzerland, the oldest confederation in Europe, offers novelties. Although small in size, Switzerland has had many of the same experiences as the United States—and over an even longer period. Its central government has acquired its powers slowly and against the opposition of cantonal politicians. The cantons still have such considerable responsibilities that the central government is weak and, in consequence, cautious and conservative. Its ability to continue an independent existence as a nation is owed more to convenience as neutral ground for the greater nations around it than to strength and coherence. It has existed as a constitutional federation since 1848, with major changes in 1874 and 1931. Its legislature is made up of an Assembly with two chambers—a National Council and a Council of States, the National Council representing the whole and the Council of States the cantons. Larger governments experiencing problems resulting from the inability of one individual, however capable, to carry out the duties assigned to him, will be interested in the seven-member council composing the Swiss executive office.

This council, although its duties have continually increased, is weakened by having a president and a vice-president who serve for one year only and who cannot succeed themselves immediately. Control over the departments is, as would be expected, not rigorous, and the bureaucracy tends to become autonomous.[10] It is weakened by having its members elected by the Assembly; also by the limitation that there can be no more than one member from any of the twenty-two cantons.

Switzerland is much admired for its ability to maintain a federal structure, allowing considerable autonomy for the cantonal governments, and is often cited as an example for others. It is, however, so special a case that its applicability elsewhere is very doubtful. Moreover, it has shown a tendency to respond, as other countries have done, to the influence of technology. The federal government does constantly expand its powers, and the cantons do lose theirs. The nation as a whole has become intensively industrialized, and its economic system is inevitably national. Then too its agriculture now employs the smallest proportion of its population of any country in the world, and this change has weakened cantonal devotion to separatism and local independence.

There are, of course, far larger nations with federal structures. The larger British Dominions, now calling themselves nations, have constitutions (unlike the United Kingdom); and all of them have states and a central government with assignments of power to each. Of these, Canada and Australia will perhaps have an easier way to integration than was found in the United States; but both have special separatist problems, especially Canada with its reactionary French province of Quebec. Both, however, are much smaller in population, even though they have vast expanses of

10. Federal responsibility is confined to enumerated powers, as in the United States, each represented by a department: foreign affairs, justice and police, interior, finance, defense, public economy, railways and post offices.

territory, and neither compares in power and influence with the United States.

India and Indonesia exist in a kind of governmental wonderland, calling themselves republics and having a central government; but in neither is that government competent for its immense duties or for resistance to separatism that periodically threatens their integrity. Besides, they are notably backward in economic development. These examples offer no suggestion of interest to others.

The Communist powers, Russia and China, are groupings of nations too; but not the sort that would be of any interest to nations not willing to accept one-party dictatorship. There are nominally separate republics, and there are periodic meetings of national representatives. Deliberation in these affairs, however, is completely unknown. The delegates come for inspiration from the party leaders in Moscow. When they have been given the word they return to carry out instructions.

Nevertheless there are interesting divisions of power between the national bureaucracy and the local officials. In these the republics are entirely subordinate except for such functions as have no interest for Moscow. And they are not effectively used as administrative agencies. Without being especially competent, because of the intrusion of ideological criteria, the central apparatus attempts to administer the entirety of the vast land as a rigidly controlled whole. The Russians have undoubtedly thought themselves strictly logical in accepting the imperatives of technology. The trouble is that they have not really possessed the necessary facilitating instruments, and have attenuated the effort by delegating tasks to political rather than administrative experts.

The comment may be offered, without too much certainty, that the United States, in one way, and the Russians in the other, have come rather blunderingly toward much the same end of national integration. On the other hand, the immense nations of India and Indonesia, both seeking union in their own ways, are, as one commentator has said, "coming apart at the seams"; and the most hopeful, a few years back, of the African nations—Nigeria—has barely escaped breaking up under the stress of tribal and religious differences.

These experiences have different lessons, hard to assess with any assurance. In India religion and custom have made integration unacceptable to illiterate and ill-nourished masses, and the magic of Indian nationalism has not proved to be a sufficiently countering bind. It lasted for a generation; but the leaders who had bested Britain in their bid for independence proved incapable of administering the nation they had created, and national loyalties have faded. Federalism, like democracy, it seems, can be safely grounded only in affluence and education. Poverty and ignorance make it impossible for citizens to raise their concern beyond the struggle against poverty in their neighborhood or village. India is a disappearing image in most Indian minds.

So far as any of these experiences have meaning for the United States in its continuing study of nation-state relations, it is that the causes of dissension and separatism elsewhere are not massively present in the United States; and such as do still exist are rapidly yielding to efforts of elimination.

There ought to be a further word in this about the Communist nations, especially Russia's galaxy of Soviet republics and associated states, extending her home borders far to the east, the south, and the west. This tremendous feat of integration during the past fifty years deserves both respect and understanding. It began with conquest or subversion and has continued with police-state tactics, and it is this that must in the end be transformed into voluntarism if the empire is to survive. Democracy is an inevitable accompaniment of the progress being experienced in those lands, and democracy will ultimately destroy the one-party system now depended on so heavily by Moscow. The West is where democracy has its centers, and looking eastward to Moscow is certain to be more and more a strained effort.

But in the West, for various reasons, democracy has had difficulties. France, democratic at heart, nevertheless found no leader able to reconstitute her shattered prestige after the injury suffered during the world wars and turned to a modified dictatorship. To the south, in Spain and Portugal, authoritarianism kept its traditional relentless hold. And the defeated Germans, struggling back to representative institutions with an extraordinary constitution dictated by American advisers using—with amazing obtuseness —the pattern of the American example, still had to escape from this imposed enormity, and rebegin where the Weimar Republic left off. The United Kingdom and the Scandinavians offered no lessons in federalism. The British had recently lost Ireland to nationalists; and the Danes, Swedes, and Norwegians had broken up their once useful union.

This catalog includes many warnings but almost no relevant lessons. Nevertheless there are perceptible forces at work that can be expected to emerge with strength if the world's effort to conquer poverty succeeds. This is not a success to be easily anticipated; hungry people who are diseased and miserably housed make the first efforts to progress with terrible handicaps; and the succeeding evolution proceeds so slowly as almost not to be perceptible in any one generation.

The prospect now is that the underdeveloped nations, except those held together geographically and racially by national boundaries, will not become nations in any integrated sense for many years to come. They may even move backward, being disillusioned by the false promises of ideologists who substitute slogans and exhortations for administrative progress.

Most of Africa and of Asia, and much of South America, is governed by dictatorships, largely military or military-controlled. They have passed through democratic and representative phases or have emerged from imperialist control only to fall into native dictators' hands. The Russians are reaching for integration in interesting ways, but without the consent that would anchor such integration in popular sovereignty. It would seem more likely to break up because of this than to progress into a rationalized whole.

It is apparent that the United States has to look, in this matter, to its own history, and to the nature of its people and its circumstances. Also something has to be said about the theory that has been clung to by Americans all along. This is the idea that separate entities can successfully exist in a union, but that union is essential to that existence. Gradually the nation has taken the place in citizens' regard that the states formerly held. By now it is a tie among them so strengthened by technology as to have passed the point of possible return.

When Blackstone said that there is and must be in every state a supreme, irresistible, and uncontrolled authority in which the *jura summa imperii* (rights of sovereignty) reside, he was speaking of Parliament.[11] But Coke, who was more familiar to the American legal scholars in 1787, held time after time that both Parliament and the king were subject to the limitations of law. And John Adams had quoted Coke as well as other authorities to the effect that "an act against the Constitution is void."[12]

This set the Constitution above all the branches of government; but it also set the courts to be the guardians of that Constitution. Strangely, almost absent-mindedly, it seems, the framers did, however, give the Congress power to determine the Court's jurisdiction. This anomaly still remains to be cleared up. But if the Constitution is supreme, and not the legislature, then that document, as it actually exists, determines where authority in the state is to be found.

It is possible, if this is so, to make distributions of power and, by amendment, to revise them, as long as these enterprises flow from the sovereign people in a legitimate grant. Since this is so delicate a matter, and so much influenced by circumstances, the process of amendment ought to be regularized.

This is strictly within the bounds and practice of American theory. What is not within those bounds is the expansion of necessary interpretation of meanings into the judicial autocracy spoken of by Dicey. The doctrine of supremacy is not an inevitable accompaniment of union if that system is understood to proceed from popular sovereignty.

11. Sir William Blackstone, *Commentaries on the Laws of England,* 4 vols. (Philadelphia: J. B. Lippincott and Co., 1856), IV, 50–51.

12. *The Works of John Adams,* ed. by C. F. Adams, 10 vols. (Boston: Little, Brown and Co., 1850–1856), II, 522–25.

The Future for the United States

A strange and tragic circumstance haunts the people of the United States. It is that they are unable to accept their fate, and so are unable to manage its further development. The historic occupation of a continent left its mark not only on the conquering generations but also on succeeding ones. These later Americans, proceeding from pioneering and from rural life into the age of technology and urbanism, began somewhere in mid-transition to look backward for their values. They could not think clearly about industrialism and city existence because emotionally they rejected it. What they saw of the future they did not like, and so they could not conform to any plans they cared to make.

This was as true of government as of other institutions. The people deified their obsolete Constitution and, because they would not change it, allowed an unstable and haphazard one to emerge from custom and unauthorized invention.

If, even as they create the future, Americans shrink from its implications and reject its characteristics, they cannot be altogether different from other peoples, especially those whose futures are far less visible, and who, in fact, live mostly in their past because they have not yet left it behind.

To the contemporary generation, and very likely in several succeeding ones, governmental tendencies toward integration hardly matter. People consider that it will not happen in their time. They may be quite wrong about this. The rule of progression has escaped from the conventional linear measurement; it has become explosive. New discoveries and new techniques are daily matters, and they spread in every direction. And an observer does not have to be very acute to sense an erosion of the old values as new realities appear. The void thus created is so serious that it involves the whole of the future. There is an awakening conviction that technology is here to stay, that it can get out of hand if it is not made to serve human purposes, and that it is already late to turn away from the old and plan for the new. But the conviction does not result in plans to match the need.

Since the only way to begin the process of catching up so far as government is concerned is by confederation, it is important to learn the available lessons about the first compact for union. From the American experience something about the dangers of arriving at union by bargaining and compromise can be learned. They have been alluded to in Chapter 2, but it can usefully be repeated that the makers of compacts had better not be representatives of fixed positions. If they are, they will use their bargaining powers not to find practical solutions but to salvage what they can of their beginning demands. A composite government established in this way will be in many serious phases indeterminate; it may have inconsistent or conflicting devices; and it may prepare the way for long-drawn-out conflicts.[13] This requires that the difficult problems be faced, and if compromise is necessary to agreement or to ratification, that provision be made for later reexamination in an amending process of the same legitimacy as the document about to be promulgated.

The new American government of the late eighteenth century was subjected to two dangers, one exigent and the other at least annoying. The danger was that independence might be lost. The empires (Britain, France, and Spain) were in an expanding phase, and no place on earth was considered inappropriate for colonization. Each of them, moreover, was located on an indeterminate American border. For sheer survival a union strong enough to erect a common defense was necessary. The annoyance was continual interference by some with the commerce of others. They were seaboard states, but some had better ports and more experienced merchants than others. There were profits taken as goods passed through warehouses and were forwarded; but, even worse, taxes were laid; and these raised the cost of living or reduced the take of merchants in the less-developed states. It was this immediate complaint, felt by merchants and plantation proprietors, that made the excuse for a series of meetings precedent to that in Philadelphia.

It was reflection on this growing tendency to the pursuit of commercial profit and his general's comprehension of strategic dangers that distinguished Washington from the Virginia and New York separatists who were doing well as things were and who confused their advantages with rightful privileges or, for political purposes, identified the two. Madison, Hamilton, Morris, and the Pinckneys, for instance, saw things as Washington did. Union was necessary to survival.

The degeneration of the Congress established by the Articles of Confederation was evidence enough of the deepening danger. As has been pointed out, that body, by 1787, was in dissolution. The revenues it "requisitioned" were not forthcoming; it had no executive; and its members, being in effect ambassadors from the states, were more often at home than in the Capital. It was absurd to call so weak an institution a government at all. Yet the recent revolution, when militiamen from all the states had served the national cause—even though that cause was only independence —was not far in the past. And Washington had been commander in chief of a "continental" army. There were strong nationalist sentiments even if geography was unfavorable and politics was local.

There had been in fact only weak national political differences until leaders were aroused by the conclusion for Union reached in Philadelphia. Then there was a storm of protest from local leaders, and the ratification contests were hotly argued. In the larger states—Massachusetts, New York,

13. This conclusion, and those following, were reached after extensive examination in Chapter 1, "General Criteria for Constitutionmaking," and Chapter 2, "Criteria Further Considered."

Virginia—there were furious debates, and acceptance was achieved by tenuous majorities. There actually was no resolution of this confrontation until, more than seventy years later, it went to the test of civil war.

This history is recalled because of its general significance. It is the usual way for unionist movements to start and the usual experience when they begin to affect old privileges and powers.

There were foreseen dangers; and there were large-minded men who, recognizing them, felt that the risks had to be accepted; but there were others who insisted that the union necessary to security was less important than the liberties they possessed in regimes of dissent and *laissez-aller*. Coming together, the two groups compromised instead of reasoning together until a substantial consensus had been reached. The majority prevailed, but a minority was left with a cause readily infused with sentiments appealing to their constituents at home. Institutions erected out of the compromise were the subject of continued controversy during the next half-century, and they were weakened by a continued carping derogation.

This was an ideal situation to be taken advantage of by private interests who were learning to exploit resources, making profitable speculations, and funding advances in technology. There were occasions when it seemed possible that the government would be entirely submerged by the overwhelming proliferation of these profitable enterprises. Its agencies were hopelessly outmatched in confrontations and, anyway, were undermined by infiltrations of financial and commercial representatives.

The chaos resulting had within it, however, a principle of evolution all its own. Laissez-faire had an inevitable end in concentration. This was because in an unregulated struggle the strong in every industry would demolish the weak. There was left, after some time, an array of giants confronting one another in a contest so destructive that they found it discreet to look for accommodation among themselves.

The final phase of this complex struggle among the financial and commercial giants, and between them and the government, has not even yet reached resolution; but the end can be forecast. There will emerge an organic whole controlled by advanced arts of administration. Unhappily this will be a cause of anguish to nostalgic citizens, but it will happen. The question is whether it will be publicly or privately controlled. If it seems inevitable that regulation must fall to public agencies, it is necessary to say that it will not happen by default. Monopolies will not become public agencies unless they are compelled to do so. And that compulsion cannot be organized if support for it is lacking because the nation's elite is looking over its shoulder regretfully at a simpler rural past and making efforts to return instead of going forward. One manifestation of clinging to the past is the maintenance of federalism—that is, states' rights—in a time of technological revolution.

From the comparatively long experience of the United States as the only large genuinely federalist republic, it is possible to make the tentative generalization that the arrangement is an unstable one, and that it ends in either union or dissolution. Under contemporary circumstances there can be no successful leagues, associated commonwealths, or federated governments in the United States or anywhere else. This is because the tensions are progressively more effectively implemented with communication systems, because geography has been transformed in significance, because the skills of administration are so far advanced, and because politicians seeking power and appealing to nostalgia are free to make use of the very facilities they denounce.

To recapitulate: in the beginning there is a bargain struck among sovereign, usually contiguous—but always somehow related—states. These concede to a central government the powers necessary to their mutual security and economic advantage. These are not the only interests; there may be others of a loftier sort; they will involve the best citizens, but not all citizens. When the agreements are made to form a union it will have been the result of bargaining, not really satisfactory to either the unionist or the separatist because each has to make a sacrifice. Hence the continuing tension.

The separatists will more and more feel the constriction of central power as the technologies are perfected that will gradually envelop the whole Union in a massive advance. Formerly sovereign units (states) become irrelevant and ultimately impotent. They will not succumb without protest, perhaps even attempts to secede; but such attempts will not be successful unless geography is favorable. Britain could hardly hold Australia or Canada in an administrative union even though their people were of a common origin and culture. The United States, however, could and did make a cause of union and defeated the threatening secessionists. By the same law it seems almost certain to absorb all near neighbors.

The federal principle is thus breached. The Union no longer possesses only enumerated powers; it possesses all powers—de facto if not de jure—if they are necessary. They will be acquired by administration, or, if it is more convenient, by judicial invention. There may be peripheral military conquests; but these are likely to have been made unnecessary by penetration and absorption, and by the holding out to neighbors of affluent prospects.

This process does not require the abandonment of a useful distribution of duties and even of powers. They cannot, however, continue to be the originial ones, since technology and geography will have made the first compact obsolete, and it will have fallen into disuse except in a symbolic sense. This situation may go on being called federalism, partly from habit, but largely to mist over the extension of central power.

The situation existing when this historic development reaches its later stages is unsatisfactory, because it is not really legitimate and so cannot be stabilized. The states can still claim autonomy even if it is mostly an empty claim. And the extensions of half-legitimate powers are made by an unsatisfactory process not really congruent with the demands of administration. Escape from this unpleasant situation is entirely possible, and the legitimization is even possible. There can be a workable distribution of responsibilities, but these can come about only in another creative act authorized by the sovereign people. That is why there ought to be other conventions owing their authority to that original source. The result will not be federalism, but will give local governments recognizable autonomy.

If instability is inevitable in compacts arrived at as federalist ones are, this fact ought to be recognized by arrangement not only for standards and limits for judicial interpretation but also for amendment and for occasional complete revisions. Only in this way can the states and localities retain any powers, even those they can most usefully administer. They will otherwise be diminished and perhaps lost to a more powerful central bureaucracy ready to assume all public duties, and only in this way can the principle of legitimacy be preserved for the Union itself.

The Future for the World

Is this a process of universal significance? Is there a law of progression dictating that the nations of the world will first federate and then enter a period of strain, emerging only when secessionists have succeeded or failed? And if they have seceded, will the painful process only resume until union is compelled?

If integration on a world scale should evolve—and the same reasons for it as there were for its evolution on the American continent are rapidly developing as technologies improve—the people of the United States ought to be among the unionists rather than the separatists as compacts are made, constitutions written, and administration begun. They ought to be counted with Washington, Madison, Hamilton, and Morris, not with Paterson, Gerry, Lansing, and Yates. And not, it must be said, with Jefferson.

To mention this last name is to wrench the emotions Jefferson so faithfully represented. He forecast—and did his best to shape—a republic of free agrarians. All that was commercial and complex was to him unacceptable, and his preferences are still dominant in the minds of many Americans. In full course toward a national organization of all economic— and even social—activities, Americans, looking backward to Monticello, do not see that estate as it really existed—comprising industries (on the scale of the time) as well as farming, and depending on hundreds of slave laborers for its operation. They see a Jeffersonian society of sturdy peasants that never existed.

The immense advantage of communism has been its acceptance of the future and the forthright attempt to reach its logical ends. Xenophobia and even imperialism have not been extinguished in Russia or in other Communist states; but there has been less talk among them of return to the good old days; and if there are expensive programs to preserve passing arrangements—such as that to prevent the disappearance of the family farm in the United States—they have been so muted as not to be heard of abroad.

This looking backward has contributed to the elaboration of values that keep people separated and certain of their own superiority. This was a sustaining ingredient of the old imperialism and will doubtless be one of the new. Americans, if they listen, can hear the beginning claims of "negritude." It frightens them a little, and it should frighten them more, not because it constitutes a real threat but because it is a reflection of their own complacent assumption of superiority and their rejection of well-established physical facts. The equality once boasted of was securely founded.

Everyone knows that between the present condition of international anarchy and even the unstable confederation of the near future there is a wide chasm filled with monstrous risks and bridged with flimsy spans of self-interest. It requires, in our generation, an act of faith to suppose humanity will make the crossing without disaster, armed as it is with frightful weapons at the disposal of political leaders who may be simply that rather than responsible statesmen.

Disasters have been avoided, however narrowly, in the past, and it may be that wisdom and moderation sufficient for the need can be summoned from among the world's leaders, even though they are officially devoted not to peace but to the increase of their nation's power. There are, of course, the contradicting instances of war, even wars that become world conflicts. But the horrors of those incidents in the past have made their impression, and it may at least be hoped that the politicians of the future will be restrained by the lessons they offer.

It is on the assumption that, however unlikely it may appear to pessimists, the coming generations will survive that crossing into a season of détente, and that more peaceful times may be planned for. Besides, in a sense, it is the thinking about them that may make the transition possible. To keep in view the far shore—escaping the monsters in the chasm—and to leave behind the irrational and nostalgic past, is really the paramount duty of the statesman, for nothing is more certain than that holocaust cannot any longer be contained. Forces unleashed for the small purposes of nations in a bargaining process that traditionally includes resorting to force will from now on end in genocide. But everyone knows now that this is true.

It is this certainty, borne in on statesmen's minds as they go about their business of serving nations, that may furnish the incentive for an armistice on the way to the happier state of better times. If this certainty could be organized into an institutionalized defense it could be the single, most worthy victory of a generation.

One thing we know: the law governing the evolution of states in relation to each other will operate only if this condition prevails in the future. It did not need to in the past; it will from now on.

Federalism, as such, belongs to a temporary historical era. It may be expected to develop European (perhaps with Eastern and Western groupings) and African (perhaps Northern and Southern) and Central and South American confederacies. But the evolution of these, it is suggested, will be similar to that of the United States. In the end it must find its resolution in union.

Some of these regions have been more or less resistant—but not immune—to technological advance; but among their states they have the requisite resources, land expanse, and populations; and the more backward among them, with help from the more advanced, can be expected to produce educated leaders, technical skills, and expertise in administration. This follows very simply from the fact of a world that has become electronically one—meaning that all will have the same news, will communicate instantaneously, and can travel rapidly among themselves. Even now there is hardly a place in the world more than ten or twelve hours from any other place; and simple extrapolation of presently known machinery will reduce this by half, then three-quarters. Meanwhile, the seeing telephone, the computer, and other such facilities will have brought everyone face to face with everyone else.

It will not be surprising if in fifty years the United Nations will be comprised of a few instead of many members: perhaps Eastern and Western Europe; Russia; China; Arabia; Southern Africa; and Northern, Central, and South America. Each of these very likely would be going through its own evolution from loose to tight confederacy, and then to nationhood.

It will not be surprising; but it will not be without its protestants. The wrench for conditioned patriots passionately opposing union—Patrick Henry proclaiming Washington a disloyal Virginian—will always be a danger. The appeal of nostalgia will not have lessened. Harlem and Watts today are called ghettos; tomorrow they may be defended as homelands. Their politicians may denounce outsiders. They may appeal for ghetto dwellers' rights. And they may have tight political organizations maintained as those of nations and states are today. These too may have their run prolonged in the same way. Nationalism has had its way with the world for several hundred years, and it has been a bloody way indeed. It had become illogical and obsolete, but what is dead or dying in reality lives on as myths men will die for.

Concerning these myths and their symbols it has to be hoped that the massive efforts being made in all the advanced nations to extinguish illiteracy and to improve education will be effective. Fifty years ago H. G. Wells illuminated this effort by calling it a race between education and catastrophe. Since he made that statement there have been two wars, both coming very close to catastrophe for the world as they were for so many of its people; but in the meantime there have been advances in education as well as lessons in the effects of war.

There is no alternative to hope; there is no excuse for not understanding whither we trend, as well as the necessity of furthering rather than opposing the forces making for integration—and so for peace.

It may be objected that the theory of federal beginnings and endings in the United States is not relevant to distant world developments. It is submitted that there is an important connection.

If the United States at this late stage in its evolution should move backward to separatism the effect on the international community would be disastrous. Only a nation recognizing its own nature, and holding out the prospect of assistance to others struggling to find their nature too, can be of use in the modern circumstances. The risk of genocide in a world moving away from, rather than toward, integration ought to be obvious, especially to Americans who have had so much to do with technological advance. That even now myth can be aroused to support a rejection of reality may seem incredible, yet there are repeated attempts at constitutional amendment having this effect.

It can only be said that the result is in doubt.

CHAPTER 4

THE SEPARATION OF POWERS

How the Doctrine Developed

Political historians trace the separation doctrine, so important a structural part of the Constitution, to Montesquieu, to Locke, and eventually back to Aristotle. They point out that Wilson, Dickinson, Morris, Madison, and the Pinckneys, as well as others, had studied these philosophers and were prepared to base their arguments on precedent as well as practicality.

It is not certain to what extent such theoretical support was really depended on by the framers. The idea of separate powers acting to counter each other must have seemed to them a natural arrangement, except perhaps to Hamilton and a few others who would have provided one of them—the executive—with royal prerogatives. One reason for ready acceptance among the majority was the recent colonial experience, and this was undoubtedly present in most minds. The heavy-handed overlordship of British governors was warning enough about executive power, and very recent responses of legislatures to emotional demands were not conducive to trust in their reliability. Nevertheless the distinguished lawyers were apt to parade their scholarship, and there is reason to believe that they did feel more secure in what they were devising for having the support of a political tradition.

Their references, to be sure, were sometimes rather doubtful. Aristotle's "three elements" did not forecast exactly the three Montesquieu recommended, and Montesquieu's divisions were not so applicable to eighteenth-century America as was often suggested—in fact they were much modified in the final draft of the Constitution.

Sir Ernest Barker, the meticulous translator of Aristotle's *Politics*, was also a commentator, and to the passage about the "three elements" he appended a note of correction; prima facie, he said, they seemed to be identical with the legislative, executive, and judicial powers of modern theory; actually, Aristotle's deliberative element was hardly a legislative one (though it had legislative functions); it was rather concerned with the executive and with some of the higher judicial functions. Similarly his magistrates, although they had executive functions, did not constitute an "executive government" in the modern sense; the "deliberative element" had overriding power in that respect. Finally, the judicial element was not a body of judges; it was composed of lay popular courts. The reader of Aristotle has to think himself back into a Greek framework essentially different from the modern design, and to abandon the model suggested by Montesquieu's theory. He cannot even allocate the division chosen by the framers to British (or previous American) practice.

Aristotle was for the framers not much more than a shadow in the background. Montesquieu and Locke were nearer and more relevant; most of the Americans, being lawyers, looked more to such British legal commentators as Coke and Blackstone for their authority. Still, they might have read with profit (and probably some of them did) Aristotle's pronouncements about constitutions in the *Politics*.[1] For one thing, he said that the study of politics, one of the "practical arts and sciences," had to consider which sort of constitution suits which sort of civic body. Moreover, the system proposed by constitutionmakers ought to be one easily grafted onto the system already in use. It was all very well to concoct ideal drafts, but ones already found to be useful ought to be studied as well, so that reform could be adapted to reality.

It might be thought, from a reading of their Constitution, that this advice had been taken seriously by the Philadelphians; no doubt they did take some account of it even if they were more mindful of certain lessons from their own past. These were mostly negative, but if they looked further in Aristotle they found in Book VI of the *Politics* a section on the construction of constitutions for democrats. It was there that he spoke of the three organs: the deliberative (he called this the sovereign one), the executive, and the judicial. These divisions had come down to the framers as structural ideas through two thousand years, having grown so familiar as to seem natural. The state constitutions arranged for such tripartite organizations. Even as colonies they had developed assemblies or councils, usually against the opposition of royal governors, when such bodies were not appointed, but were dangerously representative; and their courts showed a tendency to become more independent than the governors could approve.

1. Reference here is to the 1958 edition, translated and annotated by Barker, and published by the Oxford University Press. The above note will be found on p. 193; and Book IV, "Actual Constitutions," begins on p. 154. The references to Montesquieu are taken from the edition of *The Spirit of the Laws*, translated by Thomas Nugent, with an introduction by Franz Neumann, published in the Hafner Library of Classics, 1949.

It is often said that they learned much from Locke, and it may be true, but about the separation of powers he had said nothing. It was in Montesquieu that they found a closer textual lead for division into the three they found useful. His argument was that the legislature enacted the laws, but since it was often not in being, an executive was needed who would always be present. The legislature ought not to control this executive because if it did it could use the powers of both for private advantage. It was this reasoning that very quickly disposed of the proposal, during the Convention, for allowing the Congress to choose the executive. It was readily anticipated that even if legislators did not use their positions for profit, they would be likely to favor groups or classes; those favored would be the most numerous and most indigent. There would follow more cheapening of money and forgiving of debtors such as had happened in the hard times following the war in the early days of independence.

Still, Montesquieu had had a bias in favor of lawmaking bodies that the framers were responsive to; he had not thought of the other branches as being independent. His legislature would always have been able to resume the executive powers they had delegated because, in a "constituted commonwealth," it would be supreme. He did say, however, that when action had to be taken, the holder of the delegated power must be allowed to act, he being the only one able to make immediate response to emergency; but this should be only until the legislature could convene and consider the issue. This, it will be seen, was not at all a balance-of-power theory. It is true that he approached such a doctrine more nearly than Locke, who would always have had one power authorized to take action—even the people, if their natural rights were threatened (but he did not say how). Moreover, Locke did not anticipate a judiciary separate from the executive, because he saw both as implementing general laws in specific instances. Montesquieu did distinguish the role of the judiciary; he did define the executive as one who must maintain both internal and external security; that, however, was about as far as he went, and he explained the powers as temporary and revokable.

The division, in his theory, would not have prevented interconnection, and, of course, some balance or checking among the branches; but here he was obscure, seeming to provide for a mutual relationship without actual independence. This, however, was sufficient to create conflicting authorities. As to what might happen if they did not see things the same way, he had only the answer that they must agree; and this meant that the executive must agree with the legislature.

Bentham was one critic who objected that Montesquieu's system offered no guarantee of liberties since it did not modify in any way the absoluteness of governmental power. If all the branches represented the same group in society, as they obviously would, exploitation could go on unchecked and protestants could be stifled. Montesquieu, however, had thought of this. The monarch (the executive), he had said, would always represent an interest different from that of legislators; and they in turn, divided into two houses, one bourgeois in origin and the other aristocratic, would see things quite differently—not only from the executive but from each other. The judiciary would be quite removed and would have a detached point of view. As though he had anticipated criticism of Bentham's sort, he devoted the whole of Book XI to criminal law and its function as the protector of individual rights.

Montesquieu's other critics had been quick to point out that he not only misinterpreted Locke but misunderstood British government. There was no such allocation of functions as he assumed, either in Locke's theory or in British practice. What he had been led to finally was the impossible conclusion that sovereignty in Britain was composite, and this meant that action or change would always have to be legitimized by consensus. That this was far from true anyone with British experience could have told him. The legislature—and, of its two houses, the Commons—was, after a long struggle, becoming supreme. The executive, the monarch, was becoming merely a symbol of state, with its authority being taken over by a committee of Parliament called a cabinet, the cabinet having a prime minister as its chairman, but having a corporate existence. That is to say, the cabinet could vote, and its majority would prevail.

It was a time of transition. It was not yet clear, as it would soon become, that the prime minister, as a member of the house and leader of the majority there, would become much more powerful than the cabinet or the House of Commons. He was learning to control his colleagues by allotting constituencies, dispensing patronage, and granting favors; before long the Commons would become a severely disciplined body. The distribution of cabinet posts was the prime minister's prerogative too. Of course his party could be disestablished by a vote of no confidence, whereupon there would be new elections, but the cabinet was definitely subordinated. Control did ultimately rest with the electorate, but even in the late eighteenth century that was a restricted number of the wealthy and wellborn. There were severe limitations on the monarch, but the country was still a long way from becoming a democracy. A prime minister as the acting executive would soon be exempt from a voters' referendum for at least five years—if he so chose.

As imperial power had shown itself in the American colonies it had been peculiarly odious to this same upper class. Laws passed in Parliament adversely affected the interests of the merchants, the shipping concerns, and the plantation owners. It was done without consultation; and enforcement, by appointed governors who were more kingly than the king dared to be at home, was harsh. Britain was being transformed at home but not in the colonies. It was no wonder that public men in America read Montesquieu with eagerness. He seemed to say that legislatures, as representatives of the people, ought to be paramount in government, and executives merely agents to carry out ("faithfully execute") legislative decisions. They understood the implications of consensus as meaning that the executive subordinated himself to the legislature. They had only the problem, in theory, of making the legislators their representatives and not those of the nonpropertied classes.

They were members of the elite, most of them, and their dismay at the manifestations of democracy during the Revolution and after was still an active emotion. Having repeatedly seen legislatures cheapen money so that debtors could escape just payments to their creditors, they concluded that there could easily be too much democracy. An electorate, confined to the elite, a government with enumerated and restricted powers, and a judiciary to interpret it were arrangements that seemed to them a middle way between autocracy and democracy. It would be a government they could control. When they juxtaposed tranquillity, union, justice, common defense, general welfare, and the blessings of liberty, they meant to emphasize public order; and this extended to a concept of acceptance. They would manage things—in a just and kindly way, of course, yet with firmness. The lower classes would submit.

How It Was Adapted to the Framers' Needs

Exploitation of the structural possibilities in the principle of separation, as the Philadelphians progressed in their discussions, finally approached the fantastic. The whole, as they built it up, became an intricately interlaced framework with balanced members opposing each other with nicely calculated strengths. Separation offered an opportunity for positioning one against the others and at the same time of seeing to it that arbitrary power, if it should suddenly appear, would be opposed by another power with equally good credentials and adequate resources. It was an attempt to gain the stability so necessary to a tranquil society.

None of these balancings added to firmness or dispatch in action; they were not meant for that, and that was not something the framers worried about. Even if emergencies should arise, only awkward means were provided for meeting them. This was a serious defect, but both states' righters and the nationalists agreed on the limiting principle. Serious quarrels among themselves were not anticipated once it was made certain that the legislature, even though the most powerful of the branches, was properly constituted. The states' righters recalled bitterly the old quarrels with British administrations; the nationalists feared legislatures that might act emotionally whenever their constituents were aroused. Thus, for different reasons, both agreed on separation. It seems not to have mattered that the reasons for it were different, and it seems to have mattered even less that it left the government with very poor defenses against aggression from within or without.

This was a serious matter. The reconciling of popular sovereignty with the desire for a stronger government, one able to guarantee security, not to say tranquillity, was a problem not really solved. Security and tranquillity had been made not more, but less, secure by the war for independence. The colonies in the empire had been part of a powerful whole; the postwar confederated states had not only lost that protection but were eyed covetously by the other empires as well as the still-hovering British. Besides, under the Articles, it was not a union; divisiveness among the various states had become worse and worse until it almost seemed possible that some might be detached by a foreign power. New York politicians, at the time of the Philadelphia Convention, were holding highly suspect conversations with Canada; New Englanders regarded the Virginians as tainted with aristocracy; no one could say where the southern borders ran; and the British had not withdrawn to the lines fixed in the treaty establishing the peace.

As for tranquillity, the adjustment to independence was not easy. British discipline had ended, and nothing effective had been substituted for it. The times were hard, and the common people were not taking their deprivations well. The planters' old markets were restricted; merchants and ship owners had little business; artisans had fewer jobs; a large proportion of the population in Boston, Philadelphia, and New York was without any means of support. There had been active protests involving disorder, even riots. These were the "mobs" spoken of so often in the framers' discussions; they were not always city people; farmers too were deeply dissatisfied and in a rebellious mood.

If it is realized how conflicting demands and unsatisfied desires worked on the framers' minds, something of the deeper difficulties at Philadelphia can be understood. Popular sovereignty was not regarded as it would be among similar persons fifty years later. It was more like the Greek conception of a small elite and a much larger body of slaves. The white colonists were not slaves; many, however, had been indentured but recently and so were not far from it. And, of course, there were actual slaves whose rights were nonexistent. Only substantial property owners were to have the vote; how substantial was a matter to be decided in the various states; all, however, had such a qualifying test. Since this was so, it need not be referred to in a constitution for the Union. If it seems strange that voting for federal offices should have been left in state control, this is the reason. What seems unaccountable is that, except for certain limitations on exclusion, it should still be that way.

There was still another complication: the desire to prevent the invasion by government of personal liberties, yet at the same time to make the necessary force available for maintaining order. This was a real dilemma. No one wanted property jeopardized by the envious, and no one wanted a return of the colonial restrictions on liberty; but a force in existence and in control of the executive might be used for just these purposes unless carefully confined. As they discussed this and similar matters the framers came to see that such delicate provisions—not too much and not too little—were the peculiar opportunities of a constitution as contrasted with legislative statutes.

Revolutionary emotions were just beneath the surface, and the new nation, divided as it was, could hardly survive another Shays's Rebellion. Of course the states had police powers, and these would be left to them among the residuals; nevertheless there might be times when this would not be enough. Federal intervention might be necessary. The states' righters, however, were firmly opposed to authorizing interference *except when requested*; and after some argument, they gained the point. But the compromise was not very logical; no federal force existed or would for a long time. Only the state militias would really be available. And governors might refuse to request intervention. They might refuse, also, to allow the militia to be used in other states.

So the central government would be bound in a web of checks if insurrection should occur; it was also weakened by the provision that the House of Representatives should be chosen by district electorates with qualifications set by the states. Furthermore, the federal judiciary was confined to cases arising under the Constitution (or laws or treaties of the United States).[2]

Some exceptions were made when the framers realized how far they had gone in restricting the federal government's powers. It had to tax, for instance, if it was to exist at all; what would happen if a citizen refused to pay? And it had to do all those other things it was charged with doing in section 8 of Article II, such as, for instance, regulating commerce with foreign nations, raising and supporting armies for defense, establishing post offices and post roads, and regulating the value of money. So finally there was added the provision that the Congress might make all laws necessary for carrying into execution the duties charged to it. That was something more than a compromise; it was a recognition that the restricted powers were impractical.

Other impracticalities among the checks were, however, not so quickly recognized. Their abandonment would be gradual and mostly by an illegitimate process—not the result of amendment. The changes would in the end —a distant end—be substantial.

It is difficult to disentangle the opposing powers within the government

2. This was made worse in 1798 by the Eleventh Amendment; the federal judiciary could not accept suits brought by citizens of one state against other states.

from those resulting from the principle of enumeration. All those not specifically allocated were left to the states or to private citizens, something reemphasized and made all too clear in the Eleventh Amendment. And since growth began at once, creating new responsibilities, what was residual (that is, left exclusively to the states) was almost from the first a matter of controversy. Was each new duty beyond federal reach because it was not mentioned? Those who would construe "enumeration" strictly grew more and more bitterly determined as powerful interests became involved in issues such as the tariff, control of the currency, and, of course, slavery.[3]

There were those who would construe it loosely, thus allowing new duties to be brought within old categories and, on complicated matters, by trying to stretch further and further the doctrine of implication rather than seeking legitimacy through amendment. It was a long and bitter quarrel, neither side denying the Constitution, both sides trying to use it for their own purposes.

If the loose constructionists gained—as they did—to which of the independent branches would the new powers go? Since the Constitution did not say, each could contend for them. Some considerable part of the struggle among them concerned such issues.

We have seen that the idea of separate powers was an old one to be found in the texts of respected theorists. It has also been noted that the framers—or at least some of them—were learned in such matters. Historians have turned up lengthy quotations from Montesquieu in contemporary newspapers and pamphlets. Pennsylvania, Massachusetts, New York, and Virginia lawyers quoted him; these included Adams, Wythe, and Madison. It ought to be recalled at the same time that other philosophers were read and often cited. Among these were Locke, the French Physiocrats, and Adam Smith. The conception of the state to be gathered from all these authorities was one of limited powers. Professor Franz Neumann, in his introduction to the Hafner edition of the *Spirit of the Laws,* summarized the general view:

1. The state should interfere as little as possible with social life.
2. Whatever social changes are necessary can be made only through legislation.
3. Legislation means the enactment of fixed, abstract general rules.
4. Legislation is the monopoly of the legislature.
5. Administration is not the agent of social change; it is nothing but the concretization of general rules.
6. The judicial function is a logical one. The judge is merely the mouthpiece of the law.

The striking difference between these principles and latter-day practice is the difference between the written Constitution and the emergent one.

3. The powers not delegated to the United States by the Constitution, not prohibited by it to the states, are reserved to the states respectively, or to the people.

The one is honored and, when convenient, is appealed to; the other is lived by in the present-day nation. Not one of the principles enumerated by Neumann is characteristic of American practice. The state is required to interfere with social life; the legislature is the least creative of the branches and so almost never originates change, the executive being the source of practically all innovations; and judges do not confine themselves to being "mouthpieces of the law."

The functions assigned to the separate branches in theory, and embodied in the Constitution, have all—every one—become so seriously obsolete that if a new constitution were to be written, assignments of authority would in some respects be reversed and in all severely modified.

Still, the underlying idea of separated powers, owing their legitimacy to the primary source in popular sovereignty—a much wider electorate— would certainly be preserved. So, in fact, would the principle, at least, of checks and balances. The modifications within this structure would make it unrecognizable to the framers; much would be added or taken away; relations would be altered; functions would be redistributed. But the general outline would remain.

It would remain because it is still useful. Without it either the legislature or the executive would disappear, or be merged—as has happened in the United Kingdom; the judiciary would become an arm of the combined legislative-executive, as has happened again in Britain. It is useful in the United States for the reason it was originally accepted—to prevent the lodgment anywhere of arbitrary power. There was combined with this, in the minds of some, the confining of federal power to a very few uses— mostly foreign and interstate relations. That has disappeared; but there are few who would argue, with the American circumstances in mind, that any of the branches ought to possess all the federal power or that interpenetration is no longer useful.

One thing, however, is to be learned from American experience: there ought to be careful and explicit distribution of duties and responsibilities. And because new ones arise and old ones disappear, there ought to be periodic reassignment. This ought not to be the result of internecine quarreling; it ought to be the result of the same process that worked out original assignments.

Theory and Fact

A theory to govern the needed redistribution can be stated as follows: Popular sovereignty, to be successful, requires well-chosen instruments as well as understood purposes. If it is to survive and be effective, these requirements must be constitutionalized: that is, made irreversible aims for the life of the current statement.

To agree on policies and to keep competent agencies in existence, information, continuous discussion, and impartial electoral procedures are necessary. A precondition for these is an established acceptance of majority rule. This will give officials favored by the prevailing majority the power to mold the agreed purposes into law and to see it faithfully executed. For the making of law both the leadership of those who have special knowledge of what may and should happen and those who must carry it out are needed; so is the consideration of legislators who are in touch with the electorate. To execute it, competent administrative organizations are required; such execution as is entrusted to other than public agencies must be assimilated to general purposes by regulation under law within constitutional directives.

As to the continuous need for reconsideration of instrumentalities in a changing society, two arrangements are necessary: a judiciary for making certain that laws accord with the constitution, and provision for periodic amendment. The courts are to interpret; they are to make neither constitution nor laws; the laws must emerge from a uniquely legislative body; the constitution may be altered only in a process legitimized by the sovereign people.

This, it will be seen, is in the sharpest contrast with the theory that would have to be deduced from present practice. The received theory is largely myth and, like most political myths, is used by the possessors of power for their own purposes. Warfare among powerholders for ownership of democratic symbols accounts for a good share of upper-level activity in contemporary society. Those who do well in these struggles are naturally opposed to modernization that accords with reality when it threatens to disturb their positions. Since they control, in one way or another, most of the communications agencies, they are able to resist effectively any change of inherited institutions and customary ways except those they find agreeable.

It must be supposed that this is a condition common to all democratic societies with varied instrumentalities for carrying out the majority will. Since that will is apt to be poisoned at the source by using public resources to influence its thrust, a public interest in the dissemination of information must be recognized. This creates a difficult problem. Private media of communication often serve interests other than public ones, but public media may become mere defenders of contemporary officialdom. A way between the two is essential—a public medium free of governmental interference. Opinion can all too easily cease to be a will and become a passive registration of consent.

No democracy has found a way to make its government really responsive to general needs rather than those of a restricted elite. The seriousness of this perversion is measured by the very general conviction that leaders of all sorts, public and private, easily and frequently defect from their public responsibilities. And there are few who believe that in pursuing their own interests they accomplish those of society.

Wesley Mitchell, following Thorstein Veblen, pointed out the essential irrelevance to social purpose of business in *Making Goods and Making Money*; and many conscientious commentators have joined Walter Lippmann in the search for a *Public Philosophy* that would hold officialdom true to social purposes rather than others associated with seeking and keeping power for themselves and their supporters.

The way out of this persistent impasse has not been found. The economy in a profitmaking system has an inherent tendency to become irrelevant to needs for goods and services, just as the political system in such a society is likely to be irrelevant to the need for governance. It is submitted that the reason for this last is to be found originally in the Constitution and is perpetuated by refusal to consider proposals for its remaking. For in a democratic republic constitutions are intended to be the charters of conscience and the embodiment of reason's rule. If these have been frozen in a vanished past without means for other than a glacial flow toward the present, they will grow more and more obsolete and so less and less respected. This is especially true in centuries of dynamic movement. Illegitimate means will be found for accommodation, and since these are not referable to the constitution, there will gradually be established another sort of governance with the constitution as an honored but actually unused or distorted source of reference. No one will really know what are the rules to be lived by, and, looking at his government, a citizen will wonder how such a monstrous creation can have issued from the brief and simple charter of 1787.

The framers had disparate interests; they could not reconcile those of some with those of others; the resultant agreement satisfied no one. They agreed no better after reaching a compromise than before. This continued to be so. Like them, later generations have not agreed. But certain principles, in the years of American history, have established themselves in the minds of a majority. What were sources of contention at Philadelphia, and were either avoided or rejected, or were diminished for the sake of compromise, have gradually won their way.

Consider, for instance, democracy. The Constitution reflects the contradictory simultaneous affirmation of the people's sovereignty and a rejection of people's rule. The authors of *The Federalist* insisted that it was a republic they had made and warned against confusing it with a democracy. Clearly, there has been an enormous change; citizens now regard themselves as committed to both democracy and republican institutions, and regard them as inseparable; but this is not reflected in the Constitution they have inherited.

Or, to take another instance, consider the ambivalence exhibited then, and continued down to the present, concerning union. Federalism was a way of escaping the creation of what can now be seen by most of us as having been an inevitable unitary system. But among the framers the sentiment for nationhood was far from being unanimous. As a consequence, they conceived dual citizenship and divided sovereignty as a practical arrangement. From the first it was not seen as possible by the citizenry. Their loyalty was not thus divisible, or, at least, one was usually dominant and the other subordinate. And when events produced the physical bonds of communication and transportation so helpful to union, the preference for country over region, nation over state, prevailed. The country now having become one physically, federalism became an anachronistic arrangement.

The same can be said of separated powers, the subject of special interest here. The concept of definite assignments, clearly differentiated, began at once to melt in the crucible of change. Practical need forced reassignments, and it has been even worse in the matter of the checks and balances accompanying separated branches. As in the controversy between states' righters and nationalists, the adversaries set up by the mutual checking theory have carried on a never-ending conflict. Sometimes the president, sometimes the Congress, has seemed to prevail; and in the fierce heat of such struggles the Supreme Court has again and again enlarged its range, pretending finally to supremacy over the others. Like the Federalist controversy also, events and gradual accommodation to need have resolved this one largely in favor of the executive. This was partly because the Congress allowed itself—being immune to outside influence—to become irrelevant, incompetent, and even corrupt; also because the Court had difficulty in taking on legislative and executive functions and still remaining a court.

The original arrangement was simply not feasible. That lawmaking could be the exclusive domain of a deliberative body and that the president would merely preside over a minuscule establishment, being conciliator among the states and acting for the nation in relations with other countries, were notions that soon began to be ignored in practice.

Laws were very seldom made by the process assumed by the framers' theory. Actually, they almost always originated in the executive branch. This was because they met a need felt by one of the administrative or regulatory agencies. More often than not the Congress resisted and had to be persuaded or compelled to agree—persuaded by a special species of political bribery or compelled by presidential pressure. But parties, so prominent in the news, and so much in people's minds, had less to do with origination of laws than was imagined by those who were not close observers. Emergencies occurred or presidents responded to national needs not mentioned in party agendas. Members of the Congress were more responsive to constituents' demands than to considerations of public interest. They introduced private bills or ones for local improvements. They had to do this if they were to continue in office. Nothing in the Constitution required conformance to national interests; their duty was to their voters. The theory that the good of individuals or of scattered communities added up to the good of the whole pervaded that document. Eighteenth-century statesmen could hardly have acted on any other scheme. It dominated the thought of the time. But it was simply not true.

Separated powers as a theory was shaken out of the same box as the additive conception that resulted in laissez-faire. The important thing was to see that government did not interfere with individuals as they went about their business. If an emergency occurred there would be a coming together, a mobilization. But actually this was not provided for in the Constitution except that the Congress—not the president—could "provide for calling forth the militia to execute the laws of the Union, suppress insurrections and repel invasions." Even the "discipline" of the militia was to be prescribed by the Congress. But this militia had its permanent seats in the states, and its ordinary commanders were governors.

The federal government was not even a disciplinarian in other respects; police powers belonged to the states. True, some more general purposes were mentioned in the Preamble; but they seem wholly alien to the provisions of the Constitution itself. "General welfare" and the establishment of justice, as well as a "more perfect union," are spoken of. But only the president (and the vice-president) in any sense represented the nation as a whole; and even he, through the electoral college, owed his selection more to a class than to the people as a whole. They had their representatives in the lower house. Congressmen were allocated to districts, and they were expected to look out for their constituents' interests. It is not strange that this is exactly what they did—and, for the most part, still do.

The powers allocated to representatives were, however, not without their own checks. There was not only an upper house, originating in the states rather than in districts, and needed to complete legislation; there was also the president who had a partial veto—that is to say, he could compel laws to have a two-thirds instead of a simple majority. Representatives did have one overwhelming power: only they could originate revenue bills. This did not, as it might, include the origination of appropriations; but the hold on the one was soon customarily extended to the other.

The senators' special powers, apart from their needed concurrence in legislation, were two: they must confirm presidential appointments; and no treaty could become effective unless two-thirds of them consented. They were thus a check both on the house and on the president.

These senatorial powers were formidable. Compared with them the president, in the Constitution, seems a feeble partner. He has no real part in the legislative process, other than from time to time to "give to the Congress information of the state of the Union, and recommend to their consideration" such measures as he considers necessary and expedient. He can, besides, convene either or both houses for extraordinary occasions, or if they should disagree about the time for adjournment, terminate their sessions; but that these provisions held the possibility of being enlarged, as they soon were, into a chieftainship of legislators, no one anticipated. Clearly the president was not meant to be the tribune of the people or the planner of policy. He soon became both.

This was a breaking down of the separation principle that escaped from all constitutional restraint. It was neither check nor balance. In fact, the Congress became a check on the president rather than the reverse. He found that he was expected to conceive policies and, besides, to get them passed; but this he could not do without behaving in most unseemly ways; he could not appoint without consent, and often he could not appoint at all if the Congress insisted on preempting the privilege.[4]

Not one of the intended allocations held firm. Every one was violated, and grossly. Moreover, it was done without amendment, making the Constitution a document without force in the actual circumstances of governing. The separation of powers suffered as much as any other principle. Something was left, after a century and three-quarters—but not at all what was intended.

Departures

Any discussion of the separation doctrine is made difficult by the numerous variations in American practice—departures from pure principle. We have seen that these set up such intricate dual responsibilities and potentially conflicting powers that clear and exclusive assignments were soon almost altogether lacking. This led to differences of interpretation and, when disagreements became abrasive, to conflicts caused by changes in society and in the duties of government.

To carry out the main stated duty of the legislature, the presidency, or the Court, each branch, making its own interpretation of essential powers, sought to preempt them—when necessary elbowing others aside. Since it was true enough that in practice there did exist an area of silence or, sometimes, of anomaly, each could make its own interpretation with constitutional justification—using, of course, the convenient theory of implication. Thus, each in time established a tradition of defense for its own territory.

There is some reason for suspecting that this may have been intended by the framers. Branches busy attacking each other or in defending their prerogatives against others' aggressions would be less concerned with expanding their interferences with citizens; the conflicts would thus prevent

---

4. It was inevitable that the president's appointive powers in this system would largely disappear. Congressmen demanded that any federal official having duties in their districts should owe his appointment to them. This has been whittled down from time to time by the extension of the civil service. But all important officials are still in the patronage area. Federal judges, for instance, owe their appointments to the politicians of the district. Inevitably they are chosen from the local bar, and have more interest in local than national policies.

any from attaining a position of such authority as to threaten property rights. Such a prevention of interference was put forward afterward as one excuse for not having included a bill of rights in the original draft. What was nearer the truth was that most of the framers were fearful that libertarianism might run over into civil disobedience if encouraged by constitutional recognition.

Considerably before Marshall and his court asserted the power to decide such matters, conflicts among the branches had begun, as well as disputes about liberties. As to these last, the furor over the alien and sedition laws in John Adams's administration was a good example. In the dispute between the branches, the implied powers claimed for itself by the judiciary meant that all such differences would be resolved by the Court. This was a bold raid into no man's land. The supremacy of the judiciary, however, had its own difficulties. Bound by its own concept of proper procedure, the Court could decide only when causes were brought to it; as a result its decisions were seldom timely and were therefore ineffective. Even worse, the Court was at times embarrassed by its own claims and escaped embarrassment by such resorts as the invention of emergencies involving imminent national danger or "political thickets" it ought to avoid. These evasions were in themselves so vaguely stated that a clear rule about either emergency or the avoidance of politics could not be extracted.

Anyway, judicial supremacy was not acknowledged by either of the other branches. It has also to be said that presidents time after time relied on a Doctrine of Necessity to justify such action as seemed vital to the national interest. In effect, they defied the Court to interfere. After all, they had their powers more directly from the sovereign people than did the Court, whose justices they themselves appointed. This direct relation with the electorate was an advantage shared also by the Congress. The Congress, as well, was charged by the Constitution to mark out the Court's jurisdiction; and conceivably it could, by law, exclude the justices from deciding cases affecting the separation principle. Always in the background too was the appropriating power. An incensed legislature might restrict even the justices' salaries, or, as was soon discovered, control their number. Added to this latent power, there was the presidential control of execution. He might simply not enforce judicial decisions. Neither the purse nor the sword was within judicial control.

The Court, in spite of its claims and its occasional presumptions, thus had a tenuous hold on its implied authority and especially that having to do with directives for the other branches. Besides, in interpreting the Constitution, it was in the position of having, itself, grossly breached the lines of demarcation laid down in the Constitution.

The judicial was, however, not the first of the branches to do so. The very first president discovered that he was not merely the ornamental presiding presence evidently contemplated by the framers; no other agency of government was able to act when the national interest was threatened. The Congress could deliberate and legislate; the Court could decide causes when they were brought before it; but the president was always available to meet emergencies when time was lacking and the matter was urgent. This latent power might be essential to the very existence of the nation. The trouble was that his availability was not matched with resources. Washington was reluctant to assume unintended responsibilities, but he was repulsed when he asked the other branches for cooperation. Congressmen were reluctant to take the risk of making unpopular judgments, and the justices preferred the safer role of judging after the fact. The Senate refused Washington counsel; the Court rejected his plea for advice. He was left with no alternative but to proceed without authorization, taking the risk of being told that he should not have done so and scraping up the necessary implements and forces.

From that early time the Senate's role in foreign policy was reduced to something often described as dog-in-the-manger behavior. Sometimes the constitutional two-thirds majority needed for the ratification of treaties was withheld, sometimes ambassadors were not confirmed, and sometimes critical resolutions were passed. And most of these actions had about them more smell of partisanship than was appropriate to such serious occasions. Either that or they represented bursts of emotional xenophobia not allowable in a responsible agency.

Rejection of the Hay-Pauncefote and Versailles treaties illustrates one such type of action, and the Connally Resolution and many directive riders, such as that limiting foreign aid to cooperating nations, are illustrations of the other. The House of Representatives very often tried to interfere with the Senate and the president by passing resolutions of dissent or rebuke or by attaching riders to appropriation bills directing that expenditures be made in certain ways. These nearly always were interferences with execution or directions to appoint favored individuals.[5]

These petulant attacks on the barriers between the branches were followed by others of a magnitude comparable to the assertion of judicial supremacy. Presidents enlarged the Doctrine of Necessity, invented a substitute for treaties needing no Senate approval (the Executive Agreement), became the symbol of national leadership as well as a presiding presence, assumed the role of chief legislator, reached for control of the appropriating power through the executive budget, enlarged the functions of commander in chief to the use of armed forces in undeclared wars, and, in executing the

5. This history of interferences has been amply detailed in works such as Joseph Harris's *Congressional Control of Administration* (The Brookings Institution, 1964); and Stephen K. Bailey's *Congress Makes a Law* (New York: Columbia University Press, 1950). More will be said on the subject in later chapters.

laws, selected those laws and parts of laws they preferred to execute and, by neglect or outright refusal, did not execute others.

All this was not accomplished without resistance. On occasion there was conflict and recrimination. These always stopped short of impeachment proceedings; nevertheless, threats of such action were often the subject of congressional oratory, and in a few instances, serious but unsuccessful attempts were made to organize support.[6] Presidents have often wished they were able to impeach Congresses, and they have, in effect, done so in appeals to the public. But its members are numerous, and especially when the indictment is obstructionism, individuals are difficult to locate. Only occasionally is such a target as Representative Howard Smith of Virginia available. He, for several decades, refused consideration of executive measures he happened to disapprove from his post as chairman of a committee that controlled the calendaring of bills. Only his colleagues could have disciplined him, and they never did. This was not an unusual instance, but more often the opposition is anonymous.

The branch that, in the regard of the framers, was the first—the Congress—made many attempts, some aggressive, some passive, to invade or obstruct the territory claimed by others. Forward positions in the no man's land of the Constitution became a traditional source of contention. In these efforts, the appropriating power of the Congress was used without restraint to check the other branches. No president before Eisenhower was allowed assistance at all consonant with his duties, or even adequate facilities for carrying them out. Before Theodore Roosevelt, the president had to conduct the affairs of his office in the family's living quarters, hardly changed from Jefferson's time, and with only a few clerks for help. Cleveland's correspondence was in handwriting, and Wilson used his own typewriter; Lincoln borrowed men in uniform for clerkly duties—and was accused of exceeding his powers and defying the Congress!

These niggling restrictions were a constant handicap. But it did not prevent rural congressmen in every session from making a cause of fancied presidential extravagances. For a century and a half these were the regular stuff of legislators' oratory. Some fantastic charges seriously diminished presidential dignity, such as when J. Q. Adams was loudly condemned for spending public funds on a "gambling device" that turned out to be a billiard table he had bought with his own funds. But, like all such attacks, the derogation got much fuller publicity than the correction. In another vein,

6. The one impeachment actually attempted came about through presidential resistance to a congressional aggression that was later admitted. It was unsuccessful. Johnson's escape, however, was so narrow and the initiative so generally disapproved that no other has ever reached the trial stage provided in the Constitution. The Tenure of Office Act, which would have forced presidents to gain Senate consent to dismissals as well as appointments, was soon modified and later repealed (in Cleveland's administration).

the White House nearly collapsed from overuse and undermaintenance in Truman's time. Until it was rebuilt it was described by surveyors as perilously unsafe.

The outright aggressions of the Congress were less successful because the capacity of legislators to comprehend the multiplying problems of an expanded society was limited. There was a characteristic bafflement that prevented resentment from being implemented. The Congress itself, in effect constitutionally immune to reorganization, refused to recognize its own limitations. It continued to scrutinize budgetary proposals line by line, and to hold hearings designed to show itself as the source of the expenditures desired by the localities where its members were based. Generally, it used its appropriating power not for national but for local projects. Its lack of concern for national affairs contributed to the president's enlarged powers because only he was constantly concerned with general interests. It allowed itself to become an agency of influence for its constituents so that most of its members were engaged in matters related to favors and patronage.

Its more effective inroads on the other branches were represented by two really gross breaches of the separation principle: the establishment of a comptroller general and numerous regulatory (or independent) agencies. Because material for oversight of the executive was beyond the capacity of congressmen to gather, or to understand if it had been collected, the office of the comptroller general was instituted at the same time that the necessity for a national budget was finally, with the utmost reluctance, recognized (in 1921). This official was to be an agent of the Congress. He was to keep various committees informed of the use made of appropriated funds by the executive agencies. He was given a long term (fifteen years) and ample facilities. The first incumbent, and the one who established the procedures of the office, was J. R. McCarl, a protégé of Senator George Norris. He shared the Nebraska Progressive's rigid honesty, and he surpassed him in zeal. It was these traits, and the encouragement he had from the pleased legislators, who at last had a way of interfering with executive behavior. McCarl soon exceeded his terms of reference. He instituted the custom of preauditing instead of postauditing expenditures. This was a completely unjustified interference with "faithful execution," and it naturally galled administrative officers. They rebelled; however McCarl refused to release funds for expenditure until he had before him plans for their use that seemed to meet the intention of Congress. If he was doubtful, he consulted committee chairmen. This gave these chairmen opportunities for directing administration in detail that they had never before possessed. Infuriated presidents, one after another, protested interferences with their duty—but without result. When the Report on Administrative Reorganization (the so-called Brownlow report) was presented to F. D. Roosevelt in 1937, restriction to postauditing was recommended. The president attempted to bargain for restriction of the comptroller; but his pleas were ignored, and the nuisance was continued.[7]

The other congressional offense was of a still more consequential nature. Because it could not, itself, regulate businesses grown dangerous to the economy through size and indifference to the public interest or, at least, to the interests of powerful congressmen's constituents, the supervisory duty was delegated to newly constituted agencies. These were not entrusted to the president; for this, the excuse was made that they were not executive. The duty of these agencies, like that of the comptroller general, was to the Congress, although their members were appointed by the president. Soon the Courts were passing on their behavior, and this quickly became a means of establishing norms. The agencies were, in fact, usually spoken of as "semijudicial," although most commentators referred to them as "independent." They grew to be the largest bureaucracy of government, taken together. They had no common administrative head, no clear standards for action, and only when scandalous situations were exposed was there any check on their functions or their zeal in pursuing them.

The laws establishing these agencies did not clearly recognize that the businesses involved were using resources belonging to the people, and, lacking this, their authority to make allocations was hazy. They were handicapped also by the prevailing belief in laissez-faire; and, except when offensive advantage was taken of consumers, the feeling was that business ought to have the freedom called for in the theory. These regulatory bodies, although with exceptions, in general have had a feeble history; not only have they not controlled, but often they have themselves been controlled. This happened largely by infiltration of commissions by appointments from the business supposed to be regulated or, what was as bad, their legal representatives. The excuse for this was that no one else could really understand the regulated industry, but the effect was to use government for the facilitation of the very practices sought to be eliminated.

If this is too harsh a criticism of some officials and some agencies at some times, it does describe the rule rather than the exception; but what is in question here is not the effectiveness of the invention but its constitutional implications. It clearly violates the separation principle; it has no justification in any clause of the Constitution; and more than any other of the many branches, it calls in question the continued reliance on that principle as a structural characteristic. If it can be violated for convenience whenever the need arises, is it useful, really, in the most practical sense? That sense goes deeper than convenience or even than law. Regulation is a necessity in a plural economy, but it ought to have intentions and standards of constitutional legitimacy.

7. For an account of this interesting incident see Richard Rolenburg, *Reorganizing Roosevelt's Government* (Boston: Harvard University Press, 1966).

A Monolith?

If governmental power is to be divided there must obviously be power to divide; but at Philadelphia the curious fact was that until an agreement was reached about the division between the states and the Union, it was not certain that there would be a government; and, naturally, its structure could not be determined until that was known. After the Great Compromise, it was at last agreed that there would be a central authority; but how powerful it would be, whether it would follow the tripartite pattern, or how each of the branches would be armed were matters still to be decided. The deciding was often, but not always, an agonizing process.

It was rather remarkable that when this discussion did begin in earnest there was much less heat and much more seeking for light than there had been earlier when the states' rights advocates were attacking the nationalists' position so determinedly. About separation there was no real controversy; the principle was quickly agreed to.[8] No declaration of this sort was proposed for the Constitution; but that there would be division followed inevitably from enumeration: legislative, executive, and judicial branches would be specified, and their duties and powers assigned. No limitations were to be detailed; it was the central government itself that was to be limited in scope. But when it was said repeatedly that certain actions might not be taken, the prohibitions were located in Article II defining legislative powers; the other branches were not thus admonished except as they shared in legislation.

This must be taken to mean that, to the framers, separation implied something taken away from the primary branch, the legislative. The other branches had a lesser status, less potential power, and needed no such admonishment. The fact is that it was all done much too quickly. The presidency was not at all clearly visualized; the judiciary was taken for granted and barely mentioned; and even the Congress was not given permission to legislate in matters that were already becoming important as the nation grew.

Easy agreement to the principle of separation and to a particular arrangement for it came, as has been suggested, from mixed motives. There were lingering recollections of colonial harshness and a strong sentiment for

8. The most rigorous rule of separation previously formulated was that in the constitution of Massachusetts. It read: "In the government of this commonwealth, the legislative department shall never exercise the executive and judicial powers, or either of them: the executive shall never exercise the legislative and judicial powers, or either of them: the judicial shall never exercise the legislative and executive powers, or either of them: to the end that it may be a government of laws and not of men."

For a discussion, see C. Herman Pritchett, *The American Constitution* (New York: McGraw-Hill, 1968), p. 9.

the representative bodies that had fomented and sustained the Revolution.[9] But there were also those frequent references, during the debates, to the dangers of democracy and "mob rule." No one wanted another Shays's Rebellion or more depreciated currency. It was not easy to allay all these mixed fears and still maintain the principle of popular sovereignty. What was wanted was protection for property and for individual liberty *without* an embarrassing listing of rights that might encourage demagogues and prepare the way for social upheaval in the wake of the war for independence —sometimes called a revolution. This it distinctly was not. It was a rebellion.

The impossible was being sought: protection for individuals and property mostly against possible legislative action; yet not so much protection that debtors could escape their debts or demagogues be freed from restraint. This called for nice calculation. One of its results was the perception that the executive must not be chosen by the legislature as it was in eight of the states. That branch would clearly be supreme if it had that duty. At the same time it would be asking for trouble to have the executive elected even by a restricted electorate. After all, Shays's followers had been property owners. If the executive did directly represent the people he might become a fearsomely authoritarian figure, much like a king, not by divine right but by the manipulation of easily inflamed popular sentiment. Demagogues were to be guarded against; it was a Washington the delegates had in mind for the presidency, not a Sam Adams or a Jefferson.

The way out of this difficulty was found in the electoral college. This device removed the choice from direct popular election and placed it safely in the keeping of the elite. The character of the college was guaranteed by an electorate already confined to propertied men under existing state laws. Such voters could be trusted to choose men like themselves to be members of the college. Their choice, it followed, would be a conservative one, a principal who would share the attitude of the rich and wellborn, who would preside with dignity and restraint, yet be vigilant to promote tranquillity.

Thus legislative and executive were furnished with powers. But they would be functioning in the same government, and they might defeat the purpose of separation if they were so situated that an alliance would be likely to be formed. This possibility called for devices to ensure hostility between them. If only the legislature could raise revenues, the president would be prevented from making the expenditures he would be sure to press for; if the president could veto its bills, the legislature would be kept from passing bills arranged for by logrolling or ones providing for cheap-

9. In each of the new states the governor was elected by the legislature, and in only three states did he have the veto. There was a strong leaning to short executive terms; in ten states these were limited to one year. John Adams said of this that "where annual elections end, there tyranny begins."

ened money. Also, it seemed to be thought, legislatures might be kept from being irresponsible in other ways, perhaps by provoking foreign powers or by interfering with trade.

Not only money matters would be affected by this hostility; neither of these branches could undertake rash adventures of any sort; and neither could be too harsh with minorities.[10] But separation had really been adopted at the beginning for another reason—it was the most important ingredient of the states' rights–nationalistic compromise. Since it was to be there, however, it could be woven into a balancing system. So it was arranged not only that the president could veto legislation but also that the president's appointments must be confirmed and his treaties subjected to examination. Furthermore, since the House of Representatives would need Senate concurrence for all its legislative measures, the ebullience of that popular body would be effectively damped down by a more sedate upper house.

The framers, most of them, were very pleased with these arrangements. And they did serve well for what was intended—to prevent government from becoming oppressive. What was overlooked was that this peculiar negative conception, together with no more than a hazy focus on the presidency, made it almost impossible to formulate policy and to act on it— aside, that is, from negative policies of economy and restraint. If the government was to do anything even to protect itself, the circle of checks had to be broken out of; and, of course, the president was the first to feel the compulsion.

He was, after all, the chief of state; he represented all the people even if he was elected indirectly; he was looked to for leadership and protection. This was an unwelcome discovery for most members of the legislative branch. They turned sullen and critical, and remained that way, generation after generation. But leadership and the ability to act quickly when threats impended or opportunities were offered were so necessary in the kind of nation that soon supervened—the scattered agricultural economy known to the framers rapidly becoming urbanized and industrialized—that efficiency and security became more important than protection against swollen executive authority. When this became plain the Constitution might well have been amended to recognize and legitimize it. This not having been done, the situation that developed was one shaped by conflict and distorted by shifts of actual power. In a serious reconsideration, ways might have been found to encourage leadership, at the same time not allowing it to become authoritarian.

Since the states' rights issue was settled by events, the original reason for establishing the Senate disappeared. The Seventeenth Amendment (rati-

10. Madison said of this that "distribution and organization provided better guards than are found in any other popular government against interested combinations of a majority against the rights of a minority."

fied in 1913) providing for the direct election of members went some way toward adaptation to this reality. But no change was made in the unequal representation that had been demanded as the price of the smaller states' agreement to union. It remained an egregiously malapportioned body, some of whose members had many more constituents than others. It was cleansed of the corruption involved in selection by state legislatures; it was no longer a rich man's club; its members less frequently owed allegiance to those who had bought and paid for their seats; but still, with its reason for being gone, it had lost its original justification for existence.

In the literature of political science after 1913 other justifications were put forward: a second chamber, it was said, is a useful check on the House of Representatives; its smaller membership allows it to maintain some of the deliberation legislatures were supposed to have in classical theory, but which no longer existed in the House; and its larger constituency—statewide —enlarged somewhat its views of public problems. Evidence was adduced to support these contentions; there was more debate; many amendments were made to bills in passage; and more time was given to national interests.

It has to be said, however, that praise for the Senate ran mostly to contrasts with the performances of the House. This, as time passed, became progressively more deplorable. Its machinery was gradually dominated by a few old hands from safe districts, mostly southern and reactionary; it had an increasing phobia of opposition to executive proposals. Its exhaustive attempts to rewrite budgets it could not understand produced fantastic administrative confusion. It insisted on financing projects of local interests (a pork-barrel bill as an annual event), on filling the executive agencies with appointees who then owed loyalty to one of its members rather than to his superior, and on an elaboration of services for constituents who might be helpful in what had become a continuous campaign for reelection.

This degradation of the legislative function in the House does make the Senate seem necessary, but obviously a return of the House to decent standards of performance would erase the disparity and cancel the argument for a second house. The Senate, as merely a legislative chamber with the function of taking a second look at legislation, rests on an extremely shaky justification.

There is, however, the argument that the Senate acts as a check on the president, one of the ingenious devices opened to the framers by the Great Compromise. The checks are two: confirmation of appointments and ratification of treaties. It is interesting to see what has happened to these as they have been used in practice. It is not in all respects a favorable account, but it is not all bad either. Treaties have been too often opposed with no better excuse than irrelevant attempts to coerce the president. And the confirmation of appointments has become an unwritten agreement that cabinet members will usually be confirmed if the president will accept the senators' suggestions for appointing district judges and other federal officials who function in their states. More often than not these appointments serve to strengthen senatorial support more than the governmental services. The whole business has lost its character as a check and become little more than a frank bargaining. This balancing effect as a justification for the continuation of the Senate cannot be sustained.

These failures do not at all argue that the legislative function ought to be abandoned and somehow turned over to the executive—or the judiciary. They argue rather for regeneration, for a return to the original idea of legislation accommodated to contemporary circumstances. The failures do not argue, either, for the abandonment of separation and the balancings of powers so that none is abused. They argue, rather, for making them real and effective.

The first principle of the framers that absolute power ought not to lodge anywhere is as necessary to liberty of the citizen and of his concerns as it ever was. If the original devices have become obsolete and have been perverted to doubtful uses, they ought to be reexamined and regenerated; the intention ought not to be abandoned.

It is a simple proposition that if powers are not separate they are joined, and if they are joined, they tend to be absolute. It may be argued that this will not be true so long as popular sovereignty is expressed through elections and majority rule. Nevertheless a one-power state will have little concern for deliberation, for second thinking, or for holding administration true to established purposes. Even if such a monolith had its power conferred only for a term, that power would be so concentrated as to constitute the intolerable danger of authoritarian rule.

If these are important considerations, the separations ought to be better devised for their effectuation. Presidential leadership need not become a dictatorship; a house of representatives need not become a shop for favors; and an upper house could share the powers of both representatives and president with benefit all around. For this, some changes would be needed —longer terms, wider constituencies, a smaller membership, and restricted functions for the house; for the upper house, responsibility to a national rather than a state constituency and an infusion of tested statesmen with no other interest than the nation itself; for the president, a reallocation of duties, recognizing his inability to act as active administrator of the federal agencies, but accepting his role as chief of state, policy proposer, and guardian of the national security.

Disputed Terrain

The Supreme Court has felt itself obliged to act a strange part in the developments originating in the separation entanglement. It has undertaken to define not only the role of the legislature and the executive, but of itself.

This last is an anomaly lawyers are reluctant to recognize; when they do acknowledge its strangeness, they fall back on the singularly undemocratic justification that the judiciary can be trusted beyond other men. They cannot have it so. A power able to define itself is supreme; if the whole idea of separatism is to prevent supremacy, the Court cannot be what it apparently feels it must be. It must be limited along with the other branches.

In fact, the Constitution said this in several ways. The Court's jurisdiction was made subject to legislative determination; its members were to be appointed by the president; and there was always the need for funds that only the other two branches could appropriate for its use. Besides, the nature of the judicial process supposed that it would be confined to deciding among contenders, using the law as its guide. The law might be either constitutional or legislative, but the Court was not to create either. This being a limitation not clearly definable, there was the same temptation to expand that infected the other branches, especially when what was being accomplished was so approved by the judges' higher audience—at one time of businessmen, later of professionals. What happened was that a small reach beyond the boundary was encouraged in this way, and presently a further reach was made. There proved to be no definable end to this expansion.

The Court has had marked periods of conservatism and liberalism, not with respect to its own powers, but about political, economic, and social policies. In each phase it has had support from its elite public; this has encouraged it to expand its area of decisionmaking. When the laws were undesirable or the Constitution inconvenient, the Court cautiously made laws or changed the Constitution. This expansion has not gone unnoted; mistakes have, on occasion, jeopardized the Court's long-run ambitions. The rejection of the income tax is an example of this. In one decision such a tax was upheld.[11] But sometime later when a new law to tax incomes was passed, the Court rejected it.[12]

One of its periods of reaction was by then well under way. Of this period Pritchett remarked:

This surrender of the Court to entrenched wealth, in the same year that it refused to apply the Sherman Act against the sugar trust and upheld the conviction of Debs for violating an injunction during the Pullman strike, revealed all too clearly the judiciary's alignment on the side of capital and earned the Court a reputation as a tool of special privilege which was not dispelled for forty years.[13]

When F. D. Roosevelt's appointments became a majority, a consistently liberal view became characteristic. This was, of course, anathema to the

---

11. *Springer* v. *United States,* 102 U.S. 586 (1881).

12. *Pollock* v. *Farmers' Loan and Trust Co.,* 157 U.S. 421 (1895).

13. Pritchett, *op. cit.,* p. 209.

conservatives who once regarded the Court as the defender of liberty, but the liberals prevailed. Neither of these reputations ought to be earned by a constitutional court; they show quite conclusively that it has not been kept within the bounds appropriate to a separate judicial branch but has reached into the others for powers it may not properly possess.

As has been suggested, this sort of thing was made possible, if not inevitable, by the original indefiniteness of allocations in the Constitution and the unwillingness afterward to reexamine and redefine them when experience had shown more clearly what they ought to be. Since reexamination very evidently was not to be undertaken, the Court grew notably bolder as time went on. This tendency accelerated in its liberal phase. Such pronouncements as those having to do with school segregation, and with the reapportionment of state legislatures, would have been unthinkable only a short time earlier. This might not have been because of judicial modesty, rather because of discretion, but the restraints would have been the same. A rule summarized by Brandeis in 1936 marked out the limits then regarded as allowable.[14] The Court, he said, would not anticipate questions of constitutional law and would not decide any such question if it could be avoided; it would not formulate an interpretation broader than required by the facts; it would always try to find other grounds for disposing of the cases before it; and even when legislation was in question and doubt of constitutionality had been raised, an effort would be made to find a construction of the statute that avoided constitutional interpretation.

This may have been discretion rather than modesty or an admission of incompetence. It was, at any rate, abandoned when Frankfurter left the Court. Even before that, other justices had found it much too confining. It is not exaggerated to say that if something disapproved by the majority came within their purview the majority had no hesitancy in issuing directions to the other branches or committing them to enforcement of decrees that amounted to legislation. Discretion among the justices has been more and more confined to a few conservatives. It has been the liberals who found that their sensitivity to injustice or misbehavior easily overcame their discretion. The Constitution as seen by the Court changed more during Warren's years on the bench as chief justice than in the 150 preceding years. This trend would be reversed by the Burger Court.

What has been said here has applied mostly to issues between the Court and the Congress. The civil rights decisions affected issues neglected since the post-Civil War constitutional amendments, but they preceded legislative action by only a few years and so might fairly be said to have been unnecessary. That concerning apportionment in the upper houses of state legislatures turned on the principle of one man, one vote, something, the Court said, that was basic to democracy. But the fact is that the Constitution does

14. *Ashwander* v. *Tennessee Valley Authority*, 297 U.S. 288 (1936), 145.

not say anything of the sort.[15] The principle was an addition to the Constitution that perhaps ought to be made; but if the Court can make it, constitutionality becomes something other than always has been supposed, something made in court, not in constitutional conventions or by the processes of amendment. Either a constitution is over and above legislative and administrative law, and controlling for all citizens, or it is a mere convenience. No professedly constitutional government can afford to make such an admission.

In regard to the president, the Court was much more discreet until recently. But the startling decision in the steel case changed all that—or did, so far as the Court is concerned; a determined president in an emergent situation is still to be heard from.[16]

This case created an issue between the Court and the executive that can be settled only by constitutional clarification. The Court placed itself in the absurd position of asserting its competence to decide the limits of presidential power in emergencies, not hesitating, in doing so, to extend its own powers indefinitely. In effect, its opinions said that only the Court could decide what constitutes an emergency and what is properly to be done when one occurs.

The issue between these two branches had been in an indeterminate status since the beginning, and at various times had been critical. President Jackson said on one such occasion:

Each public officer who takes an oath to support the Constitution swears that he will support it as he understands it, and not as it is understood by others. . . . The opinion of the judges has no more authority over Congress than the opinion of Congress has over the judges, and on that point the President is independent of both.

In the steel case the issue posed so long before, and so irritating to an arbitrary court, was finally met by the justices. Not all of them wanted to see it met. Chief Justice Vinson, in fact, dissented. In his opinion he listed no fewer than twenty-five instances of similar presidential actions; all of them had been essential to the national welfare, and all of them had stood. The president's action this time had the same justification, he said, and the Court ought not to interfere. But even Vinson, supporting the president's action, refused to surrender the Court's potential supremacy. He said:

In this litigation for return of the plaintiff's properties, we assume that defendant, Charles Sawyer, is not immune from judicial restraint and that plaintiffs

15. On the contrary, the amendments saying that certain excuses shall not be used by the states to limit the privilege of voting imply that, generally, the admission to the electorate is a matter to be determined by law. And certainly the guarantee to every state of a republican form of government does not imply a particular form of representation; if it did, the United States itself would not be a republic, since the Senate is a notorious instance of unequal representation.

16. *Youngstown Sheet & Tube Co.* v. *Sawyer,* 343 U.S. 579 (1952), 313.

are entitled to equitable relief if we find that the executive order under which defendant acts is unconstitutional. We also assume that the Court may go behind a President's finding of fact that an emergency exists.

Of course, that is precisely what strong presidents, meeting the twenty-five emergencies cited by the chief justice, had maintained that the Court might not do. Although Truman returned the properties without comment, his compliance in no way surrendered the presidential position. A Doctrine of Necessity, built up over the years since Washington first applied it, was not obliterated. It could not be. If the Court thereafter regarded itself as supreme, that did not commit the other branches—who themselves are separate and independent, and who, as Jackson said, may interpret their constitutional duty as seems to them appropriate.

Preserving the Separation Principle

One justification for the separation principle is that if it were to be abandoned there would result a monolithic government. All power, it is maintained, would necessarily be concentrated in the legislature, if not at once, then eventually. This is certainly true; if it should be concentrated in the executive there would be a dictatorship, and this is rejected by consensus; and obviously, since judges are not competent to make law or execute it, they should have no more than interpreting duties. They obviously do not agree to this, but others understand their limitations very well. If this reasoning is accepted, some sort of distribution is obviously called for.

In its short form, however, the statement is too absolute. It needs further specification to show why separation as the alternative to legislative monopoly is not only practical but essential to American purposes as they have always been understood—as they are stated, say, in the Preamble to the Constitution.

A government of concentrated powers elevating the legislature to supremacy, and making the other branches subordinate, would also elevate all the weaknesses of that branch. The executive would thus become but a committee of members of one house—there could not be two houses.[17] And this committee would act as a body with all the failings of group operations, but then, because government by a group would prove impossible, dominance in administration would certainly be seized by a more competent operator. The first energetic chairman would—as he has in Britain—come to dominate both cabinet and legislature by concentrating in himself the popular support no legislative house can ever have. This last is because representatives are elected from districts and so do not have a national constituency. This chairman would then be a prime minister and

17. The less representative one would rapidly become vestigial, as it has in Britain and France, and even its delaying powers would be diminished and finally abolished by an impatient legislature.

would be looked to by the whole electorate for the fulfillment of his promises. This would permit him to have relationships with the voters without interference from legislators. It has happened that way in Britain. Policymaking there is much more concentrated than is usually admitted. The prime minister, having this general support, can and does effectively dominate the Commons. He can even determine, through party machinery, who shall compete for seats. The members thus owe their positions to him. Party discipline is strict in a sense that appals legislators in the United States, on whom party or executive restrictions weigh very lightly.

The conclusion has to be that if powers are not separated in a constitution, the government will, in one way or another, come into the control of one individual. And this will be so in even the most determined democracies. That individual might turn out to be a prime minister as he has in Britain, but he might also turn out to be a Hitler as he did in Germany. The difference between these developments was owed perhaps to national characteristics, but even if this is so there is no way of knowing how such a system would evolve in a country like the United States. It is neither a United Kingdom nor a Germany; and it cannot be denied that its size, its heterogeneity, and its discords might very soon make tranquillity again the elusive virtue it was in 1787.

Separation, in the sense of having branches that owe their independent existence to a nationwide constituency, does at least operate to keep absolute power away from the legislature where it cannot be used in operations and where it will inevitably devolve on one charismatic leader. This is a valuable negative utility for the device. Its positive virtue is that it permits the development of limited leadership by a president who is responsible to the electorate as a whole yet leaves the legislative function intact. It also makes the judiciary relatively immune from the threat of subordination by duress.

This is the way it might be, but only partially is, in the American version. As we have seen, several countering and checking arrangements adopted at Philadelphia for various reasons interfered from the first with the fulfillment of the intention. To begin with, the legislature was given the advantages over the other branches that we have seen. To the extent that this was done for understandable reasons, these reasons were temporary, and as they faded, the difficulty of amendment made it impossible to correct the imbalance; the legislature was in position to guard the gateway and would not permit revision. This tended to result in that evolution toward dictatorship that complete legislative supremacy would have started. But since the advantage was slight, it could be strongly opposed by the other branches. It did not, for instance, prevent the president from assuming the national leadership so essential to democracy in a vast area with a large population.

Successive presidents found ways to overcome legislative advantages and constant hostility, but they were ways that were not good ones for a democracy. They were, in fact, rooted in a guilty contravention of separation. In order to meet his responsibility to the electorate he had to subvert the legislature. This not only distorted the legislative process but also had the result of weakening substantially his executive efficiency. He allowed legislators privileges in his own domain—such as the control of administrative projects and personnel—that he felt could be sacrificed to gain more important freedoms to act. But this was a fatal sacrifice. The congressional appetite was insatiable. And eventually domestic administration. was substantially lost to its titular head.

The president was more inclined to let this happen because from the time of Jackson or thereabouts (the 1830s), administration had begun to slip from the president's grasp. The establishment was too big and much too complicated; he lacked the facilities; and his attention was continually directed to the more urgent duties of political leadership, internal dissension, and the responsibilities incident to the nation's increasing wealth and power. But, for whatever the reason, the planning and execution of domestic affairs drifted into the control of inherently incompetent legislators. The president's establishment grew only slowly, retarded by an angry opposition that had always to be placated by these costly administrative compromises. After 150 years of this opportunism, accompanied by a chorus of dissent, he was no longer a recognizably constitutional figure. Can Washington be imagined as a Roosevelt, a Johnson, or a Nixon?

But the other branches were no longer what had been intended either. The Congress was no longer a deliberative body. What consideration was given to lawmaking was confined to committees; these were dominated, as we have seen, by chairmen who used their special controls to bargain with the president, less with a view to wise national policy than to consolidating their own positions—or to serving the special and local interests with which they were allied.

Time and growth were the villains in these unplanned distortions of original intentions. They inevitably spread through the whole system.

Consider the judiciary for instance. It too had preempted for itself a position in the scheme of government not contemplated by the framers. It had seized the right to change the Constitution by interpretation, to restrict the other presumably independent branches, and generally to impose its views of proper national policy on the economy and the society. But the judges never had much understanding of administrative matters; and even if they had, cases came to them so haphazardly that fifty years of practice might have become established custom before being overturned by a decision. That this is no way to run a government would be concluded by the most casual observer. But those involved are seldom so disengaged that they can be critical. One of the strangest characteristics of dialogue in the United States is that the departures from the framers' intentions are not subjected even to elementary analysis.

The indictment made here need not have been possible if original mistakes had been adjusted in proper constitutional ways and if social and economic changes had been taken into consideration. Instead of allowing the Constitution to become obsolete, and thus ineffective, it ought to have been amended periodically with the indicated ends in view. Because it was not, the actual operating Constitution of our day—the emergent one—is made up, as we have seen, of excrescent growths and distorted interpretations (mostly so hazy that constant challenge is encouraged). It ought not to have happened, and it ought not only to be corrected but made impossible of happening again.

Even if a constitution is, by definition, a supreme law, it is not immutable. Even its principles need occasional reexamination. It is not argued here that separation ought to be preserved because Montesquieu favored it or because the framers adopted it; it is argued that it ought to be kept (in more logical and operative form) because it is an indispensable structural device for the United States of the present. This is, of course, provided it is wished to implement popular sovereignty and operate as a pluralistic society; and to protect, in increasingly difficult circumstances, the individual liberties so easily sacrificed in dictatorships, however they come about, and whatever name they are given.

An Integrated Whole

There is no magic in the number three, and Montesquieu did not have magic in mind when he settled on that number of branches for government. Neither did the framers; it simply appealed to their practical sense that there should be a legislature to make laws, an executive to carry them into operation, and a judiciary to decide causes brought under them. Such a structure corresponded well enough with the needs of a small nation in the late eighteenth century. Also, as can be seen, with the intention of having a government of limited impact.

But the country did not linger in a condition that made such a government desirable. The Constitution was framed, as it happened, at the end of an era, not at the beginning of one. When expansion, population growth, and industrial advance soon changed everything, when small farmers and independent artisans became a small percentage instead of a large percentage of the people's occupations, when cities enlarged and communications grew easier, government found itself in perpetual crisis because of demands it must satisfy that had not been anticipated. It soon began to respond. The president was harassed by problems he was not equipped to meet, even if they had not been inherently beyond the capacity of one man; the Congress, coming from scattered districts, was not structured to legislate properly for a nation; and the judiciary, seeing that the struggle for control by new forces was disrupting the social order, invented the doctrine of implication.

This rule was thereafter applied everywhere. It was essential to all the branches. None possessed enumerated powers sufficient to encompass their enlarged responsibilities or to cope with the private interests that multiplied so rapidly. The president had to meet emergencies he had not been instructed to meet; the Congress, violating the ancient legal axiom that delegated powers cannot be redelegated, found it necessary to pass many of its duties to other agencies with more competence; and the judiciary, not meeting any serious opposition, began to revise the Constitution so that, with as little strain as possible, it might be adapted to the new circumstances.

As time passed, these adaptations became so commonly accepted that today a literal reading of the Constitution is as uncommon as a literal acceptance of the Ten Commandments. The framers of 1787 would have been amazed to discover that their three branches have been expanded in number. These new agencies are not called branches; they have a hazy original relationship to the traditional three, but this grows more tenuous as time passes. The three added ones might easily be identified as political, regulatory, and planning. They exist, but only in an uneasy state. If they are embarrassingly present, why have they not been constitutionalized and so given the legitimacy conferred only by this recognition?

It is no answer to say that the Congress has delegated duties to them, or that the Supreme Court has acknowledged their existence. This, again, was redelegation of delegated powers. Neither Congress nor Court had the competence to do this any more than they had the competence to approve new powers for the old branches. Expressly, the Constitution had forbidden any such thing: the powers not delegated . . . *were reserved to the states or to the people.*

Avoiding the difficult question of the states' competence to surrender powers, it is possible to point out that the people have never been consulted. And they are the ultimate sovereigns. Do they want these new branches? And do they approve the new disposition of duties? They could do it only through the process of amendment, and there never have been amendments touching the structure established in the Constitution.

There are those who say that this is a comfortable situation; it leaves everything to contention among the branches and among new agencies for recognition; ultimately, for acceptance by the Supreme Court. The justices are willing to guide the nation through the embarrassments of future expansion as they have in the past. They are learned in precedent and alert to national needs. They stand at a patriarchal remove, above the maneuvers of president and Congress. The advantage of this is obvious. It leaves the settlement of large questions to an existing body and does not require the difficult and disturbing effort required for revision. Little by little the judges have made adaptations; there have been no uncontrollable convulsions; and when convulsions threaten, the justices retreat with dignity, and no harm is done.

The trouble with this is as obvious as its advantages. It leaves all the hard decisions to an elite, a legal elite removed from the observations of those democratic devices—majority rule and representation. Perhaps that is necessary or, at least, wanted; but it is a negation of popular sovereignty. Besides, if it is preferred that the nation be guided by an elite, it is certainly arguable that this is not the best one for the purpose.

It is submitted that the American people have drifted into a situation not contemplated by the framers and not given approval by any generation of voters since. What is necessary is to accept the fact that the nation has become irreversibly one whole and that this requires its citizens of all kinds to assume an appropriate relationship to that whole. The meaning of this is that they must regard with deeper respect their national responsibilities; also that they need governmental agencies competent for the complex duties of planning and managing such a society as ours has become.

In providing, separately, for these branches of government they need not, indeed they must not, be set against each other. The distribution of duties must reduce sharply the struggles within government for advantage. Dictatorships accomplish this by concentrating the assignment function in one individual. But this sets up a system of favor giving. Democratic theory holds that there shall be no favors; how far we have departed from this principle is well enough known; since the political system is not constitutionalized it operates constantly with favors and privileges as currency.

The present situation can be described as permitting competing would-be dictators to dispense favors so that their own interests may be advanced. Americans might seriously ask themselves why a senatorship is worth ten or twenty million dollars, and why the presidency is worth something like a hundred million: to whom and for what? Certainly not to the run of voters who contribute nothing—or nothing like the contributions made by suspiciously interested individuals or associations.

So far as there is stability, it is a sort of truce—an uneasy agreement—to divide powers and patronage. This is not referable to a constitution, because, in the governmental area, a respected one no longer exists; it is left to bargains among competitors who have gained office by characteristic appeals through a communication system that also may be suborned.

Are Americans proud to have their presidency out of reach for any but their wealthiest citizens, to have their congressmen owe election to a few contributors who get together sums aggregating perhaps fifty times legislative annual salaries, to have the upper levels of bureaucracy apportioned by patronage with less regard to competence than to support of patrons? And, further, are they content to have issues settled in Washington by a system of trades, bribes, and specious appeals to the electorate?

If not, they had better attend to a considered constitutional revision calculated to eliminate these conditions.

They had better think of one government belonging to them whose officials gain office because of promised competence and whose duties are assigned in a constitution suited to the circumstances of the times.

CHAPTER 5

THE DOCTRINE OF NECESSITY

The Doctrine

The Doctrine of Necessity: Power will be seized and used to preserve the nation whole. It will be seized by him or those who are able to concentrate the sustaining forces of democracy. His or their judgment will determine the necessity.

Anyone who studies the presidency quickly concludes—if indeed that was not why he began the study—that such an accumulation of powers could have come about only because presidents reached for and held powers against what must often have been fierce opposition. Such powers may not have been taken from the other branches; usually they would have resulted from governmental expansion; but some must obviously have been seized. The Congress or the Court would have felt that these were theirs, and they may have tried to keep them; but in such a contest the president would have won because after all he is the doer of our system.

Among these last there are the powers taken by the president, without regard to their presumed allocation, when necessity has compelled instant action. So Lincoln suspended writs of habeas corpus and freed the slaves; so Roosevelt ordered the relocation of the Pacific Coast Nisei; so other presidents have carried on virtual wars abroad without asking for a declaration. These were plainly seizures and were plainly not contemplated by the framers.

One difficulty has been that just as two objects cannot occupy the same space at the same time, no two branches of government can exercise the same authority concurrently. One or the other, if and when tests come, prevails. The president's advantage is that when it is he, something gets done; but when it is the Congress, something is all too often prevented from

being done; and when it is the Court, everything is stopped. Seizure or
retention by Congress or Court in time of emergency is intolerable. It has
been tried, but failure is foregone.

If, however, experience with extensions of presidential authority is
examined, in the end there is not much enlightenment; such extensions of
authority are provisional, conditional, and usually temporary; since this
is the nature of emergency they are regarded as quite outside the normal
system. When in rare instances they are extended in time, opposition to
them grows stronger and defense of them weakens. They are regarded as
momentary usurpations, unavoidable and unfortunate, but impossible to
resist while crises last. Natural opponents tend to conform, but their
tolerance is limited and there is trouble if termination is delayed. Even prolongation of a crisis with all the reasons for discipline still valid causes
more or less serious dissent, and professional politicians recognize and accommodate to the erosion of consent.

When powers are separated and not carefully enumerated, they are
vulnerable to seizure. This is true both of new duties and of emergency
powers. Since separation is a characteristic of the Constitution, one of its
lapses or, as is sometimes argued, one of its deliberate arrangements is the
ambiguity that encourages aggression. Elasticity, it is argued, prevents
breakage. It cannot have been intended that the stretching would proceed
until the strain became unbearable, but whether deliberate or not the result
is the same.

In this pull and haul a vigilant president can extend his rule over
practically all new functions, but in a time of crisis, when he seizes powers
not normally his, he holds them at some risk. Because such powers have
settled into White House control, the president cannot assume them to be
permanently reassigned. Only constitutional change could do that, and
there has been none.

Of course, if these powers are taken by a president, or for that matter,
by the Congress or the Court—for a time—usage and precedent do have a
certain effect. As presidents have become bolder, for instance, their
extensions have often seemed to be accepted; actually, none has been safe
unless clearly administrative in nature. Even extraordinary ones thought
easier to keep because they had been kept before will be challenged when
the emergency dies down. In the returning quietude the Congress will slyly
try to take back what it has tacitly let go, or the Court, by way of defining
all powers but its own, will progress to another stage in its persistent advance toward judicial supremacy. In the end the president may be no better
able to meet emergencies legitimately than he was before; if he feels
compelled he certainly will again resort to seizures; but he will experience
difficulties not much less than those of his predecessors. He will need to
marshal support, dip into his political credit, fight off dissenters, and be

prepared to give up all or most of what he has taken—very likely before he regards it as safe to do so.

The metaphor of a continual ambiguity is applicable not only to the powers that must be used in emergencies; the distribution of ordinary responsibilities is often the cause of interbranch hostilities. There are raids and counterraids, spying and counterspying, just as in any conflict among disputing sovereigns. Unless an incredible carelessness or lack of foresight is attributed to the framers, it must be concluded that they meant this to be a continuing condition. Political theorists have often found such a deliberate arrangement for conflict and disorder hard to accept. True, it was defended in *The Federalist Papers,* and this is all but final, yet when it is described to those bred to other systems it seems incredible. British observers have ventured explanations. They usually regard it as the result of a mistake. The Americans, they conclude, locked into their new Constitution old antagonisms by then resolved in Britain. Cabinet government with party discipline and parliamentary sovereignty had replaced endless struggle. King against barons and king against Parliament were centuries-old conflicts; however, these wars were over; Parliament had won. Government had been found impossible when powers were separated and independent; by 1787 the executive and the judiciary were definitely subordinated to the legislative.

There can be no doubt, however, that in America the constitutional arrangement did assume that conflict would not be resolved but would go on and on. This was in the interest of individual freedom. It was presumed necessary to prevent the possible lodgment of absolute authority in any part of government. Each was to share, but none was to dominate.

This principle of tension was almost impossible to draft, and the framers were not completely successful; but they appear not to have been at all apologetic about the ambiguity they left to posterity. It seems unlikely that they could have meant to establish chronic inertia, but perhaps this was not something they felt important; after all, government in the late eighteenth century was not expected to do much more than deal with the predatory empires. Even the domestic tranquillity spoken of was consigned to the states. They deduced from the behavior of colonial administrations that government was more apt to be tyrannical than beneficent, and this propensity was to be kept in check.

Among the baffling characteristics of their document none is more difficult to understand than the failure to make provision for inevitable circumstances. Emergency was one of these. That there would be times when ordinary processes would be insufficient to ensure the integrity of the nation, and when authority must be centered in someone or some agency, was among the probabilities either not thought of or left to be settled in future conflict. Yet there had never been a nation whose history was free of occasions when its very existence had to be defended. At such times authority always had to be mobilized, one head had to direct, dissent had to be suspended, and extraordinary disciplines had to be imposed. It is true that the recent rebellion against Britain had been stumbled through without any such concentration, but disorganization had very nearly caused its disappearance; at the time of the Philadelphia meeting a few years later, the threats on three borders approached emergency.

That no provision was made for circumstances of extreme peril with such experiences to draw on is not easily explained. Nevertheless the structure of government—the three counterposed branches and the limited central sovereignty—together with the appended rights making ample provision for individual freedom but none at all for circumstances of common danger, continued through the generations without amendment.

It does not appear in contemporary comment, and was denied in *The Federalist Papers,* that one of the Constitution's principles was the discouragement of novelty. Yet actually provision for change was omitted and substantive amendment made virtually impossible. It is tempting, because the framers are generally regarded as having had a kind of timeless wisdom, to read into their document what they did not at all intend; but it is clear that they did not mean to provide for altered conditions. The principles were regarded as permanent because they were rooted in unalterable human propensities. This was good eighteenth-century doctrine. Adam Smith said it in his *Wealth of Nations*, and its influence was pervasive among the framers. Men were selfish, but in pursuit of their own interests they would bring about the good of all—if they were not constricted. The special danger was that government would limit freedom.

This the framers meant to prevent by setting off each branch against the others, thus preventing any from accumulating dictatorial powers. Still, if, as Justice Brandeis argued, the tension among the branches was intended, and if there was no recognition that at times it must be suspended, the framers cannot easily be forgiven for not defining those times and the distribution of responsibilities when they arrived. The assembling of all the government's forces and their use in exigencies ought to have been anticipated.

Looking back at numerous national crises, it can be seen that, lacking definition, much always depended on fortuitous circumstances such as, for instance, willingness to forgo customary freedoms and trust in the president's understanding that grants of power were temporary. These in turn had always been affected by popular concern. The Congress and the Court would have problematical reactions, since they were consigning increased power to a natural rival. Actually it was clear from the first of such crises that they must give way, willingly or not, to the president; since he was given no directives and no one with whom he could share his responsibility, he must act alone, a dictator in a democracy. If this seemed undesirable when crises began to appear, it is strange that no amendment should have provided definition. Instead, what appears to have been the continuing attitude was that although there had been one crisis, or even several, there would never be another, and what was past had better be forgotten.

This was a mistake on the part of the other branches. A president who was also commander in chief was not only in possession of force but had been elected by a majority of the people and would inevitably be looked to for the protection of threatened common interests. Even the check provided by the lodgment of appropriation in the legislature would not hold him back if the danger were real or the advantage to be gained were massive —and the Treasury Department was within his jurisdiction. If this was not expected to happen it argues an unlikely misunderstanding of realities.

It is out of this positioning of the president and the ambiguity of the Constitution that the Doctrine of Necessity has developed. What presidents have considered imperative in time of national peril they have done; they have confronted foreign powers, sent armies abroad, deployed the navy in international waters, sent spy planes aloft, suspended civil rights, repressed rebellions, and used unappropriated funds; no one knows the extent of the intelligence activities directed by them, or the undercover activities of their operatives. All of these have taken on frightening dimensions under modern circumstances, but that the precedents reach far into the past cannot be denied. There are, for example:

- Washington's suppression of the Whiskey Rebellion and his somewhat roundabout arrangement that the French representative Genêt, who was preaching revolution, should be disavowed.
- Jefferson's Louisiana Purchase and his dispatch of the expedition to Tripoli.
- Monroe's *doctrine* and the Theodore Roosevelt *corollaries,* leading to numerous interventions, usually, but not always, among neighbors to the south.
- Jackson's gathering of force to suppress nullification.
- Polk's instigation and conduct of war with Mexico followed by the annexation of territories, and the strange procedures in the acquisition of California.
- Lincoln's use of force to combat rebellion; his expenditure of unauthorized funds, his suspension of civil rights, and his abolition of slavery.
- Cleveland's use of armed force to stop internal disorder; and his deployment of naval forces in the Venezuela dispute.
- McKinley's acquisition of Puerto Rico, the Philippines, and Cuba.
- Wilson's sending forces into Mexico and other small nations.
- Franklin D. Roosevelt's prohibition of trading in gold; his invention

of "national emergency" and subsequent naval actions; his occupation of Iceland; his gift of arms to Britain; and the many decisions not incidental to his position as commander in chief. Some of these were semilegitimate—but only doubtfully so.

- Truman's Korean intervention with the backing of a United Nations whose Russian contingent was absent.
- Eisenhower's occupation of Lebanon, and his limited intervention in Southeast Asia.
- Kennedy's sending of combat troops to Vietnam disguised as advisers.
- Johnson's intervention in Santo Domingo and the escalation of action in Vietnam.
- Nixon's continuation of intervention in Southeast Asia.

These are only a few of a larger number having the same justification —and the same lack of genuine legitimacy.

It will be recognized that such assumptions of power are quite apart from the expansion resulting from inability to find constitutional authority for novel undertakings. Especially in recent years despair of finding a constitutional lodgment for new enterprises has caused an increase in consignment to a newly created presidential "office." Occasionally some new agency has been made "independent" as the regulatory agencies were in earlier years, but "independent" is also a category unknown to the Constitution. These have not caused nearly so much dispute as the emergency seizures, and especially those requiring deployment abroad of the armed forces. Because these require drafted servicemen and because their costs are hideously high, they inevitably generate opposition and sometimes serious dissension.[1]

The Contending Branches

It is simply a fact of our history that presidents, the strong ones, have grasped and used whatever authority they felt to be needed in emergencies of all kinds, internal and external; and that they have either ignored or refused to give in to opposition from whatever source. Sometimes this has caused furor at the moment; at other times it has been accepted without opposition. Some of the seizures listed above were among those referred to by Chief Justice Vinson in dissenting from the Court's rebuke to Truman when he seized the steel mills during the Korean crisis, but Vinson found no fewer than twenty-five relevant precedents. The president, he reminded his colleagues, was charged with the faithful execution of the laws, and his

1. For a discussion of crisis situations and the constitutional dilemma they pose, see Clinton Rossiter, *Constitutional Dictatorship* (New York: Harcourt, Brace & World, 1948).

position required him to make his own judgment of what must be done; the Court was not entitled to intervene.[2]

In the recurrent determinations of presidents to make the nation secure, and to use all necessary means, the Court, until the steel cases in 1952, had not really attempted to prevent action while in progress; it had mostly said afterward, and rarely, that what had been done was inadmissible.[3]

The chief justice saw the decision in the steel case as a dangerous departure from this habit of restraint. What he did not say, but what was implied, was that it was another, almost final, step by the Court's majority toward judicial supremacy. Since it was always able to select its causes, and make its pronouncements after the crisis had passed and its decrees would not need to be defied, the Court had been astonishingly successful in building a tradition of final power. It had been checked only rarely, as, for instance, when its jurisdiction had been restricted while a case was being considered during the Reconstruction period after the Civil War. The Congress, fearing the punitive laws it had passed were about to be invalidated, repealed an act enabling the Court to hear such appeals.[4]

Despite such rare checks the progress toward supremacy, begun by Marshall's original assertion of the Court's duty to say what the executive might and might not do, had gone on intermittently whenever occasions were favorable. Certain legislative aggressions had been almost as bold, but not so successful because not so carefully calculated. An instance in point was the Tenure of Office Act. If honored, this would have deprived the president of control over his subordinates and transferred it to the Congress. That attempt was momentarily successful but was eventually defeated—not by the Court, however, but by congressional retreat. During Cleveland's administration a generation later, a repealer was quietly passed, but the act was by then understood to be untenable and had become inoperative.

Another kind of legislative aggression was represented by the setting up of the comptrollership general in 1921. The Congress had shown recurrent impulses to check executive expansion and demonstrate its claim to supremacy, but had found no effective way to do it except that of harassment by the withholding of funds or by the attachment to appropriation acts of restrictive riders; however, the budget was becoming so enormous, and the interferences of committees were consequently so blundering, that this could no longer be defended. Besides, the administrative agencies were largely staffed with employees recommended by congressmen and

2. *Youngstown Sheet & Tube Co.* v. *Sawyer,* 343 U.S. 579 (1952), previously cited. Vinson did not persuade his colleagues.

3. For instance in *Ex parte Milligan* in 1866, when Lincoln's use of military commissions was protested after the fact.

4. In *Ex parte McCardle,* 7 Wall 506 (1869).

were carrying out projects much wanted by their constituents. To cut the budget was often to hurt their own protégés in the bureaucracy and to offend their supporters back home.

The establishment of the supervisory office was a way to exercise control without seeming to, an irresponsibility much valued by politicians. The comptroller general was required to report only to the Congress. The first appointee, J. R. McCarl, was well aware that what he was supposed to do was to reduce the independence of the executive agencies. He very soon set up a system of preaudits, and this amounted to directives concerning the use of funds. McCarl required administrators to appear before him and furnish plans for expenditure, whereupon he either approved or issued directions for revision, sometimes with particulars, meanwhile consulting congressmen to make certain of their wishes. This interference went without serious challenge, largely because of executive fears. The appropriating branch had now found such a ready check for executive initiative that resisters were few. The administrative life was hard enough without carrying on a running battle with this new dictator provided with an army of investigators, but the burden had to be borne.

The strongest presidents, however, did presently begin to offer resistance. The preaudits made intolerable delays, and there was discovered a useful weapon in public opinion. This resource was quite as unknown to the Constitution as was the comptroller general, and presidents found that they could muster support almost every time if the cause seemed important enough. It remains the bitterest grievance of legislators that the president so invariably wins any contest with the Congress if he carries it to the people. Contrary to the theory they prefer, he, not Congress, represents the public interest—and well they know it. The comptrollers general gradually lost their early effectiveness as the extenders of congressional power. They fell back on exposures of administrative sins in postaudits, not nearly so useful to legislators, but much less obstructive to officials. The Court was inclined to ignore the separation principle represented by the comptrollership general, perhaps because neither of the other branches wanted to advance the justices in their progress toward judicial supremacy and so did not ask for opinions.

As would be expected, it is a characteristic of the continuing struggle among the branches that the one with the strongest leadership tends to prevail when no emergency exists; but it has certainly become an accustomed practice for the other branches to give way to the president in time of peril. He may, if the crisis is demanding, occupy, at least temporarily, most of the Constitution's foggy areas. Either opposition does not appear or it fades away, overwhelmed by support for the president from the electorate. The Congress simply retires from its advanced positions when a crisis is confronted and a president takes appropriate action, explaining to the nation why it must be done; and the Court finds no relevant case to decide until it will no longer affect the president's position.

Once crises are overcome, however, whether civil disturbance, peril from a foreign source, economic prostration, or deployment of armed forces to support foreign policy, the struggle is again resumed on very nearly the old terms. The congressional elders reassert their negative powers and again suggest the possibility of reprisal; and the Court cautiously entertains arguments that the president has exceeded his constitutional powers.

Such actions as he takes may indeed be reversed, their validity denied, and he may be condemned; but presidents are not long in office; and each succeeding administration tends to consider its problems unique. As for the Congress, its reactions are unpredictable because of the numbers involved in making policy and because of susceptibility to executive subversion. The Courts, by the time they have issued an opinion, find that the crisis is over— as it was in *Ex parte Milligan* (1866); or perhaps they will deliberately delay, being not so much interested in the case as in the issue. The justices do inch toward supremacy, but the unacknowledged urge is muted in emergency because it too has the weakness of not being constitutional and even discordant with the theory of separation. This is inherent. The Court cannot act, and the president can.[5]

Presidential Predicaments

There have been some successful appropriations by other branches of new duties as well as of old ones, but presidents are well aware that their predecessors have saved the Union from grave perils and have guarded its citizens' welfare as, in the circumstances, they felt they must; they know that to do it the views of judges or legislators have been disregarded; and their legal advisers, if not they themselves, know that these actions have exceeded any possible interpretation of the framers' intentions. If they have studied history, however, they also know that posterity has almost invariably been grateful. Never once before, say, 1950 had a seizure and use of extraordinary authority turned out badly for a president; and, until then,

5. This flat statement must be modified to recognize a new development. The Court has always been dependent on the executive for enforcement of its decrees. There are, however, federal marshals organized as a division of the Justice Department. This department is executive and under the president's theoretical direction, but the Court has gradually come to expect of it whatever its decrees require. A conspicuous instance is the supervision of desegregation by the federal judiciary. Marshals have sometimes constituted an invading force directed by judges. If this does not amount to the superseding of executive powers, the difference is hardly discernible. It would be the cause of a confrontation if the Court should attempt to use the marshals against the president in any way. The requirement that they should enforce immediate integration in southern schools after the president had authorized delays approached such a crisis, but the president did not make an issue of the matter.

it could have been said that never had a president allowed himself to be obstructed in the action he felt he must take. Then the steel case occurred.

This was a tragedy for the presidency, and a victory long awaited for the Court. What it did to the national security a student can hardly bear to contemplate. The defeat for the president came about because he had forgotten the uses of restraint. He had read the intimations of public support wrongly, and the Court had read them rightly. The Court had seized the opportunity and, with unprecedented celerity, decreed that the president had exceeded his powers. The weakness of his position was exposed, and he returned the steel properties to their owners. For the first time a president had been humiliated by the Court. The justices did not conceal their elation; the president retreated to embarrassed silence. He should have.

There was nothing about this seizure to set it apart from many presidential actions in the past except that the degree of emergency was not considered generally to be as it was presented. In resting ultimately on the example of Washington as he went about creating his new office, and on the precedents established by other presidents, Truman had failed to elevate his problem to the recognized emergency level or, perhaps, to see that there were alternatives short of expropriation. This was a vital difference. When Washington had made up his mind that the new Constitution required him to ride abroad in an ornate coach drawn by matched white horses, to hold levees in a fine mansion, and to withhold himself from intimate contacts of all kinds, he had set the presidency on a lonely eminence. For all time he had made it the conservator of the public good, beyond and above individual or local interest, untouchable by any partisan consideration. But he had also, by his behavior, previously as a general, and later as president, set a standard of responsible judgment that was all but unanimously recognized. This was a standard all his successors would have to meet if they were to have freedom of action adequate for their responsibilities.

When Washington took later decisions without consulting the Congress, and without the least thought of Supreme Court opinion, the effect was to establish himself as the unassailable representative of the national interest. The legislators were reduced to the objectors they would usually be thereafter. The Genêt affair and the expedition to defeat the Whiskey Rebellion were expressions of Washington's authority, but is is worth noting that he was extremely cautious about both. He sought advice in writing from his associates, making quite certain of both necessity and the knowledge of what he could count on. When he finally acted, all possible repercussions were discounted in advance and it was certain that objectors would have little or no effect.

Not all of Washington's successors were able to meet the standards he had set; not all would even understand his method; but all would be measured by him, and all would succeed or fail as they followed his patterning. Even at the time, and despite his prestige as military commander and statesman, his success annoyed some of his contemporaries, and the most unrestrained in saying so were legislators. Even though they were marked as carpers and were few, he found them hard to ignore, and one of his compromises was to allow them, without objection, to establish by law his administrative departments; but on the whole his disdain of partisanship was consistent; and his view that his own power reached to whatever he must do for national security was not successfully challenged. This was because no one could conceive that he acted against the public interest. His judgment was trusted.

Some successors, Jefferson for instance, who had been so hostile to Washington's regal style that he had resigned from the cabinet, soon discovered when he assumed the presidential office that what was expected by a people who had known greatness was a continuation of that greatness, even if with more conformity to a spreading democratic theory—a different style. He also discovered that presidents had responsibilities beyond the minimal ones he had theretofore so arbitrarily defined. His later appropriation of power in making the Louisiana Purchase remained the furthest extension of the Doctrine of Necessity until Lincoln acted to save the Union, and his dispatch of an expedition to Tripoli was a forecast of other expeditions by other presidents—those of the Kennedy/Nixon succession not excluded. For Jefferson's day it was almost as massive an undertaking.

It must be said that Jefferson was not the only ambitious politician who, having denounced such assumptions of power, found himself making equal or greater ones when he became president. Lincoln, for instance, the least hesitant of all when faced with rebellion, had, as a congressman, denounced Polk's provocation of Mexico as an excessive presidential commitment to a dangerous course.

A similar example was furnished by Jackson, who after losing to Adams in 1824 castigated his victorious opponent for various unseemly presidential initiatives; but when he in turn defeated Adams in 1828, he was quite prepared to use unauthorized force when he considered it to be necessary. Knowing that he had generous popular support, he did not hesitate to choose a novel and dramatic way to assert his powers. This fact is worth attention. His behavior in office had been whimsical, willful, dictatorial, and inconsistent; and among his careless decisions had been ones that had given southern politicians cause to think he would be sympathetic to the nullification they were preparing. When the issue was made and he realized what he had allowed to be concluded about his permissiveness, he had to reverse himself or condone secession. Abruptly and with shocking effect, on the occasion of a formal dinner, he arose to offer a toast. Glaring at the guest of honor and raising his glass, he said loudly and distinctly: "Our Federal Union; it must be preserved."

The principal threatener of that union happened to be John C. Calhoun, his own vice-president and expectant successor, and the gathering had been intended to further Calhoun's ambition. One spectator said of Jackson's words that "a proclamation of martial law in South Carolina and an order to arrest Calhoun where he sat could not have come with more blinding, staggering force."[6]

Until then Jackson had not troubled to consider how easily he could be associated with nullification. For instance, when white settlers had wanted lands owned by the Indians in western Georgia, Jackson, the old Indian fighter, had simply refused to recognize the Cherokee claim. Although it was fixed in a treaty and had been validated by the Supreme Court, Jackson had ignored repeated violations by the Georgians and defiant talk by the governor. In effect, he had refused to enforce the Court's decree.

When the South Carolinians inferred from this that nullification would be permissible whenever a state found itself in disagreement with the federal government, Jackson suddenly understood what his refusal meant. Soon after, he issued a proclamation to the effect that any further moves toward nullification would be suppressed. Actually, force was deployed and would have been used if the South Carolinians had not backed down.

This presidential sternness was so effective that it was twenty years before the issue came up again. This time Buchanan was president—a "northern man with southern views." He was so permissive that his detractors called him a "doughface." He simply let things go until Lincoln, succeeding him, did have to use the force Jackson had threatened, and for the very same reason in the very same place. He caused Fort Sumter to be defended on his own responsibility, as Jackson had been prepared to do. He explained afterward, about this and his other breaches of the separation principle, that he had been compelled to choose between disobeying one clause of the Constitution and seeing all the rest of them disobeyed.

He thus gave the recurring presidential dilemma its clearest statement. Should he disregard his oath to defend the Constitution in one way or in another? He had chosen the lesser disobedience. He intended to preserve the integrity of the Union. He would hesitate at nothing for this purpose. Emergency was his criterion, and his was the responsibility for judging its reality.

The Doctrine of Necessity relied on by these presidents has been accompanied by a kind of enabling twin—a corollary Rule of Self-restraint. Jackson, for instance, bold and vigorous as he seemed, had been cautious

6. The commentator was Isaac Hill, quoted in Marquis James, *Andrew Jackson* (New York: Bobbs-Merrill, 1937), p. 234.

in actually making his moves. He threatened the Carolinians with force, it is true, but he also offered them relief from the grievance. This happened to center in a tariff law bearing hard on cotton and tobacco and favoring New England industries. It was known in the South as the Tariff of Abominations. Furthermore, he knew he could count on support from public opinion. His electoral victory in 1832 had been overwhelming, and the inaugural rejoicings were outpourings of pent-up emotion. The frontiersmen had ousted the elite.

The South Carolina legislature was presently constrained to rescind the aggressive resolutions they had passed when the president had seemed so compliant, but Jackson's restraint had saved this from seeming to be a humiliation. Other incidents in his administration also illustrate his finesse in following presidential threats with conciliation. This latter habit is sometimes overlooked, perhaps in Jackson's case because he was sly about it. He seemed to be all violence and unreason—actually, he arranged compromises his opponents could accept—but he would not allow the Congress or the Supreme Court to interfere when he acted to protect what he regarded as the national interest.

Lincoln also, despite his boldness in extremity, tried very hard to conciliate the secessionists and bring them to accept compromise. Later presidents, before resorting to extreme measures, have tried restraint with more or less understanding that their authority could be consolidated and used only if their behavior had begun in reason and had elevated to force only when all else had failed.

Later presidents, it must be said, have not had uniform success when they have not conformed to the *rule* their predecessors understood so well. It was the cause of Truman's failure, and of Johnson's as well. Neither made sure of popular support; neither seemed willing to apply the art of conciliation. Both began with strong backing, but prolongation and escalation gave time for costs to multiply and for second thoughts to generate which permitted their natural enemies to undermine their positions. What they continued to believe they must do was not accepted by a large part of the electorate as necessary to the national security, or even to the pursuit of its interests. These were fatal weaknesses.

Presidents well anchored in popular regard have found restraint essential to softening opposition. It has tended to disarm enemies, give them face-saving alternatives, and preserve the dignity so precious to the presidency. Truman's Korean intervention was failing as his term came to an end; Johnson's tragedy was that he seized a power he did not know how to hold. Johnson gave up because his was a losing cause. Nixon, say what you will of his general intentions, knew how to find and hold at least sufficient support to allow him the freedom he needed.

Baffling Areas of Constitutional Silence

It is impossible to know whether the framers, who allowed silences to stretch across such immense areas of the Constitution, were actually aware of what they were doing or whether they realized afterward what they had done. John Jay, the first chief justice, spoke of the allocations of duty as though they were sufficiently defined:

The Constitution . . . has instituted . . . three Departments, and much pains have been taken so to form and define them as that they may operate as checks, one upon the other; it being universally agreed to be of the last importance to a free people, that they who are vested with executive, legislative and judicial powers should rest satisfied with their respective positions, and neither encroach on the provinces of each other, nor suffer themselves to intermeddle with the rights reserved by the Constitution to the people. . . .[7]

Madison, arguing for ratification in *The Federalist Papers* (No. 47), was not so clear; but he did defend the system of checks. He quoted Montesquieu to the effect that there could be no liberty where the executive and legislative powers were united "in the same person or body of magistrates," or "if the power of judging be not separated from the executive and legislative powers." But, he commented, Montesquieu "did not mean that these departments ought to have no partial agency in, or no control over, the acts of each other."

Each having "partial agency" in the others was, of course, so ambiguous as to become avoidance. To say so much was to avoid defining the powers of each, and gave no help in determining how far each could go if circumstances changed—and especially if emergency should arise. The first to test the indefinite principle might be said to have been the Congress when it passed the Judiciary Act in 1789 and then invaded the executive by insisting on the prerogative of establishing the first departments. The Court, however, was not far behind. Marshall's assertion of judicial supremacy came in *Marbury* v. *Madison* (1803); but then the president—Jefferson— made his advance. He had only the slightest of authorizations to make the Louisiana Purchase. He was thus committing funds without specific congressional consent. Actually, before the Constitution had been in effect for a generation all three branches had violated this organizing principle of its government.

It must be reiterated, since that is in question here, that presidents have not invariably been successful in seizures of power. Conspicuous instances have already been cited. If they tend to prove the rule rather than

7. *Correspondence and Public Papers of Jay,* ed. by H. P. Johnston, III (New York: Putnam's, 1891), p. 389. This reliance on self-restraint will be developed further.

to discredit it, they nevertheless offer lessons. One not precisely in point, but still an attempt to enlarge the presidential power, was Roosevelt's proposal for "reforming" the Supreme Court, all too obviously to force its acceptance of his domestic policies. In demanding that it be reorganized he violated the Rule of Self-restraint; and the popular support he had evidently counted on proved to be almost nonexistent. Among the reasons he gave was the complaint that the old men making up the Court were out of touch with the contemporary world and that younger men were needed. Since both Brandeis and Cardozo were the most noted of judicial liberals, and both were elderly, this was regarded as so sophistical as to insult the intelligence.

Roosevelt's was a curious mistake for so experienced a politician to make, but perhaps not so curious when it is recalled that only a few months before he had had a reelection majority unique in presidential contests. He obviously had expected that anything he asked would be given on penalty of political punishment by those partisans who owed their successes to him. He ought to have anticipated that congressmen, who regarded him as being in the last years of his incumbency and were always alert to oppose presidential initiatives, would balk. He ought also to have been aware that the very size of his unprecedented victory would be an added annoyance among many legislators. He was careless; he neither made sure of his backing nor resorted to the conciliation he could so easily have used. He was badly defeated.

There are other examples of such carelessness or faulty estimation of circumstances. The most conspicuous have already been mentioned: Truman's seizure of the steel plants in 1952 and Johnson's escalation of an already unpopular involvement in Vietnam. These miscalculations were fatal for the presidents who made them. If the precedent they furnished had continued to prevail it might well have proved to be disastrous for the nation as well.

It is easier to explain the Truman failure than that of either Roosevelt or Johnson. President Truman was not experienced, nor did he have secure popular support. When what he regarded as an immediate crisis had to be overcome, he did what he understood his predecessors to have done; but his estimate of the necessity was not one that seemed to justify seizure of the steel properties; and, to make matters worse, he had had no warning that the justices might have ambitions of their own. There did, however, happen to be a majority who regarded themselves as quite capable of correcting the other branches. All might be supposed to be independent, but this the justices could define—each for himself. Only the Court's own position was thus invulnerable. It could say that president or Congress had exceeded their powers; but who could say that the Court itself had gone too far? Conceivably, even if the Congress should use its authority to limit the Court's jurisdiction, it might be told that in the circumstances it could not do so. This, in effect, would be what Justice Warren would say at a later time in the Powell case.

The justices had not before shouted into the particular silence they now shattered. True, Chief Justice Vinson was joined in a vigorous dissent by two of his associates, but even he affirmed the Court's power to decide; he simply thought its decision mistaken. There was very nearly unanimous approval of the majority opinion among other legal scholars. And it was not unusual to hear variations on the earnestly expressed gratitude of libertarians that presumptuous presidents could be rebuked.

The practical consequences of this seizure were fateful beyond measure. Consider the situation of the Court as the arbiter of emergency: it must have a case to decide, one which must have been submitted by adversary procedures; in all probability, the time consumed would allow crises to do what damage they were capable of; and the Court's opinion might well issue in the debris of some disaster. It is an untenable position.

Accepting the certainty that no government can survive without some final resort in extremity and that the American government will not allow itself to be destroyed by simple inaction, it must be concluded in spite of the Court that there will be an assumption of power and that it must be by the president.

This requires reiteration of the observation that what has happened or has been said in this realm of silence simply cannot ever be taken as final; this is as true of Court decrees as it is of an unenforceable law or of presidential responses to emergency. The branches are formally coordinate, and successful forays by any branch are interesting and informative—each adding to a body of experience likely to be claimed as a precedent. They have been referred to voluminously, but they have never determined subsequent decisions to act or not to act in emergency; and it is certain that they never can. When action is in some way vital to the life of the Union, that agency of government able to act will act and will be approved. Indeed, if a president did not respond he would be marked in history as recreant to his trust. Pierce and Buchanan, who had concourse with secessionists, are, in any judgment of presidents, the weakest; and it is because they did not do as Jackson had done and as Lincoln felt he must do. They failed to preserve the Union from its most serious challenge when it could have been done short of war.

It is not argued that the deployment abroad of armed forces in pursuit of policies not sustained by reliable majorities are in the same category of necessity as the defection of the secessionists. The threat may well be remote even if real, but when does a threat become imminent peril? The Constitution gives no help, and clearly the Court must not be allowed to say.

It is one of the most baffling of all the areas of silence. What can be said about it is only that as things are it cannot be wholly occupied by any branch; that only amendment can make assignments more explicit, but that meanwhile the Doctrine of Necessity will continue to be relied upon; that presidents will act as their judgment tells them they must; and that they will succeed or fail according to their abilities and the circumstances of the time, and according to the uses they make of the Rule of Self-restraint. So far the nation has had extraordinary luck.

Balancing the Powers

Several times during the long hot summer of 1787 in Philadelphia the gentlemen meeting there reverted to discussions of the executive. It was realized that he (or "they"—the singular was not immediately decided on) must have at least the minimum power to perform the "executive" duties; but these were not at all sharply visualized, and the sentiment for preventing them from becoming extensive or arbitrary was strong enough to overcome the arguments of those few who would have preferred an approximation of the powers held until recently by British royalty. Because there was no possibility of agreement on specifics the whole matter was left to experience—but without really saying so. Beyond the statement that the president would be commander in chief, the allocations were cloudy; and even the commandership was not so clear as it seemed at first. Did he command forces only when they were in the field? If so, who sent them there? Obviously the provision that the Congress must "declare" war did not cover that. An invasion could occur without any declaration; so, in fact, could an insurrection. Was it reasonable to have an army without a head until it had been deployed for combat?

Such arguments broke out over other clauses. What did "advice and consent" mean? And there was some doubt that the treasury was finally meant, after discussion, to be a presidential department. There was strong argument that it should be responsible to the Congress, since only that body could authorize expenditures. Because these instructions—and many others—were hazy, no one could have described the criteria for the behavior of a president after it had been decided that there should be one. Even about his length of service there was no agreement. His terms were to be four years, but no limit was set on their number. In the end this too was inconclusive, and the electorates of the future were left free to decide. Presumably an undue reach for power would result in defeat, and its justified use would be ratified by reelection; but this is not apparent from the discussions. This was the sort of avoidance that in the future would cause so much controversy.

The early presidents, Washington, Jefferson, and their successors, in such indeterminate matters adopted their own customs. As to terms, Washington set the limit at two; and for 150 years there was no serious suggestion that an amendment should make the limitation constitutional. Not until the second Roosevelt asked for and got a third term was the tradition actually disregarded, although it may be recalled that Grant had indicated a willingness to go on after his second term. Protracted incumbency by Roosevelt so annoyed partisan detractors that as soon as Republicans acquired enough support they carried through a limiting amendment—the Twenty-second.

Even considering the reaction to Roosevelt, aggravated by weariness from the responsibilities left by the war, the adoption of this amendment was remarkable. Either massive agreement or general indifference, together with professional maneuvering, had always been necessary to overcome the formidable obstacles to amendment. In this instance it was Roosevelt's own overconfidence and peevishness while his long-frustrated political enemies were working energetically among their professional colleagues. In the absence of other changes, however, the defeat must be counted a grave mistake. Second-term presidents, who may not again be candidates, are four-year lame ducks. As this implies, their claim to leadership vanishes; their party status is lowered; and, especially, they cannot be—what has become vital to accommodative changes in society—powerful initiators of legislation. The Congress will not listen when they propose. The Twenty-second Amendment was an additional strengthening for the obstructive propensities of the legislators. Since its ratification, forward movement in a second term has been unknown, and governmental responses to newly appearing problems have been slowed.

If this alteration in comparative powers is to stand, it is imperative that other changes be made. The problem is this: if the president is no longer to exercise legislative leadership there will be none, or at best it will be weak. The nation cannot afford to have the president ignored. Since he cannot again ask for votes, his party's machinery will not be available to him—its leaders will be searching for their next candidate—and he will no longer be able to marshal public opinion for proposals he will not be able to carry through. The important members of both houses—party leaders and committee chairmen—are devoted, anyway, to slowing down or preventing legislation, not to passing it. For their own fortunes they have no need to press forward, since they come from safe districts and have their positions because of seniority, not because of ability. By any assessment the amendment was a mistake. It cannot very well be reasonably explained how the number of professional politicians—two-thirds of both houses, and three-quarters of the states' legislatures—could have attacked the system with such savagery, leaving it crippled and leaderless. Unless some other source of initiative can be found—and it can be found only by amendment; it will not come from the legislature—creeping obsolescence will be accelerated.

It is surely remarkable that in no other important respect has Article II of the Constitution been amended; particularly, that there has been no recognition of inevitably recurring emergencies. If it was realized by the framers that powers must in certain conditions be extended, the realization did not make its way into the document. Arguments had to do with ordinary necessities, not extraordinary ones.

Looking back, it can be seen how completely the office was shaped by its incumbents. Washington established a regal presence; Jefferson doubled the nation's territory by unauthorized purchase; Jackson assembled a force to preserve the Union; Lincoln "violated one clause of the Constitution to preserve the rest"; Wilson committed the country to making the world safe for democracy; and Franklin D. Roosevelt invented the "state of emergency" to provide freedom of action—he even elaborated on this and first asked for a "limited emergency." Authorization for any of this cannot be found in the Constitution. So perhaps it is not strange that the extraordinary threatening conditions should not have been provided for. But since there have been many minor and several major ones since, it is remarkable that there has been no move to constitutionalize the inevitable arrangements to meet them, to define their character, or to differentiate the requirements for various circumstances.

If the Constitution, as it was left in 1787, did not authorize presidents to meet emergencies, it also did not forbid them to do so. Of this omission, whether deliberate or not, all the strong presidents have taken advantage. As we have seen, not all even of these have correctly calculated the reverses they might later meet or the resources they might count on for keeping the powers they may have assumed. Some have succeeded in avoidance; some have grasped the nettle and have done what they must; some are now rated as weaklings; others became and remain national heroes.

Concerning this, Theodore Roosevelt made some often-quoted comments about his powers. As he read the Constitution, he said, the president was supposed to be as strong in his behavior as the circumstances called for. This was decried by his successor, Taft, who felt himself limited to clearly prescribed duties. These antithetical views still stand unresolved by the legitimization of either. Yet Wilson had said the same thing, but in words other than those Roosevelt had used; and later presidents have accepted the activist position. So, it seems, has the public, judging from the comparative position in their regard of, say, Theodore Roosevelt and Taft, or a later Roosevelt and Hoover. Even later presidents, however, seemed to prove the need for constitutional rule. Their behavior demanded it.

It may be recalled that Washington was cautioned by John Jay, the first chief justice, about being too weak and conciliatory. And there have been many presidents—Jackson and Truman among them—who have be-gun by saying that they intended to defer to the other branches only to discover how fatal this could be. They usually have ended up more belli-gerent than others who at the start had been more wary of potential opposi-tion. These recovered rapidly and thoroughly from their early illusions, but others like Buchanan and Grant never grasped the responsibilities of leadership. Theirs were comparatively uneventful administrations, but both left legacies of neglect which ultimately led to destructive events.

It has been all too easy for Americans generally to accept the deceptively simple theory that theoretical separation involves recognizable allocations: the Congress to make laws, the president to execute them, and the Court to judge their concordance with the Constitution. This derives from an extra-polation preferred by legislators who have always regarded the House of Representatives as the sole repository of genuine democracy. Presidents, over and over, have reminded them—sometimes sharply as Jackson did—that if they meant to talk of "representativeness," it was the president whose warrant came from *all* the people; no legislator represented more than a district or, at most, a state.

What was said in *The Federalist Papers* about the distribution of powers was true; none was given to one branch alone. Each was to share the responsibilities of the others. To what extent each branch must share respon-sibility and how much each must keep to itself was only hazily defined. Ambiguity would continue to be the most subtle but most pervasive charac-teristic of the essentially unchanged document. The intention was that the Congress was to make laws, but that the president was to recommend such of them as seemed necessary to him. He might also veto them; but even so, he did not have the last word, for the Congress might still prevail by mus-tering two-thirds majorities. In practice this from the first has meant that most legislation originated with the president and was approved (or not approved) only by the Congress.

Moreover, the Constitution said that the president was to see that the laws, once made, were faithfully executed. How could he do this unless the Congress voted him the funds to do it with? In addition, the Senate must confirm the appointment of his officials. Also, the Senate was to furnish "advice and consent," a phrase never fully explored, but taken by senators, when they are in favorable bargaining positions, to mean that their advice amounts to command; and actually, for many appointments, the president does have only ministerial status, something completely true for minor judicial and many other federal positions. Furthermore, senatorial com-mitteemen often demand to be "equal partners" (in J. W. Fulbright's phrase) in the making of policy, this last being an extrapolation from the word "advice."

Concerning all these arrangements it must be insisted that ambiguities remain unmodified, since none has been clarified by amendment. They are recognized only as long as they can be defended. The Congress, for instance, has never been content to confine itself to legislation; nearly all presidents have had to fend off administrative interferences. So persistent has this been that one authority—Charles Warren—once gave a lecture called "Presidential Declarations of Independence." He began by saying that one neglected phase of constitutional development ought to have more attention: this was the sturdy struggle of presidents, throughout our national life, against congressional encroachments.[8] He marshaled dozens of illustrative incidents, beginning with Washington's refusal to disclose his instructions concerning the Jay Treaty in 1796, and running on to the rather surprising reply of the usually compliant Coolidge to a Senate resolution demanding the dismissal of his secretary of the navy: that "the dismissal of an officer of the government is exclusively an executive function." There followed only silence; there was no evidence of contrition. The congressional attitude seems to be that there is no harm in trying; sometimes, if the president is caught off balance, the attempt succeeds.

It was Professor Warren's conclusion that congressional belligerence was encouraged by a general historic assumption that the Congress is somehow peculiarly and especially related to popular sovereignty—"a belief that congressmen themselves are fond of inculcating." But, he argued, the fact is otherwise. Congressmen are devoted to local and special interests; any attention to national problems is coincidental and results only from presidential insistence. It is he who is the tribune of the people.

A Legacy of Ambiguity

That the branches should have reciprocal relations was a prevalent idea easily traced to such theorists as Montesquieu and generally accepted by the literate gentlemen who dominated the Convention—or, at least, the influential lawyers among them. In practice, however, it proved not to be a workable guide for the behavior of officials. Like so much else in the Constitution it allowed members of each branch an interpretation, not necessarily acceptable to the others. The ambiguity invited controversy and sometimes conflict. When any one branch undertook duties it felt intended for it, the assumption was frequently challenged by one or both of the others. This became acute when the interpretation was insisted on. If it became coercive it was fiercely resented. It might or might not really threaten the others and disarrange the whole, but it so often did this that each branch became sensitized and defensive. Early in the history of the Constitution a condition of constant irritation resulted which has never been cured either by amendment or by restraint.

8. *The Bacon Lectures* (Boston University Press, 1939).

The Congress enlarged its limits easily. Much more often than the presidency it claimed positions it could not sustain, and it seemed always to be inserting capricious directives into legislation bearing on administrative behavior. Very often these were submitted by the president because of the numerous retaliatory devices used without scruple to maintain the general legislative position. The Congress was convinced that it was meant to be supreme. This went back to the Continental Congress, and although it had been largely responsible for the futility of that body, the framers could not bring themselves to reduce stringently the legislative directives. After all, Englishmen were then just emerging from centuries of struggle with absolutism, and legislatures had been the principal subduers of royal dictators.

It was not so strange, in this tradition, that the Congress should assume the extraconstitutional power of creating the executive establishment and the court system, since neither could operate without appropriations. This was an advantage neither could match. Anticipating future reprisals when funds were needed, administrators submitted to unreasonable demands with only formal protest. In this way the Congress reached a position of superiority.

In the struggle to occupy the no man's land of the Constitution, the claim of legislators that they embodied the democratic virtues was very often a cover for obstructiveness; but relying as it did on a centuries-old suspicion of executive power, it was hard to discredit in the popular regard. Nevertheless a clever president—Jefferson—discovered a way to outmaneuver objectors; he created a party, many of whose members were legislators, and through it developed just such a domination as was spoken of by Madison. By methods doubtful perhaps in their ethics, he imposed a discipline that brought both branches under his domination. For him, and for his successors Madison and Monroe, the method succeeded. It depended, however, on their numerical superiority over the contending Federalists, and held only because the older group was in a slow decline. When party rivalry became a more even contest and party lines were less compulsive, the branches could not be held to one loyalty. This appeared early when the Court remained Federalist even in Jeffersonian times; it affected the Congress as soon as the presidency fell to another party. It remained a condition nothing was ever done to correct and, as we have seen, was often cited as a virtue.

There have been times since Jefferson's when the executive and legislative branches seemed to have adjourned their traditional hostility and acted in concert; however, the conditions for these have occurred only rarely and, merged in the average, have been exceptions rather than the rule. When a party has won an election after being in the minority, its president usually has a "honeymoon." While this period lasts and the president is high in popular favor, he can demand that the Congress act promptly on the legislation he has promised in his campaign. He finds, however, that in a matter of months this concordance disappears, legislation is delayed in committees, and the opposition of those whose interests may be injured becomes effective again. This has been true, since the Civil War, even when one party controls both the executive and the legislative.

Other than this, presidents get their way without obstruction and delay only when a crisis of some sort occurs. At such times congressmen are submissive. They pass consenting acts without debate, they resolve that emergencies exist and allow the president to take responsibility, then they look the other way while the president does what is necessary. It will be he and not they who will be blamed for failure or for public disenchantment. If the measures taken succeed, the congressmen have been patriots supporting the national leader; if there is failure, they can join in the chorus of detraction, disclaiming any part in the proceedings.

Jefferson was only the third president, but he was one of the most sophisticated. Also he was a theoretical democrat, but one who understood when democracy had to be managed. He knew how to get his way in spite of the constitutional provision for congressional check. For him, and for others in his position, there were advantages available to offset those possessed by the legislature. Of these the most important was that he was but one and the congressmen were many; then too, they represented localities only, and he the entire nation. They were therefore always divided and vulnerable, and he could use his executive apparatus without consulting anyone. He won in interbranch struggles because he knew how to hold congressmen under the obligation he had created even before his election. They had the illusion of having been consulted because they were spoken to. His apparatus for this purpose amounted to deputies in the legislature who conveyed his wishes to the faithful.

Some later presidents used—or tried to use—the same method, and most learned to trade executive favors for congressional support; very seldom, however, has there been so tight a party organization. When occasionally it exists, presidents are able to follow Jefferson in shaping policy to their own views. Such compliance, however, has been infrequent and always ephemeral. Nearly always the good relations break down.

Nonetheless, some shrewd observers have spoken of more recent presidents as chief legislators. Professor McBain[9] and Mr. Louis Brownlow[10] concluded, indeed, that he had become more important in this role than as the chief executive mentioned in the Constitution. It should be noted, how-

9. Howard Lee McBain, *The Living Constitution* (New York: The Macmillan Company, 1937).

10. Louis Brownlow, *The President and the Presidency* (Chicago: Public Administration Service, 1949).

ever, that since this role is not explicit, and has never been recognized by amendment, reliance on it has been responsible for the unhappy frustration of most presidents in the twentieth century—and of some even before.

If it were successful it would be a development the framers had hoped they had made impossible. When in full operation it has obviously had a devastating effect on the separation principle, so much so that it seemed sometimes to have disappeared. Such a condition seldom lasts, however, and when it fails and hostility recurs, governmental processes come almost to a halt.

In this connection it will be seen what effect the Twenty-second Amendment had. It reinforced the separation and made coordination of the branches more unlikely. It did this by emasculating the president as chief legislator, at least for the whole of his second term, and returned obstructionism to its old effectiveness. It can almost be said, looking at the patent lack of wisdom in this amendment, standing alone, that attempts to amend the Constitution in a way to make separation more definitive are certain to do serious harm. Such partisan and partial patching as is represented by the two-term limitation is quite likely to result in the encouragement of delay or even paralysis.

Still, encroachments on the unoccupied no man's land, without modification of the Constitution, have often been as bad. It can be seen, in this context, how fatal it would be to accept the Court's claim to the definition of *necessity*; or, to cite another instance, the permanent existence of a comptrollership responsible to the Congress. Loud though these assertions may be, however, and important though the extraconstitutional changes may seem, they have not become part of the structure. After all, they lack the essential legitimation of basic law. Even what the Court says must be accepted as law, may, if it proves unwise, be allowed to languish.

It may be said with confidence that no such limitations will prevent presidents from doing what they consider to be required in emergency; it may even be said that none will cause them to hesitate. The Twenty-second Amendment, becoming part of the basic law, had a more subtle effect. It made the president much weaker for the second four years of his presidency. It has already been seen how his support from the public fades as he approaches the end of his incumbency. He would have far more difficulty in assuming and keeping emergency powers. The situation, if a crisis should arise, has become one likely to cause acute internal dissension.

It is unthinkable that the emergency power should ever pass to the Congress. The effrontery of one congressional initiative—the Tenure of Office Act—called out President Andrew Johnson's indignant rebuke in a veto message (March 2, 1869). It was not only a rebuke but also a half-conscious recognition of both the Doctrine of Necessity and the Rule of

Restraint. His words were those of one who had good reason to know all about congressional aggression, but since he was not a philosopher he did not recognize the source of his own weakness:

> It cannot be doubted that the triumphant success of the Constitution is due to the wonderful wisdom with which the functions of government were distributed between the three principal departments and to the fidelity with which each has confined itself or been confined by the general voice of the nation within its peculiar and proper sphere. Whilst a just, proper, and watchful jealousy of Executive power constantly prevails, as it ought ever to prevail, yet it is equally true that an efficient Executive, capable . . . of executing the laws, and within the sphere of Executive action, of preserving, protecting, and defending the Constitution of the United States, is an indispensable security for tranquility at home and peace, honor, and safety abroad.

This was an eloquent enough statement, but it was not a realistic assessment. Johnson was alarmed at the dissolution of the classic barriers, a process that would seem even more alarming to later literalists; these often have a version of the Constitution in their minds not to be found either in the document or in the practice of the government it founded.

In spite of this message, Johnson's veto was rejected. Later, in a cooler time, the act was quietly repealed. The Congress was forced to recognize its own incapacity, even if not in words. In fact the flow of speeches by legislators denouncing executive dictatorship would go on and on, and there would be indignant presidential rejections of congressional incursions on the executive domain. The contest, of course, could never be won by either because there was no designated end. There could only be an advantage gained, then lost; or one lost and later regained. Everything remained ambiguous.

Still no one suggested that demarcations and assignments ought at least to be made more clear. And no one seemed to realize what damage had been done by the one amendment in all American history that had made doubtful the power of presidents to act in emergency.

Tilting the Balance

All of this had a special significance when presidential assumptions of power began to overweigh the balance and to be prolonged beyond easy tolerance. Looking back, one can see the enlargement to have been developing as technology began to make central command possible. Communications became instantaneous, genocidal weapons loomed in the background of every negotiation, and executive extension was called for by the immediate and exigent nature of decisions.

It was not much more than an adventure when Wilson dispatched marines to Vera Cruz, and there was not much excitement when dictators in the small republics around the Caribbean were disciplined. These actions violated the principle of self-determination, but they were pictured as giving governments back to their people. Some purists worried about the Theodore Roosevelt corollaries to the Monroe Doctrine. These assumed that the United States had a duty to make neighboring nations behave in civilized fashion—to honor their treaties, for instance. The long occupation of Haiti seemed extreme, but this was an exception. Generally, no extraordinary expenditures were required and the occupations were soon over. Besides, before the time of radio and television the electorate was not widely enough aware of what was being done to develop very solid opinions.

It was when interventions were not for the purpose of restoring order but in pursuit of global strategy that the emergency powers strained their customary bounds and began to be widely criticized, and the strain was increased when television correspondents accompanied invasion forces with daily pictures and comments. Reporters depended mostly on bad news to hold the interest of their constituents and were naturally resentful of any limitation by the military. Expeditions of such massive size as those to Korea and Vietnam could not be sustained as mere exercises for temporary effect. They were given an arbitrary cast, they went on too long, and they were too distant for the threat to be credible. Their reasonableness was challenged continuously and effectively by large groups of newsmen who were knowledgeable in getting attention and by dissidents who seemed to have nothing else to do.

It was argued by some doubters, when Korea got under way, and again when South Vietnam was massively supported, that such enterprises should be undertaken only after declarations of war—avoided by presidents because such action would require other nations to make choices. A nation formally at war cannot allow others to supply the enemy; if they do they are in effect belligerents. When Vietnam came in question this became an even more important consideration. The Russians went on supplying their Communist friends, at the same time maintaining their representation in Washington. The two nations had an important common cause in keeping nuclear weapons away from lesser powers, and it was important that explorations looking to a treaty should go on. Belligerence became something determined by policy. A declaration of war would have made this impossible.

Another consideration was naval strategy. It was judged by successive presidents, from Truman on, that although air power was becoming vital, control of the seas was still necessary. If Indonesia, Malaysia, and Thailand should become Communist, the growing Russian navy would control the narrow Asian passages and would shut off access to the Indian Ocean. The loss of Vietnam and Thailand would close the Strait of Malacca and bring all neighboring waters under unfriendly control. A declaration of war would force choices on these nations they had no desire to make. It would also require the American navy to challenge the Russians who were supplying the North Vietnamese through the port of Haiphong, and it would involve confronting the Chinese in their own waters. It was a peculiar in-between time. Naval supremacy might be giving way to new weighings of comparative power in the air, but the resistance to a final conclusion was formidable.

Altogether there was ample reason for avoiding a classic declaration, but this left presidents with all the responsibility. Those who argued later that successive ones had exceeded their allowable powers ignored the changes in international relations they were urged to consider. What critics relied on during the later stages of escalation was revulsion at home among peace groups whose numbers became formidable. The disaffection spread and deepened as it was admitted that a military victory was impossible. The strategy of containment had been generally approved. The nation had for a generation been developing a deep fear of Communist subversion, and anything to check the spread of first Russian, then Chinese, expansion was acceptable. The dichotomy between the "free world" and the "Communist dictatorships" was accepted in ordinary communication, but the continued involvement gave time for opposition to grow. The draft of men to serve so far away and in a conflict intended only as a holding action was a difficult policy to accept, especially among those likely to be drafted.

Opposition came first from the alienated liberals who sought to rely on their own interpretation of the Constitution. They denounced the adventure as illegitimate and suggested intervention by the Court. What was demanded was that customary judicial discretion should be abandoned and the president told that he must not do what he was doing. Anyway, it was argued, the judiciary had extended its reach in recent years across the barriers of separation, and there was no longer any recognized limit. The Court had defined not only the powers of the other branches but incidentally its own. It might do so in this instance.

It was in the course of this argument about the president's assumption of power that the Court gradually began to recognize a situation that might well be an opportunity for itself. Having several times decided that the other branches could not do things they had done, and having had its opinions generally upheld, could the Court not make a decision now that would end all question concerning its supremacy?

Until 1952, there had been only after-the-fact admonishments as in *Ex parte Merryman* (1861), *Ex parte Milligan* (1866), and *Ex parte Endo* (1944). But when Truman returned the steel mills to their owners, thus giving way to the Court, the Doctrine of Necessity, used by so many presidents, became a more doubtful reliance. Presidents, it appeared, could never know, until the justices told them, that a compelling necessity had arisen—or what they could do if it had.

That the Court had gone too far might, of course, be shown when the next emergency arose. Chief Justice Vinson's twenty-five occasions when presidents could not have waited without jeopardizing the national security for a case to make its way through labyrinthine procedures to the Supreme Court had been convincing; the opinions of the other justices had been loose and wandering. The circumstances, however, had favored the judicial boldness Vinson deplored. In a showdown the president had allowed himself to be caught with a weak case and without the support of effective allies. The Court, presented with a long-sought opportunity, had taken full advantage of it. It was Truman's weakness, however, that did the real damage. When the next emergency came the Court would have less hesitation in rebuking the president.

Since there was no definition covering spread or length and no one to share the presidential decision, we became dependent on credibility; and credibility is a difficult matter for estimation. The nation's defenses and even its deployment of strength depended on uncertain support, never quite definable, and subject to veto if trust in the president declined. That was where use of the Doctrine of Necessity had positioned the country after Korea and after the Court's decree.

Intervention Makes Apprehension

During the later stages of the Johnson escalation in Southeast Asia certain of the justices showed signs of lying in wait. It was now apparent that a succession of presidents had too long and too confidently pushed a traditional doctrine beyond any formerly understood limit. If the Court entertained a cause and found one of the presidents to have exceeded his powers, public opinion might well desert the president. The conflict in Vietnam was even more unpopular than the still-lingering one in Korea. Moreover, it was now widely felt that the whole Asian involvement had been a mistake. It was hard for Americans to accept a virtual war undertaken with no intention of winning, only of checking the expansion of an undeclared enemy into faraway nations whose friendship was not easily seen as vital to American security. Even the so-called hawks found it difficult to argue convincingly for continuation, much less the increased forces urged by some Johnson advisers.

There was something hypocritical about the justification for so enormous an effort. To the citizen who saw his sons drafted and his taxes increased, it was obvious that there was a war going on. A half-million fighting men on foreign soil—and this not a war? It had not seemed so unreasonable at first. Communists were overrunning a resisting people; self-determination was being violated. It was permissible to send advisers and supplies; but when collapse was imminent and combat troops were sent, it was war; and wars are to be won, not just used to stabilize a confused political situation. The resisters—the doves—began to gain the initiative. The Court would have substantial support for finding that the presidents, acting without the "declaration" of the Constitution, had usurped the prerogative of the Congress. Johnson's Tonkin Gulf Resolution was already pictured as a contrivance; the Court might easily find it to have been a subterfuge.

Was the Vietnam involvement different from Jefferson's expedition to Tripoli, from Lincoln's attack on Sumter, from Theodore Roosevelt's deployment of ships at Panama, from several occupations of Haiti and the Central American countries, from Wilson's disciplining of Mexico, from Roosevelt's occupation of Iceland, from Eisenhower's landings in Lebanon, and from Johnson's in Santo Domingo?

The public could see one difference, at least: those other expeditions had been short and successful; this was prolonged, was hideously costly, and, worst of all, had no clear definition. Of course Pershing had not caught Pancho Villa, but generally speaking the military undertakings justified by the Doctrine of Necessity had been sharply defined and quickly ended. The Korean venture might be an exception, but it had had the imprimatur of the United Nations, even if the Soviet Union had been absent when consent had been given. Vietnam had only the supporting tradition of self-determination, expounded by Wilson and become an article of faith to American officialdom, together with the policy of containment growing out of the fear that communism might spread. These were accepted as policies; but were they worth the cost?

To make matters worse, self-determination for South Vietnam presently began to be interpreted as an attempt to keep a corrupt regime in power and the nation from being unified. This was the thesis not only of Communist sympathizers but of numerous isolationists who are glad of any opportunity to question presidential attempts to "man the walls of liberty" unless those walls were erected along this continent's coasts or at most not far from its shores.

Then, too, the fear of communism was no longer the activating motive it had been for some two generations; the Soviet Union had been stabilized for a long time, and although relations with its representatives were always exasperating, many crises had been lived through. Coexistence seemed possible if only because it was obvious now that the Russians were more old-fashioned imperialists than ideologues. Nationalism was forgivable, and even imperialism could be dealt with by compromise.

If the twin apprehensions had served at first to justify the intervention in spite of the Korean lesson, they no longer impressed a disillusioned public. The truth was that no campaign in American history had so lacked incentive for those who must support it—and for the soldiers who were required to fight. It should be added that there were fewer who desired to have their nation dominate the seas. Few Americans by now recalled Mahan,[11] and if they had read him they would not have been persuaded. The air age had arrived, and if military strategists did not calculate its requirements, others did.

The insubstantial support for an adventure so many thousands of miles distant and the violation of the traditional military aphorism, often repeated, about not "getting bogged down in Asian jungles" were, together, actively erosive. The latter rule, that the army should never be engaged on the Asian mainland, had undermined support for Korea. Even MacArthur, previously a firm opponent of invasion, had not known when to stop once involved, and had gone on and on to disaster. His initiative only proved the rule. This experience ought to have been a sufficient lesson, yet presidents, whatever warnings the wiser generals offered, stubbornly preferred the advice of belligerent ones and persisted in an operation of unexampled military risk. Since it was also one depending on outworn appeals to public opinion, it created an opportune situation for a well-deserved rebuke.

After Johnson gave up to public opinion, the Court would have something like massive approval for any move it might make. The consequences of practically extinguishing the president's emergency powers would be quite lost in popular relief from a frustrating situation—just as had been the case when Truman seized properties in pursuit of a cause not believably vital to the national interest.

Nevertheless, seizure by the Court would be a shift with unpredictable consequences. The unquestioned power of the commander in chief to deploy the armed forces in support of policy, and especially to send them abroad when, in his judgment, it must be done for the protection of American interests, would for the first time be called unconstitutional. In the steel case the Court had checked the president in a domestic matter; if it now ignored the irrelevance of a declaration of war and asserted its own right to say what constituted an emergency in confrontation with foreign enemies, the nation might conceivably be made helpless to defend itself. At least, the Court would have done what it could to bring this about.

It could be guessed that the only practical result would be that the president in exigency would have to make more certain of his popular support; but what might be worse, he would be more dependent on approval by his military advisers. If it is thought desirable that the military should always be controlled by civil authority, such a dependence would be a serious erosion of the principle. There were indeed reasons for rejecting

11. Alfred Thayer Mahan (1840–1914) is best remembered for his lectures on naval history and tactics from which grew his notable studies, *The Influence of Sea Power upon History, 1660–1783* (1890) and *The Influence of Sea Power upon the French Revolution, 1793–1812* (2 vols., 1892). Because Mahan wrote at a time when manifestations of imperialism were worldwide, his work influenced the policies of Germany, England, Japan, and the United States.

resort to the Court for definition of emergency and for monitoring the behavior of those who must act when one arose.

Undeclared Warfare

The question whether the "wars" without declarations in Korea and Vietnam were ventures different in kind from those traditionally carried on by presidents needs some exploration. They are obviously not to be explained as comparable to insurrections or domestic crises, nor are they in quite the same category as interferences in neighboring small nations where disorders may have occurred.

The nation was certainly not threatened with invasion from North Korea or North Vietnam; its security was jeopardized only if a very long run and several remote contingencies were considered; but this long run and these contingencies were the ones used for justification. The most vocal of such advocates of intervention, beginning in the Truman administration and carrying over into that of Eisenhower, was John Foster Dulles, first a special envoy and then secretary of state. It was his assumption that if the Communists were not stopped they would go on expanding and eventually the nation's very existence would be threatened. This, brought forward into the present, was made to seem an actual threat.

The appeal of this pronouncement, aside from its reliance on what by then were well-developed fears of infiltration, was to the tradition that American wars must be fought overseas. Not since the War of 1812 had it been necessary to fight enemies on this continent. Roosevelt's strongest plea for intervention in the prewar period of 1939–41 was that bombers based in the West Indies could reach a dozen inland cities with devastating effect. Suddenly the implications of the new weaponry were understood. Invasion was not a matter of armies landing on beaches. The peril could be seen gathering in places scarcely heard of before.

It seems, in retrospect, a strained argument that an attack on South Korea by North Koreans was an invasion of territory the United States was compelled to defend; but it can be understood how Eisenhower and Kennedy, having inherited Truman's cold war, could see it differently. It has to be recalled that during the world war recently concluded, the nation had assumed responsibilities far beyond those of even the recent past. Japan's defeat had required an occupation not yet terminated. There were revolutionary movements throughout Southeast Asia as the old empires were being liquidated. The United States had urged those evacuations, and it was not unreasonable to oppose the occupation of the newly independent nations by even more ruthless imperialists. Sentiment called for their support, but when the Dutch and French had been expelled, the Russians and Chinese were obviously prepared to move in. They liked to call their sort of imperialism "liberation" and their own occupation "self-determination," but it was a peculiarly cruel domination wherever it succeeded, and it horrified those to whom it was reported. Even the remote prospect that once all Asia had fallen to the dictatorships centered in Moscow and Peking there would be an attempt to "liberate" the Americas by the same subversive methods was enough to justify opposition to it whenever it appeared.

At that time Russia was the more active nucleus of the new imperialism, but when MacArthur made the mistake of crossing the 38th parallel and approached the Yalu he brought into action hordes of Chinese; it was suddenly no longer possible to consider Communist China a disorganized and sprawling conglomeration of regional dictatorships. The leaders of Mainland China who had expelled their predecessors became a threat as real as the Russians. Their methods were the same—subversion, terrorist infiltration, then dictatorship by local traitors under the leaders' direction. It was peculiarly repulsive that honored symbolic words were appropriated by the Communists for their own purposes. Liberation was the first of these; it replaced conquest. But dictatorship was called "peoples' democracy," and the revolutionists nominated themselves as patriots and used the word to discredit existing governments.

John Foster Dulles and those before and after him who regarded "liberation" as something to be stopped where it was, and, if not defeated, at least contained, at first had overwhelming support. The invasion of South Korea was an offensive so characteristic of the Communists' intent that repulsing it was an almost automatic reaction. Without examination it was assumed to be a Russian threat.

Added also to the enemies' sins was the rejection of religion, and this made them a threat not only to free government but also to the freedom of worship so deeply embedded in Western tradition. At that time any leader who showed the least disposition to permit expansion of Russian or Chinese power, or to deal with those countries in any way, would have found himself in trouble with, or at least disapproved by, an overwhelming majority of the American people. The most useful political tactic of the time was that of aggressive opposition wherever and whenever subversion showed itself—no matter how far away.

Strategic considerations played no part in the formation of the resulting policy; fears and revulsions were dominant in American minds; and warnings of the size or cost of the involvement being undertaken—and there were some—had no effect on policy. Whether or not presidents shared such thinking, they had to respond to it; Eisenhower was influenced by Dulles, except that Eisenhower consistently refused to approve his secretary's proposals for intervention as would a general who had been schooled in the tradition of continental defense. Kennedy, later, listened to successors of Dulles who exploited his military naïveté in this as in other unfortunate adventures. So the nation assumed the duty of keeping the new imperialists within their own borders, and it became a settled policy. For a generation or more it had been believed that somehow the Communist heresy could be stamped out. President Wilson, as long ago as 1918, had sent an army to Siberia to assist in doing just that. But mistakes had been made in later years. Russia, having been a wartime ally, was not opposed at first in making satellites of bordering Eastern European nations, and soon it was too late. China had been allowed to be taken over by revolutionaries and was lost to the democratic alliance. Containment was a weak successor to extinction, but it was regarded as the furthest and final compromise. It simply must be enforced.

These brief references to some three decades of confused and, on the whole, disastrous happenings are given only to explain how it was that a succession of presidents felt themselves justified in sending large armies to distant places solely on presidential responsibility. They were certain not only that containment was correct but also that public opinion required such implementation whatever the cost. Wartime military facilities and their supporting munition industries were still not fully dismantled, and the Congress was anxious to increase rather than diminish appropriations. The draft was still effective and army complements expansible; the navy had huge fleets in both oceans; deployment in Western Europe and around the Mediterranean was still complete, and this was true in the Far East as well. Whether there was a declaration of war or not, the sentiment of the legislative branch was clearly belligerent.

Only as short a time ago as the early 1930s President Roosevelt, ignoring most indignant protests, had had to abstract funds from public works appropriations for the modernization of a few naval vessels. Out of the same fund a few begrudged millions had been allocated to mechanization of the army. But in the 1950s incredibly costly nuclear weapons were making all others obsolete, and there was no hesitation over these costs. Soon, however, the chance to extinguish the Communist threat by preemptive attack passed; the Russians began to have nuclear capability. Talk about coexistence began to undermine the containment policy, but it was accepted reluctantly, and years were yet to pass before it would seem sensible—even inescapable—to most Americans.

Meanwhile the Communists became more and more confident, and more truculent as well. This had the usual effect of causing reaction. Americans were not in the mood, during this period, to take anything from the enemy without response. Exchanges in the United Nations between Acheson, as Truman's secretary of state, and the opposing Russian members reflected this. Hardly ever has there been such extended resort to extravagant mutual vilification, obviously approved by the principals of both—and presumably also by their constituents. Each felt compelled to give as good as he got. The great powers seemed poised and ready to have it out. A little later Dulles, borrowing a Communist locution, spoke of "liberating" Eastern European nations from Godless terror, just as Communists spoke of liberating all those peoples who were being ground under the heels of the imperialists.

If Truman did not hesitate to throw armies into the path of invading North Koreans, it was because he was carrying out what he could be certain was a popular mandate; if he did it without a declaration of war, he had not only the consent of the United Nations but also that of a compliant Congress. The United Nations acted, of course, while the Russians, in a fit of petulance, had absented themselves from meetings of the Security Council; but the resolution served for presidential justification. It was settled that Communist expansion should be opposed; after it was opposed in Korea, intervention in Vietnam had a justifying precedent. There was, indeed, a series of treaties requiring it, or, at least, ones that were so interpreted. The Southeast Asia Treaty Organization (SEATO) had been one of Dulles's masterpieces.

This is how things appeared to Truman's successors; each of the succeeding four, Eisenhower, Kennedy, Johnson, and Nixon, saw their duty in the same way. It began to be questioned when the Korean business went wrong and Eisenhower accepted armistice conditions made acceptable only by his military reputation. The questioning was soon raised to shrill opposition when Johnson sent more than a half-million men, mostly draftees, to protect Vietnam—and did it without consulting the Congress, except, it must be noted, by way of the Tonkin Resolution, but that was yielded by an enthusiastically supporting Senate. The anti-Communist sentiment was still overwhelming, and reliance on it seemed entirely safe.[12]

The Doctrine and Military Nightmares

To make the scene complete, the liberal clergy, during the Johnson years, began to maintain that the "invasion" of Vietnam was "immoral." How could the soldiers of a democracy be sent to prevent a people from overthrowing their usurping government and installing one of their own

12. The so-called Tonkin Gulf Resolution, passed on 7, August 1964, was recommended to the Senate by its Committee on Foreign Relations and passed with only two dissenting votes and with none in the House. Senator Fulbright, as chairman of the committee, had some subsequent difficulty explaining his part in the affair. He said later that he had been misled by the administration, but this left him open to question about the ready acceptance of information.

The important thing, however, is the practically unanimous acceptance, even by those who later became "doves," of the containment policy. In the campaign of that year, Johnson was the more moderate; Goldwater was for an immediate all-out attack on North Vietnam, for instance, and Johnson spoke of restraint in enlarging an already costly interference.

The Tonkin Resolution was repealed in 1971.

choosing? It was quite forgotten how stirring to the conscience it had seemed when President Kennedy had notified the world that Americans would "pay any price, bear any burden, meet any hardship, support any friend, oppose any foe, to assure the success of liberty." It was precisely to assure this success that he had sent fighting men to Vietnam to supplement Eisenhower's "advisers." What had been, in its beginning, as morally meant as any undertaking in American history was now denounced as wicked because, by a curious twist, the invasion of South Vietnam from the north had suddenly become a civil war. Moreover, the Vietcong were merely trying to free their people from a tyrannical regime; their murderous tactics were justified as incident to liberation from imperialists.

As this transformation of liberal opinion took place it involved the Doctrine of Necessity in unexpected opprobrium. The presidents who had taken emergency measures to repel the North Vietnamese became the suppressors of liberty. There was no respected general to cover retreat from Vietnam as there had been from Korea. That whole adventure was now an aberration of presidents, unchecked and unconstitutional. Suddenly opposition to presidential assumptions of power became a liberal cause.

Because the president is commander in chief and because the military is called on to enforce presidential policies, the generals are usually blamed when they do not succeed. This is more true when the president is a civilian and presumably an amateur. That the chiefs of staff advised either Korea or Vietnam is unlikely considering their strong traditional aversion to deployment on the Asian mainland. There is evidence that they considered Cuba a threat and did not oppose the Bay of Pigs, but that venture was arranged by the Central Intelligence Agency's taking advantage of Kennedy's naïveté as well as his own personal overblown authority. The debacle really occurred because the military was not in charge.

There is reason to believe that as far as was possible most generals resisted at least Korea—and very probably Vietnam. There is, for instance, the statement of General J. L. Collins that the joint chiefs offered such counsel: Korea was of little strategic value to the United States, and any commitment to the use of military force there would be ill advised. It seems incredible that the chiefs of staff of the 1960s would have abandoned the position held by their predecessors in 1949, especially since the rejection of their advice had been so disastrous. What happened when a half-million men were engaged and the problem was not to advise on involvement but on ways to win was another matter.

It is of some significance that Collins's book carried the title *War in Peacetime*.[13] The Vietnam deployment, like that in Korea, was one of those missions military men dislike. They were not supposed to produce a victory,

13. Joseph Lawton Collins, *War in Peacetime* (Boston: Houghton Mifflin Company, 1969).

only to check the invaders; it is the professional's business to defeat an enemy, not to hold him within bounds. If they could have used the tactics needed to win, they would at least have had a chance for credit in a venture they must have undertaken reluctantly; as it was, they had to defend a country whose long borders were open to the enemy.

If Vietnam was a military nightmare, and if war could not be declared, the presidents who sent the armed forces must take the responsibility. In taking this responsibility they had to stretch the Doctrine of Necessity beyond any precedent except the weak one of Korea. Not surprisingly, this action proved to be beyond popular tolerance.

Whether sudden or not, and whether attributable to the failure of ventures into the Asian jungles, there followed for the first time a formidable reexamination of the deployment abroad of armed forces by presidents, justified only by the presidents' assessment of the national interest. There was not much disposition at first to associate this with the doctrine they acted under. A few critics—Senators Morse and Gruening, for instance —tried to maintain that the expedition was obviously war when no war had been declared, but no one listened to these protestations. References to precedent were sufficient refutation. The more telling attacks were those reciting military ineffectiveness in spite of the huge effort, but the liberal objections centered on the corrupt South Vietnam government and the immorality of opposing liberation.

What was not suggested, at least with any audible emphasis, was that the authority the presidents had relied on to justify such a futile—or immoral— venture ought to be reconsidered. The proposal, soon heard, that the "war" should be stopped by the Court because it was not a war was an unthinking resort to what seemed a ready means. This would not rationalize the emergency power every government must have in reserve, setting standards for resort to it and establishing a procedure for invoking it. Transfer to the Court would merely consign it to a branch incapable of exercising it. This consideration, however, did not come into the discussion.

The steel case might seem to have effected just such a transfer, and that was undoubtedly the intention. It may confidently be said, however, that it did so only in that one instance. It was not a genuine emergency, and Truman was unwise to have relied on its being taken as such. In the interest of the executive office he ought not to have given the Court such an opportunity. At some future time, if an actual crisis should occur, one generally recognizable, a president would act as presidents have always acted —unless, meanwhile, some structural changes had taken place. It might be more difficult, but it would be done.

Unless Tripoli, Sumter, Mexico, Haiti, Korea, and all the rest were unconstitutional uses of presidential power, neither was Vietnam. It was unwise, but it ought rather to be argued that it *should have been* rather than that it *was* unconstitutional. That two presidents, neither to be rated as below average in judgment or dedication, proved to have so little strategic sense does argue that presidents cannot be trusted in these circumstances with the definition of "necessity." Only two lodgments would be worse: in the Congress or in the Court.

Justices, as has been intimated, can always afford to wait. The position they intend for the Court has to be protected from the danger that the Congress may sometimes use its power to limit jurisdiction. Besides, there are always some who share the Brandeis/Frankfurter belief in judicial restraint—keeping out of the "political thicket." A check would certainly occur if there should be a decline in respect for judicial wisdom. The Warren Court took risks so considerable that when the chief justice retired, a petition calling a convention to restrict jurisdiction lacked only one state for its activation. It was not a time to push further toward complete judicial supremacy, but some justices were thought to feel themselves thwarted in the most favorable opportunity of a generation.

One other consideration of importance is relevant, and especially for those who urge intervention by the Court. If it should proceed into this new territory, it would be reversing itself—that is to say, former Courts—in a most embarrassing way. Of course reversals are far from unknown, but this would involve the separation of powers and, as has been noted, would not only prohibit certain ones to the president but would transfer them to itself.

There has never been an instance of interference with the president's deployment of the armed forces. Two early decisions explicitly rejected the possibility. Justice Story[14] did say that the presidential power was limited to actual invasion or the imminent danger of invasion, a remark extraneous to the decision in question, but what followed was fully germane: "the authority to decide whether exigency has arisen belongs exclusively to the President and his decision is conclusive upon all other persons." That was in 1827; in 1849 Chief Justice Taney[15] denied categorically that a presidential decision to call out the militia could be questioned. Thereafter, those were the controlling views.

Reviewing the history of incidents involving the use of the armed forces for various purposes, Professor Pritchett reached the conclusion that the presidential powers extended far beyond uses of the militia in domestic crises, upheld in Taney's decision: "Obviously the courts have no power to examine decisions of the President to use the Armed forces outside the country. . . . In fact, a 1966 study listed 162 instances where the President instructed the military forces to act against enemies without congressional

14. *Martin* v. *Mott,* 12 Wheat. 19 (1827).
15. *Luther* v. *Borden,* 7 How. 1 (1849).

authorization."[16] The word "obviously" used by Professor Pritchett was justified by every relevant precedent; the justices have been known to ignore conclusions of their predecessors, to say nothing of inferences drawn from their refusals to interfere (one of their prerogatives being that they can choose freely among the causes they will entertain).

Korea and Vietnam might be regarded by a contemporary Court as ventures of such magnitude as to have taken on a difference in kind; that, in fact, a whole people was subjected to perils no one person, even a president, should be able to decide must be risked. Besides, his decision being subject to challenge, as these incidents proved so conclusively, the making of policy took on an uncertainty no nation could afford. Withdrawal from the commitment of men and materiel to such an undertaking as the defense of South Korea or South Vietnam became in itself a movement so vast as to divide the nation into hostile factions. No policy of such scope, it became clear, should be adopted unless the agreement to it is substantial— much more substantial than the consent to the Southeast Asian ventures.

If these are reasonable conclusions, they argue that dependence on the Doctrine of Necessity ought to be reexamined. If presidents have assumed powers not granted them by the Constitution, and have adopted policies of the gravest consequence on their own responsibility, and if, further, these decisions have been proved by experience to have been on occasion gravely mistaken, then indeed the authority for making them ought to be reexamined.

They ought to be considered not in the controversial heat of demonstration and counterdemonstration, but in the solemn procedures of amendment. Far more serious national decisions might well at any time lie just ahead. It was almost intolerable to endure Korea and Vietnam, but these were nothing to confrontations with powers equally well armed and even more convinced of their moral missions. It will not be enough to limit presidential initiatives; those initiatives will have to be—and will be—taken. The question is whether they ought to be located elsewhere, shared by others, preceded by preparations for making them, limited by definition—all that sort of thing. The controversy over Vietnam—acerbic as it was—did not touch the real issue.

The Doctrine and Presidential Fallibility

The recent experiences referred to here suggest that the Doctrine of Necessity should not expand further as a presidential monopoly. It is elementary—but not at all irrelevant—to say that the president is only one person and so shares the potential weaknesses of all human beings. The

16. C. Herman Pritchett, *The American Constitution,* 2d ed., rev. (New York: McGraw-Hill, 1968), p. 379.

president may fall ill and be more or less incapacitated as were Wilson and Eisenhower, may lay dying indefinitely from an assassin's bullet as did Garfield and McKinley, or may suffer physical changes that impair his judgment. There is, besides, continual strain calculated to wear down the most resistant physique and to warp the most calculating judgment, and there is no constitutional interlude for recuperation.

Then, too, the president must always be conscious of having been chosen (usually) by less than half the voters, and of being viewed with a calculation by the others that readily turns unreasonable and may often become hostile. That this can happen rapidly when staying power and motivation are tested by reverses in the field or the need for sacrifices at home the Asian experiences show all too certainly. It has been noted that what began as a moral commitment to self-determination was interpreted when costs mounted as immoral prevention of self-determination. The presidents who had made the decisions could not support them with public understanding. The forces in the field could no longer feel themselves fighting for their country; they were, indeed, made to feel that they were fighting against its wishes—or at least against those of loud and numerous protesters who, so great was their revulsion, did not hesitate even at subversion. This was a miscalculation a president ought not to have made alone. A democracy may make mistakes, but fatal ones ought not to be made for it by fallible individuals—even presidents elected by all the people.

These are facts and circumstances known to everyone. Yet nothing is being done about them, and they are not even much discussed. There is, of course, the fugitive suggestion, earnestly put forward by concerned citizens, that the Court should intervene. They see that congressional declarations have become unlikely. Future wars promise to explode when events reach a certain climax; in fact, the last declaration *before hostilities* was at the beginning of the Mexican War in 1845. The refusal of a declaration could change nothing. In World Wars I and II the Congress was merely asked to "recognize" hostilities; harassment by dissenting committees has amply shown its futility, yet it is the only legislative participation in the progress of events—except, of course, the voting for appropriations, and this even dissidents usually do.

That the wish for responsible policymaking should suggest such a professional body as the Court for the purpose is not strange, but it is nevertheless impossible. Justices can only reject commitments, they cannot make them; and such commitments are sometimes urgently required. The Court cannot participate in any active sense; it can only, with austere disapproval, enter a demurrer; and for the national purpose this is futile.

Nevertheless the position of presidents has become impossible. Even those willing to make decisions without hesitation—as Truman was—cannot carry through undertakings unless they are immediately successful.

If the policy has not been made with public participation, resources of determination and willingness to supply will not appear, and the president will find himself isolated and even powerless except to command troops in the field who are unhappy—perhaps even rebellious.

Experience has exposed some unhappy traits. The more a president is criticized the less likely he is to share his information or listen to those who dissent from his policy. Legislators are, at first, easily used as support rather than opposition; this was shown by the little-considered passage of the Tonkin Gulf Resolution; but that this is uncertain backing, the retreat from this consent clearly proved. The president in usual instances has only to assert the existence of a crisis; no one, lacking his information, wants to oppose emergency measures for the protection of the nation's security; on the other hand, politicians are very quick indeed to leave the president in isolation when dissent begins to spread.

It would not do to furnish subordinates who might advise the president in emergency; he now has them with such status as can be given mere advisers. They do not modify his responsibility for choosing among the alternatives they perceive. Their conclusions may or may not be accepted. Actually, they usually present choices among several well-supported alternatives, and they may confuse rather than clarify; but it is at this juncture that argument becomes commitment. This was the process meticulously described in at least three of the Kennedy emergencies—the Bay of Pigs, the sending of combat troops to Vietnam, and the confrontation with the Russians who were deploying missiles in Cuba.[17]

The limits of the advisory role are definite. They show how easily mistaken judgments can be made in spite of efforts to assemble voluminous facts and engage the best counselors. Kennedy listened, then approved the Bay of Pigs; he listened again, then sent troops to Vietnam. It is now known that in this instance he chose between J. K. Galbraith and General Maxwell Taylor. These were not the only ones involved, but their accounts show how emphatically they differed from each other. The third instance—choosing to prevent the deployment of missiles in Cuba—was successful. The score would have to be put down as one out of three. Considering the consequences of mistakes when genocidal weapons or faraway wars are involved, this is indeed a frightening percentage.

Johnson, in his time, listened and consented to escalation, thus involving himself and his successor in a dilemma that forced Johnson's retirement and had at least one other consequence: the worsening of relations with the world's other nuclear powers who were supporting the North Vietnamese.

17. For moving accounts of these Kennedy dilemmas see Theodore C. Sorensen, *Kennedy* (New York: Harper & Row, 1965), and Arthur M. Schlesinger, *The Thousand Days* (Boston: Houghton Mifflin Company, 1965).

It has been suggested that the Congress might be ingenious enough, when considering appropriation bills, to entrust the nuclear establishment to an independent authority. The precedent of the regulatory bodies is cited. These were placed quite outside the executive establishment. They were, however, to carry out new duties, nonexistent in 1787, and did not represent something taken away from the president. To make them "independent" was to do something not forbidden by the Constitution, but it violated the separation principle by making what amounted to a fourth branch.

It would be quite another matter to set up an independent security authority. This would infringe the powers of the commander in chief, especially if its head should be authorized to share decisions concerning the use of weapons.

It is true that the Constitution has that provision concerning the appointive power, and just how far it might be stretched to allow such a departure is difficult to say.

Article II, section 2, after indicating that the president shall appoint ambassadors and so on, goes on to say that he may also appoint "all other officers of the United States, whose appointments are not herein otherwise provided for, and which may be established by law. *But the Congress may by law vest the appointment of such inferior officers, as they think proper, in the president alone, in the courts of law, or in the heads of departments."*

This seems to allow the Congress indefinite control over governmental appointments and frightens the incumbent head of any executive agency who reads it. It is only one source of what has been referred to here as congressional advantage; added to the exclusive power to tax and to appropriate, it gives the branch a bargaining power much superior to any the other branches can muster. It is, of course, weakened by the inability of several hundred legislators to gather majorities for the interferences.

In contrast to this broad power of the Congress, the president's designation as commander in chief is specific. How could the nation's most potent weapon be segregated and entrusted to others in open defiance of this provision? Even if provided in a law that generals should be appointed by someone other than the president, thus in effect making the military department independent, the president could still give them orders. And it is hard to conceive a commander in chief with no power to appoint or discharge his officers.

On the whole, the abstraction from the president of the sole decision-making power in the use of genocidal weapons does not seem constitutionally a practical suggestion.

There is something else. The more this Doctrine of Necessity is studied, the more impossible it seems that its availability can be restricted if peril to the nation becomes actual. It will be possessed by some agency of government, and it must be one able to act without delay. In the new and dangerous world, suddenness is a characteristic. Dangers can arise almost instantaneously. There have been months and years to prepare for every war in the past. The condition of safety now is that all preparation for it shall have been made in advance. Armies must have been recruited and trained; weapons must be at the ready. Their activation is simplicity itself; a button pushed, a switch thrown, and the commitment is made. How this contrasts with 1787 is indeed startling when seriously considered.

What have become crucial are the preliminaries, the provocations and confrontations leading to activation. In this, others could share with the president; but it must be accepted that such formalities as declarations are obsolete and that uninformed legislative harassments are extremely dangerous. The need is for national agreement on policies defining generally the national interest, and then for multiple judgment on such issues as the approval of the Bay of Pigs and the "escalation" in Vietnam.

The separation of powers, as Brandeis said so clearly, is a legitimization of friction; but what he did not say is that its inevitable consequence is dependence on struggle and bargaining to produce decisions, and that these do not result in dependable ones. It is foreign to the nature of this process that it should end in cooperation or coexistence.

On another level it must be recognized that it is desirable to have debates and to have policy formulations issue from them, but that it is quite another matter to have debate when the firing of missiles may be in question. It is too late then for anything but the judgment of trusted individuals. That there should be more than one of these, and that they should not have been exhausted by work, harassed by political adversaries, or impaired by physical weakness, are precautions of the most elementary sort.

These are the background requirements of a safer kind of decision-making. Specifically, the president should be relieved of many domestic duties, and should at least share his emergency powers with others—a few and clearly peers.

Considering the Doctrine of Necessity itself, the practical suggestion may be made that the dangers from it have come from lack of recognition that it inevitably comes into operation at certain junctures. It is assumed, in spite of all the evidence, that no emergency will ever again arise; therefore no preparation for it need be made. This refusal has a reason, of course; it is that emergency does not fit anywhere into the scheme of 1787. In order to be met, such emergencies must be treated as extraordinary departures. They are embarrassing, since they seem to indicate a systemic insufficiency. They are really never recognized and so are never regularized.

There has by now been enough experience not only to support the conclusion that emergencies will recur but, as well, to make such classifications as will make ways of meeting them realistic. There are some quite obvious differences, and others would appear from study and discussion. For instance, we have seen the president checked by the Court when he attempted to impose domestic disciplines; but we have been told by Professor Pritchett that no check on the president's use of armed forces abroad is possible.

Surely one check has been found in the case of Vietnam. It is opposition from public opinion and demonstration. But to regard this as the only resort is to admit that dissension must tear the nation apart in order to force a reconsideration that would have been provided for if emergency were anticipated and resorts when it occurs were provided.

As a beginning it might be well to analyze the experience with the Roosevelt declarations of limited and full emergencies. To be sure, they were completely extraconstitutional—that is to say, they allowed the president to do things the Constitution would otherwise not have permitted. These might be made constitutional, and actions allowable in either situation might be defined.

Declarations of emergency might take the place of the obsolete declaration of war; they might differentiate between domestic and international crises, allocating such powers as might be appropriate. Any declaration would have the consent of others than the president, thus making certain that the decision was not his alone.

There would, however, still remain the ultimate crisis of attack from without. As long as there is free deployment of intercontinental missiles it is impossible to do much else in advance than admit that the president, with perhaps a few designated associates, must have complete freedom. The emergency could present itself instantaneously, and if any response should be made it could not be delayed for discussion. This, however, differentiates itself from the Vietnam involvement sharply enough. For that venture the Doctrine of Necessity ought not to have been relied on. There was time for discussion, and delay might have saved the nation later humiliation.

The suggestion here is that in present circumstances it is unrealistic and dangerous to go on assuming that emergencies will not happen. It should be assumed, on the contrary, that if they are inevitable, they ought to have appropriate study leading to the legitimation of the means they will require to be used.

CHAPTER 6

THE RULE OF SELF-RESTRAINT

Checks and Balances

It is not often recalled how much the success of the American system of government relies on restraint—*self*-restraint by those in each branch who feel compelled to enlarge the powers they already possess, or who are tempted to infringe the prerogatives of those in the other branches. Perhaps this forgetfulness occurs because restraint is a negative rather than a positive requirement of social relationships. It is not even explicit. Democratic theory supposes it to be felt and to be respected, but warning signs seldom exist, and there are no prohibitions other than canons of mutual trust. Restraint grows weaker as numbers multiply and the sense of mutuality declines. This is as true of those in official positions as of ordinary citizens.

Such a statement has to be modified by recalling that the framers furnished the tripartite system of branches with the well-known "checks and balances," and these, as far as they go, are positive enough. They show a certain realism about political affairs, but their prohibitions are sparse and indefinite. They have become less prohibitory as time has passed. When adjustments to circumstances have had to be made they have been interpreted as excuses for obstruction. This is always doubtfully legitimate.

The counterpoised powers are capable of bringing initiatives to a stop but are not effective in promoting them. The result is often the accumulation of dissatisfactions until explosive acerbities develop. Then the weakness of the unstated obligation to be reasonable allows impulsive action to be taken, and this may be the cause of lingering irritation rather than compromise and accommodation.

The few imposed restraints represented by the Constitution's checks are thus not helpful if a government of service and action is wanted. Not enough was said about limits, or demarcations; nothing at all was said about the resolution of inevitable conflicts, or the giving way of all to the need for meeting an emergency or getting ahead with a needed action. A method for compromise might at least have been laid out. All is left, as things are, to struggle, and since it often escapes mere settlement of one issue and becomes a chronic belligerence, unmeasurable but very serious harm results.

This situation has gone on developing for nearly two centuries with no attempt to relieve it. All branches have been guilty—but not necessarily equally so—of encroachment on areas they were not expected to occupy. Sometimes, but not always, this has been done with excellent motives, but often these have not been even remotely related to the public interest. We know that the Congress tries to manipulate the executive, and even to control its personnel and its operations. It has excused this by persistently citing the obsolete theory that the legislature is the "real" embodiment of "the people," and that in a democracy, since the people are sovereign, their powers are passed by election to their representatives. This allows legislators to claim moral responsibility for controlling the other branches.

The legislature alone does indeed have the constitutional power of appropriation; but it is one thing to furnish funds and quite another to use them, and a reasonable recognition of this difference might be thought possible; but even when a certain recognition of their own inherent ineptness occurs to the lawmakers, they may still feel themselves called on to specify how administrators shall act. This may—and often does—become so detailed as to approach actual direction of operations. This is all too easily done when appropriations are made, and sometimes under some such rubric as investigation or the requiring of reports.

The incursions of the presidency have come about in a different way: responsibilities are naturally consigned to the president's office because he is a national leader with the power of a majority behind him; and because, as the nation's affairs have grown more complicated, the multiplication of these responsibilities has been inevitable. Several presidents— notably Jackson in a famous controversy—have reminded the Congress that presidents are elected too, and not by the people of a district or a state, but by all the nation's voters. And it is certainly true that the president, with only the sketchiest of constitutional directions, is blamed, or given credit, for nearly everything that goes on in the country—certainly its foreign relations, its economy, its good order, and the welfare of its people. It is an amazing concentration.

All these duties either are extrapolations from the few specified in the Constitution—such as the appointing of ambassadors and the making of treaties, taken to mean that foreign affairs are his responsibility—or are merely assumed, as are his credit or blame for the behavior of the national economy. Since the beginning of the twentieth century the promise of prosperity has been prominent in the appeal of every successful candidate, whether or not he had the means to achieve such a desirable condition; and hard times will usually defeat an incumbent, as it did Hoover.

Tranquillity can be found as a general statement only in the Preamble, not among the specified objectives; but if domestic peace breaks down and there is trouble, the president is expected to intervene and restore order. Very soon, however, following whatever action he takes, there arise heated complaints because he did not prevent it, or because what was done was arbitrary; but these, coming after the crisis is over, are of no more than historical interest.

It will be recalled that welfare is mentioned twice in the Constitution, once in the Preamble and once again among the directives for the Congress. This last mention occurs in a curious clause, following one about the taxes, which are, it says, ". . . to pay the debts and provide for the common defense and general welfare of the United States."[1] The context would suggest that this was intended to be an amplification of "defense"; it does not mention people, only the nation. But "general welfare" has been expanded latterly to mean care for individuals; since the New Deal people have looked to the government for relief in time of hardship—something that would have been inconceivable to the framers—and comparative benefits are as much an issue in modern campaigns as prosperity was in earlier ones. Nor are relief and general welfare any longer closely associated. Americans have long since learned that affluence is not shared, unless law compels it, with those who are somehow excluded from earning wages or salaries. Welfare, indeed, has become one of the most settled—and costly—aims of government, and parties win campaigns by promising to enlarge it.

Since this is so, and since they are politicians, presidents try to meet the expectations of the electorate and incidentally make good their parties' promises; and they cannot do this without using the means first massively assembled by F. D. Roosevelt. This, however, is recent. Cleveland, for instance, became very unpopular in his second term (1892–96) because of a lingering economic depression, but no one suggested seriously that he should do anything about it. Hard times simply went on until recovery came in a slow and unaided climb. This, even then, and however unjustly, was charged to the president. It was the source of Cleveland's unpopularity and in the succeeding campaign was the most prominent issue.

The Populists in the Midwest believed that clinging to the gold standard was at least partly responsible, and their crusade for "easy money" became so considerable a political movement that it captured the Democratic party

1. Article I, section 8.1.

and made Bryan its presidential candidate. He made a formidable campaign on this issue alone but was defeated by McKinley, who was a "hard-money" man. The simplistic Populist theory of the way to ensure economic progress did indeed depend on governmental action—the printing of money without gold backing. From that time on, the parties divided on the means for maintaining prosperity. The Democrats offered the discipline of "the interests," particularly "the Wall Street barons," as one of their objectives (the other being cheap money). The Republicans contended that high tariffs and the gold standard were the only sound policies. Presidents were elected on these issues and could not have done what had been promised without taking new initiatives.

When these responsibilities were assumed, presidents had no more definition of the means they could properly use than of the actions they ought to take. It is reported that when Justice Brandeis voted with the Supreme Court majority to reject Roosevelt's National Recovery Act in 1935, he slyly sent word to the president that nothing in the Constitution limited the power of the Congress to tax and spend. By then this was not a new way of interpreting the welfare clause—Roosevelt had from the first assumed that it allowed him to offer relief—but to Brandeis it seemed indefinitely expansive and, indeed, a sufficient substitute for the new arrangements among industries Roosevelt had been trying to impose as recovery measures. The way to assist the poor, Brandeis was suggesting was not through industrial self-discipline and voluntary reemployment but by distributing direct benefits. This was not much different from the Populist policies of half a century earlier, except that the Populists had not contemplated direct relief but had relied on cheapening money as a way of increasing the purchasing power of the poor. Roosevelt had hoped to give up the handing out of what his detractors called "doles" if only factories could begin running again, giving workers jobs. A coordinated reemployment effort failed, whereupon he undertook to manipulate the price of gold, thus raising prices and enabling frozen debts to be liquidated. In all this the legislature, after authorizing it, passively watched the expansion of presidential power.

The nation, suffering recurrent breakdowns, was at this time finding its way tortuously into the century of technology and organicism and had to do it not only by trial and error but also within the confines of a basic law that had not contemplated any such development or foreseen any governmental responsibilities while it was happening. The economy of 1787 had not even been a horse-and-buggy one; it had been one of tracks through the wilderness and horseback riding or coastal travel in sailing boats. That of the twentieth century was continental. The country was crossed by railways, factory employment was outrunning that in agriculture, and the cities were growing beyond their old confines.

Adjustment to these changes was not assisted by any constitutional recognition—that document remained firm and fixed—and until the Court had been reconstituted by new appointments after 1936, not much was reinterpreted except to make it firmer and more fixed. The series of anti-New Deal Supreme Court decisions in the 1930s illustrated the difficulty. Plainly a good deal of legislating was going on outside the legislature. Laws —or rules and regulations—were being made not only by officials of government but also by officials of industrial and other institutions such as corporations and labor unions. Whether these were allowable depended on the practical necessity for them—unless the Court decided otherwise. The question was a double one: whether the Congress could delegate its power to make laws as it had tried to do with the National Recovery and the Agricultural Adjustment acts, and whether other agencies might simply assume that they could make such laws—whether they were called orders, rules, or regulations—as seemed necessary.

There accumulated a large corpus of what was called "administrative law." It was really regulatory orders. Unless the commissions and boards where the orders originated could be called legislatures (or paralegislatures), these were not laws in the usual sense, but they did "have the force of law." They were illegitimate in the sense that the Constitution had not contemplated them. Perhaps they should be called "nonconstitutional." They existed only because the Supreme Court had not determined that such powers to legislate could not be delegated. But it had said just that in the New Deal cases. Cardozo's famous phrase "delegation run riot" indicated that the Court reserved the power to say what kind of delegation— and how much—would be approved. This provided no dependable guide, and subsequent decisions provided none either.

Presidents themselves legislate a good deal by way of executive orders, but they have the excuse of a constitutional duty to see that the laws are faithfully executed. The regulatory agencies are nonconstitutional newcomers to the governmental complex, established by a Congress whose desire to control outruns its ability to do what it desires; the agencies are creatures of baffled legislatures.

The Court had never been bothered by serious questions of delegation before the New Deal innovations; but in its zeal to oppose Roosevelt's efforts, it suddenly found that not he but the Congress had exceeded its powers to delegate; and it was simply assumed that delegations it approved were permissible but others were not. How these decisions were made no one could say. This was clearly beyond the Court's constitutional warrant, just as was the Congress's establishment of such agencies and delegating to them lawmaking and administrative powers it could not itself use but wanted to deny the executive. The regulation of business was undreamed of by the framers; but of course it had not been forbidden; it was a vast area of unoccupied territory. It should have been distributed, together with directives for its administration, in a constitutional revision.

Technology simply could not have grown as it did in the century after the Civil War without a concurrent expansion of governmental operations, but in the allocation of new territory among the three branches there was bound to be contention. Challenges were presented by one situation after another. When something new had to be done, the president might act, or, if his relations with Congress at the moment happened to be good, he might consult congressional leaders before acting. Whatever resulted the Court took the position that it could judge whether: (1) action ought to have been taken, (2) if it had been taken, the Congress should have consented, and (3) whether the constitutional authority to consent existed. The Court did decide when cases came before it and the justices cared to consider them. One thing was made quite clear: the final determination belonged to the Court if for some reason it chose to intervene.

Tortuous legal procedures usually prevented decisions of this sort from being made at the time when they might have interfered in critical situations. Emergencies were usually overcome before opinions were rendered; but these did serve for guidance on future occasions. They did not actually prevent the application of instant remedies, and often contemporary presidents or legislatures regarded them as minor annoyances. This was only partly owed to legal delays. Much of it was caused by the discretion allowed everyone in a society so fluid and so frequently in turmoil. Self-restraint was all very well when no one was hurt; but when there was public demand for constraint, politicians were likely to respond without much attention to likely Court objection and even less to the unwritten but all-important rules supposed to govern all officials just as they did all citizens in their private relations.

Presidents, in the view of both the Congress and the Court, were the worst offenders, the greediest grabbers of power as the expansion of government activities went on; but it could reasonably be said that their position and their responsibilities made them so. Since they were elected by all the people they owed their constituents whatever it was generally felt was owed them. This, decade by decade, was more welfare, more order, more certain justice, more tranquillity—and especially, after the trials of depression, more economic security. As politicians they tried to respond, but in doing so they found themselves bound by irritating restrictions. Their constitutional powers were completely inadequate. They could meet only a few of the modern claims on their office. Order was a matter for local authorities; tranquillity required arrangements first between employees and employers and, beyond that, the establishment of an elaborate program only the Congress could legitimize; justice was not usually a federal responsibility; and welfare required specific legislative appropriations from a Congress dominated by Conservative leaders.

It was for such reasons that presidents reached for the position of chief legislator as well as chief executive. They achieved it because the

Congress was so little responsive to national needs. Its best efforts were devoted to serving *its* constituents—the people back home who wanted public works, subsidies of various kinds, or favorable treatment for supporters. Their demands seldom had much to do with national issues. Being both initiators of legislation and executives, presidents became more and more the central figures in the nation; and because they acquired in time so much power they felt less and less restraint about simply taking more to supplement what they had. Restraint, with modern presidents, became a matter of conciliating the other branches to the minimal extent necessary for avoiding embarrassment and frustration.

Then, of course, there were recurrent emergencies. These seemed to follow one another with only the briefest interludes of relaxation—of "normalcy" as Harding called it. If depression did not require unusual measures, foreign involvements did. Both were resented fiercely; both demanded immediate and drastic response from the president. They could be met only by takeovers of power; one of these was precedent for the next, until finally the presidency was almost constantly engaged in actions not contemplated by the Constitution (or any of its amendments) and frequently engaged in controversy with Court or Congress. Both were reluctant to consent; and the reluctance when an emergency persisted for some time, and the president continued to meet it, rose to harassment and charges of usurpation.

The checks and balances of the Constitution, for all these reasons, have operated more effectively on the Congress, and even on the Court, than they have on the presidency; this is true, also, for the unwritten and amorphous Rule of Self-restraint, so elusive but so important to the constitutional scheme. This, again, is because changes requiring adjustment have become nationwide and only the president is a national representative. What he does may be only to recommend congressional action, but it cannot end there. If the something—whatever it is—must be done, and if the Congress refuses or is dilatory, it must be done anyway; and the president sees to it—or tries to see to it—that action is taken. The Court he could always ignore, until, in 1952, it showed a new celerity in procedure and interrupted Truman while action was still going on. He had scarcely seized the steel mills before he was told to return them to their owners.

The Rule of Self-restraint is badly shattered, often, by such confrontations. Whether necessity is about to develop or continues to exist is decided by the president. This is because it is he who feels the pressure most quickly, and because he is responsive; and what must be done to avoid or prevent trouble he must in the end decide. Often there is no time to consult the Congress. Customarily in such situations, however, he does call in the leaders and listens to what they have to say; but he also listens to his own consultants. These are not the cabinet any longer; and they are members of the Security Council only in matters affecting relations with other nations. It is a group, organized by the president himself, according to his own notions of the assistance he feels he must have; and it is often added to by others he calls in for particular purposes. Finally President Nixon set up a Domestic Council as the counterpart of the older Security Council. It had long been wanted by presidents.

At Nixon's accession there were auxiliary bodies; some, like the Council of Economic Advisers, had been authorized by the Congress and were not new (it had been included in the Full Employment Act of 1947). The Security Council was established by executive order. Presidents have gradually won funds for such purposes, but they must be used with discretion, and they are never adequate. Before F. D. Roosevelt there was no such apparatus for assisting in decisionmaking. That the elaborate organization of information and counseling does exist, however, has sometimes given the public confidence in the presidential assumption of powers and has intimidated critics. Sometimes, again, it has had the reverse effect. The president cannot always depend on his helpers to be anonymous or expect them to be accepted by hostile partisans.

The existence of a presidential establishment of this sort is relatively recent. It was first organized in 1938 as a result of recommendations made by Charles E. Merriam, Louis Brownlow, and Luther Gulick for the reform of administrative management. This was the first of several such inquiries into the president's difficulties. It urged the addition of researchers, secretaries, consultants, special advisers, speechwriters, and the like. Presidents before had had informal helpers, the most notorious having been Jackson's "Kitchen Cabinet." But Wilson, for instance, even during the First World War, still wrote his own speeches on a battered typewriter and depended on a very few intimates for advice—Colonel House being the best-known. Even Hoover, the most experienced of chief executives, had very few assistants, and he, too, laboriously put together his own speeches, something no later public man would consider doing.

The presidency has become a formidable office. There is a real question whether it has not acquired too much *unshared* power, and whether, if there are no constitutional changes, it will not be compelled by circumstances to assume more and more. There will certainly be increased demand for services; there will be no diminution of congressional obstruction; there will continue to be emergencies; and the Court is likely to be more determined in its definition of permissible powers.[2]

Americans ought to consider carefully what can be done about this. Evidently a self-imposed Rule of Self-restraint is no longer effectively

2. An examination of this presidential apparatus, with articles by members of recent presidential staffs, has been edited by Thomas E. Cronin and Sanford D. Greenburg, *The Presidential Advisory System* (New York: Harper & Row, 1969).

operative in any of the branches, and evidently there are reasons reaching deep into continuing social and economic change why this is so.

The Undefinable Virtue of Restraint

Actually the Rule of Self-restraint was never effective in the way the framers must have expected it would be. All the branches, in the very first years of the new government, began to encroach on the prerogatives inferentially or even specifically assigned to the others. Since the limits were mostly indefinite, they could be—and were—readily ignored when another branch happened not to have good defenses or when it did not move at once to protect its prerogatives.

An instance of this was the establishment of the executive departments. Instead of appropriating funds to be used by the president in setting up such departments as he judged necessary, the Congress assumed the power to name them; and instead of merely authorizing them, it went on to specify the detail of their structure. It went even further in starting off the judiciary. In the Act of 1789 the Supreme Court was limited to sittings in the capital; it was specified that all suits before it must be conducted by an attorney general (whose office was created); and, after a struggle between nationalists (Federalists) and states' righters (Democratic-Republicans), it was provided that there should be two judicial levels: district courts in every state, and regional circuit courts to be presided over by Supreme Court justices traveling to their assignments.

The Congress discovered thus early what an advantage it had in its control of the largely undefined taxing and appropriating powers; it could be seen also that these would be used to invade the other branches—without much recognition of their responsibilities—whenever its majority cared to do so. This meant something more than the assertion of prerogatives by a whole governmental body; it meant that powerful individuals, in control of committees, could have their way with the executive—or that part of it they had use for.

Presidents were no more restrained. Beginning with Washington, they found it more and more convenient to interpret generously such duties assigned in the Constitution as that to negotiate treaties and to "appoint ambassadors, other public ministers and consuls." This they quickly expanded into substantial control of relations with foreign governments, and in time almost complete control. It could be said in their defense that this was forced on them by the other branches. The Senate, for one thing, refused to admit that "advise and consent" meant the sharing of responsibility. The president was to take the initiative, leaving the Senate free to reject drafts of treaties one-third of its members found objectionable, or to refuse confirmation of presidential appointees.

When John Jay, the first chief justice, refused to give an advisory opinion concerning a foreign issue, he left Washington to a lonely interpretation of his own. Since the new president was deeply concerned to set the government on proper courses, and since threats on all sides from the old empires were actual, he was soon dealing with the representatives of other nations as though the sole responsibility were his. He continued to be uneasy lest a small group of senators negate any agreement arrived at, thus diminishing the respect so badly needed by the administration; nevertheless he negotiated and agreed as though he had no such fears. So began the president's predominance in foreign relations.

The Court was established with the most meager language of any branch. To begin with, nothing was said about its duties or the numbers of its members; then there were to be "such inferior courts as the Congress may from time to time ordain and establish"; and, worst of all, in all cases except those "affecting ambassadors, other public ministers and those in which a State shall be a party," the Court was given appellate jurisdiction limited by these words: "with such exceptions, and under such regulations, as the Congress shall make." This meant, plainly enough, that the legislature, by majority vote, could reverse the Court's judgments and even make further ones impossible by removing them from judicial reach.

For both the presidency and the judiciary, there always loomed in the background the provision that "all bills for raising revenue" must originate in the House of Representatives. This distinctly did not say that all *appropriations* must originate there, but it was quickly assumed by members that the power to appropriate was included in the power to tax. It became a custom fiercely defended even against fellow legislators in the Senate, and of course the other branches were completely dependent on funds voted by the House. In all their most treasured plans, they had to undergo the suspicious scrutiny of committees in the House. The difficulty with this was that representatives were much more devoted to district or state interests than to national ones, and this made them hostile to federal plans.

This preference for expenditures on local projects originated in another principle of the Constitution—that members from many districts, coming together and bargaining, would in the end arrive at a result favorable to the national interest. This was a variation of the additive theory then prevalent in economics. Adam Smith's famous theorem will be recalled; the butcher, the baker, and the candlestickmaker, he said, each following his own interest, must end by furthering the interest of all. It was natural, perhaps, that this should be transferred to politics.

Holism, the opposite of fractionalized enterprise, was represented by the eighteenth-century monopolies granted and protected by kings and emperors. The colonists had had enough of *them*. At any rate the whole nation was given no constitutional center as the American structure was being put together—except, of course, that the president was chosen by the entire electorate and was removed from local affiliations.

The exclusive taxing power of the representatives would not have had such serious consequences if it had not at once been escalated into detailed examination of proposed expenditures, and if these had not so easily become interferences with administration. Appropriating in detail furnished the opportunity to suggest employees for spending the funds proposed to be appropriated. Before long the departments were largely staffed by bureaucrats who owed their jobs to congressional sponsors rather than to their official supervisors, and whose tenure was secure as long as their patron remained in office. The sponsor saw to it that authorizations for the jobs he had caused to be filled were not altered.

It remains to speak of the judiciary in this same connection. The real shocker was produced by Chief Justice Marshall in 1803.[3] This decision was such a bold assertion of expansive judicial powers as to constitute an all but complete abandonment of the restraint depended on by the framers in writing the Constitution. It amounted to a defiance of both president and Congress. The chief justice was obviously more intent on asserting the paramountcy of judicial power than in keeping to any governing principle, and the effect *within* the central government was to be felt from then on. When Jefferson, for reasons of his own, failed to challenge the Court, the precedent stood.

Marshall, along with his fellow Federalists, had been losing popularity for some years, and the new party of Democratic-Republicans had won the election of 1800. This was largely Jefferson's doing; he was a remarkable political organizer, and he was now the president. He intended to diminish national powers in favor of the states; and within the federal government he meant to make the legislative branch stronger. The nation, if Jefferson had his way, would soon be returned to the old arrangement of the 1770s and 1780s. It was what the states' righters at the Convention had meant to do. What they had lost there in 1787 they would win by replacing the Federalists with their own partisans. After eight years of Washington and four of John Adams, whose centralizing tendencies Jefferson repudiated, the government would be "returned to the people."

Marshall had been appointed by John Adams as one of his last acts in office, and this made the Court the only remaining branch controlled by the Federalists. Marshall meant to make it a stronghold, but to do this he must assert its power to reject acts of the Democratic-Republican legislature as unconstitutional. The document itself had not conferred any such power; but, said Marshall, it must have been inferred; how else could the Court decide cases in accordance with the Constitution? How else could

3. *Marbury* v. *Madison*, 1 Cr. 137 (1803).

the Constitution be "the supreme law of the land"? Actually Marshall put it this way: If the Court should be asked to approve a statute it believed contrary to the Constitution it "must either decide that case conformable to the law, disregarding the Constitution, or conformable to the Constitution, disregarding the law"; it must determine which of these conflicting rules governs the case. This, he said, was "of the very essence of judicial duty."

What the framers had actually said was probably meant in another way. The words were: "The Judical power shall extend *to all cases*, in law and equity arising under this Constitution. . . ." This could more easily have been thought to be a protection from other courts—those of the states—than from the other branches of the federal government. The so-called supremacy clause, saying that the Constitution of the United States, its laws, and its treaties were "the supreme law of the land," did not confer further powers on the judiciary. The implied powers invented by Marshall rested alone on the stated power to try all cases arising under the Constitution.

This was an inference, but an enormous one; still Marshall cited it, asking whether the Court was forbidden to look into the Constitution when a case arose under it. He also noted that judges took an oath to support the Constitution and concluded that it would be immoral to compel their violation of a document they had sworn to support.

The unmentioned difficulty with this was that legislators and presidents were also sworn to uphold the Constitution. With the same reasoning the president might well refuse to enforce what he regarded as an unconstitutional law or even to recognize the Court's interpretation if it differed from his own. In fact, at a later time, Jackson said precisely this, denying that only the Court could say what the Constitution meant.

There is still controversy about this. But although no other acts of the Congress were rejected by the Court until the Missouri Compromise was voided by the Dred Scott decision in 1857, between that time and 1964 seventy-two were held to be unconstitutional, the climax coming in 1935 and 1936 when a reactionary majority handed down twelve such decisions.[4]

Then again during the later period of the Warren Court when the justices took to "legislating" it was repeatedly in difficulties over the supremacy issue. Of this Pritchett remarked that "the institution of judicial review emerged unscathed"; but "it should be obvious that the exercise of such powers would not have been tolerated in a democratic government unless it had been wielded with a reasonable measure of judicial restraint. . . ." About this it must be said that the justices interpreted the term "reasonable" so freely that on several occasions they barely escaped congressional action

4. C. Herman Pritchett, *The American Constitution*, 2d ed., rev. (New York: McGraw-Hill, 1968), p. 165; a fairly full discussion.

limiting their jurisdiction. Actually, they were extremely bold in asserting their powers—quite as bold as either of the other branches had ever been. Their recognition of a duty to be restrained in the interest of constitutional integrity was far less than the framers must have counted on.

The reasoning from so brief and vague a statement as that in the Constitution to the assumption that the Court might tell the other branches what they might and might not do did rest on an extremely insecure foundation; and the judicial assertion of such a power constituted a refusal to acknowledge the essential principle of restraint. Judicial extensions were tempered to what the justices considered acceptable at the moment, but this was no more than expediency.

The struggle for dominance in the continual contest for supremacy that had begun in Washington's time became, with interludes, recurrently more intense as time passed.

Restraint is, indeed, a subtle and undefinable virtue, essentially dependent on willingness to respect it without further advantage than the traditional reward of virtue or, to put it another way, the reward for honoring an understood principle of the basic law. Since men, in their private or their official lives, so often refuse this respect, and do behave in such ways as will further their own ambitions regardless of damage to the general good, protections against their refusal have been devised. Some of these are merely reminders of duty, calculated to encourage self-discipline; civil relations have always been dependent on schooling of this kind furnished by family, church, and all other social institutions. Obviously the framers thought these fundamental. They also thought them sufficient.

A good citizen, it was assumed, should participate in politics at least to the extent of becoming informed on public issues and using the vote intelligently. According to the theory taken at its full meaning, this, taught from childhood and reinforced by tradition, would make a self-regulating citizenry. Everyone should be able to presume that his own decent respect for the rules would be matched by his fellow citizens' similar respect. If such recognition of mutual duties had been as successful as the framers seem to have anticipated, Americans would have had a peaceable society and could have got along with the minimal legal directives. True, some checks, soon to be further examined, were taken by the framers—but not many. The assumption, as can now be seen, was much too heavily depended on. But why, in defiance of all experience, should it continue to be depended on?

That the reliance has failed and instead has become a source of weakness is all too apparent. The departure is not measurable, and the part of it attributable to the weakness of educational and other efforts at inculcation of respect for it is not measurable either; but the failure is an important source of divisiveness and, for long periods, has been the cause of active and damaging hostility.

It may be premature, however, to conclude that the principle is unworkable and that all hope that it can be relied on at all must be given up. Disillusion is certainly widespread, but this may not be because latent virtues and loyalties have been extinguished but rather because they do not find practical uses. Perhaps the system has been allowed to become obsolete and is no longer an expression of the common will or even that of a majority, but—more likely—it has fallen into the control of those who count on others' virtues yet consider themselves exempt.

Both these unfortunate developments seem, in fact, to have happened. As to the double standard of public morality so evident now, it emerged in full sight of everyone and has been allowed to proliferate as though in itself it had some admirable quality. Citizens are naturally tolerant of their politicians, even of their own representatives. They expect them to contrive, to bargain, and to shape their behavior in ways advantageous to themselves. Everyone knows that capitals swarm with lobbyists and public relations practitioners whose business it is to contrive favorable deals for their clients. Everyone knows that behind façades of virtue the principals in government, especially legislators, favor financial supporters. It is this that has turned "establishment" into a recognized term of opprobrium.

As to obsolescence, the nation seems to have locked itself into a system resistant, almost impervious, to changes in the basic law. This seems to have been done in pursuit of the very virtue it has in the end thwarted. When loyalty to institutions is insisted on, it is too often loyalty not to their purpose but to an embodiment of the purpose—a branch, a department, an agency. The government is meant to be representative, but the House of Representatives comes nowhere near living up to its name. In the nearly two hundred years since its first meeting, it has not made one concession of any importance to those who have insisted on its ineffectiveness and the need for reform. Its members are still elected from districts and still have two-year terms; it still is controlled by committeemen with no qualification other than seniority, still has only the feeblest ethical requirements, and still makes automatic objection to presidential proposals but finds it difficult to generate any of its own.

The young are asked by their elders to respect such institutions, not only federal but state and local as well; when they find respect impossible, their responses are essentially virtuous. They want something very different. If they do not speak of reconstruction in the sophisticated language of those who have studied government and have some ideas about what must be done to recapture the loyalty it once commanded, it may be because they consider the present institutions not likely to be useful in any reasonable assessment of the future and with any reforms that seem probable. Perhaps they are right. It is a suspicion that this is so that most annoys their elders, even those who understand their disillusions.

It is less easy to sympathize with such critics because they offer so few suggestions for the effective conduct of a high-energy system with more than 200 million members. Somehow it must find appropriate agencies for its operation. It is too late for reversion to a fractionalized society, far too late.

The framers erred in relying so heavily on self-restraint to keep the branches within acceptable bounds. Each had reasons for expansion—good reasons, incumbents could argue—but when the expansion of one invaded the assumed prerogatives of others, clashes were inevitable. There did in fact result among them the kind of struggle that tended to make each lose sight of the public interest and concentrate on its own prestige.

The worst offender, because of its inflated assumption of more authentic representativeness, was of course the Congress. Contributing to this general assumption was the arrangement for election from districts for the House of Representatives and from states for the Senate. If any part of the legislature had been elected at large it might have generated an interest, at least among those particular members, in the country as a whole; but no such arrangement was made. Especially the House had such short terms that a member was barely seated in Washington when the next election demanded attention. He had to claim, almost at once, that he had extracted some benefits from Washington for the people back home. Each member was tempted to set up a kind of service organization for his constituents. His staff attended to these demands; he himself worked for projects favored by his supporters, and measures of interest to the nation were considered only as they might affect his chances for reelection—that is, if they resulted in something for his locality or were much favored by his supporters.

Legislators were, in other words, placed in a curious situation by the Constitution. They were expected to legislate nationally and to use restraint in relations with other branches, but they were given no incentive for doing so, and many for not doing so.

Disregard of the Rule

Looking back, Americans can have no very good reason for thinking that the framers' reliance on self-restraint has been justified. At the least it must be said that the dependence has prevented many serious national issues from reaching settlement. Moreover, there is reason to believe that the lessons have been obstinately resisted. They do not prove that such reliance is impossible, but they do indicate that the limits of its practical governance are narrower than the framers anticipated.

Diminishing compliance has caused each branch to arm itself with legions of soldiers—who, in the military, would be classified as regulars, guerrillas, and special forces. They are to be found everywhere in Washington as they are in state capitals and in the neighborhood of city halls. The Washington troops are best known because they are so thoroughly reported on by correspondents. As a result there is little secrecy about what goes on, and what is not known is shrewdly inferred by experienced watchers. This tends to make aggressors somewhat more cautious. Nevertheless the continuing dissension has sinister effects for a working democracy.

Lobbying has become something more than the representation of legitimate interests. Those who may be affected in one way or another, by legislation or by administrative actions, are entitled to push their own views; but there now exists an overwhelming force of professionals, most not even pretending to have any interests except those of their clients. Because they have such generous funds at their disposal and can promise congressmen such real help in forthcoming political contests, politicians are tempted to accept their offers of alliance; worse, they become advocates—for pay of one kind or another, not of money, of course, but pay nonetheless.

It does not make matters much better to argue that they are only responding to demands coming to them from their home districts or states. For one thing, except in issues that do not matter, these constituents' interests, so often spoken of, are not those of a majority, and certainly not those of the poor and the disadvantaged whose need is greatest. For another, it is inconceivable that the trading between representatives or senators from Nebraska or Maine with others from Illinois or California can result in anything of advantage to the nation as a whole. It may have been so in the late eighteenth century when the country was small and districts and states had little to expect from the capital, when there were no vast private enterprises subject to regulation, and when there were no extensive public works and no governmental services except a primitive postal system.

A nation of 3 million along one seaboard has needs very different from one of more than 200 million occupying most of a continent; but the containing framework has not changed, the rules are the same, and the trading follows the same pattern. Specifically, the Constitution still assumes that restraint will be relied on; individuals and corporations pursuing their own interests will not go beyond unstated but understood limits. The body politic is, so to speak, assumed to be present in everyone's mind. Neither society nor government really rests any longer—if it ever did—on that assumption; but the Constitution, except for civil liberties, still does not recognize any change. Notably there is no mention of duties owed by each to others; and duties are the specifics of restraint. At an earlier time it may have been enough if people left each other alone and if government did not interfere; but in modern circumstances, being left alone and not being interfered with can mean neglect and hardship for the poor and, for the more fortunate, permission to carry on exploitative activities.

It did not much matter if Washington found the Congress hostile to his suggestions, if it insisted on determining his administrative organization, or if its members traded among themselves for the few perquisites, projects, and jobs available. There were no legislative staffs to contrive clever moves; legislators lived modestly, and since they were most of the time at home, they really represented the majority who asked of government only that it be invisible and silent unless the nation was threatened in some way.

All this changed as congressional constituencies grew, and it became easier for growing enterprises to influence government. As staffs proliferated, and legislative sessions became longer—finally continuous—nothing, literally nothing, was done to protect the general interest so rapidly being lost in the massive transformation. Since legislators stayed in office by "doing something" for their districts or states, if they did more for some than for others, those favored were generous with financial support. Well over a hundred years after the immense industrial expansion during the Civil War, what the historian Brooks Adams called "the degradation of the democratic dogma" was still going on. The process was often enough described. Nevertheless it caused no considerable indignation, and certainly no reform. Representation turned from reality into myth, and the Capitol became a cockpit of maneuvers, quarrels, and bargainings. These came to be accepted as an inevitable part of a continuous political contest. That the government of a great continental power should be continually at the mercy of those in pursuit of their own private interests made self-restraint inoperable.

The results occasionally made their appearance in crises of one sort or another, and at such times something of national importance was done. The Great Depression was such a time; and Social Security was an acknowledgment of the need disclosed by its hardships. This was a confused acknowledgment, proceeding not from reconsideration of men's relations to each other and the changed role of government but from fear of political punishment. Not one word of the Constitution was changed, and not one was added to guide economic relations. Of course, the expansion of industry went on anyway quite outside the reach of basic law. The rule was that anything not forbidden could be done. Since there were few forbiddings, and those mostly directed at government, the Constitution lost more and more of its relevance to what was taking place. During the regime of the Warren Court there were generous extensions of civil liberties—that is, forbidding governments to invade rights—but there were few economic or social directives. The era succeeding the depression was a bonanza for big business, and its managers made the most of their widening opportunities.

One original provision did serve to modify the political situation. Since the president was elected by all the people, he *was* a symbol of the whole. This, however, was not enough. He became the source and the advocate of most new legislation, but he still could not get much done, since he had to deal with legislators who had no reason for interest in his measures and who resented their loss of respect and their inability either to generate initiatives or to get credit for anything of importance. Besides, by now their connections with the most conservative of their constituents were fixed. These, generally speaking, simply preferred that nothing be done, and so the Congress became more and more obstructive.

If democracy must depend on decency among its citizens and its organizations, apparently it cannot be left simply to voluntary compliance with unwritten rules. It is not enough, it seems, to make professions; performance may very well not follow. It is necessary to say that if democracy is to survive, then this and this and this must be done, and this and this and this must not be done.

The framers, however, did not proceed on any such assumption. It was their conviction that if government was prevented from doing injustices, constricting rights, and imposing hardships, it would follow that free men, in their dealings with one another, would take care of all the rest. They would conduct their relations fairly because each would check those with whom he dealt. They would even care for one another, should care be needed. Can it be imagined, at the utmost stretch, that Washington's or Jefferson's government would have provided a social insurance system or have considered the establishment of agencies for the regulation of businesses? It was enough then if government did not somehow contrive oppressive taxes and regulations, as they considered colonial governments to have done. It would have been found especially offensive if government had impressed citizens for armed service. They would volunteer if they regarded the cause as just and the threat to the nation serious; but if they became impatient or if there were crops to be harvested, they would simply go home. In any case, they agreed to serve for no more than a few months.

The Civil War, half a century later, was a crisis of attitudes and necessities. It was a long time coming on, but when it broke out it generated measures no one would have believed possible until then. For the preservation of the Union, men were drafted; but it was only when volunteers proved not to be sufficient, and, it will be remembered, there were serious riots among the draftees. Also, it was provided that anyone with $300 could buy a substitute. He could then get on with his business—which, during the war, was very profitable.

A terrible trauma, however, did result from the determination of the South to separate itself and to go its own way. Southern politicians, counting on a fictive righteousness and a belief that the North would not really organize for suppression, carried the crisis to the ultimate confrontation. A series of permissive presidents—"Northern men with southern views" —had for some time taken them into their cabinets. Traitorous speeches were made in the Congress, and there were defections to the rebels. During the preparatory years restraint was trusted far beyond its capacity. It was taken advantage of, and it became necessary to resort to compulsion. The lesson was that restraint has to be recognized by both sides of a controversy or conflict results; but it was not a lesson well learned—for instance, it was not carried over into labor-management arrangements until many horrendous episodes had been experienced.

In the years of industrialization that followed, compulsion was used so reluctantly on employers that, looking back, one can see that it was regarded always as an exception to a rule. The rule was that everyone did as he pleased and was constrained only when he pushed his interests beyond tolerance, as the southerners had done in 1860. The community had to be outraged enough to compel the decent behavior necessary to getting along together. Even then it was done reluctantly, and the measures used were temporary.

In the sporadic wars between employers and employees in the years when the factory system was growing, no serious conciliatory or disciplinary measures were taken until the 1930s. Self-restraint was very little respected, and finally the situation became intolerable and rules had to be imposed confining and civilizing disputes.

Still, in spite of so many instances proving its fallibility in large matters and small, voluntarism was not given up as a principle of association. It could not be. To have abandoned it would have been to admit that the alternative—conflict, or the threat of it—was to be relied on. It became a principle with exceptions. Industrialism operated in such ways as to make it seem sometimes no longer useful at all. Employers and employees in the factory system each took all the advantages possible, each trying to weaken the other and coming, frequently, to open battle in strikes and lockouts. The same was nearly as true of farmers and the processors of their crops. The industrial giants, because of their influence on government, were successful for decades in setting limits to employees' behavior. They were repressed if they struck, and jailed if they used force. The courts enjoined them, and federal marshals enforced the injunctions. The flaw was that there were more employees than employers, and since employees could vote, they finally brought enough pressure on politicians to overcome the influence of their employers. Then there came collective bargaining and a system of rules for the conduct of both combatants, but it was after more than seventy-five years of reliance on self-restraint that was growing progressively weaker.

Somewhat the same thing happened when farmers were exploited. They too finally overcame the advantage of the processors to whom they sold their crops and established the principle of parity. Their returns for effort were thereafter to be kept at a norm, but this was not made law until fifty years after they first began to protest—sometimes violently. The Populist movement finally engendered a farm bloc in the Congress with cohesion enough to exert legislative power, but again it was not until the 1930s that it succeeded in imposing the Agricultural Adjustment Administration as a continuing way of ensuring fair treatment.

Great schisms like these do, at times, grow intolerable. Restraint breaks down, conflict results, and limits have to be recognized. Machinery for conciliation is invented; standards are imposed.

What was found impossible as a reliance anywhere else in society without rules, equally enforced, continued to be relied on to govern the relations among the branches of government. It was embedded in the Constitution.

Extensions of Power Become Precedents

When the framers constructed a barely outlined framework whose filling in could be done only after experience with the operations it controlled, they must have supposed that following generations would have the sense to make these additions explicit by revision as they became necessary. If they did not suppose this, they were much less practical than there is reason to believe from their other arrangements. Their dependence on voluntary restraint was far from total. There were, for instance, the "checks and balances."

The framers thought of these as automatic. Any aggression would trigger its own opposition. A president who, in the opinion of the legislature, went too far would soon run out of funds and find that more were hard to get. In the most important matter of all—war—only the Congress could give permission by making a formal declaration. Although he could "make treaties . . . and appoint ambassadors, other public ministers and consuls, judges of the Supreme Court, and all other officers of the United States," treaties made by the president could be made final, and his ambassadorial appointments confirmed, only if the Senate agreed. Moreover, there is a curious limiting provision in the Constitution as to appointments; the "all other officers" phrase continues with the following: ". . . whose appointments are not herein otherwise provided for, and which shall be established by law. But the Congress may by law vest the appointment of such inferior officers, as they think proper, in the president alone, in the courts of law, or in the heads of departments."[5]

A literal reading of these limits to executive freedom horrifies present-day students of public administration. The Congress apparently could take away from the president all power of appointment and vest it in his supposed subordinates, and if that should happen his authority to manage affairs would simply vanish. Occasionally, still, some legislator rereads this passage and does offer an amendment to an appropriation bill, or a rider to other

5. Article II, section 2.2.

legislation providing for some such directive. A department head with considerable support, say a secretary of agriculture, may be specified to appoint the administrator of a new agency within his department. This did actually happen in the instance of the Agricultural Adjustment Administration, and it has happened in other later instances. The understanding, usually, is that the appointee will be suggested by the legislator who initiated the amendment, thus confirming a liaison ruinous to executive control. The president might as well not exist.

Actually, the president does most of the upper-echelon appointing, and it has become customary not to refuse confirmation of his cabinet appointments. Federal judgeships other than Supreme Court justices, however, are, by custom, patronage for senators. Presidents who ignore their suggestions find themselves opposed thereafter in more important matters. They seldom do. The Supreme Court is an exception. Very often appointments are scrutinized at length. Hearings are held, the appointee's credentials are questioned, and his attitudes are often more important than his competence. Control of the Court's majority, especially since it has transformed itself into a legislating body, has become a contentious matter.

The Court might be supposed, from the language of the Constitution, to have the least opportunity of any branch for extending its reach. The first sentence of Article II establishing the judicial branch says that there shall be one Supreme Court, but it says nothing at all about the number of its members or their qualifications. These are obviously at the discretion of other branches, since the president nominates, and the Senate confirms. There might be any number of justices, and they might have the most various qualifications; they need not even be lawyers, to say nothing of having had judicial experience.

A little later there is the provision that the Court shall have appellate jurisdiction "in all cases arising under the Constitution"; but then the document goes on to the strange reversal that says "with such exceptions, and under such regulations as the Congress shall make." Clearly the Court is at the mercy of the legislature in more respects than its membership. To make it more insecure, there is its annual need for funds whose only source is the Congress.

It is the more remarkable that, without changing one word of the Constitution, or adding one word to it, the Court has been able to establish itself in a position of final dominance over the other branches. It can and does tell the president and the Congress how far their powers extend, and this has the effect of granting to itself the powers forbidden to others. According to its procedure, however, a case has to come before it after originating in a lower court, and has to be argued and then decided in camera—by a majority among the justices. At the end of this lengthy procedure the emergency may well have passed. Presidents have usually proceeded on the assumption that if the Court did object it would be too late to affect presidential action. More will be said about this in a later chapter.

As late as 1970 President Nixon admitted that he was looking for a "strict constructionist" to fill a vacancy on the Court. This locution obviously did not mean what it had meant in the years when states' rights were the center of controversy. The South had then been contending that the states were sovereign and the federal government had only those powers explicitly granted to it. Strict construction was presumably repudiated by the Union victory. What President Nixon meant was something different. He wanted the Court to accept literally the words of the Constitution concerning the Bill of Rights. The Warren Court, he felt, had read meanings into its provisions not at all intended by the framers. Criminals were being overprotected, school desegregation was going too rapidly, and somehow the Court had made the "equal protection" of the Fourteenth Amendment, intended to protect the freed slaves, mean "one man, one vote." There were other citizens, not at all in sympathy with harsher treatment of accused criminals and very much in favor of integration, who felt that these were matters to be decided politically and not judicially. The justices were thought to have stretched the Constitution's meaning far beyond its most elastic limits. The ends sought might more legitimately have been reached by legislation or, if necessary, by amendment. The Court was not a proper legislative body or authorized to amend. Liberals approved the Warren Court's behavior; but if justices could be found who would read the Constitution strictly, that would not matter.

Latterly, as any reader of contemporary comment must be well aware, neither the Congress nor the Court had been generally regarded by the public as a serious enlarger of granted powers. It was the president who was given, or who had taken upon himself, most of the responsibilities created by the country's growing size and complexity; and especially he had moved to meet emergencies of all sorts with whatever means were needed. And presidential respect for restraint had seemed to grow less and less as crises followed one another. Each successful extension had been regarded as precedent, so that each new meeting of an emergency was less inhibited than the last.

It is not so important to ask whether the president has been a worse offender than the Congress or the Court as to note that all have regarded the custom of restraint as something to be ignored unless there would almost certainly be formidable objection. It would be useless to deny, however, that presidential offenses have been more conspicuous as well as more numerous. Recent examples are too well known to require more than mention, beginning, say, with several of F. D. Roosevelt's actions when the Second World War was in prospect but when resistance to American involvement was strong and the Congress was reluctant. When Roosevelt took defensive measures he judged the Congress would not authorize, he obviously relied on the "political doctrine" expounded by such justices as Brandeis and Holmes, especially, to keep the Court from interfering. At that time the doctrine seemed to be respected.

Later Courts, although many of the justices were appointed by Roosevelt, would not have been so compliant. They decided many issues their predecessors would have avoided. The test seemed to be whether the causes were ones they happened to approve. Formerly the president might have had trouble with the legislators but not with the justices.

As presidents extended their reach there were growing complaints, but for a time there was no really serious opposition. The Congress, because of its lawmaking and appropriating powers, did watch closely everything the president did. It was meant to do this, but in foreign policy, especially, it seemed helpless. As in so much else, however, the real situation could not be deduced from a literal reading. The Congress was often intimidated. Concerning this, and quoting John Marshall when he was a member of the Congress, Professor Pritchett has pointed out how often the Court, as well as the Congress, recognizes presidential primacy.[6]

The Congress either granted or acquiesced in the use of powers it would have objected to if used in domestic matters. Although the Constitution says so little, it does make the president the only official contact with other nations. It directs him to appoint American representatives abroad, and he must conduct negotiations if he is to "make treaties." Allowing him to decide whether other governments should be recognized or whether their diplomats should be accredited was not a considerable stretch.

The Congress was not consulted when Roosevelt negotiated an exchange of envoys with the Soviet Union in 1933, after a period of nonrecognition extending back to the Revolution of 1917. The appointment of an ambassador of course required consent, and it was given with reluctance on the part of some senators who nevertheless felt it impossible to reject the president's arrangement. This was an illustration of the presidential use of prestige with the public to induce senatorial compliance. Similarly, the long refusal to recognize Communist China was a decision repeated by presidents from Truman to Johnson, and Nixon's reversal was a purely presidential initiative.

Perhaps the furthest extension of presidential power, without consultation, is represented by Eisenhower's landing of marines in Lebanon and Johnson's intervention in Santo Domingo; but it is not necessary to look far back to find precedent for these in numerous interventions of a similar sort. They were mostly in Caribbean and Central American countries, and had the cover of the Monroe Doctrine; but the actual invasions were mostly

6. Pritchett, *op. cit.*, pp. 356–57.

undertaken by presidents without authorization or, sometimes, even consultation.

These are extensions of power in dealings with other governments; but as Pritchett points out, the disposal and use of armed forces has always been regarded by the Court as a presidential privilege. Tyler used both army and navy to protect Texas when the treaty of annexation was pending, and many other incidents followed—such as, for instance, Theodore Roosevelt's "taking" of Panama and Wilson's interventions in Mexico. Even though Congress was given the power to "declare" war, presidents, as commanders in chief, have made it practically impossible to withhold declarations. In fact the only formal declarations in modern times have been after war was an obvious fact, as, for instance, after Pearl Harbor had been attacked.

Another notable extension of presidential powers has been in making agreements with other nations without asking ratification of the Senate. These have taken the place, many times, of treaties requiring Senate concurrence and obviously were resorted to for this reason.

On the whole, it is the president, who can most credibly be accused of ignoring restraint. That there is always the excuse of emergent public interest is not really a reason for having allowed the habit to grow until it enormously enlarged the office itself. Still, nothing happens, or does not happen, for which the president can be excused from carrying the responsibility. This was not the framers' intention, and it has created a dilemma that only reconsideration of the Constitution itself can relieve. If it does become apparent that presidents no longer recognize self-restraint as a virtue applicable to their office, and will go as far as public tolerance will permit, then only a change in the basic law can act as an effective check. Even that, as we shall see, is not consonant with democratic procedure. Each member of such a society, and especially its officials, is assumed to recognize the restraints imposed on him by his membership.

The unwillingness of government officials to exercise self-restraints has found its furthest expression in the attempt of each to limit or undermine the ability of the others to oppose: the president by appointing compliant justices and by effective lobbying for his proposals, the Congress by filling the bureaucracy with favored appointees, and the Court by presuming to tell both what they may and may not do.

Court Violations of the Rule

One way of approaching this issue is to ask what the situation would be if self-restraint should no longer be depended on at all and enforced restraint should be the rule. It can be seen at once that as a constitutional principle enforced restraint would be impossible.

The Constitution and its supporting statutes would gradually become a mass of specific directives for behavior, allowing only a minimum freedom for individuals; the guidance of moral codes, customs, and the recognition of others' interests would no longer be depended on. If government officials and agencies had their duties specified in detail, initiative would be effectively smothered. Some nations (India, for instance) and some states (among them California) have constitutions of enormous length and specified detail. The logical development would entrust immense bureaucracies with making rules and immense police forces with trying to see them enforced.

Between these extremes there are all degrees of freedom. It is quite possible to think of some individuals and associations as being expected to behave well and some having to be confined within definite regulations; and there might well be special constriction for those most likely to exploit others. Buyers may be protected from sellers; those with disabilities may be sheltered from those who prey on them. Evidently a good deal of this will have to be done, but how much can be done without passing over into restrictive conditions is not a question easily answered.

Considering this question in relation to government, the first—and most important—need is to recast the directives of all three branches and to add perhaps two others: planning and regulatory. The one would exist to discover and define national intentions, the other to guide private enterprises in the indicated direction, meanwhile protecting individuals and the environment from careless or intended exploitation. Unless self-restraint has lost all its influence in people's affairs, clearer definition and self-government in enterprise should at least be tried.

It is not difficult to understand why the framers judged their checks and balances to be sufficient so far as government was concerned. Human nature was no different in the late eighteenth century than it became later, but the relations between people *were* different. Many problems grown insupportable since were not then visible. Most controversies were solved without legal intervention; at least it was not expected that such as there were would involve the federal government, although many might involve the states. At that time the federal government had no police powers, and no more than a half-dozen cases reached its Supreme Court during its first decade. There was an interval when there was no Court at all because no appropriation had been made, and it was not much missed. It was when population grew, communities became crowded, the demand for services increased, and public policies affected more citizens that the definition of duties of each branch became important. This too was when the expansion of each into new territory became notable.

The level of tolerance for dissenters could be high when they could reach only a small—and usually a neighborhood—audience. It is true that throughout the eighteenth century there were riotous mobs in New York, Philadelphia, and Boston whenever something displeased the local demagogues; and the upper classes, so well represented at the Convention, were very much afraid of them. There was undoubtedly more interest, among the predominant framers, in good order than in freedom for dissent. Those who might have insisted from the first on a bill of rights—for instance, Sam Adams, Henry, and Jefferson—were not present. However, it was seen by the Federalists that checks to authority were necessary. Their own interests might be affected if officials could act without legislative or judicial warrant. They were fairly satisfied with the compromises they had made between liberty and control—and doubtless discomfited by the further liberties they were forced to concede in the first ten amendments. These were appeasements. The ratifying conventions were more libertarian than the Convention's majority had been, and there was a demand that rights should be spelled out. The promise of these liberties was really a condition for ratification in several of the state conventions. All ten of the resulting amendments were limitations on government, not on individuals. They were specifications of areas in which self-restraint was considered to be enough, and government was forbidden to interfere.

The sparse population and self-sufficiency of rural communities during the eighteenth century account for more of the Constitution's characteristics than is sometimes recognized. Similarly, its obsolescence is largely accounted for by the growing population and large agglomeration of people, and this seems not to be recognized either. At least there have been no amendments to acknowledge the change. People might not have trusted one another more in the old circumstances, but the betrayals of trust were less serious and were held in check by the immediacy of neighbors' disapproval and by informal punishments. These controls of aggression were well understood, and they operated satisfactorily. If goodness did not suffice, the certainty of communal displeasure did.

Criminal law, enforced by an ever-increasing body of officials, grew in correlation, during the following decades, with population increases and urban concentrations. As self-restraint failed, compulsion had to be substituted for it. The criminal law still assumed that those accused were innocent until proved guilty, but the increasing number of the unruly would have to be apprehended and taught that they must behave as they were expected to do. There were more rules and more punishments for breaking them. The displeasure of neighbors no longer held offenders in check. The police and the courts had to take over.

Precisely this same theory can be seen in the Constitution—applied to institutions, of course, not to individuals. But the president would be a person; so would legislators be persons; and judges, as individuals, would be even more respectful of custom and civilized expectations. So officials representing the branches were not expected by the framers to be in continual contests. Justice Brandeis was never more mistaken than when he said that the framers had expected intergovernmental frictions. What they expected was that officials would understand their situations and conduct themselves with respect for the situation of others. A different condition, arising from unforeseen historical developments, put the check-and-balance mechanism to severe tests, so severe as to hamper governmental operations. The conflicts among the branches, regarded so benignly by Brandeis, have turned out to be a very poor way of establishing the limits of power.

It was assumed that the president, in executing the laws, would not unduly expand his powers; the legislators would not interfere with administration; and the Court would adjudicate cases coming before it without any expectation that either president or legislators would exceed their powers and so make it necessary to say that they had gone further than the Constitution allowed.

It has to be recognized that this expectation began to be disappointed almost at once. The aggressions of each branch, resulting in friction and often in open disputes, became more numerous and more difficult to resolve. New situations, requiring more of the president, making more temptations for the legislators, and opening vistas of power for the justices, ought to have resulted in reconsideration of the excessive reliance on self-restraint. It has been said, and may be repeated, that harsh and confining rules for the branches would violate the spirit of a pluralistic and democratic system. They need not go that far for officials any more than for individuals. A nice rejudgment to find a compromise between demanding reality and a desirable principle will not be easy. It is, however, insisted that if it is not undertaken the nation is all too likely to find itself resorting more and more to administrative restriction, and might finally lose its traditional character.

Like the expansion of laws against violations of unspoken custom, the Constitution ought to have expanded in this direction with the weakening of voluntary restraints. The president, the Congress, and the Court ought to have agreed on a more precise definition of their powers to accord with the changes in their duties and responsibilities.

Instead, it being left to ordeals of strength, a bitter and continuous struggle to control newly appearing services has resulted and threatens the principle of voluntarism.

The framers, as is well enough known, were not democratic; but they lived in a society where relations were well understood and were respected. Soon changes everywhere would destroy this understanding and erode respect for custom. The framers did not anticipate this. They made amendment so difficult that constitutional growth simply did not occur. Still, something had to happen, and what did happen was that the Court became the adjuster. It assumed to tell the Congress when it had exceeded its warrant;

similarly, it undertook to restrict presidential powers. In attempting to mediate, it extended its own powers to inadmissible limits.

This part of the Court's activity was an even more curious violation of the Rule of Self-restraint than the violations by the other branches, because it could not have felt forced by circumstances to interfere. The president had to take action in emergencies sometimes so critical that the life of the nation was involved; the congressional aggressions came from the understandable demands of their situation; but the Court's invasion of the other branches' territories was purely political—a reach for power.

There is simply no way in latter-day society of making realistic the whole range of self-restraints relied on by the framers. They have not been, and will not be, respected. They will have to be modified, a process that, like the growth of law to meet new violations, still can leave much to the recognition by each of what it can decently do; but they must mark out new limits, set new standards, and say, particularly, what the new code requires of each.

Diminishing Voluntary Restraint

More than this will be necessary. It is clear that the degeneration of voluntary restraint has been caused not only by changing outside circumstances—more dangerous emergencies, new needs of people, and the like—but also by the nature of the institutions established in the Constitution. Neither executive nor legislature was fitted for resisting the urge to expand; each was indeed made belligerent by its nature and its situation. The Court was in position to take advantage of these excesses, and when it was called on to interfere it could further its own more subtle program of dominance.

This does not mean that the principle of separated and interdependent powers was a mistaken one. It was, on the contrary, essential to a system intending to leave all possible to voluntarism; and, so far as it is still practical, voluntarism still ought to be relied on for the same reason. There have been certain influences making for moderation in the aggressiveness of all the branches. They have not entirely overcome their strong impulses to dominate; but many instances of self-restraint can be cited to indicate further possibilities. Let us speak of them.

Very few presidents have undertaken emergency measures without previous consultation with the Congress or, at least, with congressional leaders. Jefferson did send naval forces to contend with the Barbary pirates, but he got congressional support for further operations against their bases. Polk certainly provoked, even started, the Mexican war but presently asked for a declaration. Wilson, sending expeditions to Mexico, was most high-handed of all, acting, as he felt, for undisputed moral reasons; but Truman, intervening in Korea, had the legitimacy of a U.N. Security

Council resolution—the Russians having made this possible by absenting themselves some months earlier, and there being a treaty giving the Council peacekeeping powers.

F. D. Roosevelt, preparing for war but speaking of "defense," got from the Congress something called a Declaration of Limited Emergency, later expanded to Unlimited Emergency. Under this authority he proceeded to actions just short of belligerency. No provision of the Constitution grants the Congress this power; it was a recognition that it ought not to be left out entirely when fateful decisions are being made; but the declaration was completely extraconstitutional.

Johnson, escalating the Vietnam involvement, asked for and got the so-called Tonkin Gulf Resolution from the Senate, supporting his intervention. At best, this was a doubtful warrant for warlike acts; but it did involve the Congress, to its later embarrassment, in attacks on North Vietnam. The resolution was a broad one and was subsequently used beyond any intention the nearly unanimous Senate could have had. The feebleness of Johnson's claim to consent for what followed in subsequent years was an indication of presidential belief that in the modern world of nuclear jeopardy congressional consent for the use of armed force had become a mere formality. Nevertheless, it was a recognition that presidential power is still a conditional one. It can be diminished by popular resistance, and can even vanish in electoral defeat. It can be kept only by majority approval.

It was clear that this was so when President Nixon ordered the invasion of Cambodia to protect the American flanks in South Vietnam. He asked no one, he informed no one in advance, and afterward he acknowledged no duty to have done so. He was mistaken, and very hastily, and at great pains, he made his case with the Congress and the public. Only by putting a date on ending the invasion was he saved from the same situation Johnson had found untenable.

These are examples of emergency action, of course, and they affect only one area of presidential behavior. Civilian, or nonemergency, expansions have been far less arbitrary and more restrained, although still important. For instance the president's responsibility, now generally accepted, for the health of the national economy is something quite recent. Every depression before that of 1928 and later was simply allowed to run its course. It is true that Republicans since McKinley had been claiming credit for prosperity and blaming hard times on profligate Democrats; also the Democrats had cure-alls such as cheap money and regulation of monopolists; but measures such as those taken by F. D. Roosevelt in 1933, especially the sequestration of gold, would have been inconceivable. When Roosevelt asked for what seemed horrific appropriations to be used for relief and public works, he demanded lump sums to be parceled out under his direction with practically no directives. The Congress was frightened and granted his demand, but, again, it had afterthoughts and within a short time was reasserting its restrictive powers—even beyond their normal limits. Several New Deal agencies established by executive order were refused funds and in this way forced to liquidate.

To use another example, the regulatory agencies, added to under F. D. Roosevelt's prodding, were and are presumably independent; but their policies are notably affected by presidential preferences. Presidents appoint their members; but commissioners' terms are fixed, and the Court has said that the president cannot remove them. Nevertheless, Johnson called them together at his accession and advised them to be reasonably decent to the industries they supervised. This was strange coming from a Democrat, and one with Populist antecedents at that, and it did not originate in any general consultation among his party leaders. The agencies were already accused of being too kind to the businesses they were supposed to control, and might have expected to have been rebuked for that; but Johnson had his own reasons, and he meant to enlist businessmen in his causes—not to irritate them. His dictum opened years of collaboration that lost him much of the liberal support he normally would have had. It was a personal initiative, a presidential expansion. He had no justification for giving the agencies advice of any sort; but he could, and he did.

This particular expansion, like many others, was bound to happen. The regulatory agencies had no constitutional legitimacy. Presidents with new responsibilities for the economy felt that they could not allow each agency to behave in a maverick pattern with no relation to the whole. It was, in nature, much like the president's position as chief legislator. He had, by Roosevelt's time, become not only the suggester of legislation but also very nearly its only originator. Very few laws of any importance came from any other source. In rapidly changing circumstances, successive administrations were judged more by their legislative accomplishments than by anything else; and periods were identified with presidents, not with his colleagues or with the legislators.

There are, we see, many and sufficient reasons for the abandonment of presidential restraint in emergencies and for its erosion in everyday circumstances. It has not happened because presidents wanted to be dictatorial; it has happened because they were expected to do things they could not do unless they possessed the means. In such crises, however, it becomes easy to grasp too much, and easy to hang on too long. It is usually at later stages of liquidating emergencies that annoyed legislators suddenly discover the invasion of their prerogatives, and justices decide that presidents have exceeded their warrants.

As has been noted, conciliatory gestures are made if there is time and not too much opposition, but consent of this kind is no more constitutionally warranted than the president's original action. Johnson's Tonkin Resolution was not a legitimate substitute for a declaration of war; it was merely an acceptance, by the senators who agreed to it, of a presidential initiative they considered necessary for meeting an emergency. It was a weak measure of restraint, but not a really serious one. Johnson would have gone ahead without it, but it seemed to involve the legislature in his subsequent actions —in the public view, at least.

In this instance full advantage was taken of one of those temporary attacks of xenophobia to which the Congress is so susceptible. American ships had been fired on. This was intolerable. The presumptuous attackers must be taught a lesson. Contrast this, however, with the feeble response somewhat later to the seizure of the *Pueblo* by North Koreans, an outrage to naval traditions that might well have resulted in a violent recapture effort. By that time, however, Johnson had exhausted his credit with the Congress and the public. His inaction was accepted with no outburst of indignation. He must have felt that if he had taken extreme measures he would have risked more determined opposition to the now unpopular involvement in Asia. It was the first time an American ship had been captured at sea without reaction. The ship was never returned. Such humiliations are not easily forgiven a politician.

Congressional violations of the Rule of Self-restraint are less spectacular than those presidents almost invariably have resorted to in emergencies; and they are not motivated in the same way. The Congress is never "saving the country"; it is merely preventing the expansion of power by a dictator in the White House. Only a few times in American history has the Congress frankly sought to assume executive powers, the most notorious being the attempt to interfere in the management of the Civil War and the following Reconstruction. It even sought the impeachment of President Andrew Johnson for resisting its determined vengefulness.

More often the Congress merely opposes and hampers the executive by attaching conditions to legislation, something easy to do anonymously in private bargaining. A favorite method is specific instructions about organization for administration—where agencies shall operate and what appointments shall be made. Also, the period of funding is often limited, forcing the administrators to return frequently for renewed authorization. Then it will be found that if members have not been consulted about patronage and other details of management, renewal will be very difficult.

It is in the course of these negotiations, given the respectable name of compromise, that corruption creeps in. Special interests likely to be touched by threatening legislation take full advantage of their rich opportunities. In return for contributions to campaign funds and other assistance in maintaining a local organization, congressmen, who must soon run for reelection, get amendments, special exemptions, and a watering down of provisions they find objectionable. It is not unusual for bills submitted by the president to be amended a hundred or more times as legislators bargain, trade, and maneuver for changes demanded by their supporters. Inquiry has often disclosed that legislation is actually written by lobbyists, and either is substituted for bills submitted by the administration or is added by amendment. In a count during the late 1960s one law firm in Washington listed itself as representing twenty clients, most of them with very large interests likely to be affected in some way by legislation. Among their many associates were some of the most skillful draftsmen in Washington. This has become a system, but it all happens in offices and committee rooms—never in public. It limits the subsequent administrators of the laws, relegates the public interest to a place lower than that occupied by private interests, and so passes congressional powers to those who have no recognition in the Constitution.

A variation of this process, more convenient for both private interests and congressmen, is the provision of ownership interest in enterprises likely to be regulated. Some forty members of Congress were counted in 1970 who owned stock in financial institutions subject to public control. A dozen of these were members of committees in which legislation was processed. Any citizen or any association of citizens has the right to be heard, but do they have the right to legislate or to control the legislative process?

This subtle subversion is a constant trial to the executive branch; but that branch has no constitutional warrant for legislating, or even for influencing legislation beyond advising the Congress of what is needed. For this the president can rely only on the passage in the Constitution that says that "he shall from time to time give to the Congress information of the state of the union and recommend to their consideration such measures as he shall judge necessary and expedient." "Recommend" does not mean to draft, to insist, or to bargain for; nevertheless this has become one of those areas in which struggles crucial to the public interest go on with no rules, with no chance of open debate, and with the president at a disadvantage.

The reach of each branch for the power to make laws is constant and never settled for more than the instance being fought over. To counter lobbyists, the administration, offering legislation, often asks for more than it expects to get, then compromises or develops supporters of its own among members who have been given favors in other bargains or are promised ones in the future. One of the most unlovely characteristics of the legislative process, when it comes to light (as it often does), is the way consent is secured. The public interest, efficiency in operation, effectiveness for the stated purpose—such considerations are quite lost in the contest between lobbyists for the government and those representing interests with something to gain or lose.

When the Court is considered in this context it is all too apparent that it often ignores the need for restraint. It justifies this by invoking a kind of inverted logic. It rebukes the other branches for grasping what it is reaching for itself. By confining the other branches within its own conception of their powers, the Court necessarily seizes for itself the power of definition. It can do this because it finally interprets the brief and ambiguous directives of the Constitution. The last word must be said at some time about the meaning of meager constitutional passages written long ago, but when interpretation is persistently so difficult that justices cannot agree, the matter ought to be resolved by amendment.

The Court offends in another way equally doubtful when it says what the Congress meant in passing legislation. This is not interpreting the Constitution as it claims the right to do. It is legislating by doing the Congress's business.

There have been many justices who have been properly reluctant to invade what one of them defined as "political thickets," meaning public affairs subject to electoral decision. In this view, if the other branches exceeded their powers the voters would soon rebuke them; they would not be returned to office. Holmes was one justice who insisted that the Court should grant the legislature's right to experiment with solutions to democracy's problems. He, however, was usually in a minority. That he turned out to have been of later majority views only underscores the likelihood of judicial fallibility.

We see that the branches have all assumed powers they can claim only by extensions or inferences, sometimes extreme, of the Constitution's spare directives. The resulting conflicts are costly. It is no novel conclusion that amendments, necessary to escape obsolescence, were made so difficult as to be impossible in serious matters. Amendment was exclusively entrusted to the legislative branch, and that branch has the most interest in preventing modernization. As has been suggested, this must have been on the theory that the legislature is uniquely representative, and this in turn must have followed from the colonial experience with royal governors.

If this is so, the theory ought long since to have been abandoned and a different amending process adopted. To amend the amending clause is, however, one of the most difficult of all changes. It opens all other clauses to reconsideration, and this is what is most feared by the presently untouchable Congress. It will have to be undertaken, it would seem, in a general revision.

"Admirable Brevity" and the Rule

A Rule of Self-restraint must have been the result of what is often called—by those who by now ought to know better—"the admirable brevity of the Constitution." It is easy to be brief, and safe enough too, if there are well-understood areas that need not be defined. The British are brief to the point of extinction. The brevity of the framers was not a virtue so much as simple recognition that in a society with common ancestry and accepted morals not everything need be specified. Also, the delegates must have been tired of compromising as they were forced to do so often. Finding a middle way is a wearying process at best, and in a Philadelphia summer it must have caused unbearable irritation.

Lincoln is reported to have replied to a question about the proper length for a man's legs by saying that they ought to be long enough to reach the ground. Asked about the Constitution, any serious student would have to say that it no longer reaches the ground the citizen must stand on. It leaves him suspended in air, swaying and swinging, perhaps colliding with others. As for government, it provides uncertain and constantly more irrelevant directives.

When this is said, however, it must be added at once that the distinction between constitutional and statute law does need to be carefully observed, the Constitution defining principles, the statutes providing for operations as required. As to this it can be asserted categorically that the only way to preserve this distinction is to lengthen the legs until they do reach the ground; that is, to enlarge the Constitution until it gives adequate directives for statutemaking in an immensely enlarged and more complex society. It ought not only to be enlarged but also to provide for further enlargement from time to time. It can still, however, be distinct from statute law.

To state principles briefly is not enough when their reach and application is not obvious. When objectives have to be conjured up out of the mists of history they may well be one thing to one interpreter and another thing to others. We know how often this has happened—even among Supreme Court Justices.

A useful metaphor in speaking of the limit of powers might be to speak of their frontiers. Any American will understand the confusion prevalent in an unknown and empty country just being occupied. There will be rivalry to possess certain of the more valuable areas, and settled conditions will be slow to arrive. There will be ad hoc governments, and only careless formulation of rules, enforced, often, by vigilantes.

The struggle to occupy the no man's land of governmental powers left by the framers has gone on for the better part of two centuries. It is long past time for its possessors to award titles and organize against invaders. It is time for civilized institutions to be established and for their activities to be regularized. Adventurous forays into unoccupied territory and the use of force to displace inconvenient homesteaders are frontier occurrences, not those of settled territories.

In such a civilized condition what is necessary among governmental agencies is quite like what has been found necessary in private relationships

—each may proceed freely until objection is made by another whose rights or liberties are threatened. Usually the knowledge that these limits exist— that others have similar rights—is still enough. Asked to define this situation, almost any citizen would say that an individual brought up decently and taught the rules of living in society will, as a matter of course, respect others' rights; but he would add "not always"; and for those who do not, there must be legal limits. This is indeed so. The limits have been worked out over many years of experience with violators, and they continue to be elaborated as conditions change.

This becomes a complicated matter in an industrialized society, as contrasted with the sparsely populated and rural one of the eighteenth century. But even giant corporations, powerful as they are, must often be reminded that others' rights are to be respected; also, that they have a duty to the public as well as to stockholders.

This is not so in government. The same principle is depended on, but there have never been any imposed limits on the powers of the branches, no progressive adaptation to conditions. Their behavior remains as anomalous and indefinite as it was when the Constitution's words were first written. The branches are independent. The president may expand his powers until checked by objections from Congress or Court, and then only for one instance. He is quite free to try again. So with the Congress. As for the Court, its air of finality protects it from any but the most massive outbursts of indignation, and it is left to test the climate carefully for possible resistances.

Officials representing the branches all seem to have a similar attitude about this, a quite different one than they have as citizens. They recognize no limits. They engage in the most outrageous maneuvers to outwit the others and consider themselves virtuous for having gone beyond what was before allowable.

There is a strange similarity in this with the contrasting morals exhibited by men in their different capacities. The most honorable and upright of men in their capacity as representatives of their countries will lie, deceive, and commit almost any other offense and think themselves virtuous in proportion to their successes. So it is, it often seems, with representatives of the branches. They will resort to means they would be horrified to be charged with as individuals.

It is quite obviously necessary to recast the constitutional provisions limiting each of the branches; but it is still better to state only principles in such a document, together with such directives and standards—and there are some even in the overly brief document of 1787—that can be made relevant to latter-day conditions rather than those of the beginning republic.

For the Congress some very simple ones would be helpful if not sufficient, such as, for instance, saying that appropriation acts may not include administrative directions, that the budget may be revised only by whole titles instead of line by line (thus removing the old abuse of arranging detail to accommodate political supporters), and that the Congress may not vest appointive powers in subordinates to the chief executive (as it may now do).

For the president, having in mind the necessity for action in emergency, the consent of a special standing committee of the upper house on national security could be required to give consent to any drastic action he believes ought to be taken. Emergencies defined—as they have never been—might be anticipated and the limits set for executive action.

Again, if the president may not check the emotional propensities of legislators responding to public hysteria, and if he may not deal promptly, and sometimes secretly, with emergencies, the country may very well find itself in danger. The Court, too, must be able to dispense justice without interference from those who have other ends to serve. It must be the guardian of the Constitution as long as it stands unamended and must be able to reject invasion of the system it establishes.

Told firmly and in sufficient—but not in elaborated—detail what is and what is not expectable, the representatives of each branch would be supplied with the directives they now lack. They would not have the support of those strange alien morals that permit the commission of outrages in the name of official duty.

When one branch goes so far as to usurp the powers of another, the occasion is clearly one for constitutional definition. Self-restraint has failed. Nevertheless, to the extent possible, it is better to rely on it. This is because the borders are necessarily ill-defined and are always changing. To set limits at all would make it likely that further limits would be devised and that they would become strict and permanent. This would make government so constricted that obstructionism would be a common condition and adaptation to changes in society would be even more difficult than it is now.

For instance, consider legislation. There is constant temptation for regulatory agencies to enlarge the limited powers entrusted to them when statutes are passed. Most laws assume that a mass of rules will be formulated by administrators. It is also assumed, however, that the regulations will be intended to make the laws effective, not to change them. When administrators exceed their powers and add to them or subtract from them, adequate congressional supervision is often impossible; and until some flagrant excess is brought to light, nothing is done.

The situation is often even more complicated than this. Since regulations are extensions of statutes and are drawn up by the agencies entrusted with administration, the separation-of-powers principle is compromised. The law, except in broad outline, is written by the executive branch. Simply by the growth and complexity of the society being controlled by law, the Congress has indeed lost much of its ability to deal with it, and has consigned the duty to the executive.

Is it necessary to conclude from this that the separation principle has become obsolete? Demarcations have certainly become more difficult to define, but it also has become more dangerous to define them in any such permanent way as would be involved in constitutional change. It is much better to rely on a principle of self-restraint, even if refusals to recognize its canons are hard to punish. If violations are serious they may be checked, even if the checking is late and perhaps costly.

On the other hand, the separation principle can be defined and the limits stated more clearly than they were in the Constitution of 1787, and the restraints expected of each branch can be better understood.

PART
TWO

THE STRUCTURE

CHAPTER 7

THE ELECTORAL PROCESS

The Illegitimate Party System

The government of the Federal Union was to be a Republic committed to majority rule, and yet no scheme for the selection of representatives (executive and legislative), or the development of policies for the guidance of officials, was included in the Constitution. Since no means for the conveyance of the voters' preferences to lawmakers or administrators was provided, the representatives soon became less representative of national interests than of local ones.

Like some other arrangements, those for the selection of officials seem to have been omitted because they were not thought to require definition. The federal establishment was to be outside the reach of partisans. Since the electorate was restricted to a small percentage (perhaps 5 or 10 percent) of white males over twenty-one, only responsible men, in considering mood, would make the laws; and others like them were to choose officials. Responsibility was equated with the ownership of property, and this eliminated many citizens. Gentlemen would agree; at least gentlemen of the same race, religion, and interests would. There was need to guard against the thrust of the unpropertied—and therefore irresponsible—masses, and one way was not to allow them the vote. These restrictions go some way to account for the framers' neglect to specify electoral procedures.

The formation of opinions, and expressions about them, together with elections, constituted an important part of practical politics in 1787, as later. There were already many traditional devices and methods in use for these purposes, and they were known in all the states. Some had evolved through the centuries until they seemed to *be* republican government. This was true of majority rule and of representation; it was also true of districted constituencies and, as has been noted in a former chapter, of separated and balanced powers. There was no thought, anywhere, of universal suffrage; and majorities and minorities were both made up of propertied gentlemen.

It does seem strange now that no arrangements for political discussion, or for election, were thought necessary for the new Union. The gathering of the electorate into parties, and decisions among them in contested elections, going on so energetically in the states, already had the characteristics of later politicking; but it was evidently expected that they could be confined there and would not be projected into the federal system.

The unreality of such an assumption might have been anticipated. Ambitions already reached beyond localities and states. People of like mind were anxious to control the central government for various purposes, and the adoption of national policies immediately caused dissension. Already there were regional divisions about matters consigned to federal oversight. The conclusion that these would be properly considered by locally oriented representatives was always an untenable one.

For a century or more small farmers had had a quarrel with southern planters and even inland pioneers, and merchants in the seaports had had their own ideas about tariffs and other commercial arrangements. These and other differences obviously had to be settled nationally. From the beginning of Washington's administration they had partisan supporters; and even before that, conservatives and radicals had been carrying on oratorical and pamphleteering campaigns quite unrestrained in language about national policies. The conservatives were much of a mind with the Loyalists who had gone into exile; they considered the radicals levelers who, if they were allowed to vote, would fill governmental posts with incompetent and perhaps radical individuals. As was indicated in *The Federalist*, this fear of common men had a decisive influence in the Convention. A republic but not a democracy; there was open admission that this had been the intention.

During the discussions in Philadelphia there had been voluble dissenters, and why the highly visible causes of future trouble were ignored and no means of conciliation provided, it is not easy to say; but perhaps the best guess is that the framers meant to exclude the questions not substantially agreed on by all Americans. Or it may be that the conservatives, prevailing, considered that their preponderance would be projected into the new regime. Their several devices for this purpose may have been considered sufficient for the purpose.

What is certain is that from the very first the arrangements for confining "faction" (as it was spoken of in *The Federalist*) to the states were futile. Washington, endeavoring to keep the presidency above controversy, was distressed and finally dismayed to find himself the head of a party as well as of the nation, and to find that he had an active and even vituperative opposition. His dignity, vain as he was of it, was not nearly so precious to him as the office he was trying to create; it was a deep disappointment that it should have been so assaulted. He did not succeed in protecting it. It has to be said also that no subsequent president has been more successful in resolving the dilemma of his dual role as party head before election and national representative immediately afterward—especially since he must again think of his party's fortunes every two years, and this is not to mention his own continuance in office, if he so desires.

When is a president the paramount representative of all the people, and when is he head of his party? True, he has a formal presidential writ, but how legitimate is it when not much more than half the voters have consented? How can he pretend to represent the whole when so many citizens did not favor him and do not approve of the policies he has said he would try to effectuate? The chaffings and carpings can be very serious at times, and in a general sense they may be significant; but the Republic would not have survived if they had very often been so deeply felt as to cause vital cleavages. Only once have national divisions been fatally irreconcilable, with a powerful minority determined to rebel openly and by force against the decision of the majority. The Civil War was an agonizing lesson in one essential of democracy.

The agreement to accept agreed policies, even when majorities are thin, has ever since been recognized as a condition of union among a sufficient number so that it has been an important element in continued civil life. Some national elections have been very close indeed, with the victors having less than 1 percent more votes than the losers. And no recent election has resulted in a majority of more than 64 percent.[1] The losers, since the expansion of the electorate and the increases in population, have numbered many millions, enough, if they had refused acceptance, to rebel with some reason for believing that they might prevent the winners' induction. But it has not happened. The calmest weeks known to the United States are often those just following a national campaign. The losers do not pretend to be satisfied; they grumble and view with alarm; but they do bow to the decision of the electorate and make what adjustments they must.

This acceptance, grown customary, is the stranger because of the new majority's equivocal position. The president-elect has been its leader, but now he must act for the whole electorate—including the minority. He cannot very well abandon those upon whose votes he was lifted to his position—especially since he will depend on them to support his legislative program. The winners, it will be expected, will jubilantly take over all positions of power (if the party has been out of office), create a new establishment, and exclude members of the losing party. There will be dismissals. They will include, in theory, all policymaking officials, along

1. This was in 1960; in 1964 it was 62 percent. F. D. Roosevelt's majorities never reached 60 percent.

with those other agency heads within the president's appointive prerogative. Even the Supreme Court will change as the justices come to the end of their service. This seems to deny that a new president's concern is for all the people.

Happily, the changeovers do not happen quite that way. An illustration of the actual process is furnished by one of the most deplored evacuations in recent history—the one following the election of Eisenhower in 1952, following twenty years of Democratic incumbency. There was much criticism at the time, but actual displacements in the upper levels of government were later calculated at about 10 percent, not very different from some earlier transitions. The Jacksonians, most notorious of all incoming administrations for ruthless displacements, removed in the first year, for partisan reasons, not more than 9 percent, and in their first term not more than 20 percent. Those were times when it was still credible that anyone could fill any office, and it was the period when the locution "spoils system" came into use. But its actual effects then and afterward were exaggerated. Losers can be querulous and can command sympathy even when their personal troubles do not much affect the system.

Party differences in recent decades have tended to become blurred. Certain large policies have become common, even those fiercely fought over at an earlier time. Examples are well enough known. The sporadic battles between workers and employers amounting to small civil wars over wages and working conditions, lasting until the 1920s, soon disappeared as issues likely to erupt in this way. The income tax and comprehensive social security ceased to be causes of controversy. The Populist uprising that brought Bryan three party nominations faded away; during the same Cleveland-McKinley-Bryan era there were not only rancorous rural protests but also other furiously contested issues having to do with the protective tariff and the soundness of the dollar; both were meliorated by time and common sense. There were campaigns in those days too that turned on the question of national expansion. Politicians in Communist countries still find it useful to denounce American imperialists, but no candidate for generations has actually advocated the acquisition of further territory. The "dollar diplomacy" of prewar days is sometimes exhumed reproachfully by minorities, and there are some economic penetrations of other countries, but even these are modified by aid to poorer peoples.

So old differences disappear, and new ones with similar divisive potentialities arise less frequently. The national parties tend to compete with each other mostly in claims of competence to do the same things—attend to national security, seek peace, and enhance the well-being of all. These involve no more than differences in method or degree. An illustration of this is furnished by the controversy during the Johnson administration about the Vietnam involvement. The president's opponents, seeking to oppose increasing commitments for Vietnam, had to contend with Johnson's profession of reluctance and his much-publicized offers to enter into negotiations. No one, he insisted, was more anxious for peace than he. The debate turned on the narrow issue of his earnestness and sincerity in seeking opportunities for negotiation, or for accepting ones others believed to have been offered. He seldom spoke of the issue without reiterating his desire for disengagement. What he obviously sought to do was to usurp the consensus for peace while still pursuing his method of attaining it. He was not successful, but this was more because the operations were unsuccessful than because the objectives were questioned.

Another relevant fact is that many of the government's expanded operations are highly technical and those who conduct them necessary to their success. For the most part even the heads of agencies having to do with welfare, education, the development of power resources, space exploration, and the like are apolitical. Their work is not much affected by changes in party control. The expansion of their agencies or their conduct may be questioned, but politicians who try to criticize or defend them are soon lost in complexities they do not understand and can find very little profit in declaiming about to the electorate.

The divisive issue of states' rights and the expansion of federal power still lingers in many minds. The support for stricter construction comes largely from bureaucracies in the states determined to keep control of education, welfare programs, police powers, and the like. Their incompetence is, however, a source of all too obvious weakness; their pleas have not been convincing, especially in national electoral contests. Time and circumstances have attenuated the venomous hostility of partisans even on this issue. And no party is willing to be marked as dogmatic about it; there has, indeed, been something of a reversal. At the time of the Civil War, and for years afterward, the Republicans found it profitable to contend that Democrats had been, and probably still were, secessionists and not to be trusted. The fact is, however, that Republicans have for a long time been more critical than Democrats of federal expansion and the erosion of state autonomy. It was they who raised the issue of revenue sharing, for instance, the ultimate commitment to stronger states and weaker federal government.

This issue seems inextricably involved with that of free or regulated enterprise. Republican interest in states' rights originates in the demand of supporters for easier regulations than are imposed by federal regulatory agencies. Differences between the parties, however, have attenuated and, like so many others, have become ones between extreme wings of both. The Democrats have always claimed to favor *small* business and accused Republicans of favoring *big* business, but this is not at all the same as differing about hostility or friendliness to business in general. Public ownership has very nearly dropped out of the interparty dialogue, although clearly the technological situation has made it more and more feasible, especially for public utilities. These were once designated as objects for expropriation by the Democrats, but that was when the party had a heavily Populist membership. This too, along with states' rights, has diminished as an appealing issue. The nation has settled into acceptance of a pluralistic economy conducted largely by private corporations and dominated by giants among them. True, the tightness of regulation is often in question, but it too, although sometimes a party issue, is not a satisfactorily differentiated one. Neither party has succeeded in keeping the regulators from favoring the regulated.

So the parties lose distinctiveness. Still, something remains. There does tend to be a persistent, if not always obvious, difference in orientation. The Republicans have fallen into a pattern generally more acceptable to business, especially big business, protectionist and conservative about fiscal matters. They have been less inclined to support strict regulation, less generous about aid for the poor, less equalitarian; also, more xenophobic. Because it is their constituency, the Democrats have been more solicitous of small business and family firms; they have been more protective of the rights defined in the First Amendment; they have favored low tariffs and easy money; they have worried more about poverty and disadvantages; and have tended to be more responsive to local views, and less interested in national affairs. These differences, however, are often confused, complex, and misty; they are not always the same, or always visible; and often the parties seem temporarily to have reversed their positions.

The two-party system, having these rather uncertain general contrasting characteristics, can be traced far back, even to preconstitutional years. The Federalist and Democratic-Republican differentiation did not begin the well-known quarrel between Hamilton and Jefferson across Washington's table. They had been distinctive attitudes in Colonial America. The tendency toward the blurring of contrasts, however, has gone on for most of the time since the Constitution became effective except for periods of intensive support for one or another position, such as, for instance, the enlargement of the electorate in Jackson's time and the Populist campaign against the money power.

The administration of Monroe from 1816 to 1824 is often spoken of as an "era of good feeling." There then seemed to be agreement on nearly every issue. Even this era, however, was interrupted by controversies from time to time, and other placid periods have been similarly vulnerable to dissent; but a return to consensus has to be indentified as a persistent trait of American political life, perhaps its most notable one—until the serious divisions following Roosevelt's death.

It should not be forgotten, however, that there have always been parties other than the two large ones, made up of particularist advocates—

of abolition when slavery was an issue, of greenbackism when cheap money was widely demanded, of socialists and laborites from the 1890s on, of prohibitionists, and even of vegetarians. These, even when minuscule, have been extreme and vociferous. Some have appealed to a certain number of voters, but none has attracted enough votes to threaten the larger two. Only a few times have third parties really offered a challenge. These were times when the big two had very nearly lost all differentiation, when the Democrats had become almost as conservative as Republicans, or when Republicans, like their Federalist progenitors, had become more a sect than a party.

Three times, in 1912, in 1924, and in 1948, Progressives organized parties and affected elections. Each time their appeal was to those dissatisfied with the older parties' indifference to certain issues and their unwillingness to placate a considerable number of voters, but invariably the old parties, after an election or two, absorbed the new—being stirred to compromise by the loss of support. Even Republican inner circles were somewhat disturbed by these influences, but usually the Democrats were more responsive. Then, having won an election or two by accepting the program of the dissidents—yielding something to labor or to farmers— they were presently being accused by the Republicans of radicalism (successfully too), showing that they had, in the view of a majority, overly accommodated. They lost then to McKinley, Harding, Coolidge, or Eisenhower, and, after an interval, to Nixon.

Professional politicians, recognizing this persistent return to the center, are reluctant to accept innovation, or even sectional or ethnic demands for favor. They see more profit in not offending anyone than in satisfying the demands of a few. This, being inconsistent with appeals likely to make campaigns lively, is modified somewhat by candidates who, once they have captured the nomination, must make all those speeches and issue all those statements. But even candidates, taking professionals' advice, are reluctant to frighten or offend, and appealing issues are often lost in generalities. The other party is castigated, if it is already in power, as radical, corrupt, or inefficient. Only occasionally do genuine issues break through, find advocates or opponents, and affect an election. Presidents, entering an office, often owe debts but seldom have mandates.

It is true that several times there have been serious departures from consensus. Strict or loose construction, already an issue between Whigs and Democratic-Republicans, ran on into the states' rights controversy and came to climax in secession. In that conflict the Republicans claimed to be Loyalists and this made all Democrats dis-Unionists. This was a useful political ploy long after the war; indeed, the Grand Army of the Republic was identified with Republicanism until the last veteran died. Not until 1884 did the Democrats succeed in electing a president, but he won because the overly confident Republicans had sunk into the worst spell of corruption in American history, giving Cleveland, who was offered as a man of notable integrity, his chance. He overcame, but barely, his Democratic affiliation—made worse by his not being himself a veteran.

These issues, it will be noticed, did show a conservative-progressive difference between the two dominant parties; but neither held exaggerated attitudes for long and soon returned to a nearly neutral position, claiming only to be most staunchly in favor of popular positions. At the end of his career Cleveland was happy to see McKinley defeat Bryan, who had embraced the revolting idea that money need not be "sound." The Cleveland faction had lost control of the Democratic party through indifference to rising farmer and labor demands for attention to their needs. But they were quite satisfied with Parker, who succeeded Bryan as the Democratic choice. The professionals had taken the party back to the center.

This tendency of the two permanently dominant parties to return to the positions favored by most voters is thought by some observers to be responsible for a stability never possible when divisions are ideological and sharp. This is a favorite theme, for instance, of Walter Lippmann. Other nations are pointed to as being unhappily subject to chronic partisan battles and to rapid changes of government. In these countries belligerent legislators excoriate each other, form and re-form coalitions, and, when they temporarily gain power, dispatch leaders in quick succession. Theorists, ignoring these lessons, have nevertheless often advocated ideological groupings for the United States; and several minor parties have had such origins—Socialist or Communist, most notably, but at other times extreme rightist or leftist, under one or another label. But voters have quite steadily shown a preference for accommodating within their two largest parties the widest range of such differences with only slight conservative and progressive tinges. Even these cannot be distinguished in every campaign, although the din of combat may be clamorous. The center has, for politicians, an attraction that ideologists have been quite unable to overcome.

So it has to be accepted that in practice national politics has assumed a permanent two-party form, and that it is approved by the electorate. That it has no constitutional basis and only the barest legal acceptance cannot alter the fact of its existence. But this does not mean that constitutional recognition would be objectionable. There are, indeed, indefensible results from the extralegal activities of party organizations that would not be accepted in any rigorous assessment.

The Needed Changes

The government, it has been endlessly promised, will always be of, by, and for the people. If this promise has any reality, it implies general participation and can be tested by such a criterion. In this it comes off badly.

The framers, of course, had the more limited conception embodied in the Constitution. Not everyone was to participate in the symbolic act of voting; in fact only a few were, and so only those few would be represented by the government of the Union.

What differentiates the Constitution from the earlier Declaration is that the framers were making a government, and the signers had been making a rebellion. The sentiments of the equalitarians were good for enlisting patriots in a cause, but not, as the framers saw it, for the practical matter of governing. Besides, only the powers necessary to the common functions of a federation were conceded to the central government. Most affairs of immediate interest were left for the states to regulate, or not regulate, as they chose. They could arrange as they liked about the privileges of citizenship. They could even determine the conditions of voting for members of the federal Congress. The president of the United States was to be chosen in an even less democratic process.

Subsequent developments were of a kind obviously not anticipated by the more influential framers. In the terms we have used they would be Republicans. But elections, after the first three, would be won by what would now be called Democrats. The equalitarianism of the Declaration was returned to by Jefferson (who had reservations about the Constitution) and his successors, and it was deepened and extended by the Jacksonians. This period lasted until a Whig was elected in 1840 after the Federalists, who had made the Constitution, had disappeared. The Federalist Constitution was in fact less and less suited, as this democratizing went on, to the Americans' circumstances or ambitions. They intended to shape a nation of free and equal citizens, participating in government but not controlled by it except in the general affairs of interstate and foreign relations, and helped only in the most general sense—every man was to do what was necessary for himself and his dependents.

Thus, in spite of the Federalists' intentions, there were forty-four years of approximate equality and democracy in a growing country. It was a period, also, of gradual recognition that if elections were to continue and to provide a workable government, some considerable accommodations would have to be made. All voters would have to be educated, for instance, if participation was to result in wise choices both of officials and of policies. So there began the educational project that has taken more capital and effort than any single other ever undertaken by any people anywhere. It was not at first a government project. It began and grew as a local movement and was for a long time supported by the local and private resources alone. But it happened everywhere.

Concurrent changes in these years also gave the federal government an importance the Democrats deplored even while they were creating it. The states began to lose their hold on affairs of national scope. But as new powers were assumed by the federal government no changes were made that would extend democratic controls beyond the states. Participation in federal functions became more difficult as it became more necessary—if democracy was to remain a reality.

The evolution of representation has to be considered in this connection. There is a law or rule involved here: literal representation becomes less possible as constituencies grow larger. At some quite early stage it must pass over into delegation and cease to be representation except in a derivative sense. In local meetings policies can be determined; also, officials can be elected with the expectation that they will carry through the approved policies under the watchful oversight of their constituents. An official who departs from instructions will be replaced by a more promising candidate.

How many voters can be represented in this way? If the number fifty is suggested it is certainly large. If the number is larger than this the official can neither be instructed nor be held to performance. He must be allowed freedom of judgment; he is no longer representative in the original sense.

Other changes occur too as constituencies enlarge. A small assembly can argue until it reaches consensus or an approximation of it, reducing its minority to a few. A large one cannot do this. If it is very large, or if it covers an extensive area, it cannot even meet. What numbers are involved here are somewhat determined by facilities for meeting, as well as distance and the difficulty of movement; but under the best conditions, consensus will be more difficult to reach and minorities will be more numerous as constituencies enlarge in number and area.

However reluctant, voters will be compelled to allow elected officials increasing freedom. This changes the characteristics of suitability. What will be required will be not merely an automaton who will carry out instructions but an individual believed to be capable of representation in a higher sense. His appeal as a candidate may have elements of conformity to constituents' attitudes; as to usual and known beliefs, these may be marked, but he will have to be given latitude in many matters not yet much discussed, and even some that, because of obscurity or novelty, will never be understood.

It was because of the fear that democracy would cease to be effective in these circumstances that fixed terms were adopted by the framers. Representatives would be required to submit themselves for rejudgment at stated times, usually after short intervals in office: In this way they could be kept under fair control by the majority. For the Senate and for the president longer terms were allowed than for members of the lower house, the idea being that these were dealing with matters of more intimate interest.

It was still hoped that representation could be actual. But gradually another custom evolved and became important as a kind of substitute for direct instruction. This was an enlargement of delegation. It operated in conjunction with the device of majority rule. For majority rule to succeed, constituents have to agree that persons and policies wanted by more than half will be accepted by the less than half.[2] The minority has had its opportunity to argue and has not prevailed. If someone *has* to be chosen or if some decision *has* to be made, it has been agreed time out of mind that the larger number must be allowed to determine.

This, in American development, has been a rule accepted even in the most divisive circumstances. Giving way has become a national characteristic not understood or practiced where there is no commitment to democracy. The rule was not embedded in custom without hard lessons—and even the suppression of dissenters. There have been rebellious minorities, made up of those who believed themselves right in spite of having been outvoted and who have refused compliance. But the rule has become so obviously essential to governing that dissenters are few and, with differing degrees of consideration, have been willing to conform if not to consent.

There is the strange comment to be made about this that dissenters and withholders are generally those who would be expected to be most loyal because most committed to democracy. Such attitudes, they dislike to acknowledge, arise from a belief that their judgments ought to prevail over others, however heavily in the majority, because they are somehow worthier. Others are not only mistaken but ought not to prevail.

Disobedience of this sort is always a problem of democracy, and no clear rule determines how far it may be allowed to go in action. Individuals are expected to form opinions and to express them. Freedom of speech is a precious right. But at times when decisions must be made, and majorities make them, noncompliance or interference is in some way limited.

This is especially true when national security is involved. There is a difficulty here which is common to all times and places but is particularly troubling in a practicing democracy. Suppression is very easily abused. There have been incidents in our history, now regarded as regrettable, when conformity not only in deed but also in thought has been demanded by demagogues and supported by majorities. The conclusion about this has to be that latitude for dissent must be wide, and the smothering of minorities must be forbidden. There is no way to secure these necessities except by constitutional provision. It has been proved again and again that legislatures will be carried away by fear or fervor unless controlled by the firm rule of constitutionality.

Like representation, a general law governs disobedience; it is that it

2. Majorities may be any percentage over 50. The division at half is a practical arrangement with a long history; but even in the Constitution there are provisions requiring a two-thirds or three-quarters majority—as for senatorial confirmation of presidential appointees or for the initiation of constitutional amendments.

cannot be allowed to interfere with operations decided on by majorities. If it did, no operations could take place. Government, it is believed, cannot be paralyzed because an individual or a minority determines that it knows best and tries to force compliance with its will.

So considerable are the departures from democratic theory in large constituencies, and so difficult the problems of consent, that improved procedures for reaching decision in the modern state are desperately sought. What has happened, because these efforts have not been successful, has appalling aspects when they are looked at analytically. The federal government has a legislature whose members do not and cannot in any simplistic way represent their constituencies. This is true in spite of the members having been elected by majorities of those voting. Those majorities may consist of individuals who, in spite of the vast effort at education, have little knowledge of issues or acquaintance with the candidates, and who, if they did, would not be able to choose wisely among policies. Also many issues are bundled together, and there is too little provision for assembly and discussion. Appeals for votes are often specious, especially since the spread of television, and since campaigns are costly, hidden private interests are able to prevail over public ones. The candidate who is elected may have been more sold to his constituents than chosen by them as the theory requires. In no sense can it truly be said that the system is "working" as it was intended to work.

The degradation of the democratic idea inevitably results in the selection of officials and the adoption of policies for which the electorate feels little responsibility. Many of those who vote for a president and give his party a congressional majority feel quite free to repudiate the policies adopted along with those who were elected to make them. This at its furthest extreme involves active civil disobedience; there are all degrees of dissent short of that, ranging from mere expressions of disapproval to loudly voiced criticism.

A variation of this, owed to the device of the stated term, is the allegation that officials have departed from commitments made when they were candidates. What shall a disillusioned voter do in these real or fancied circumstances? He sometimes merely grumbles; but if he is much discommoded, or if he dissents violently, he may resort to demonstration or, in extreme cases, to the disruption of order.

This is a feature of political life that needs more study than it has had —not that suggestions for remedy have been lacking, but that none of those experimented with have proved adequate. Really drastic ones have not been tried; partly, at least, because of the inertia so characteristic of accepted practice. In several states referendum and recall have been tried. And some theorists have proposed that definite terms be abandoned for indefinite ones of the British sort on the assumption that government no longer trusted by the electorate ought to be replaced at once. Primaries, used in some states, are another way of engaging citizens in active participation and making more certain that they understand issues. These have not notably succeeded because they have been confined to states and, moreover, are in several states merely preferential rather than binding. National primaries, preceded by dialogue, might be more useful.

None of these is a cure for the alienation of minority groups or individuals whose real objection is to governance by majority rule. Consulting conscience or believing in the superiority of their own judgments, some citizens always feel justified in nonsupport, opposition, or even disobedience. Majority decision, however, does seem inseparable from democracy; allowance having been made for freedom of expression and full access to facilities for communication, the rule cannot be abandoned without accepting dictation by a minority.

There then remains the question of *what* minority. The framers' answer was that only property owners should be allowed to vote. They, it was thought, would have a stake in the national welfare of such importance that it would result in active attention to government. This was so serious a departure from democratic principle, and it answered so little the demands of the later widened electorate, that all such exclusive restrictions were soon abandoned. By the Jacksonian era privileges were opened to the poor along with the rich. Unfortunately this also comprehended the careless and ill-informed along with the concerned. Actually it created a residue of uninterested eligibles amounting to at least one-third of the whole.

This is the largest proportion of nonvoters in any professedly democratic country.[3] Efforts to engage their interest have amounted sometimes to campaigns. Getting out the vote has been regarded generally as a contribution to democracy; however, there have always been doubters about this who say that the addition to the electoral rolls of large numbers, who have little interest or knowledge can hardly improve the element of reason in choices.

A more frequently approved approach has been the suggestion of multiple votes. Ranging, say, from one to ten, those most likely to make informed and intelligent choices would count the most in making choices; and those with demonstrable disqualifications would count the least. This might not—probably would not—assure the consent to decisions of those citizens who insist on nonconformance if they happen not to be suited. But it would give them less assured ground for active disobedience. As things are, they can say that officials elected for a term have departed from promised performance. Very likely they may have, since many issues must

3. As will be noted, this is not wholly owed to disinterest. An unknown but growing percentage is ineligible because of residential and other restrictions imposed by law.

have taken on new color, or even newly appeared, since election. This could still be claimed if the device of stated terms were to be kept. Dissenters could still maintain that democracy had not had full recognition, since the principle of consent to policies had been violated. But they could not say that they had not had the weight appropriate to their concern and ability in making choices at election time.

The further recognition of participation as an essential of democracy would seem to involve much more elaborate provision, in an enlarged electorate, of facilities for discussion, of organization for the formulation of policies and the development of candidates for office. It would be a further recognition of the need for improvement if some sort of recognition in voting were awarded for proven political interest. Whether there should also be a recognition for probable wisdom as an elector is another question. It is one, however, with many advocates and deserves at least consideration and experiment.

Any serious study would, however, have to begin by asking what method is to be used in determining exclusion or voter rankings. It would be repugnant to the democratic principle if some were able to rank others merely on their own judgment. Consignment of such a duty to an unimpeachably detached body with only the national interest to serve would seem to be the only tenable answer.

The Decline of Participation

One clearly recognizable purpose found agreement in so many American minds and has continued through so many succeeding generations that it seems in retrospect to have transcended all difference and dissension. It has been true of all regions, of rich and poor, of farmer, worker, industrialist, and merchant. That purpose is the making of education universal. Participation in social, economic, and political affairs depends on it. Education would make everyone equal, and nothing else would keep them equal. Any educated individual could hope to succeed in business, or could rise from laborer to manager. He would also be equal to any other in the affairs of politics—deciding about policy and selecting officials to effectuate it. There might be differences about the issues of the year or the generation —states' rights, tariffs, monetary management, foreign relations, labor organization—but no one differs about the need to educate the young. Differences are mostly about the kind of education needed.

A farmer or small merchant, for economic reasons, could do with the celebrated three R's; however, clergymen first, then lawyers, and doctors, and later scientists and those devoted to the liberal arts became eligible to go much further. After something like a century, it became usual to think of high school for everyone. It was at about this point that the dream or purpose seemed to fail. Not everyone, it appeared, was, after all, equal. A considerable percentage was simply not capable of going beyond arithmetic to algebra, or beyond the Indiana poets to Robert Frost. Physics, chemistry, and biology could not be understood without preliminary mathematics, and a student who could not read would never know why Shakespeare was a genius.

It was also discovered that many young people were incapable of reading and understanding explanations of the policies proposed for national consideration. These were complex, and they required extensive knowledge of geography, history, and economic possibilities. Such young people would become eighteen and could then vote. But were they democrats in the equalitarian sense of the word?

The making of the democratic dream was certainly not the whole reason for the beginning and the persistent support of education. But it always had an equalitarian relevance. Free enterprise, it will be understood, was also democratic. The conception was individualistic; it relied on competition, on getting ahead in a system governed only by the ability of one individual to succeed above others. There was a philosophy about this; classical economics centered on the marketplace, where freely competing producers offered their goods and services to consumers. He who had the best product and the most reasonable price attracted the most customers. The others did not prosper. The rewards were a profit or a loss, and no sympathy was wasted on the loser.

The analogue of this in politics also depended on freedom of competition among equals who offered themselves for election, displayed their wares, and were chosen or not chosen. It was a rule of the system that he who attracted a majority got the position and with it both the power to dispose of the perquisites of office and the responsibility that went with it. If he performed well during a given term in the view of his constituents, he would be reelected; if not, he would be defeated and another would take his place.

But just as in economics the conditions for perfectly free enterprise never actually existed, so in politics all the conditions for free election never existed either. In economics the marketplace could be, and usually was, controlled in some way; some producers had advantages over others, perhaps even a monopoly or something approaching it; less often, a consumer might have a similar advantage. And there were ugly features about the struggle to lower costs, best one's competitors, and control the market. All these had eventually to be regulated in one or another way. So in politics; parties developed machines and bosses; bosses manipulated elections by distributing appointive offices, dispensing favors, and, often, by subverting election procedures.

Almost from the first in the United States, and at least from the time of

Jackson, the word "politics" had a connotation of foul competition. Anyone engaged in it was suspect. He was a low fellow, or if a respectable citizen become candidate, he must be subservient to the low fellows in the clubhouses and back rooms where the bosses and their helpers worked.

Periodic revolts against this system were as characteristic of American politics as were depressions in economic history. When the machines became too flagrantly corrupt a hero would appear, denounce the corrupters, and, using his charismatic appeal, gain enough votes to throw out the rascals and establish a new and honest regime. These reform convulsions were an expected feature of municipal and state governments. One of the most colorful periods of general revolt occurred just after the turn of the century and is generally known by the name given it by Theodore Roosevelt. The group of exposers—including Upton Sinclair, Lincoln Steffens, R. S. Baker, Ida Tarbell, Gustavus Myers, and a few others whose work was mostly published in S. S. McClure's magazine—produced a literature climaxed by several historically valuable books: Upton Sinclair's *The Jungle;* Steffens's *Shame of the Cities*, and later his *Autobiography*; Tarbell's *History of Standard Oil*; and Gustavus Myers's *History of the Great American Fortunes*. While the exposures were running their course they were repudiated by Theodore Roosevelt as "muckraking." Like the man in Bunyan's *Pilgrim's Progress,* Roosevelt said, they were so busy raking the muck off the floor that they could look no way but downward.

This reaction of Roosevelt, whose career was built on repeated offerings of alternatives to the persistent corruptions of political life, was quite typical. Unpleasant accompaniments of progress did exist; but there was, after all, the enormous credit of progress itself. Somehow the system worked out beneficially. Roosevelt did not go so far as to suggest that the accompaniments were indispensable to the benefits, but his many compromises with corruption have led later commentators to some such conclusion about his private views.

The muckraking outburst did show one thing all too clearly: economics and politics had become inseparable. The source of political corruption was clearly business. Merchants paid for municipal favors, bought state franchises, kept congressmen on secret retainers—numerous revolting ways of controlling government came to light. When it was necessary, elections could actually be bought through the political machines and their bosses. There was no doubt about all this; the exposures were complete; but there was no very strong public reaction. People seemed to accept it as usual, perhaps inevitable. In an earlier generation Cleveland had got a much more vigorous response to his denunciations of the system. He had risen from the mayoralty of Buffalo, where he had cleaned out a ring of boodlers, to the governorship of New York, where he had challenged and defeated Tammany's chieftains, and to the presidency. His rise on a tide of indignation had been unprecedented—from mayor to president in two years. And all simply because he was honest.

A generation later, however, corruption was again usual; there seemed to be a weary acceptance of political sins, as though they were part of free enterprise and democracy; if freedom was wanted, its accompanying corruption must be tolerated. Anyone in politics must be part of the dirty business that went on. This caused revulsion among respectable citizens. They kept away from it—except, of course, to pay the fees for protection demanded by the bosses. The most sedate and respectable merchants and financiers regarded this as a regular necessity. They preferred to think about it as little as possible; often they contributed to both parties or factions and hoped not to be harassed. If they needed favors or franchises their agents made deals for them. If there were qualms, these were not allowed to interfere with practical arrangements.

Later generations have from time to time reassessed the situation, asking what, in view of this cynical habit, had become of the equalitarian dream. Were we only mythically a free people, committed actually to accustomed corruption? Had the notion that education, a free press, and a vigorous dialogue would sustain free and incorruptible institutions been abandoned?

It seems curious indeed to say so, but while investment of effort and capital in educational facilities was being increased and the techniques of education were improving, uncertainty about why it was being done seemed to deepen. There was no longer the early simplicity of intention. Part of this was owed to an uneasy feeling that the transmission of knowledge from one generation to another was not enough; this may have been the most important cause; certainly as the requirements for participation in the affairs of industry and finance were raised, proportionally fewer and fewer were able to meet them. Equality was obviously no longer a recognizable fact. It was no longer a tenable aim either, as dropouts at every stage showed.

But part of the disillusionment was the perception of what was happening to the democratic dream. Equality was still assumed in certain ways. Every adult in his right mind could vote, and everyone was theoretically eligible for office. But to pretend that all were fit to vote, or that all were able to fill the immensely demanding posts of modern government, was hypocritical. It simply was not true. No one really believed these things anymore, but no one wanted to admit that so old a justification for democracy had disappeared. About the whole subject there was a kind of mass agreement not to think. And because no one could accept the fact, nothing was done about the new situation.

Should democratic government be abandoned? If so, what should take its place? Perhaps the answer was that it had already been given up. Why was it that only sixty percent or so of those eligible bothered to vote? The embarrassing fact was that a good many of them did not feel that it made any difference what was decided or who was chosen, and therefore they saw no use in participating. This was more true in the upper than in the lower reaches of political life. Matters having to do with local arrangements—property taxes, zoning, schools, and other facilities—were discussed with some passion, and decisions were made in fully contested elections. But about state officials and national ones there was an obstinate indifference. This might not be guessed by the furor that went on during campaigns, but it was indubitably registered in the statistics of participation.

An ever lessening number went to meetings, engaged in dialogue, or, when the time came, voted. This was a circumstance well calculated to allow small, well-financed, and determined groups to control nominations and win elections. Far-leftists lacked one of these characteristics: they were few enough and determined enough, but they could not match the resources of the extreme rightists. These, whose hold on the Republicans was more secure as campaigns became more expansive, were, again, so uniformly opposed to the welfare programs wanted by the majority that they could seldom muster enough votes to win—at least nationally. But by the sixties they had begun to win in some states, and soon they were compromising their principles.

This struggle between extremists to capture votes of the majority nearer the center went on mostly within the parties. When an extremist won a national nomination for the first time in 1964, he was defeated by an enormous margin. Extremists are resistant to lessons of this sort, but professionals are not. Time after time they have persuaded conventions to reject their preferred choices for moderates more likely to attract ordinary voters. This moving toward the center makes for dull campaigns and confines dialogue to issues of no considerable moment. It is, in fact, hardly a dialogue at all.

The relevance of this here is that the long-continued effort to educate everyone seemed to have had a disconcertingly reverse effect. The extremists on both flanks were the best-educated. They had views about policy and meant to see them adopted. It was almost equally disconcerting to see that these were the individuals who were least willing to accept the conditions of democratic existence. They were even disposed to ignore its most elementary rules. On the one side, police-state suppressions were acceptable; on the other, civil disobedience went to the length of disrupting debate and interfering with rights they professed to believe essential.

Certainly the educational effort of nearly two centuries had not produced a working democracy. The continued formal existence of democratic institutions in spite of the attacks from both extremes was owed to the least educated, who regarded both with skepticism. Measured by American professions, there was something very wrong about this. The life of reason in politics was simply not emerging from the schools and colleges, and it seemed least acceptable in the nation's graduate institutions and among the intellectuals.

Perhaps this was only seemingly so. Perhaps the decisions were growing harder and more strain was being put on minds not, after all, grounded in the necessity for tolerance, dialogue, and respect for majorities. Perhaps it was the extremists on whom the educational effort had least effect, and the immense center was, after all, better grounded in a tradition the others thought themselves not called on to respect. Americans, anyway, were not abandoning education. Larger and larger amounts of capital and effort were devoted to it. It was evident to any observer that the people no longer knew why, and no longer looked for the same results. Earlier there had been two clear reasons: (1) education would enable children to grow into competent competitors with one another, and (2) children would thus advance the economy and even the society. This had once made them understanding democrats, capable of operating a simple government that was satisfactory to free and equal citizens.

There was no longer the same trust in this support for, and constant renewal of, the traditional institutions of the Republic. People were appalled by their condition. Plenty, they had attained—or the possibility of it—but security, equality, tranquillity, loyalty, and even liberty seemed all the time to be in more jeopardy. Americans had many things; comparatively they were wealthy, but in a way they seemed to lose what traditionally they had worked and sacrificed to attain.

The Renewal of Dialogue

Is it necessary to accept this apparent failure as final? Or is it possible to think of a renewed educational effort that may emerge, as far as politics is concerned, in creative dialogue? It will be argued here that it is at least worth trying. This is not only because the alternative is so appalling but also because the possibilities are so apparent.

Changes will, indeed, have to be made, some of them unwelcome and costly. This is because the society is no longer small, contained, isolated, and simply organized, but on the contrary is immense, overflowing, and complex. It will be necessary to learn how to be pluralistic yet integrated. If this sounds paradoxical, it is because, stated baldly, it is. Yet both pluralism and integration are conditions we are committed to accept and go on with. It may be difficult, but it is not impossible if each is taken with modified and realistic meaning. And not the least of incentives for trying is that either pluralism or integration, taken alone, and literally, is a denial of the American intention—pluralism (laissez-faire) because it would be an application of old theory to new conditions, and integration because it would be an abandonment of democracy.

Our government is deeply and permanently involved not only in our security but also in our welfare. It has been pointed out repeatedly that the Constitution we live under was framed before these circumstances existed, and that no amendments have effected the changes indicated by the new conditions.

The renewal of genuine majority rule in decisionmaking and in the selection of policies would require:

1. That there be everywhere facilities for discussion of issues and choice of representatives, together with organized communication within parties.
2. That there be equality of opportunity in politics as well as economics.
3. That there be freedom for judgment among representatives, and that they should therefore be secure in office for their terms, but that they should be open to petition.
4. That elected federal officials should have constituencies more consistent with national responsibilities.

The first of these requirements would involve a suitable organization to administer the provision of meeting places for discussion and for conventions, as well as places of election.

The second would involve campaigns of limited length and with equal access to facilities for communications. It would also require that public funds be provided for the costs of campaigning, and that contributions from private sources should be prohibited.

The third would require suitable terms of office for representatives, and also provision for petition on questions arising during these stated terms.

The fourth would require a reorganization of districting and election procedures.

Such changes might make political activities matters of public rather than private responsibility. As things have been, the whole process has been outside the law—at least of federal law. Primaries exist in some states; but they have been more significant in some than in others—that is to say, some primaries are binding and some merely preferential, the real choice being left to state conventions. State conventions, even though they choose federal candidates, are not regulated uniformly and not at all by federal law.

In some states the formation of third parties is made practically impossible by fantastic requirements for registration or for putting candidates on the ballot. In other states, long dominated by one party, even the second minority party operates under severe handicaps imposed by state laws. Strangest of all is the continued existence, since the ratification of the Twelfth Amendment in 1804, of an electoral college whose choice of president and vice-president is governed wholly by custom. Its members are under no legal compulsion to respect the popular choice; and, in fact, have on occasion refused to respect it. This awkward device, intended to prevent rather than facilitate democratic decision, is an anachronism.[4]

The Fourteenth and Fifteenth Amendments (ratified in 1868 and 1870, respectively) together with the Nineteenth (ratified in 1920) have established the principle that all adult persons may vote, but these are short and inadequate directives to state lawmakers. What is needed is the assumption of responsibility by the federal government for the election of its officials and for the preparation of its policies.

These procedures ought not only to be established firmly but also to be administered by federal officials. Politics has become much more generally important as time has passed. It is often suggested that it can no longer be left to politicians. But this statement needs examination. If it is not to be a politicians' monopoly, to whom will its machinery be entrusted? The more important it is the more dangerous it would be if it were managed by amateurs or part-time practitioners. There is nothing inimical to democracy about professionalism in politics except that the institutions provided for it furnish unexampled opportunities for the seizure of power and the use of it in the service of private interests.

Since most of those who would displace the politicians if they were dispossessed without institutional reforms would come into control from those same private interests, it is hard to see how this would improve matters. It might be better to think of improving the profession, and indeed such improvement has begun. Entry into politics at local levels is no longer confined to otherwise unemployed ward heelers. The expansion of higher education has affected politics as well as other occupations. A growing number of congressmen and senators once were practicing political scientists, and if the proportion of lawyers in the membership has not become less, the lawyers have become something better than the average of other generations.

When Grover Cleveland, in 1855, made up his mind to become a lawyer his uncle persuaded a Buffalo firm to let him sit in its outer office and run errands for its members. The only attention given to his training in the law was permission to read from the meager store of books on the office shelves. It took him five years to prepare for bar examinations. And when he had passed he was woefully uneducated otherwise. He undertook the governorship of New York and then the presidency with no more knowledge of the

4. President Truman refused to support its elimination because, he said, it usefully exaggerated popular majorities and assisted in the ready acceptance of election verdicts. It does do that, and more. In 1912, for instance, when there were three candidates, Wilson had 6 million popular votes, and his opponents, Theodore Roosevelt and W. H. Taft, between them had 8 million. Wilson had 435 electoral votes and his opponents a total of 94. Another more usual instance occurred in 1936: F. D. Roosevelt had about 28 million votes to Alfred Landon's 17 million; Roosevelt had 523 electoral votes and Landon only eight. At other times, as in the election of J. Q. Adams and of Rutherford B. Hayes, the electoral vote has negatived the popular result.

affairs he would administer—although by then he had a lucrative practice —than any individual who might have been chosen from a crowd. He was intelligent, but he had to learn on the job.

It has to be said that nearly all other governors and presidents have learned on the job. They may not have been so completely unprepared as Cleveland, most of them; but then many of them have not been so intelligent, either. It is hard to think of a president since the Civil War, with the exception of the Roosevelts, who did come to the presidency in any sense prepared. It is true that some came from the legislative branch, but an examination of their learning periods would show them to have been longer than those of others who came, say, from governorships or from the army. The early days of Truman and of Kennedy, for instance, were disastrously inept. A year, or even the two years needed by Truman, can no longer be afforded.

The escape from these intolerable dangers for a great nation lies, however, not in the improvement of individuals; that, important as it is, can never be enough if the realm of politics has grown beyond the capacity of individuals to manage. As has been repeatedly pointed out, the vast corporate agglomerations now in substantial control of economic life have long since learned that individuals cannot stretch their abilities, however brilliant they may be, to the actual running of their enterprises. Corporations of any size have escaped from the charisma of earlier days when entrepreneurs were better known than politicians. Who knows now who are the chairmen and presidents of the concerns whose reach stretches over almost the whole of the nation, and perhaps other nations as well? These are, anyway, not decisionmakers in the old sense. They have very little choice after their technical planners have presented them with their findings. They may have had more influence when they were a good deal further down in the hierarchy.

If the government is thought of as the biggest firm of all, it is appalling that few of the managerial advances adopted by the economic giants have been adopted. The system is still headed by officials chosen for charisma, not for ability, and the results are as may be expected. Since the interweaving of economics and politics is so intimate, the better-managed corporations use the government for their own purposes to a degree fast becoming intolerable. They arrange for appropriate legislation; they constantly influence the regulatory bodies set up as protection against them; they infiltrate the bureaucracies; they sell so much to the government and are so dependent on it for services that they cannot afford to have its management left to amateurs.

It is for these reasons of control and exploitation from without, as well as the recapture of citizen participation, that institutional changes are indispensable. If participation cannot reach to managerial problems, it *can* set up dialogues about what is to be managed and in whose interest. Besides, government has other affairs to consider than economic ones. There is welfare; there is education; there are the uses of power in a world of independent nations. These are questions citizens are affected by either directly or indirectly and ought to inform themselves about.

It is not at all difficult to imagine how this participation might be arranged for. It would only be necessary to use familiar organizational arrangements: an administrator responsible to a body with only national interests; assistant administrators for each of the qualifying parties (usually two and seldom if ever more than three); facilities made available for local meetings and for regional and general conventions; shortened campaigns with equal access to communication facilities; and national primaries to choose among the candidates suggested by polls.

It would be necessary to extend this systematic reform by constitutional directive to all governmental entities—that is, to states, cities, counties, and townships, with appropriate modifications. The organization must be nonpartisan and removed from the control of the incumbent administration, operating purely facilitating machinery. Its anticipated effects would be to end the suborning of representatives by private interests and to create an informed majority by the stimulation of discussion and the holding of conventions to adopt platforms and designate candidates.

How Free Can Decisions Be?

It seems to have escaped any official recognition that in much of government as in private corporations the tendency has been to diminish the areas of allowable choice. Certain decisions, many of them vital, are no longer really open to alternatives—that is, without severe penalty for mistakes. When it can be shown, without appreciable margin of error, that a policy will, if adopted, be wholly inconsistent with another already in operation, the only reasonable choice to be made is whether to abandon the first and adopt the second. They cannot *both* be adopted without negating each other. Yet the present system often results in just such absurdities.

A further extension of this reasoning is of importance to democracy. Some choices depend on knowledge not possessed—sometimes not possessable—by the electorate in general. And some others are made sequential to a train of events or facts, and to adopt a policy inconsistent with these would be to choose chaos over order. This, of course, is what the arts of planning have been developed for—to assess the facts and conditions of ongoing events and to point out congruent policies. Alternatives often exist; these are large choices of ends; but ends, once chosen, do point to appropriate means. To deny this—to disapprove necessary means—is to prejudice or perhaps make impossible the attainment of the wanted ends.

This situation has hardened as the social system has become more complex. Facilities for the discovery of the most useful means have vastly improved, and this tends to present conclusions more and more difficult to escape. This suggests a serious modification of democratic choosing. There are many areas, indeed, where the rather random expression of preferences may inhibit the attainment of ends. So what people want may be something for which they are unwilling to sacrifice something else. This, indeed, is a very common democratic dilemma, and only the careful marshaling of evidence and general agreement to accept reasonable solutions can avoid practical paralysis.

Discussion is most usefully centered on ends; the means are often, though not always, best considered after technical study. But, in many instances, choices cannot be made with any hope of accomplishment unless the cost of the means is made plain. Misunderstandings about costs have been the cause of many dissensions as administrators have tried to do what they have supposed they had been directed to do. When the costs begin to be apparent, those who have expressed emphatic desire for the result often defect. Planning administrators have learned to present costs along with alternatives so that such disillusionments will be minimized. Once a commitment has been made, however, it is illogical to skimp the resources for accomplishment or to make a late change in choice and so incur the penalties of waste.

These generalizations may be made clearer by some illustration. Some dramatic ones are available that reach a grand scale. Consider for instance the Homestead Act of 1862 opening unoccupied land west of the Mississippi to free settlement. Its terms resulted in a wave of migrants who claimed quarter sections and began farming operations on the same pattern they had been familiar with in the East. But the Great Plains were subject to droughts, sometimes of many years' duration, and plowed land was lifted by winds that swept the prairies. The topsoil drifted into ridges or blew away into the East, and millions of acres once able to support Indians and buffalo became the Dust Bowl of the twentieth century and had to be reclaimed. But the Homestead Act has been extremely popular; there was no doubt of its having been the result of majority choice.

Another illustration of a similar sort is the encouragement given to small farmers in many successive congressional acts beginning in the 1930s. The family farm, a flood of florid oratory proclaimed, was the foundation of American civilization. It was there that the virtues of thrift, individual initiative, and independence were nurtured. At immense cost in subsidies small farmers were kept in business. But they did not stay; in a generation their numbers had diminished by half; and soon that half had again been halved.

This effort was a clear refusal to recognize that agricultural techniques had made it possible to depend largely on powered machines and to economize on labor. Units of increased size, more highly capitalized, enabled farmers to escape the hard conditions of the old farm—dawn-to-dark working days, dependence on the vagaries of weather, and helplessness before the attacks of pests and diseases. The larger operator could live in town and commute to his land—and he did so in millions. The ones who attempted to hold on in homestead fashion found themselves unable to compete and often ended as employees in the nearest industrial establishment. Many, also, drifted into the slums of the cities. It was a painful transition for the victims of ill-conceived encouragement and was endlessly costly for the nation as a whole. But it was clearly a majority choice.

Still another illustration, familiar to everyone—although the lesson seems not to have been learned—is the competition among cities and regions to attract industries. The reason for it is obvious. Members of chambers of commerce want the city to expand. They also want an occupation for their laborers to relieve unemployment, becoming more burdensome as dispossessed farmers move into town. They begin by offering free sites, special loans, and tax remissions. What they get is what might have been expected—a special version of the sweatshop. Only those manufacturers are attracted who are interested in lower wages than they would otherwise have paid, and, of course, in the privileges. The general result is a level of living for workers that might be expected from subnormal wages. And the merchants find that the buying power they had hoped to exploit is less than they had hoped for.

Competition for industrial location has been such throughout the rural areas that the privileges for absentee manufacturers have tended to increase and costs to the community along with them. These costs, or a good part of them, are passed on to the wider community. Federal antipoverty programs multiply in imaginative variety, and enormous efforts have to be made to salvage something from the unplanned chaos. It is difficult to refuse assistance to those who are in trouble. It seems much more difficult to anticipate it and make rescue unnecessary; this would be to deny the virtues of free enterprise and competition so often and so persistently confused with initiative and creative endeavor. But that penalties attach to chaos many hard lessons have shown.

To use an illustration of another sort, it is instructive to consider the organization and operations of the typical large corporation and then to compare it with the typical city—and, indeed, to federal operations.

Corporate planning is generally of such a sort that decisionmaking by individual executives is reduced to a minimum. What can be done with the resources available is explored with extreme technical care. It includes not only production—that is, an assay of facilities, workers, and materials—but also the capital available and the market for the product. It extends to the possibilities of growth also, whether by means of research and invention or by the assurance of an extended market. The sums allotted for research are about matched by those for consumer persuasion.

Each report in this process is made by trained personnel and is subject to review by boards or committees, so that when it is passed along for consolidation with other reports it is fairly invulnerable to criticism. And when the corporate officers are reached, their part is reduced to that of general policymaking. Day-to-day administration is carried out at levels far below them and in ways they have no need to examine. There is very little left of the bossism that once characterized economic operations. It would be disastrous for an executive officer to interfere with actual operations, and he is prevented from doing so by corporate rule. He may remain an inspirer and leader of the enterprise, but in fact charismatic individuals are feared and usually eliminated long before reaching the top levels of management. Most executives have once been technicians themselves and understand that the conclusions of the review committees must be respected. Integration, smooth operation, is the corporate ideal. The executives are not perhaps altogether anonymous, but they are seldom known outside the corporation and its contacts. They are not public figures listened to as were an older generation of Rockefellers, Fords, Fricks, Carnegies, Schwabs, and their contemporaries.

But government has none of this quiet and competent quality. It is invaded by oratorical characters who may have a shrewd idea of the voters' wants but usually no idea whether the satisfaction of those demands is feasible. Irresponsibility is a general characteristic. Whim and caprice often determine decisions; and the uses of power—and the power available is tremendous—are apt to be blundering and wasteful.

Much of this is because government has become the largest of all productive organizations without the recognition that these operations are sharply different from those it was earlier supposed to carry out. The framers expected it to make equitable arrangements for living together in a simple society. These were negative where they were not merely permissive, and they were not meant to be disciplinary—except in emergency. Aside from national security, the summoning of people and resources for any purpose was not contemplated. Public education was not yet thought of, for instance, much less responsibility for welfare. But new duties piled up. Public lands could not merely be owned; they had to be managed. Agriculture eventually was something more than a scattering of farms in an endless countryside; it became a source of food and fiber and had to be brought under control. The provision of homes could not be left to private enterprise, and government had to intervene, to encourage and assist. So with numerous activities.

Some of these—as in the instance of agriculture and housing—were intricate interweavings of public and private enterprise, requiring the most delicate judgments for success. But whether it was government management

—as of the forests and parks—or private and public—as in housing or banking—the possibility of planned and competent organization was jeopardized by the intervention of the politician who sought and gained the status of director without possessing the competence demanded for the duty. It is a tragedy of historic democracy that the kind of talent required for getting political power is a disqualification for using it in the modern circumstances of government.

All this requires a reorganization of political appeal, and of the uses of various talents. If government is to carry a heavier and heavier load of duties, it must be organized for the purpose. Purposes and means must be separated. The appropriateness of general dialogue about ends and purposes is involved too. Like the corporate decisionmaker, the responsible participating citizen may well be given the expertly prepared materials necessary to wise decisionmaking, examined and certified by committees he has helped to authorize. It will be necessary also to recognize the penalties of interfering with integration. And ways will have to be found for delegating the decisions logically necessary to the ends designated as desirable.

The Fallible Majority

One conclusion from the many examples available is that majorities can be, and often are, mistaken; that is to say, they in time will be shown to have been unwise. This is as true of unregistered public opinion as it is of elections; opinions approaching consensus may still be wrong by this criterion; but electoral majorities, needing only slightly more than 50 percent, will naturally turn out to have been mistaken in many more instances.

There can hardly be any doubt, to cite no other presidential contests, that Seymour, then the capable governor of New York, would have been a better selection than Grant in 1868, or that Cox would have saved the nation the humiliations imposed on it by Harding after 1920. And innumerable similar instances can be cited from state and municipal histories. Majorities refused several times, at twenty-year intervals, to approve the rewriting of New York State's obsolete constitution. California, among the states, rejected by referendum a liberalizing amendment concerning discrimination in housing. Many more illustrations of fallible judgment will occur to an observer.

On the other hand, observers will recall that majorities have been right on many occasions. And it may well be that they have more often been right than wrong. The question is: how serious are the consequences of being mistaken, however few the mistakes may be? It is quite possible that one wrong decision may be more significant than many right ones. It depends on what is at stake. Deciding whether the federal government ought to make domestic improvements, whether tariffs should be raised or lowered, whether to have a managed currency or a gold standard—these are large issues majorities have decided in the past, and the nation has survived. In all these matters the decision has at one time gone one way, and at another time has gone another way.

Decisions affecting war or peace, the acceptance of responsibility for welfare, the disposition of national power, or the protection of human rights have been made too. They involve a different order of consequence. A wrong decision on such matters might well involve results embarrassing to the nation for a generation or more. Some few of this sort have carried the possibility of disaster.

As has been noted, such issues do not often come to a vote. Only occasionally is there an opportunity to decide on important and distinctive policies in national or even state elections, the reason being that candidates become less and less willing to take sides; the request for mandate is avoided except in the clearest cases of consensus, and then the contenders usually differ only in degree, not in principle. Whether majorities would opt for human and foresighted policies, or would reject them as too costly or too radical, is seldom known. Politicians prefer not to offer them such an opportunity. When on rare occasions the chance is given, however, majorities are quite apt to be wrong on both counts. Xenophobia, radical hatreds, penuriousness—such illiberal emotions are all too easily expressed in secret ballots.

Apologists for the mistakes made by majorities used to say that people had a right to err and to suffer the penalties if they proved to have been wrong. But there have been majority decisions so disastrous that they hardly seem humanly allowable. If the choosing of a president, an event more exciting than most, and more apt to draw out a substantial percentage of eligible voters, can be mistaken by almost any test, in spite of having followed the most thorough discussions known to political life, decisions involving obscure or complex issues are much more likely to be settled unwisely.

There is the complication about this that national elections are referenda about issues only to the extent that parties and candidates have been committed to them. And since commitment is softened habitually and stated frankly only when consensus has pretty certainly been reached, questions of great moment may escape being really brought to vote. What the majority feels may be inferred only by what happens in a still later election—as, for instance, when Hoover was defeated in 1932 after having won overwhelmingly in 1928. He had been a conservative, standing for sound money, high tariffs, individual responsibility for welfare, and friendliness to business. The depression following almost at once after his election was, however, judged to be the result of these very policies, and he was turned out after four years. The majority had been wrong to endorse him in 1928 if it was right to reject him in 1932. That four-year interval was a terrible ordeal, but, at that, not as terrible as some other might be in the future.

What is the significance, in modern circumstances, of this occasional perversity? If the right to err and to pay for it was something less than calamitous before 1945, the same cannot be said of certain issues since that time. This is particularly true of one portentous question: Has humanity —or a majority of it—the right to choose a course certain to end in its own extinction? This is no longer an empty speculation to be quieted by citing the old democratic clichés; it has not been since Hiroshima.

Skepticism induced by the caprices of the electorate and the imcompetence of elected politicians induced Henry Adams at the end of his long life to write *The Degradation of the Democratic Dogma*.[5] It was a deeply pessimistic assessment of democracy's failure. At the very least it posed questions that clamored for answers and still do. The central question, among many others, is whether a largely ignorant or irrational electorate ought to be entrusted with decisions affecting not only its own members but all life on earth. More carefully formulated, this question may be put as follows: in a season of history when human folly may well lead to actual cataclysm, can the risk involved in majority rule be tolerated?

This naturally leads to the further speculation whether improvement can be hoped for so long as the way is closed by a Congress devoted to local and private interests. As has been suggested, there is more involved in this than was contemplated in democratic theory. It is not a question only of people making mistakes and paying for them; it is a question of making mistakes and requiring *others* to pay for them—and perhaps an ultimate price.

It will have to be admitted that absolute elimination of risk is, like most absolutes, not within possibility. What can be considered as practicable is its substantial reduction. Concerning such relief there are certain suggestions to be made. Changes must, for one thing, be institutional in nature; and these must be looked for where the dangers center—in domestic institutions and in those of the world community. They can come, it would seem, only as the result of forthright research and experiment with substitutes calculated to ensure progress with reasonable safety—progress being defined broadly as movement toward the improvement of the human situation.

5. Published after his death when it had been put in final order by his younger brother, Brooks Adams. Henry Adams died in 1918, Brooks Adams in 1927. The period studied and written about preceded the Civil War; the period Henry Adams lived through was considerably later. His home was across Lafayette Square from the White House, and he was a familiar of the most prominent statesmen of the time, John Hay and Theodore Roosevelt among them. He was not heartened, as Woodrow Wilson was, by the presidential house-cleaning of Cleveland after the years of Grantism. McKinley, bland and vacillating, letting the nation in for the "splendid little war" against Spain, so popular and so wrong, was only another count in his indictment of democracy. Brooks, his brother, who studied and wrote about economic events, saw the same erosive forces at work in the industrial system.

Perhaps the Adams forecast is still to be fulfilled; but the later decades of the century promise to be different from its first decades; and there are some improvements Adams would not have expected.

It ought to be considered probable, however, that the weighing of what must be given up against what will be gained will always be difficult. These decisions will continue to involve uncertainties as well as fallible and irrational judgments. Many troubles have arisen out of a social evolution so much the natural expression of men's desires and capabilities that it is clearly these that will have to be modified, countered, or, hopefully, sublimated so that they come to a different result. It can be taken as given that the decisions themselves will have to be made initially by the same majority that has to be convinced of its own fallibility. The new or revised institutions will have to be *its own*; the sacrifices and disciplines will have to be voluntary (even if a limited involuntarism is accepted as part of the change); and the limits of involvements will have to be understood and accepted. If they are not, support for the new arrangement cannot be counted on.

What has to be won over is a majority with a weakness—or so it seems from its history—for insisting on keeping what it wants without paying the inevitable price, without accepting uncomfortable disciplines, and without much altering institutions to which it has grown so accustomed. The United States is prosperous, its citizens will feel entitled to say; its abundance is unexampled in all history; its power reaches around the world. There are inconveniences, inequalities, and yes, even dangers, but Americans are a people who have always eliminated inconveniences, lived with inequalities, and overcome dangers. These successes, it will be said, can be continued without drastic change; indeed, drastic change involves risks to prosperity and freedom. The dangers will simply have to be met as they always have been—by avoidance or, if there is a challenge, by resistance.

As to resistance, our military planners are proud of having kept wars fought with foreigners far from our own country, on the other side of wide oceans. They can be trusted to go on doing this, it will be said—as is evidenced by the border incidents of the long struggle with China and Russia. Fighting in Southeast Asia, supporting and arming allies in Europe, preventing foreign penetrations of our own continent and South America—these are examples. Behind its strategic ramparts the nation can go on as it has done—spending what it has to for its necessities and trusting the statesmen and the military to implement the continuing tradition of isolation from actual conflict.

It would seem a simple conclusion that if genocidal weapons are possessed by several nations, agreements among them to control their production and distribution are the least precaution that ought to be taken. Nothing short of world integration and the abolition of such armaments will wholly eliminate the threat, but it might be considerably reduced by mutual agreement. This, however, would involve the abandonment of war as a final recourse in international disputes. It follows that if war is not available there must be other means of settlement. When bargaining fails, arbitration must be accepted. It cannot be said to have been fully demonstrated that a majority would disapprove of merging sovereignties, but public opinion has run heavily against the least surrender of national freedom to act.

The point about this is that a mistake, if the issue should be posed plainly, might lead not to bearable, if annoying, costs, but to complete annihilation. No question in national experience has ever gone quite to this ultimate test of majority rule. But it has now to be answered: Can a majority be allowed the privilege of committing a nation to extinction? And with it, moreover, the rest of humanity?

If the answer is that this is an inadmissible privilege, the further question is: To whom or to what agency shall the security of the people be entrusted? And how is this entrustment to be achieved in a democracy? Perhaps the dilemma here is not so intractable as it seems. If a political organization existed, the avoidance of such issues would be impossible. They would be thoroughly explored. The danger and ways to escape it would be clearly connected, and the necessary delegation of authority to compromise might be made acceptable.

If delegation is required to an agency with a mandate to do what may be necessary, consent to it would be necessary; moreover, it would have to be irrevocable except by constitutional process. Otherwise it would not be invulnerable to sudden majority caprice. This indicates the necessity for an instrument of government more permanent, less vulnerable to ills of the flesh, and representative in a larger sense than a president who is at best one fallible individual, who is a party leader, and who may have been elected by a less than one-percent majority.

The Incompetent Voter

Robert M. Hutchins once said: "We might as well make up our minds to it. If our hopes of democracy are to be realized, every citizen of this country is going to have to be educated to the limit of his capacity."[6] He went on to say that he did not mean "trained, amused, exercised, accommodated or adjusted." He meant that every citizen's "intellectual power must be developed."

If that could be done, he felt, the simple faith he recalled from his Brooklyn childhood would perhaps return. That was a time when Americans were moving toward civilization of the dialogue, toward a time when "everybody talked with everybody else about everything . . . nobody tried to get

6. In an address entitled "Is Democracy Possible?" at the Sidney Hillman Foundation, New York, N.Y., Jan. 21, 1951.

his way by force or fraud . . . " and "everybody was content to abide by the decision of the majority as long as the dialogue could continue."

The trouble was that progress toward the ideal was being interrupted in important ways. He was hearing some disturbing dissents: from farm leaders who thought democracy had little application in union politics; from lawyers who said that democratic control of foreign policy was impossible because the Constitution forbade it, and anyway, the technical problems were too delicate for decision by ordinary people; and by friends who objected to pleas for "getting out the votes" because persuading people to vote "when they did not know what they were voting for was not helpful, and might be harmful, to the objects I had in view."

At almost the same moment in history Aldous Huxley was troubled by the same general foreboding.[7] "We know," he said, "that in a very large and complex society, democracy is almost meaningless except in relation to autonomous groups of manageable size."

He went on to say that life in cities had become "anonymous, atomic, less than fully human," but nevertheless cities had steadily grown more huge; and more and more of every nation's affairs were managed by bureaucrats of big government and by business. In practice, he said, "the problem of over-organization is almost as hard to solve as the problem of over-population. In both cases we know what ought to be done; but in neither have we been able, as yet, to act effectively upon our knowledge."

It seemed to Huxley that since democracy could be effective only in small groups, there must be a return to them; and if this could not be done all society's problems would only grow worse. He did not, however, offer any way of making them operative in a technological and integrated society. Since this is the society we have, and are likely to go on having because existence depends upon it now, his was largely a cry of despair. Huxley's was not a lone voice. He spoke for many others who felt the same despair.

If it is in the society we have—industrialized, urbanized, integrated— that we must find a way to make democracy work, that is the problem to be addressed. Can citizens be assured of a say in decisions vital to them, or, if they are indifferent, can they be made interested? If not, democracy is indeed impossible. Are these difficulties completely insoluble as Huxley thought—or are there possible accommodations?

There is, at least, one condition of workability to which little attention has been given. If the electorate has a significant proportion of incompetents, no effort to create a dialogue will succeed. They will not take part because they cannot; they will continue to use their voting privilege as they so often have in the past—as directed by a boss with interests to serve, or in response to their own caprices.

7. Aldous Huxley, *Brave New World Revisited* (New York: Harper & Row, 1958).

In a way this is the result of predictable forces. In another way it is a measure of unrealistic assessment. In their willingness to participate, as well as their capability of understanding, it was always obvious that equality among citizens was unreal. The framers and their contemporaries knew better. In the states as well as in federal arrangements, the electorate was severely restricted. Only those were to vote who had reason for being interested in public affairs and who, by achievement, had demonstrated that interest. By using the standard of property ownership they could claim to be realists. And even though there were dissenters, this argument prevailed. In spite of the radicals during the Jeffersonian succession, suffrage did not become universal until Jacksonian times nearly four decades later. Then an equalitarian era began, with its assumptions which ran even to equality in ability. Anyone could not only talk to anyone else about anything, but anyone could do anything that anyone else could do.

Those were the days when public decisions did not jeopardize the continuation of human life. Some of them did cause results that had to be paid for by later generations, but evasions and hypocrisies allowed people to go on believing that what seemed profitable at the moment would turn out to be best in the long run.

An example of this was the belief in free competition as a regulator of economic affairs. Because they practiced freedom and liked it, citizens refused to see it as a protective screen for the capture of the economy by big business. The capture might not have been so bad if it had been done under public auspices; but because it was carried out under the rubrics of laissez-faire, it could go on until the familiar two hundred corporations dominated the economic system. Freedom had destroyed itself. There were, at length, some few entrepreneurs left in America, but their share of the economy was slim and growing slimmer.

Somewhat the same thing happened in politics. By the late nineteenth century, because every man was equal and could vote, the real power had gravitated to a few bosses. They, in effect, owned the city and state governments; and to only a somewhat lesser extent controlled the Congress as well. This was accomplished, as it had been in economics, by persuading people that democratic institutions were still working. The Congress became a satrapy governed by a few chairmen of committees from safe and conservative districts. No change was even suggested in the district system, in the length of terms, in the composition of constituencies. One proposal for internal reorganization was approved and immediately contained by the establishment, so that things went on as before.[8]

This political degeneration was caused by the same forces that were at work in the industrial world: growth of population, specialization leading

---

8. This was the La Follette-Monroney Act of 1946.

to complex organization, the growth of bureaucracies, and the substitution under deceiving rubrics of narrow and protective values for the once effective ones of simpler times.

The truth is not to be escaped; if democracy is to be attained—that is, if citizens are to participate in the decisions they are affected by—it has to be with modified devices. The pretense has to be given up that what is failing is succeeding. There has to be a reappraisal of institutions so long regarded as democracy itself, when, in fact, they are only facilitating devices—and ones that have long since become obsolescent.

It even has to be acknowledged that the voting privilege is one that, even if born to, has to be kept by the ability to use it capably. Exclusion for the nonpossession of property is not a criterion relevant to modern conditions. But neither is its opposite. There is no virtue in being without possessions. It is elsewhere that we ought to look for eligibility tests. Perhaps none that is satisfactory can be found, but it is all too obvious that universal admission to voting privilege needs justifications it does not now possess. Merely because it has been adopted ought not to bar reconsideration.

It has to be recognized that in a complex world some issues are beyond the comprehension of some people, and that to have them making decisions by guess, by prejudice, or on advice can be fatal to the commonwealth. What is required is a separation of the specialized or complex issues from those that make commitment to values and directions. There is no reason why thoughtful citizens cannot determine what they want without knowing precisely how it can be attained. There is no reason why the technicians cannot be given directions. Just as the military in our system is under civilian control, so too can the corporations that do our producing be brought under public direction.

Dialogues concerning these matters could take place with some prospect of effectiveness if they were specifically arranged for, if they were participated in by competent voters, and if the agencies for implementing the decisions were responsive and suited to the purpose. This is a formidable enough prescription for a more democratic future, but there is a more formidable one remaining: what to do about the incompetent. The indifferent voter may be stirred; the one tied to a machine may be freed; but a congenitally incapable one cannot participate, and pretending that he can, and allowing him to go through the motions, is to consign political decision to chance.

This widespread condition has generated a strong tendency to turn away and ignore it—partly because voter-qualification is a state matter, and state laws have been directed to purposes of their own. When the framers provided that, for members of the Congress, "the electors in each state shall have the qualifications requisite for electors of the most numerous branch of the state legislature," they consigned federal elections to the diverse judgments of state lawmakers who were not otherwise concerned with national interests. Some made the restrictions affecting blacks and women that were eliminated by the Fourteenth, Fifteenth, Nineteenth, and Twenty-fourth Amendments. These amendments, however, had the effect of extending suffrage, not of restricting it. In none is there any standard of eligibility; there is only the prohibition of certain exclusions.

Reformers, scandalized by the abuses of boss-controlled elections, were responsible for a restrictive campaign of another sort. This resulted in registration laws in most states fixing the length of residence in state, county, and voting districts necessary to eligibility. By 1956 five states required a residence of two years, thirty-two states required one year, and eleven states half a year. The required residence in counties and districts was, of course, less, but still restrictive. By 1960 there were estimated to be from five to eight million otherwise eligible voters who could not vote in the presidential election of that year because they had moved from one place to another. While the registration laws were being passed to prevent manipulation of elections, American mobility had been increasing.

These statistics were used in President Johnson's message to the Congress in 1967 proposing a new Presidency Voting Act which would provide that citizens might not be denied their vote in presidential elections if they had become residents of states before September first of the voting year. This, if passed, would reduce the requirement to three months. It would, that is, if it was declared to be constitutional.[9]

A democrat can have no objection to the elimination of restrictions that reduce eligibilty for such reasons as being without property or having moved. But this does nothing to meet the objection that wider admission of the incompetent reduces the choice to change. If patently extraneous influences do affect large numbers of voters, further widening of the electorate will merely make the average that of a larger number. This was the subject of controversy during the period when restrictions were being removed in the early nineteenth century, and this very argument was fallen back on by the Jeffersonians—that an average of many judgments, however ill-informed and however influenced by irrelevant motives, is safer than government by an elite who will always shape things to their own advantage.

---

9. A Presidential Commission in 1963 presented some interesting figures: the percentage of votes cast by those eligible was much higher in the late 1800s than it was after the registration laws were passed. In 1876, 85.5 percent of the adult male eligibles voted. In contrast only 44.2 percent voted in 1920. It never reached 60 percent in the F. D. Roosevelt elections, and was only 62 percent in 1964. There were immense differences among the states. In 1960 Idaho's participation was 80.7 percent, and in Mississippi it was 25.5 percent. The question of constitutionality would seem to be covered by Article I, section 2.1, saying that the qualification for voters should be that for electors of the most numerous branch of the state legislature.

This is still the justification most relied on by equalitarians. But it does not meet the objection that a democracy relies on the free decision of its voters with the underlying assumption that they are not only free but competent and informed as well. It is clear that they cannot even be informed if they are incapable of assimilating information. It is hard to resist the conclusion that another sort of restriction is called for, one relying on at least elementary tests for intelligence and perhaps evidence of interest in participation.

If it seems that there is in this a hidden suggestion that arbitrary rules of eligibility be imposed, it may be answered that a rational inquiry concerning qualifications is a good deal less arbitrary than the fixing of an age limit. The problem in fixing restrictions is the making certain that they are made for the purpose of creating a competent and informed electorate and not one that is weighted in favor of any views or any interest but that of the nation. This could be accomplished by an assembly having only the national well-being at interest, and it could not be done in any other way.

The Uses of Dialogue

Since mankind emerged from a stable relationship with his environment he has more and more risked falling into what Sir Geoffrey Vickers has called an "ecological trap."[10]

The fear is that human beings may make one mistake too many and disappear as other species are known to have done.

The opportunities are many, the warning signs are difficult to read, and the disciplines of avoidance are hard to enforce. What may seem advantageous at the moment to those in position to decide on it may turn out to have been fatal for the commonalty. The decision may have been reached for any one of many apparently good reasons; it may even have been responsive to impulses regarded as virtuous; and it still may turn out to have been mistaken.

We are at a time when we begin to recognize the more obvious of these. Conservationists have been alarmed for a long time about the exhaustion of irreplaceable resources and the wastage of replaceable ones. Demographers have been equally alarmed about the continuance of unchecked reproduction as death rates have declined. Planners have warned repeatedly that the arrangement of habitations and working places was leading to a congestion soon likely to approach paralysis. Sociologists have viewed with alarm the displacement by power and machines of vast numbers of workers in nearly every occupation. Geologists and geographers have studied warily the clouds of dust and smoke spreading over the earth

10. In a lecture at the London School of Economics and Political Science, Nov. 22, 1966.

and are wondering whether such factors may not raise temperatures, melt the polar ice caps, and inundate the continents.

What man is doing as he races into a future whose circumstances are drastically altered in unprecedentedly short times happens too fast for evaluation of the effects. The development of agriculture from nomadic beginnings was accomplished in slow changes spread over millennia. The growth of a metropolis such as London, Tokyo, or New York was at least spread over a century or more in its most troublesome stages. But communications and transportation went into their later phase in about half a century. Access to unlimited sources of power, water, and perhaps food may take, again, half that time. And, as everyone now living knows only too well, genocidal weapons appeared in what seemed no more than an instant to those not aware of advances in basic science.

It is a commonplace that all these technologies had a common origin in old discoveries and old theories, and it was always foregone that there would be a progressive acceleration as the areas of knowledge were widened and as they became available to more individuals of high intellectual capability.

It is this prospect, we are now in a position to see—cannot possibly avoid seeing—that has caused the concern of Vickers as well as others. The possibilities are so vast, the knowledge so specialized, the language of communication so unintelligible to others than specialists, that it is next to impossible for anyone, even if seized with concern and having the requisite intelligence and education, to foresee what traps may lie no more than a decade or two ahead. The time given for avoidance has become terribly short.

Then there is the difficulty of communication, partly owed to specialization, partly to interferences. Each group of specialists, these days, has a language of its own; and in one way or another barriers are raised against the transmission of what one knows and others might like or need to know. If it is true of technologists themselves, it is many times worse when they try to communicate with the lay public. They do, after all, share much mathematics among themselves and are familiar with the technique of phrasing their problems in computer language. But the voting public does not use this language.

In the present world, also, there are interferences. Corporate secrets are hoarded fiercely. And this fierceness cannot be compared with that among nations in the name of defense—all of which is apt to lead to the prohibition of any communication at all.

Quite apart from these security precautions, if the climate was such that anyone could talk to anyone about anything, there might either be nothing to say or no intelligible way of saying it. This is so serious a challenge to the idea of democracy, and creates so enormous a risk of unanticipated catastrophe, that it appears to warrant the emergency creation of facilities for a renewed political dialogue.

It may not be possible to increase the intellectual powers of the individuals who, in a democracy, must make decisions; but it will be possible to reduce ignorance and increase tolerance. And if dialogue can be organized, better understanding may lead to wiser choice of policies; but that dialogue will have to be purged of the specious appeals that characterize it now, and it will have to be clear that mandates have been given and will be observed.

In considering political organization it is necessary to recall the importance of leadership in democracy. People choose leaders, customarily, rather than policies. They may not even be very clear where the candidate they vote for stands on many issues, since, so far as he can, he will try to be ambiguous in his appeals for votes. Often candidates are voted *against,* and this serves to elect their opponents. This happened to Hoover in 1932. He had allowed the paralysis of depression to deepen without doing anything effective to check it; and although there was no considerable demand for Roosevelt, he was elected.

This propensity for choosing agreeable persons rather than ones who have the requirements for filling positions of power can be made use of for democratic purposes. Candidates' parties, and they themselves, can be made to take more definite stands and thus lessen the ambiguity they prefer. It may even be hoped that candidates will survive the primary and election tests for better reasons than they have seemed to in the past. This might be one result of induced dialogue, since dialogue does not thrive on personalities but does on issues.

If elected officials thus carried mandates into office with them, the disenchantment that so often sets in after honeymoon periods might be to an extent avoided; and there would certainly be less excuse for civil disobedience. It could not be claimed, as it so often has been, that candidates elected because of promises made had gone back on them.

An even greater gain would be the power that would accrue to leaders because of the mandate. The opposition of private interests to policies thoroughly discussed and clearly represented by the leader would be weakened. This power would make itself felt also in dealing with other nations. As things are, in foreign capitals the estimate of popular support for an American administration often determines the relations of those countries with the United States. Their estimates are often mistaken because of a tendency to believe what it is preferred to believe, and because of reliance on defective intelligence; but it is an important element in the making of international arrangements. Reducing doubt about support for administration policies would make an enormous difference in the relations of the great powers to one another.

In spite of any democratic gains of this kind that might come from continuing discussions of policy, there still do remain difficulties owed to the arcane nature of technology; and one of the reasons for establishing a national organization publicly paid for and supervised by federal officials is that permanent facilities and continuous encouragement might lead to enlightenment. This does not result from the casual and sporadic dialogue of the present, which dies out after elections and revives shortly before the next one. It consists largely of specious appeals by parties and candidates for support. The intention is not to form judgments but to persuade, and to do that not by educating but by bamboozling.

Losing parties fall into lethargy. Their headquarters are closed; their candidates disappear. The winners settle into office and at once begin considering how to stay there. Instead of offering leadership, this system results in the attempt to guess what people want and to satisfy the demand. There is no organized dialogue, much less a civilized one, between the elected official and his constituents. Such as there is confines itself easily to communication with the private interests who can use the official's influence in the capital—often very much against the public's interest. Constituents may, and do, make demands; but these do not come from the sources of most need.

Worst of all, the demands made on representatives have no national orientation. A legislature elected from districts will neglect nationwide issues simply because these are not what he has been chosen to pursue. He will have promised "to do something" for his district. He will contrive to do it if he can by maneuvering for advantage. He will be so occupied in this way that he will neglect to inform himself about larger matters and will vote on them, when they are presented, without any real preparation.

A proposal for facilitating continued discussion on general as well as local issues might make an appreciable change; if supplemented by other devices, it might make a considerable one. Candidates for federal office, for instance, might be expected, if defeated, to become part of a working opposition, paid, and given facilities to go on until candidates are chosen for the succeeding election. Their duty would be to act as leaders. They, as well as incumbents, would then have a base for renewed appeal. The exchanges generated would in themselves constitute something of a dialogue. Each might make use of research and the interpretation of technology by experts; issues now beyond discussion, because beyond comprehension, might be brought into the area of political decision.

It is suggested then that national legislators be elected from wider constituencies, some even at large, not only to give their interests a national cast but also, as will be necessary, for longer terms so that the present preoccupation with reelection may be somewhat relieved.

What has been said has had to do with federal or national matters, but there is an obvious need for constitutional standards in state and local politics. A dialogue is similarly needed, and election procedures need to be under a general rule. It has been noted that there are wide divergences in the procedures for voter qualification. These are as serious for local elections as they are for federal ones.

The message of President Johnson proposing his Residency Voting Act of 1967 offered the figures of "between five and eight million" voters made ineligible because of "unnecessarily long residency requirements," and this was before the admission of eighteen-year-olds. The proposed act would affect only federal elections; constitutional amendment would be needed to affect others. New standards are equally needed for those, and in some states this has been recognized, but the more backward ones have shown no softening toward newcomers. It was reformers who caused the stiff laws to be passed in many states, and it is a later generation of reformers who are now trying to reverse their predecessors and get back on the lists those voters excluded by earlier laws.

It may be true that the abuses sought to be cured by the earlier restrictions will not return. But it may be doubted that the change has been sufficiently drastic. When registration was quick and easy, bosses could herd temporary residents to the precinct polls and often, in fact, herd them on to other precincts. But the real trouble was not the exclusion of recent residents. There was carelessness in preparing and checking lists. And voters were only too willing to cast their ballots as they were told to do in payment for favors received. These favors might be, and sometimes were, simple payment in money; more often they were what the boss was able to do in crises in the lives of poor families—a small loan, help in getting a job, easing some regulation, or perhaps intervention with a demanding landlord.

These were eliminated by Social Security and by federal assistance for welfare services begun in New Deal days and steadily expanded year by year since that time. The city bosses who supported Roosevelt through his three campaigns for reelection awoke late to the realization that he was depriving them of their stock in trade. It is the welfare office that helps out now, not the boss in the back room of the party's clubhouse.

With voters freed from the compulsions of boss rule, there is now an unexploited opportunity to set up contracts between politicians and their constituents on quite another basis. Some of them have seen this. Mayor John Lindsay of New York with his store-front offices tried something of the sort. But it ought not to be done only with private party funds and only by one leader. In this case representatives tend to serve a local ombudsman purpose until the next campaign approaches. And, in fact, they are not much more than a modern version of the clubhouse. Such facilities ought to be open to all, subject, of course, to considered rules. They should be places for holding an organized dialogue. Schools make convenient gathering places for the purpose, and there could be no objection to their use if the dialogue was open and fairly regulated.

The civilization of politics at the local, state, and national level is quite possible with the resources available. It does depend on other changes such as federal intervention in education (with well-considered decentralization of administration). This would make the schools a federal property, and their maintenance a national responsibility, so that their use for the political dialogue could be encouraged. Other changes, primarily for other purposes, would also contribute—such as the standardization of state constitutions and city charters by constitutional rule, and the reforms of legislative bodies that are so long overdue.

The whole would, however, be quite impossible without the institution of an *electoral branch* with its powers and duties specified in the federal constitution.

It may be as well to say here, at the conclusion of this chapter, that it is simply not possible to think of change anywhere in institutional arrangements without serious consideration of the effect on other parts of the whole government, and that this is especially true of politics, since in a democracy it underlies all else. If, for instance, there should be changes in legislative or executive duties, the incidence of voter interest and impact might be considerably altered. What would not be altered would be the voters' duty to use their best judgment in making decisions. For that purpose they ought to be provided with adequate facilities for discussion and with uncontaminated information.

Since this is true, and since there have been changes in all three traditional branches, it follows that the political system ought not to be left behind as it so far has been. Essentially, the election procedure and the presentation of issues for decision remain as they were in Jackson's time. The changes have been minor. And such as have occurred have not enlarged, but rather diminished, voter competence and participation. It is this that is proposed to be remedied by constitutionalizing the system.

CHAPTER 8

ASSESSMENT AND GUIDANCE

Constitutional Enmities[1]

It is admittedly difficult to distinguish what national issues may appropriately be decided without an elaborate structure of justification. There are such. Figures, beyond the most elementary ones of number and distance, help very little in deciding how much land ought to be set aside for the recreation sure to be demanded by future millions. Such figures help even less in determining how much to spend on explorations of space or of the deep seas. Ought the arts to have public support? How much should be spent on special cultural enterprises? Marshaled facts are not decisive in such matters—helpful, but not final.

When it has to be determined whether funds will be allocated for such purposes, the contribution budgeters may make is fairly obvious. They may estimate what funds will be available for everything, and how much ought to be used—or must be used—for essential commitments already made, or ones likely to be made; they may go further and say that proposed expenditures will have probable results or, at least, quote authority for such statements, thus establishing alternatives and making choices more rational. There is, however, a deceptive simplicity in putting it this way. It is easier to cover the possibilities with a generalization than to see how the proposed thing or process may emerge into reality. Where statistics are available, where comparisons can be made with some certainty, it may not be so

1. The argument in this chapter that foresight is indispensable in a complex and burdened society was elaborated, with reference particularly to Puerto Rican experience, in *The Place of Planning in Society: Seven Lectures* (published by the Puerto Rico Planning Board in 1954), and in numerous articles during the years since 1925.

difficult; however, figures often are not available or, if they are, do not contribute substantially to decisionmaking.

If the surgeon general reports that the spread of a disease will be stopped if preventive measures are carried out, if the chief forester estimates future deficits of wood, if the sources of water are reported to be nearing exhaustion or that the planned provision of schools will be insufficient, in such matters the inspection of figures is imperative—not decisive, because the needs are variables, but helpful. By putting together such demands, it can be determined what appropriations would have to be made available if all of them were to be satisfied. But since this will always add up to more—probably much more—than expectable income, there is here an area of conflict to complicate the relative uselessness of many facts and figures.

Besides, there have to be estimated the excesses owed to the anxieties of the surgeon general, the forester, the educational administrator—and all the rest—who have responsibilities to meet. They are always afraid of insufficient support. In a national establishment of modern size and complexity, each agency tends to become isolated from most of the others, so that competition with others is not a direct and acute rivalry but more a sense that since funds are limited every means must be used to divert whatever can be managed to their own uses. Precaution enlarges requests, and since it is taken for granted that when sharing is decided on, allowances will be restricted, it is a rule that more must be asked for than can be expected.

Then there is the administrative tendency to exaggerate demands merely in order to keep on expanding, reaching for new territory and new power. The larger the sums obtained, the more important are those who obtain them. The Washington phrase for this is "empire building." Calculations are used in this struggle, but they must be suspect because of their origin—and are seldom decisive. Estimators at the center cannot trust such sources.

The heads of agencies are endlessly ingenious in justifying demands and in bargaining for their support. Because their organizations have long since expanded beyond any possibility of control by the nominal executive —the president—each feels free to find support among all reachable allies. These are to be found most easily among congressmen who like to claim credit for the initiation and continuation of projects their constituents favor. Legislators, after all, do vote the funds and, it may be recalled, may make appropriations whether or not there will be the funds to meet them. One attribute of sovereignty is the manufacture of exchange media; how much is manufactured is effectively separated, in the American system, from any consideration of what will be needed for the total of appropriations. Inflation may result from this ignorance, but its costs will be spread over the whole population—even future generations of it—in rising prices. Since this is so, and the consequences are not traceable to the careless appropriators, inflation is not apt to check the tendency to vote more than already exists. Legislators cannot really be blamed. None of them knows whether projects he votes for may exceed the government's ability to pay; or, if he has some notion of the difference, it comes from unreliable sources. The budget certainly does not tell him. Its estimates are only for expenditures.

Finding allies in the contest for appropriations is an easier matter, because congressmen are free to reach anywhere they like. A member of Congress can always find a reciprocating individual or group in the executive establishment. Through such a connection he can do a good deal for his supporters. He can even influence the projects submitted. These may be for the location of facilities in his district, or perhaps for special activities such as the study of a crop disease (from agriculture), perhaps for expanded park facilities (from interior), or perhaps for aids to local health authorities (from health, education, and welfare). The variety of these mutual interests is astonishing. And working relationships are easily set up and maintained.

Then there are connections, verging on corruption, but innocent by custom. Favors extracted from administrative agencies may even enlarge bank accounts. A congressman's vote may be used as he likes. The reasons for it may be suspected but are seldom exposed. When a congressman attains influence in committees his price advances, and his anonymity becomes practically invulnerable.

The system is at best irresponsible. What is undertaken is determined not by an assessment of comparative needs within a safe estimate of income but by comparative pressures from those at interest. It can be seen that an intervener—such as a planning agency must be—would disrupt this procedure and the relations it nourishes. It can be seen also that this would be resented. Congressmen, administrators, and favor seekers would find it an intolerable nuisance. They would try their best to prevent any move toward its establishment, and if it did come into existence, the circumventing maneuvers would be ingenious and, if necessary, forceful.

Budgeting efforts have suffered continual harassment from both executive and legislative circumventers. And neither party to them has given up. The Congress still treats the budgeters, after half a century, with contempt, and without having the necessary facts and without being in any way expert, it makes its own determinations. For this purpose its appropriation committees have in recent years been elaborately expanded, and long hearings have been held, but what emerges has only the most remote relation to an integrated whole. It is shaped to the prejudices, the caprices, and the particular desires of congressmen trading among themselves and with members of the executive departments.

The many years of agitation and denunciation of irresponsibility preceding the establishment of the Bureau of the Budget in 1921 finally ended in the following way: the Congress gave way, elaborate budgets began to be submitted, but its committees continued to rest on the constitutional right to appropriate. What emerged in authorizations served the politicians' purposes about as well as in the past. They do after all represent the people, as they often remind their critics; and the people have not told them directly to respect a program devised by the presidential bureau. After all, it is their own creation; the Constitution says nothing about it. What that document does say something about is that no expenditure shall be made without legislative authorization. It also says: "All bills for raising revenue shall originate in the House of Representatives."[2]

Resting on this, and lacking any directive to accommodate expenditures to income, the representatives feel no compulsion to balance the two. There has naturally grown up a running appraisal of this procedure. Involved in it are grave consequences for the economy. For instance, continued deficits may result in inflation, or continued surpluses may mean that public expenditures are too limited. Clearly, there ought to be an assessment of needs and an accompanying estimate of the resources available for meeting them. This could be made compulsory only by constitutional change, however; and, as we have seen, only the Congress can initiate amendment.

No one has ever been able to appraise the damage done by trading and maneuvering—the things not done that should have been done, and the things done that might better not to have been done (or were, at least, not essential). There might have been more interest in control if responsibility could have been assigned for consequences. The legislator who insists on a favorite project, or who prevents the adoption of others, is usually hidden in a committee. Appropriations often are passed by voice vote, and any congressman can always say he was on the side that later turned out to be the better one for his purposes; there is no record. Then, too, the results are slow in showing themselves. The guilty and the careless are usually long gone when consequences finally appear.

It is the contention here that this, if persisted in, can lead to something like national bankruptcy. It will never be called that by the political leaders who have participated in its happening or, more accurately, did nothing to prevent its happening. But what else can it be called? In spite of growing productivity, Americans have grown into the habit of paying themselves more than they produce, and inflation in the last few decades has stolen at least half the value from fixed incomes—from long-term creditors, pensioners, and insured (including receivers of incomes from the Social Security services).

In the enormous expansion of recent times, politicians have lost any

2. Article I, section 7.1.

concern they may once have had for prudence; appropriations and the income to pay for them are separated by such a massive confusion that all connection has been lost. Those who make appropriations are not associated with the procurement of income except in the most tenuous and extralegal way. Irresponsibility on a scale that escapes the imagination pervades the government, running as it does into sums almost immeasurable by customary symbols.

Once the politicians had grasped the uses of imbalance to stimulate enterprise and had made their own simplistic interpretation of it, they chose to assume that it justified expenditure beyond income not only in times of slack activity but also under any circumstance. True, there have been spasms of retrenchment when conservatives were temporarily in control; what this usually has meant has been a reduction in the welfare services which they resent anyway, and not in the expenditures favored by their sponsors. The pork barrel is never neglected. There has never been much slackening in the flow of appropriations, only occasional changes in their specifics.

Estimating, as a device, offers the opportunity to make the lacking connections. Affluent as the nation has become, the spending of more and more billions year by year in excess of income will have the same penalties as though the nation had remained poor. A nation undertaking more than it can pay for is asking for delayed trouble. Of course, excess is not always so deplorable and may even be necessary as an expedient during sinking spells of the economy. But if what is to be done is important enough, the funds for it usually can be found without resorting to inflation.

For politicians it is far more difficult to raise taxes than to lower them, but lowering as well as raising is called for in the theory of fiscal management. To establish priorities, to bring governmental enterprises and payment for them into immediate equation, to make rational choices possible, and to put those who refuse them on the defensive—these are the possible contributions of a planning agency.[3]

Merely setting up such an agency will not have an equating effect between income and outgo. It has to be recognized that there can be no real guidance unless there is an overhauling of the Congress and the presidency. As these institutions now exist, they will not allow a guiding agency to operate any more effectively than they now allow the budget to serve its intended purpose. Let us see.

The president, having before him only the facts—multifarious as they are—of his own budgeters, with responsibility for projecting expenditures only for one year ahead, will usually follow their advice. The budgeters will have no incentive to consider what ought to be done other than what is

3. "Implementing the General Interest," *Public Administration Review,* Autumn, 1940.

laid out so extravagantly in the demands of existing agencies, and they will have no expectation of respect for their efforts by the Congress. They will provide the president with only a contracted list of expenditures. In this situation he will project novel undertakings against an opposition he knows can only defeat him. He cannot be an effective allocator of funds and energies. Such departures as may occur to him when he is campaigning will be treated with hypocritical respect by the nearly invisible, but also nearly invulnerable, members of congressional committees, who, when not hostile, are indifferent to presidential preferences. If he prevails it will be a small allowance compared with appropriations for the projects that the legislators themselves favor. Besides, they can depend on allies in the executive agencies with notorious ability to dilute presidential orders.

It is a system corrupt in a subtle sense, since it is, by old standards, even defensible. There are still those who say that the best system is an additive one, with its projects originated by those with close links to the electorate, and with a hold on the executive agencies. Of course the reality is that the "electorate" is actually comprised of their supporters, and their activities are camouflaged by the theoretical position of a president who is called "chief executive" but who is helpless to administer the present overgrown departments. The actualities of government compared with the assumptions about it are startling—and become more so as time passes.

The congressional brokers will have been able to appropriate for a multitude of improvements. They will have made many supporters happy, and they will have stifled any suggestions for changes in the arrangements for authorizing expenditures. There have never been any changes in them, not really—only a few seeming ones. Actually, in their position, they need only be alert to one danger. This is that there are those who have a missionary impulse to expose. Such individuals have more opportunities as the old system fails to cope with the disorder of capricious growth. But if they have nothing more to offer than rebukes to the corrupt, they will not contribute much to reform.

It is amazing how easily such threats are smothered and how efficiently investigations likely to result in critical appraisal are consigned to the anonymity of reliable committees. The muckraker (to use an old but useful term), if he cannot be bought off by being taken into the circle of cooperators, can at least be ostracized and shut off from communication with potential supporters. At an extreme he can be labeled subversive, a serious charge during recurrent periods, especially within, say, ten years' distance from a war. Usually, however, exclusion from important committees and other evidences of disfavor will be enough.

What is proposed here, beyond exposure, is institutional change; without it an estimating agency would inevitably find itself interposed between favor givers in government and favor seekers on the outside. These last, of course, are the ever present lobbyists. In an impersonal system, lobbyists would have little place—something they know very well. They are nourished by successes in suborning legislators and administrators. They are paid to do this by their principals, and it is done with professional skill. There are substantial returns they can make for those favors they wangle for their employers; moreover, most of their activities have come to be regarded as quite legitimate. In important instances they are not simply individuals arguing for their principals; they are organized agencies having generous funds for their operations. Taken altogether, their number is many times that of the legislators—and sometimes seems as large as the executive establishment itself.

What these efficient lobbyists offer congressmen is the solidifying of support at home, but also they find ways to supplement incomes insufficient for Washington living; and, incredible as it may seem, they even maintain liaisons between legislators and appropriate bureaucrats. They are extraordinarily successful in identifying themselves with those who have the disposal of funds and favors. It is a massive establishment entangled with every motor impulse of government. To uproot it seems more than reformers could ever manage. The truth is that it has come to be regarded as an extra branch of government. To oppose it with a comprehensive alternative is to propose ending an institution as typically American as representation; indeed, it has become a part of the representative system. Private interests likely to be affected by legislation or by administrative regulation expect not only to present their views but also to further them, and they see nothing wrong in the effort.

The allowable extent of this furthering is indefinite. How would the word "favor" be defined, or "support," or "assistance," or, for that matter, "interest"? Occasionally there is exposure of scandalous extensions by those who do not stay within the unwritten rules. The mutual giving and taking does sometimes become "bribery," but this crudeness seldom appears. Why should money change hands? Campaigns can be paid for by contributions, and the distinction between what is spent for campaigning and what for personal bills is easily confused. As for the bureaucracy, manipulation of the budget is always available to keep its members properly respectful. A congressman has little difficulty in adding or subtracting some inconspicuous item when appropriations are being considered. Projects and jobs are easily eliminated by an interested legislator.

No one with the slightest knowledge of governmental affairs will find all this strange. To a fresh observer, however, its acceptance as a system must seem bizarre. It goes against all the canons of decency; it denies the sworn duty of officials; it makes many operations of government ridiculous and others of them suspect. But its uprooting and the substitute for it of an assessed way to dispose available resources will require comprehensive reforms quite outside the assessors' scope. They can only be ready with an alternate system when one is called for by a disillusioned electorate.

Meanwhile their readiness is a constant threat, and resisters are busy elaborating imaginary objections. Guidance, it is said, requires centralization in Washington, with a bureaucracy dehumanized, insensitive, and intent on getting and keeping power over people's lives and over their enterprises. That just the opposite is true seems difficult to argue with any effect.

To make use again of the biological analogy, with the reservations always due when analogies are appealed to, it may be pointed out that no bodily organ could function except in a random and blundering way without a brain, and one, moreover, fully developed and working. But given proper direction by this directing organ, each of the other organs contributes to an integrated whole. That this is true of the social organism, in at least somewhat the same way, it is more true to say in a technological age than in any former one. Lacking a place where demands are received, related to other demands, and put in context with general intentions, governmental programs simply proliferate and become, in the end, random and often mutually canceling conglomerations of operations.

A useful illustration of this is the multiplicity of contemporary welfare agencies. They were created in response to an obvious need and in time of growing affluence. But put together piecemeal over a period stretching from the thirties to the seventies, several hundred of them separately provided with funds constitute a chaotic and self-defeating system. There was a general impulse to assist the disadvantaged, but there was no resolve to find out what the causes were, what the remedies ought to be, and how available resources ought to be distributed.

There was also a confused urging to decentralize, together with a kindly impulse to entrust those to be helped with a part in administering their own assistance. Conflict and dissatisfaction resulted. The problems have increased in size and seriousness faster than the means to cope with them.

Uncoordinated responses to pressure or to emergency have their own penalties. They begin by repeated amendments, slipped into legislation as it is processed by congressional committees. Afterward, agencies authorized without much relation to others already in operation simply proliferate. During the period of expansion, rivalry and duplication are operating to check the effectiveness of every agency. All are discredited because no attempt has been made to assess the whole and to assign each a part.

How might it have been different in recent decades if there had been an agency for estimating and guiding?

A welfare assessment would have been made and the dimensions of the problem determined. There had been massive migration to the cities with consequences there of crowding, competition for jobs, and poverty, and there were other unhappy readjustments in the agricultural regions. There was no mystery about this; that it was going on was well known, and its gravity was well publicized. But instead of a general program to meet the situation, numerous meliorating acts were passed. They consisted of separate projects intended to relieve the victims of specific pressures. There were housing acts, acts providing income for deserted mothers and children, for training restless youths, and for expansion of educational and health facilities. The number of these finally added up to scores. Because the operations were inchoate, the concentrations of the displaced eventually erupted into the riots of the middle sixties. Expansions of police forces and other means for the suppression of violence were then required. These amounted to a denial of the original intention.

The nation had no early warning system, but it had a very effective one for resisting the changes necessary if the warnings had penetrated the politicians' minds. It might even be said that there were, finally, unmistakable signs even if the massiveness of the problem was underestimated. But politicians were in positions requiring them to think of other matters. They had to be reelected quite soon and so had to consider their constituents' needs, local needs; worse, these were the needs of special constituents with influence, ones they were linked to by long association. Somehow it was more important to compensate farmers for cooperating in a national adjustment program than to look out for the laborers being displaced by the new agricultural technology. The farmers had an effective lobby; the workers had none. This was typical. It was true of labor, of manufacturers—of whatever.

The effect was the opposite of what seemed to be expected. The problem needed to be met on a national scale. It began in a different place from the one where its consequences showed themselves. It did not require administration by nationally operated organizations, or by a series of them; but it did require national funding, allocations, and standards. Its management could not be centrally controlled; it was not only too big but too various. It reached into different regions, climates, and cultures—and these differences required sensitive administration.

When this need for decentralization was finally understood, there were further difficulties. The cities where the problems were had no direct relations with the national government. The states stood between the givers and the receivers, and there were endless interferences.

Most of the difficulties might have been overcome if, during the early Roosevelt years, the frightening depression had resulted in some real reforms instead of reconstituting the obsolete system. If, at that time, when the displacements were just beginning to assume the proportions of incipient disaster, guidance had been instituted, resources allocated, priorities established, and the necessary administrative organizations set up, the later years might have been much more equable.

Once the problem was made clear, and its requirements recognized, the part of the national government and that of regional governments would have been obvious. It was not done. Whether the systematic changes necessary to the operation of a complicated society can be accomplished in somewhat the way those of 1787 were brought about by disillusioned patriots, it is impossible to say. Not, probably, until the dissatisfactions become so prevalent that the repercussions reach those who have the ability to direct reform—a majority of voters. These may then find latter-day Washingtons, Hamiltons, Madisons, Wilsons, and Franklins—constitutionmakers, able and willing to accept responsibility comparable to that accepted by the framers.

Governmental Estimation and Guidance[4]

If the government's agencies are expected to reach objectives, it seems a simple conclusion that those objectives ought to be clearly defined. Also, it ought to be known how they can be approximated with the resources likely to be available. Incredible as it seems, these intentions are not now known, and the resources for reaching them are no more than wildly guessed at; we have seen, moreover, that there are those who do not even want them estimated. Since estimation is a technique for assisting both in identification and in realization, and is not wanted by those who prefer uncertainty, it will be adopted as a governmental institution only against the hostility of many existing institutionalized powers.

As far as the general government is concerned, there have been some concessions. Rudimentary guidance does exist, but it is not of an organized sort; such as there is has forced its way into use in clandestine ways and has done no more than assist harried administrators in defining direction for some, but not all, of the various agencies. Planning for the whole has not been accepted; it is, in fact, not even discussed by those who might be expected to feel the need for it most.

The budgeters naturally found that annual allocations for projects whose construction costs may extend over at least several—and perhaps many—years require a forward look. This may be unauthorized, perhaps kept private; but figures cannot be materialized out of nothing; if there is a project to be undertaken its total cost must be estimated or the increment for one year cannot be known. So, actually, a good deal of long-range projection is done. Not, however, being legitimate, it is not put together with any general view of the future. Officially the government never has a general sense of direction, what the alternatives are, what the costs will be, or whether income will cover the expenditures. It is not required to know;

4. That guiding must have an independence comparable with other branches of government was argued in "The Fourth Power," *Planning and Civic Comment*, Part II, April–June, 1939.

by custom it is even required not to know. This must be taken to be all too characteristic of a democracy desirous of the yield from technology without accepting the disciplines for its direction.

Several devices are recognized as useful by those who hope for further development of estimation and guidance: budgets, zoning, acquisition and strategic placing of public facilities (rapid transit, streets and highways, government offices, and so on), and the placing of private undertakings. These are illustrations. They have been used mostly by local governments in the United States; but in such noncommunist governments as Britain and France patterns for transport and communications have been made, satellite cities have been built, forests and parks have been set aside, and, if necessary, administered; whatever is nationwide in reach has been centrally controlled. What has been done in those countries can be taken as experiments in the way all will have to go eventually. It can be said of them that to the extent they have been guided by conceptions of the whole, they have succeeded. Observers are ready to say of them now that if a general conception of what the whole may and ought to be had not been accepted, there might have been many improvements—parks set aside, excellent highways built, efficient communications—but they would not have constituted a consistent recognizable and operative whole.

It will be recognized that some of this has been done in the United States. There is a "national" highway system, there are park and recreational areas, forests have been set aside, and waterways are a federal responsibility. Gradually such physical matters have become a national pattern. What is lacking is a general linking of all these together. This must extend, also, to productive facilities if protection against many hazards of social life is to be sought. What is amazing is that with so much specialized effort by agencies with particular objectives, an operating whole has not been allowed to materialize.

To point out the utility of using the techniques of estimation, including direction in the interest of the whole, is not to suggest that technicians ought to determine what is to be done. Bureaucrats in European countries have not had such dictatorial powers. What they have done has been to confine discussions to reality, exclude impossible alternatives, and eliminate many causes of conflict. In no country is there any suggestion of a return to preplanning chaos, nor is there any feeling that liberties have been lost.

It could have been expected that had everything been decided by the technicians there would have been a rigid and confining environment with little recognition of regional differences, and without much possibility of experiment and adaptation to the legitimate preferences of people. But no advocate of guidance in democratic countries suggests such a position for his agency. He does recognize, however, that there is needed a conception of the whole as well as attention to people's preferences. A guiding scheme must satisfy both these criteria. If it does not it will not serve the special purposes of a pluralistic society.

It is exactly these criteria that both executive and legislative officials still reject. It is true that estimating for the whole would take from them their ability to favor particular supporters. To bring what may be promised for campaign purposes within credible limits often reduces the politicians' appeal. And attention to other people's preferences annoys those whose demands are ignored. The attempt to please everybody is the oldest of political ploys. It is given up with the utmost reluctance.

There is evidence, however, that the customary gestures are not as useful as they once were—even to candidates for elective offices. Televised campaigning is apt to expose partiality. Having done something remarkable for one area may not prove it was taken from another, but comparisons become inevitable when such claims are heard by several audiences. Even a small congressional district may include resentful losers in contests for favors or public works. The pork barrel in affluent times is generous, but it cannot include *everything*; and what has been left out is apt to prove embarrassing when all its contents are known. Senators have even more difficulty in explaining, if they have to, why enlargements for a naval yard went to Charleston instead of Bremerton, why the interstate highway system missed one city and passed close to another, why one river was dredged and another was not, or why an agricultural experiment station was established in one area rather than another.

In the same vein of frustration, a president enumerating his favors to the Northwest cannot escape being heard in New England and along the Great Lakes. He has the added difficulty, although his party associates must share it with him, that he may have joined in spending so much, and so unwisely, that the benefits are lost in the inflation following large deficits. This, added to the resentment of those who may expect to be taxed to meet such expenditures, is likely to make continued popularity chancy and political lives short.

There are politicians who have seen that they might be better off if the center of attention were to be shifted from their favor-giving powers to their concern for the nation. If none can give their constituents what has to be taken away from *others'* constituents, or paid for with embarrassing deficits, they can represent themselves as devoted to commonweal instead of the *local*weal. It is suggested that this shift might go further. Representatives' new problems might be reflected in the structure of government as well as the demands of technology. It might become more appealing to advocate advancement for the whole than for the parts. Common sharing and fair sharing are supposedly virtues that exist, and perhaps they would exist if a way to invoke them could be found.

Estimation and guidance, as spoken of here, welded into government would assist in making such an overdue shift. But it could scarcely be done unless institutions were to be altered with this in mind. Legislators would have to be relieved of the necessity for nearly continuous campaigning and would have to be given reasons for centering on the national interest rather than local ones; also they would have to be put in position to respect their party commitments instead of using them, more often than not, to prove how much warmer their regard is for their supporters' interests than for those of the country as a whole. The president, too, would need to join with them in national thinking rather than in nurturing a coalition of voters in order to keep himself and his party in office. His situation would need to be appropriately modified.

Disintegrative tendencies, such as those referred to here, are imposed by the allocations of power to be found in the governmental structure. They were put there by constitution framers who believed in them. It may be argued that much could be changed if all concerned should suddenly become aware that the nation is one, if the president abandoned the Jeffersonian method of bribing legislators, and if the legislators agreed to honor the national budget and look to future commitments—all, in other words, converting themselves into statesmen instead of contriving politicians. But why should it happen when personal careers and party successes are more likely if it is *not* done? Is it unrealistic to expect such conversion? The separatist pressures emerge from traditional institutions.

Still, there is the fact that the old methods are far less effective than they were before the country was industrialized, before communication was instantaneous and transportation nearly so, and when government had fewer responsibilities for welfare. With the hard exposures of publicity in the modern modes, candidates cannot, as they wryly acknowledge, "talk out of both sides of their mouths." And the doctrine that anyone can do anything is no longer tenable about government jobs any more than it is about private ones.

It can still be contended that a separation of powers is necessary to the American scheme. If one were dominant, it would have to be the legislature whose place in government would not allow it to be either an effective executive or a fair judge of its own behavior. It is now argued further that an assessing and guiding power is necessary because executives or legislators are, in the nature of their positions, incapable of comprehending national interests. The whole nation, through technology, has come to be one community; it must have the institutions it needs to act like one. Separation of powers need not mean aggressive opposition of each to the others.

Assessing and guidance must, of course, have the same independence as the other branches. This will not be complete any more than theirs is; but the need for correlation, for conjuncture, now so necessary, cannot otherwise be met. There is no means or method provided now for formulating a program of national concern. It is proposed that this lack should be remedied.

Concerning most matters there is no need for competition. Matters having to do with finances, with physical resources, and the like are not too abrasive if approached with respect for facts and reason. Even about policies derived from facts, the suggested agency would do no more than indicate tentative conclusions. One man's reason might not be another's, but departure from the plainer indications would certainly be made difficult.

Consider, for instance, the assignment of priorities for expenditure—once probable income has been established. There are no absolute criteria for choosing alternatives among thousands. What will be lost or gained by certain choices can be shown, but what cannot be done is to say that education shall be preferred to public health, or space travel to transportation on earth. Such choices will still be consigned to public argument. The dialogue, however, ought to be more reasonable because of the information supplied by the planners and because, as far as it can be done, the alternatives will have been clearly and factually presented.

This is a very special kind of contribution, one not so important in a less crowded and affluent country or one less well equipped with technical devices and their skilled operators. In simpler and less complicated circumstances, a government might not get into trouble because it proceeded from uncoordinated initiatives, or because it acted from prejudice rather than conclusions from assembled data. But that is no longer true. A government may now get into very serious trouble from acting in that way; it may waste its resources in massive amounts and allow really horrendous situations to develop: undertakings beyond its capacity, vast neglects that accumulate until crises exist, inflation that steals from those who can least afford the loss.

It may be argued, therefore, that some guidance has become necessary —perhaps for the survival of the nation, and certainly to a more successful management of its affairs. And comparative independence in its operations is dictated by what it has to do—that is, to discover and understand facts, trends, and forces. Its relations with the older branches are indicated in their need for common objectives and the wastefulness of not accepting them.

To recapitulate: the founding fathers' concern for balance among government branches in order to avoid the lodgment in any one of them of an overpowering authority began a contest for power now grown so serious in its consequences that it must be stopped. The legislature and the executive struggle lengthily while matters of great importance await decision. Much of the area of that struggle is unsuitable and could be avoided by removing the subject of argument. This removal is possible only by making the data and the needs so plain that quarreling becomes unnecessary—or even absurd. This has gradually been recognized by students of government if not by the politicians themselves—as is evidenced by the reluctant acceptance of budgeting.

To go on, it ought to be understood that such a branch, being inserted into a government made up already of traditional branches, must take something from each, as well as add something novel of its own. Here the question arises whether there must be constitutional reconsideration. If each of the traditional branches should make concessions willingly, it would be less necessary to insist on amendment. What they must concede is, in each case, precisely what they cannot any longer—or perhaps never could—do successfully, and they will be better off for having shed the responsibility. But such realities are only reluctantly recognized where political prestige is involved or where imperialistic sentiments are outraged. This reluctance alone would make constitutional change desirable. Also, as will be argued, there is no really good reason for its avoidance.

On this question of constitutionality, it must be understood what the new agency needs to take and what the old branches must give up. In New York City, for illustration, there is (1) a Planning Commission, a para-legislative body to examine and pass on plans, (2) a Planning Department to make the plans, and (3) an Appeals Board where it is determined whether plans have been ignored, or where exceptions are warranted.

New York, as it happens, is large enough, and has problems varied enough, to offer a general example. In the 1930s the rewriting of its charter was undertaken by a singularly enlightened group of citizens who saw the need for considering the city as a whole, and for the recognition of planning as a way of seeing to it that the whole was regarded as superior to any of its parts. This body recommended a commission to be appointed by the mayor, for terms longer than the mayor's own. The commission was to consider the proposals coming to it from the technical staff working under the direction of the department head (in this capacity, a member of the mayor's cabinet, who was also to be chairman of the commission); and it was to sit at stated times for public hearings, when all those who were interested might comment on the proposals of the commission.

The commission and the department have been in operation since 1938, long enough for instructive experience. The charter provided that the physical layout of the city should be forecast, together with the regulations and the public expenditures necessary to its achievement. The commission was given custody of the city's official map and had to consent to any changes in it. It was also to originate and administer regulations determining the kind of uses to which property might best be adapted. Also, it was to make the capital (or improvement) budget for the city.

Together these represent responsibility for the appearance and efficiency of the city's institutions and the use of such resources as are in prospect.

The position of New York City as a port, or as a financial or cultural center, is not likely to be questioned; but even these may be developed more effectively if the port has generous facilities, and if education, housing, water supplies, and all the other municipal works are financed according to an accepted scheme.

The concept has proved practical except that it was not made mandatory that the duties imposed on the commission should be adequately supported. Except for salaries specified in the charter and certain engineering duties necessary to the custody of the map, the commission was never given proper funding. Both mayor and council saw at once that planning was dangerous to their prerogatives, and they had no scruples at all in thwarting the intention of the chartermakers. Private real estate interests, also, traditional enemies of any controls likely to make speculation unprofitable, have been effective in frustrating the commission's attempts to carry out its directives.

The first duty of the commission, according to the charter, was to produce what city planners call a Master Plan—an ideal projection of the city. All projects submitted by public agencies would be measured by their accord with the plan. The funds for such an effort were never made available, and the commission went on for decades with a kind of ad hoc advisory role. Finally, after many promises, the making of a plan was entrusted by contract to a private enterprise and now exists in several large and detailed volumes. The commission was at last furnished with the indispensable tool for its future work.

Like New York City, the nation has representative government with branches needing the same kind of integration; and like the city, it needs to control its physical changes and allocate carefully the funds necessary to carrying them out. A national planning agency, like that in New York, would have no absolute powers; it would not make decisions by itself, but it would have some say in them. The operations of government ought to be, as a result, more objective and less capricious.

The lessons from the New York experience are available for both encouragement and warning. The commission has demonstrated usefulness in anticipating the future, but it was frustrated in its attempts to organize its work.

The borrowing from the other branches suggested here is not so novel a suggestion as at first appears. In cities, in states, and in the federal government as well, the old divisions are not so rigid as they once were. Numerous bridging concessions have had to be made. In New York City it is difficult to tell whether the Board of Estimate is executive or legislative. It acts as an upper legislative chamber, but on it there are such executive officers as the mayor, the comptroller, and the presidents of the five boroughs, as well as the president of the Common Council. To a classicist this departure from the usual tripartite division would seem very confused; yet it works very well.

In the federal government, also, there are similar arrangements; among them are such commissions as interstate commerce, federal trade, power, and communications, all with responsibilities that once belonged to one of the old branches. Another kind of body is the Federal Reserve Board, whose powers include the supervision of banking but also, through its regulations of credit, exert a real influence on the whole economic machinery of the nation.

These few illustrations at least show that a proposal for assessment and guidance would not breach the barriers in any novel way. Provided what is proposed to be done is not something unreasonable or fearsome, it need not be regarded as theoretically objectionable or difficult to operate.

Wholes and Parts[5]

Perhaps we should see just what a planning agency, sited at the center of the government complex, might contribute to getting agreement on a program for the future.[6]

That program in the end hopefully will become a materialization of national ambitions set out in explicit terms for inspection. What has before been inchoate and doubtfully understood may in this way become the object of discussion and finally of choice among alternatives. One of these may well be so obviously superior that disagreement about it will be slight. This can result from the full exposure of the reason for it over a sufficient length of time, together with such changes and compromises as appear reasonable. But it should be of a different order from the usual uninstructed polarization on such matters.

Some issues will be more difficult than others to resolve. This will be because many do not lend themselves to factual descriptions, or it may be a result of continuing disagreement never settled because of deep unresolved differences. There is likely to be more controversy about the size of educational, welfare, or defense establishments than about necessary quantities of food or fiber, water, power, transportation, and the like. But even about matters with the least consensus, such a display of factual material as may be gathered together, with estimates of consequences from alternate choices, would assist in arriving at majority decision. And majorities are all that can be hoped for in most instances.

5. The subject of this section was treated more extensively in "Governmental Planning at Mid-Century" by the author (with E. C. Banfield), *The Journal of Politics*, May, 1951.

6. Cf. "The Utility of the Future in the Present," *Public Administration Review*, Winter, 1948.

This is what it all comes to: the planners will have said that if what is proposed is projected into the future the result will be what is shown. They will have said also whether it is really attainable. If it is not, and scattered debris of failed undertakings should be left along the way, how much will have been lost in wasted expenditure and missed opportunity? And will the social costs be more than the community ought to pay for private individuals' gains? There are heavy penalties for wrong decisions, some already being suffered in the United States. There are, for instance, slums, polluted air and water, exhausted soil, destroyed forests, inefficient services, insufficient welfare allowances—all the result of not having measured costs against expenditures in prospect.

Such failures, as things have been, have too often not come to notice until too late, and, besides, the alternatives have never been made visible. A planning scheme would present continuing alternatives, factually and in such detail as might be available. Attainable development, with social costs deducted, would thus be brought into view. Its components could be inspected and priorities weighed. As the future gradually became the present, the plan, approaching year by year, under discussion repeatedly, could become something decided on with relevant considerations in plain view.

A calculated schedule of expenditures would have been arrived at. These the central agency would not have originated so much as put together from the many proposals coming to it from various localities and regions. Each of these may always be depended on to formulate its own demands, and they are likely to be more than can be allowed within the resources available. In a city they will include, as has been suggested, such varied works as schools, streets, sewers, playgrounds, port, railway, power, and light facilities, housing—all the activities and institutions needed for urban life. Some of these would be publicly and some privately provided. If they were public, they would appear in the improvement budget; if they were private, they would at any rate be estimated and the social costs appurtenant to them already estimated. Would a new housing development require sewer extensions and the extension of streets? Would a private office building create traffic problems? Would a movement of population require public utilities of all kinds to be extended to one place and abandoned in another? Would expanded air traffic make new facilities necessary, and at what inconvenience or requirement of expenditures?

In the nation, as contrasted with a city, plans, instead of actually locating most improvements, would need do no more than indicate the need for, or the limits of, their development. For instance, requirements for power, communications, reclamation, conservation, and facilities for education and health would be estimated, priorities established, and provision for them included in the improvement budget. Even if many were to be private, their sufficiency could be measured. If they were not large enough some kind of decision about enlargement would have to be made with all the fringe involvements taken into account; if they were too large and expenditure on them not justified, their development would be counterrecommended.

Important decisions, as we shall see, would not be for the technicians to make either at the very beginning or at the very end. Problems looming in the future and their solutions would be described, together with alternate solutions, in the projections; but the plan would then be subjected to long and intense scrutiny as a whole, and would very likely be revised again and again.

It will be understood that the process outlined here would actually never be so neat. It can be imagined that the lobbyists' efforts to influence development, now concentrated on legislators, would be transferred to other decisionmakers whenever it seemed worthwhile. If any possible way to do it could be found their projects and arrangements would be worked into the proposal—added to it or subtracted from it as it continued to be discussed. There would be harassments, demands, denunciations, charges of favoritism, and even, perhaps, corruption. In all this the planners' protection must be that facts, made inescapably plain, speak, more or less loudly, for themselves. This, of course, is not true of intricate jointures, delicate relationships, narrow conclusions, and the infradecisions made along the way. But dangers of this sort can be minimized by making the processes public and holding public hearings repeatedly.

Such a branch of government as is described here must first do the simple preliminary work of putting together estimates of demands and of resources. Although other national agencies, and other governments, will have statistical staffs who will have gathered enormous collections of data, these naturally will carry a heavy load of interested justification; consequently, the raw statistics presented will not, in themselves, yield the necessary priorities. The planning agency, although it may prefer not to gather facts itself, must sometimes assemble them, and must very often recast those it has not actually had to gather.

Perhaps this may be stated again in other words: if the agency is to serve as the "central considering complex" of an organism, especially one so immense and so intricately woven together as a nation, if it constantly receives masses of materials, and if it is to bring them into a comprehensive whole, it must operate somewhat as the mind does in an animal organism— that is, as a place where information is received, stored, and sorted out, and where recommendations for action are then formulated. Its memory bank (store of knowledge) will provide useful precedents, and will enable it to make suggestions that accord with the general policy of the organism, indicating also what had bettter be done if that policy is to be carried out.

This is, of course, an oversimplification. There are many intermediate, tangential impacts and much worrying about them before anything resembling even a tentative project can materialize. If the first approximations are made for some years ahead, and are revised each year as new considerations arise, they should become more and more realistic. This, of course, is because, as later years approach, their necessities will become not only more quantified but also more visible. When the operational year approaches, the project may be quite different from its appearance six or twelve years before, but the differences will be the result of plans having been revised over and over as new facts have emerged and further discussions have had their effect.

In a biological organism the mechanisms for this kind of direction are inborn and automatic. They may be improved by training, but the physical basis for them already exists. In social organisms the mechanism has to be created, not merely improved. Not that governments, industries, and other social organisms do not, from the very first, possess certain means for making decisions and creating general policies. They may very well start with agreed objectives—as the United States started with commitments to "union" and "tranquillity." But keeping to the purpose and furthering it in operation, guiding by reflection, and achieving coordination will have come about only indirectly and in response to particular needs. They may have been forgotten or neglected by many, and may be lost by simply not pursuing policies appropriate to their ends. None will have more than piecemeal projections until the need for direction forces the creation of special devices.

An undirected social organism will act as is determined in a contest among political representatives who will have mixed motives, will have powers derived from complex sources (perhaps only seniority), and will have private or local interests to serve. Besides, when they have been only tangentially arrived at they can have no more than the haziest view of potentialities. It must always be recalled that the constitutional business of lawmakers in the American system is that of looking after the interests of their districts, not the interests of all.

Since organisms will move inexorably into the future whether or not it is an agreed and planned one, there is constant need for allocation and direction; it is not made less by imbalance among the forces *within*, where an organ grown strong for some special purpose may force other organs into its service—thus swerving the progress of the whole toward its own ends.

This last is especially true of governments. Any American, to illustrate this point, must have read about the corruption of city government by utility interests in the first decades of the nineteenth century when it sometimes seemed that whole cities were exploited for their profit. Occasionally some interest has gained enough power, even in Washington, to swing public policy upon itself as a fulcrum. The farm bloc, powered by the Farm Bureau

Federation, the Grange, and other organizations, was an instance of this, lasting for two long generations. But so also there have been—and are—various other lobbies serving the manufacturing, the banking, the real estate, the food processing, the patent medicine, the trucking, and numerous other interests. Labor, gaining power, has been as neglectful of its duty to the whole as the commercial interests it once denounced; its lobby became quite as formidable as any and quite as self-centered. In this contest to dominate government the most favors go to the strongest, not to the one most likely to assist in creating a viable future. The setting up of processes for guidance would at least move these contests to a relevant object. Instead of buying support by corrupting legislators and administrators, lobbyists would have to prove a case for inclusion in a program calculated to further the country's interests. And in doing this they would meet head-on the calculations of an agency staffed with those who, over years, have accumulated immense stores of knowledge.

In its fact-analyzing and arranging activity the agency may become in these ways an indispensable part of the organism. Its intimacy, finally, with all the various and complicated operations and their effect upon one another may at the end bring the agency to an understanding of what contributes to or detracts from the whole, how parts fit with other parts, how the interlocking has come about, and how necessary each is to general operations. This would leave the lobbyist with much less leverage than he customarily has had.

In principle, local and national governments are in similar situations; and, one day, a government of the world will face the same challenges. Size and complexity do make differences, but not in devotion to the organism and in concentration on keeping it to its purposes. These virtues must be made more, not less, operative by the institutions shaped by their demands.

The finding and establishing of purposes is, of course, no simple matter. Its difficulties will be discussed later; but, generally speaking, it is not for the assessing agency to do, at least not by itself. It can facilitate by making visible the possibilities, and by showing what is impossible or is most likely to turn out well. It may point out alternatives within a whole, but it should not try to do more. A people's future, so far as it is susceptible of change from old commitments, ought to be settled by their representatives, not by the representatives of an idea—not even so important a one as optimum yield from social effort.

The many reports issued by the National Resources Planning Board during its comparatively short existence from 1933 to 1943 were exemplary analytical exploration. They amounted in sum to an inventory of resources and of national potentialities. Unfortunately the board of those years never had any independence, or even, for that matter, any clear terms of reference; and as a consequence, it never went beyond researches and conclusions from them. It never operated as a planning agency. But even its putting together of a whole view was found repugnant by a majority in the Congress, and when the chance came in 1943 it was abolished by the deletion of its funds from the budget.

This was obviously because there was a hint of priorities merely in the pointing out of possibilities. Besides, it was attached to the presidency and thus added weight to his recommendations. Congressional caprices were correspondingly reduced by some appreciable increment. This was intolerable, and the president was not, in the end, able to keep the board in existence. That the circumstances were peculiar must be admitted. The war was coming on, and to put it plainly, Roosevelt was trading his New Deal ventures for a preparedness the Congress was reluctant to finance. At any rate, the operations of the National Resources Planning Board ended without ever having advanced beyond giving the nation new self-knowledge. It never acted as a coordinating agency. It might have had a better chance to survive if it had been independent. This would not have overcome the objection of the numerous and powerful antiplanners, but the board would have been freed from involvement in the struggle between the old branches. It might in time have proved its utility and have been allowed to evolve into a genuine assessing operation.

The New York Planning Commission did not have the handicap of belonging to the mayor as the National Board belonged to the president. The commission was made independent by the charter. Its members were amazed to discover, in a city whose corporate existence had gone on for several hundred years, how little knowledge it possessed about itself. It had no reasonable estimate, for instance, of its probable growth in the succeeding decades—although methods for such a forecast were by then available. Conclusions about size made an enormous difference in every decision. How much water would need to be supplied, for instance, in twenty or thirty years? Some judgment about this had to be made because it requires twenty years or more to carry out such enormous works as will furnish a supply for so large a metropolitan area. For a supply to be available in 1980, work must have been begun in 1960.

Some sort of forward look is taken, because it must be, by all departments charged with long-term projects. The Water Department of New York made its estimates; so, for that matter, did other agencies. For the nation, the Corps of Engineers and the Reclamation Service were continuously engaged in ten- and twenty-year projects. Their estimates could always be found, when compared with others, to disagree by as much as 50 percent. What such a diffused arrangement guaranteed was that when twenty years had passed there would be a too generous provision of some facilities and a shortage of others. The funds used for the overexpanded ones could well have been used to remedy the shortages, but nothing like such an equalization could be carried out until there were means for regarding the organism as a whole rather than as a conglomeration of uncoordinated enterprises.

That central considering function some agency should supply. For any social organism, it may be supplied in the same way; but for government not to use such an available means of knowing itself is to make certain that there will be many costly mistakes and, always, unsatisfactory performance.

When the Congress simply refused further appropriations for the National Resources Planning Board, there were still those who found it absurd that so immense an organization as the central government should have its activities authorized by caprice, and particularly those having to do with economic undertakings. Involved in this, for instance, was control of the business cycle now grown so familiar. Even congressmen readily conceded that the intensifying extremes of boom and bust had become intolerable. The unemployed now had to be taken care of. It would be better to reduce their number.

Going on to the afterwar years, the adjustments incident to the peace frightened everyone. As a consequence of this concern, something was done. What was called the Full Employment Act was passed. Of course it had in its prologue a commitment to free enterprise. This amounted to a disclaimer of any intention to allow any planning to be done. It was a planning act, nevertheless, a curious and ineffective one, but one that reluctantly recognized a necessity.

The times were peculiar. In war's aftermath the country was finding its way into peace with all the disruptions usual in such a convulsion. It always seems easier to organize for war than to disestablish the organization it has caused to be set up. This is perhaps because war scares legislators, and allows administrators to follow the logic of their responsibilities. When an emergency occurs the government behaves as though the nation had suddenly become a whole. Disestablishment after the emergency return it to the mercies of entrepreneurs acting as though a whole had never existed. The immediate penalties in 1946, for instance, were such serious ones as inflation and extensive unemployment.

At least some gesture had to be made. Full employment was passed. It provided for a Council of Economic Advisers intended to be of assistance in "stabilization." This meant the avoidance of fits of activity followed by sudden and stubborn paralyses. These successive up and down cycles had become familiar throughout the industrialized world. But in recent years economists had been saying that they were avoidable and suggesting how they could be controlled.

It was President Hoover, when secretary of commerce, who had caused serious studies to be made and published under the editorship of Wesley C. Mitchell, the director of the National Bureau of Economic Research. Postwar disturbances of the economy had given Hoover his chance to do this, and it had been done impressively. There could no longer be any doubt that depressions were avoidable. In fact, preparations for averting the next one had been made. An office to prepare plans for the expansion of government activity when private enterprise slowed down had been set up. Also, Hoover had recommended the fiscal changes necessary to preparedness. He had seen and deplored the weaknesses of the country's financial organization. But he had been president only a few months when the consequences of the Harding-Coolidge permissive policies showed themselves. Early panic extended into helpless inactivity. The economic system simply slowed down to a near stop. The plans made for expansion were minuscule compared with the massive need. The banking organization began to crumble. And when enterprises took measures for their own protection, they were ruinous for the country.

Hoover fought a losing battle until he was replaced by Roosevelt, who did some further patching but was able to get only fractional recovery from the profound sinking spell. It was the war that rescued the economy, but it was paid for by inflation. This was inherited by Truman, who, advised by businessmen, removed war controls without the slightest realization that they had been holding down a potential explosion. It came immediately. Prices jumped; debts expanded; there were labor troubles as workers felt the pinch. But presently a level was reached at an elevation requiring every part of the economy to make new adjustments. It was an uneasy accommodation with nothing much done to avert more extremes of expansion and contraction.

There had been certain changes. Roosevelt had insisted on certain reforms of the financial system, and Social Security measures guaranteed a minimum of spending power for the economy. Bankers could no longer speculate with their depositors' funds, and there would not again be the complete disappearance of people's power to buy. But that these were not enough, everyone knew.

There had been spreading through the professional community—ever since Roosevelt's reluctant injection of artificial purchasing power into the economy through relief, expanded governmental enterprise, and deflation of the currency—the realization, grown from the seed of Hoover's reports in the twenties, that the economy could be stimulated or damped down by monetary and fiscal measures. The Federal Reserve Board could do something as it was now organized; but the Congress still had the power to control expenditures, and it was completely unresponsive to warnings.

It was to assist in controlling these economic expansions and contractions that the Full Employment Act was passed and the Council of Economic Advisers set up. It was an early warning device. The advisers were to set a watch on the indicators of activity and suggest actions calculated to avert abnormal rises and falls. Unfortunately, it was not made clear whether the advisers owed responsibility to the president or to the Congress. The council chose the president; but the Congress had been provided with a joint committee to consider the council's reports, and this it did. But other legislators paid little attention, and after a few years it was apparent to everyone that what had been done was not sufficient. The council had no powers at all. It could not even command attention. But it was all there was.

During Eisenhower's eight years in the presidency, there were three serious sinking spells, none reaching the depths of the Great Depression—obviously because Social Security furnished a minimum of buying power. But never in all the conservative years was the budget balanced or inflation stopped. The "honest dollar" promised by the Republicans steadily eroded. The economy was still manipulated by professional speculators at the expense of the lowest-income receivers.

As 1970 approached there was ample evidence that palliatives had failed. Inflation would go on; every group with some economic weight would force favors from the economy—and the unions, now grown strong with the protection of their new laws, would use their strength not for further stabilizing measures but for getting overgenerous shares from an unstable economy.

The unions' attitude was a general one. Businessmen, for instance, preferred to depend on their own forecasts of coming events, and their ability to outguess slower competitors, to furthering progress toward a general system of orderly and controlled advance. There would be rises and falls of activity, checked before disaster by rudimentary devices. The Congress would appropriate when stagnation threatened, but it was slow to compensate pensioners or others with fixed incomes whose livings were made precarious.

It is suggested here that it is widely enough known what needs to be done. Assessment and guidance begun years ahead, and brought to a conclusion in an annual budget, would supply the needed advance within available resources; planning would link objectives with the means for attaining them; it would protect the incomes of those now defenseless; it would stimulate a dialogue—now completely missing—concerning national intentions, and would relate these intentions to the likelihood of their materialization.

This is the argument made here for giving up the futile devices of laissez-faire, favorable only to speculators, and accepting the calculated assessment of needs and resources available through a new agency of government.

The parts can be made parts of a whole, not centers striving to turn the whole to their own uses.

The Putting Together

Thus far the duties of an imagined agency have been no more than suggested. There is more to come, most of it for various reasons both involved and difficult—sophisticated in a technical sense—but also requiring sacrifices from political leaders impossible to find in their usual habit. What is required is no less than a giving up of inflated promises and favor giving, the bread and butter of representative government. And this is a good deal to ask, too much to ask of legislators themselves—an admission that it can come about only through constitutional amendment.

It will be seen that such an agency would necessarily have much to do with decisions about matters politicians are accustomed to take positions on without really having the solid information they should have before making commitments. Worse than this, politicians will too often summarily reject information that happens to be inconvenient. Unless they are miraculous guessers, and unless their interests just happen to fit into a scheme of general benefit, their promises are bound to be inappropriate. They offer what cannot be delivered or, if it can, ought not to be invested in. It is understandable that a candidate should speak airily of projects he intends to see undertaken if and when he is elected. Such promises are notorious for not being fulfilled, since they are so often impractical or so alien to general policy—and they are not always forgotten. Many a second campaign has been lost by comparing promises with records of accomplishment. It is quite possible that politicians are better off if they are deprived of such fallible appeals, but they have shown no sign of realizing this.

The roughed-out sum of demands or expressed preferences, emanating from the executive and going on to the legislature as a budget, is far from the integrated whole that ought finally to be shaped. And now it has to be said that it is impossible for such a whole to appear until the impact of what is proposed has been estimated. This is not only the immediate costs. There will be many others, even ones long delayed, and there must be a weighing to see that what results will be a net gain. Cost effectiveness, as engineers mean it, must be extended to include social costs. The automobile must be charged with air pollution; the airplane with the decline of railways; high-rise buildings with congestion; new housing with the subsidiary facilities the public must provide; agricultural practices with soil erosion and, as well, with city ghettos.

Every undertaking, or nearly every one, has this sort of attached disadvantage. Those who do the undertaking, often including governmental projects, are never anxious to include such costs in their estimates; but the planner must.

The inevitable matching of the total cost with available resources will come at a later stage of consideration, but it must come. Can what is wanted be paid for? If not, what must be deleted? It is feasible to estimate population some years ahead; certain resources may be opening up, or may be nearly exhausted; power potentialities may be considerable or limited; industries may be growing or declining; transportation and communication may be changing; even climate may be showing persistent hostility or may, on the contrary, be coming under control. These are necessary considerations, but they should not be represented as easy to follow through. The measurements involved are often uncertain, and when they are, technicians must be content with the establishment of probabilities. Fortunately, for the purpose, although a wide deviation may seriously affect the result, a smaller one may not; still a skew somewhere in the material may result in an unacceptably larger deviation in the result. A leaning tower of Pisa may begin with a slight mistake in laying the foundation. How important a mistake is likely to be is an important factor that must be determined.

Considering this, it can be seen how serious it may be if an irresponsible political promise is forced into the calculations and everything else has to be adjusted to it. Because this is a fair description of the usual procedure in American political organisms, it is not really strange that a state of near-chaos has resulted.

To complicate matters still more, it must be noted that legislation passed in another jurisdiction may make adjustment necessary (as when the central government requires cities to enter on a program of sewage disposal to end pollution of harbor waters or when, on the other hand, it underwrites some of the welfare services the city cannot afford to match). Either sort of impact necessitates a subtraction from, or addition to, the city's obligations and must be represented in its list of expectations. Rising standards may make new demands on local administrations; there may be considerations of public health (as when the federal government in 1946 had to improvise a vast preventive campaign against the spread of hoof-and-mouth disease from Mexico into Texas, and not only incurred enormous expenses itself but disrupted the economy of Mexico and imposed subsidiary costs on Texas). Many illustrations will occur to the experienced reader; in most cases, it will be recalled, there has been scant connection made between the requirements and provision for their expense. The Congress, for instance, often refuses appropriations to match its earlier authorizations, a habit depriving administrative agencies of the ability to see even one year ahead.

These are quite usual uncertainties owed to impacts from outside. Those entrusted with the execution of programs thus affected will present their own estimates of the support they ought to have, including expenditures beyond their own capacities unless these are appropriately enlarged. What is needed to escape such difficulties is not only surveys of resources but estimates of the results likely to occur from the carrying out by each agency of programs certain to affect others, not forgetting that all will be affected as well by externals. It is not necessary to insist further that the whole will be skewed this way or that by each decision of those persons who are uninformed or who have self-interests; and it can be guessed how frequent the appeals to emotion will be and how often there will be denunciations of those who proceed from public premises.

In any case, when demands and estimates have been brought into comparison with the possibilities, it will very likely be found that if every activity should be financed as its promoters and administrators propose, or even as a tolerable standard would require, the outlay would exceed total income, perhaps far exceed it; and at this stage, in any rational system, a balance of proposed expenditures and incomes will have to be sought.[7] There will then be agonizing reductions.

It will be recognized that if this is to be at all adequately accomplished, it can be done only by highly sophisticated methods. The personnel that would be staffing an agency with such duties will need to have a command of calculating and measuring techniques used only in the most advanced industrial enterprises but so far known rarely in governmental operations. Much of the calculation will, of course, be consigned to powered machines, and the setting of problems for these machines will be a skill in itself. It may as well be recognized, too, that the operations of the agency here being discussed will be many times more complicated than those ever before undertaken. There are in existence mighty industrial empires, but none is more than a fraction the size of many governmental departments. Besides, all, even the largest of these, will be subordinate in the colossal national entity.

When it is considered that private operations affect governmental estimates so importantly that they must be known and allowed for, the conception may seem to have exceeded any possibility of being reached in reality. This will be said, always has been said; the only answer to the contention must be that what is contemplated is no more than exists now in deliberately disjoined operations; and that bringing them into relation, even if with only moderate success, may reduce the damage from the customary blundering. Something conjunctional must be done; and that something, if it does not make some sort of holistic sense, will be far short of what it could be.

If all this seems impersonalized and mechanical, it actually is less so than appears in a brief description. Besides, it must be pleaded, this is not the place for such considerations, which properly come both before and after the estimating procedures. Before expenditures are programmed there ought to have taken place general discussion resulting in a concept of intention with its relation to the whole (something to be enlarged on later).

---

7. This need not be an *annual* balance. The idea of a yearly settlement of this sort has no logic. The forces at work may not mature in so short a period, and it may well be advantageous to incur deficits for longer periods to maintain the momentum of the economy. On the other hand, there may be times when the building up of surpluses may be desirable. The fetish of the annual budget often prevents realistic governmental programming. Nevertheless, the rule guiding decisionmakers ought to be one of balance. If expenditures exceed outlays, the eventual result must be payment by those who did not make the choice.

The organism does not merely exist; it has missions to carry out. In determining what exactly these missions are or should be, the planning agency will have helped by organizing the materials for judgment; but as has been indicated—and must always be kept in mind—the agency will not do the defining. It may be decided, for instance, that the modernization of cities requires the checking of growth at the periphery and the encouraging of renewal at the center or, alternately, the building of complete satellite cities. Or, for other illustrations, a nation, coming to a realization of its geophysical situation, may understand that drastic changes in policy are necessary if its resources are to be conserved; it may be realized that its food supply is endangered, that its posture in the world requires revision, and that its social services are inadequate. Many such decisions are ones to be discussed and then made finally with the help of calculations, but they are not to be made *by* the calculators.

There ought gradually to emerge—as a result of what may be prolonged, repeated, or supplemented studies and discussions—an accepted notion of the organism, with its parts properly related to the whole. This will be something more than a mere design, just as a living individual is more than his anatomy. The whole may then take form somewhat in the way a photographic negative, when developed, begins to show detail after detail until finally the picture is complete. It is to be recalled that the factors in this not susceptible of quantification will, through discussion, have been assayed and have thus become large considerations.

The ethos of San Francisco is not to be confused with that of Chicago or Philadelphia, and its preservation will have become an accepted aim. Similarly, nations have recognizable and precious characteristics. Each organism will have spirit as well as physique, sometimes so plain that it is easily caricatured. Philadelphia is represented as dull and conservative, Chicago hustling and careless, and San Francisco spectacular and worldly. Such descriptions may owe more to general perceptions than to measurement; the continental largeness of the American nation is in strong contrast with, say, British insularity and French self-containment.

When such qualities become recognizable, however, they will not be intelligible to others unless there is such particularization that they may join in the making of decisions concerning the future. However repugnant it may seem to objectors, this future, if it is to be materialized, has to be shown in budgets, in charts, in maps, and in other descriptive materials; only in these ways can matters be exposed for discussion, with the future thus generating a directed motion toward itself.

It may well be discovered in such assessments that what is wanted is not what currently exists, needing perhaps a little added here and there, but a very different form—deficiencies and neglected possibilities being what they are. There will remain unsettled questions about what is really wanted, but a practical way to compromise such differences has been found in majority rule. So, in effect, although the questioning may not stop, if all agree to accept what the majority wants, the whole organism may gradually understand its destiny and set its course in that direction.

True, those who stand to make or lose something from projected change are apt to muddle such decisions deliberately, especially when hard choices are involved; as, for instance, when more schools have to be weighed against more street improvements in a city; or when, in a nation, more water development has to be weighed against added funds for highways, or when welfare expenditures seem to limit educational expansion. Because these are complicated choices, there has to be agreement on certain standards to guide the rulemakers.

Such agreements are important in decisionmaking; they are preliminary to the work of those who must submit a comprehensive estimate with indi cations of possible alternatives. They must expect to explain every item, and they cannot do it without frequent reference to anterior criteria. When these are available the estimations are within a protected area. Definition of such values is a quite different matter from operating within them. The one is not planning territory—at least not primarily; yet even here they may have an influence on the dialogue—but the other is within the territory. There may be controversy about the statement of intentions, but the central agency must have it in order to continue its work. Does the nation, for instance, mean to have fair sharing of incomes; devote, say, 5 percent of its territory to recreation; have a free health service; make its education open to all; live at peace with other peoples, but maintain an adequate system of defense; rid itself of ethnic separatism; require that industry be managed in the public interest; make its cities places of pride; furnish effective governmental services?

Such questions, and others of the same sort, must be described as premature. They are the ones to be settled in political dialogue and then to be taken as presented for planning purposes. This is, of course, not a simple matter either. There will be differences, and the indispensable device of majority rule will not stifle minority dissent. The planning agency must expect its operations to be troubled by harassments from those who will continue to maintain that the decision was wrong and may not be accepted as a premise. They will oppose proceeding on the assumption that the decision is acceptable. And minorities have many advantages in a democracy, especially in preventing conclusions from being reached.

Still further trouble must also be anticipated. Such decisions may never be put to a vote because their formulation is uncertain and confused. Code words such as equality, freedom, security, and the like are agreed to, perhaps, but the variety of interpretation may well include a term that is inconsistent or even contradictory. Such a term, for instance, is free enterprise. Does this include freedom for *all* businesses, or is it necessary to restrict some so that others can be free? Clearly, if this is done, there is no general rule of freedom.

If, however, the estimating agency can operate in spite of such ambiguities, it will find itself compelled to be the sole or, at least, the most devoted protector, in a plural society, of the whole—whose integrity is essential. In this duty it will find itself resorting to such objectivity as will either avert controversy or settle on such differences as do not cause distress. Much may be assumed to be in this way agreeable; but what may not must not prevent the submission of a comprehensive proposal. That, after all, is the purpose of planning. The construct must, by then, command such respect that the burden of proof will be on the dissenters rather than the proposers.

The varied kinds of information to be gathered, mastered, and fitted together having been fully discussed, the organism should be generally understood and its needs (for operations and for development) substantially agreed upon. Such an accomplishment will have required many cooperating specialists: geographers, economists, anthropologists, students of politics, as well as engineers and architects. Variegated expertise will have been directed to one end.

The geographer has a specific knowledge of the environment possessed by no one else. Northern areas have severe seasonal changes, but they are not uniform and the differences need refinement; there is plenty of water but a shortage of sunshine. The Southwest needs water, but its heat is often excessive. The cramping of New York City between waters very early gave it checkerboard streets; but Los Angeles, being able to spread out, has done that to excess. The United States has had a continental stretch quite different from that of smaller nations. These facts and forces impose conditions the geographer will insist must be recognized.

It is the responsibility of the political student to understand how organizations are related to one another and how all of them together form the larger whole. A city, for instance, although it will have character and individuality, is, after all, part of another government—indeed, of at least two other governments—and it is related ultimately to the world. What the state or nation is, or may be, or does, or may do, to affect the city itself has to be estimated and allowed for. There is usually very little the smaller organism can do to change the policies of the larger; and even if it could, no more than mutual accommodation, requiring adaptation on the part of the city, would be required. This is true in different degree of neighbor nations. Each affects the others.

It has to be recalled here that what is being spoken of is not a static proposal but a progressing development, put forward tentatively, for perhaps twelve years from the present, gradually shaped and matured by discussion in each of the succeeding years until it emerges as a commitment into the present. It should, in fact, become the annual budget to be proposed to the legislature for authorization. There will have been repeated objections, supporting arguments, restudies, and rearrangements. In this way it is possible that most differences will have been eliminated or compromised; at least a majority will have given its consent to most settlements.

Since we are speaking here of all this being done by an agency within government, political affairs must have attention. What will be done will be decided by people and their representatives. It is essential that a public agency shall remain public and shall find support in wide general acceptance of its proposals. Admitting this, realities still have to be faced, no matter how disagreeable. The plan must take on fiscal reality: what can best be done with the resources at the disposal of the organism, and what ways of enlarging those resources may best be adopted.

These are the social considerations; but the agency must also make a physical assessment of the present and the future. Streets, buildings, waterways, and other facilities become real only when they have been reduced to chart, map, design, and ultimately specification. It is for the engineers to express, in specific symbols, the possibilities described generally by others. Very often in the past the whole job of planning has been entrusted to these physical arrangers. The results of this have been unfortunate when the engineer had no sufficient directives; also, he is inclined to think restrictedly of physical arrangements. What he has arrived at often has been found not to be feasible for economic, political, or even psychological reasons. Even though a design may be neatly laid out, it may not be approved by a majority of those who must use it. There are hundreds, even thousands, of engineer-made "master plans" for cities and for developing nations, drawn up, published, and put away in files, never to be heard of again because social and political considerations have not been taken into account.

This is another way of saying that the engineering/architectural contribution comes last rather than first. Designs need to be made only for something likely to be done. Planning, anyway, as has been intimated, is a continuing function, not a sporadic or periodic one. Engineering is in the end necessary to a final materialization. Decisions cannot be made without it, but neither can they be made unless the engineer is directed by others.

To suggest that every planning body must have a full complement of specialists is to ask for perfection. Many times—as in the smaller cities, for instance—such a proposal would be impractical. Besides, a good many other necessary contributions have not been mentioned—those of statisticians, accountants, administrators, lawyers, draftsmen, experts in public health and education.

Smaller organisms can rely on consultation for many such services, and there is the further possibility of joining together. But it is no exaggeration to say that any large social organism must have experts in all these various fields, and a national agency, such as is under discussion here, is even more dependent on a varied staff of specialists.

It remains to be said that estimating per se is also a skill of a specialized kind. There must at a late stage be those who will make a whole out of the materials presented to them, putting to its appropriate use advice from all the experts. To make intelligent use of geographic, economic, political, and engineering data, a technician in each of these fields is not required. One person obviously could not become capable in more than one or at most two of them, but he can learn to proceed from the center outward, to become concerned with wholes rather than parts. To be a planner is to operate as a coordinator whose first care is that the gestalt shall remain in good health and shall proceed on its intended way.

What has been said here may seem too obvious to need statement. That it needs saying is, however, shown by remarking that it cannot be found anywhere. Its necessity has been just as obvious for many decades, but its acceptance as a public function has never been seriously considered. There have been a few exceptions to this in the American system. No more than two of them (New York City and Puerto Rico) have been properly conceived, and these were promptly made ineffective by politicians who found them intolerable. These exceptions represented the public interest, not special ones; but representatives of districts consider first their particular constitutents and, as has been said, among these first the ones they depend on for support and for continuance in office.

Knowledge is not the problem; every necessary fact is known. Expertise is not the problem; it is easily found in this time of technological richness. What is lacking is an arrangement of institutions favoring the interests of the gestalt, not ones so seriously opposed to it that if they can prevent it they will not allow it to exist and, if it does exist, will prevent it from operating effectively.

Anterior Concord

There is one relevant concern mentioned but not yet opened for discussion here. The procedures thus far described are really ways of implementing or narrowing values already hardened into convictions; or, if not quite that, at least gestating in the collective mind and therefore certain to materialize. Many of these can simply be taken by planners as assumed. They are not entirely exempt from reconsideration, but often they are, or may seem to be. Their conclusions have been innocent of any rational tests; nevertheless they may well be deep and lasting ones, subject only to influences running far beyond decades, or even centuries, into the past.

The existence of these beliefs is indisputable; moreover, questioning them is made difficult by their acceptance through such extended time. Yet there is the complication that they do evolve. In addition, if not really evolving, they may take on appearances in such contrast at different times as to make them unrecognizable. As a result, they may be traceable to their origins only with considerable difficulty. Their origins will, however, have given them characteristic qualities, and they will be dominant within wide and seemingly various cultures.

Actually, these beliefs are seldom accepted with unanimity; it is difficult to know when substantial consensus actually exists. Resting thus on uneasy support, they are frequently challenged. But every professing democracy must proceed by majority consent, and it is therefore necessary to discover whether majorities actually exist when socal values are translated into programs of action.

Objectives may be defined by an elite (for instance, a constitution may be written *for* a people rather than *by* them); but there must be ratification. It is in this process that consent is tested, and the test may not be a dependable one. It is preceded by dialogue; and political dialogue rests on claim and counterclaim; it is frequently shot through with specious argument; and its protagonists, having something to gain, may be more interested in confusing issues than in clarifying them. What is brought to a vote may be thoroughly confused, and the emerging majority may not have concluded what in the circumstances will prove at all wise.

It is one of the contributions of planning that it may measurably improve the rationality of the dialogue. This it may achieve by establishing realistic terms, thus making conclusions more relevant to issues. It may be argued for the development plan that it is an unexcelled device for reaching decisions that nature and reason will not reject and that majorities will accept.

The complications are baffling. Among the more or less fixed values or assumptions, some are always traceable to original myths or later misconceptions. If bizarre and fanciful notions are widely current, politicans are likely, nevertheless, to advocate their promotion and realization. If these are mistaken and, if implemented, simply irrelevant to the issues it is assumed they represent or explain, and whose materialization will give satisfaction, the consequences may be serious. Long and massive efforts may follow, and enormous expenditures may be made—only to end in frustration. This too is something the planning procedures are useful in helping to prevent.

For an example of this in American experience, consider the frontiersmen who had a severely restrictive biblical code of behavior. Their beliefs required them to live in friendship with their fellow men, but the conditions of their environment required the maintenance of the force necessary to establish their claims to property and to maintain conformity in morals and customs. The frontier is regarded in retrospect as more violent than peaceable, more individualist than cooperative. But the violence was not the ideal those people meant to reach. It was the only way they found for keeping peace. It was unfortunate, but necessary. Religion was for Sunday; the sheriff or the marshal was for the rest of the week. And if the lawman was distant, each citizen then became an enforcer.

When the time came to establish more orderly government, very many fierce propertied men resisted. They preferred to depend on their own reserves of violence to maintain stable conditions. They were skilled and courageous; the law was slow, and its penalties were uncertain. Yet frontier deference to its religious leaders was unexceptionable. They professed peace and compassion, but the practical decision was for swift and not too careful repression. Disturbers were enemies and deserved none of the mercy the preacher expounded in his discourses. The underlying urge was toward order. Independent violence was only the means—even when it seemed to be an end in itself. If there was paradox, it confused not only the outsiders; the people themselves sometimes seemed to forget what end was being sought.

A similar example is furnished by free enterprise, an ideal closely allied with frontier individualism. Every person could operate in his own affairs pretty much as he liked as long as there were not many others who were trying to do the same. But when the land became populated and some enterprises grew so large that they could suppress others and could exploit consumers, the time had obviously come to abandon free enterprise. Instead, the attempt was made to *enforce* it. Enforcing freedom was much like using violence to establish peace. The means used came to replace the objective in a good many minds. Businessmen's rights to do as they pleased clashed continually with competitors' and customers' rights. Moreover, it made order in economic affairs impossible. Because of the ensuing chaos, violent cyclical disturbances recurrently disrupted the whole economy. A dozen serious ones during the previous hundred years climaxed in the paralyzing breakdown of 1929.

The Great Depression was much more serious and persistent than previous ones; it was not cured until, a decade later, preparations for war excused collectivization and, for the duration, the abandonment of laissez-faire. This could not be done in the name of order and stability, only in the name of national security. Some traces remained after the war, but still it was not acknowledged that the free habit of business had caused the breakdown and that the only preventive was the opposite. Such of the collective effort as did remain was enough to prevent further disasters of comparable scale. It was never admitted, however, that collectivism had been substantially accepted, and, consequently, institutions appropriate for its containment were not created.

Intentions, it will be seen, have to be exhumed from overlays and deviations. Ways of reaching desired ends must not be mistaken for inner determinations; if these are not discovered and accepted as anterior to any planning effort, then that effort will be futile. What is planned for can succeed only if it is helpful in realizing deeply held desires. The kind of freedom that injures others cannot be allowed the entrepreneurs of society.

Larger and deeper freedoms than Americans were used to—especially the enormous one of liberation from want—began to be defined by F. D. Roosevelt. But this security could be had only by making it a first claim on productivity, thus displacing profits.

Profits, claimed for generations to be the motivating force of enterprise, must also be understood as likely to destroy the ends they are supposed to bring about. The ends beyond are the ones to be sought. Profits may very possibly have to be sacrificed. In their place, organized skills, managerial direction, and, of course, planning may fit the anterior demand. A beginning was made—without saying what its further effects were—in the Social Security system. This established a prior claim on productivity for welfare, with profits taking a lower place.

Other permanent guiding principles are to be discovered by sensitive searches. They are not really obscure. They are compacted into words and phrases, some of such antiquity as to run beyond any knowledge of their origins. Democracy itself is one of these, and associated with it are many others describing the conditions of the utopia approved by the Sunday conscience. Some such would be individualism or independence, equality, justice, honesty, loyalty, and freedom. Other words associated with these by long usage are representation, majority, and patriotism. These have been, separately, the subject of repeated explorations; and many inquiries have been devoted to uncovering the core within deceptive shields of profession. Ends are obscured by praise of meretricious custom.

By being so compacted and so hidden, such ideas are apt to have ambiguous interpretations. They accumulate exegeses as their expositors torture them into the shapes they find useful. Nevertheless, a people with open communications and a common educational system seems finally to understand their essence. This understanding may be come back to only after departures and in spite of misuse by aliens in the culture, but it does finally emerge. The typical American westerner, for instance, was not the gunman, the overbearing cattle baron, or the habitué of the colorful saloons so often seen in films; he was a hard-working settler who, with his long-suffering wife and children, wrestled with a hostile environment to make a living and establish a stable community, who listened to the preacher on Sunday and acknowledged his moral teaching. If this pioneer fiercely repulsed, with force if necessary, any infringement of his rights, property or otherwise, it was not because he believed in a violent society. It was because he regarded violence as an unfortunate but necessary way to peace and order. The danger was that violence as a means would prove effective enough in those circumstances to last over into quite other circumstances, becoming organized and relied on and emerging finally not as a means but part of an accepted code of conduct.

In spite of such dangers, underlying principles of this sort are stubbornly maintained. Violence, for instance, is frighteningly in favor, although it is clearly recognized as wrong. It is the order that violence was intended to keep that is really wanted. Such values are likely to reemerge from the confusions created by misguided attempts to support them in ways that deny their validity. It would be hard to find a word embodying such commitments without a history of such vicissitudes. Independence for frontiersmen could not have the same value when the frontier had disappeared and they had become settled citizens. What was essential in independence had to be separated from what had once been its necessary support. It now has taken on other defenses necessary to its survival in a later environment, yet the frontiersman's descendants often seem to feel that they can and ought to recapture a literal situation possible only in isolation.

The core of this belief is that a person is to do what he holds to be right and be rewarded for the doing. Since urban man cannot succeed in being an individualist of this sort he is likely to feel frustrated. Sublimation does not come easily. He may arrange to keep his liberty of thought; this, however, is far from satisfactory even when he succeeds, and succeeding is difficult. That it was what was essential anyway he is slow to admit, and usually he does it only tacitly. His actions, even his expressions, may be seriously limited. But if he understands what is essential, he will not give up the right to think as he likes but will stay within the constricting rules of a crowded civilization. These rules may prevent others from oppressing him as they also prevent him from forcing others to allow him privileges. It is hard to hold this version of freedom in high regard; much of it may be lost in conforming to the necessities of an urban environment; still, when time has passed, something is there. It has somehow survived. It may be enlarged. It may even be more satisfactory than before.

Equality is not perhaps so difficult. It is easier to understand that rules pertinent to the prairies are not those appropriate in a city. Traffic regulation is not needed until there is traffic, and obeying stop signs, resisted at first, is soon accepted. So with sanitary arrangements; and compulsory education came hard for some, as did safety precautions, protection for consumers, building codes, and neighborhood zoning.

It is obvious that everyone cannot do what the gifted technician does; nor can everyone expect to have a position comparable to his. If this is so, what becomes of equality? Even Jefferson knew very well that it could be defended—indeed could be preserved—only in an economy of scattered small farmers with minimum demands on ability and minimum public arrangements for defense, transportation, education, and the like. Inherent inequalities were at once exposed when impossible demands were made on the less capable, and when isolated situations made earnings less than for those closer to markets. Shaping national policy so that small enterprises of this sort would constitute a national system became difficult. A succession of equalitarian statesmen tried, but failure set in at once; and industrialism was in full development even before the Civil War. Employers and workers were inherently unequal; so were workers of various skills.

What *could* be held on to was equality *of opportunity*. Much later this was expanded to include equality *in sharing*. This was redefinition, and not readily recognizable for what it had once been, but at bottom it represented a holding on to an old essential; and it was on this plea that it gradually became embodied in law and custom.

How does a people decide that liberty, equality, justice, and order are values they must not allow to be taken away? How do they decide to manage the arrangement of their institutions so that, whatever the difficulties, they can still be free, equal, and secure? Or can they do it at all in a hostile environment?

It is evident that they often fail and fail dismally, even if not permanently. They allow themselves to be crowded into slums, to be separated into groups with more and fewer advantages, to be treated in all their affairs with substantial differences.

Even in the midst of failure, however, the intention does survive and the search does go on for ways to reestablish and maintain the evasive values. It sometimes becomes a despairing search, and is apt to be lost in mistaken diversions. There are times when what is necessary to be done may seem to have been made impossible by the piling up of obstacles. Many, perhaps most, of these obstructions have been created unthinkingly, or, more accurately, have been allowed to develop because their consequences were not anticipated. Or perhaps immediate advantages outweighed warnings, if there were any, about long-run disadvantages. Often disasters are simply not associated in people's minds with their own undertakings. When this is true, consequences are seen too late and even convulsive efforts at repair are futile. Social costs are seldom assessed in advance, and very often are not assessed to those who cause them.

A century or two of changes not considered in the context of their consequences has burdened the latest generations with problems that need never have appeared. Measured by still-surviving intentions, disaster is not too strong a descriptive word for some of these. It is certainly possible to condemn some efforts, undertaken in honest enough pursuit of accepted values, as massive and costly mistakes.

When people, at least some people, realizing that liberties were being lost and that equality was quickly disappearing, undertook to check the decline, they were late. Advantages had been appropriated by a few who denied them to others, and they not only seemed secure in their possessions, but they had for defense the traditional values of individualism. There were objections; and attacks were pressed with persistence through several generations, always failing and always renewed. This was sometimes because the alternatives suggested were repugnant or because they seemed to rely on unacceptable disciplines. But it was usually because a man must not be prevented from doing what he liked with what was his.

The example of independence in business is instructive. The ideal was freedom to pursue any enterprise an individual might undertake. Shrewdness was to be rewarded with profit, but because the more successful used their freedom to smother their competitors, the paradox at the heart of free enterprise was gradually exposed. Success did yield power for one to suppress others, and it was used ruthlessly. When this became evident it was thought that the disadvantages of those who were losing in the competitive race could somehow be overcome and equality so restored (a scheme with its own inner paradox); or—another choice sometimes advocated—competitive enterprise might be abandoned and either of several collective schemes adopted.

As we know, the first was chosen. Monopolists—that is, suppressors— were excoriated. When legislators became convinced that suppression of monopolists would be agreeable to their constituents, and when enough were themselves free of lobbyists, ways were sought to deprive the offenders of their advantages. Two general ways of doing this were considered: competing unfairly could be prevented, or expansion of the more powerful could be limited so that equality in competing would be restored and maintained. Both had the same end in view, but there was furious controversy about comparative effectiveness. Because there was no conclusive answer to this, and because the ends sought were the same, both began to be adopted as governmental policies in the eighties of the nineteenth century.

An antitrust law was passed and several times strengthened. It provided for the breaking up of any combination threatening competitive freedom. Theoretically this would force the return of equality; because all would be small, all would be equal. The paradox of a *forced* freedom was ignored by the evangelists of atomism. After nearly a century of maintaining a costly war against the trusts, enlarged repeatedly and injected with new energies by successive legal initiatives, it had to be acknowledged that American business had become far more concentrated, and so more impossible for small rivals to compete with, than it had been a century before. With the intention of weighting advantages in favor of smaller enterprises, a Small Business Administration was set up. It was to make "soft" loans to those who were unable to get credit from private sources. The big businesses were to have putative rivals boosted into competitive equality by government.

All this attacking of the large and bolstering of the small enterprise was not enough to check growth in scale. Surveying the industrial scene after a century of mixed encouragement and suppression, an observer might have concluded that monopoly had thrived on the policy intended to destroy it. A few enterprises—some put the number at four hundred, some said it was nearer to two hundred—effectively dominated the American economy. Small enterprises were disappearing with increasing rapidity.

The massiveness of this policy failure and the cost of persistence in it were beyond imagining; but this seemingly inescapable conclusion had no effect, or not much, on the majority conviction that the effort must be continued and even intensified. The reasons for this were those hinted at above. There was, of course, a whole legal establishment earning fees from both sides of antitrust operations. Some defended violators; some prosecuted them. None examined the futility of the whole notion. Their operations simply grew larger and more involved. But the deep source of the impulse was not defense of lawyers' interests; it was the persistent belief in equality spoken of above. The repeated attempts to achieve it by government action were evidently mistaken, but the belief was not attenuated.

The other attempt to civilize a system of enterprise whose existence was conditioned on its *not* being civilized was the effort to regulate—that is, to make rules—for the control of public utilities first, but other businesses when it became necessary. Standards would be established for their treatment of one another and occasionally, although this was less important, their treatment of consumers. The regulatory agencies, commissioned for this task, were usually born in indignation, sometimes in the wake of scandal. They invariably began with vows of harsh discipline, after having been resisted by armies of lobbyists who always claimed loudly that free enterprise was being restricted, not restored. How could a businessman be free if the government was interfering with his operations? The history of this attempt is, again, a sad one. The regulators set to discipline the businessmen were easily tamed. After a few years they inevitably constituted an immense bureaucracy, but it was usually of more assistance than annoyance to those intended to be regulated.

Something like half the energies of the federal bureaucracy (some said more, if all the adjunct activities were included) became engaged in this generally approved effort. Free enterprise was to be sustained by limiting its freedom to compete. The expectable result was that liberty ended in the stifling of liberty, and in the process both legislator and administrator were alike corrupted.

The conviction persisted, however, that if this was a way back to equality, government must continue to follow it. And doubts that it *was* the way back, nurtured by an accumulation of embarrassing facts, received some—but not enough—attention. The end was too desirable. Presently, too, the means became profitable. Businessmen could handle the regulators; the congressmen pleased their constituents by gentling any crude attempts at enforcement; the bureaucrats naturally liked their jobs; and the public, not understanding the complicated language of camouflage, made no sustained objection.

Was it possible to have avoided the beginning of efforts that would end in furthering the result they were intended to make impossible?

There was a time when progressive reformers seemed to see that the course they were about to enter on had internal contradictions. Their literature at the beginning of the century advocated government ownership, at least of common facilities: communications, transportation, warehousing, the furnishing of power, and, perhaps, banking and insurance. The reformers would not ensure competition, however fair; they would abolish it.

Another alternative was conceived and made into law in the first administration of F. D. Roosevelt. It was the result of realistic assessment of the older efforts. This was embodied in the National Recovery Act. For various reasons, its implementation was never consummated. It was fought so strenuously by lobbyists for industry and by the progressives themselves, by no means ready to abandon trustbusting and regulation, that when the Supreme Court declared the act unconstitutional it was abandoned. Small revisions would have satisfied the Court's objections, but Roosevelt appeared to be sorry he had ever thought of it. He at once bustled the old antitrust division of the Department of Justice into new life and got additional regulatory legislation passed. And NRA was indeed forgotten. The old methods were restored. Their massive failure was ignored.

These events are noted as an example of error on a truly grand scale, persisted in and even enlarged in spite of obvious evidences of failure. The point to be made is that there are decisions that even the most efficient planning would affect only tangentially. They would be taken even if demonstrably wrong. Planning is more a way of making such determinations more effective than of avoiding them when they are mistaken. What emanates from deep impulses embedded in tradition, and is reinforced by professional interest in continuance, will not be likely to be avoided by any planning procedure.

Or will it? There is obviously at least something more to be said.

Accommodative Processes

The analogy between individual organisms and social organizations is a useful one; it would be a mistake to press it too far, but both do have physiologies, and both have interrelated systems. Both also have more or less measurable inputs and outputs, both are affected by outside forces, and both can improve by taking thought or by having thought taken about them, and by making the adjustments suggested by careful consideration.

It is easier to identify these similarities if the individual is compared with a city rather than a nation. The city, once a primitive settlement, has persisted and grown, and for reasons comparable with those of biological entities; but nations are constructs whose natural borders are easily overrun or subject to negotiation; they therefore have comparatively insecure identities.

A person exists as himself through a life cycle; even a city may not do that, although cities have been far more permanent historically than nations. Most have grown; few have disappeared. But nations have been conquered or have grown by conquest; some have been totally obliterated; others have been enlarged. They do not have cycles or norms to be measured against in estimating their situation. It cannot even be told whether they are new or old because the scale of measurement is not known. Empires have been notoriously unstable, hardly to be called nations at all. Fractionalization by revolution has occurred; splits have resulted from wars (Germany, Korea, Vietnam).

It is hardly necessary to offer further examples. No Western nation has had an unbroken identity for long. Italy and Germany did not exist until the middle of the nineteenth century. There were only nominal nations in Africa until the twentieth century; the United States became a vast continental rather than a thin seaboard nation during the same century. At that time it seemed that consolidation might be the rule; but the British Empire has since broken up, and there are nationalist movements even within France and the United Kingdom. What may happen in the future is not at all clearly forecast by what has happened in the past.

This observation is of some importance if it is desired to make improvement in the human condition by taking thought. Systematic planning cannot be satisfactory unless a concept of the whole exists, and unless it can be understood how the systems operating within the whole are related to each other in one entity. The essential in any effort at improvement is that each shall make an optimum contribution to the life of all; but it is often difficult to tell how the national "all" is made up, and, as well, whether the contribution of its parts can be made more than a reluctant minimum.

A nation, then, may be an open system in a sense that a biological individual is not and, in a lesser sense, that a city is not. The influences coming in upon it are from more directions, are more various, are less easy to evaluate in advance, and may make more serious alterations in its composition. For these reasons, in making plans, the procedures used by scientists, say, operating with closed physical systems, are inapplicable— or at least applicable only with drastic modifications.

One scientific method—that of experiment—can be used as a social methodology only by imaginary projection. It is true that what are called "experiments" are often tried, but they are not the genuine thing. It is difficult, and usually impossible, to set up parallel alternates for comparison. Consequently, results cannot be attributed definitely to causes. It is true that social studies have made good use of "as if" and "one thing at a time" methodologies, and that these have proved helpful; but proof, in the sense used by the physical scientists, is not definitive.

This does not mean, however, that the characteristic blundering of political decisionmaking cannot be improved. What is wished or what suits someone's interest can be separated from what is factual, and what is factual is more easily agreed on in the presence of such multifarious and instantaneous calculations as are made by powered machines. They may well eliminate a large percentage of the guessing that now influences the making of policy.

A social organism is not expected to reach a condition of "normality," an "equilibrium," but rather to remain fluid, to evolve even when it still remains a recognizable whole. It may be a concept more than a reality, but as such it can be treated as an entity for planning purposes. Its outputs and inputs can be measured and the one maximized while the other is minimized. It can, in other words, have improved direction. It can make the most of what it will have, and its citizens can become more prosperous and secure as a result.

Mention of intelligence and its uses in national policymaking calls up consideration of the most intractable of all the impacting forces. This is the response of human minds to challenge, or their seeming vagaries as they operate on the materials their minds select. This uncertainty has both internal and external aspects. Ambition to expand, for instance, is latent in a nation and only awaits a leader with power to marshal support and gather the necessary force; he may well change the boundaries, and perhaps the very nature, of his country. Empires have grown out of such expansive movements, and they have been broken up by rebellions led by similarly forceful politicians.

There may also be internal changes from similar unforeseen sources. The discovery and pertinence of fossil fuels could not well have been foreseen very long in advance, nor could their successor source of power in nuclear energy. But both were the cause of profound disturbances. So, in other instances, have been the increase of productivity in agriculture from unexpected improvements in cultivation, and in seeds and plant material. It seems to have become likely as time passes that such discoveries will succeed each other more rapidly and make accommodation to them necessary. When these will happen is more predictable as communications improve, but their incidence and impact is still difficult to estimate in advance and within tolerable risk of error.

What will occur to some intelligence is not always and wholly mysterious; when some need becomes obvious, it is likely to be met; but that it was obvious is likely to be a conclusion arrived at by a limited number of individuals; and general preparation for the advent of discoveries has usually been lacking in the past. It may be that there was nothing remarkable about what was discovered; but the accommodating apparatus of the organism about to be disturbed was not alerted; and nothing was done to avert unfortunate—or to take advantage of favorable—possibilities. Perhaps there was no accommodating apparatus for the nation. Certainly the United States has had none.

Scientific discoverers have routinized procedures for their part in these processes, but they unfortunately finish where the accommodations must begin. The social inventor does not have such reliable methods. This is largely, of course, because the physical scientists work within closed systems and he may not. Their analyses may be complicated, but they can be isolated from interfering factors. This is not true of social estimates, especially—as has been suggested—of national ones. There is no norm, no constant state; on the contrary there is, and will be, continual flux. The situation to be sought and worked for is one that is developing out of the present, and will go on into the future, the result of many forces, some of them emerging from intelligence and so, by definition, unpredictable. There is a tidal flow, fed from sources at least in some part beyond human control or even comprehension—at least present comprehension.

These considerations do not demonstrate that national planning in an open society is impossible; it is not that. It is difficult; it cannot be done by using the so-called scientific methods; but it can be done well enough to be useful. With the use of sophisticated calculators, by bringing together the devices and arts of the social studies, and by allowing for the unexpected, approximations can be made, and made accurately enough, for dependable guidance or, at least, for better guidance than can be applied without such assistance.

The essence of the method, it will be seen, is the isolation of such of the oncoming impacts as may be estimated, giving them weights, assigning probabilities to the guessed-at emergent ones, then going on to fit these together in a mutually effective whole. In this way what may have seemed an impossibility may become progressively something less than that.

It is allowable to say that it is better to make this sort of effort than not to make it. Such a statement may not be satisfactorily provable, but it carries a formidable weight of practical evidence. The future becomes less mysterious and progressively more predictable as the procedures are repeatedly used. It is admittedly more difficult, for the reasons suggested, when the planning effort is for a nation rather than, say, a city. Confinement to borders is difficult, and it is unreal to consider the nation as an isolated functioning organism. But this, too, is not beyond imagining. The concept may be elusive, it may not be held constant or be confined, yet government does form an operating matrix, and its planning agency may act as its guiding intelligence. As it moves into the future there will be measurable, as well as elusive, impinging forces; as a system it will have to mesh with other governments in an inescapably related world system; but if borders are theoretically closed, and impacts on it are carefully estimated, a useful working model may emerge as a national plan or system of plans.

Engineering analysis as a technique can be used whenever a going process is to be dealt with; it can be used with some effect, however complicated the meshing operations may be. Even if interconnections or contributing energies are observable only with sophisticated instruments, conclusions can be approximated. The difficulties are not so formidable, either, as they are sometimes pictured. For one thing, mechanical calculation has made it possible to quantify situations formerly impossibly complex. For another, it is better understood than formerly that establishing ranges of error makes absolute—or even extremely close—accuracy unnecessary when the result affects programs or projects with broad ranges of effect; and this is the character of many large public undertakings.

It has become customary, for instance, to estimate future population in this way, and with good enough results. The calculation will proceed from alternate assumptions of birth and death rates, and the assumptions themselves will be given weights of probability. As the future comes closer to the present, repeated examination will refine the conclusion, narrowing the probable error. The figures necessary to planning welfare, educational, and other programs will be sufficiently dependable for all practical purposes —and certainly far better than guesses.

Still, the difficulties are sometimes formidable. The origin of functions important in social organisms are not all of them known. There remains the source of uncertainty in human minds. Who can say, even, whether these will proceed to an indicated conclusion once they begin to work? Some conclusions are foreshadowed, it is true, but only tentatively. And once in a while something massively consequential will emerge, surprising everyone concerned, even, sometimes, the discoverer.

A bacteriophage much like the antibiotics was expectable; but it was decades after *Arrowsmith* was published before penicillin actually appeared; Leonardo da Vinci foresaw the airplane, but it did not arrive for centuries; once the gene was isolated at least some control of human nature became inevitable, but who could say how soon, or how effectively? There are intimations of most such developments well ahead of their arrival. The ubiquitous automobile might have been foreseen when the first Pennsylvania oil field was opened, and certainly when the internal combustion engine became usable; but there were no planners to warn of coming effects; and anticipation was confined to those who saw ways to make a profit. They did so without thought of social costs. As such eventuations approach they become more familiar, or they might, if there were an anticipatory apparatus, and their consequences ought first to be speculated about and then measured in prospect. This is planners' work. They learn more about it with experience.

The automobile stands as a warning that when adjustment to novelties does not come until after they have caused such disturbance that accommodation simply has to be made, the costs can be very high indeed. There can be expected institutional and individual resistance to accommodation; but it will have to come and will be disastrously upsetting if what needs to be done to receive it is not anticipated. It may be better to reject it or to keep it closely confined.

Planning, of course, is a procedure for prospective management of what is about to happen. To establish a means for adaptation is to make sure, for a reverse purpose, of what has always been the worst block to the civilizing process. There is opposition to change from all those who have formerly taken advantage of novelties and are settled into favorable situations. But a customary impediment—an institution, with all the prestige of custom—may become an instrument for welcoming rather than blocking what is to come if it promises well, and for making use of it. Such an institution may represent, for the organism, a way of incorporating and adjusting, or even confining, the arriving novelty so that it fits a culture, enhances it, and does not become destructive. On the other hand, it may make possible a counter to unfavorable developments seen in the offing. It may serve both these purposes, and both are invaluable.

To illustrate: new discoveries in the building arts may make possible structures of hundreds of stories. The planner would object to building them unless some way of getting their users to them and away from them were apparent. If, in other words, they would entail more social costs than private gains, he would not agree to their construction. The central agency will insist on attention to these maverick ventures; social systems are extremely vulnerable, especially in a pluralistic regime, to such impositions. Unfortunately they can be defended very effectively as admirable initiatives. For limitations on such freedom defenders have to make a very solid case. The estimator is to supply the evidence. Further he should not go; but the caution he can supply is an indispensable condition of such phenomena as immigration to completely unaware cities; the rapid expansion of automobile production; control of deaths without control of births; the advent of airplane travel without arrangements for terminal facilities. These are ready warnings from the recent past—or they should be.

To recapitulate: a social organism becomes a system of systems. A biological individual has a circulatory system, another for the transformation of nutriments into energy, still another for directing motor responses. He has, in fact, numerous identifiable systems operating within the general organism. They interconnect, support one another, and constitute, taken together, an individual. The individual is vulnerable, but also is provided with means for resistance. Disease works within him, and harsh forces beat upon him from without. But his systems are to an extent manageable and may be manipulated to mobilize defenses against his enemies, and even dangerously rapid change. The source of this management of his relative security and prosperity is his mind. And, of course, his central management is marvelously effective. But the disruption of one of his systems may occur in spite of his mind, a fairly capricious instrument all too likely to fail him. It happens all the time. And if one system is allowed to fail, the rest will tend to falter. But the mind does manage relations with the environment—in the getting and consuming of necessities, in ordering relations with other individuals, and so on. Here, it must be noted, there is more than a mind; there is conscience, and there are, for instance, sympathy and love. They must somehow come into the calculations.

Here, it will very likely be said, the analogy between individual and social organisms ceases to be useful. Qualities are now being spoken of, and these are unique to the particular makeup of human beings and more elusive even than intelligence and initiative. Men, at least most men, are kept from criminal behavior by a conviction that it is not right, that it violates a kind of compact with their fellows: It is necessary to get along together, and it cannot be done unless agreement to certain rules is recognized. Indeed human beings cannot get along well unless there is, beyond agreement, a feeling of solidarity, of mutual care and responsibility. This may well extend to serious concern for others; individuals find themselves not only refraining from disapproved behavior but, perhaps, actively engaging in public service without expectation of more reward than comes to all in improved situations.

It will be seen, then, that the analogy may well extend to the social organism with some usefulness. The incentives are perhaps weaker and the relations more tenuous, but they are strikingly similar. The individual guards his physical being and controls his behavior in the interest of his ambitions. The social organism may guard itself, as well, from deleterious arrangements and may deliberately be guided toward objectives.

The immediate point about this of interest here is what is lacking to fill out the effective operation—this is the collective mind to match that of the individual. This the planner and his agency will hope, if allowed, to supply. They have the capability.

There is, however, a final difficulty, and it may well be the worst of all. There are the unexplainable differences in the attitudes of those who will be affected by the arrangements. Some will welcome and some will resent anything novel. About the old and accustomed there arise cults, marked by refusal to accept and to accommodate to any change. The automobile was thus rejected for a generation. It was sought to be suppressed rather than welcomed with a program of facilitation. The telephone was certainly received with misgivings. Because of these attitudes there was something like a conspiracy to ignore such important novelties, and what is ignored may not be turned to civilized uses. So, now, there are those who deplore adventures into space.

Planning, as an accommodator, an adjuster, is thus dependent on unsure support. If, however, its uses can be understood for what they are, if novelty can be recognized as inevitable, it is an institution capable of averting undesirable consequence and immensely reducing social costs.

Cost Effectiveness

Estimation and guidance have been described as an adjustment of men to each other and to their environments. This is not too bad a definition; the terms do, however, need some extension. For one thing planners are more than just explorers; therefore, they must have a concept of organism, one expected to become operative. In addition, they must take account of suborganisms within a larger whole and also in seeing them operative, too.

This accepts as inescapable the condition that no men and no societies live alone but always in company; and it is always a company with connections, customs, and ambitions. All of these are subject to advice, pressure, and leadership; they are therefore constantly changing, and sometimes changing unpredictably.

It follows that planners must expect to assess the impact on their organism of internal and surrounding influences and must indicate, as well, how these may be usefully modified.

There are, in the first place, other governments to be dealt with: if the planning is for a city, these will be the state, the nation, neighboring cities and states, and even other nations; if it is the nation, there will be lesser jurisdictions, other governments, the world as a whole.

There have been times when more than half the budgets of the largest cities for purely municipal activities have been met out of funds provided by higher levels of government. This was particularly true during depression years (1934–40) when only the federal government could command adequate revenues. A city, unlike a nation, cannot long operate with a budgetary deficit. It soon exhausts its credit, just as an industrial enterprise does, and goes bankrupt. So in hard times, and even in other times of crisis, there is a peculiar dependency on the larger sovereignty. This the planning agency has to take into account, estimating what, exactly, can be expected in the way of assistance. Otherwise no intelligible forecasts can be made.

Since American cities get their charters from states, they are dependent on them for definitions of their taxing power, for the composition of their government, for their right, as a matter of fact, to do almost anything—including planning. In spite of a formidable home-rule movement during the last few years, growing out of resentment over the exploitation of cities by rurally dominated legislatures, the art of maintaining a workable relationship with a parent-state government is still unsatisfactory. Then, too, state governments invariably interfere in any relationships the cities may need to establish with the federal government. Being so largely obsolete and unnecessary, the states are likely to be extremely jealous of any threat to their prerogatives. For the city, ways of holding on to federal ties without incurring costly ill will from state officials are always hard to find. Mayors and governors seldom see things alike.

And also, a city's officials must maintain relationships—economic, political, social, and others—with nearby communities, perhaps in other states. New York, Philadelphia, and Chicago, for instance, supplement one another in many ways. Hundreds, thousands, of daily planes, trains, buses, and automobiles link them; and New York, being a port, has a stake in the fortunes of other ports, even foreign ones. Some compete; some cooperate. Their ships and planes come to its harbors and airports. The planner for such an entity has a special need to be understanding about relationships.

It is obvious that this is true, too, in a vastly enlarged way, of a nation. Self-sufficiency, even for a continental country, has long since become impossible. This is shown by even a casual inspection of budgets for recent years. The proportion of expenditures going for national defense, payment for past wars, assistance to neighbor nations, and the like bulks large in the whole. It will be seen quickly enough how necessary it is to understand not only the organism itself but also all of its many inescapable ties with others. The planning agency must deal constantly with matters that can be described only as international.

The relationship dealt with by a planning agency must be expressed in measured terms. Expression will be by way of maps, showing where it is expected that physical things will be placed, and with budgets, expressing volume anticipated; and there must be a time schedule for development. These will be the materialization of three dimensions—place, time, and volume—the essentials of any plan; and all of them must represent the congealing, for a given moment, of forces and trends otherwise seldom brought into such definite relationship. The conjuncture will not last; influences from within and without will work on it continually, and the form will be shattered even as it crystallizes. But for the instant, and for the purpose, the members of the community will be given a holistic view of their organism. Moreover they will be able to see what it may be expected to develop into, and this will allow them to judge whether it is something they approve or do not approve. And, if this moment is seized, its showing will have an effect on the future not to be had in any other way. The presenting of a reality held momentarily for inspection, but constantly expected to escape, is as considerable a challenge as analysts and synthesists may ever have.

What has to be comprehended is the whole organism with its interlocking systems shown separately—but also together. Each of this multitude of systems is actively using energy and materials, and each is returning a contribution. This may be in a product to be finally consumed, or it may be in a product to be used in further production—either that of tangible goods or that of contributions to well-being, not material, but still supplemental to the attainment of objectives, whatever they may be. Examples are food and shelter, machines and power for further use, and recreation. Separating final from feedback production is in itself complex; in fact, the relationship is such that the temptation to rely on engineering devices alone for establishing plans is very seductive. There are, however, significant contrasts between methodologies appropriate for a mechanical analysis and those needed for planning.

There are, for instance, such differences as these:

1. The planner must evalute systems whose elements include unpredictable or emergent impacts and influences; the engineer deals with closed systems whose norm is equilibrium.

2. The planner must set up priorities among future alternatives. The engineer engages in the solution of problems, with one answer—the correct one—expected to emerge in quantitative terms.

3. Planners' choices will affect coming relationships in ways not quantifiable in advance, and, perhaps, not even in the present. The engineer will find one choice better than others, with the risk that its merits may turn out to be specious.

Alternatives must bear on the maximization of selected objectives for the organism; this will depend on definitions he cannot always have in advance; they will be made in expectation of results; but the results in turn depend, to an extent, on the definitions. This inevitable circular effect makes quantification difficult.

With appropriate reservations planners may make good use of engineering analyses, recognizing that their usefulness is limited. They will be of most assistance in reaching the answers to questions within the limits of identifiable systems. For instance, analysis could distinguish the best kind of transportation for a nation if the test could be confined to cost effectiveness and there was no escape into aesthetic or other nonfactual preferences. Or it could establish the cubic space of classrooms needed for an expected number of students if there was acceptance of a fixed ratio between student and space, and if differences in instructional methods were known.

There are, however, indefinables usually present, and their quantification must come from social agreement as well as engineering data. It will be seen that much the same usefulness would apply to most social objectives—always provided they could be expressed in realistic terms and were not overwhelmingly determined by other than factual considerations. Actually, hardly any can be defined in such a way except by some sort of political agreement.

Engineering methodology is, however, useful for presenting alternatives. It will show, for instance, how much any choice other than the most efficient in yielding product will cost. If no more than caprice or prejudice is involved in another choice, or if it appeals only to a minority, the statement of cost effectiveness can be a check on extravagance. Such conclusions, in any society governed by free politics, expose the loose promises of politicians; they would be useful for this, if for nothing else.[8]

In attempting the extremely slippery materialization of a plan, a "matrix" of values is spoken of. The values themselves are derived mostly from anterior considerations beyond the planners' own proper scope. Still, some undoubtedly form around the material assembled in the course of planning work. As a result of comparing the cost effectiveness of alternatives, the superior value of one may be demonstrated, and that opted for will at least be realistically assessed. If a less effective choice is made it will have to be on other grounds.

Carrying on this process in a series of hearings with anterior values stated and their effect shown by analyses, the matrix may become a fitted system, capable of producing maximized satisfaction. Not everyone will be pleased, but this is true of all social decisions. If the most satisfaction for the least cost emerges, the objective of planning will have been reached.

It is quite possible to expect too much from these processes. However judicious the establishment of its institutions may have been, governmental planning in a pluralistic society can do, and should be expected to do, no more than form this matrix of many interacting systems, each with considerable free play and each originating in sources with changeable characteristics. To complicate calculations still more, there will be some feedback in the larger comprehensive system as well as in the subsidiary ones, and this will have an effect on the eventual recommendation.

8. A discussion of the differences between planning and engineering analyses, coming to somewhat the same conclusions, can be found in A. J. Catanese and A. W. Steiss, "Systematic Planning—the Challenge of the New Generation of Planners," *Ekistics*, 26: 178, Aug., 1968. In this connection cf. also M. C. Branch and Ira M. Robinson, "Goals and Objectives in Civil Comprehensive Planning," *The Town Planning Review*, Liverpool University Press, Jan., 1968.

What has to be visualized at best then is not a truly finite process. It might become more definite if it dealt only with factual cyclic phenomena —even accepting the complication of feedback; but actually it has to deal with something different—a continuous stream of elusive phenomena only partly quantifiable.[9]

It has also to be remembered that planning for a nation, and especially if we speak of one of the world's largest, will encounter added difficulties from sheer size. These may be expected to have increased, exponentially, from those of a simpler situation. There are those who would say, indeed, that further effort to comprehend will then have become counterproductive.

This, of course, is to surrender when challenged with complexity. With precybernetic equipment this would have been inevitable. Mere gathering and ordering of data for inspection would have been impossible. That, however, is no longer the limitation it was a short time ago. Still, the availability of instant survey does not automatically indicate the wisest decision among alternatives. It may not even be a certain guide to cost effectiveness, since the incidence of emergency can be reduced to only expectable percentages, not always to be trusted. And in situations involving most of a varied continent and more than 200 million people, unreliability is a high risk.

Comprehensiveness has these limitations, and they will be hard to overcome. The matrix, at best, will not be a hard intricate device that functions with mechanical perfection, but will have a structure of numerous parts (because constantly being expanded and improved or perhaps losing effectiveness). It will be able, however, to make policy choices wiser ones —on the sense of maximizing the results from inputs of natural forces and human efforts. This, at least, is something.

It will be seen how limited, yet how indispensable, such a feature of government will be in the highly technological future. Without it, reliance must continue to be put on the caprices and constricted interests of politicians and on the majority consent of an uninformed electorate. The procedure now is that a course is adopted in the hope that it will succeed well enough to be approved. It is true that the adoption may be owed to something more than intuition; the calculation may have been very shrewd, but it will have been shrewd not as a cost-effective solution but as something with appeal to the uninstructed who vote. If the project succeeds (is approved) the politician may ride on it; if it is not, he fails and the project is liquidated.

This could be defended as an experimental method of finding ways into the future if it did not begin with the wrong intentions—that is to say, with the intent of politicians' purposes rather than those of the nation. It re-

9. On this point, see Yehezkel Dror, "Comprehensive Planning: Common Fallacies vs. Preferred Features," in *Essays in Honor of Jac P. Thijsse* (The Hague: Publications of the Institute of Social Studies, 1967).

sembles the producing of goods by laissez-faire industrialism. What is produced will answer the consumers' needs only incidentally; the real effort will be to make profits. Similarly, the nation may benefit from the politician's behavior, but only as an incident of his effort to attain and stay in power and get advantages for his supporters. What any experiment of this sort can prove will be only that it did or did not keep a person or a party in office. And that is not the governmental purpose.

The processes of estimating intend to take from the politicians this ability to experiment with society and to substitute for it a more sophisticated method, dependent on calculation, systems analysis, and such proof of cost effectiveness as can be reached. That these are difficult techniques and will become reliable only with earnest effort is admitted. That they are necessary to a reasonably defensible advance into the future is the planners' contention.

Operative Estimates

If it may be assumed that the central agency does have the capability of doing what has been described here, and will be allowed to do it, we may go on to consider projections into the future and the making of accommodations to unexpected circumstances. It must always be kept in mind that ongoing processes cannot be frozen for very long; besides, they are not necessarily under control. Emergencies cannot always be anticipated, and objectives may change. The inspection of alternatives may in itself be a cause of change. Smooth and rapid amendment must therefore be provided for, still staying within known capabilities and still having care for the integrity of the whole.

Recalling that there is a practical difference between forward plans and immediately operative ones, it will be understood that changes in the one will be less serious in an operating sense than changes in the other. When the long-range plans are revised in some important respect, the change will affect a future budget but not the current one; actual revision can be put off until the next annual submission has to be made; but if it should be necessary to increase expenditures during the course of the year, a procedure for opening and revising the budget must be provided for. It is less likely that reduction will become necessary than that additions will be required, but a procedure for the one will be available for the other.

Such possibilities require so firm an insertion of the agency into the government complex that its communications will be smooth and rapid. Even the annual budget must be flexible. Stiffness of structure might result very soon in absurd misfittings. Even the closest possible projected approximation to what it is possible to do with what now exists may be affected by some change. It must always be subject to revision, but this must be done without injury to the other organs or the whole.

The statement of common objectives, represented by a plan, is an obligation of all concerned; it should not only make unconsidered changes difficult but should also prevent members of the organism undertaking incompatible programs on their own. One of the benefits of management guided by a plan is that all efforts are merged in a coordinated thrust. Even if perfection is not reached in this, immense gains may result from approximation.

It could indeed be said of forward plans that the benefit from them is not so much that a forecast future may be expected to develop as that centering on agreed objectives will unite the operating agencies in the present. The energies of the whole organism may thus be pulled together for what needs to be done.

It is in view of this that emphasis must be on the central agency rather than on the plan. The plan is a device used by the agency; but in using it, the agency may still retain the capability of adapting each system to every other, thereby reaching an optimum effectiveness. The agency plan will monitor all changes; only it, therefore, should authorize revisions if there is good reason for them, and if the changes can be absorbed in good order. It is not for operating subagencies, acting unilaterally, to ignore the plan when change is indicated, going their own diverging ways; it is rather for the agency to indicate whatever adjustments are necessary.

The development plan will thus have flexibility, but the possession of freedom will make necessary precautions for protecting the organism. Otherwise the idea will very soon spread that it need not be taken seriously, and the gains to be made from coordination will be lost. So it must be insisted that the adopted plan be respected by the operating agencies until change has been reviewed by the central agency in a provided procedure, and that adoption be made with this review on the record.

It ought to be said, again, that orderliness will become more difficult as size and complexity increase, and that in a modern central government it may well appear to be beyond human contriving. The reply to this is that the complex circumstances will not become simpler if left alone but will continue to proliferate, and that the results of disconformity will become more massive until they somehow come under control. There is a temptation to allow the vast operations of the government departments to proceed toward the execution of concepts arrived at by their own disparate methods simply because their synchronization seems so difficult. All may have desirable ends; but the probability is very high that among them there will be interferences and duplications, as well as that they will make excessive claims on limited resources. The result will certainly be the disordering of priorities. Worse, the stronger among them will be able to force the rest into conformity.

Opposed to the arguments against attempting to plan, there are, then, exigent reasons for making the attempt. Besides, techniques are known to improve as the need for them grows. It is a rule of development that problems tend to stimulate attempts at solution. This is, of course, because the worst challenges frequently attract the best abilities. The very existence of an agency dealing with prognostics increases the probability that the techniques it requires will be invented and will be improved.

In the federal agencies, as in other great enterprises, this has already begun. Projections are already being made, not on the scale needed for direction, and not for the whole, only for the parts, but with enough technical success to contradict the despairing conclusions that the problems are beyond human capability.

Flexibility and integrity (or variation and unity) may seem contradictory, but actually they are natural and are universally found together. The flexibility allows the integrity to maintain itself when circumstances are altered and accommodations must be made; it also eliminates one of the arguments used against the making of any development plans at all—that they impose fixed and frozen limits when change may be desirable. Actually, such limits are imposed by present procedures, and the existence of an estimating agency would make changes no less easy but much less disruptive. Budgets, according to present procedure, after having been passed by the legislature, cannot be changed until another budget is submitted and passed at a fixed later time. Practically, there will have been loosenings, accomplished by supplementary appropriations; these simply legitimize refusals to conform; they are made without comparison with income available or their effect on other commitments.

The executive agencies will cooperate more willingly if they know that they will not be expected to go on carrying out operations suddenly become obsolete, or to undertake new ones within an already fixed budget. Attaining this double quality of flexibility and integrity is difficult; it is possible only if all revisions are authenticated by those who shaped the plan, and who understand the complex relationships of the operating agencies.

If the illustration of New York City is used, it can be seen how this actually works. The Planning Commission has a schedule fixed in the charter for submitting the next year's improvement budget to the mayor, who in turn transmits it to the legislature (the council) once a year. There will have been hearings, both public and private, at close intervals, timed so that opinions expressed in them may be taken into account. To a person who reads the charter and the regulations only casually, there may seem to be an overinsistence on scheduling and impossibly short intervals between important decisions; but these are the result of the inexorable passage of time, not of human arrangement. When the year ends and a new one begins, a new budget must be ready.

In order to meet this obligation the commission and the mayor must meet their deadlines for passage of the budget to the legislature, but also the legislature must allow it to become effective unless a two-thirds majority finds objections. Even then it may not substitute its own version, but must return it to the Planning Commission with its preferences noted. The commission will then reconsider and resubmit.

It may be noted that in this process, legislative veto is used. An affirmative vote is not required. The use of appropriation measures for favor giving is thus made difficult. It should be remembered in all this, too, that the commission is itself a legislative body (technically a paralegislative one), not an executive one. It does not make plans or shape the improvement budget—the department does that—but it does consider, and finally gives approval to, what the department has done. Thus half or more of the legislative work has been done before the larger legislature is asked to approve. This makes the restriction imposed on the lawmakers more reasonable.

If the whole or a major part is rejected, or if a change is made necessary by an emergency, the commission, in reconsidering, uses its already adopted plans for reference.[10] Enlargements or changes now asked for are compared with the already formulated scheme to see how the whole, so carefully fitted together, will be affected. If more funds are required, and none are free, they will have to be subtracted from some other undertaking. Either this, or borrowing will have to be resorted to and a deficit incurred. It is in scrutiny of this sort that the effect of change on other arrangements will appear. Revisions are traditionally a favorite way of getting something administrators and legislators could not get in more regular ways; the planning agency is a check to these conspiracies.

The comparing and altering process is what is meant when it is said that the plan must be *administered*, and that it will not be effective unless it is. The planning agency must be allowed to say to the other agencies just what will happen to the whole if any of the parts is altered; it must be able to object when alterations are not proved to be necessary; and the burden of proof, when alteration is contemplated, should be on the proposer. The legislature is the final decider; but its decisions can thus be made substantially more responsible.

For an understanding that flexibility can be actual, it is important to repeat that the planning *commission* has not made the improvement budget but has accepted it, after scrutiny, from the planning *department*, and that this is properly a paralegislative act. The commission will be smaller than the usual legislative body but will be specialized and informed. Its scope will be limited, and its powers not final; but if it has a constitutional place in the scheme of government, and has therefore to be respected, it can

10. It is customary in city planning to refer to these as "master plans." It is more descriptive, in larger contexts, to call them "development plans," thus indicating their flexible, yet firm, nature.

remedy the worst charges now made against the legislators' handling of development. The decisions it makes—the adoption of the plan, and the checking on large revisions—may be reversed by the general legislature; but if this can be done only by a legislative veto and if more than a simple majority—two-thirds or three-quarters—is required, a rigorous reform of present procedures will have been accomplished. Since the commission represents a whole constituency, and not just part of it, and if it has relatively long terms, it will discourage legislative irresponsibility. Its interest in integrity will be enforceable.

Supplemental legislatures for such purposes are not, in fact, novel. The regulatory commissions of the federal government have such legislative powers, varying in extent; however, because they are not constitutional but statutory, they are usually insufficient. This is because the Congress is reluctant to accept the principle of legislative veto; but unless it does, delegation to paralegislatures cannot serve the purpose intended for them. Failure really to regulate businesses is notorious; and a good part of the reason is that the Congress, having delegated some of its powers, still continues to inferfere capriciously with administration. Lobbies operate through congressional allies to keep the agencies under threat. If the lobbyists' legislative friends had to contend with a commission representing solely the public interest, deviations would be much more difficult and regulation might begin a new and more effective regime.

As for flexibility, development plans for twelve and six years, laid out in yearly increments, with each remade annually, would be a tenable model for central government. Approximations made some time in advance would become more realistic year by year through restudy, discussion, and public hearings. The whole, thus repeatedly made, would become more realistic as its increments were revised over and over. The plan would be the development budget for the nearest year.

Any governmental program is made up of many projects continuing into the future, sometimes for decades. What can be added to these in each annual period will necessarily be only part of the whole. It will also be judged by the commission, not as an outsider would judge it, but as a contribution to what is already an ongoing scheme repeatedly worked over by the members of the commission. For the years furthest ahead it would hardly be defensible, but it would be much more so than any less-studied program could possibly be. Because much of the whole would be made up of commitments already made, new undertakings would have to be justified as additions to the whole—not merely as desirable initiations. Once begun, they would make it impossible to undertake others only a very little less desirable and perhaps, on consideration, even more desirable—that is, unless those others were to be undertaken irresponsibly with funds not actually in prospect.

The New York City scheme has been in effect since 1938. It has been derided and undermined by mayors and city councils. And its promise has been only partly fulfilled because opposition was made potent by one serious omission from the charter: the commission was left dependent on the other branches for its funds. Because of this it has not been able to create plans and to administer them effectively. What was never really begun could not be expected to have succeeded.

There is another available example. In Puerto Rico, in 1942, a Planning Board was established with much the same position in the governmental system as has been described here. That is to say, it was made semi-independent. Its relation to the governor and the legislature was that of a body able to assemble the materials for a development plan to be sent to the legislature, through the governor, and to go into effect unless vetoed by the legislature; if vetoed, in whole or in part, the plan was returned to the Planning Board for revision and resubmission.[11]

For some years, with the difficulties to be expected in the dislocations of wartime, the scheme promised to be useful. The board was appointed, a staff was assembled, and operations were begun. The situation was, of course, peculiar, and to the extent of its peculiarity not relevant to the problems of a national planning establishment. Puerto Rico had been attached to the United States since the Spanish War in 1898, but its government had become semi-independent in all that had to do with its own affairs. Its constitution was an organic act of the United States Congress and, since no Congress can commit its successors, could be amended or repealed at any time. Local legislation was not likely to be interfered with, however, unless there was serious cause.

The congressional committees with insular jurisdiction did not approve the changes being initiated in Puerto Rico during those years. However, the government of the time had been elected on the promise of drastic reforms, and the Planning Board was one of the reforms. It was to direct the distribution of resources. Congressional committees investigated and issued denunciations, but the board's operations proceeded in orderly fashion and, with the support of both executive and legislative branches, became the central organ of a much-delayed reconstruction for the depleted insular economy. It was an unusual circumstance, of course, that this support could be counted on, and the reasons for it will not be detailed here.[12] They were roughly of the same importance to a beginning for Puerto

11. The genesis of this act is recounted in the author's *The Stricken Land* (Garden City, N.Y.: Doubleday & Company, 1946; reprinted by The Greenwood Press, Westport, Conn., 1968), *passim*. See index. The theory of its operations is described in "The Place of Planning in Society," Puerto Rico Planning Board, 1957.

The theory has been elaborated in *The Fourth Power* and other publications cited above.

12. They are described in *The Stricken Land*.

Rico as a constitutional amendment would be for the United States.

It was another circumstance that interrupted the Planning Board's progress. Another governor presently found the board intolerable and, because he controlled the legislature, got the act amended. Of all the destructive possibilities available he chose the worst. It was, however, the one most agreeable to him as an elected executive who meant to make himself the source of all good things to his electorate. The amendment he insisted on having passed moved the planning agency into the office of the governor.[13] This was the end of the agency's usefulness. It continued to exist afterward only as another adjunct of the executive office, most of its efforts going to support for successive governors' initiatives, some of course useful, but some also intended purely for political advantage.

This experience is cited here because it illustrates the same point made about the New York Planning Commission—that the executive and the legislature, between them, will smother any attempt to institutionalize planning if they are able to do so. Only if planning is institutionalized can it have the usefulness claimed for it. Like the freedoms in the Bill of Rights, planning can be given a certain security only if protected from politicians. Their careers are furthered by victories in public conflict in matters they ought not to decide. Only anchorage in a constitution can prevent these causes from being settled in political contests rather than by rational consideration.

It has been noted that, in spite of the politicians, some clandestine prognostics are being experimented with in the federal government. Resort to them has been forced by the expansion of governmental responsibilities with long maturation periods. The representatives of the budget who testify before congressional committees in support of presidential submissions are often asked what projects will cost. Committeemen expect them to say what the commitment is for the future—this in spite of their unwillingness to authorize any study of the future calculated to yield the information they demand.

To answer such questions there would need to have been investigations of projects submitted by the whole federal organization. These have an enormous range. There will be a plan for a welfare system to meet the needs of an increasing population; similarly, health, education, and military facilities will have been projected; the regulatory agencies will have to be provided for; in fact, the multifarious enterprises of modern government are not at present brought into an authorized conspectus; what is done, of this sort, is fragmentary.

Will a planning system grow out of these beginnings? It must now be understood that prognostics of this nature are not, in their nature, planning.

13. This transfer was objected to in *The Place of Planning in Society.*

They are forecasts. Their relationship to the operating agencies is only that of assembling data and, usually, reducing demands before a general submission is made to the Congress. After the first attempts at this sort of thing under the Act of 1921, the Office of Management and Budget was established in 1970 to regulate appropriations for the administrative agencies; and with the president's support it was able to present a comprehensive estimate of needs within his notion of what ought to be done and how it ought to be paid for. It included estimates of capital projects as well as operating expenses. This, of course, was something, although, as has been said, the Congress yielded it little respect.

The first of these—what ought to be done—had, unfortunately, no firm basis. It was said, in the president's messages, that some activities ought to be started or stopped and some expanded or contracted. He was likely to have campaigned for election by promising to do some of these activities, or adopted them subsequently for another reason. But it is the literal fact that a modern president never really knows what he is talking about. Concerning the financing of what is to be done he knows almost nothing. He cannot get information from the budgeters. They have no knowledge of future income. What he gets is from experts in finance who, on the other hand, have no information about what new undertakings, and their scope, are in the executives' minds. The ultimate result in all but a few of the thirty-five years preceding 1970 was a deficit made up by borrowing; and of course there was consequent inflation, so that people subsequently paid in increased prices for this irresponsibility.

The federal government, then, has no planning system, and no agency with "planning" in its title. The larger cities, all of them, do have planning agencies; but except for New York City, mentioned here, none has an operating agency fixed in its government. What is meant by planning, so far as city officials are concerned, is not even budgetmaking; it is physical arrangement. The devices most used are the city map and a set of zoning regulations. The so-called planning agencies lay out areas for various kinds of use—housing (one-family houses, apartments) small or heavy industry, and the like. They advise the real authorities whether applications for enterprise are within the rules and, if variances are requested, whether they ought to be granted. This is a useful advance over the older free use of property for anything its owner supposed he would find most profitable, but it is a deception to call it planning. The agency may be allowed to suggest where schools, parks, hospitals, and other facilities ought to be placed, where streets ought to be extended, and where sewers are needed. But unless these public facilities are projected in connection with the income necessary to protect the integrity of the organism they are part of, their efforts cannot have the results spoken of here.

The conclusion has to be that nowhere in the American governmental system is there scope for the the planning techniques now theoretically available. The contrast with large businesses is startling. These enterprises do bring together the elements of their future—the projects and the financing. And their executives are more planners than administrators. Their acceptance of the careful and elaborate estimates coming to them is taken for granted, but industrial and commercial enterprises are not managed by politicians of the governmental sort.

It is to be noted, however, that various developments have tended to change the attitudes of politicians. They are more limited all the time in their ability to dispense favors and interfere in administrative matters. Their putting together of future activities with the sources of income is also becoming at least a matter of discussion. An operative planning agency may not be so far in the future as the present lack of it might suggest.

The extended activities of the Office of Management and Budget have a name. They are called the Program Planning Budgetary System (PPBS); they do require from the operating agencies a clear definition of goals, an estimate of future costs, and they are instituting demands for studies of alternatives. These are advances over older techniques; what they lack, of course, is any relation to revenues, and any required respect for their budgets from the Congress when appropriations are being made.

The extensions are toward planning, but they fall a good way short of reaching it.[14]

Paralegislative Examination

If it is assumed that a development plan has been put together, that it is specific for the year to come and more general for further years, that the plans the Planning Department have made have been laid before the Planning Board, where they are to have their first outside consideration—then the contribution of the technical planners will have been made and their work concluded unless review is requested.

But forwarding by the Planning Board is still to come, and this will be a very important occasion, since when plans go to the executive, they can, thereafter, in a proper system, be rejected only as a whole or by great parts, and only with certain conditions, by the general legislature. The integrity by now achieved must be protected from the disruptive attacks still likely to come from political adventurers and their allies who have less interest in good order than in their own fortunes or those of their supporters.

Members of the board will be familiar with most of the plan's provisions from continual contacts with the staff as its assembly has proceeded. About items at all doubtful, investigations will have been made and special

14. David Novick, ed., *Program Budgeting* (Boston: Harvard University Press, 1967).

hearings held. As the engineers, the fiscal experts, the geographers, and others have been brought together, there will have been a good deal of critical probing. The board's members will not have participated in this, but they will have been kept informed.

When the plan has been fully discussed, the chairman must have the authority to declare it finished and ready to be sent on even if there are dissenting members, and even if they are a majority. Otherwise the schedule might not be met. Dissenting comments may be included, but the date for submission must not be missed. This compulsion may seem harsh, and in a sense it reduces the members to the role of advisers, but the government must go on operating. There must be plans, and they must be ready on time. And, of course, dissents may be as vigorous as members care to make them.

When the executive (mayor, governor, president) has made his examination, he in turn will transmit the plans to the legislature, with his comment. What follows has been described: the twelve- and six-year plans for the future will be in effect unless they are disapproved, and the same is true of the more specific annual development proposal or budget. Only this last will become law. It may be rejected as a whole by the legislature, but if parts are disapproved they must be large parts, not small ones—whole titles, not items—and the disapproval must be by more than a simple majority.

The planning agency would be useless without the protection afforded by these restrictions; they are meant to prevent both executive and legislature from manipulating expenditures. A road here, a park there, a navy installation in Charleston, an army camp in New Jersey, a public health hospital where it is not appropriate—distribution of government facilities in this way will no longer be possible.

It is easily seen why any limitation on their ability to give such favors is objected to by politicians and why they are bound to resist the establishment of a planning agency. But it is easily seen also how vital it is—why, for instance, the citizens' commission in New York City, working out the charter's provisions, regarded the legislative veto as essential and insisted on its inclusion. It indicates why, also, they established the requirement that if the legislature objected it must be to large items and by more than a simple majority. The commission intended to destroy the habit of trading, so long indulged in by those in charge of appropriations. They were justified. No real controls would be possible without protection of this kind.

The differences between the forward plans—perhaps for six years and for twelve—and the operative annual budget are striking. Those for the longer terms will be submitted in regular course and will have been prepared with care, but they will be controlling only in a cautionary sense. That is to say, they will indicate what it is intended to do when the future arrives. Private venturers will be guided by these plans, but will be free to do as they like except that departures will be at their own risk. If they use property or capital for some undertaking in defiance of the plans, private venturers will have no claim if subsequently they find their capital misplaced or their property required for a public purpose.

Only that part of the annual budget involving improvement or new ventures will be administered by the board. Its submission to the legislature will have been coincidental with that of the operating budget put together for the executive by the budgeting agency. Only serious reopenings would need to be reviewed by the board for their effect on the general situation. What constitutes seriousness, in this sense, would need to be clearly defined. Any change less than this might be left to the budgeters.

If one thing more than another is supposed to be a virtue of democracy it is that every citizen may participate in decisions. Reiteration of this, heard so often, may in itself be evidence that there exists some justified doubt; and the suspicion grows as population size increases. Actually many, perhaps most, public decisions are initially made *for* people rather than *by* them. They are, of course, made by chosen representatives; but representation can be hollow, and often is. Thus, voters, although they are legally sovereign, do in fact lose their participatory privileges.

Corruption creeps in when the surveillance of principals becomes impractical. An elected representative may "sell out" without being discovered, or he may be influenced by the well-known means lobbyists use. A private interest with something to gain is always present. Enough has been said about this sort of thing in another place; the evidence need not be detailed here. Its significance, however, for representation ought not to be overlooked. Legislators simply ought not to be so tempted. We see, in considering decisionmaking, that keeping representatives true to the public interest has been wholly neglected; and that public participation is no longer generally actual.

It is obvious, however, that the need is for something even deeper than faithfulness to trust. Instructions to representatives may be mistaken. Many social catastrophes—wars, famines, depressions—remind us that millions of people, even majorities, can be wrong too. Mistakes involving massive penalties are owed neither to legislative unfaithfulness nor to the nonparticipation of citizens. They may be clearly traceable to complete misconception of social and economic forces and their probable consequences. Whole nations, whole groups of nations, have, for instance, needlessly been led into wars. Examples of error on this order are known all too well by those who have lived through recent decades. Errors concerning even human survival, it is widely suspected, may have been made.

One of the ironies of this is that often those who were chosen representatives at the time, and empowered to make decisions, will no longer be present to suffer the penalties. They may be in retirement or perhaps, as in the case of Nazis and Fascists, may have been destroyed in the holocaust their errors brought on. Still, the consequences extend far into a future they do not share with posterity. Europeans will be paying for decades to come for the support given the dictators by their ancestors.

Among the devices of democracy most in need of revision is the means for participation. One of the contributions of the planning suggested here is the facilitation of dialogue. Perhaps the problem may be stated in this way: representatives need more freedom in making choices; but at the same time, their constituents need more protection against their errors and their propensity for corruption. There must be some means of ensuring that choices are more wisely and honestly made.[15]

What planning may contribute to the decisionmaking process is determined by such considerations. Facts, forces, and trends may be assembled into a whole; the probable results of variation in joining various elements may be estimated; sufficient objectivity may be given to the description of alternatives so that choices may at least be made with more knowledge; and those who finally make choices may be rescued from the temptation to make them with a view to local, personal, or lobbying interests.

There is no escaping delegation, and it is not practical to instruct representatives in more than the general desires of constituents. Expressions of more specific wishes are likely to exhibit selfish demands, and without knowing whether they are attainable and how they compare in urgency with possible others. Up to now there have not been discovered, or at least not been put to use, devices at all adequate for making sure that the decisions will be better made by representatives than they might be by mass meetings. If he were free, a city councilman, a congressman, even a mayor or president, might be a better decider than an average one of his constituents, but as things are, he is pulled and hauled by so many irrelevant influences that his judgment is likely to be overwhelmed. Yet he carries a continual responsibility.

This situation might be improved, it is argued, if officials should be equipped with such proposals as are represented by well-prepared plans for the whole, and if they were compelled to suffer the consequences of refusing to accept them. That, indeed, was the purpose of those who wrote New York City's charter. It is an example, as has been said, of what may be done in any representative government.

Planners do not make final decisions, but the executive or the

15. Consider, for instance, the case of atomic energy. Not enough information is made public for decisions to be made about it; a few officials are making them. The theory of popular sovereignty depends on public discussion and final popular decision, but these are shut off for reasons of "security." Actually there is no participation whatever in potentially disastrous decisions.

legislator who would argue against the solid factual construct presented in such plans—as are suggested here—would need to marshal something more than prejudice, local interest, or personal advantage. He would need to bring against it new facts or a deeply felt conviction that it was mistaken; he would need to argue against it in public; and the opposition would be to an intregrated conception already exposed to extensive hearings. What will be passed on to governmental colleagues will already have had a more public judgment than has been available in the past.

It may be imagined, now, that a planning agency has been set up in such a way that it has sufficient independence to operate as a central referral organ, that it is divided into planmaking and decisionmaking divisions, that it has done its preliminary work of research and conjecture, that plans have resulted and been forwarded to the executive, that he in turn has made his comments and passed them to the general legislature, and that legislators have scrutinized them and have allowed them, without veto, to become effective.

As has been indicated, there is still the possibility of alteration. An emergency arises. There is a flood or a drought; there is an outbreak of disease and sudden and extensive health measures must be taken; there is crisis in the nation's foreign relations and new defense arrangements are necessary. How may the adjustment be made?

All the income expected to be available has been allocated for the period covered by the budget. Yet new expenditures are urgent. The old way of finding funds would have been to appropriate without regard to resources, thus making it necessary to issue bonds and to risk later deficits. This has been done so often that practically all modern city charters and many state constitutions have finally included strict limitations on borrowing. There are, of course, no such limitations on federal borrowings, and deficits may be, and often are, incurred. They may become a habit. There is usually no excuse for it, since the taxing power is available for any expenditure within the limits of productivity. Still, if the emergency is really overwhelming and sudden, then it must be met.

The old methods, it may be assumed, have been abandoned. There is now a planning board. The emergency having arisen, the legislature refers its proposal for appropriation to the budgetmakers. If this exceeds the limit allowed it will go to the board for a report on its future effect. If it seems essential, resources will be reappraised. Something will be taken from here or there among the allocations previously made. When the resources have been found, or if the emergency is great enough to warrant deficit financing, an amendment to the plan will be forwarded to the legislature precisely as the original was sent. The legislature, by consenting (majority vote), can make the amendment effective at once. If necessary, the government's fiscal officer may arrange for borrowing; or if borrowing has not been necessary, but only reallocation, the new conditions are immediately effective. It is as though an individual, in order to meet an emergency, had redistributed his available resources or had decided that he must borrow.

At any rate it will be seen that a plan can be flexible. Alteration is not at the disposal of a politician under some sort of pressure; nevertheless, if essential, it can be made. The more usual case will be for slight readjustments. In a city some street has caved in from the breaking of a water main, or a bridge has collapsed, a school or a hospital has burned; in the nation some locality is beset by disaster—hurricane, flood, or epidemic. In such circumstances, assuming there exists a contingency fund, there will be no need for referral to the board; but if the necessity should be extremely costly, the board will make an examination to determine its effect and will make recommendations. These could be overruled by the legislature (by, say, a two-thirds majority), acting with mayor, governor, or president, but that would be comparable to the reaction of a biological organism whose directing apparatus had not been consulted for some action it is to take. It would be a very unlikely occurrence. It has, in fact, never happened in New York City. With proper estimation of risks and establishment of reserves, its happening in the nation ought to be no more than a remote possibility.

City planning agencies are practically always given the primary responsibility for designating zones—that is, the establishment of rules for the use of property. There are, for instance, residential, commercial, manufacturing, and other similar areas, broken down into subcategories, as when dwellings may or may not be of the apartment or the row-house type. The rule may also require compliance with certain sanitary or even aesthetic standards not reached by the general requirements for property uses.

Such regulations have often been influenced by real estate developers desiring to protect exclusive neighborhoods, but they can be very useful in the rational public control of land use. They are, in principle, useful precedents for similar directives of any organism. A nation in search of itself will have more need for something of this sort than local governments—if only because of its life-and-death responsibilities. As an organism comes to maturity and possesses a concept of its own nature, as it seeks the means to concentrate its forces in avoiding degeneration and realizing its potentialities, it will set up norms and standards for access to resources; and it will direct all efforts, including those usually called private, to these ends.

There are those who object strongly to any suggestion of regulated development for a world or a nation—though not, anymore, a city—but protest probably will not affect matters much. The technological situation has left no choice. Recognition that opposition is hopeless may very possibly be responsible for the savagery of objectors. There are those—and not only those who have something to lose—who see in a self-conscious social matrix a kind of monster likely to stifle all human initiative. There are others, however, who see it as the logical outcome of efforts to make a complex system work.

If commitment has already been made to social management on the largest scale, to go on arguing against its wise direction is futile. It is apparent that the nation is beginning to organize for planning. The outlines are broad, still; but they will be filled in by thought and experience as new operations proceed.

The Future in the Present

It has been suggested that an important result from appraisal of future resources will be to draw together developmental efforts in the present, so that one purpose may guide what is to be done. Certainly one reason for past differences about what ought to be undertaken is that the future has never been visualized. Not only private enterprisers but also governmental agencies have in the past habitually gone on as they liked without reference to what was being done by others. It is entirely possible that for their own purposes they would not conform to others' intentions, or to a general plan, if they did have the knowledge. This is the nature of entrepreneurship. But without the knowledge they certainly cannot be expected to conform, and it would be ridiculous to require it.

Much more than lack of prediction, or of confidence in it, has been responsible for this. There are also differences about preferences, and they are not easily reconciled without some organization for the purpose. Besides, what is preferred may be affected by skepticism about attainment, somewhat as a citizen's voting is influenced by polls showing the standing of candidates. Will there be sharp changes in illness, birth, and death rates, and how will this affect all kinds of arrangements for housing, schools, hospitals, and so on? Will the internal combustion engine be superseded; will there be new sources of electric power? What will be the effect of new discoveries in building methods and materials? Will higher education take on new patterns, perhaps making campuses obsolete? Will the future food supply be significantly altered by harvests from the seas? Will new communications devices reduce drastically the movement of individuals from place to place?

The answers to most such questions are at least foreshadowed some time ahead, and fair accommodation to them may be made in the interval before their arrival. But there will be those who will be opposed to their adoption or to conformance with their requirements. Such persons may have vested interests, and others may see disturbing changes as inherently undesirable. There are in these differences the causes of enormous inefficiency and waste. Much energy may be misdirected that might better be used in cooperation. At the least, there ought to be means for arriving at agreement far enough in advance to obviate most of this disruptive conflict. Actions taken without some resolution of purpose, some estimate of available resources, some concentration on an agreed program, will in the end come to very little.

Change cannot reasonably be assessed and, if need be, opposed unless its nature is recognized and its consequences estimated. It must be recognized, of course, that there are many uncertainties—even of fact—and then there is appearance of unanticipated developments. Who can say, for instance, what the population of any specified locality—a city, a region, a continent—will be in twelve years? The continental estimate will be the easiest, since it depends so much on the crude birth and death figures. The region and the city will be more difficult, since for these there have to be estimates of migration, and migration is much affected by new demands or compulsions set up by discoveries. The cotton-picking machine and the jet engine are examples of this. Then there is the mysterious attraction of urban life. Take it altogether, prediction has to be admitted to have an element, sometimes a large one, of uncertainty.

Because of this, and because medical treatment will probably be changed, such a question as, for instance, how many hospital beds will be needed, and for what diseases, is hard to answer. Facilities for transportation and communication, sources of power, food supplies, construction materials—all these and many other objects of use and investment are also subject to changes difficult to estimate. Unforeseeable they are not, but unpredictable with satisfactory accuracy they are.

Then there is the emergence whose source is man himself. He goes on inventing, making discoveries, fitting things together in new ways, improving the techniques of management, and just simply changing his mind. He also makes decisions through the political institutions he has adopted, and these, being operated by politicians, are something less than predictable; nevertheless, they affect the distribution and uses of resources. Man may decide to progress in one direction or in others; he may stifle advance by controls or encourage it by subsidies. He is quite capable of applying these controls without knowing or even caring what the consequences will be. He is all too likely to ignore unfavorable ones if they affect others and not himelf, or even if they will not appear until he is gone.

Because no one can really say from one year to the next, not to mention one decade to the next, what the incidence of these changes will be, especially in a pluralistic society, it seems to many that planning is impossible. It has to be admitted that, of many changes, neither the source nor the rate of specific ones can be predicted; nor can the effect of one change on others always be calculated.

Not much mention has been made here of feedback effects, but this too is a source of uncertainty with its own complications. Who can say how much more productive an economy would be, for instance, if recessions should be eliminated? These recurring pauses involve big losses from idle capacity. Measured in productivity, this might amount to a large percentage of the national potential; in goods it might substantially affect the levels of living, and this in turn would certainly affect workers' productivity. The difficulties of measurement, so of production, and so of planning for control are obvious.

In such chaotic ongoing relations why bother to plan? Because, the planner argues, it will be demonstrably better to plan than not to plan. That is to say, the consequences of attempting to know and to manage will be better than leaving everything to chance—the random operations of free ventures. If the effort is made, many uncertainties will gradually yield to calculation or control; some decisions will be made more rationally; some wastes will be avoided; some better uses will be made of energies and resources; some gains will be made in welfare.

Consider somewhat further an example: the numbers of people a decade or two in the future. If a certain number are already born, a certain number may be expected to mature. But in the two decades following the introduction of antibiotics many more matured than had been estimated, and the proportion of older to younger was considerably altered. This could have been foreseen as soon as the effect of new medicines was known, but preparation for it was not undertaken until the results exerted pressure through the reluctant and uncoordinated agencies of government.

More disturbance in the world, it may well be said, has resulted from the relatively recent decline of the death rate than from any other general cause in all history, unless it may have been the Flood. The disturbance, most of it, resulted from the saving of lives without preparing for the inevitable consequences: the necessity for raising enormously enlarged numbers of children and providing for them in adulthood. Antibiotics were a dramatic climax in a long war on disease, a breakthrough; and breakthroughs are the despair of predictors. But this one made its consequences felt almost immediately, and it could easily have been seen that it would.

Another similar problem impends: practical contraception will have effects that will move predictions of birth rates into a new order of speculation—that of preferences of couples for children. Until new modes of analysis are undertaken, estimates will be confused; but it can be seen that the consequences will be of the same order as the conquest of death.

Let us see, however, what one continental nation might do to mitigate the effects of population changes if it had a planning agency authorized to devise and maintain, say, a twelve-year plan.

The agency would have been aware of such disturbing discoveries or methodological novelties as insecticides, antibiotics, and contraceptives. Supposing the nation to have been at the year 1952, and that it was making a plan for twelve years ahead—until 1964. In 1952 the new medicines were multiplying the effects of new insecticides (capable of eliminating malaria, then the world's most prevalent disease), and death rates were being dramatically lowered. At about the same time it was becoming evident that cheap and practical contraceptives were about to come into wide use. It would have been estimated that a dramatic lessening of children's deaths, already begun, would go on; also, that life would be prolonged for the elderly. In twelve years there would be increased numbers of people aged one to twelve, the incidence depending on the probable distribution of controls. And the number of the aged would be increased by those who (except for prolongation of life) would have died.

Both these changes made new adjustments necessary. To complicate matters, however, the useful lives of the elderly would be prolonged by proper care, adjustment of retirement ages, and conditions of work. New investment would be required; but there would not necessarily be a net loss, since their contributions could be substantially increased. As for the children, fortunately, when they came to maturity they would become active and creative citizens; that is, they would if their future were planned for, but not if they were allowed simply to crowd unexpanded homes, schools, and other facilities. At the least, an immense increase would be indicated in facilities for nurturing and educating them and making provision for their entry into adulthood.

In this particular period dramatic changes were occurring in agriculture as well. The combined effect of better breeding, pest control, and applications of mechanical power were multiplying yields per acre. Concurrently laborers and small farmers, no longer useful in agriculture, were migrating to the cities.

Taking the date chosen here, it is quite obvious that recognition of the changed forces at work was late, that adjustments were fatally slow, and that the consequences were inevitably tragic. Ghettos in northern cities resulted directly from the migration of ex-farmers. The Rusk brothers notified the world in the early thirties that they had a practical cottonpicker; the tractor had already replaced horses; marketing was transformed by trucking. Expulsion from the farms then began, and the receiving ghettos began to be crowded. There was resistance to governmental housing, and there were never nearly enough living places. Educational facilities were provided too slowly; so were all other urban facilities. The cities did not expand so much as become more crowded. There was a consequent feedback in unemployment, alienation, and crime. There was plenty of food, but there was difficulty in its distribution, so that there was malnutrition in spite of surpluses.

A central agency in any year with responsibility for looking at the twelfth year ahead might have had an inaccurate estimate of death rates, migration, the coming burden on city facilities, and the distribution of food; but it would have made *some* estimate, allowing for the percentage of error that seemed reasonable. In the next year it would have been able to make a better one for the twelfth year to come, but by that time the trends would have been better established. Facts would have been still more dependable And for each of the twelve years between such terminals accuracy would have been improved. And meanwhile, looking ahead to successive twelfth years would have been improved by experience.

These successive plans for the further years would have been warnings. It would not have been practical or necessary for them to have had the force of law until they had become annual budgets. This distinction is of some importance. After five or six years of work on the plan for twelve years in the future, with repeated studies of all estimates, and with ample hearings to fix public preferences in the presence of known facts, the six-year plan should have had a considerably improved dependability and might well have been made binding on governmental agencies—and at least a guide to private enterprise—and the annual budget would be a commitment of resources.

Even then, however, the possibility of amendment should not have been difficult to arrange. If, when revisions were indicated, they had been consigned to the planning agency, where accommodations would have resulted, both the plan and the revisions would have been rationally arranged. It would have been made certain that what was changed had a measured and tolerable effect on the organism. The integrity of the whole would have been protected while the change was being accommodated.

As for private enterprises, the effect of the plan might in some respects have been discouraging, in others encouraging. These effects would have been transmitted through government's regulatory agencies or, perhaps, through subsidy-giving ones. But planners and managers of enterprises would have been as well aware of the twelve-year studies, consolidated into a plan, as were government agencies, and would have been able to make adjustments in their own plans accordingly. If they had chosen not to do this, the penalties would have been deliberately risked, and they would have had no legitimate complaint.

All this long preparation would have come to a conclusion in a completed budget. By that time the forces at work and the alterations they must make in present institutions should have become recognized realities.

It ought to be recalled that this process, however, is much more than the gathering of data and the projection of trends. At every stage some preferences will be brought to bear, and if the course of development is not desirable, deliberate efforts to guide it in another or a modified direction may still be made. The planner, as we have seen, does not supply values; he does, however, have something to say about their cost and their yield, if there is a cost or a yield; about alternatives, if there are such; and, generally, about the materials of judgment. And he may join in the dialogue, and in final choices, in ways appropriate to democracy, having his say, asking for consideration of his calculations, but not being in position to demand it. He would be able to get attention but not to impose the acceptance of his conclusions, to say nothing of his proposals for the future.

CHAPTER 9

THE PRESIDENCY

The Conception and the Reality

"President" as a name for the highest official of the new federal government was easily come by. It is true that until almost the end of the Convention the office was referred to as "the executive," but this was because it was doubtful whether there ought to be several persons or one; it was, of course, not possible to say what they, or he, ought to be called until this was settled.

In the delegates' own experience there was only the British monarchy for a model. Naturally, after their recent rebellion, they would not have a king. But also they had seen the difficulties of committee administration in the Continental Congress. In spite of this, another trial of congressional control was advocated by a number of equalitarians, but its failure had been too apparent for acceptance by a majority. Then, too, it was argued that prerogatives could be moderated: he (or they) could be elected with stated terms, powers could be limited, and checks could be provided. The Convention was gradually won over to the view that there could be a non-monarchical executive, and that a single one would be best.

The name derived ultimately from classical sources—the Latin *praeses*. Actually, officials with this title had been lieutenants or governors of provinces—not more than that. And in England, presidents had presided over councils or courts. The Continental Congress had styled its chairing official in this way, perhaps to emphasize the merely presiding connotation. Similarly, in several of the states (Delaware, New Hampshire, and South Carolina), executive councils chose one member to be president. He was *primus inter pares,* as Madison put it; that is to say, he acted with others even though he was first among them. He was not a single head.

So it was a familiar enough term, but until it was adopted by the Convention it had never been used as the title for a powerful official acting alone. The framers' president was to do more than simply preside, as though the administration were an ecclesiastical chapter, a court, or even a council; but how much more was a question not easily determined. If he was to be responsible he must be able to decide quickly and act promptly. It followed from this, but only after much argument, that one would be better than several. Yet no one wanted him to have authoritarian powers. Even when the drafting was consigned to the Committee on Style there was ambivalence about this.

When, during the closing days of the Convention, "the executive" became singular and began to be referred to as "president," it had been only after it was seen that the position was unique. Its occupant was to take part in legislation through his recommendations and his veto; he was to be commander in chief; he was to manage all dealings with foreign governments; and besides all this, he was to see that the laws were faithfully executed. Only in this last was he executive. Yet in the Constitution this was the *power* he was given. That he was actually more was recognized by calling him president. Perhaps the name had inappropriately survived, but tired delegates could think of no other.

It was Charles Pinckney, a South Carolinian educated in England, who first proposed, without giving it a name, that there should be what he called "a vigorous executive"; but James Wilson followed at once. He moved that a single person should be chosen, a proposal that stirred something like consternation among the delegates, or at least a thoughtful hesitation. It was distinctly reminiscent of monarchy; indeed, it evoked the image of George III. Were they really considering a monarchy? The nine states in which there were single executives, called governors, seemed not to be a wholly applicable precedent; and "governor" was never considered as a title. The delegates were discussing a nation, not part of one. Governors belonged to the states.

There followed an interesting exchange; Sherman, Randolph, and Franklin were opposed to a single incumbent. Cataline and Cromwell were spoken of, and the royal reference was always in the background; but the argument of Pierce Butler, who spoke of plurality as a sure source of divisiveness, and Dickinson, the eminent lawyer who backed him, prevailed over that of Mason, who wanted a three-member executive with one to come from each of three regions, and of Franklin, who feared that a single head might be "fond of war," and that he might fall ill. Why not, suggested Franklin, elect a council for life? If the choice should be for a single one, "the first man put at the helm would be a good one," he said, "but nobody knows what sort may come afterward." He was looking at Washington, but he was really concerned about later perils of physical incompetence. It was a practical consideration of more weight than was accepted by the others.

The vote was seven to three; New York, Delaware, and Maryland voted "no." But Washington, who had said nothing at all, voted "aye" (according to Madison); and there was no reversal of this decision as there had been of many others. The remaining discussions about the presidency had to do with other matters such as procedure for election, duties and powers, and the succession. The name softened the kingly reference, and the several checks obligated him to consult.

The drafts all avoided speaking of a chief of state, but this avoidance was an equivocation. The framers knew what they had done, and there were some to whom it seemed dangerous. The others—the majority—left further definition to the future. It has never been made in the legitimate way of amendment. The presidency has grown by accretion.

Washington, having been chosen in the first awkward election, with everyone's concurrence except that of John Adams, who found it difficult to accept second place even to the great general, went on to fill out the silences left by the framers. The executive duties, specifically mentioned, were not enormous then; but becoming the chief of state, so tangentially inferred, was a responsibility Washington took with the utmost seriousness. He understood that this must be his first concern. And it was as the symbolic head of government that his impress on the office was most permanent.

After seeing what he made of the office, the citizens of the new nation might have been expected to legitimize his conception of the presidency by amendment. But no word was changed, except in the manner of choosing, until a whole century and a half later the limit of two terms was imposed in annoyed legislative reaction to the second Roosevelt's four elections.[1]

Washington, riding abroad in his coach and four, appearing at ceremonies in formal splendor, holding solemn levees—even if in a mansion he had to rent with his own funds—and opposing stiffly the predatory powers on every border of the new nation embodied the fierce pride and determination of the patriots who had won independence. Adams, succeeding him, understood the office in the same way; but whereas Washington was tall and imposing, Adams was short and pompous, and was far from carrying the same image of nationhood to the frontier villages and backwoods farms. He was fiercely American, but his posturing barely escaped being ridiculous; he was easy prey to Jefferson and his Republicans, who had quite another conception of the office.

This third president, who had departed Washington's official family because of its monarchical resemblances and had been even more annoyed by Adams's pretensions than by Washington's, used his genius for intrigue and political conspiracy not only to get Adams out of the presidency and himself into it, but to alter its character. He set out to show what a democratic chief of state should be. Actually he was gracefully aristocratic in

1. This Twenty-second Amendment was passed by the Congress in 1947, and ratified in 1951.

appearance, and his affected simplicities only showed that he could afford to dispense with the outward show of gentility; it did not detract from his natural dignity. He was never ridiculous. And the changes he made were more superficial than was realized.

His presidential style might have been affectedly common, but Monticello, with its large acreage and two hundred slaves, was no plain farmer's enterprise; and the mansion in Washington was still no ordinary dwelling. He may have reduced the ostentation of Adams, but that he was chief of state no one could doubt. Also, his plainness did not keep him from a cultivated appreciation of the arts. He had an unusual talent for architecture; he was, in fact, a gentleman. He also had what was reputed to be one of the best wine cellars in the nation, showing that he had learned more than revolutionary doctrine in France. Still, he did a good deal of damage to the office.

He preferred to get his way by maneuver in the Congress rather than by asserting presidential prestige. When, however, Napoleon, in a moment of weakness, offered the glorious opportunity to expand the country's territory beyond the Mississippi, he acted at once. To do so was contravention of all his principles, but he did not hesitate. It was the most considerable precedent, until that time, for an already discernible Doctrine of Necessity: the president possessed the only emergency power when something had to be done at once and without discussion. From Jefferson's behavior there could be deduced no clear line of development. He seemed to say one thing but to do quite another. What a president *was* became a blurred concept.

Still, if Jefferson's conduct in office had an appropriately democratic cast, and if he fancied himself a revolutionary in the French manner, he still let nothing interfere when the national interest was involved; and of all the characteristics of the office, this was the most important. The president had the reserve powers. When the nation needed to act, he was the one who acted.

So Jefferson, after all, reinforced this part of the Washington tradition. On the other hand, he did fasten on the presidency one damaging custom that was to survive. This was presidential lobbying. He knew how to get his way by acting through his party lieutenants in the Congress, and every president since has had to do the same. It was undignified, it led to something uncomfortably close to corruption, and it involved the office in affairs no chief of state ought to countenance, much less be engaged in; but the ambiguity of the Constitution, together with Jeffersonian preference, certainly allowed it and made it permanent.

The Jeffersonians who followed—Madison and Monroe—inherited this mixed tradition, but Washington's showed through Jefferson's style; and after their four terms, and the one of John Quincy Adams, the presidency was fixed in the minds of Americans as a curious but unique blend of prerogative and maneuver. Monroe and Madison tended to a gentility and dignity that Jefferson, watching from Monticello, seemed now to approve. Monroe's administration has come down to later generations as an "era of good feelings"—the revolutionary style was muted. But politicking was something a president must do.

It was Jackson, coming from the West and ousting the second Adams, who changed even the style. He thought it too Virginian—that is to say, effete and aristocratic—and his frontiersmen upset the routine of government. He himself shocked the staid capital society. But Old Hickory was no democrat. He knew how to tie men to him, how to lead, and how to defeat his enemies; but the policies were his, and he was as domineering as his roistering youth had indicated he might be. He behaved in a manner befitting a head of state—as he understood it. But a good deal of what he did was done through lieutenants on Capitol Hill.

Jackson's kind of show was not the elegance of Washington; but if it included spittoons in the drawing room, and dashing sorties rather than dignified progressions, it nevertheless was a presidency of ruthlessly applied power. He took nothing from any detractor or even any opponent. He was chief of state, and he never let anyone forget it—especially the Senate and the Court. The president, as he often reminded them, was put there by the people, all of them, as the others were not. The whole nation was his constituency, and he meant to act accordingly. When Calhoun, his vice-president, took a separatist line, he was publicly reproved; and when the South Carolinians persisted in secessionist behavior he let it be known that he was prepared to suppress disloyalty by force. He kept the nation together, and he countered the seaboard traditions with the aggressive ones of an amateur military genius. Americans had been reaching far into the continent's interior even in Jefferson's day; and the conquest was consolidated when Jackson's protégé and successor, Polk, took California and everything in between.

Washington, in age, agonized over Jefferson and his French ideas, but he died before the new party took over the government. He might well have approved Jackson and Polk, even if they were not so well behaved as he would have liked. After 1845, however, the equalitarianism of the frontier began to have a really devastating effect on the presidency, perhaps because it passed to weak incumbents. Between Polk and Cleveland (1845 to 1885) a succession of mediocrities occupied the office, with Lincoln the only exception. And, except for his performance as commander in chief, Lincoln was not much of a president. Some of the others were worse than just misfits; they were disastrous. Fillmore, Pierce, and Buchanan allowed southerners to think they might have their way, and so a war came on that Lincoln had to meet as best he could; and after the war, the fatal attraction for military rule—a strange democratic paradox—induced the voters to begin choosing a succession of generals. Grant, Hayes, Garfield, and Harrison were all of that rank. Even Arthur had a general's commission from the state of New York. McKinley, as far along as 1896, three decades after the war, had been a major; and Bryan, his opponent, had been a colonel.

Cleveland was the only exception in this succession, and he won because Grantism had become another name for corruption, and because Blaine, his opponent, was deep in the business of selling favors from high office. Even in the new century Theodore Roosevelt campaigned for his various offices as a superpatriot with his Rough Riders at his back. The generals, after Grant, were, however, all too obviously of brevet rank. They had had a few years in the field but had come home to be used by astute party managers. There were no more Washingtons.

The presidential image had become politicized. Later candidates were so besmirched by the opposition during campaigns that when they came to the presidency they could no longer pretend to have the whole nation for their constituencies. Frequently a victor could claim only that a few more than half the voters had wanted him, and sometimes not even that; there were several minority presidents. Hayes clearly did not even win; Cleveland lacked a plurality both times; so did Wilson; and, coming closer to the present, Kennedy and Nixon.

Yet the Washington style persisted and tended to recur. This was because it must. A president was there, in the White House, for four or eight years. Whatever the Constitution had neglected to say, he *was* the chief of state. He represented the Federal Union to foreign nations; and because the Congress became more and more obsolescent, he became more and more the source of innovation, of accommodation to a changing world, and the disposer of the nation's resources.

This last was nothing like an absolute power, not by any means; but it was something every president, even the weak ones, had on his conscience —even those who were more subservient to private interests than they should have been. Even the weak ones occasionally roused themselves to fight for public causes, making such a stir and gaining so much support that reluctant Congresses were moved off center.

The presidency developed some startling characteristics as the nation changed from agricultural to industrial, from rural to urban, as it grew from 20 million people to 200 million, and as the sources of national income changed from individual enterprise to the sophisticated exploitation of natural power by large-scale organizations. These new characteristics could be described generally as the acceptance of wider responsibility for the welfare of a national constituency and the development of means for meeting that responsibility. The president was chief of state now in an entirely new sense.

These new vast responsibilities came to the president by default. And since there was no legitimate accommodation to what was happening, his facilities for meeting them were enlarged only reluctantly. They were never sufficient. A corporation whose activities expanded a hundredfold, and were changed radically in character, would meet the challenge by successive reorganizations, by the addition of devices for large-scale management, by making arrangements for integration and overhead planning, and most of all, for the delegation of responsibilities.

How different it was with government! The world situation and a domestic revolution made it essential that the president be active chief in both realms. His daily decisions affected relations among jealous and sometimes hostile nations and among equally jealous and hostile citizen groups. Because this involved security and identity for the country, or for immense economic or social interests, they could not be neglected. What could be neglected was everything else. And that everything was precisely what the Constitution meant by giving him the executive power. His duty to be chief of state might have to be inferred from evasive clauses in the Constitution, but that he was to see that the laws were faithfully executed was a direct charge.

The Constitution was never altered. What enabled presidents to meet their expanding responsibilities was wholly extraconstitutional. They began to assume, as Theodore Roosevelt explained that they must, powers suited to people's expectations. He finally asserted that he could do anything the Constitution did not say he could *not* do. This meant that he was going to stretch and extrapolate and assume. His immediate successor, Taft, was outraged and said so in a series of lawyerlike lectures,[2] and his exaggerated rule of restraint became the Republican party line. But it was a losing contention. Adherence to it accounts largely for the Democratic victories of later years.

The other branches—the Congress and the Supreme Court—sought to do something similar. Their implied powers became immensely greater and sometimes entirely different than could be told from a reading of the Constitution. But the presidency was enlarged to far more than life size. It became again the splendid office it had been in Washington's time. His coach became a fleet of limousines; his slow progressions became swift flights in airplanes; his levees became social seasons; and his pronouncements came to all ears not by addresses from balconies but by television.

Of course, if all branches were going to expand, using each its own judgment, some collisions were likely to occur—and they did. They continue to occur, and the area of uncertainty created by these claims and counterclaims is by now very extensive and very important. In some ways this is

2. At Columbia University in 1916, published by the University Press as *Our Chief Magistrate and His Powers*.

much worse for the president than for the others because he is the source and the mover, the conceiver and the initiator. Congressional expansion means more obstruction; court expansion means neither innovation nor accommodation. Above all, the president has become the source not of tradition and of ideology but of the people's well-being. Or, if he is not, there is no other, something the people realize quite clearly and hold him responsible for.

He is the people's man, and they watch him constantly. His every move, every thought even, is communicated to the corners of the nation. They share his decisionmaking, or they try to; and if they do not like it, they protest loudly. Hardly anyone says a good word for him, but why should anyone? It would be like praising oneself.

The Constitution did not make such a position and still has not legitimized it. But there it is.

The Splendid Misery

Many commentators have deplored the heavy burdens of the president; and nearly every president has himself complained to associates at one time or another that the overwork, the intolerable strains, and the selfish pressures he must withstand are too much to ask of anyone. Although, curiously enough, the tasks most complained of are not ones imposed by the framers, his sphere of duty is still formally defined by their Constitution—formally, but not actually. The reluctance to amend, and the difficulty of the process, has, in this instance as in others, forced amendment by usage. Presidents have done what seemed to be called for, sometimes with reluctance, often against opposition. But the greatness ascribed to several derives from undertakings not originally expected of them. Rising above the Constitution is nearly always a virtue in the estimation of posterity, if not of the contemporary public. There have even been instances—as that of Lincoln in suspending writs of habeas corpus—when constitutional prohibitions have actually been ignored.

This amendment by indirection may be a good way to improve a constitution; some students, including most lawyers, think it is; but it is not the way we profess to believe in, and usage, whatever else may be said for it, does not constitute a reliable body of reference. It can be looked to as precedent, but it cannot be defended to protect liberties any more than it can define responsibilities. That is to say, one president's constitution may not be another's; and the same is true of citizens. Each of them, as things are, may have a constitution, or part of one, of his own; and it can remain his own unless or until the Supreme Court invalidates his interpretation and substitutes its version. And in numerous instances this has proved to be temporary. One Supreme Court cannot commit its successors.

The presidency, because it was so briefly outlined, has been peculiarly subject to this varied interpretation. It has been pointed out that Jefferson, for instance, believed the legislature to have been given superior powers and even thought they ought to be enlarged. His annoyance at the first president's kingly style, cautious as Washington was about carrying out the duties before him, was fed by knowing he could get his way by using his party and making sure that members of the Congress were subject to its discipline. It was roundabout, but very effective. Presidents since have not often had the same success because few have had Jefferson's ability to organize and work through subordinates. Even when a president has this talent, it is a costly and awkward way to make progress. Nevertheless it has been fastened on government so tightly that nothing but amendment will change it.

Its operations often seem reminiscent of those used by British monarchs who subverted early Parliaments, a comment that would have horrified the framers, but is certainly owed to their arrangement. Money is no longer the persuasive, but there are other rewards of equal value. And presidents must move congresses or be derelict in their duty to the nation.

Especially in time of change and recurrent crisis laws must be written or rewritten in emergent circumstances. Commenting on this in the thirties, H. L. McBain noted that executing the laws was "of small moment":

> Our Presidential campaigns, to the extent that they are conducted upon any clear-cut issues of policy, are fought out normally upon the record of legislative achievements and proposals for constructive legislation ahead. We elect the President as a leader of legislation. We hold him accountable for what he succeeds in getting Congress to do and in preventing Congress from doing.[3]

Since party discipline is necessary to this method of procedure, and since presidents do not have effective political authority, it has been a way more and more departed from in recent years of crisis. Professor Burns has pointed out that the party system is no longer what it was in Jefferson's time or what it is still assumed to be. There are, he has said, two Republican parties, the presidential and the congressional, each with different general policies; and the same is true of the Democratic party. Both have been split in the same way for many years. The congressmen have not felt that they

---

3. H. L. McBain, *The Living Constitution* (New York: The Workers Education Bureau Press, 1927). See also Louis Brownlow, *The President and the Presidency* (Chicago: Public Administrative Service, 1949), and *The Presidency* (Chicago: Public Administrative Service, 1947), wherein Brownlow spoke of the president as the *chief legislator*. Brownlow also was coauthor of a report made to Roosevelt in 1937 about administrative reorganization. This report began a series of studies that continued through the Truman administration. The later ones were organized by former President Hoover, and some of the recommendations were eventually adopted. But they were not directed to this problem of leadership and of the president's dependence on legislation to implement his promises and those of his party.

were under party discipline and so need not respond to presidential requests. They have constituencies with narrow views of policy, and this has made progress in national legislation difficult. They frequently make coalitions with one wing of the other party—whichever is opposed to the president— and refuse his requests. Because party discipline is lacking they suffer no penalties for this apostasy. In such instances their price for supporting the president is very high, perhaps impossibly so. Presidents, whether Democratic or Republican, are left with much to explain when they are candidates for reelection and have no accomplishments to display.

Were McBain and Brownlow right? Are presidents judged largely by legislative successes or failures rather than their own executive accomplishments? Both Truman and Kennedy would be judged to have been failures by this test. It would be an exaggeration to say that this is the only measure of success, and even deadlocks have had their own uses. They have opened the way to executive behavior that a generation ago would have been judged impossibly authoritarian. Kennedy risked war in a confrontation with Khrushchev, and both Truman and Johnson carried on wars without a declaration and against vociferous opposition. But these were only more conspicuous instances. Presidents may now act in disasters under assumed emergency powers, and they may commit the nation to other policies of many kinds that would not have congressional approval. This is not a new development, either; it has been a growing tendency, forced by constitutional limitations.

Presidents do not hesitate to address the nation and and say that "we" are going to do this or that, and the term is used as the royal "we" was once employed. They are able to make good their promises if they succeed in arousing public support. Lend-Lease, the Marshall Plan, the Truman and Nixon doctrines, like the Great Society, were presidential initiatives implemented by an often cramping Congress. But such achievements require enormous and tiring efforts. Even in economic affairs, presidents have found themselves blamed or praised for events—such as depressions—they had no power to affect; and they have acted accordingly, simply assuming that they did have powers never assigned to them. Their actions are seldom repudiated if the public has been informed. It is when special appropriations are asked for that they may be checked and sometimes stopped by balky legislatures. Even congressmen can be impressed by overwhelming events requiring drastic action and may give way to presidential demands. This happened when Roosevelt threatened to use "war powers" to meet the crisis of panic in 1933. But such occasions are rare and occur when disaster is already imminent, not when it is only anticipated.

Presidents, speaking collectively, have advanced, in these ways, into completely unmarked territory as conditions have changed; and those who are most admired have not hesitated to do what seemed to them to be called for, regardless of legitimization. But why should this be necessary? If the Congress has fallen into a state of chronic and obstinate opposition, and if reasonably quick reaction to events is necessary to the nation's welfare or security, why should not the situation be recognized in the Constitution and appropriate readjustments made?

The answer is all too easy: not enough of those with the power to do it want it to be done. First, as has been noted, the gateway is guarded by the Congress itself, and any readjustment is certain to affect congressional prerogatives because that is where most of the trouble lies. But second, there is a pervasive distrust of the people among the elite groups of the nation; this is especially true of its intellectuals. They have fallen into the habit of trusting the Supreme Court to recognize emergent situations and to reinterpret the Constitution accordingly. This seems to them a much better way of updating the Constitution than entrusting it to a more popular process.

The danger in this becomes apparent, however, when the Executive does something they find they cannot approve, and the Court, limited by its procedures, cannot come to the rescue. An example has been furnished by the warmaking of Truman and Johnson. The Constitution said that only the Congress could "declare" war. But it did not say that the commander in chief could not use the armed forces abroad in any way he thought necessary. Opposition to such ventures as Eisenhower's in Lebanon, Truman's in Greece, and Kennedy's in Vietnam and Cuba is ineffective. The Supreme Court may say, some time later, as it did in *Ex parte Milligan,* that what has been done cannot be done.[4] But presidents will always risk this displeasure if security is at stake.

Even the presidents who have pushed furthest into new territory have wished for a legitimacy they did not have. They depended on substitutes of doubtful authenticity—such as the United Nations resolution of support for the Korean Resistance, and the so-called Tonkin Resolution relied on by President Johnson to justify escalation in Vietnam. But neither they nor their sometimes extremely critical detractors have offered a remedy.

It has been suggested that one possibility is an amendment giving emergency powers to a guardian body with the president as its executant. This may not be the only alternative, but it is put forward as one suited to American circumstances. Whether the Congress could ever be brought to agree is another matter. Perhaps for this, as for other reasons, a tour de force will someday be required.

In later stages of presidential expansion the American people have been aware that their president, exhausted and harried, was working into the nights directing military operations of half a million soldiers at the opposite

4. Wall. 2 (1866), 109, 352, 517.

side of the world. This, however, was only one among his other responsibilities. President Johnson, for instance, was also deploying lobbyists on Capitol Hill in the attempt to persuade a cantankerous Congress to go on with his antipoverty program and extend aid to needy nations, or he was fending off hordes of lobbyists who wanted protection from foreign producers (after years of negotiations for reciprocal trade). He had to do all this because he had to have appropriations as well as ratifications or confirmations. He was locked in an obsolete system. Nixon's situation was no better. He had to end an impossible involvement abroad while the Congress paid no attention to his domestic recommendations, and he lacked the public support needed to compel attention.

The president has become, in the national view, neither a chief of state nor a chief executive. He does not sit up nights to direct the domestic departments. Even their emergency problems do not have his close attention; some of them get no attention at all. This is inevitable. When any president assumes his role as director of foreign relations, and even more when he is actively commander in chief, relentless demands are made on his time and effort. There are crises concerning the national security. Young people may be drafted into hazardous service; risks must be taken; if sacrifice is involved, there is sudden question about the nation's purposes. He is expected to explain what these are and how the responsibility is being met. While he is doing this, and while eager political enemies are watching for mistakes, he must direct his diplomatic corps or the military in operations he has no knowledge of and no training for. Hardly any of the American presidents have known much about other countries. Many have never been abroad. But even if he makes no gross errors, it is impossible for a president to satisfy everyone; and in a free society a few dissenters can make very loud noises.

Harassed presidents during every war have wished themselves anywhere but in the White House. President Johnson evidently felt that in Vietnam he had to do what was most difficult of all—exert a *restrained* pressure, something inevitably objected to by vocal extremists, both left and right. His objective was not simple. He wanted aggression stopped, as he explained over and over; he wanted to substitute civilian processes for military ones. But he had to deal with more and more dissenters on both flanks. There was talk of a credibility gap, something he got into, as other presidents have, by trying to persuade people to see it his way, and in the effort manipulating facts to suit his intention. Dissatisfaction mounted. The respect a president needs declined.

The presidency had often been "laid on the line," as Kennedy put it at the time of the Cuban missile crisis, by incumbents in Johnson's situation. The real trouble was that they felt it was what they had to do in spite of all objection. And all of them, Johnson included, must have had awful moments, as Lincoln did, when they themselves were not certain, yet were committed and unable to withdraw.

Look behind the events: the president was still only one man; he was a civilian controlling a vast diplomatic or military operation; he was not doing much of anything else effectively; he was worn and unhappy, and because of this he fumbled. Dissenters wanted to force him, by civil disobedience if necessary, to pull back—in Johnson's case, to "deescalate"; those with another idea meant to make him do more—attack unmercifully, lay waste a whole land, and destroy its people.

All this, however, was not new. It had happened not only to Lincoln, but to Wilson, to Roosevelt, to Truman, and to Kennedy. The president must hold the line of policy and must carry people with him. None has ever wholly succeeded in doing it. Lincoln had his radicals, Wilson his few willful senators, Roosevelt his Dewey, Truman his MacArthur, and even Eisenhower his McCarthy. Nixon finally had to give way on Vietnam.

It has long since become obvious that the presidency is not constituted to carry the duties it has assumed, perhaps not half of them; certainly not half when wars impend or are being undertaken. By Roosevelt's time, even before the Second World War, the situation had become appalling. There were some two hundred separate agencies whose administrators were supposed to be under his direct supervision. Some of these were much more important than others, of course, but all had a claim on his time and judgment. Naturally, those with work to do that could be regarded as critical were given the most attention. The others, to put it plainly, were neglected. They had to be. It was what the public good required. Mathematically he could not have had five minutes a week with all of them, even if he had no Congress to deal with and no foreign affairs to worry about.

Remedies were sought; as a result of the Hoover studies, there was a good deal of shuffling around. There was some consolidation; a few agencies were abolished. The number of those responsible directly to the president was reduced. But the national expansion was accelerating, and the responsibilities of government were proportionately increasing. And, actually, more agencies were added than could be abolished. The burdens increased inexorably. And, of course, the number of things the president should have done and did not do multiplied. What he did do, he could give minutes to when he should have given hours. His decisions were less and less his own because he depended more and more on subordinates. And this, becoming known, made him vulnerable to his detractors.

For the presidency, even in peacetime, an individual of special genius is required just for administration. The essential has to be sorted out not only from the trivial but also from the important. Delegation has to be precise and instructions sharp and understandable. Also, there has to be an energetic follow-up. Such duties, however, require the kind of talent and interest politicians do not have. There is a shrewd old saying that what it takes to become president unfits him for the office. It is more or less true —true because he is expected to be an executive, not true because he is also expected to be a democratic leader. But the one can easily destroy the other. It usually does.

It must be said that presidents have struggled manfully in this unhappy situation. But it must be said also that every one of them has failed. Not one has escaped severe and sometimes devastating appraisal. If it seems inhumanly cruel to have put an individual in a position where it must have been known he would fail and then have pilloried him for not succeeding, it is what the United States invariably does to its presidents, and, sad to say, without understanding, pity, or even decent tolerance.

Reorganization schemes directed to other than the real difficulties cannot improve his situation. If an individual is not, and never could be, an executive, no reordering of his duties will help him to become one. On the other hand, no one who is a gifted executive is, in the first place, likely to become president; and, in the second place, likely to succeed in the president's other duty of being national leader. It is a genuine dilemma.

Failure in leadership seems to follow when parties adopt nonpoliticians as their candidates and succeed in electing them. Hoover was one of these. In spite of his great reputation as an administrative expert, the problems of the depression required all his energies. Eisenhower was another. He adapted for the presidential office a staff system brought from the army. As a result the executive agencies ran more smoothly than they had ever run in the past. But during his eight years in office the government seemed to be on dead center. Depressions of some severity recurred every few years, and recovery from them was slow. The deflationary propensity of the businessmen he depended on for advice allowed the economy to sink into slackness. And the Republican party became moribund.

Popular affection for the general seemed almost untouched by his inept direction of affairs; after his first two years, he always had a hostile Democratic Congress to deal with, and nothing of importance was done. Problems accumulated. They were left for his unhappy successors.

The state of our institutions requires that the electorate choose between an individual who cannot be an effective president for one reason, or another individual who cannot for another reason. The question is whether a separation, a reordering, cannot be made, one that will give the nation a chief executive who will manage foreign relations, an administrator who will attend to the management of domestic affairs, and a leader who will sense the nation's needs and see that they are met.

Such a separation is not easy to conceive, since so much of what a leader must get done involves administrative apparatus. If it is not done, or is not done well, it will inevitably discredit his administration. Yet there are wide areas of government activity that a chief executive need not concern himself with, and would be better off for not having to. He need not be responsible for the welfare services or any other similar ones: forestry, customs, internal revenue, aids to education, agricultural research, and urban renewal. These are illustrations. Of course, if he is not to have these in his charge, and the responsibility is to be lodged elsewhere, the terms of the problem suggest the need for a chief executive relieved of such duties —although, since everything must fit together, he cannot escape a general responsibility. This would require a reconsideration, in modern terms, of the framers' intention concerning the presidency.

The president *must* be chief of state; he must have the powers appurtenant to that office. It may be that by taking away from him the duties he is least suited to do, and that inevitably bring him personal grief, his great office can be enhanced—rather than diminished.

The Hazard of One

Benjamin Franklin was not invariably so wise or prescient as his reputation would have us believe. At one time during the Constitutional Convention he had read for him a speech (he was not able to stand for long) arguing that the proposed executive should have no pay. Any good citizen, he thought, ought to serve because of public spirit, not because he was to be paid for doing it. His contention did not commend itself to the delegates after it was pointed out that all except the wealthy would be excluded.[5] Somewhat later another of his arguments did not find acceptance either, but, unlike that about compensation, it should have been taken seriously. This was his warning that a single executive, being a human creature like everyone else, would suffer all the usual ills.

The Single Head may be sick. Who is to conduct the Public Affairs in that case? When he dies who are to conduct until a new election? If a Council, why not continue them? Shall we not be harassed by Factions for the Election of Successors? Become like Poland, weak from our dissensions?[6]

During the subsequent years experience with the single executive decided on by the framers seems to substantiate Franklin's fears. He might have mentioned some others if he had lived at a later time: for one thing, if there had been eight-year incumbencies, regarded as normal after Washington and

5. It should be said that at the time Franklin was thinking of an Executive Council. Could there not be found, he asked, three men willing to serve their country in this way?

6. *The Records of the Federal Convention of 1787*, ed. by Max Farrand, 4 vols. (New Haven: Yale University Press, 1937) I. This is supposed to be Franklin's own draft of the speech. It went on to consider instances, notably that of confusion in Holland after the death of stadtholders.

Jefferson had set the two-term precedent, there would have been, by 1972, twenty-two presidents; but actually there were thirty-six. Of these, eight died in office. This is very nearly a quarter (W. H. Harrison, Taylor, Lincoln, Garfield, McKinley, Harding, F. D. Roosevelt, and Kennedy). Of these, four were succeeded by vice-presidents who were then able to be elected for a term of their own (McKinley by T. Roosevelt, Harding by Coolidge, F. D. Roosevelt by Truman, and Kennedy by L. B. Johnson). This is half.

Of the eight who died in office, four were assassinated by firearms, and two others narrowly escaped, a hazard evidently intensified with the years; none of the first fifteen was a victim. It has long been known to those entrusted with presidential security that there is no way of preventing assassination by a determined attacker who is willing to risk his own capture in the attempt, and that the risk is increasing with larger crowds, more efficient firearms, and a wider distribution of weapons.

But death in office is not the only risk from having a single executive; of equal concern is the likelihood of crippling illness and of mental deterioration. The latter is sometimes difficult to establish, but there is reason to believe that several presidents suffered some degree of mental failure while in office (Madison, Jackson, Buchanan, Andrew Johnson, Harding, and F. D. Roosevelt). Besides, it may be recalled as undoubted fact that five presidents lay ill for some time, leaving the office practically vacant (Taylor, W. H. Harrison, Garfield, McKinley, and Wilson); also that several suffered incapacitating incidents while in office (Cleveland and Eisenhower), though they eventually recovered. For this reason some presidents have made compacts with their vice-presidents to take over in such circumstances. But such arrangements have no claim whatever to legality, and vice-presidents have been understandably reluctant to assume a responsibility they had no power to carry.

There is no reason to think, according to medical opinion, that there has been any change in susceptibility to degeneration. W. H. Harrison might not have died of pneumonia, or Taylor of fever, probably typhoid; but these were the only presidential deaths that later became preventable. There has been little if any modification of the causes that carried off Harding and F. D. Roosevelt; and since the likelihood of assassination has increased, the prospect of keeping presidents alive has not improved, nor has the probability that their judgment will remain sound and that their health will endure.

When these facts and probabilities are considered in connection with presidential responsibilities in the contemporary world, there is ample reason for concern. It is the commander in chief who decides (in spite of the Constitution) that the nation shall go to war, who directs strategy as Roosevelt did in the Second World War, who decides whether genocidal weapons shall be used, as Truman did, or even takes over tactical decisions, as Johnson and Nixon did. There was involved in the Vietnam decision the nice determination of bombing targets that would effect interdiction of men and materials to the south, yet ones so restrained that China would not be provoked into entering the conflict. The direction was maintained daily, almost hourly, from an operations room in the White House. The hiatus if the president should be incapacitated, or if his judgment should falter, might well have caused disaster.

These, however, are only the decisions involving, one way or the other, immediate calamities. Others hardly less critical have also to be made by this single individual, so clearly subject to ill health and accident, so likely to have weakened judgment, and, without any stretching of capabilities, called on to meet immense enlargements of responsibilities. He has to propose and to carry on exhausting struggles for legislation needed by a complex and changing society; he has to conduct the relations with other nations as the head of one grown to be the most powerful and affluent in the world; he has to think of internal security, of citizens' well-being, of productivity and fair sharing in the economic system, of the interests of posterity. And besides such responsibilities as these, he has others he cannot constitutionally avoid for the conduct of affairs only somewhat less consequential. Among them is the duty of making appointments to the Supreme Court (and other federal courts) and of choosing heads for the executive departments, members of the regulatory agencies, and his own numerous staff. Besides all that he has to carry out the one duty named in the Constitution—see that the laws are faithfully executed.

No president, except the very first, in his earliest days, has been able to meet his obligations to the satisfaction of all—or nearly all—of his constituents. He has had to be satisfied if he could keep the support of a majority. And if it is considered how relatively less demanding were the duties of Washington than are those of recent incumbents, that a president is able to accomplish even as much as he does seems miraculous. Washington was reelected easily enough, but he left office finally in a storm of unrestrained abuse engineered largely by Jefferson, who meant to succeed him.

Jefferson and his immediate successors did somewhat better; they had easier times and a more secure consensus for their weak-executive policies. The nation was rural, loose-joined, and uncentralized. Not much was expected of the president. But there were unhappy incidents, as when Madison, left with only a weak defense organization by Jefferson's economies, suffered the disgrace of abandoning the capital during the British attack on it in the War of 1812 and allowing the mansion to be burned. But even worse presidential troubles began when Andrew Jackson, as a candidate, attacked President J. Q. Adams with such spiteful energy and drove him from office. After Monroe no incumbent had any surcease from attack.

It now came from enemies who had gathered strength from coalitions of dissidents and were able to make their administrations ones of continuous and often vicious attack. Think how terrible life must have been for Lincoln, for Andrew Johnson, for Cleveland, for Taft, for Wilson, for Truman, and for Johnson; and these were only the worst instances. Even the placid McKinley had his troubles.

It is quite factual to say that no modern president, and hardly any of the nineteenth-century ones, had any relief from harassment. Sometimes, much more often than is pleasant to admit, these attacks became malicious and even vile. Resort was made to every device of rumor-spreading, character assassination, and hate-mongering. Restraint was not a popular virtue, and the presidential target was highly visible and entirely unprotected.

What is important about all this is, for the purpose here, the toll that known hazards, accumulating responsibilities, and continual criticism must have on the physique and the mentality of one individual who has no more resources of health, stability, endurance, or resistance to strain than any other citizen. Presidents have not been unusual in any physical or mental sense—or at least most have not. They have had the talents peculiar to the political profession, and this may be associated with the capability of absorbing punishment; but on the other hand they are predisposed to fatigue in unpleasant application to paper work and the almost unlimited necessity for straining to understand issues beyond capability of comprehension except by those who have given much of their lives to them. And by fifty-five they have lived for years in a way calculated to sap even the strongest physique. It is impossible for a private person to realize what it must have meant to have undergone the strains of repeated campaigns, and especially the final one for the presidency, and to have kept up the exhausting but essential communications with numerous influential people and associations. No one can arrive at the presidency in any but an exhausted state or recover in it the resilience he needs.

It may be a vague realization of the inherent weaknesses and incapacities of professional politicians that have led Americans so often to turn away from politicians and choose others for the presidency. These have usually been generals, ones who have taken on heroic size in the public mind. There have, in fact, been no fewer than eleven generals who have become president. Some of these, to be sure, were hardly military professionals. Washington and Jackson were examples of military heroes who were as much noted for other accomplishments; Hayes and Garfield were civilian soldiers (brevet generals) in the Civil War—but heroic ones. Taylor, Grant, and Eisenhower were the only soldiers in the professional sense. All had their reputations from brilliant victories.[7] All, it must be said, turned out

7. The other generals were: Taylor, the two Harrisons, and Pierce, all with temporary rank, and Arthur, who was commissioned by the governor of New York.

to be woefully deficient in office. Except for Harding, they would probably rank lowest among all the presidential line in the estimation of most historians.

It must be concluded that the solution for the presidential dilemma cannot be found in any of the resorts so far adopted. The heroes have failed; and the professional politicians have proved, with a few exceptions, incapable of meeting their responsibilities. The statistical and historical evidence, along with the known facts about human capability and the probability of incapacitation, all argue that Franklin was right. And of course Madison had noted the same reservations.

But to marshal such evidence and make the inevitable deductions is not to suggest an alternative; it is only to prove that a single president is an unreasonably poor way of providing for the duties he is expected to perform.

As Americans looked back from the sixties while Johnson was president, they had to be aware that Johnson himself was a former coronary patient; that Kennedy, his immediate predecessor, had had physical disabilities and had been assassinated in a senseless attack; that Eisenhower had had two heart attacks and a serious operation and had been incapacitated for months at a time; that Roosevelt had died in office of a cerebral hemorrhage and even before his first inauguration had been shot at in a Miami crowd.

The insecurity of life from fifty-five to sixty-five and the peculiar hazards of the presidency have been amply demonstrated. The insecurities and hazards are not declining either; they are becoming more usual. The argument for the pluralization of the presidency, if it could possibly be contrived, is not a forced one; it makes itself clear. The conclusion is inescapable.

The British Solution

For the problem of the increasingly unsatisfactory American presidency, the British solution has repeatedly been proposed. This has not always been for the same reason. Recent dissatisfaction has been caused by the president's overwhelming burdens, his unsatisfactory administrative performance, the fact that he is a poor risk, and the statistical probability that he may not be able to meet one of the nation's increasingly dangerous crises with unimpaired vigor. The real alarm, however, should have been aroused not so much by his incompetence, or by the likelihood of disability, as by the generally ambivalent conception of the office. It is not so much that the president cannot meet all the demands on him as that he is kept back by a growing tradition of forbearance while expectations of accomplishments have increased. Americans want their president to be amenable where their own interests are concerned but to be stern where others' interests are likely to be affected—and also to be wise and capable when great matters are at hazard.

It has often been noted that the Republican party's conception of proper presidential conduct was reversed after the Civil War. Until that time its predecessor parties, the Whigs and the Federalists, had been, above all, Unionists, believing in a strong central government and, as a result of the secession controversy, in the relative subordination of the states. But during and just after the war, and largely because of it, industrialism expanded rapidly and began to take on the characteristics so familiar in the twentieth century: corporate organization; large-scale production, often dominated by a monopoly or a near-monopoly; the cultivation of markets by stimulating consumption; the penetration of industry by financiers who determined overall policies, and the overrunning of state boundaries.

It seemed necessary to the expanders of industry that it would not be interfered with by government. Big business regarded people as customers who ought to pay prices that yielded profit, or as workers who were lucky to have jobs and ought to work for wages that did not unduly increase costs. Generally, people's interests were viewed as subordinate to those of owners and managers. The difference in attitude became serious when the Populists began their long war on monopoly and when progressivism in various forms manifested special hostility to the larger businesses. The excesses of railroad speculators and the effrontery of the oil, sugar, steel, and other industrial combines created something like a minority uprising.

Antitrust laws were passed and later repassed in enlarged form. Wilson was elected in 1912 on a platform of refined progressivism. It was not hostile to business, only to *big* business. But bigness was the essential characteristic of efficient production and the stimulation of demand. The Congress, in spite of efforts to subvert its members, manifested a fairly constant enmity. A majority of its members came from old Populist districts or from others where workers were strong; and most of the time its committees were chaired by rural members. Even Republicans among them were unfriendly to the trusts and positively hostile to Wall Street.

Big businessmen discovered that it was much easier to get their way with presidents by means of convention manipulations and help in campaigns than through members of the Congress. But even with their own men in the White House they were not safe. Legislators were often activated by constituents' complaints. On the whole, Washington was not business territory. State governments were, however, less devoted to any general public interest. Especially their legislators saw no threat from deals with the lobbyists of the corporations, or, if they did, trusted that their constituents would be indifferent. They had the disposal of many favors: franchises, easy labor regulations and rate structures for public utilities, access to the public lands, and, most of all, the chartering of corporations.

State capitals, from the eighties on, swarmed with lobbyists. They often outnumbered the public representatives, and they lived in far more luxurious circumstances—ones they were glad to share. The instances of exposed bribery in state capitals were so numerous that eventually they came to be expected. The corruption was the subject of a secondary run of muckraking by the same group (McClure, Steffens, Tarbell, Baker, Sinclair, and others) who had recently exposed conditions in city government.

It will be recalled that for no other reason than that he was an honest man in the time of loose public morals, Grover Cleveland went from the mayoralty of Buffalo to the presidency in two years, irritating the Albany ring of lobbyists and bosses on the way. He was as completely ignorant of a president's duties as he had been of a governor's, and he was an unsatisfactory president in every way except that he was incorruptible. This was, again, in the eighties. (He was elected the first time in 1884 and, after a reversion to Republicanism with Benjamin Harrison, again in 1892.) He was, however, a conservative, fearful of the Populists who were working up to the control of his party and wholly in sympathy with his New York contemporaries. He was, in fact, less a Democrat than a mugwump—that is, a member of the elite who was shamed by the low state of public morality but not disposed to injure business.

He never held with most of the tenets of his party, except that he became converted, through study, to the lowering of tariffs; and this, paradoxically, alienated many of his associates who regarded his views on this subject as an inconvenient exposure of their hypocrisy. Defections from this cause were responsible for his defeat for reelection in 1888. But because of his integrity and his cleaning out of corrupt pockets in the federal establishment he was rated as a "strong" executive.[8]

This was the time of transition in conservative principle, Democrats and Republicans alike, from strong to complaisant presidents. The parties were more and more closely aligned with industrial and financial institutions. Still, all was not happily arranged. It was very difficult to control state legislatures; but productive organizations continued to expand, and the growing ones were no longer confined within state areas. Besides, the federal government was more and more exercising the rule that jurisdictions preempted by federal power were closed to state authority. This made it more than ever necessary to see that presidents were disposed to look the other way as business infiltrated government.

The thrust of the industrialists' and financiers' reach for public power had to include the Congress as well as the presidency. This had been made difficult by the change from the choice of senators by state legislatures to popular election.[9] The way around even this difficulty was obvious and had been for some time. It was through control of the Republican party, ap-

8. See also, by the present author, *Grover Cleveland* (New York: The Macmillan Company, 1968).

9. Accomplished by the Seventeenth Amendment, ratified in 1913.

parently in permanent possession of a majority. This effort emerged into the open when Mark Hanna undertook, in effect, to buy the election of McKinley in 1896. Hanna was a big operator himself, and he set out, as he confessed, to amass such a campaign fund from his fellow businessmen as had never been known. He spoke of it as "frying the fat" out of the corporations who ought to see how much a friendly president meant to them.

McKinley's campaign, with Mark Hanna's management, came just at a time when the Populists had succeeded in capturing the Democratic party and had an effective candidate in Bryan, who ignored the tradition that presidential candidates ought to maintain a dignified silence after being nominated and after writing a formal letter of acceptance. He spoke everywhere, and was immensely effective. It really looked as though he might win the 1896 campaign.

But McKinley—and Hanna—beat back the threat, and the Republican party resumed a control that had lasted now since the Civil War. Cleveland had been an interruption, but except in the area of protectionism he had been no threat; in spite of increasing agitation for regulation and for the breaking up of monopolies, and in spite of the Wilsonian interlude when the financiers were thrown into a panic by the Federal Reserve Act with its decentralizing effect, Republicanism and big business were to go on controlling. Only the inherent paradox of business, that the single-minded pursuit of profits will never allow consumers sufficient purchasing power to keep productive facilities in full motion—resulting in the Great Depression—dislodged them at last in 1932.

Then there began a new era; the big businessmen were forced to change their tactics. They had to accept the necessity of full employment and high wages, and even of collective bargaining; they had to understand that Social Security was not so much philanthropy as an economic necessity; and they had to agree that the time had come when government was something they must become part of in a responsible way. In the new generation many of them did grasp these ideas, and a slow regeneration, largely under Democratic auspices, began.

Because the professional Republican politicians clung to the old notions, labor became Democratic and small businessmen began to defect. These, added to the remaining Populists in the South and West, ended the majorities the Republicans had had until the 1930s. The Democrats now had the solid majority. The Eisenhower incident did not count in this any more than Cleveland had counted in the Republican monopoly of the last century. It was an interlude only. And actually it was Democrats who turned the election for Eisenhower, as it had been Republicans who had turned that for Cleveland in 1884. It was defecting partisans who made the difference in both instances.

But with the influence on government of big business, with the emergence of regulatory undertakings, and with the immense bureaucracies necessary in varied welfare undertakings, the president's task grew to proportions never before imagined. No corporate official, however big his organization, had duties of such magnitude; and the president's roster of assignments was added to year by year. It is most strange to consider that the person of whom so much was expected had very likely never before in his life managed any enterprise, even his own campaigns. A president competent for his duties became even more improbable in the last half of the century than had been the case during the first half.

These decades, also, brought affluence and power to the nation, inundating the chief of state with responsibilities for the affairs of other nations as well as his own. There were not only repeated wars, or threats of war, large and small, there was the need to support or discourage governments everywhere in the world whose policies were friendly or unfriendly; and there was the need to assist less fortunate nations whose situation moved American consciences even when no real interest was involved. And no president could be indifferent to the penetration by American capitalists of other nations' economies. He might favor their activities or deplore them, but he had to meet repeated crises—large and small—caused by their intervention.

If only one percent of the people were enraged by presidential policies, one percent of 200 million was enough, when organized and well financed, to constitute a noisy opposition. Focused on television screens, it could be mistaken for far larger disaffection than it actually was. Demonstrations, with the president or his secretaries as the targets, became one of the novel—but nearly unbearable—burdens of office. It was hard to represent a majority with minorities clamoring to get their way.

It became more and more obvious that the president could not carry all these responsibilities and resist both the insidious favor seeking and raucous dissent. He must neglect some to give attention to others, especially ones that aroused active agitation. He was continually dragged out; daily he risked his safety, his health, and his ability to weigh decisions. Even the physical disorders he must neglect, because he had no time to avoid or cure them, were unbearably wearing. Not the least of his worries was that he was expected to have the endurance of a superman. Some way out must be found.

One of these ways had been found by the British under the weight of imperial burdens; the executive was made an arm of the Parliament. A similar solution was proposed for the United States by, among others, Woodrow Wilson, who soon became noted among political theorists. In *Congressional Government,*[10] conceived while he was a graduate student

10. Boston: Houghton Mifflin Company, 1884.

at the Johns Hopkins University, he suggested a somewhat modified version of parliamentary (or cabinet) government; and was taken with the utmost seriousness by a generation of fellow academicians. The book ran through fifteen editions and was still being read when his *Constitutional Government*[11] was published. This later analysis gave up the theory he had found so popular in the earlier one, which had been that something approximating the British system ought to be recognized as essential to the intentions of the American democracy. The fact was, as he had seen it, that the Congress had an impregnable situation among the branches. Because this was so, the executive would never be able to achieve the independence necessary for fulfilling its prescribed purpose. The Congress would always obstruct and delay with bland irresponsibility, and an advancing nation could not afford stalemate.

Wilson argued that if the Congress had the power it ought also to accept the responsibility. If it did, it would be forced to develop initiative in place of obstruction. The executive and legislative branches balanced each other so well, as things were, that either could block the other; but neither could move the other; and the contest had become a main preoccupation with both. The British, in contrast, by making the executive responsible to the Parliament, in effect a committee of its members, had developed a reasonable and effective means of meeting governmental responsibilities. Changes decided on by debate in Commons became the policy of the prime minister and his cabinet.

A review of American experience at first caused Wilson to believe that comparative weakness in the executive office had become permanent. He recalled the troubles of Andrew Johnson, who, faced with a Congress of post-Civil War radicals, was very nearly removed from office for not agreeing with its majority about Reconstruction after the war. He went on to consider Grant, Hayes, Garfield, and Arthur, all mediocrities when measured by Americans' expectations; none developed into a leader; none was able to move the Congress. These were his conclusions when he was a graduate student writing the dissertation that became so influential.

But almost immediately afterward, Cleveland became president and interrupted the succession of weak and permissive presidents. Students of Wilson's thinking believe that Cleveland's facing down of congressional opposition revolutionized Wilson's view of the presidency. This is probably true; but it must have seemed to him questionable when McKinley succeeded Cleveland and reverted to the Republicanism of the 1860s and 1870s. He missed the point that Cleveland's strength was more negative than positive; he had not been a dynamic leader even if he had cleared out corruptionists and faced down those who would have exploited the government. But perhaps he had shown Wilson that a president *could* lead

11. New York: Columbia University Press, 1907.

if he determined that he should. Even though Cleveland had shown strength only in crises, had believed in keeping out of legislative affairs, and had seen no reason to regulate the economic system, his interventions had sometimes been electrifying. McKinley may have seemed to Wilson a lesson in contrast.

There is also a hint that by the time Wilson delivered the Columbia University lectures in 1906 that were printed as *Congressional Government,* he was experiencing his first secret hopes of one day becoming president himself.[12] At any rate he now felt and said that the president had advanced far beyond his literal position in the constitutional structure. He had become the leader of the people and possessed the means for coercing the Congress if his popular support was solid.

There were subsequent theorists who continued to be discouraged with the evenly balanced powers of the system, and some who continued to feel that the British solution was a way out. It even seems that Wilson, after frustrating experiences in office, reverted again to his view that a parliamentary system would be better. Concerning this, it has to be said that American commentators, when they make this suggestion, seem much more convincing when they criticize the Congress than when they appraise the British advantages. The Congress more than the president is at the center of the American deadlock. But both are undoubtedly involved.

Most perceptive observers have come to agree that the British precedent is better suited to the peculiar conditions it was invented to meet than it would be to American conditions. The prime minister, at the head of a majority in the Commons, has become the determiner of policy in every aspect of governmental activity. Moreover, he has developed ways of coercing its members that reduce them to near-helplessness. He is even able to determine who shall become members by assigning constituencies among them, and he can enforce his legislative wishes by exclusion from party prerogatives if consent to his measures is withheld. He has even been known to cause expulsion from the party, and this almost inevitably brings a political career to an end.

It is not a dictator that is needed in the American situation, it is a representative of an informed people who is chosen by them to become leader, and who has the means to carry the Congress with him but not to coerce it. He should not need to coerce because congressional members should have instructions similar to his, and they might if their constituencies

12. The most extensive explorations of Wilson's development have been made by Professor Arthur Link in several books; other comment has been made by many students, including the present author: cf. *The Enlargement of the Presidency* (Garden City, N.Y.: Doubleday & Company, 1960), chap. 36; and *How They Became President* (New York: Simon and Schuster, 1964), pp. 339–55.

were more like his own than they are at present. They, like him, should be subject to party discipline, because parties ought to be the vehicle of public desire, and because majorities ought to exist for a reason.

The president should also have the protection of a clear mandate with means for renewing it (perhaps by referendum). This would furnish the protection he must have from the civic disturbances caused by small minorities seeking to force acceptance of their views, or from interests demanding favors.

The other much-praised characteristic of the British system is the separation of the executive from the chieftainship of state. It is often imagined that this is achieved by retaining the monarchy. It is apparent, however, that the monarchy has left to it only the emptiest of ceremonial duties. No royal suggestion concerning policy would be allowed; contact with the foriegn diplomats who pay their respects is purely formal; and initiative in counseling with political leaders would be regarded as an intolerable interference. Such a position would be of no use to another people, especially a people who look to their chief of state for leadership, not merely for symbolic unity.

The problem is rather to take away from the splendid and useful president the duties he can no longer perform, to free him for the responsibilities he and no other can assume, and to support him in these by providing seconds, substitutes, and counseling peers who will share his now lonely and awful authority.

Efforts at Reorganization

The several reorganizations of the executive establishment during the 1930s and 1940s were in the end disappointing. They did result in the movement of some bureaus (Food and Drug to Health, Education, and Welfare; Public Roads to Commerce, and so on), the abolishing of a few agencies, and generally better overhead management. But since it was a time of expansion, and since most of the support for the various reorganization efforts came from those who had supposed that economies could be effected, the effort in that convulsive form was abandoned.

Such task-force attacks on the enormous central conglomeration of agencies were succeeded by intensive internal studies and more sophisticated rearrangements. There remained much dissatisfaction, but most of it was because of congressional unwillingness to authorize change rather than lack of agreement among experts about what ought to be done. There can be no defense for bringing together such disparate functions as those involved in health, education, and welfare, or in making urban renewal secondary to housing in another. Public roads have no discoverable relationship with other bureaus in the Department of Commerce—and so it goes. The groupings into departments are more understandable than they used to be, but there are still numerous anomalies.

A chief executive with relative freedom to arrange his administrative agencies as seemed best to his own staff would doubtless make many more changes, and most of them would probably be improvements. But as long as the Congress has to consent and may object, other considerations than effective administration will dominate the arrangements. It has been explained that this is not an explicit but an implied power. It is one, however, so closely related to appropriations that it has gone unchallenged since the first departments were set up. Several times a president has persuaded the Congress to free him for making rearrangements, but the permission has always been temporary and with the proviso that there should be a congressional veto.

What would be gained by more executive freedom is, however, not very much in comparison with the accumulated problems of the presidency. The time has come for considering much more drastic solutions. One of these is that there should be created an entirely new executive branch for domestic affairs to relieve the president for his other and, for him, more essential duties. He cannot escape being chief of state; perhaps he also ought to keep control of some departments related to this; but not all of them need his immediate direction. And if they did, they could not get it.

It has been explained that these duties have been progressively given up. The nation's security and welfare are involved in the larger decisions the president must make, and in the arrangements incidental to them, and this absorbs his energies. First things have to be put first.

Not at any time during this century has any president actually acted, except sporadically, as the supervisor of all the departments. Modern presidents are driven to choosing department heads and leaving practically all the rest up to them. When it is necessary to enlarge or diminish the mission of a department, the president intervenes; and when it is desirable to undertake new governmental responsibilities, he must head the movement to undertake them; but about their actual conduct he cannot possibly know very much. There are too many of them; their duties are too varied and often too technical; and his judgment anyway does not have an administrative cast.

One result of this is that direction of the department often passes, in a kind of informal and sporadic way, to some member of the Congress who has a particular interest or acts for one, and is influential among his colleagues. It has been explained that he takes no responsibility, but that he makes it his business to know what is going on and is often more knowledgeable than the president about its affairs. He makes demands on officials, watches the progress of its appropriation requests, tries to direct its policies, and may come to be known as its unofficial dictator. Such legislators are the despair of all officials. This, of course, is not a legislative function, but it is a folkway of the federal capital. And the president is in no position to do anything about this invasion of his domain.

Another result of the president's overload is that department heads tend to become advocates of the interest they represent—agriculture, commerce, labor, and so on. As such, they at worst become ambitious to replace the president or to oppose his policies if these happen not to please their supporters. Since they have this support, the president may hesitate to discipline them for fear of losing leverage with the congressional bloc they, in conjunction with a strong lobby, may have developed. To say that they are then subordinates in an executive establishment is to use an empty word.

Still another consequence is that members of the cabinet cease to be of use to the president as consultants. Presidents since Hoover have either stopped having cabinet meetings at all or have reduced them to a formality. They hesitate to let such a separatist group know anything confidential outside their own spheres of action. There is some escape from this in appointing secretaries who have no such affiliations; but this is taken as a rebuke by labor, for instance, as in the case of Roosevelt's Perkins, or agriculture as in the case of Kennedy's Freeman. More generally secretaries are appointed to hold or gain the political support of powerful interests, and the president is less their master than their evasive associate. In any case they too are only incidentally skilled in administration, and their vast establishments are necessarily left to be run by civil servants.

It is patently absurd to expect that the president can well decide what airports shall be enlarged, what the allowances ought to be for abandoned mothers of small children, what explorations the Geodetic Survey ought to undertake, whether the production of wheat ought to be enlarged or contracted, how tariff schedules ought to be arranged, or what should be done to keep the country free of tropical fevers or hoof-and-mouth disease. These, and a thousand other decisions of a similar sort, are important to the welfare and convenience of the people and to the economy, and they deserve something better than five minutes of a harassed president's time on rare occasions.

He ought not to have such matters on his mind at all. For one thing he will not be guided by the usual administrative standards. His decisions will be political, in large part, and so far as they are purely administrative—that is, after they have been undertaken and consigned to an agency for execution—they are better for being abstracted from political influence. As long as they are in this area, they are likely to be used by both president and the Congress for whatever advantages there may be in choosing their personnel or in carrying out their missions. This will amount to interference and would better be eliminated.

This does not mean that the question of undertaking them, or the scale of their operations, ought not to be discussed and decided in the democratic way. What is to be undertaken is a question of general interest, and the public ought to be in on the decision or, at least, in on the delegating of it; but how the mission is to be carried out is an administrative matter, and it ought to be left at that, with, of course, ample resort for those who have complaints. If it is not done well according to instruction, or if it produces hardship, the means provided for correction ought to be relied on. Then it can be discontinued, its administrator can be relieved, or its instructions can be modified.

What happens at present, in contrast with this, is that a program is undertaken at the president's initiative, perhaps in response to agitation and urging, perhaps because he himself conceives it to be desirable; there will have been the usual struggle to get congressional approval, and the expected bargains will have been struck concerning patronage, the location of installations, and careful amendment to favor or exempt important interests. Then when operations begin under mutilated legislation, instructions will be confused, administrators handicapped, patronage seekers half satisfied, partisan opposition aroused, and secretaries of departments will proceed in their own way either because they respond to pressure or because they cannot get clear directives. Worst of all, the president will be held to account.

It will be recalled that this was the situation of F. D. Roosevelt as the efforts at recovery were undertaken in the thirties under the rubric of the New Deal; and memories still linger of the engagements he had with the Liberty League and with the conservatives who accused the WPA of boondoggling, and of the Chicago *Tribune's* weeping about the killing of little pigs undertaken to reduce the surplus of pork products. The same risks were undertaken and for the same reasons, by President Johnson three decades later. His Great Society designs were in large part attempts to carry out the projects left over from the interrupted Roosevelt regime. Johnson's presidency was risked for the success of a program certain to have enormous difficulties and to have the same unhappy but inevitable characteristics as the boondoggling of the New Deal.

It is suggested that the president be freed from responsibility for such undertakings after they have been decided on by the Congress. He need not be required to put his great office in pawn because an antipoverty program is offensive to middle-income taxpayers who incline to think that the poor are responsible for their own plight and ought to be left abandoned in their slums. He ought not to be involved in small departmental quarrels, in settling strikes, in arbitrating among departments, in scandals emerging from congressional conflicts with bureaucrats, or even with the choice of personnel for any but the positions of real consequence to high policy. As things are, mischance or maladministration in Detroit, Oakland, or Philadelphia, likely because of vague direction, of financing that can be counted

on for no more than an emergency period, and of inherently difficult undertakings, can be charged directly to him. Newspaper and television reporters
rush enthusiastically to the scene of failure, and a heretofore indifferent
public is shocked at the disclosures.

As a system it is not good enough; something ought to be done about
it; but no administrative polishing up and refurbishing will have much effect.

What is needed is revision of responsibilities, partly of the presidency but
also of the Congress. If there were more party responsibility, gained by
induced dialogue, together with the working up of policies in a series of
conventions, and the election of representatives on some other than a small-
district scheme, there would be a very different attitude toward the legislation needed to meet the enlarged responsibilities of government.

There would also be a very different organization of the executive
establishment. The president would not be placed in jeopardy through the
criticism of administration as he so often is at present. It would be understood that he has another responsibility—that of leadership and national
representation. True, he would be held accountable for the general success
or failure of governmental undertakings; but the responsibility would be
shared by the party, by its representatives in the Congress, and by a separate
administrative organization.

The present procedure has its advantages when the program is popular.
It belongs to the president, not to any congressman (unless he has deliberately chosen to identify himself with it). If it succeeds, it adds to presidential stature, gives him prestige and powers, and concentrates in his person
the trusteeship of the nation. If there is failure, however, his involvement may injure his ability to carry out other all-important duties. The
chief of state, in his dealings with other nations, ought not to be weakened
by administrative failures or even dissensions about domestic policy.

As long as he is thus involved he will continually be bothered about
such matters and will take such precautions as he can to isolate himself
from their effects. This is apt to result in further estrangement from his
departmental heads. He will not discipline them because he will not dare
—it has become a rare occurrence for a secretary to be dismissed; they
will, however, be exiled to their departmental offices; and it will be known
that they are not in his confidence. Since he is still the constitutional chief
executive, however, he cannot separate himself from general accountability
for what they may do.

It is not a happy situation for a nation to have its chief of state feel that
he must daily watch the opinion polls to see whether he has lost a percentage
or two in the scale of public favor. These polls are published not only in his
country but abroad, and they have become a constant preoccupation of
foreign leaders. When the percentages fall, they feel that their bargaining
position is improving. They may, at an extreme, anticipate a change in

administration. These conclusions may be dangerous. Others are notoriously apt to mistake the meaning of such expressions in a democracy, and they are apt to make judgments costly to themselves as well as to the American people. The Germans have twice in this century judged that opposition to intervention in their wars would prevent the president from actually acting against them. In 1967 the North Vietnamese and their supporters again made such a judgment.

Elements of the Presidential Assignment

It ought to help, in discovering what is essential for the presidency to do, and what might be assigned elsewhere, to identify more particularly its present assignments. When this is done it appears at once how impossible a conglomeration of duties and powers have accumulated in the White House. It is not conceivable that any individual could carry all these responsibilities and exercise all these powers. But it is also seen what is less and what is more essential to be done by the presidency.

It is true that many assignments are inextricably part of a web. They may have been assumed by default; they may have been taken because they were convenient for others; they may have come to the presidency by that process of implication spoken of before—the extension of a static constitution. And they have been interwoven with existing duties. Yet, if the effort is made, some sort of separation can be made that will not seem too unreasonable. The president, then, acts

—as *chief of state, external affairs:*
> The gathering of intelligence and projecting of other nations' intentions.
> The conceiving of foreign policies and their day-to-day management.
> The conduct of diplomatic affairs: appointment of officials, ceremonials, and interviews.
> The making of treaties and executive agreements, and struggling for Senate ratification.
> The supervision of economic affairs: loans and gifts, military aid, technical assistance, tariffs and trade.

—as *chief of state, domestic affairs:*
> Formulator of national social policy: welfare, education, health, conservation, the development of sciences and the arts.
> Formulator of national economic policy, including fiscal and monetary arrangements to ensure prosperity; policy toward various organizations in economic life—unions, corporations, and other associations; the special developmental needs of regions, and of

various occupations such as agriculture, industry, commerce, and finance. Regulation of independent organizations.

Guardian and conservator of resources.

—as *national leader:*

Using all the media of communications available to explain policies to the public and especially to those who elected him, gaining other support if he can. This support is the real source of presidential power. If he can keep and increase it he can manage the Congress, maintain discipline within the government, and keep the party apparatus vital. If he loses it, the Congress will increase its obstructiveness, loyalty among his subordinates will fall off, the party will become fractionalized, and public order may be threatened by civil disobedience of more or less dangerous degree.

The ability to meet the demands of this function varies enormously and for inexplicable causes. When complaints begin, they are hard to check, and their nature will become more and more unreasonable until they reach attacks and allegations that have little or no relation to their source. He must avoid this.

The possession of leadership qualities required for this national duty enables a president to establish such a rapport with supporters that his mistakes may be excused, lack of executive ability may be forgiven, and he may do whatever he and his advisers believe to be necessary for the national good.

—as *chief of party:*

Immediately after nomination (and the preliminaries may have run through several years with increasing intensity) candidates must accept the general formulations of the platform, and enlarge and explain them to the electorate; a campaign organization must be chosen and directed, and the lead must be taken in raising the funds and appealing to influential supporters.

If elected, the president-elect has become automatically the center of party activities, determining policies, paying off debts, establishing a headquarters and seeing to it that the party apparatus is kept intact for the next campaign. Supporters must be rewarded and foundations laid for future needs.

As head of party, the administration's record will be the issue in his or his successor's campaign for reelection; he must always consider how it will affect party fortunes.

Throughout he must have remained sensitive to the traditions of his party, have conciliated its leaders in the Congress, in the states, and in localities, and must have tried to establish discipline for the effort promised during the campaign to translate promises into accomplishments.

—as *chief legislator:*

Influence must be used tactfully to see that the organization of both houses will be friendly to presidential proposals and will be useful in the struggles to come for legislation.

He must deal as best he can with the inherent hostility of the legislators to his initiatives and try to overcome the obstructionist bent of the Congress. He must also bargain actively with congressional leaders, giving personal favors, dealing with prejudices, trying to maintain some sort of contact with more than 500 members. Especially he must gain support for national projects, usually by granting his own support for local ones.

—as *commander in chief:*

He must direct the organization of the military forces for all the duties they may be called on to carry out; in this he will have the difficulty he will also have with other departments, that their secretaries (in this case supported, perhaps, by prestigious generals and admirals) will have plans and projects other than those he and his party prefer.

He must, nevertheless, enforce the traditional rule that the military can have no foreign policy but that which exists to serve civilian purpose.

In case of war, he must direct strategy, coping with the military demand for victory when the civilian objective may be marely resistance to aggression or the establishment of a situation in conformance with the nation's interests.

—as *head of the Federal Union:*

The relations with the states must be managed with tact as integration proceeds, the states losing powers but being asked to assume more duties.

—as *exemplar:*

This is the most difficult as well as the least measurable of presidential duties, yet it is perhaps as important as any. He is supposed by the electorate to be the custodian of the nation's traditions, its honor, its general commitment to posterity, and its integrity. The weight of this duty is felt more than any other. It is recognized by those who speak of even the most unlikely presidents as "being seized of office." It transforms them from ordinary mortals—sometimes weak ones—into dedicated servants. Yet it is a quality that the process of selection makes most difficult to find, and one, also, that many presidential duties tend inevitably to undermine. There is continuing curiosity about presidents' lives, their families, their circumstances, and the traditions they represent. Criticism from these sources may transfer to politics and even affect presidential capability in his other duties.

—as *holder of residual powers:*

It has been explained that many times in our history, presidents have assumed powers not granted in the Constitution and have exercised them during emergencies. It is improbable that a time can be anticipated when such reserve powers may not be needed. How he may be relieved of their weight has long been a difficult question.

—as *selector of personnel:*

He must choose his heads of department, judges of the federal courts, and all officials everywhere in government occupying what are called policy positions. In spite of relief from minor appointments by expansion of the career services, he must still make hundreds of choices and presumably supervise the work of his appointees, replacing those whose service is unsatisfactory. In this he is peculiarly bound by political considerations, and they may have nothing to do with the capability of appointees. Many administrations have been handicapped by such appointees.

—as *supervisor of regulation:*

The regulatory agencies are sometimes spoken of as "independent," meaning that they belong to none of the branches. They are recent (since the 1880s), and they are an exception to the principle of separated powers. They are created by the Congress but do not necessarily report to it except as seems politic. But the president appoints their members and therefore has much influence on their policy. Besides, his presidential record is affected by their behavior, and he often exerts influence on their decisions. Their situation is anomalous, but unless they are more or less in harmony with the administration, the president is bound to interfere.

It will be seen that any such attempt to classify has to be modified by the inevitable interplay of forces and the interweaving of responsibilities. It is impossible to separate very clearly the duties of a *chief of party* from those of a *national leader.* A *selector of personnel* affects every policy he may attempt to direct by the appointments he may make. A *chief legislator* becomes a bargainer, using his whole executive apparatus to get from the Congress what, as he sees it, the nation needs. A *commander in chief* can use the military and his agent in enforcing policies of all sorts, even undertaking undeclared wars.

In all these duties the president has enormous powers, and at the same time only those he can persuade others to allow him, a paradoxical situation noted by practically all shrewd observers of the presidency. If he loses his prestige, his popularity, or his credibility, it is known instantly everywhere and especially in the Congress and in his own executive establishment, but also everywhere in the world where he must act. Demand for acceptance of the measures he proposes drops off, and the Congress, sensitive to the change, becomes more fractious than usual. At length, if the weakening goes far, he is simply defied and new legislation comes to a stop. His appropriation bills will be cut up and perhaps even rejected; and his own subordinates will begin to separate themselves from him, their sudden independence showing itself in the carrying out of his directives as they themselves prefer.

With the electorate strongly behind him it is all different. His associates work together with enthusiasm; they find the Congress reasonably cooperative; and other nations are respectful. The press is subdued. There is little carping and obstructing. Everything goes his way. He has only to ask, and others around him hasten to serve.

The power he has or does not have is extraordinarily evanescent. It is not an ability to give orders because he is the chief executive; it is the ability to give them because he represents in his person the will of the people and because those who must act with him recognize his supremacy.

This peculiar situation makes it necessary to adjust institutions to it as a reality. The national government ought not to proceed without a majority; but if the majority is wrong—as it can be—those responsible still ought to be able to rely on constitutional authority adopted in procedures reaching deep into the national conscience and embodying considered wisdom.

To make this authority legitimate the government in office ought to have what the government does not have now, a mandate from the electorate. It has been said of every modern president, except Eisenhower, that he was doing or attempting to do things he was not elected to do—or, conversely, that he was not doing things he was elected to do. This is one reason for suggesting the inclusion in government of an agency to organize discussions of important issues so that some sort of party consensus could be reached. If this were done, platforms might become more specific and less evasive, and candidates might similarly be committed more clearly to promises made during campaigns.

It is a saying among professional politicians that candidates do not win the presidency—their opponents lose it. This is a shrewd observation. But as a rule dominating campaign strategy it leads to the election of presidents who are committed to nothing because their main effort has been to avoid offending any considerable number of voters. Presidents often find them-selves vulnerable from the same cause that is supposed to have elected them. They attempt to do something, and it is at once said that they were either not elected to do it or had been expected not to do it. If they intended such a policy they concealed it from the voters, and this was an underhanded way to treat an electorate.

Since only the president is elected by all the people, and only he is responsible for the varied duties outlined above, it is inevitable that in some sector he will be thus accused. Once this sort of criticism starts in one place it spreads very easily to others. This is because it has to do with character and credibility. Nothing is so dangerous to a person with all these varied and awesome responsibilities as that he should have his integrity questioned. To have genuine power he has to have undoubted and unchallengeable honesty, disinterest, and dedication. He cannot be suspected of giving favors, of amicism, or of getting his way by subterfuge. Yet, as we know, he has almost daily to use all these doubtful devices in order to get done the things his conscience and loyalty tell him he must get done for his country.

It is a supreme irony of our institutions that we place the president in a position like this. He must be the nation's mentor in all these respects, yet he cannot fulfill our expectations without constant departure from them. The burdens of the presidential office must be made man-sized, not hero-sized; human-sized, not god-sized.

Dispersal and Strengthening

Going back to the classification of presidential duties (*chief of state,* external and internal; *exemplar; leader; party chief; holder of residual powers; chief legislator; commander; selector of personnel; executive*), it is evident that if the presidential system—in contrast with the parliamentary (or cabinet) system—is to be kept, the presidency must remain supreme in some of the categories. Several, however, can be shared, and in others the president can be replaced altogether. The duties are already far beyond one person's strength and are rapidly becoming more so. If it is true that in the interest of making him more capable of doing what is essential he ought to have relief from what is only important, ways must be found to do just that.

No more of the powers as chief of state, either in foreign or in domestic affairs, can be shared than already are; but there can be a different sort of body to share them with. If there were a legislative house with a genuine and central interest in national rather than state or local problems this would be supplied. Members of such a body would have no further reason for dictat-ing executive appointments or for diverting appropriations.

An elected president would have to be head of a party, but he might be relieved of its worst problems. For instance, there would be clearer mandates on important issues because of the dialogue induced by the operations of a new election system. There would be means of communication with party members through a permanent organization; and there would be relief from the troublesome chore of financing. It could be expected that there would be much closer ties with party members, but also that the opposition would conduct itself more reasonably because it too would have leaders and a continuing internal dialogue.

One legislative house ought to be entirely nonpartisan. Like the House of Lords, it might delay but not originate legislation. Also, it might become a sort of advisory council on national policy. These are matters discussed more fully in the accompanying chapter on legislative reform, but here it may be said that with the proposed changes in both houses the familiar obstructive impulse, arising simply because proposals may have originated in the executive branch, would at least be lessened. President and legislators would, for the first time, have mostly common concerns. Stalemate might occur, but it would not occur for partisan reasons or from the tropistic reaction of a legislature constitutionally set against the executive.

One of the serious difficulties all presidents have had has been the public knowledge that they are always having to give something to get something. Outsiders wonder whether what is being given is of interest to them, and whether what is being gained is worth the price being paid. Such operations are carried out in a kind of semisecrecy with all involved using the media of communication covertly to show themselves in the best possible light. At present there is a contest between wary antagonists who tend to think of advantage rather than the objectives being gained or lost. There is no ethics of interchange. And the public policies tend to become lost in the techniques of carrying on these sophisticated political controversies.

For the president to be forced into this sort of dealing is a certain source of suspicion and disaffection. All the concealments, the representations that are only partly true, and the efforts to gain influence by managing public opinion lead finally to a feeling that the president, at least, is engaged in maneuvers and manipulations inconsistent with the integrity of a national mentor and the dignity of a chief of state. There will always be those who will claim that he has lost in his trading, that he has been untruthful in telling what has gone on, and that he has used the presidency for purposes demeaning to the office.

It has often taken a kind of blind trust among followers to believe that the president was contending for the public interest in the best possible way, and no president has been able to keep a majority following of such convinced loyalty. Franklin D. Roosevelt came nearest, perhaps, but even his followers fell off in number from one election to another. And even before his first term was over, the familiar campaign of disparagement had begun.

It increased during his second term; in fact, that term began with a bitter battle between himself and the Congress. During the campaign for a third term it took on the demeaning characteristics other presidents have suffered. He himself, as an old campaigner, expressed amazement at the unrestraint of his opponent, Dewey.

If the party apparatus can be used to carry on such conflicts in public, presidential manipulation and frequent confrontations with congressional opponents can be eliminated. Such occasions have more often happened when domestic policies have been in question than when foreign relations have been involved. But the one is certain to affect the other, and trading about one almost inevitably involves the other. Roosevelt gave up a good part of his New Deal in persuading the Congress that military appropriations must be greatly increased as the Second World War approached. This repeated Wilson's experience in the earlier war; he had had to give up his whole program of progressive reforms in exchange for congressional support.

Presidents, during the postwar periods, when more and more world responsibilities have devolved upon an unwilling people, have all had trouble getting appropriations for foreign aid, and that trouble has uniformly had to be smoothed out by giving up important domestic projects. The conclusion must be that the bargaining process brings everything into one trading area.

In very large part, the recalcitrance of the Congress in all such matters has been owed to the situation of its members: their local constituencies, their short terms, their vulnerability to lobbyists for private interests, their frustrations when they make decisions they are not qualified to make, their need to interfere in administrative operations they cannot control, and their defensive internal organization. Presidents, as chief legislators, have had to recognize these characteristic obstacles and to take such measures as they could to overcome them. Their resorts have not been consonant with the character we like to assign to the highest office in the nation.

Presidents have had to begin by shaping their cabinets to please important legislators, perhaps choosing several from the Senate. They have hoped in this way to smooth the way for legislation by using the traditional senatorial-club spirit; sometimes it has had some effect, particularly in the beginning; but they have always found that politicians have been placed in executive positions they could not possibly fill satisfactorily, and often found too that they had taken rivals rather than cooperators into their official families.

Two organizations have been set up to handle the demands of congressional partisans, one to parcel out jobs and the other to organize itself as a presidential lobby. This lobby ordinarily prepares the way by giving favors, arranging for patronage, and working out such arrangements for congressional collaboration as can be managed. The loss in this has been far more than just the inefficiency involved in employees unfit for their jobs; the employees have realized that their duty was to their patron, and that their political services for him must be their first consideration. Because the merit services have been expanded, patronage has grown less available in recent years; but presidents who have expected to be relieved of this nuisance have found an unexpected new one in the search for other ways to please demanding legislators.

In a society of accelerated change when the need for responsive legislation grows more acute, the task of presidents who must try to meet their obligations by getting legislative programs adopted has grown increasingly difficult. If they had no other duty this would take all their time and energy. Roosevelt in his last terms, Truman throughout, Eisenhower after his first two years, Kennedy during his truncated administration, Johnson, and Nixon were able to make only a minimum success of this part of their obligation. It might also be said that nothing was really done to establish in legislation the adjusting mechanisms necessary to the vast social changes created by new technologies and movements of populations. The result was, in Johnson's administration, a series of accumulated problems. In 1964, however, he came into office with a majority willing to follow his lead. This was because extremist reactionaries had captured the Republican party and, by being defeated, allowed the new Democrats to dominate the Congress. But the advantage did not last, and by 1966 he was having to deal with a Congress more obstructionist than any for some time. As the inner circle of conservatives regained its power, it seemed willing to use it more ruthlessly for having been deprived of it during a short interval. Nixon, of course, had a hostile Congress from the start.

That this sort of bargaining, with counters whose values are loaded with public consequence, is not something chiefs of state ought to engage in seems hardly worth arguing. Certainly if any way out of such demeaning activities can be found it ought to be considered. It seems inevitable that escape must be found in a simultaneous reorganization of the Congress and the changes suggested here for the presidency.

For this purpose those departments having to do with domestic matters might be organized into a group: Departments of Commerce, Labor, Agriculture, Interior, Health, Education, Welfare, Transportation, Housing and Urban Affairs—and such others as may subsequently be created— could then be abstracted from immediate presidential supervision.

There are reasons, however, for thinking that the presidency ought still to retain immediate control of the departments having to do with high policy—Foreign Affairs, Treasury, and the Military (State, Treasury, and Defense, as they are now designated). These are the departments involved in the premier duty of chief of state. The responsibility for dealing with other nations, for attending to fiscal responsibilities, and for guarding the nation's security cannot be sloughed off. Such matters could be attended to more faithfully if there were relief from domestic administration. In a sense the presidency must always be in charge of foreign relations and of the treasury, and it is a precious principle that the commander in chief shall be a civilian. This cannot have much meaning unless the military *department* is also controlled.

It could only be a relief to the presidency if duties as *selector of personnel* were largely removed to another jurisdiction. Some distance in that direction has already been gained in recent massive expansions of the civil service. But there do remain many "policy positions" the presidency must control. The president now appoints not only cabinet secretaries but sub-cabinet undersecretaries and assistants. These appointments could be left to those with immediate responsibility for the work to be done. There are also the appointments to the courts, and these could be left to the chief justice, who might perhaps be elected, but for a long term.

These proposals, taken as a whole, are suggested to free the presidency for the supreme duties as chief of state, mentor, national caretaker, chief legislator, and commander in chief. Even for these areas, individuals of tremendous physical vitality, endurance, and dedication will be needed. So much so that ways must be found to facilitate presidential activities.

The establishment of several new branches has been hinted at; it may be said here that one reason for their organization is, again, relief of the older branches from obligations they have not met and cannot meet. It will be said that this would be a serious departure from the traditional tripartite system. It may be answered to this that it has already been departed from. The enormous regulatory bureaucracy, for instance, exists in a constitutional limbo. Its agencies have been authorized by law, but the delegations of authority have been such as no reading of the Constitution could possibly legitimize.

These duties have been taken from all the branches. But none takes, or can take, full responsibility for its actions. All are reviewable by the courts; all have their members appointed by the president with the customary senatorial consent. All make administrative law within ill-defined limits. And all are admittedly unsatisfactory for their intended purposes. But as things are now, if there is a dereliction of duty it is without fail charged to the president. If duties were constitutionalized the president's responsibility would at least be considerably modified. He might appoint a chief regulator as he now appoints a chief justice, but he would not be involved in regulatory decisions any more than he is in those of the Court.

The same is true of assessment and guidance, a function now scattered clandestinely among several agencies and never brought into the consideration of next year's or the next decade's governmental programs.

A whole new agency would not only relieve the presidency of a duty to be foresighted in matters it has no competence for but also would supply what is now lacking—a comprehensive view of the future to be reached through the actions of the present. The distribution of available resources is at present subject to the urgings of various political individuals, tempered by such factual material as may be supplied in a somewhat casual way. And it is, of course, the subject of bargaining among all of them for the advantages they may have in mind. Gains in this have been made by the efforts of the budget personnel, but their efforts have to do with the immediate future, mostly, and although they try to look ahead—without having been authorized to do so—because they must, it is not the kind of look taken by an organization charged with the specific duty.

The failures of foresight incident to this haphazard arrangement are charged to the president, just as economic depressions are charged to him, without his having any constitutional duty to control the dispositions they result from.

With these changes it is possible to outline a picture of the presidency purged and rejuvenated, fit for its highest responsibilities and relieved of duties it ought not to undertake.

CHAPTER 10

THE LEGISLATURE

The Congressional Position

> All legislative powers herein granted shall be vested in a Congress
> of the United States, which shall consist of a Senate and a House
> of Representatives.
>
> —Constitution of the United States
> Article I, section 1.

If by "All legislative powers" the framers meant what the words seem
to mean, they were not being exact. For in other sections (7 and 8 of Article
I, and 2 and 3 of Article II) the president was also given what are
certainly legislative powers: in one instance to veto measures passed by the
Congress, in another to make recommendations, and in still another to
make treaties "provided two-thirds of the senators present concur";[1] and
the judicial power was extended to "all cases . . . arising under this
Constitution, the laws of the United States, and treaties made . . . under
their authority."[2]

In fact, only one exclusive power was allowed the House of Representatives: to originate "bills for raising revenue."[3] But even then there was
the proviso that the Senate might "propose or concur with amendments

---

1. Article II, section 2.2.

2. Article III, section 2.1. It has been pointed out before that no law made by
the Congress was securely valid until the Supreme Court said it was in accord with
the Constitution; but only the Supreme Court could say (according to the Court)
what the Constitution meant. So lawmakers could not know in advance whether they
understood it as a majority of the Court did. The Court thus joined in making not
only legislative law but, in an expansive interpretation, constitutional law as well.

3. Article I, section 7.1.

as on other bills."[4] And since these, with their amendments, might become laws, the president's veto still could be exercised.

Not long after the new government was installed the president's recommendations became the source of many important legislative initiatives; after the party system was developed, they became almost the only source —at least of important ones. Numerous bills were introduced by members, but those likely to be adopted were the ones proposed by the president. There came to be a certain ambivalence about this. The Congress disliked being told what to do and bargained strenuously before yielding, but it turned contrarily peevish when the president did not submit promptly drafts of measures the country was expecting. If a congressional session was notably futile, the president was blandly blamed, and his administration was spoken of as having failed. And if a session was reasonably productive, the president claimed the credit.

By the end of the nineteenth century the president was being regarded as the chief legislator. Theodore Roosevelt started the new century as very nearly the only initiator—although there were some vehement objectors. From that time on, if the president was not anything like a monopolist of legislative power, he was the most important user of it. The initiative had passed to him, and it did not return to the Congress.

As for the judiciary, it will be recalled that as early as 1803 (in *Marbury* v. *Madison* [1 Cr. 137]) Chief Justice Marshall made plain what he understood to be meant when the framers said that the judicial power should "extend to all cases, in law and equity, arising under this Constitution, the laws of the United States, and treaties made, or which shall be made, under their authority."[5] His reasoning was that the Constitution was the supreme law of the land, that the members of the Court had sworn to uphold it, and that if laws passed by the Congress and signed by the president conflicted with the superior law of the Constitution, they simply were null and void. Similar oaths taken by the president and all the members of the Congress were ignored; but these individuals could, and occasionally did, claim to understand their duties under the Constitution quite as well as the justices could. When interpretations conflicted, the words of the Constitution actually offered no way of choosing whether Congress, president, or Court should prevail. It is one of the curiosities of legal history that the Court has substantially made good its claim to be what amounts to the final legislative power because it makes superior law by decision. Presidential rebellions and congressional indignation have sometimes prevailed, but a strong tide of opinion rebukes any affront to the Court.

4. Article I, section 7.1.
5. Article III, section 2.1.

These remarks are not made as a comment on the undoubted inconsistency of the Constitution, but to show that legislation for the Union was from the first regarded as something that should not be left wholly to legislators. Powers were separated, but they were also made interacting. This was true of the legislative as well as the executive and judiciary. But in successive incidents of conflict the Congress has lost more and more of the initiative until finally it possesses very little.

The framers did not have in mind such a simple division of powers as would be implied in the statements of the more aggressive occupants of federal offices. These claims were to the effect that the legislature was to make laws, the executive was to carry them out, and the judiciary was to determine the constitutionality of everything done. These pronouncements were most emphatically made at times when conflicts had arisen, such as, for instance, that between President Andrew Johnson and the Republican radicals who controlled the post-Civil War Congress. But since on that favorable occasion impeachment of the president failed, no other has ever been tried. The Tenure of Office Act he was accused of violating was finally repealed, and this closed the attempt of congressional leaders to seize exclusive power. Since then, taunted occasionally by being called "rubber stamps" for presidents, Congresses have reacted with some spirit; but time and its events have been against them. Their unreformed bodies have not been able to maintain a credible position of relevance to the swiftly developing complexities of society. They have sunk lower and lower in the public regard and in actual power.

It is most curious to realize, in view of this, that intentionally or not, the Congress was originally given preponderant powers. In the process of separating and balancing, the framers meant each branch to share its powers in some respects with the others, and the whole was meant to be in balance; but actually the legislature was given certain strategic superiorities. For one thing, it had very nearly absolute obstructive abilities: nothing could compel it to act if it preferred not to act. Then, the procedures it adopted concentrated this power in the persons of a few committee chairmen. As has been noted, these were inevitably members with the seniority of a long service owed to repeated election from safe constituencies, and safe constituencies were nearly always conservative ones.

The ability to obstruct was reinforced by relative freedom of its inner circle from the pressure of general public opinion, of party discipline, or of presidential pleasing. The only force recognized by these elders was the threat of exclusion from governmental favors. They did give way to logrolling offers, conceding something to colleagues from other districts when they could get something for their own; and they did succumb to presidential promises if they considered that he could carry them out. Otherwise, their situation was impregnable—negative but unreachable. They were even able, as a body, to resist all but the most powerful gatherings of public demand. Only pressure from their own constituents could move them.

It is a kind of paradox that a branch of government with an original preponderance should have lost it in such an important matter as the initiation and sustaining of national policies, and that it should fall into a posture of sullen obstruction. But the fact is that almost all changes, or reforms of consequence, requiring legislative commitment are by now, and have been for a long time, more likely to originate elsewhere than in the legislature. And such proposals become laws only after arduous efforts to persuade reluctant congressmen. These efforts usually begin as movements among groups of concerned citizens who, in long campaigns, gradually make an impression on public opinion, finally persuading the president that his own prestige will be enhanced by taking up the cause. Sometimes these efforts have gone on for a generation or more before he and they could finally move the Congress. This was true of such governmental reforms, among others, as the merit system for employees, the establishment of a budget, and the setting up of the various regulatory agencies.

Even when the Congress has finally given way, it has almost invariably been with reluctance; and always the thrust of the legislation has been blunted by amendments softening its effect or sheltering private interests from its requirements. No regulatory body has had the capability intended by those who advocated it, and some have been turned more to the uses of the interests sought to be regulated than to that of the public.

This is because the sheltered position of safe members makes them callous to the public interest and open to the lobbyists' many means of persuasion. It is not necessary to document this situation here; it is done every day in the media. During every year there are exposures of connections between favor seekers and legislators, all sufficiently publicized, but only a few result in embarrassment to members.

The exception to these observations is furnished by emergencies, and sometimes by presidential honeymoons, when general euphoria exists and Congress may not yet have settled down after some disturbing losses. The Congress practically abdicated in panic just as President Roosevelt was taking over from Hoover, and a series of measures was passed that the controlling conservatives soon regretted. Some survived the crisis, but many were later repealed or emasculated. More productive honeymoons occur when presidents have won notable majorities and have campaigned for mandates. The Congress then, feeling some party obligation, may be compliant for a time. But the softness never lasts long. President Wilson struggled during most of a year for acceptance of the Federal Reserve Act; Cleveland lost out altogether in attempts to lower tariffs, although it was a traditional policy of his party; President Johnson, after his triumph in 1964, bringing in with him numerous new congressmen to replace older members, made an unprecedented success of his Great Society legislation, but in 1966 he lost his collaborators, and the Great Society began to languish.

Partly the obstructionism is owed to lobbying, a system that has grown to proportions every observer remarks. It is deplored, but no one advocates any reform beyond the requirement of disclosure. The lobbyist is generally regarded as a subverter of decent procedures, but his capacity for evil depends altogether on the willingness of legislators to be persuaded. There is only the most elementary code of ethics for either legislative house; and the favorite defense of the most outrageous offenders is that what they have done is common among their colleagues. Their indignation is addressed to the point of unfairness. Why me, each asks, and not the others?

It might have been expected that abuses would gradually disappear under the glare of televised publicity when that medium became common. The difficulty with this expectation was that the rewards of corruption had increased as private interests had become more likely to be affected by what happened in Washington. The ingenuity of lobbyists and of their respondent members of the Congress is proportional to the increase in the hazards. Besides, some old and long-accepted dodges are nearly untouchable.

Lawyers and professional "consultants," for instance, who are also legislators, have long "worked both sides of the street." Bills are introduced and pushed, or others are opposed at the request of lobbyists. It is often found that a sponsoring member belongs to a partnership back home whose client is the interest to be affected by the legislation. He may protest that he is an inactive partner, and so he may be for the moment; but that he expects to gain from his legislative activities later, if not at once, is taken for granted.

If it is true that the latest Congress is usually the worst in these respects, it is because corruption pays better all the time, and because it is exposed no oftener than before. Senator Morton of Kentucky said of the Ninetieth Congress that seldom had the repute of the Congress stood so low.[6] Senator Clark of Pennsylvania elaborated on this theme on several occasions, and Senator Smith of Maine came close to denouncing her colleagues. These modern senators may have been right, but honest legislators have made similar remarks about most congressional sessions since the beginning.

President Roosevelt said of the wartime Congress of 1944 that it was wholly devoted to private interests. There were "pests who swarmed through the lobbies of the Congress and the cocktail bars of Washington,

6. *Newsweek*, July 24, 1967.

representing . . . special groups as opposed to the basic interests of the nation as a whole." They had, he said, "come to look upon the war as primarily a chance to make profits for themselves at the expense of their neighbors—profits in money or political or social preferment."[7]

The successor to that Congress (the Eightieth) was denounced by President Truman in his 1948 campaign as a "do-nothing" body; it refused his requests for legislation because of lobbyists' pressures. A conservative coalition had opposed successfully every important measure the president had proposed. But the Eightieth was no more corrupt than other Congresses. The degradation was a condition of the institution. The president —Truman in this case—could win an election by denouncing the Congress; but he could not alter its makeup, improve its ethics, or get from it a better performance.

In recent history the single exception to this record of obstruction and favor giving was the Eighty-ninth, elected with President Johnson in 1964. The circumstances were special. The old-line Republicans had abandoned their rule of picking not the candidate they preferred but one who they thought could win; and in a moment of weakness they had nominated Senator Goldwater. He had represented them so well that his defeat had been massive, and many congressmen had gone with him.

Many measures passed by the ninetieth session were the same ones Roosevelt and Truman had tried to get passed. Others were advances into welfare, urban reorganization, education, conservation, and the like. The lobbyists tried their best, and their congressional servants did emasculate many of the measures by amendment; but the accomplishment seemed miraculous to those who had become reconciled during nearly a whole lifetime to congressional obstinacy. Success proved to be temporary; the obtuseness concerning national needs and the catering to special interests returned after the next election. Things after 1966 were as they had always been.

The conclusion has to be that the problem is a constitutional one. The Congress is neither properly representative nor properly situated in the governmental complex.

Just as speaking of the president as chief executive obscures his real position and powers, so speaking of the Congress as the legislative branch obscures its position and powers. It is and does much more than this implies. But much of what it does is inimical to good government. This is because it is ill-named and ill-organized. It is suggested that in a reorganized government it be constituted and organized on a somewhat different plan. If it is conceived that there ought to be a legislative branch, a forthright attempt to create an effective one ought to be made.

7. *Public Papers* (1944–45 vols.), p. 34.

Lawmaking

Any convinced democrat would agree that laws should *not* be made by those who execute them, because it is so likely they will be made to suit the executants; and executants ought to get their orders not from themselves but from representatives of the people they are supposed to serve. Dictators promulgate arbitrary edicts; free people make their own. This, at least, is the theory. Yet the fact is that many important laws in our democracy, and most of those with direct effect on citizens, are actually made by those who administer them. How did this happen?

It is suggested that the weakness of the Congress is largely responsible. Legislators are simply unable to make relevant laws governing a technological society. But because they refuse to recognize their own disability they resort to unrecognized and, consequently, unsystematic delegations. What is referred to here is the vast body of administrative law, now operative everywhere in society and especially in economic affairs. Rules and regulations made pursuant to generalized acts of the Congress by administrators affect every individual in his usual pursuits, as well as every corporation as it goes about doing what it is chartered to do.

It is recognized that regulations must define the impact of laws on those they are meant to affect. If laws were detailed and rigid their administration would rapidly become impossible, if only for the reason that a dynamic society changes so rapidly; but flexibility in delegation needs to be governed by directives and standards that make it impossible for bureaucrats to take advantage of their situation. They can and do, as things are, impose regulations convenient to themselves but inconvenient to those controlled by them. This has become so frequent an abuse that some governments have adopted ombudsman devices in recognition of the public's right to be treated fairly by its own servants. There ought to be minimum need for such protection. Even if laws for a complex society cannot be detailed, they can be relevant and consistent, they can reduce bureaucratic abuses, and they can be directed to the general interest instead of to private ones.

As to congressional incompetence for the delicate task of legislating, it must be recognized to be inevitable in the circumstances imposed by the Constitution. Senators and representatives are by profession politicians. A large proportion of them previously were lawyers, and the rest may have been many things but hardly ever administrators of sizable organizations. When laws initiating federal action provide for effectuating agencies, these agencies may, and often do, employ thousands of civil servants. Putting that many individuals usefully to work is in itself no task for an amateur; and if the agency is a regulatory one, or has to do with welfare, defense, conservation, or similar activities, it is a very unusual legislator who will know more about the duties to be undertaken than that a general result is expected. How to reach that result is necessarily left largely to newly appointed administrators. And when the law has passed through its inevitable congressional battering, it may well emerge almost unrecognizable to its sponsors and very nearly unintelligible to those who must execute it. Many, sometimes most, of the congressmen have been more concerned to deflect or soften its effects than to sharpen its directives and provide for the disciplines it requires.

The reason for this is the familiar one that districts or states are represented in the Congress but not the public as a whole. This turns legislators' minds immediately to the effect any proposal may have on their particular constituents. Worse, they are alerted by interested lobbyists to its effects on a small selection of constituents, perhaps even on no more than one—that one being a campaign contributor, an individual important in maintaining a home organization, or the client of the member's law or consulting firm.

If the Constitution is studied it will be seen that this concentration on local issues was made inevitable by the districting of constituencies. Only most unusual disengagement can make a member more responsive to national needs than to those of his particular constituents. It was assumed by the framers that an assembly of such representatives would pursue each of the interests of those who elected him. This was his intended duty. But it was also assumed that the interests of each locality would, in the processes of legislation, somehow produce something consistent with the general good.

This was the exact counterpart in politics of Adam Smith's reasoning in economics. Each, by pursuing his own interest, would contribute to the good of the whole. This additive concept is fundamental to the arrangements in the Constitution for legislation. It was departed from in the presidency in a kind of practical recognition that holism was necessary to nationhood. But it was not the controlling thought in forming the legislature, nor was it in continuing the separate sovereignty of the states.

It is not too much to say that politician-legislators are inevitably incompetent to understand administration, just as administrators make poor politicians. Since this is so, even the best laws, intended to determine what should be done, cannot and ought not to attempt the determining in detail of ways to do it. There always has to be a book of regulations governing the work of the executive agencies; but without clear directives from the law these regulations necessarily make assumptions preferred by administrators. And the Congress is incompetent even to do this. It will be seen that there is a constitution-determined dilemma whose inevitable result is that bureaucrats have far more freedom to write regulations, and even to determine policies left inchoate in law, than they ought to have. The aphorism that no law ought to be written by those who execute it is impossible to follow. The Constitution made it so.

We are not concerned here with the large part of the regulatory book having to do with internal management but only with the part that affects the activities of those who are to be in some way regulated. The rules may be of life-and-death concern to those affected. They inevitably violate the principle of participation we have spoken of before—that no one should be forced to obey rules he has not had a part in making. This does not mean that he may not be required to do or not do things he objects to— obviously he may—but it does mean that he shall have been heard and, if overruled, it shall have been in a procedure also established by a majority after discussion. This principle has been lost.

When an official of the Internal Revenue Service compromises a debt owed to the government because of unpaid taxes, he acts according to a judgment of his agency. The limits of this judgment are defined in his instructions, but the law he works under must give him this discretion. There cannot be a law made for each of thousands of such delinquencies. But think of the differences it makes to the taxpayer!

Similarly, when a regional forester allocates grazing rights to public land he acts within his general instructions but on his own responsibility. He knows that what he decides is subject to review by his administrative superiors, but still he has to act as seems to him fair and discreet in the special circumstances of his area with all its conflicting claims.

The same is true of any other applications of general law: allocators of water rights, awarders of concessions and licenses, determiners of valuation for many purposes, imposers of penalties for the infraction of administrative rules, the distributors of welfare benefits, those who decide how highways shall be routed, where housing shall be located (and, in both these last instances, whose properties shall be expropriated), and where travelers shall be forbidden to go. Anyone, from his own experience, can add almost indefinitely to such a list. Not all, or even many, considering the number, are actions taken by federal agents. But when they are *federal* they are apt to affect a large number of people or very substantial interests.

One of the complications of administrative behavior has to do with the discretion necessarily left to those with immediate responsibilities. They would not be human if they were not in some degree susceptible to influence from those whose objections may be heard sympathetically by their superiors, or to the pleas of those who are most insistent and troublesome. There may also be a sympathy for one individual that may involve injustice for others.

If there is criticism of bureaucratic rigidity, this is the explanation. Public administration is a hazardous occupation, and it is made worse by the interferences of those who made the original law authorizing the disciplines so often subject to complaints. There could be no objection to general legislative investigation of fairness, of departure from established rules or favor giving; but when members of the Congress hear from their constituents they are apt to call the administrator to account without looking into the matter; and the implication may very well be that *their* constituents ought to be treated as exceptions.

This, again, is natural to the system imposed by the Constitution. The congressman wants the support of the complainer. He does not know, and has no sufficient means of finding out, whether fairness is really involved. It is only too easy to blame the administrator. He, as much as others, is responsible for making *bureaucrat* a word that signifies woodenheadedness, obstinacy where rules are involved, and inflexibility. But, in fact, these are the virtues of a merit service. And congressmen know it better than anyone else. They simply must have scapegoats, and these are the most defenseless ones available. There is often an engaging frankness about this—amounting sometimes to a conspiracy. The congressman is severe for his constituents' benefits; the bureaucrat knows it is not meant; moreover, the rebuke he accepts in silence counts as a favor for which he may some time expect to be compensated.

This, then, is typically the way laws are made and administered in our complex system. They are subject, in their first general phase, to the pressures of reformers, lobbyists, or the prejudices of those who prefer the status quo. And the congressman is always conscious that he must please his local supporters. Under these influences legislation emerges confused, inept, or so amended as not to reach the intended result. It is then consigned to those who must interpret it, make the rules for its administration, and see that it is applied or carried out. In this process delegation is, and must be, very wide. The lawmakers do not know much about the processes they are initiating. They have a draft from the president and are urged by his lobbying assistants to act; they hear contrary opinions in their hearings; they are under pressure from lobbyists for private interests who have amendments to suggest when attempts at outright stoppage have failed. Some of these amendments may be adopted; there may even be amendments to the amendments; and there may be added irrelevant riders.

There are legislation services in which experienced assistants make sure that drafts are in proper form, that they do not conflict with other statutes, or that they do not, in effect, amend them. But these experts are not always listened to. The lobbyists have lawyers too, skillful ones who are continuously busy. The final wording of laws originates as often in the offices of counsel for private interests as in any governmental office. When amendments are introduced this is usually their origin, and it can be taken for granted that their intent is not to further the public good.

It is, then, inevitable that laws for a continental nation of many millions shall be highly generalized. The best laws, in fact, hardly do more than state the end in view and establish the standards to be applied in enforcement; but this they may and should do carefully and fully. Mostly they begin in a felt need of some sort, perhaps for a public service or a grievance requiring correction; there may be abuses to be stopped or fairness in transactions to be defined and enforced. It would be dictatorial to exclude those likely to be affected from being heard as the law takes shape, but there can be rules about this. Presentation of a case is one thing, bringing pressure to bear is quite another, and worse, of course, is blackmail or bribery in its many diverse and elusive forms. The principles of participation and representation, still essential to democracy, cannot be honored as things are done now. Their constitutional embodiment must be thought out anew. Meanwhile there is a sinister drift away from belief that they can ever again be effective. This is, of course, to despair of actual democracy and to accept a new sort of legislation for private interests—and perhaps some hope that conflicts among them will result in the public good.

Participation by the individuals or interests affected will have to be reduced to taking part in political processes at their beginning in local meetings, in the selection of representatives, and in making known, when hearings are in progress, the views of themselves and of others who think as they do. This may not correspond literally with the democratic commitment to give everyone a say in decisions affecting him; but it is inevitable in a vast and complex society; and it can, in fact, be made very effective. The desire to have that say is responsible for the present accumulation of lobbying devices at the later stages of lawmaking. The inevitability of unfairness because of differences in resources—maintenance of permanent lobbyists can be so expensive that only interests with much to gain can afford them—makes it necessary to regulate the process. Fairness to all concerned can be best achieved by organizing discussion of the issues and proposed measures in local meetings.

There are other reforms, however, that would contribute to the same result. Lawmakers themselves—their qualifications, their conditions of work, their constituencies, their terms of office—all need examination.

Kinds of Complaint

There is a remarkable similarity in the opinion of the public about the Congress in whatever period an examination is made. For this there is the very good reason that its behavior has been remarkably uniform. The congressman, in the view of pamphleteers, commentators, and cartoonists, is a blow-hard orator, swinging his arms and denouncing opponents during campaigns, continuing his windy but slyly corrupt career in Washington.[8]

The legislator is typically supposed to have little scientific knowledge and a deficient understanding of economics, a primitive concept of administration, and no concern about any of these. The annual pork barrel, however, is another matter; about that he is pictured as emoting earnestly, subsequently claiming credit for local improvements while at the same time deploring taxpayers' burdens. His favorite target for denunciation is the bureaucracy, but he never acknowledges that it is generously salted with appointees on whom he has insisted. He pads his office payroll with relatives, and he spends the taxpayers' money on extravagant junkets to far places with only the faintest relation to any possible legislation. To make an impression, he hauls up before the investigative committees defenseless victims he can browbeat with impunity for the edification of his constituency; but he ignores procedures calculated to extract information of any value. The numerous dedicated and capable members of both houses who try to serve the country faithfully seem to be quite lost among the noisy demagogues listened to by commentators.

This view of the typical member is so settled in American opinion that it has all the attributes of a stereotype. When once a fixation of this sort hardens, it creates a tendency to conform. Behavior illustrating what the public expects to hear is considered newsworthy; behavior of another sort is ignored. This is a particular fault of the privately owned and managed communication systems grown more influential with television. It is hard on the Congress and not always deserved. Also it has served to prevent the kind of reform likely to be remedial. There is little recognition that congressmen find themselves in situations calculated to make them the individuals they are supposed to be, or that efforts to emerge into a different atmosphere are not apt to be found credible.

All that is said here about the faults of the Congress, it must be insisted, is the fault of the institution, not of the individuals. It would be possible to enumerate many disinterested initiations, many struggles for public improvements, many useful reports of committees that stand to the credit of individuals or small groups of congressmen or senators. But all of them are caught in the requirements of their occupation. The Constitution determined that they should be districted, should have short terms, and should find it difficult to assert leadership or conceive adjustment to change. Circumstances have set them in opposition to the president and made it necessary to become negative, obstinate, and often destructive. As

8. The art of political oratory was best characterized by President Harding, one of its most adept practitioners, as "bloviating"; this he engagingly admitted was almost his only claim to superiority over any of his competitors. He was a passive senator and a bewildered president, but he could bloviate indefinitely on the hustings without making commitment on any issue or to any policy that anyone within hearing was likely to disapprove.

to amendment likely to improve the nature of the Congress, those individuals who understand the obsolescence it has fallen into never have enough influence to open the closed gates. These are guarded not so much by the Congress as a whole as by the inner circle of elders whose suppressive power is very nearly absolute. There is no person in politics who deserves so much sympathy as a public-minded member of the House of Representatives who finds himself fenced in by traditional rules, who sits as a junior on committees automatically controlled by old-timers, who may introduce laws but has no expectation whatever that they will be noticed, who cannot even speak in the chamber where he has a seat. All this is less true of the Senate than of the House, but not much less true. If a junior is allowed to speak there, it will be to an absent audience. And it is notorious that the elders have ways of putting in their places nonconformists among the newcomers, or even those elders who have not made their way into the inner circle.

The truth is that there are always a few dedicated members who carry a sense of public responsibility into day-to-day proceedings, and who manage to extract something of general value from the chaos of private attritions on the treasury and constant underminings of administrative and regulatory efforts. That this has been true far into the past can be learned by studying congressional history in almost any decade; but in every decade, also, the stereotype is quite as visible as it is in the present. And there is always evidence to sustain it.

It should be noted that in every session since the 1930s there have been in the House responsible and intelligent members meeting occasionally to exchange views or listen to experts, and that they have often been able to have some effect on the worst legislative essays. Both parties, and sometimes independents, are represented. Numbers vary, the turnover among reformers is rapid, and occasionally they get down to a very few; but La Guardia was harassing Hoover in 1932 with his small company of Progressives, and although no such talented leader has since appeared, there is always someone who cares to hold the group together.

Nevertheless contemporary sessions show the familiar characteristics. For instance, the Agriculture Committee of the House recently voted unanimously to censure a member who called attention to the scandal of appropriations for the Farm Bureau, a nationwide association of businessmen and farmers begun for the purpose of lobbying for farmers' benefits but now become one of the country's largest insurance businesses, with other profitmaking side ventures, but still tax-exempt and still receiving a subsidy. Congressional support in many rural areas was obviously threatened by questioning the validity of the Farm Bureau's claim to federal support.

About the same time the chairman of the Senate Finance Committee found it possible to favor senatorial friends who were large investors in bank stocks. This he did by using his committee for the support of measures calculated to keep down competition from new banks and thus increase the profits of existing ones.[9]

Then, in the same month, a senator was discovered to have protected a notorious labor racketeer who was being investigated while the senator's law firm back home received fees for defending the same individual. Also a representative was accidentally exposed for having received thousands of dollars as the proceeds of a benefit dinner, something not unusual in itself, but this particular dinner was promoted by the officials of the postal workers' association, and the representative was chairman of the Post Office Committee.

A short time later, a newsman revealed that a congressman, in his capacity as a private individual, owned a laundry, and the manager of his plant was on his office payroll; the laundry had a contract with a nearby Air Force base. This same congressman also had hired the local printer in his hometown so the taxpayers could pay his printing bills. It seemed ironic to the newsman that it should have been this representative who offered an amendment to reduce aid to the depressed areas of Appalachia, and that, because there were seventy-two absentees—forty-five of them Democrats—the amendment should have passed.

These are actual illustrations, among many, of incidents that came to light within a short time. This happened to be the session also made notorious by the disciplining of Senator Thomas Dodd and Representative Adam Clayton Powell. But, as was often noted, the actions in both instances were considerably softened by the consciousness of many other legislators that their own behavior had been only slightly less censurable. The difference was that their positions in the establishment were more secure.

Senator Dodd's ardent defender in the proceedings was the same chairman of the Finance Committee, who did not hesitate to point out that there were no rules, not even any ethical understandings, to support the censure motion. It was true, and when the motion had been passed there still were no standards for reference. It was recalled occasionally that a proposal indirectly bearing on the ethics issue had been pending for some two years—pending but buried in committee.

This reform measure was a renewal of Senator Monroney's effort to "streamline" the Congress. A bill, jointly sponsored by himself (then a

9. A dispatch from Washington (*National Observer*, March 8, 1967) by J. R. Dickenson furnished the sort of news to be read almost daily. Speaking of the Finance Committee chairman: "It works something like this. Senator X is approached by a well-to-do corporation or individual that wants a tax break and is a potential source of campaign funds. The Internal Revenue Service disallows it, but it is tacked on to a tax bill as an amendment. The Finance Committee chairman has the power to accept these, and it is a never-ending source of political IOU's."

representative) and Senator Robert M. La Follette, had actually been passed in 1946. This is the same law spoken of above as having been "contained." It was not directed primarily to ethical deficiencies, but was intended to make congressional business more efficient. Among other changes, it drastically reduced the number of committees and provided an entirely new procedure for considering the budget. The first of these provisions was evaded by the prompt creation of subcommittees whose effect was to add one more step to an already clumsy procedure; the second— intended to recognize and implement intelligently the executive budget— was simply ignored. There were protests; but no one knew what could be done to congressmen who refused to obey their own laws; and, in fact, nothing was done.

Senator Monroney found this behavior of his colleagues painful, but being a quiet man and not accustomed to denouncing anyone, he awaited another opportunity. He waited, in fact, for ten years, meanwhile going on to the upper house and becoming its majority leader. From this position he began a new effort to persuade his colleagues that they ought to impose some degree of self-discipline. He assembled five other Democrats and six Republicans who seemed similarly interested, and after many months of conferring they agreed that the Congress was overworked, uninformed, and inefficient. If it became more efficient, they said, it would be less overworked. If it had more funds and could hire more assistants, it would be better informed. This last was a special attraction; other senators were envious of the Kennedy from New York who had a staff of thirty-seven.[10]

The proposed bill had other features, such as a provision for computerized reviews that would enable each standing committee to offer an annual report on the effectiveness of legislation it had approved. An added attraction was the reduction of committee sessions to no more than four a week.

Altogether, the changes would add no more than a few million to the congressional budget.[11] But Senator Joseph Clark, one of Monroney's colleagues, wanted a good deal more, and said so in spite of smothering indifference among the bill's proponents. He offered twenty-six amendments, most of them more likely to annoy than to soothe, since they went to the more serious causes of obstructionism. For instance, one amendment proposed that committee chairmen should give up their posts at the age of seventy. Most chairmen, as Senator Clark very well knew, were past seventy already; also, he knew that committee majorities might by-pass

10. He had so many because he was able to pay for extra ones himself, but then he had something else in mind than being a mere senator. So, perhaps, did many others, and it would be nice to have the taxpayers equalize their opportunities.

11. Congressional expenditures in that year were $135 million; the Monroney measure would add some $5 million. It was only a little later that the House passed (by voice vote so that no one could tell who had voted for or against) to increase expense-paid journeys to their home districts from five to thirteen in each year.

their chairmen and report bills even when the chairman was opposed. These were direct attacks on the seniority rule that fixed legislators from safe constituencies in chairmanships, kept them there indefinitely, and gave them dictatorial powers.[12] Other amendments proposed by Senator Clark recognized the ethical issues that had caused Senator Morton of Kentucky to remark mournfully, a short time before, that the reputation of the Congress had now fallen to "an all-time low." But Clark spoke to an empty Senate when he defended his amendments, and it was obviously felt by his colleagues that he had breached the decorum of the club.

Senator Monroney's bill was like other "reforms" that have given members more funds, more assistants, and more investigative capabilities. Nothing pleases a legislator so much as more money to spend, and nothing gives him so much of the attention a politician craves as a well-publicized investigation with himself in the role of people's advocate. But the Monroney bill, made into law, even if the Clark amendments had been appended, did not go to the sickness of the Congress; it merely made its members more comfortable. It would not close off the source of public disdain. It could be anticipated that the criticism would go on with tiresome sameness until an institutional change had been made.[13]

The continuing criticisms illustrated here by incidents in the ninetieth session offer the possibility of classification. This need not be confined to current happenings. It can as well be done by studying the persistent and uniform disfavor manifested in any decade of the past as strongly as in that of the present, in the cartoons of Nast as well as those of Herblock or

12. How serious this safe-constituency problem is can be understood by knowing that (again in the ninetieth session) of sixteen Senate committees, thirteen were headed by senators from small towns in rural areas; and that of twenty House committees, sixteen chairmen came from similar districts. The House chairmen had been reelected from ten to twenty times, and the senators were serving their fourth (or more) six-year terms. This situation had prevailed since the 1930s; before that the Republicans had held the chairmanships; this favoritism had been useful to big business. Democratic chairmen were conservative, but in a somewhat different way.

13. The final report of the joint committee on the Organization of the Congress was published as Report No. 1414, 89th Congress, 2d Session. Remarks about the bill and the report here are necessarily brief. The report discussed in some detail the complaints about the Congress and offered some remedies under the following headings:
1. Committee procedures should be lengthened, their jurisdiction realized, and assignments to them should be revised. Also their staffs should be augmented.
2. The review of existing laws should be strengthened.
3. Conference committee procedures should be modified.
4. Fiscal controls should be strengthened and office allowances increased.
5. The legislative reference service should be strengthened.
6. The *Congressional Record* should be improved.
7. A joint committee on operations should continue to study procedures.
8. A Committee on Ethics should be established.
9. Lobbying regulation should be tightened.
10. Scheduling procedures should be improved.

Mauldin, in the comments of Mr. Dooley as well as in those of Jack Anderson or Art Buchwald.

Such a list would be something like the following:

1. Obstructionism, reaction, ignorance, and lack of initiative.
2. Interest in local rather than national needs.
3. Subservience to lobbyists.
4. Preoccupation with reelection and the use of legislative influence to maintain home support.
5. A persistent tendency to amicism and nepotism (no standards have ever existed for competence among congressional employees).
6. Escape from responsibility: voting in committees is private, and roll calls in the House are avoided whenever possible so that credit can be taken or blame avoided as seems ultimately most creditable.
7. A disposition to panic in crises and to run for cover, leaving responsibility to the president, who will then be blamed if things go wrong.
8. An incorrigible habit of interfering irresponsibly in executive operations by attaching conditions to appropriations, attempting to dictate appointments, or specifying where and by whom operations may be conducted.

If this consensus of appraisal is unfair to many legislators, some of the fault is theirs for belonging to so irresponsible a body without audible protest. In its long history it has never been reorganized or reformed, its worst habits have been protected, and its ability to play its part in modern government has steadily declined. Nor has any member within memory offered suggestions for change that would in any way affect congressional powers.[14] The Monroney "reforms," if adopted in full, would do something to modify obstructionism but not very much; other faults might be improved under scrutiny but, again, not very much. The really basic difficulties would not be touched.

The reason for persistent congressional ignoring of an increasingly embarrassing obsolescence is not hard to identify. As a body it is answerable to no one. Individuals may be elected or defeated; the membership changes; but the body itself possesses an impervious repellent instinct that appears at any suggestion of disturbance. Efficient smothering devices go silently to work at any hint of change; and after a first airing, nothing more is heard of annoying proposals. Only rarely are such voices as those of Senators Clark or Smith heard in either chamber; and these are usually silenced by the disciplines the old-timers know so well how to apply. Appointments to important committees are useful in this; admission to the inner circle of policy

14. The exception to this is the La Follette-Monroney bill of 1946 that would have stopped the nitpicking changes by committees in both houses of the executive budget. The bill passed, but, as has been said, it was afterward ignored.

determiners is reserved for conformists; privileges are withheld or restricted; investigative subcommittees are chaired by others with the attendant favorable publicity; and legislation wanted by the executive is channeled to those whose names will be associated with popular measures.[15]

This resistance to change could not be so uniformly successful if it had not been established in the Constitution. A potential discipline for the president was provided in impeachment, and he must always ask for appropriations. The Supreme Court may not only have its jurisdiction restricted by law, but it has to extract from the Congress its annual appropriations, after perhaps humiliating hearings. But the Congress has none of these disadvantages. It has only to sit tight; there is no other power that can affect its behavior in the slightest. It makes its own rules; it may or may not discipline its own members; there is no way of getting a hearing for legislation proposed by the president or anyone else unless it pleases the congressional inner circle of longtime members. Also it may take its own time; bills are pocketed in committee, even when they eventually have to be passed, for indefinite periods while bargaining about amendments goes on; and frequently the bills are never heard of again.

To be sure, the public takes a rather jocose view of its cantankerous legislative bodies. There is more cartoonists' humor than reformers' vituperation about the monotonous comment. Legislators are viewed with resignation. There is no way to make them behave in a more efficient or even a more seemly manner, and so they have become an expensive and exasperating, but accepted, appurtenance of democracy.

One thing about them is conspicuously true. They are the embodiment of representative government, and indeed of equalitarianism, no worse and no better than the people who tolerate them. This reputation, even among those who elect them, is doubtful; but that is the way it is wanted to be. There are no qualifications; anyone can become a congressman, and the membership is liberally salted with ignoramuses, with backcountry lawyers, with henchmen of city bosses, with all kinds of frankly local demagogues, and with, at worst, a few who are careless even of legal limitations and occasionally find their way into jails for using public resources to their own advantage. But as long as they are members they share with all others the luxuries, privileges, and powers conferred by the Constitution on its favored organ of government.

It is, of course, because of its sheltered position that there have been no really serious attempts to check the increasing inefficiency of the Congress. There have been many more or less thorough reorganizations of the

15. Footnotes in history books can result from this last sponsoring privilege: the McKinley and Smoot-Hawley tariffs, the Glass Act, the McNary-Haugen Act, the Connally Amendment, the Taft-Hartley Act, the Smith-Landrum Act; there are a few of these in each session, and considerable prestige is attached to selection for nominal authorship.

presidential establishment, at least of its executive apparatus. These have been warily approved by the Congress, except when any suggestion was made that some change might diminish the hold of the legislature on administrative operations. But nothing of the sort has even reached the suggestion stage for the Congress.

It will be recalled that nothing in the Constitution decrees that the addition or elimination of executive agencies shall be done by law. It might well have been left to the president under the same rule of implication used by the Court in declaring acts of the Congress or of the executive to be unconstitutional. The power was seized by the legislators, and the seizure was made good through their hold on appropriations. There is always a severe limitation on executive attempts to reshape administration.

Executive obsolescence is, however, conspicuous, and many changes have had to come. President Roosevelt even succeeded in persuading the Congress to accept the principle of the legislative veto of reorganizing plans; but this was granted only for a limited time, and there were many exemptions. For instance, it was insisted by its friends in the Senate that the Forest Service should not be affected by any of Roosevelt's changes. Similarly, the military has usually been protected from unwanted presidential reorganizations.[16] The executive, compared with the Congress, has been much changed to meet the demands upon it. The Congress has been exempt by its own defensive wish; and, curiously enough, the literature of political science, although there are many descriptions of congressional procedures, has very few suggestions for reorganization beyond a few internal changes calculated to make members more effective in doing what they should not do at all.

Effective cures for the long and devastating list of deficiencies must evidently go beyond anything the Congress can ever be expected to do for and to itself. The deficiencies have only to be regarded thoughtfully to see that obstructionism, for instance, is an inherent trait, that legislative initiative, as things are, will never appear (and ought not to in present circumstances), that any body not subject to appraisal from without will become frozen (the safe, lifetime members are indifferent to the weak position of more exposed colleagues), and that members elected from local constituencies must necessarily be indifferent to large national problems

---

16. In a recent bill one provision gave the chiefs of staff stated terms of four years, something they have always wanted. It is obvious that this affects materially the freedom of the president to really act as commander in chief and gives the military a protection it ought never to have in the American system.

This is a more sinister change than appeared at first. It made possible an alliance between the chiefs and the chairmen of House and Senate committees that began at once to show itself in pressure on the president to accept the judgment of the chiefs and their xenophobic allies in the Congress. It was a combined influence he had to recognize in all his decisions.

and even to the public interest. These are conditions of continuance in office, and, as in other occupations, continuance is the first consideration for professionals.

A kind of examination other than any likely to come from the Congress itself will have to provide remedies, but it can confidently be predicted that any reforms will be fought with all the weapons politicians possess.

Legislative Improvements

Is it useless to expect that better laws will be made if the federal law-making bodies are reexamined, reconstituted, and thus adapted to contemporary circumstances? Or does the institution merely reflect the general and systematic incompetence among it practitioners, and somehow the wish of democracy not to be systematized or even to have too much integrity? It is a fact that these bodies are as they originally were, and that they have always been notoriously unsuited to lawmaking. There are still two houses with their original and duplicating powers; their members have the same terms and are elected from districts and from states as they were in the beginning.

If this seems incredible considering the difference of present conditions from those of the eighteenth century, it is nevertheless so. To modify the shape given the legislative bodies by the framers, only internal adjustments have been made to accommodate a larger number of members. But laws are a democracy's way of meeting contemporary needs. The nature of these needs is well enough known, and it is known that they are clamorous. They result from the expansion of territory, the increase of population, urbanization, industrialization, and the involvement in a world of independent nations made smaller by technology. But legislators with the same powers, the same hold on their offices, and the same local constituencies must be depended on to solve them if, indeed, they are to be solved at all.

As everyone knows, increasing American abundance has been accompanied by resistant and humiliating forms of poverty; this has become, through neglect, something even a reluctant Congress has had to recognize, but, of course, without really attacking its causes. There are familiar secondary problems arising from crowding, water shortages, pollution, and the exhaustion of resources; there are others caused by technological advances—for instance, the new devices for transport and communications. There is a continuing replacement of men by powered machines that should have opened new opportunities for personal development but have not because facilities are lacking. About such problems, discussed every day in the news media, the Congress shows an awareness only when the problems become acute; then, in a panic it is apt to do either the wrong thing or a merely meliorative one.

It is obvious enough that if change is not anticipated its incidents may be more destructive than beneficent. It is also obvious that progress in accommodation is not always what it seems to be, especially in an economy whose operations are entrusted to individuals or corporations. A publicly owned industry need not be controlled by an elaborate apparatus to ensure that it has regard for the future; but a private one must be regulated, and the regulators must have technical capabilities equal to those possessed by the organization.

What needs to be done is to find a way of making laws appropriate to such needs, and of doing it not as emergencies arise but in time to forestall them. Since the problems are national their solutions must be national. Legislative attention ought to be centered on such problems rather than on the needs of localities. The additive concept has long lost any usefulness it may once have had. Improvement does not result from the satisfaction of local demands but by bold national adventures that encompass in due proportion the local projects. The extracting of funds to satisfy demands not related to one another in a whole could be made impossible by a calculated assessment that would assign priorities according to usefulness.

The placing of congressional followers in the federal services, a diminished but still considerable practice (whenever a new agency is authorized there is a drive to exempt its employees, or a large number of them, from the merit system), could be stopped. As for constituents' demands, they might better be voiced in political meetings provided for in a political organization.

The deplorable preoccupations of congressmen can best be eliminated by making them unnecessary or impossible, and this can be done only by reorganization. Wider constituencies would enlarge legislators' perspectives and encourage them to consider national issues, and if some were elected at large and others from considerably enlarged constituencies they would acquire a national or at least a regional orientation now so conspicuously lacking. Election from districts makes it difficult, not, as it should be, easy, for a lawmaker to think of the nation as a whole and of its situation in the world. Longer terms would reduce members' preoccupation with re-election, and governmental assumption of election costs would free them from binding ties to private financial supporters. A smaller number, or a different organization of the committee system, would bring back the debate that was supposed to be an important preliminary to legislation.

The worst vice of the Congress as it is at present constituted, partly owed to incidental and irrelevant interests, is the attempt of members to control what they ought not to control, to interfere in matters they can only confuse, and to incorporate in legislation directives for the executive departments and regulatory agencies that originate in the urgings of lobbyists, in prejudice or caprice, or in the demands of bureaucrats who, for one reason or another—perhaps in response, again, to their lobbying friends—wish to change the directives they work under.

These are the sources of the amendments that appear in multitudes as long-considered measures are finally brought to formal hearing in committee rooms. They are also responsible for the continued refusal of the Congress to accept executive budgets, which have been prepared by an expert staff familiar with the work of all the agencies, and after the budget officers of the agencies themselves have studied their own needs. They are still received by the lawmakers as though they were merely the attempts of bureaucrats to expand their establishments. They are usually attacked, however, not with a view to economy or in conformance with a general policy, but in the attempt to find projects congressmen prefer for reasons of their own or to eliminate ones they dislike. The bargaining that goes on between the more influential congressmen and well-placed bureaucrats is one of the most ignoble proceedings of the present system.

Programs undertaken with the expectation of development over years may be cut off or emasculated in these trading sessions. Others may be enlarged for no better reason than their popularity with those whose desires must be catered to. These last are likely to be either local politicians who are their supporters back home or those who have something to gain and are willing to make a return of some sort. Most of the outright scandals involving legislators have arisen from such relationships.

The Congress, also, whenever it can, denigrates or humiliates the executive branch. An illustration of this is the most recent incident in the long war between the branches over disclosures. The executive has always defended the right to secrecy, and every strong president has at some time refused to give committees of the Congress information they have demanded. The reasons for this are obvious. When decisions are being made, information from many sources is assembled. If made public, it would close many of these sources. Disclosures are therefore made in confidence. This is infuriating to publicity-seeking politicians, and they are always trying to make inroads on the principle.

A new Freedom of Information Act went into effect in 1967 requiring all agencies to prove a legitimate reason for withholding information, not only that asked for by the Congress but by any citizen. The Courts were given the power to decide whether security was essential. This had the result of shifting the burden of proof from those who wanted information to those who withheld it. This would not be recognized by a president in any serious matter, even if told by the Court to conform. But in lesser matters it will be embarrassing and might seriously hamper the making of decisions.

It was discovered soon after the passage of this act that the Congress had exempted itself from its provisions. This was one more illustration of what has been said here—that the Congress has an inherently favored position and is willing to protect it by using its constitutional power with the utmost ruthlessness and with complete indifference to any complaint about unfairness.

Other illustrations of this favored position are easy to find. The success of the so-called antipoverty program was largely measured by the use the city bosses were able to make of it. Attempt to extract it from their control in some places made its renewal each year an agonizing ordeal for its administrators; politicians regarded federal assistance to the poor as a threat to their organizations unless they controlled its administration. Similarly, bills for aid to education have been impossible to get passed until their control has been guaranteed to state officials. The resistance of these educational bureaucracies to innovation is notorious. They are traditionally subject to the veto of the most reactionary individuals in their jurisdiction.

Repeated attempts to eliminate or reorganize the National Guard have met with adamant congressional opposition. It is an expensive establishment, mostly paid for with federal funds but controlled by the states. It is thus a valuable political asset, making only doubtful contributions to national security. Similarly, Department of Agriculture research scientists have never been able to maintain an effective national center because the Farm Bureau lobby, allied with state agricultural colleges, has insisted that the funds be divided among all the states, thus giving less than enough to each and not enough that any can carry on the kind of research required. The National Center at Beltsville has been systematically starved.

These illustrations are typical of the same sort of behavior in many other fields. They result, over and over, from the same sensitivity of lawmakers to those who are in a position to make demands on them. It is a behavior that will not change unless its causes are removed. Only an institutional reform will do—something that will recognize that the nation is an integrated whole with essential duties to its citizens. This involves the giving up of additive attitudes and the acceptance of holistic ones, which does not fit very well the American preference for *laissez-aller*. This, it can be argued, is a surface difference and not a deep one. The interests of all have become very much the interests of one as civilization has developed. What is necessary is to devise institutions recognizing the situation and making sure that the one is always included in the all. And this cannot be done unless it is forthrightly undertaken.

It has always been clear enough what were the causes of congressional fallibility; but nothing has ever been done to remove them, largely because the causes, if not the results, were so generally approved. Furthermore the internal changes made from time to time have made matters worse rather than better. Pay has been raised, staffs have been increased, facilities have been elaborated. But if all these, as has so often been pointed out, have gone to making more effective activities that should not happen at all, then they cannot be called reforms.

Congressmen can now maintain better liaison with their home supporters, they have finer quarters and more suave assistants to meet and soothe constituents, their speeches are written for them by professionals, they are kept from egregious errors by liaison with the Library of Congress (why should a *national* library be called the Library of *Congress*?), they are able to interfere more effectively with administrators, and generally they can devote their best efforts to fending off potential competitors for their jobs. But these activities are quite irrelevant to the making of laws for the nation; worse, they are mostly calculated to torture them out of shape, to blunt, or sometimes even reverse, their intended effect. As a consequence it has to be said in all seriousness that the improvements in members' prerogatives in recent years have made them better able to do what they should not be able to do at all.

Nothing has yet been said of the disability caused by numbers. It has been pointed out that the House of Representatives spoken of by the Constitution was visualized as having so few members (sixty-five) that actually debate was possible; and the Senate, of course, would have had a much smaller number (twenty-six). When expansion reached 435 for the House, and 100 for the Senate, the possibility of debate was no longer a reality.[17]

As in other instances of important change, no constitutional amendment followed. There was no consideration of the basic reason for a legislative body and no attempt to see whether representation could not be made real even for so large a number of constituents. There was only the freezing at the number of 435 and the organization of standing committees with the accompanying rule of seniority.

In *The Federalist Papers* (No. 55) Madison made a remark that might well be considered in any serious overhaul of the representative system. "In all very numerous assemblies," he said, "passion never fails to wrest the scepter from reason." And again: "Had every Athenian been a Socrates, every Athenian assembly would still have been a mob." What constitutes a "very numerous assembly" is not very much different now

17. Since 1912 the membership has been fixed *by law* at 435. In contrast with the first Congress, whose average constituency was 30,000, the average after the census of 1960 was 410,481. A law of 1941 provided for a method of equal proportions; that is to say, the average population for each representative was to have the least possible variation between one state and another. The reapportionment of districts after each census causes some anguish, since some seats disappear and others are created. But the growth had not been stopped soon enough. The number had already made dialogue impossible, and discussion had disappeared into committee rooms, where it was closed to the public at the committee's convenience—and this usually meant at the convenience of its chairman, supported by a small circle of equally safe inner-circle members.

from what it would have been in Madison's time. Electronic devices and enlarged halls have mostly made exchanges more formal and have tended to freeze fixed positions. There is a good example of this in the Assembly of the United Nations. It is the reason Churchill insisted that the House of Commons be reconstructed, after its destruction by bombing, on the same plan and with the same capacity as before. It was important to facilitate debate.

Perhaps it is inevitable that legislatures should become more and more places of registration for previously determined policies. If this is so, then the proposals for widespread organized dialogue are very much in order. And even if a revised committee system should make serious consideration a reality instead of a fraud, committees ought to formulate their legislative proposals as representatives, in some sense, of their constituencies and not of bosses, machines, or predatory interests.

It is with present evils and potential virtues in mind that newly organized bodies for the making of laws are proposed in what follows.

A Congress of Representatives

The framers intended the legislature to have first place in lawmaking for the nation; there can be no reasonable doubt of that. When it was said in the Constitution that the Congress should possess the legislative powers, the statement was too emphatic not to have been meant. These powers were not exclusive, but they were primary. The president could veto, but his veto could be overridden; and his only other duty was that he should: ". . . from time to time give to the Congress information of the state of the union, and recommend to their consideration such measures as he shall judge necessary and expedient. . . ."[18] To be sure he could convene extraordinary sessions and in case of disagreement he could adjourn them to such time as he should think proper. But these powers have never been of much use except occasionally to emphasize his belief that certain measures were urgent and that the Congress was being negligent.

As to the judicial share in the legislative process, no reading of the Constitution justified what has nevertheless happened: that the Supreme Court should become the highest and final legislative body of the nation.

It is not too much to say that both president and Supreme Court now have legislative powers almost as important as those of the legislature itself. The one possesses the initiative, and the other makes the Constitution and has the final word. But it was clearly not intended to be so, and there is still reason for thinking that it ought not to be so.

If theorists are right to say that the executive ought not to make the

18. Article II, section 3.

laws it executes because that way lies tyranny, similarly the Courts ought not to make the law they judge cases by because that way lies judicial autocracy. Presidential recommendation is one thing, but executive pressure is quite another; and interpretation is one thing, but creative enlargement is quite another.

Both these kinds of behavior now exist largely because the Congress has proved unable to fulfill the intentions of the framers. Of course, there may well be doubt whether an attempt should be made to reconstitute an effective legislative branch. There will be those who will say—who do say— that the situation of the present has been reached by an evolution natural to all institutions, and that it should be allowed to go on evolving as before. Further, that the executive knows the nation's condition as no member of Congress can, and that the Court is by any test wiser than the lawmakers.

It may be that the alternative to a let-alone policy is by now so shocking to defenders of the presidency and more especially those of the Courts that it will not be entertained. The argument is elaborately defensive. This, however, may be because the Congress is thought of as it now is, and as it now behaves, and not as it was hoped it would be, and would behave, by those who conceived it. Back of this it has to be considered that it was imperfectly constituted to fulfill the framers' intentions; and consequently, that timely amendment might have preserved its usefulness.

It is at least interesting that the fiction of congressional lawmaking is still, however empty, stubbornly maintained, and that presidential proposals and Court interpretations appear under camouflaged rubrics. Occasionally a representative or a senator rereads the Constitution and finds his situation far from what seems to have been intended; but as things are, any protest he may make is useless; the facts are damning. So the Congress becomes more and more obsolete, and inevitably its original powers are more and more attenuated. In sheer desperation it is reduced to a negative-minded and defensively reactionary body.

Suppose, however, there is imagined a Congress made really and effectively representative—one organized to meet the demands of the nation as it now exists. Such a projective effort might yield quite a different view. As to being representative, the lawmakers must have the nation, not local districts, as their constituency. As to organization, they must be prepared to conceive measures needed by a complex society and must be given the capability of framing the laws it calls for.

To make the Congress more representative in a nation whose problems are so generally countrywide, the election of members from localities and states would need to be changed; if congressmen had the same constituency as the president they would have the same interests. They would, in fact, be elected to do the same things. Instead of responding to nagging from home districts and attempting continually to get something exclusive for their supporters there, they would be able to join in planning for the nation and in accepting responsibility for its policies.

To make the Congress more capable of initiating and carrying through legislative projects its organization would need to be changed. It would need to be made possible for leaders to develop who were responsive to national demands in the same way that the president now is, and if they were furnished with competent assistance they could largely replace the present system of accepting projects from the executive and then instituting a complicated and tortured amending process.

It is not easy to suggest a way of nominating and electing members at large; but there should be no insuperable difficulty if, as has been suggested, there existed nationwide machinery for inducing dialogue and discovering political talent; and further, if there were a public assumption of campaign expenses and a drastic restriction on the period of active campaigning.[19]

Not to depart from the tradition of bringing regional and local concerns into the national forum, it might be provided that a certain proportion of the primary legislative house be elected at large on a ticket approved in a series of nominating conventions held by qualifying political parties.[20] The other members might be elected from regions larger than the present districts. Then, in the organization of the House, it might be provided that the chairmen of standing committees should be elected by their committees but must come from the one-third of those elected at large. If these chairmen were provided with ample assistance for putting legislation into shape, many more finished laws would result.

Some such arrangement would relieve members of the constant demands made on them by constituents from restricted localities, would enable them to resist lobbyists' blandishments (they would not be dependent on them for campaign funds), and would enable them to give their attention to the national problems now so badly mauled in the amending process. The rule of seniority, so long an incubus, would need to be abandoned for majority decision in choosing chairmen and in forwarding legislation to the whole membership for voting.

Proposals for legislation would still frequently originate elsewhere, but not so frequently as now, because members would be of a different quality and have a national orientation. The present curse of obstinate obstructionism would be lifted: for one thing, there would not be the present monopoly

19. A Gallup poll once made some such suggestion to a representative sample of those who were listed in *Who's Who*. The question asked had to do with running for the Senate, and nearly one person in four answered that if campaign expenses were paid he himself would run.

20. Ones having had 10 percent of the votes cast in the last election might be a way of determining qualification.

of strategic positions by representatives from rural and backward districts; for another, there would not be the refusal, now so frequent, to recognize party commitments that run against peculiar local prejudices or interests; and for still another, the present jealous resistance to any initiative originating elsewhere would give way to cooperation in common endeavor. A representative's position would depend not on obstinate opposition to the president, or on favors won for campaign contributors, but on the general approval or disapproval of the party's conduct.

One very necessary end would be furthered by such an arrangement—the recognition of party commitments and of responsibility for seeing them carried into legislation. Arguments might be about how best to get things done rather than how to prevent them from being done at all or being done in ways that would injure some sheltered interest. If these commitments had been the subject of discussion in the induced dialogue of party meetings, and the platforms adopted in national conventions really resulted from the gathered opinion of the electorate, there would be a common promise of action and a common reason for fulfilling the promise.

All this machinery for discussion and arriving at agreement would have seemed impossibly expensive and complicated in any former time. But several mechanical aids are now available, and taken together they make it possible to reach decisions among scattered and numerous citizens who once were reached in the old town meetings. There are facilities that offer an entirely new way of stretching out areas of communication; there are transportation facilities that make it possible to get over formerly unheard-of distances; and there are rapidly developing techniques of opinion gathering that may give democracy a dimension it never has had in the past.

With such reforms, it is quite possible to make legislatures really representative again. Legislators representing districts would no longer be dependent on a flood of letters or telegrams of doubtful authenticity. A legislator could find out what his constituents were thinking by polling them; if permanent public machinery for it existed, this could be done very quickly and cheaply. It can be seen how this affects the reason for short terms. The framers thought frequent elections were necessary as referendums; representatives had no sure way of knowing whether they were approved until they found out by being reelected or being defeated by an opponent who offered alternatives. But they would know—or could know—if selective polling were done, where they stood with their constituents.

Further than this, computerized election procedures might make it possible to have frequent and meaningful referendums, and if recall or special elections became necessary, a permanent political organization could organize them with almost no extra expense. They are expensive now because they have to be undertaken anew on each such occasion, and places have to be adapted that are used ordinarily for quite other purposes.

It is possible to think of an automatic recall provision in election laws. If approval of a representative's behavior fell below an allowable percentage as shown in polls, his position might fall into jeopardy and an election be required.

The recall procedure might be applicable to the conduct of a whole administration as well as to individual representatives. It ought not to be made easy; that is, a small minority ought not to be given the power to harass a large majority. But an administration that lost the support of, say, 50 percent of the country's voters as determined by approved polling devices might well be required to go to the people for a renewal of its mandate. With the facilities available at present and those foreseeable in the future, such a special referendum might be carried out with surprising expedition.

This, and the other arrangements mentioned here, ought to have the effect of keeping the party's and the administration's mandate positive and strong, enabling it to override opposition and ignore attempts to obstruct and mutilate the legislation necessary to the mandate. But its most important effect would be the restoration of the congressional responsibility to the national electorate it is supposed to represent.

If it is the essence of democracy—as has been contended here—that every citizen should have an appropriate voice in decisions affecting him, there must be a way, under contemporary circumstances, to make that voice heard. It cannot be done directly in national assemblies (or even in state or city meetings), but it can be done in local meetings where issues of general interest are discussed and where representatives are chosen and instructed.

To have a voice does not mean to have the only voice. It does not even mean that decisions will be made as everyone would prefer. The mandate given the representative chosen may not be satisfactory to many—to nearly half, in fact; what democracy guarantees, and all it guarantees, is that the citizen shall have a voice. For his part, if he does have a say, he tacitly agrees to majority rule. If decisions go against his preference, he can have no complaint.

The national representative in a legislative house, chosen after ample discussion of issues and full exposure of candidates' views, is certain only that he goes to his duties with majority approval. Dissent has not been stifled; the minority has merely lost control of policy. It may in time prevail because the alternative that did win may be proved wrong, but for that the minority must wait. Loyalty to the democratic scheme requires conformance in act even if not at all in thought or word.

It cannot mean, either, that the representative has more than the general instruction of his party's commitment. He cannot be expected to be an automaton. There may be emergencies; circumstances may change; specific proposals may seem to him inadequate or not in accord with the interests of his constituents. About such matters he will use his best judgment, knowing that he will be answerable at the next election—or perhaps even before.

He may find out, if he thinks it necessary and relevant, what his constituents think. He may find out even if he does not think it necessary, because it would certainly be one of the important duties of permanent party officials to set questions, gather opinions, and transmit them to representatives. For this the technology is adequate. The opportunity for legislators to trade their services for the support of special interests ought to be much reduced.

A representative in these circumstances ought to emerge from the half-light, under suspicion, into the full light of responsibility to the national electorate.

A Body to Represent the Nation

There is ample reason for proposing the substitution of a differently constituted and differently functioning body for the present Senate. It will be recalled that it was not something wanted in its present form by anyone in the beginning. Equal representation of the states was a compromise calculated to cool the tempers of delegates from the smaller ones. But if it did emerge from the Convention in a bargain, there were other reasons for its acceptance. For one thing, there were many precedents. To go no further back, second houses existed in all the states of the Confederation; so the suggestion did not seem bizarre. But more important, it would be a check on the more impulsive popularly elected House because of being more securely anchored among the propertied and wellborn.

It has been explained that fears of legislative irresponsibility were very much present among the framers. The debtor classes in the new country were always trying to cheapen money so that their debts could be met in currency of reduced value. Farmers and small inland merchants were burdened with mortgages; besides, transport to market was expensive, and the markets themselves were limited. City buyers controlled the prices paid for produce; the bankers made loans at rates appropriate to the risks; and farmers' purchases of tools and such materials as they had to buy came high. Hostility to towns and townspeople was usual, and to the cities and their people it was often bitter. It must be remembered how enormous a majority was rural—more than 90 percent of the population lived on the land or close to it.

Naturally, if voting was general among such citizens, their representatives would pursue their own interests. They would be hard on merchants, moneylenders, and shippers—indeed all the more affluent citizens. It has often been pointed out that the framers were largely professionals: those who were employed by, and were part of, the elite as lawyers and agents. Some, however, were themselves merchants, large landholders like Washington, or speculators in western lands; but it was the lawyers who had to be depended on for drafting and advising because of their skills. Randolph's July Proposals became the center of discussion for the later proceedings, and Gouverneur Morris drafted the final document for the Committee on Style. They were distinguished lawyers; and so were Wilson, Dickinson, Mason, the Pinckneys, Rutledge, Madison, Wythe, Hamilton, and others. They consistently outtalked and outmaneuvered the politicians and merchants.

It was not at all strange that the proposal for an upper house to provide second thoughts, to weigh, and perhaps to reject what came to them from the representatives should be agreeable. Also, it was an added attraction that it would share the president's powers—would be a check on him as well as on the House of Representatives.

So the Great Compromise, as it is usually called, did not concern the need for such a body so much as its composition. The argument was whether it should be elected from constituencies of equal numbers of voters—as was true of the representatives—or whether it should establish equality among the states by giving each the same number of members. The proceedings, hung up so long by the politicians from the smaller states who saw themselves being dominated by those from the larger ones, could resume only when this equality was conceded.

The Senate, as it emerged, was an undemocratic arrangement giving some more weight than others. The compromise quieted these politicians but otherwise was a loss to representative government. The desire of the elite for a protective body could have been as well satisfied by a Senate with membership proportioned to population—provided it was not popularly elected. The inequality proposed by the Paterson plan was resisted by Bostonians and Philadelphians, but they really had little to lose in giving way.

It is strange that a house agreed to because it would be a check on popular representation should have survived into the equalitarian period following the ouster of the Federalists by the Jeffersonians, and that it should have outlasted Jacksonian leveling, populism, labor organization, and all the other advances of democracy, very nearly intact. The one change, of course, was that its members, instead of being chosen by state legislatures, have, since 1913, been popularly elected. But they still represent state constituencies, and some of these have many more people and much more territory than others. California, New York, and Texas still have no more senators than Vermont, Mississippi, and Maine. This malapportionment is highly visible, but objection to it has never been serious.

It has to be said that a notable change followed from the popular election rather than choice by the legislatures. Useful legislation has had a better chance of approval there, and senators have become at least somewhat more nation-minded than the representatives. But the defects owed to its origin and to its malapportionment, and those resulting from its sensitiveness to its own prerogatives, are still notably present. And it can at times be even more obstructionist than the House of Representatives. A few senators, or even a single one, have been known to defeat measures wanted by large majorities. The filibuster is a device made possible by a self-made rule not reachable from outside.

Even its apologists would admit that the urban conglomerations of the country have been neglected by the Senate. And certainly its concern for national issues has been notable only in contrast with the parochialism of the House. Moreover its interferences with the executive have been even more of a nuisance. No president can appoint a federal official of any importance to serve in a senator's state without allowing one or both senators to dictate who shall be chosen, with the frequent result that even federal officials are more state- than nation-oriented. And a fierce concentration on local interests is visible in every year's appropriations. Also, the forcing of political appointments on administrators is even more rapacious than the demands made by representatives.

Another legitimate complaint is that neither house will consent to have joint hearings with the other on usual matters of business. These inquiries take so much of the time of busy executives that the work of the department is considerably and uselessly hampered. Part of this is publicity seeking. Separate hearings allow chairmen, particularly, to harass, publicly, bureaucrats who are always vulnerable, since they are not politicians and have no followings. These proceedings in both houses have tended steadily to lose relevance to legislative issues and to become forums for legislators' appeals to their constituencies or, worse, for the edification of those who have some private interest to further.

If the House of Representatives were to go on as it has been, unreformed, a reduction or change in the powers of the Senate would be a disaster for government. But assuming that there had been such a reform, and that the House had become a more representative body in the sense described here, a change in the makeup and the powers of a second house would be most useful. It could become the embodiment of national intentions at their most thoughtful level. In this interest it could act as a consultative body to the originating house, to the president in his capacity as chief of state, to the judiciary in its constitutional work, and to the regulatory and executive bodies who are doing the work of government.

With this in mind it is relevant to speculate about what the reformed second house might be like and what its responsibilities might be.

The first criterion would be that it must have a more national, that is to say, a more general, orientation. It must put first what is best for the whole —not for any region, not for any interest or group or individual, but for the nation. It would watch out for the well-being of citizens, and thus have a bias toward fair sharing and open opportunity; it would think seriously of conservation, of ecological permanence, and, of course, of international arrangements. It would have a special interest in order under law and of the devices essential to democracy—education, uncontaminated information, and participation in the dialogue of politics. Described in these terms, it can be seen how far we are from having such protection at present.

There is an aspect of the presidency that could well be transferred to such a house. This is the important but almost indescribable exemplar function. It could be the representative of posterity in the present, showing the way to well-considered policies concerning well-being and security.

Only the president is such a national representative now. Even reconstituted, a body to represent the nation could not attain a sense of responsibility to the whole; it would have regional interests; its membership would inevitably be numerous and would be influenced by immediate rather than distant dangers, by the solving of problems rather than escape from them, by the operation of institutions rather than their reconstruction.

The president, although he is elected by a general constituency, owes his office to a party and its adherents rather than to the whole electorate. He must supervise the most delicate diplomatic negotiations and, sensing the approach of crises in the nation's affairs, do what he can to avert their ill effects; but he must always do it with a view to his party's welfare. Even if he should be relieved of the intolerable burden of domestic administration he would still not be able to detach himself from the immediate and to consider the distant. Or, to put it another way, he must always deal with events, but not often with their causes. It is for this reason that a second house, different in nature, is proposed.

Such a house would not originate in regions, districts, or parties. To keep its national concern intact, members would have to give up any other preoccupation, and each would be dedicated to national well-being. Its members would need to be mature, proven, and dedicated. They must have given up permanently any ambition for further fortune or position. They must come from various occupations and so have had varied experiences; they must have survived the trials of getting ahead; and they must never have to consider the possibility of losing their positions as a result of their opinions or their decisions.

It will be seen that these are much like the qualifications for justices of the Supreme Court as it has always been known; and indeed, the second house would be another sort of supreme body. But it would not, for instance, be made up exclusively, or even mostly, of lawyers, and its duties would not be professional as are those of the justices. It would not decide cases except in unusual instances of review, and it would not originate laws. It would be an adjunct and consultative body, but it would share the president's powers. It would not interpret the Constitution, although it would help to remake it from time to time. It would not have executive duties, but it would be the mentor of the president and other officials.

This second house might well be entrusted with an explicit interest in the emergency powers now so often, and so riskily, exercised by the president. The Doctrine of Necessity has developed without constitutional warrant because in every government there must be residual authority. Action must be taken in crises without delay, and sometimes it is action that is drastic. As things are, only the president is in position to act, and his decisions are taken alone and on his own responsibility. This is neither fair to him nor safe for the nation. Such final authority ought to be shared. At least decisions ought to be shared and authority delegated rather than seized.

It would be well if this second house were kept small, say some such number as seventy or eighty—well under a hundred. In such a body, with perhaps fifty or sixty usually present, there could be actual and orderly dialogue, kept to essential issues; and the decisions reached could be as nearly reasonable as any human conclusions are likely to be. Indeed, this would be the source of this body's power—that it represented reason at work on the matters troubling a confused civilization. It would have stated powers —of reviewing laws in course of passage and of joining in presidential decisions that ought not to be made exclusively by one individual. But its real power in the nation's life would emerge from the undoubted dedication, experience, and wisdom of its members. They would be the best the nation could produce, and they would have promised to use their talents exclusively and permanently for the public benefit.

In the sense understood by the literal equalitarians of the nineteenth century, such a house would not be representative. In its disengagement from local affairs it would be more like the first conception of the framers. Their Senate had its power not from the people directly but from the state legislatures, themselves elected by a very restricted electorate; it had what were then regarded as long terms; and it shared presidential responsibilities as the House of Representatives did not.

Not more than half of the proposed body's membership should ever have been elected to public office, although they might have been elected to private ones—if corporations, associations, and labor unions are regarded as private. Many would have shown their distinction in other ways. They would have been dedicated public servants or exceptionally able private citizens.

But the resemblance would, in other ways, not be close. If any were elected they would represent national constituencies, but many might become members in somewhat the same manner as justices now become members of the Supreme Court—by appointment. Not all need be appointed by the president as his free choice. The chief justice of the United States might appoint some; others might become members at the end of other service. All, however, should have occupied places of trust and, having concluded that occupation, would bring their accumulated experience to a final public duty.

As is often remarked, there is now no place in government for the losers in electoral contests. They must return to private life and perhaps even make a living as best they can in some new occupation. This would be a way of making use of them. Executives of private or semipublic corporations and of nationwide labor, religious, academic, or philanthropic organizations would be other sources of membership. So, naturally, would the professions. And not only presidents and vice-presidents who had finished their terms, but secretaries of state, or of defense and of the treasury, as well as some senior legislators, might become members. It might be provided that labor unions, producers' associations, and religious bodies should agree on restricted panels for appointment of a member from among their number.

It remains to say something more of the powers appropriate for such a house. It might not only be the repository of the emergency powers now so completely possessed by the president, but also might, in other ways, be the consultative council so much talked about in the Convention of 1787 that was lost in later discussions and compromises. It might be a final place of appeal in matters of constitutional concern going beyond interpretation; it might even constitute from its members a permanent constitutional commission to suggest amendments and prepare for major reviews at stated times—say once in every generation. The purpose would be to prevent the basic law from falling into uselessness as has happened to so much of the present Constitution.

The legislative function of this house would be that of reviewing laws coming to it from the originating house before going to the president for his approval. If they were disapproved, the originating body would have to act again.

This house, if made responsible for a *watchkeeping* service, might act collectively as the national ombudsman. It might gather intelligence on its own initiative and respond to complaints from citizens' associations regarding the operation of national agencies. It would seem an appropriate duty.

Watchkeeping, acting as collective conscience, and possessing as much wisdom as the nation can gather, this second house ought to have the disinterest in anyone's fortunes and the interest in everyone's welfare that is needed in every nation's life. The institutionalizing of this collective virtue has been lacking in our government. It could not emerge from a theory of *laissez-aller*. There have been many patriots, many heroes, many reformers; most, however, have been centered on one cause, the welfare of one group; few have had the detachment combined with concern so much needed in modern circumstances.

The conception, to repeat, is of a body dedicated to the national interest and having powers appropriate to guardianship. It ought to provide second thoughts, but not to prevent, or even much delay, legislative action; it would advise and assist the president in matters of importance; but most importantly, it would act as watchkeeper for the nation's future and as the expositor of its conscience.

CHAPTER 11

THE JUDICIARY

The More Ambiguous Branch

In another place it has been argued that a government of separated branches, carefully made interdependent, is desirable in American circumstances. This is so, it was said, because the only alternative would be a government of one branch with the others made subsidiary; and this, in a democracy, must be the legislative branch. It could be expected that there would follow anonymous decisionmaking, chaotic administration, trading for local advantage, and diversion of interest from national affairs to private or local ones. An examination of American legislative behavior is quickly convincing that these—and other—weaknesses would appear and become intolerable almost at once.

It is true that the behavior of the Congress can be improved. As has been suggested here, a certain number, perhaps a third or a quarter of the whole, might be elected at large; terms also might be lengthened; and working committees, necessary in a large assembly, might be organized to reduce the stealthy obstructionism so characteristic of membership assigned by seniority. Then, too, the second house—the Senate—might be chosen in such a way that it would act as guardian for the general interest. This virtue would be assured by providing that its members be drawn from the country's active associations or from those who have served in positions of trust.[1] Some might be appointed from panels chosen by their associates in national organizations, thus making certain of their credentials as representatives. Others might be former officials who have served out their terms.

---

1. For instance: labor unions, professional associations, scientific and other learned societies, conservationist, planning, and consumer groups, manufacturing, commercial, or financial associations—none, of course, either political or religious.

433

All ought to be required to give up all other occupation and agree to serve for life. This, it might be hoped, would be a body well able to relieve the president of some responsibilities he must now carry alone. It would, as well, serve as a cautionary complement to the popularly elected House.

A legislature at its best, however, cannot act as chief of state or as an executive. Its nature requires it to be a representative and deliberative body, coming to conclusions in a way different from that used by those other officials, and with another end in view. To give it other than lawmaking duties, especially the control over administration its members are so likely to demand, is to ask of it something it is not constituted to do. The result of all such arrangements, when they have been tried, has been unhappy. Sometimes, as in the instance of the Continental Congress under the Articles of Confederation, the results have been disastrous.

The legislature, then, can be given a more general orientation, and it can be made more harmonious with other branches by arranging for it to concern itself with its real business and stop reaching for powers it will misuse.

The American Congress, during much of its experience, has done what is suggested here as its peculiar vice—conspired and maneuvered to appropriate and hold powers it ought not to possess. Apart from having interfered by demanding appointments for supporters, it has also successfully dictated organization for administrative duties. Actually its influence has been used to maintain mediocrity in the bureaucracy its members are so fond of denouncing. Also it has almost invariably shown itself to be irresponsible or xenophobic when it has prevailed in contests about national policy.[2]

Constitutional revision, it is concluded, ought to respect the principle of separation, but ought to be much clearer about the assignment of responsibilities—especially keeping representatives of localities from dominating national policies. Since it has been shown by experience that the particular institutional forms adopted in 1787 will not achieve the advantages and avoid the dangers of separation, the possibility of a better arrangement for the legislative branch and the presidency has been suggested here. Further, it has been argued that improved ones will not be useful for all time to come. No reason has been found for keeping each generation from having its own constitution.

2. Examples are not difficult to cite. There were war hawks in the 1840s; there were secessionists in the 1850s; there were radical reconstructionists after the Civil War as well as the Committee on the Conduct of the War while it was going on; there were imperialists at the turn of the century; there were years of resistance to international organization, climaxed by refusal to ratify Wilson's League of Nations. There was the Red hunt after World War I. There was the xenophobia that worsened the cold war. There was resistance to the New Deal that lasted until Johnson's Great Society and then proceeded to emasculate that program. It is a consistent record of reaction, tenderness for special interests, and dangerous insistences on provocative policies, foreign and domestic.

Going on, we must consider the position of the judiciary in a government adapted to the immediate future. In a preliminary way it ought to be recalled that the executive suggested here differs from the presidency as it now exists. Only certain departments ought to be left to the president's immediate supervision, and those the ones he will be intimately concerned with as head of state: the operations of government that cannot be abstracted from his general responsibility. Others might be grouped for a different kind of administrative supervision.

If that were the arrangement, congressmen, surveying and remaking budgets of the departments, would not be interfering with a political opponent or the head of their own party; they would see an administrator getting on, or trying to, with authorized government business and would have an interest in its improvement. Resistance to the congressional propensity for interference—one of the worst problems of present administrators—would be much blunted. Executives could keep their minds on the best way to conduct public business rather than ways to buy off politicians pressing for local projects, for the protection of influential constituents, or for jobs to keep their supporters happy.

It may have been that the framers, however favorable to the principle of separation, were uncertain of the territory each of the three branches ought to occupy, and that they expected experience to determine the definite allocations they could not agree on in prospect. Practice, it may have been thought, would have its effect in either of two ways: through amendment, when it was clearer what the assignment ought to be; or in the accommodations each would make to and with the others as conflicts arose and compromises had to be made. Gradually, it may have been thought, a working relationship would be arrived at and peace would be established. Thus many vague arrangements would be made specific by mutual agreement.

If the first, the use of amendment, was depended on, however, the initiative was lodged in the wrong place—the legislature—and ratification was left to other legislators in the states. Legislators were thus positioned in the gateway and were given defensive weapons, just as though others were not involved and ought not to have some part in making progress. Recall that amendment must begin with a resolution voted by two-thirds of both houses; and that ratification must be agreed to by three-quarters of the states' legislatures. Members of the other branches were not given an effective part at any stage. Worst of all, the people were not to be consulted; no provision was made for referendum.

If it is true that constitutional law is, or ought to be, the deliberate and studied expression of the people's will, and if, in theory, it is superior to common, statutory, or administrative law, failure to legitimize it undermines its foundations. The least a people's involvement ought to require is referendum, something easily enough arranged. Leaving the whole matter to the lawmaking branches identifies constitutional law with statutes, the particular creations of legislatures. That amendment was made difficult, by requiring enlarged majorities, does not affect this. More than any other provision, this confusion of the lawmaking processes has been responsible for the increasing cloudiness of the Constitution and uncertainty concerning the meaning of its clauses.

It should be noted, for what significance it may have, that one alternative procedure for amendment was provided by the framers. It was, however, even more awkward and more under legislative domination. Apart from its centering again in the legislative branch, the wording of this clause was indeterminate and has caused much academic speculation. What is provided was that "on the application of the legislatures of two-thirds of the several states, [the Congress] shall call a convention for proposing amendments. . . ."[3]

There are, about this, at least these unanswered questions: Does it mean that the Congress *must* call such a convention? If so, how is it to be constituted? With whom as delegates? With what rules? And what is meant by the words "for proposing"? Does this last free the convention, once constituted, to propose and adopt *any* amendment? Or may it act only on the original petition? Furthermore, what if the states' resolutions should not have identical terms of reference? Would this invalidate the call?

No one knows the answers to these questions, and no one knows by whom they were expected to be answered. It is only certain that if there *were* answers, they would come from the Congress with the Supreme Court hovering in the background; and the essential distinction between constitutional and statutory law would still not be recognized.

If the Committee on Style intended this ambiguity, it was certainly successful; moreover, what was meant is as uncertain today as it was in 1787. Experience, if it was depended on, was choked off before it could operate. None of the amendments so far adopted did begin as proposals from two-thirds of the states' legislatures.

When, in the 1960s, dissenters from the current trend of Court opinion attempted to use this clause for the first time to discipline the justices, neither those who wished to use it nor anyone else involved knew whether the Congress, if petitioned by the state legislatures, was *compelled* to call such a convention, or, if it was, who might do the compelling. Nor did the discussions clear up any of the other difficulties. There was discussion about the selection of delegates and about the limitations, if any, on the acts of such a convention, but it was not agreed whether proposed amendments would still have to have approval from both houses of the Congress and three-quarters of the states' legislatures as was necessary when they originated in the Congress.

3. Article V.

Whatever criticism may be made of such carelessness by the framers, or what answers may be proposed for the questions left open, it is beyond argument that amendment was placed almost entirely at the discretion of the legislative branch—of the states or the federal government—and also that this excluded the other branches and the people at large from the most important of the devices for repairing the erosions or misinterpretations of the Constitution. Since this is so, the inevitable obsolescence goes on unchecked after nearly two centuries.

The other devices—if they can be called that—of Gouverneur Morris's committee may have been deliberate in another sense, being the result of unresolved argument. They consisted, in fact, of silences—ones that were left to be filled with contending voices. In such contests the loudest voice may well prevail over the one with the best case for winning. All the branches have shouted into the constitutional voids, and each has had successes and failures quite unrelated to the merit of its contention. None, however, has been so effective, it may be argued, as those of the judiciary. It could choose its own time; it could rely on the convenient rubric of "interpretation," but most important of all, it met a need for finality in adversary actions. These proved to be superior accouterments for success in the battles among the branches.

It was a defensible position that neither the president nor the Congress ought to make constitutional law; and both would certainly be doing this if an executive order or a statute should not harmonize with the Constitution but would in some way alter its substance. And since the gateway to amendment was virtually closed, these actions and enactments had somehow to be retruded. The Court, in making itself a sort of perpetual constitutional convention, was doing something indispensable. Of course, its conclusions lacked the legitimacy of ratified amendments, but its occupation of the position was tolerable. It should be insisted, however, that it was tolerable only because a method more consistent with popular sovereignty had been made practically impossible.

In a general reconsideration of scope, comparable with that of 1787, no such procedure for constitutionmaking would be acceptable. It is the one, of all others, that belongs to the people in an almost mystic proprietorship. If properly charged by them, a small body of their elite may propose; but they themselves must somehow finally make any constitution legitimate.

It will be said that such validity could not be attributed to the work of the framers. The delegates were sent by the legislatures with instructions originated by them, not at all by the people; but at least ratification was by specially elected conventions. Thus principle was fairly well honored. Actually, however, the principle had not yet taken shape. It is since then that the American intention to become a democracy has been affirmed.

If it is not true that democracy is meant to be perfected, professions repeated over and over are false. If the rule of popular origin is acknowledged, present procedures must be brought into question. Constitutional law is being made in the most *un*democratic way imaginable—by a majority of nine appointed justices as far removed from popular influence as could well be contrived.

The Court by the 1950s was not only asserting that it might tell the president what he could and could not do, and the Congress what laws it might and might not pass, but without serious objection, it had assumed certain superlegislative functions. It was passing laws the Congress had refused to pass and the president had never recommended, and it was doing this regularly whenever the other branches failed to act as the Court felt they should. It was enforcing these laws, too, pressing into its service the lower courts and the Department of Justice. It used subordinate judges and an army of marshals; but also, when necessary, it required the president to use military forces—and he complied.

In the matter of segregated schools, for instance, federal courts were not only warning school authorities that they must integrate; they were telling them when, and in what particular ways, it must be done. It is difficult to distinguish this from mandamus, and it would logically lead to further directives. The president and the Congress would soon be told not what they might *not* do but what they *must* do and how they must do it.

All this expansion of judicial power rested on the authority of the clause saying: "The judicial power shall extend to all cases, in law and equity, arising under this Constitution. . . ."[4] It is relevant to ask whether any cause, of any citizen or association of citizens, who may object to something done by the president, the legislature, or some local agency, is a "case." The Court has assumed that this is so, and has gone on to decide against (or for) one of the parties, thus putting other branches of the federal government and all local governments in the same situation as any defendant. True, it has been cautious about saying what the other branches *must* do, but it should be quite obvious that the use of the mandamus is being approached.

It seems strange, at first, that the Court should be able to make the Constitution an instrument of its predilections refusing some issues and accepting for decision only those it chooses, at the moment, to consider, and then saying what they mean. For such selectivity and such latitude of judgment there must be some reason beyond mere convenience. It would be more expectable that the legislature, after the long battle of the branches, would have possessed this privilege exclusively; it did after all have the enormous advantage of determining the Court's jurisdiction and could, by simple majority, keep for its own decision any issue it liked. Or perhaps the

4. Article III, section 2.1.

presidency might have resisted more vigorously than, for instance, President Truman did in 1952 when the Court virtually deprived him of emergency powers.[5] He does, after all, have all the instruments of enforcement if he chooses to use them and deny them to others.

Both the Congress and the president, however, after the Reconstruction quarrels in the 1860s, began to give way before the Court's assumption of authority. In those years this authority was used to protect property and defend business. But in the thirties a majority of liberals brought on a conservative uprising over the Court's extension of its authority. Questions then were raised about the bending of constitutional provisions to the changed view of policy. And threats began to be made that if the justices persisted their jurisdiction would be curtailed.

Separate and independent power for the Court was still, as it had been from the first, subject to legislative modification. Yet the threat of using it had not, until recently, been serious. Even the Roosevelt scheme for modifying the Court's opposition did not propose this resort. Rather it depended on the enlargement of membership by the addition of younger justices— meaning ones of the president's persuasion. But the likelihood of restricting jurisdiction was becoming more real.

It is to be recalled that the president and members of the Congress swear to uphold the Constitution, and not as the Court sees it, but as they see it. They occasionally feel that such an oath requires them to use their own judgment and, if necessary, to follow it in spite of the Court's view of the matter. This, in fact, has happened in the past. Lincoln suspended the writ of habeas corpus in spite of Justice Taney's objection. In Lincoln's view Taney was a rebel sympathizer. The Union came first. Taney regretted his lack of enforcement facilities, but actually he had none. Lincoln prevailed, but that is not the present state of things. Presidents need emergencies comparable with the beginning of war to ignore the Court with impunity.

Even emergency is no longer an adequate foundation for executive action. If it had been, President Truman would not have complied with the Court's order in 1952. Had something happened lately? The nation was again engaged in a distant conflict and the president had found that its security, or at least its success, was jeopardized by the failure of workers and employees in steel mills to agree. A prolonged strike could not be afforded. He therefore seized the properties. But when the Court said he must, he returned the mills to their owners. He had, they said, exceeded his powers. Neither then nor later did he even comment.

Supineness did not seem in character for Truman, and besides there was a vigorous dissent from Chief Justice Vinson, protesting the decision of the majority. He cited no fewer than twenty-five instances of similar

5. In a proceeding commented on in earlier chapters: *Youngstown Sheet & Tube Co.* v. *Sawyer,* 343 U.S. 579 (1952).

presidential actions in the past, all found acceptable. If this decision should stand, he said, presidents thereafter would have to deal with the Court's displeasure in every emergency. Yet Truman did comply. Why?

The answer has to be a political one. It must be found in a long history of successful attritions by the Court vis-à-vis the presidency. Truman had to give way, as Lincoln did not, because the Court had made for itself a position superior in prestige to that of the other supposedly equal branches and had so formidable a force of supporters that the president felt unable to defy them. Even the Congress, in which fellow protesters might have been found, was almost unanimously against him. Truman was a politician, and this was a politician's recognition of his limitations in such an encounter.

There was, however, another and deeper reason: the inherent dilemma involved in the separation principle. If the branches are interdependent each must have a place where there is finality, an end to discussion, a conclusion. If all three branches are faced with the same question, and if they differ, all three cannot prevail—one must be given way to. Otherwise, there will be unresolved conflicts and insupportable confusion. This may be intolerable in some situations where there *has* to be action. The Court may in the end find itself again in Taney's position. This is a consequence of separation we shall need to explore further.

The Costs of Interdependence

It was inevitable that a president should take the lead in issues of national importance, and this became a custom almost from the first. He will have campaigned for the more important ones; and others, appearing later, are very likely to depend on demands only he is compelled to stand sponsor for, since his constituency is the only genuinely national one.

The framers created this situation, however, without really supporting it with subsidiary provisions. Even as commander in chief, presidents have had to enlarge their stated powers—or, perhaps more accurately, have *felt* that they had to—and success easily led to expansion no individual ought to be entrusted with. Indisputably, they alone have the responsibility for disposing the armed forces; and this they carefully reserve for themselves. It has been agreed that command in crisis must center in one person, and that he must be a civilian and must be an elected official. But the disposition of forces, the definition of their mission, and their direction in action is a group of powers so undefined that presidents have been able to use them for unintended purposes; and these readily extend to policies whose conclusion may leave no alternative but the use of force. On occasion presidents have substituted their own authority for declarations of war, said by the Constitution to belong to the Congress. Without such a declaration other countries have been invaded—in recent years, Siberia, Lebanon, Korea, and

Vietnam, not to mention neighboring nations such as Costa Rica, Mexico, Haiti, and Santo Domingo.

In every instance, in spite of protests, sometimes widespread, the presidents have prevailed and have used the armed forces as they thought best. There may have been objection by citizens; members of the Congress may have had reservations; the Supreme Court, however, has been cautious about intervention. It has been true in several instances that as a result war has in fact existed without being recognized in any formal way.

The language used by the framers was changed from "make" war to "declare" war when it was argued in the Convention that it might be necessary to repel invasion or suppress insurrection and that time might be lacking for legislative consideration. This, presidents have assumed, freed them from asking legislative permission to act; and, of course, from congressional supervision during the action—something too chaotic to contemplate. An interesting line of decisions has centered on the extent of a president's powers when war does exist. They are accepted as very broad.[6]

To consider the expansion of the presidency somewhat further, there is also the gradual enlargement of his legislative responsibility. It will be recalled that in the Constitution this was moderate. He was directed to recommend such measures as he judged "necessary and expedient" because of information he might have on the "state of the Union"; he could "on extraordinary occasions" convene both houses, or he might adjourn them; but apart from these powers, he was given only that of veto, and this was not final, since it could be overridden by a two-thirds vote. Most presidents have been at one time or another thus rebuked.

Nevertheless the president quickly came to have the premier legislative position. He had to use devices not contemplated in the Constitution, but

6. A brief review of the Court's attitudes about the war powers can be found in C. Herman Pritchett's *The American Constitution,* 2d ed., rev. (New York: McGraw-Hill, 1968), chap. 19. A negative view has often been expressed, as, for instance, by Francis D. Wormuth in *The Vietnam War: The President versus the Constitution,* published as an Occasional Paper by the Center for the Study of Democratic Institutions (April, 1968). But what is and what is not constitutional is not so clear as Wormuth would have us believe, and is not in agreement with Corwin's exposition in *The President: Office and Powers, 1787–1957,* ed. by Edward S. Corwin, 4th ed., rev. (New York University Press, 1957). Wormuth might more convincingly have argued *not* that Vietnam *was* unconstitutional but that *it should have been.* This, as is so often the case, was an avoidance of pleading for amendment and a choice for "interpretation." If it was felt that instances of involvement were unwise uses of presidential power, the Constitution might be made to say so clearly, not made to say so by construing its words to mean what the commentator prefers them to mean.

Generally speaking, the reasoning of Hamilton about the war clause has been approved. It was his view that if a foreign nation makes war on the United States, the Congress need not recognize it with any declaration: war already exists (*Bas v. Tingy,* 4 Dall 37 [1800]). The extension of this to any aggression by other nations affecting interests of the United States had not been seriously challenged until disillusion about Southeast Asian involvement became general.

within a few years the expectation that he would use them and, indeed, would always assume responsibility for national policies was no longer seriously disputed. This duty, once assumed, was easily enlarged. He became the principal source of innovation in the governmental establishment, and since the current administration was identified with him, it gained support or lost it because of his performance. It is customary now for presidents to speak in almost royal terms of what "we" will or will not do. The Congress resists, of course, and what "we" do usually turns out to be much less than the president proposes; but the Congress has lost the initiative.

This was not anticipated by the framers. When they provided that the president should make recommendations to the legislature it was not regarded as indicating an exclusive source of national policy; and the interpretation of this directive was the subject of considerable discussion, and sometimes dispute, before the present situation came into existence. In the long period of weak presidencies during the nineteenth century, and in the theory developed by the Republican party at the insistence of business interests, it was contended that the Congress was to make policy and the president to carry it out. He was designated as a *chief executive* and ought to confine himself to duties indicated by the title.

This was the theory of the radical reconstructionists after the Civil War, and it has remained the view of conservatives. In spite of this theory, however, strong presidents, wherever they appeared, asserted their leadership and actually did become chief legislators. Occasionally presidents reverted to the view that their office required them to refrain from influencing the Congress. President Eisenhower held to it tenaciously and tried to avoid pushing for legislation. It is still a favorite theme of campaign orators, evidently possessing as much popular appeal as ever. This may have been in reaction to the complexities of modern government. It is always an agreeable thought that what is sophisticated can be made simple, and that the control of events can be returned to the common man. But if politicians make specious appeals, the responsibilities of government require central management; and the states have never developed the competence assumed to exist in oratory.

Still the return to "the people" of duties developed to meet modern needs continues to have its appeal. What is not mentioned is that the "return" often would be to a state bureaucracy larger than the federal one of a few years ago, or to local governments with doubtful ethics, staffed with incompetents. The operative idea of those who insist on decentralization is that they will escape the stronger and longer reach of federal power when they prefer that their operations not be looked into.

The natural reaction of congressmen to presidential initiative has always been hostility. They must attempt to please state and local bureaucrats whose desire is to escape federal supervision or a response to the desire of private interests to be regulated by those they can most easily influence.

The Congress, unwilling to give up its prerogatives, but unable to make accommodations to change, is harassed by local bosses. It resents both its own futility and the president's assumption of responsibility. This, in turn, makes it susceptible to lobbyists who flatter and offer support, and causes its members to turn more and more to what it *can* do—interfere in the departments and demand favors for friends and supporters. Members often declaim about centralization and the evils of bureaucracy, but they notably refrain from acting as their speeches would require them to do.

We have located the source of this hypocrisy in an interdependence not clearly defined and so subject to continual struggles for position as new responsibilities for government develop. This was worsened by giving the Congress an allocation of power it never has been able to use with consistent respect for the public interest, and sometimes without respect for the ordinary virtues. Many theorists have despaired of finding any resolution of these difficulties. They must continue to despair, it is argued here, until they recognize that large questions of this sort are best left to amendment when serious accommodation to new problems has to be made. It is contended that as important changes have appeared—such as presidential expansion, congressional retreat into obstructionism, and the assumption of legislative duties by the Court—amendment ought to have been resorted to for redefinition. The president ought to have cautionary advisers in his vast duties, and the Congress ought to find the mission it is competent to carry out. Moreover, and this is the contention here, the Court ought to interpret, not expand, the Constitution—at least not unduly and not permanently. Expansion involves the making of constitutional law, and this the Court ought to do only within the limits prescribed for its authority.

Even in the clearest instance of power originally assigned to one branch, the other branches are usually involved. This mutual involvement was, of course, intended. It was the framers' way of preventing the lodgment of unchecked power in any part of government. It was so much depended on that a Bill of Rights was not considered necessary and was added only when libertarians refused to be convinced that it was sufficient.

The interconnections have become more intricate as government has expanded into new areas not anticipated by the framers. And it would always be so in a government of separate branches continually being required to accept new responsibilities. Even the president's control of the armed forces, one of the most expansible powers, depends on the willingness of the Congress to provide funds and the agreement of the Senate to high military as well as civilian appointments. When the president disposes forces abroad, and they become engaged without a declaration having been requested, he is uneasy unless he has evidence of support. The so-called Gulf of Tonkin Resolution was used as justification by President Johnson for intervention in Vietnam, but it was used defiantly and without assurance. Actually the resolution was only an added gesture of consent; appropriations had already given approval as they had when Polk was carrying on what was at first an undeclared war against Mexico and when Lincoln opened hostilities in the Civil War.

Whatever a minority might say, the voting of money bills by a majority allowed the action to proceed. Lincoln, who was a congressman in Polk's time, fulminated against the president's aggressive action, but he voted for the appropriations that permitted the war to continue. If the Constitution was being stretched, both branches were involved. So with the later objections of Senator Fulbright and others to the Vietnam involvement. The necessary funds were overwhelmingly voted.[7]

There are complicated issues when the Constitution is being expanded, and at the time it may be impossible to foresee what precedents are being established. When there is an undeclared war, for instance, or even a declared one, there may be such subsidiary matters as interference with civil life: control of prices and perhaps of wages, prohibition of strikes, rationing of materials, courts-martial for other than military personnel, seizure of facilities for production or transportation and communications system. Even more difficult to avoid are questions having to do with the drafting of military personnel, and such actions as were illustrated by the evacuation of all Japanese-Americans from Pacific Coast areas in 1942.

It is almost impossible for any power to be held within the sole disposition of one branch. Not only the president assumes legislative powers; the Congress frequently reaches into the presidential realm. For instance, as has been mentioned here, the Congress attaches conditions to appropriation bills amounting to directions for their use, providing that funds can be spent only in certain ways and in certain places, sometimes only by certain people. And, in extreme cases, it requires the president to seek approval of his administrative dispositions before proceeding to execution.

The president may refuse; he usually does; then controversy results. There were several such incidents in the Eisenhower presidency. The Congress, at the insistence of military lobbyists, provided funds for projects not requested, and the president announced at once that he would not comply. There was the expected outburst from indignant legislators, but

7. In the Prize cases (2 Bl. 635 [1863]) Lincoln was upheld by the Court. The action had to do with the capture of Confederate vessels; approval was arrived at by interpreting the conflict as insurrection, bringing about a state of war whether declared or not.

A later decision (*Ludecke* v. *Watkins,* 335 U.S. 160 [1948] held that a German national could be deported under an old Alien Enemy Act supposed to be operative only when there existed a declared war. A majority held that the president's action could not be questioned. There have been other decisions tangentially affecting the president's powers; but generally the Court has been reluctant to check their expansion.

Eisenhower rested calmly on his military reputation—and he prevailed. Presidents, in fact, almost always prevail if they are firm. There is no easy way to discipline them, and such issues can usually be compromised. The Rule of Self-restraint operates quite successfully when time calms excited tempers.

In such controversies it was, in former years, the policy of the Court to avoid deciding for either the president or the Congress. More recently, as we have seen, it has been more willing to accept the role of final decider even when it meant extending the Constitution in some respect—and incidentally claiming for itself an unprecedented power it obviously could not use.

What emerges from a long history of such controversies is that although the allocation of powers is impossible to define in permanent terms, agreement among the branches on priorities ought to be possible. Dispositions of duties, agreeing how, and to what extent, modifications of assignment are to be made, ought also to be possible. But the Constitution did not provide any of this specification. It could hardly have made rules for situations not yet actual; and for this reason, if no other, experience has had to be relied on. It has been costly; conflicts have erupted again and again; and relations have been so exacerbated that other more important projects have been interrupted or neglected; but, lacking amendment, what else could be done?

Instead of there being a dependence on conflict and compromise for settlement or, more likely, in the end, judicial intervention, amendments ought to settle the more persistent disagreements. These are sometimes the most important questions of a generation, fully constitutional in nature, and they ought to have the consideration given to solutions not possible by legislating or adjudicating.

One of the axioms of traditional political science is that constitutions ought to be general and flexible, not detailed and specific; and this is a tenable rule if they are intended to last indefinitely, and if a convenient way of arriving at conclusions about specific issues is provided in the document itself. It is submitted that agreement to reconsideration at intervals would obviate the objection to reasonable specificity. An enormous gain would come from quieting the quarrels arising from lack of definition. It is, indeed, contended here that revision is the only way of allocating responsibilities and of giving constitutional law its proper authority.

If amendment is made too difficult, some agency has to substitute its desires for the law that is lacking—and has to do it by superior strength. That agency then becomes a constitutionmaker. When this happens there *is* no authentic constitutional law—that is, none arrived at by legitimate processes, and none that may not be changed in the next conflict between claimants to power.

When this is the method depended on, only two levels of statutory law are left; and neither is dependable. Indeed all the issues raised by each agency's attempt to carry out its missions are left unresolved, since every move it makes, or nearly every one, either conflicts with another agency's thrust into the same territory or constitutes a threat to be countered by vigilant bureaucrats who anticipate and fear losses of authority.

It should be said, however, with some emphasis, that there will be many matters at issue among the several branches not possible to be settled finally by any one of them and that this would still be true even if there were a recently revised and reasonably specific constitution—not so many, and not such difficult unsettled issues, but still some. Perhaps not all of these ought to end up in the Court, but it seems a natural place for them to be settled, and, in fact, the most satisfactory.

The Court in consequence becomes the arbiter in many matters its members are not competent to settle. It ought not to legislate; it ought not to interfere in matters consigned to the president. How can it be kept to its own work and not become another contender for undefined powers? In American experience the Court's expansions have been as audacious as those of the other branches. Finally judicial supremacy has become an inflated concept, inappropriate for the kind of government Americans are committed to: representative democracy.

A remedy has already been suggested: considered and more frequent definition of all allocated powers, including equally careful delineation of those assigned to the judiciary. It has been remarked that the framers were gravely at fault to have left this whole matter open, even, seemingly, to have overlooked it. By allocating the start of any amendment to legislatures alone, the Court was inadvertently put in a position it ought not to occupy and cannot continue to occupy decently in a democracy. To repeat: there ought to have been provisions for occasional amendment and for periodic reconsideration of the whole; and the revision ought to have had the legitimacy of reference to the people whose creation it is.

Not all the delegates to the Convention in 1787 were legislators. Some were, and others had been; but all its members were prominent and representative citizens, and many were lawyers. True, the meeting was authorized by a resolution of the Continental Congress; that body, however, had so nearly ceased to exist that its authority was no more than nominal. It is to be noticed that when the Convention submitted its document for ratification it specified that it should be by conventions in the several states, not by the states' legislatures. This was a tour de force comparable with its provision that nine ratifications instead of thirteen would establish the new constitution. No agreement was asked for from the Continental Congress. This was strange, and it is accounted for only by the practical expiration of that body. It was simply no longer there.

This precedent was not followed as it might have been in devising the provisions for amendment. That the legislatures were made central to the amending process had the consequences deplored here, one being that any changes in representation or in the legislators' procedures were made practically impossible. They were relieved from the need to be much moved by appraisals of their deficiencies or even of their personal behavior. And it is a fact that during all the time since ratification there has been no change, other than redistricting and enlargement, in the makeup of the Congress and only such changes in procedure as were convenient to members. It ought to have been anticipated that the Congress would fall into inertness and disrepute. Its deliberative usefulness vanished, it fell under the influence of local and private interests whose concern for the nation was minimal, and it assumed duties it could not do well, and ought not to have done at all—even if they could have been done well.

About all this the Court has had nothing whatever to say. The Congress could not be sued for inefficiency, and a mandamus could not be issued when it refused to act. So the most serious problem affecting government has been beyond judicial reach. The Court has often said what the Congress might *not* do, as we have seen, but it had no way of saying what it *must* do. Only amendment could do that, and amendment was entrusted to the body likely to be incommoded by any change.

Sometimes, however, the Court, conscious of approaching crises, has eased them with legislation of its own as convenient adversary actions appeared among the hundreds available for review.

The Congress so often ignored its obligations to the Constitution and so often made laws contravening its provisions that if the Supreme Court had not seized the power to declare its acts unconstitutional, the nation would have been entirely at the mercy of capricious or self-seeking politicians who were able to dominate its decisions. Students of government are nearly unanimous in approving Chief Justice Marshall's assertion that the Court must logically be able to invalidate legislation that, in the opinion of its majority, does violate higher law. That this is a way of making alternate law is considered less objectionable than that the Congress should go unchecked.

There must, however, be a better way and one with positive reach. It is suggested here that interdependence be more closely defined and more carefully considered. In the often unfocused and frustrating complexities of the struggles to occupy vast no man's lands, the judiciary has allowed itself to arrive at an indefensible position. It has seized powers it cannot use; it has assumed to legislate even when it was no more than anticipating impending congressional action; and it has become political in a partisan sense. As much as any part of government it needs reorientation.

This, it is argued, does not essentially alter its duty to interpret the

Constitution, or even, sometimes, to act as final arbiter; it merely narrows the range of its decrees. There must be a conclusion to differences among contending powers; however conflicts are redefined by amendment, they will still appear. The constitutional Court is the proper place for their settlement. In the end, if they are serious, they should result in amendment; but meanwhile the Court must carry the responsibility. There really is no other way in a government of interdependent powers when the Rule of Self-restraint proves insufficient to prevent successful aggression.

It might, however, be a Court constituted in a different way—and so more reliable for its duty.

Protecting a People from Themselves

Certainly an important reason for having a constitution is that it protects the people who make it from themselves. Because it also makes a government, it establishes the institutions for doing what people want to do together; and this is important too. But its commitment to self-discipline and common endeavor must be said to come first.

It follows that virtue in such an ordinance consists in its explicit statement of what men owe to their fellows and what their fellows owe to them. Yet this is not nearly enough; its reach must extend inward to convictions capable of surviving crises when there are temptations to disregard them. Such deliberate resolves become matters of honor and loyalty. They are capable of holding people together, creating a bond they are willing to protect, when summoned, with their lives and their fortunes. Americans in past crises have shown this willingness, and their Constitution has been the symbol of their resolution. If their resolve has weakened it is because the bond is no longer so deeply respected.

When an official takes office it is the Constitution he swears to uphold; when a foreigner becomes a citizen, it is the Constitution he is expected to understand and undertakes to respect. How central to national life these sparse clauses are! Yet how willing we are to allow their life to be drained away! And how inevitable the result in disaffection and even alienation!

For a people with such an acknowledged devotion to the symbol of union, it is tragic that no practical means was provided for periodic review in the spirit of 1787 and by chosen representatives with the same command of support. Since no human instrument is relevant to all circumstances, none is able to span generations and keep its definitions intact. It cannot be expected, if unchanged, to command the depth of adherence it once had.

When an oath to uphold the Constitution is taken, anyone who knows the document well knows that parts of it cannot have been included. Anyone who has had experience with it knows that some provisions long ago lost their relevance and that others no longer are taken to mean what they say.

Even the newly naturalized must think it strange that there are two senators from each state, however small, that the president is given the executive power but is not designated as chief of state, that the legislature may alter the jurisdiction of the Court, and, strangest of all, that neither industry, education, nor means of communication (for instance) are mentioned. They must think it very strange indeed to learn that when officials do swear to uphold the Constitution they are known to have reservations and intend not to uphold but to disregard some parts. And all students know that there are irrelevant clauses (such as the Second Amendment), and that changes are always being made not by the method provided, but by subterfuge, by attrition, or by interpretations amounting to new provisions.

Irrelevancies and omissions are the more serious because of general dependence on the symbol. Falling into the way of paying attention to the Constitution's principles only when it seems convenient and of not finding in it any wisdom about troubling matters is to risk a general suspicion of emptiness. It is likely to separate the old from the young—the old holding to an unexamined loyalty, the young impatient with the discipline of out-worn rules. It is likely to separate those who have studied it with some care and know its deficiencies from those who hold it in blind reverence and resent any suggestion of revision. It is likely to alienate those who discover that its dictates can be evaded by those who are clever and devious, but that they are harshly enforced for others.

All these reservations and recognitions of obsolescence are, however, superficial. That some amendment is so obviously needed has not destroyed the symbolic usefulness of the Constitution, even one so mutilated by time; and in fact the Constitution of 1787 has kept its central position in the American scheme.

The knowledge that what is assumed to be in the Constitution has actually departed is resisted. Awakening to the reality is guarded against. But it is shocking when forced into recognition, and it was expectable that ways would be found to soften such disclosures.

This perhaps accounts for tolerance of continuous attrition, and for the avoidance of overhaul in the spirit of 1787. To suggest a new convention is to call in question the work of the most revered company in all American history. One practical difficulty with this is that attritions do not make a complete scheme. They come from accidental attention to problems it has become impossible to ignore, or from expansions wanted by officials who must fulfill their contract to serve. But in the end the conviction must spread that the controlling law is no longer wholly valid.

The general wish to guard the symbol was illustrated in the 1950s when many of those who testified before the House Un-American Activities Committee repeatedly identified individuals as "Communists" because they lacked "respect" for the Constitution. Anyone was free to dislike or to disparage officials, but not to speak ill of an old document. This has always been the prevailing attitude.

It is obvious enough, when pointed out, that the circumstances and needs of early republican days were quite special. This was more emphatically so because the first government was failing and was being abandoned. The Articles of Confederation, in effect for only six years, had restricted the central government to such a severely limited authority over internal affairs that it was hardly a government at all; and as for foreign affairs, negotiations for trade treaties with France, Spain, and Britain were failing because those nations had no confidence that the individual states would respect agreements made by representatives of the Confederation. The United States was, to foreign observers, only doubtfully a nation.

The Confederation did, in fact, offer telling examples of suspicion among members of such a community and of ways to enfeeble general authority. There was one legislative chamber but no other branch; there was no chief of state, and no executive; and the judiciary had authority only to settle disputes between states and to deal with crimes on the high seas. The delegates to the single chamber were chosen by the state legislatures and were paid by them. Each state, regardless of size, had one vote, and a two-thirds majority was required for the passage of laws. Even about this minimal grant of power there had been long hesitation, and it had diminished in practice year by year because the states had the fatal habit of competing to escape contributions.

It will be recalled that Franklin had been the author of a so-called Albany Plan in 1774, and that he had pressed his proposal in the years following. This would have united the colonies for defense, at least; indeed it was inspired by the British weakness in frontier wars with the French and the Indians. It carried somewhat further the loose scheme worked out for relationships during the century preceding by providing for a grand council whose delegates would have been chosen by the assembly of each colony. Its president general would have been appointed by the crown. It would have raised troops and collected taxes, but each colony would have been left with complete control of its own affairs.

The plan, however, was satisfactory neither to the colonists nor to the British—the colonists because they were mistrustful of each other, and the Crown because so much local autonomy was considered dangerous—and although it was much discussed it never reached adoption.

By 1776, however, when the colonies were ready to declare their independence, some sort of union was obviously necessary if the declaration was to be made good; and after the resolution was offered, a committee was at once appointed to draft articles of confederation.

There were immediate difficulties. John Dickinson, the chairman, could not get agreement on representation, on the apportionment of contributions for expenses, or on state claims to western lands. Since it was a condition that all should agree, and since the last, Maryland, held out until 1781, these dangerous early years had had to be passed through somehow without any government at all.

When the Confederation did come into effect, and the rebellion had to be made good against British repression, Washington, as commander in chief, was frustrated by the continuing attempt of each state to contribute as small a share as it could of men and money to the common effort. When the war was over, this propensity continued to be a fixation. By 1786 when the resolution was passed authorizing the meeting that became the Constitutional Convention, and the states chose their delegates, the Continental Congress had barely enough energy to authorize the call.

Under the old articles, the Confederation had been no more than "a league of friendship" among sovereign states; but the friendship was seldom visible, and antagonism was a more conspicuous characteristic whenever delegates met. The most immediate problem for such prominent citizens as Washington, when the degeneration had reached practical impotence, was the lack of any regulation for commerce among the states. But what was actually most important, generally, was that no measure could be taken with any expectation of its execution. State governments were to attend to all administration. They did as they pleased, and what pleased them was what profited their commercial citizens and their taxpayers.

It was clear to most of the framers, from experience with futility, that the central government must represent its citizens and not the states as interveners. It must be able to tax and to dispose of the funds it collected. Yet this conviction, when it was understood by the state politicians, assumed the proportions of a social convulsion. The fear of authority went beyond the politicians too; the war had been fought by state militiamen, and citizenship was understood as Pennsylvania, New York, or Virginia citizenship. The Union now being spoken of was a vague conception and, to such resisters as Patrick Henry, a repulsive one. To farmers—and most citizens were farmers—state capitals were remote enough; a national capital might as well have been across the sea. Roads were nonexistent, and there were no means of communication other than horses ridden through the wilderness or sailing boats making their devious way along the coast, around promontories, into bays, and up and down rivers.

Yet all the states repeated, in the terms of reference issued to their delegates, that they were to attempt the forming of "a more perfect union." The lesson of separateness had had its effect—even if not on everyone, and even if its cure was not agreed on. It was, in fact, not well learned; the people of 1787 were like people in all times and places in wanting relief from ills wtihout paying for it in either money or discipline.

This was the underlying problem the framers had to deal with in every discussion; and the Constitution does show this strong reluctance to allow a central government powers that would diminish those of the states. It was made certain that only carefully specified powers could be exercised by it. The residual powers were left with the states. The granted ones were regarded as formidable in the circumstances of their granting, but they would be only minimal in the next generation. And soon the states were resisting union—those of the South more than those of the North, but all with some determination.

Besides, there was the curious prolongation of federalism represented by the keeping of these residual powers by new states as they began to be formed and admitted to the Union. Obviously they had not granted part of their sovereignty to the central government; they had not existed then; yet Alaska and Hawaii, when they became states, joined the original thirteen in having all the powers bargained for so effectively by the local-minded minority at Philadelphia 150 years in the past.

The regrettable but persistent attempts of state politicians to get advantages, and pay as little as possible for them, shows plainly enough in many clauses. Yet the Washingtons, the Hamiltons, the Wilsons, and others of the nationalists kept steadily to the conviction that a constitution must exhibit the other impulse toward the essential institutions of union. They were to make a government with a stronger central authority than had existed before. They can be thought of as representing the eternal struggle of man to be better and larger than he is. At Philadelphia they prevailed—but only to an extent. The compromises were serious.

The short four hundred words of Article III vesting judicial power "in one Supreme Court, and in such inferior courts as the Congress shall from time to time ordain and establish," shows the inheritance from the Articles of Confederation as much as does Article I establishing the legislative branch. Disproportionate attention was paid to controversies arising between citizens of different states, but so strong was the state spirit that in 1794 the Congress resolved by the necessary two-thirds vote in both houses that the Constitution should be amended to provide that no citizen could bring suit in federal court against a state other than his own (it was ratified in 1798).

Rutledge had argued in the Convention that no inferior federal courts were needed. State courts could conveniently hear all cases in the first instance; but Madison, who had been insistent on including the inferior courts proposed in the Virginia Plan, argued for a larger judicial establishment, one "commensurate to the legislative authority"—meaning that federal courts should judge all cases arising under federal law. Presently we shall look at the results of compromise between these views that left to the legislature important controls over a supposedly independent judiciary.

There was difference of opinion, arising from the same opposed views, about the appointment of judges. Randolph proposed that they should be elected, but this did not appeal to the lawyers; and quite early (June 5) Wilson proposed that they should be appointed by the executive. This proved more agreeable, although Madison wanted them appointed by the Senate. There followed summer-long uncertainty. In July Gorham's motion for executive appointment failed. A few days later Madison's preference for Senate appointment was approved, and this was the way the provision went to the Committee of Details and the way it issued from that committee. It was not until September that another committee of eleven recommended that appointments should be made by the president but with Senate confirmation. There was objection by Wilson, who was bothered by the mixing of legislative and executive powers, but with Gouverneur Morris's support, the report was accepted.

This uncertainty all through the summer, centering on jurisdiction and appointment, was reflected in the clauses included in the final draft. The judicial power was to be vested in one Supreme Court and in such inferior courts as Congress should establish. This power extended to "all cases arising under the Constitution." But it was agreed, after some discussion, that not everything necessary had been said, and there was added, in a later Article (VI), the so-called supremacy clause. This warned all state judges that the United States Constitution and its laws were the supreme law of the land, "any thing in the constitution or laws of any state to the contrary notwithstanding."

The question of most importance was not even considered. The distinguished lawyers among the delegates evidently overlooked the probability that the Constitution, especially a reluctantly specific one such as was now to be adopted, might have different interpretations. Immense gaps were being left to be filled in, but there was no recognition that this might become a problem.

If, as later was asserted by Marshall, even the powers of the branches were left for definition to the Court, it was done by inadvertence. No one suggested that the Constitution was to be filled out in this way, much less extended to issues not yet foreseen. Whether it was intended that the Court should, through judicial review, interpret the Constitution is not so much in question as what might be added. If cases arising under the Constitution were, all of them, to be decided by the Court, it must be allowed that the judges' understanding of the Constitution has to be their guide. Several difficulties about this have already been noted. The clauses not being explicit, the judges often do not agree among themselves about their meaning, and frequently there are minority opinions challenging vigorously the reasoning and conclusions of the majority. This makes for an uncertainty added to by the inability of any Court to commit its successors, and there have been numerous instances of reversal.

Then, as has been noted, there is the oath taken by other officials to support the Constitution, presumably as *they* understand it, not as the judges do. This has always had the possibility of precipitating confrontation —and several historic ones have occurred. Generally speaking, the "strong" presidents have refused to give in to the Court. Among these have been Jackson, Lincoln, and the Roosevelts. They seemed to have established presidential independence until Truman gave way in 1952. Even this presidential surrender left the situation uncertain; presidents cannot commit their successors either. Only amendment can establish a clearer apportionment of powers.

The most frequent difficulty, however, has turned on the expansion of interpretation into rewritings that amount to new clauses, a process intolerable in a representative democracy but inherently likely in a scanty enumeration of directives. This can go, indeed it has gone, so far as the making, almost week by week in some periods, of new constitutional law simply by extrapolation. Marshall's theory of implied powers, necessary to the implementation of others, has applied exclusively to the Court in the first instance: that is to say, the Court has allowed them for the other branches, but only as its majority understands them or finds them reasonable.

It has been suggested why this must be unsatisfactory; it does not respect the elementary criteria for constitutionmaking. The first of these criteria is that, since it is a people's law, it should be created by them in a solemn and considered process. It should be more binding than statutes, and it should be clear enough to make evasion as difficult as possible while it is in effect.

But where is there a discernible line to be found between what is interpretation and what is the making of new law? This puzzling question, never having had an answer, has favored escalation from judicial review to judicial supremacy. What is involved here, it must be realized, is an inherent dilemma of separated powers—that no two of them can prevail in a confrontation, and that there must be a way to resolve such conflicts.

It is said about this that since there must sometimes be a conclusion— that some disputed questions simply cannot be left unresolved—they had better be decided by the Court. It is argued that the Court's principal preoccupation is with the Constitution, and since the judges are the least likely of all officials to be influenced by momentary emotions so strong that principle may be ignored, they are the most likely to decide in the public interest; but hardly any student familiar with the Court's history contends that this duty is invariably performed in such a spirit.

Every historian notes periods both of reaction and of liberalism, very distinct and quite suddenly changed by new majorities resulting from a Court appointment or two. And it seems evident that the justices, far from being dispassionate and disinterested, have been very intent at one time on bringing about change, and at others on preventing it at any cost; also, they have had strong views about the departures to be allowed. It cannot be denied that during long periods some interests and some individuals have been more sedulously protected than others. During the better part of the century after the Civil War when economic expansion was taking place, the justices' preoccupation was mainly to allow business its way, to protect industrial properties, and to repel attacks on its freedom. People, in conflict with things, were nowhere in the judges' minds. It is equally clear that late in the 1930s a period was entered on when welfare was uppermost in the Court's concern. The government was undertaking vast new responsibilities, and the justices, after serious study of public opinion, came around to allowing the expansion. Somewhat later what is often described as a libertarian era began. This was characterized by a rediscovery of the Bill of Rights and its application in ways undreamed of at an earlier time. The Court, borne up by obvious popular approval, entered now on its most unabashedly legislative phase.

Legislative is not precisely descriptive, although it is often used. The Court was not making statute law; it was making constitutional law, something legislatures may not do. The awkwardness of adversary action made expansion difficult, as it had always made the Court's mission difficult; but it was pursued persistently.

Protecting people from themselves requires the rejection of every attempt of some to constrict the rights of others and the enforcement of every stated duty owed to the spirit of justice by citizens and officials alike. It requires that independent powers granted to the branches shall extend only to the specified limits. That the courts must have a special responsibility in this confinement is by now well recognized. But this is not something that can be expected as an outcome of ordinary adversary actions. Judgment in such issues ought not to be dependent on the accident of relevant cases arising at convenient times, but the Court has seen no other way to proceed.

Enterprising lawyers discovered in 1968 that a law passed 101 years before had prohibited discrimination in housing. This happened to be an issue the Congress had been struggling with for something like a decade without knowing that a statute already existed. A Court not bound to adversary judgments would not have had to wait for lawyers with a convenient case to present the question for judgment.[8] It has to be concluded, it would seem, that issues would better be presented in a different way, perhaps by the officials themselves, asking for advisory opinions; also, that this is no more than an assumed duty of the Court. It rests on the argument of Marshall that it must have been intended by the framers. If this is so, there can be no reason for not legitimizing it. And the only way of doing that is by an action of the people.

Concerning such issues it may be said that they would be reduced to a

8. *Jones* v. *Alfred H. Mayer Co.*, 389 U.S. 968 (1968).

minimum if more frequent revision was provided for. Mostly they arise because the Constitution itself has not been modernized. If there were revisions in each generation such questions would be settled in the amending process rather than by the doubtful assumption of powers likely at any time to be disputed.

People do need protection from themselves. But it should be validated —that is, granted deliberately by them in procedures such as that undertaken by the framers and agreed to in majority ratifications.

The Court as a Constitutionmaker

It has been recalled that a common instruction for the delegates to the Convention in Philadelphia was the achieving of "a more perfect union." Almost immediately after ratification there *was* a closer union, but "perfect" would be an inflated description of the relations among the states. Still, the central government did begin to regulate trading between citizens of different states and did begin to conduct foreign relations with somewhat more confidence. Also, when the first ten amendments were ratified, and the restraints on government were, at least to an extent, clarified, its direct authority over individuals in certain matters began to be accepted.

The central government required taxes and expended them. It began to build roads and operate a primitive postal system; it assumed financial responsibility for debts incurred in national causes and set up a bank for fiscal management. But a farmer in western Pennsylvania would hardly have noticed any change and must have been as surprised as he was annoyed when excise taxes were laid on the corn liquor he made for sale in the towns. He proposed, in fact, not to recognize any restraint until Washington, in the first trial of strength, set out with something of an expeditionary force to teach him a lesson. As the army approached, the moonshiners disappeared into the hills—and the challenge to government faded away. But the president had made his point. There did exist a national government.

The Court established under the new directives began to review cases coming to it on appeal. There were not many in the first years, but the position of the judiciary among the branches began to be defined by two of its early chief justices. John Jay refused to give Washington an advisory opinion, thus confining the Court's work to adversary causes; and John Marshall (in 1803) asserted that the Courts might define the vague clauses limiting the activities of the other branches. When, in *Marbury* v. *Madison*, he declared a law passed by the Congress to be invalid because the Constitution did not authorize its enactment, he began the rewriting of the Constitution. It has gone on ever since.

This assumption of power by the Court, like the aspirations of other branches, was not "perfected" at once. There were long delays, and acceptance of the Court's opinions was sometimes reluctant. Concerning differences about interpretation, there were, in the worst instances, civil disturbances amounting to insurrection. It was, after all, a loose society, locally self-sufficient and not often affected by governmental controls. But the direction was unmistakable. It was toward an integration made possible by the Court's determined stance, and this was so even after Jefferson's Democratic Republicans came into control of government. His ideal nation of small farmers and artisans in a loose association began, slowly at first, but with accelerating rapidity, to be a more closely knit and a more organized system. Each part began to recognize gradually its relations to every other part. Policies became national; the states lost their monopoly on sovereignty; people became citizens of the United States rather than of Virginia, New York, or Vermont.

The American Constitution, not being fully accepted, has had to be persistently supported by those who have understood the importance of union and have agreed to the main thrust of a document defining its ends and the means of their realization. The necessities of nationhood were not easily imposed on dissenters even after ratification was completed in 1788. There were still those who were willing to take advantage of others' more serious dedication—the familiar withholding problem. Even while the struggle was going on it could be seen that the future had not been made secure for union. Votes to ratify were sometimes close, and large minorities left over from the controversy were still not reconciled when the new nation became a fact. They continued to hold back for a long time; they had successors in other generations; occasionally there were heated exchanges; once there was war; and, even after that, the right of the states to interpose appeared again and again in political exchanges.

It ought to have been expected that parties would form around issues certain to be hotly disputed, but the framers either did not anticipate them or hoped that the contenders would be welded together by necessity. When Jefferson's Democratic Republicans opposed the Federalists' view of presidential—really of central—power, there was one best way to make the opposition effective, and it was taken; they got control of the government by using the means provided in the Constitution. Of course they made some additions not contemplated by the framers, but these were not actually forbidden. It was only when Jefferson occupied the presidency himself that he discovered how realistic Washington had been. By the time his successors—Madison and Monroe—had stretched the party's domination to a quarter of a century, the Union had evolved quietly into a well-recognized entity. Its detractors had done what its friends could not do. The need for cooperation had prevailed.

While Jeffersonianism was finding its rather devious way to union, the

Court had been holding the line for the framers' conception. The Constitution they had created was not meant to be a democratic document. Its institutions were elitist; Jefferson merely arranged participation of those less qualified to participate. Suffrage was gradually extended and managed through party organization. He was able to do this because the framers had left the definition of voting qualifications to the states. He and his successors reached into them for support and broke down their restrictions. It took half a century; but when Jackson was through, property ownership was no longer a condition, and most white adult males could vote. The Federalist party disappeared because its philosophy had passed into general acceptance and was no longer a cause to be defended.

Even this enormous accomplishment of the democrats could not make their system viable. It needed informed voters to make it work. The nation, after nearly two centuries, still had not discovered how to implement equality without entrusting the nation's decisions to its least capable, and most selfish, citizens. They persistently constituted a majority. Still, the Court did what it could to protect its integrity and to see that the individualists were kept from breaking the ties of union. It was consistently nationalist all during the nineteenth century—with some interludes such as that during Taney's chief-justiceship.

The average competence among the politicians of that century was markedly lower than that in most other occupations, and a lack of integrity went with a lack of ability. At the beginning of the new century muckrakers were able to expose such widespread incompetence and such morasses of corruption in local and state governments as to cause wonder that any government at all had survived. There had been, however, and there continued to be, occasional spasms of reform. They occurred, when things got too bad, in nearly every city in the country and, although less often, in the states. Tom Johnson, Brand Whitlock, and "Golden Rule" Jones are heroes in this history. But the resumption of undercover rule by notorious bosses occurred in regular succession to such periods. They were so much a part of the system that eradication ran head-on into the opposition of the most respectable power dispensers. Politics was an extension of business by other means. Structural improvement depended on reforms that were never made in the development era. The Constitution was prostituted to the dominant cause of profitmaking.

Corruption was nearly as bad in the federal government as in those of the states and cities, although these were the ones most thoroughly exposed by the muckrakers. The postwar administrations were so sunk in public indecency that "Grantism" became another word for the exploitation of government by its enemies. Yet Grant was the dominant figure in political life for more than a decade following the war, and his two terms as president were very nearly extended to a third. On the whole, it is justifiable to say that those in control until Cleveland checked their operations by defeating Blaine in the campaign of 1884 were in the lower order of public morality as well as capability.

This was only government. Business in this period assumed rights and privileges not to be found in the Constitution. Its leaders established for themselves a kind of second government, more powerful than the legitimate one and quite innocent of a defensible ethic. Worse, this was accepted by the Court; and the rise of industrial power was guided and guarded by a succession of solicitous majorities among the justices.

About the federal principle accepted by the framers there were radical long-lingering differences, and they were a torment in each of the governmental branches. But the worst divisions of the half-century before the Civil War centered in the old discord between nationalists and states' righters: "loose" versus "strict" construction of the Constitution—whether the federal government was to have only those powers conceded to it by the thirteen states or was to have those necessary to the other prescribed undertakings. These undertakings were the implied powers appropriated by Marshall for the Court when the other branches were dominated by those who favored states' rights and deplored central controls.

Even when it had been conceded that the government must have more powers than had been mentioned, there were angry controversies both in the Congress and among political contenders about every extension of their reach. Down to the actual beginning of the Civil War more passionate political oratory dealt with this than with any other public question. Strict constructionists by that time were claiming the right of secession—surely about the limit of strictness. As the war approached, even the Court faltered in its nationalistic bias. Taney, the chief justice, was a southern sympathizer and would have prevented Lincoln's defense of the Union if Lincoln had not ignored him.

The passions evoked by these adhesions could be settled only by force, it seemed; yet even the resort to war did not conclude the argument. National authority was still reluctantly conceded. The states still had reserve powers not given up until new confrontations were precipitated. Incredibly, perhaps, so late in American development, Eisenhower tried to reactivate this opposition to federal controls. And even after him politicians continued to find states' rights a popular issue when others failed to excite the electorate. It could so easily—even if falsely—be equated with decentralization, and even with independence, individualism, and liberty.

Differences over the separation of powers within the government could not very well run to civil war. The president never attacked the Congress on Capitol Hill with his army. The public, in fact, was seldom aware that conflicts were in progress. But the acerbities were nevertheless bitter, and their settlement had consequences of importance even if outsiders were never much concerned.

About these the Court had almost as convinced a view as it had for a period about the protection of business. But it usually left the president alone and confined itself to declaring that laws were in accord or not in accord with the Constitution. This involved the president in the sense that he had signed them, and usually, in fact, had sponsored them. This, however, was different from finding that something done in the execution of his office exceeded his constitutional warrant.

Constitutional ambiguity was thus consequential far into the future from 1787. The serious issues of principle left unsettled and consigned to political processes with no adequate provision for dialogue went on complicating all relations among citizens. If amendment had been made possible, even perhaps mandatory, when issues were clearly seen to be of constitutional importance—that is to say, matters of principle—there might have been accommodation. But as the amending process was left, with the way blocked whenever the one-third of both houses or one-quarter of the several states' legislatures might object, there never was another convention for general reconsideration. Issues had to be settled by the Court when it thought it could prevail, but sometimes they expanded into conflicts impossible to settle finally—even when the Court announced that conclusion had been reached.

If legislative and administrative law belong to a different order or authority than constitutional law, the implementation of principles to be found in the Constitution is a transcendent responsibility. If that law was ambiguous or if it became obsolete, neither the Congress, the president, nor the Court could be guided by it. So all began, soon after ratification, to create enactments that momentarily passed for constitutional law. They were not really respected, being subject to continual attack, and were frequently altered with changes of membership on the Court or of inclination among the justices. The process is still going on and seems, with time, to have become highly regarded. The resultant conglomeration is spoken of admiringly as the "living constitution." Perhaps it lives; but it is a low order of life, hardly to be differentiated from nonexistence.

Constitutional law is, however, so necessary that, lacking means for amendment, a better way than the invasion of its body by statutes or administrative regulations had to be found. This gradually came to be the role of the Supreme Court. It was not meant to make constitutional law, either, any more than Congress or the president was meant to make it; but a Court, on the whole, was generally conceded to be better for the purpose than either of the other branches. It was assumed to be less partisan, more disinterested, wiser, more reflective. It had no other duties to perform. Its judges were appointed for life and, by a custom generally respected, were untouchable. The provision that its jurisdiction could be determined by the legislature was sometimes a threat, and there was occasional menace from attempts to enlarge or reduce its membership, but it proved resistant to most of these attacks, protected not so much by its own constitutional position as by a genuine necessity for a higher law, even if one not wholly valid.

The idea of a constitution made "living" by Court activity would have startled the framers and outraged most of them. They may not have considered carefully enough their arrangement for amendment—they certainly did not—but they did provide for it and must have expected that the provisions would be used. Since the "living" conception is, moreover, so nearly equivalent to having no constitution at all, it undermines the conception of a higher law created in a special way. If the Court can make of itself a legislative body, even if in a more protected position than the Congress because its opinions cannot be vetoed by the president, its decrees cannot be genuinely constitutional. They become added parts of the Constitution in the same sense as acts of the British Parliament, and can be changed in the same way.

Very few legislative bodies have the Court's freedom in choosing causes it will consider. None need pass laws not approved by its members, but the consideration of issues cannot be avoided if influential members are moved to press for action. The Court chooses cannily among possibilities and blandly avoids issues it prefers not to confront. Mostly it succeeds unless it affronts public opinion too seriously. In recent years, when it has restricted the powers of the other branches, attempts to strike back have failed, although disaffected contenders have not always been so supine about it as President Truman was in the steel case.

Whether the Constitution would be more useful if the Court had not allowed itself to become its extender is problematical. It can be said that great issues would have had to be settled by amendment, and that an overhaul of the amendment clause would have been necessary. To this there would have been active opposition; but once it had been accomplished and legitimate procedures had been resumed, the Constitution would again have become the repository of the considered principles needed in a democracy.

It is quite true that much of the Court's work has introduced a needed flexibility. Many controversies have been damped down, and this has been a contribution to civil peace. On the other hand, it must be recalled that constitutional law made by the Court is not really respected even by itself; it tends to become, like any other law, tentative and temporary. This is a downgrading that in the long run may be extremely serious.

On the whole it has to be said that if the need for a constitution is granted, it ought to be made (and remade) by procedures conferring an unassailable legitimacy. For this purpose it would need to be much more specific than that devised by the framers, thus allowing the Court to confine itself to actual interpretation. Also it ought not to leave controversial issues undecided. One such avoidance resulted in the Civil War. Others have started prolonged disputes.

It has been concluded for the purpose here that in a general reconsideration the possibility of almost unlimited expansion of any power ought to be controlled. As for the judicial branch, it ought to have the same powers it has now—even most of those it has merely assumed—but their exercise ought to be constricted by closer definition not only of its own responsibilities but those of the other branches.

This applies also to canons of justice and of mutual relations among citizens. Rights and duties defined for eighteenth-century circumstances could not be expected to be relevent for an extended future. They ought to be redefined, but not usually by the judiciary. Here again, whatever the Constitution provided would inevitably require interpretation. But this ought to stop short of enlargement. Most such questions ought not to be available for Court determination. They ought to be consigned to the procedures of amendment. It ought to be made, if not easier, more frequent.

The Courts in Context

As in other parts of our argument for a renewed Constitution, it is suggested that the judiciary be fitted to a conception of the whole—the putative whole, not the existing one.

When the Supreme Court, during the nineteenth century, was forced into the situation (or, at least, felt logically justified in assuming it) of becoming the final legislative body, the balance of powers was badly upset. Until then the Congress had been the custodian of equilibrium because of its several advantages; when Marshall's decree went unchallenged, custodianship was transferred to the Court; it now had the advantage. There it was held, somewhat uneasily, because not legitimately, from then on. It would perhaps be more accurate to say that what the Constitution had given the Congress, and had been taken by the Court, could be kept by the justices only on sufferance; but it proved to be a long sufferance and a fairly successful one.

The aggression was undertaken and carried out by Marshall not because he meant to make the Court something the framers would have disapproved; on the contrary, he was—like them—a nationalist, and there were those who were intent on breaking up the Union. He thwarted what he regarded as a conspiracy and kept the framers' work from being destroyed.

Marbury v. *Madison* (1803) initiated a direction that Marshall's successors have followed since; when his opinion, for the Court, declared a law to be repugnant to the Constitution, he was claiming the power to say what the Constitution *was*. When interpretation stretched almost imperceptibly into intervention, and the Court, following Marshall's beginning, expanded review until it became a rewriting, it could, by indirection, shape the government to its conception of what it should be and do.

Or could it? For the most part the new position was exploited with due caution; nevertheless, gradually, and at opportune times, powers were abstracted from both the presidency and the Congress and were, by simple implication, added to those of the Court. This was done by reproving the other branches for having exceeded their constitutional warrants. To illustrate by a later instance already referred to, the Court in 1952 defined the emergency powers of the president in such a way as to leave itself in the position of determining in any future crisis what could or could not be done to protect the nation. In an earlier time it had used the commerce clause to reject the Congress's definition of regulatory powers and substitute its own. This served to impose its own notions about the freedom of employers to treat their workers as they pleased. And, of course, it had other effects as well—all agreeable to business interests.

Then, when the Court had begun to write a comprehensive concordance to the Bill of Rights and to fit its extrapolations to the amendments adopted after the Civil War, it had made important changes in criminal procedure. It was, moreover, completely unembarrassed by its reversals of decisions arrived at by former majorities. Just as a legislature might recognize that times had changed and old laws ought to be abandoned, the Court reconsidered the constitutional laws written by its predecessors. For instance, the income tax was rejected at one time and found acceptable at another; and the "separate but equal" rule for Negro education, once approved, was subsequently disapproved. These were not rejections of statutes; they were reversals of constitutional interpretations. If nothing else did, they showed that the Constitution's clauses were not much more dependable than congressional statutes. Either could be given new meaning without the validation of amendment.[9]

We have seen the reasons for this assumption of the power to revise the Constitution. Between them, the Court and the Congress made it imperative that some way be found for adapting the Constitution to changed circumstances without destroying its authority.[10]

Certain alterations of governmental structure, such as the addition of new branches for electoral management, for planning, and for regulation, if adopted, would make it necessary to reconsider the position of the ju-

9. One such reversal was more embarrassing than most others. In 1920 (in *Evans v. Gore*, 253 U.S. 245) the Court decided that judges need not pay income tax because it would amount to a reduction of salary forbidden by the Constitution. But in 1939 (in *O'Malley* v. *Woodrough*, 307 U.S. 277) Frankfurter wrote a majority opinion saying that the tax made inroads upon the independence of judges was "to trivialize the great historic experience on which the framers based the safeguards of Article III." From then on the judges paid taxes, but whether the one or the other interpretation was correct it was impossible to say. Only amendment could make certain. And this was true of most reversed decisions.

10. On the Court's assumption of the power to legislate, Adolf A. Berle's *The Three Faces of Power* (New York: Harcourt, Brace & World, 1967) is eloquent. According to Berle there was a revolution going on, and the revolutionary committee was the Supreme Court.

diciary in the whole scheme of government. Its peculiar disability for legislation or administration would be recognized, and it would no longer shape public policy in decisions arising from random adversary actions. It would, however, assume an enlarged importance as interpreter, cautionary adviser, and guardian; and it would still, within a narrowed range, continue to interpret. When this involved defining presidential or congressional powers it would be authorized to do so. It would do this by continuing to decide finally not only causes brought to it from lower courts by way of its circuit courts of appeal but, as well, by deciding issues arising from controversies about duties of the other interdependent branches. Its supremacy would thus be recognized and made legitimate; but, because the Constitution would no longer be immune to change, the Court's important decisions would themselves be subject to a higher authority—that of the people, who hitherto have been able to reach the justices only indirectly. And what was done in the way of interpretation would proceed from an authority granted in the Constitution and granted recently.

The present objection to judicial interference has arisen largely from the Court's willingness to fill out the clauses allocating powers. The Court's interpretations have been too broad, because unlimited. It is necessary that as many as possible of the constitutional silences be ended: that definitions known to be needed be supplied. The clarity thus obtained would, expectably, narrow considerably the Court's role as arbiter. More frequent revision would settle interbranch conflicts within a reasonable time. The Court then would have the same responsibility when conflicts did arise; however, they would be ones soon to be considered in the higher process of amendment, and, anyway, their number ought to be much diminished as time passed and clarification proceeded.

There are, besides, administrative considerations. Accommodations to growth have been made in the operating agencies of government by expansion and modernized management. The Supreme Court, however, has changed hardly at all. It still conducts itself much as it did in its first years, each justice participating in every decision, however complicated. When the chief justice chooses an associate to write an opinion it becomes not his opinion but that of all the members—unless they dissent or unless they concur for other reasons. When this happens they write opinions of their own, and in critical cases there may be several. Merely in the nature of time and of human limitations there can be few such concerted efforts. Of the hundreds of issues available, only a small number are so carefully considered during each term. This may be sufficient; but the probability that constitution writing by such a method is, in modern circumstances, complete and completely careful is simply incredible.

More special courts would be useful not only in disposing of a larger number of cases but also in selecting those coming to the highest court. It would be better to have only serious constitutional questions reserved for the highest bench.

The present Court's multifarious obligations make a formidable list—too long, it may be suspected, to assure enough attention for the more important ones. It must consider both criminal and civil cases, accepting or rejecting appeals; and if constitutional issues are involved in these actions, the Court must study them against a long historical background. As things have been, cases it does not accept for decision are rejected in a process that cannot possibly be thorough because of their number and diversity.

One result of rearrangement ought to be clear distinctions among legislative, administrative, and constitutional law; this, in turn, would make it possible to respect the appropriate processes for each. That the highest Court has fallen—or been pushed—into the way of making all three kinds of law is unfortunate; it would better be kept to its proper work; it would be better, too, if there were benches for the different duties of the judicial branch, with the highest being more concerned than at present with the guardianship of the Constitution—that is, making sure that the behavior of private individuals, of officials, and of legislative bodies accords with its clauses. If these had been adopted by amendment, within a recent past, they would, in a far more real sense than before, represent the common will. It would be neither a manufactured will nor an obsolete representation of it, but one reached in an open and thorough dialogue and disposed of, if clarification should be needed, by referral to the legislative branch; or, if new laws seemed to be required, to the procedures of amendment. Amendment is conceived as possible to arrange and prepare for, and ought to be depended on to keep the fundamental law alive and relevant to contemporary circumstances.

For adversary actions coming up from the circuit courts, it seems a practical proposal that most should be disposed of in a high court of appeals. There might also be a court of rights and duties and an administrative court with several specialized benches. The one would be a place of resort for those who believed their privileges as citizens were abridged, or who felt that others were not meeting their obligations. In restricted circumstances such a court might have original jurisdiction; but the restrictions, in so large a country, would need to be severe. Most complaints ought to be settled in similar courts of lower jurisdictions and come to the national court only on appeal. The administrative courts would see to it that if regulatory activities and administrative operations were not kept to their stated purposes, there would be relief for aggrieved parties. Besides these, there might be courts of claims against the government, involving patents, taxes, customs, and the taking of property.

If from these benches, appropriate constitutional questions were selected and passed along to the high court of appeals, most would be concluded before reaching the High Court devoted to the Constitution. It is suggested that such a division of duties might lighten the work now done by a single court and that justice would be furthered by a much needed expedition. It would also furnish a particular place of resort, not now available, for those with grievances in their dealings with the administrative bureaucracy, as well as those who feel themselves harshly treated by the regulatory agencies whose responsibilities could not be met without controversy.

To recapitulate, it is suggested that there might be: a High Court of the Constitution; a High Court of Appeals; a Court of Rights and Duties; Administrative Courts; Courts of Claims.

So that he may be able really to preside, it would seem practical for the chief justice to be excused from sitting with the High Court of the Constitution unless it seemed to him necessary, but if he did, his vote should count as two. His duties might well extend, however, to the original appointment of judges and to their assignments, which would be made easier if there were available to him a larger number of associates than will sit in any case—perhaps thirteen, with nine constituting a full bench. This reserve would also provide much-needed depth of consideration for important issues. Justices might be freed for as long as necessary for study, returning to the active bench only at the completion of their work.

Taking the appointive duty from the president and giving it to a chief (or principal) justice would make it reasonable that he should be elected, perhaps by his peers. If he had a long term—perhaps twice as long as that of the president and equally representing a national constituency, he should be guided by the same general interests. Also, having one long term, he would be free of any partisan obligation. His would be a position of dignity and influence with far more than merely judicial implications. He would be recognizably the principal justice *of the nation*, not merely the presiding officer of the court; and he would not be a political judge.

This position for the principal justice would make it more reasonable to continue in the judiciary the duty of deciding, as issues arise, to whom responsibilities belong and how far they reach—in other words, to intervene when necessary in delicate decisions concerning divisions of power. Since this must be lodged somewhere in a system of interdependency, and must probably be in the court, judicial authority would at least be legitimated, clarified, and narrowed.

It is conceived that by this and other arrangements, the troublesome question, so often raised, about the Court's allocations of power to itself would be resolved as well as it ever could be. As has been insisted, it is essential for this purpose to provide for a frequent reexamination of the Constitution. If the Court tended to enlarge its scope unduly as it restricted the other branches—an almost inevitable tendency, checked now, in practice, only by the discretion of the judges, or by the threat of congressional interference—the next constitutional convention could make its own re-definitions. That this should be about twenty-five years in the future would seem a sensible arrangement.

It ought to have been seen at once after ratification in 1788 that allowing the Court's jurisdiction to be determined by the Congress, instead of by amendment, would be an invitation to future controversy. Such an arrangement gave vast power to a body unlikely to use it for furtherance of justice or for the general good; and although the prudence of successive Courts, with this provision always a latent threat, has usually served to evade confrontation, it can never be known what decisions must have been determined more by the need to suit the known sentiments of judiciary committees and congressional majorities than by legal requirements or considerations of justice.

It would not be unreasonably difficult to prescribe jurisdiction in a more frequently amended Constitution. The argument is often heard that if the Court spread itself too widely, an aroused Congress would reject its aggression. Apart from the likelihood that its rejections would be in the wrong causes, the fact is that the Congress has seldom acted to limit the Court.

To this generalization there are some important qualifications, arising from issues so important as to involve the whole nation—as when the Federalists wrote and passed the Judiciary Act of 1801. This reduced the number of justices to five (when the next vacancy occurred), so that Jefferson would not be able to make an appointment. At the same time more district courts were established and staffed with Federalist judges. The Jeffersonians, when they succeeded to control, at once adopted a new act (in 1802) after repealing this "midnight judges bill." They also added a seventh justice in 1807. By 1864 the number of justices had been increased to ten, but during the congressional quarrels with President Andrew Johnson there was a reduction to seven.

These disciplinary efforts of the Congress had very little concern with the administration of justice or care for the integrity of the Constitution. They had more to do with that "taking care of the situation when the Court got out of line" spoken of above. The "line," however, was that preferred by the more influential members of the Congress. The acts, most of them, represented one of the anomalies of the American system. Successive manipulations of the Court have been exercises of the same sort spoken of before—reassertions of legislative supremacy.

It has not been necessary, usually, to propose and pass reorganization acts for disciplinary purposes. All governmental agencies must have funds, and the amount and use of the funds may be prescribed. This crude but useful fact allows the Congress to determine the functions and size not only of administrative organizations but of the courts as well. And congressmen's peculiar allegiances make it likely, all too often, that national purposes are absent from their calculations.

There was a formidable threat to the Court's assumed powers in the 1960s. It came about because a sudden access of liberal views annoyed congressional conservatives who, by seniority, had become committee chairmen. They proposed, in a comprehensive bill, to restrict the Court's jurisdiction in several areas. Some were eliminated as the bill progressed through the houses, but some of those retained were obvious rebukes to the Court for its liberalized interpretation of the Bill of Rights. It raised again the problems involved in separated powers. There was no doubt that the Congress was authorized to make the proposed restrictions. There was, however, protest from the legal fraternity and, in this instance, from most liberals. What the Court's recent opinions had done, it was said, was what the Congress should have done. That recent decisions had made the Court more than ever a legislative body, and so had interfered with the constituted one, was conveniently overlooked by those who approved the expansion.

It could be seen, as this issue was discussed, how much judicial supremacy, reached through many years of cautious attrition, was dependent on public acceptance. It really had frail support.[11] This served to revise a long-held confidence among liberals that the Court could be depended on to set right national policy on disputed questions.

The controversy of those years was a needed reminder that the expansion of the government, as territory enlarged and the population grew, had from the first been controlled by the Congress, and that when judicial supremacy was spoken of, there had all along been, so to speak, a superior supremacy. The Congress could not abolish the Court, but it was not compelled to furnish it with funds; conceivably, it might reduce its membership to one; and it might, if sufficiently aroused, restrict jurisdiction to innocuous issues outside all possible controversy.

It is not intended to suggest that the power to tax and spend should be taken from the Congress. It is, however, suggested that appropriations should not become an agency of interference in matters outside proper congressional competence.

It has always been an interesting speculation (since *Marbury* v. *Madison*) that some day there might be a massive confrontation between Court and Congress. At the extreme, it could be supposed that the Congress had passed a law severely restricting the Court's jurisdiction or its

---

11. What the offended conservatives proposed was to reverse, by statute, several opinions enlarging the rights of accused persons. But in the background there were the other grievances mentioned here: notably interference in racial segregation, in religious invasions of schools, and in the reapportionment of state legislatures to reach equitable representation.

membership, and that following this, the act might be declared unconstitutional! Such a possibility was publicly speculated about as the Congress
debated what amounted to overrulings of the Court.[12]

It *was* careless of the framers to have left this possibility of confrontation open. Duties ought to have been more clearly prescribed, and the
obligation to make appropriations ought to have been made definite. In a
revised Constitution this, at least, ought to be accomplished. The Rule of
Self-restraint was obviously depended on, but its potency was badly strained
in such situations.

Correction of this mistake is more important than any particular complaint from aggrieved politicians in the other branches about the aggressions
of the Court. It has to do with allocation of powers belonging to the
branches and the necessity for reallocations as circumstances change. It is
suggested that the agencymaking of the Congress shall be limited to consenting or not consenting to proposals of the administering agencies; that it
shall discontinue the practice of remaking budgets each year line by line;
that it shall be required to provide for the effective operation of the
agencies established by the authority of the Constitution; and that this
effectiveness shall be determined, if need be, by another house. If the Court
is to make judgments of this sort in a government of interdependent powers
it needs this protection even more than the other branches. Self-restraint
is not enough.

This would imply that further reorganizations of the court system,
except for those made by constitutional amendment, would originate in the
courts themselves, as administrative changes would originate with the
appropriate presidential or executive agencies. The representatives would
debate changes and might refuse appropriations, but would not originate
changes, and, once authorized, constitutional amendments would not be
killed by the simple withholding of funds without consultation.

Furthermore, jurisdiction would not be determined by the Congress but
would be left to the Court within the limits prescribed in the Constitution
itself. It is always to be recalled that reconsideration ought to be carried
out in a thorough way at least every generation, and that the gateway to
interim amendment ought no longer to be blocked by the necessity for
legislative permission. There would then be constitutional law apart from
and above common laws, statutes, and administrative regulations. Also
there would be legitimate foundations supporting the position and powers
of each branch.

12. There was wide popular interest and a good deal of commentary. *Time*
magazine (May 24, 1968, p. 59), for example, said: "Though some legal scholars do
not agree with the *Miranda* ruling, virtually all of them believe that legislative attempts
to overrule constitutional decisions by statute establish a dangerous precedent. The
fact that the Court might later overrule the overruling . . . simply adds to the potential confusion."

This is perhaps too simplified a statement of what would occur with the changes proposed. But it may be hoped, with some reason, that amendment would occur when amendment was indicated, that it would be recognizably constitutional, and that the authority of the Court would be concordant with, rather than hostile to, that of the other branches.

A Simplified System

It has been noted that some important silences of the Constitution have been filled by judicial voices. More remains to be said about selectivity in the Court's exploitation of its opportunities. There are difficulties in the ambivalence of important provisions as well as the omissions of ones needed for clarification. The difficulties have persisted, although, as would be expected, custom has come to govern some. Besides, the Court has voluntarily abstained when it might have claimed jurisdiction. Such abstentions have not been many, but one has had continuing significance.

Article III might well have been taken advantage of, since it seems to contradict itself, thus making possible the choice of one alternative rather than the other. The Court seems deliberately to have accepted a distinction between "judicial power" and "Supreme Court." This made the article seem to indicate a range of jurisdiction the Congress might authorize the Court to exercise.

Only a few sentences apart, in sections 2.1 and 2.2, of Article III, there are these two provisions: "The judicial power shall extend to all cases, in law and equity, arising under this Constitution . . ." (2.1) and ". . . the Supreme Court shall have appellate jurisdiction, both as to law and to fact, *with such exceptions, and under such regulations as the Congress shall make*" (2.2).[13]

It will be seen that the second of these clauses seems to take back what the other confers—or, perhaps it should be said, limits it so severely as to give the other doubtful meaning. The judicial power is made to extend to *all* cases arising under the Constitution, but the Supreme Court can have jurisdiction over only such cases as the Congress may approve. If the Congress prefers not to have certain matters considered by the Court, it may put them beyond its reach, and even those accepted must be judged "under such regulations as the Congress shall make." Many of these have been made, giving the Court an initial handicap when the Congress—say, by passing a law repugnant to the Constitution—has to be told it may not do what it has done. The Court has assumed that, in judging a case, it still may declare a law invalid. But if this offends the Congress, the disputed statute may be put beyond the Court's power to reject. There is

13. Italics are mine. The phrases quoted are not the whole of either section, but the remaining language distinguishes between cases to be taken on appeal and those to be taken with original jurisdiction; they do not affect the allocation of powers.

nothing, either, to prevent this from being done retroactively, thus making the Congress a Court as the Court has made itself a legislature.

When the first Judiciary Act was passed in 1789 it was made clear that whatever the Court might think, as far as the Congress was concerned the first clause was to prevail over the second. The Congress clearly meant to keep for itself all the implied power it could read into the Constitution. The Court acquiesced; since then, nine reorganization acts have been passed.[14] Some of these merely changed the number of justices (called judges in this section of the Constitution),[15] but others have interfered extensively with the Court's position in the judicial system.

At almost any time after the passage of one of these acts, and especially the first, the Court might have insisted on identity with "judicial power." It was, after all, "supreme"; it might have insisted that such an act was invalid, since it would prevent the Court from considering *all* cases arising under the Constitution.

In fact, the Court did not do this, and never has done it. The reason may well be that the Congress might retaliate in the many ways—some of them brutal—at its disposal. The Court may well have felt unable to sustain itself in such a struggle. This, however, is speculative; what is fact is that the congressional interpretation has been acquiesced in by the Court, and in a succession of opinions over a long time. The Rule of Self-restraint has been effective.

Early Judiciary Acts relieved the justices of the duty to ride circuit and hold court in various localities; some established or enlarged the circuit and district courts. Presumably the justices favored these changes, but others limited their jurisdiction—and this cannot have pleased them. This situation, like others, is still uncertain. How far the Court may go in accepting and deciding cases is always a question requiring repeated diplomatic judgment. Having accepted the Congress's domination, it has resorted to thrusting forward and waiting to see what reaction follows. If it is severe, retreat must be arranged before the Congress acts to exclude from its jurisdiction the case or cases at issue.

This was what was taking place late in the 1960s after the Warren Court's advances into new interpretations of the Bill of Rights had offended many powerful congressional leaders. It had also been the effect of a dramatic retreat after the overthrow of several New Deal measures in the 1930s.

Such problems were old ones. Difficulty had appeared at once after

14. In 1801, 1802, 1807, 1837, 1884, 1891, 1911, 1916, and 1925.

15. It was the Judiciary Act that made the presiding judge chief justice *of the United States*. For this there is no constitutional warrant, but it is not difficult to understand why the Court has never found occasion to say so. On the other hand, the significance of the additional words in the title has vanished because of the Court's failure to claim an identity between "judicial power" and the Court. A chief justice *of the United States* would seem to be more than the presiding officer of one Court.

the passage of the first of the Judiciary Acts. Although "inferior" courts were mentioned in the Constitution (section 1 of Article III), and it was said there that the Congress was "to ordain and establish" them, it seems to have been assumed that these would be federal courts of appeal just below and subsidiary to the Supreme Court; but the act provided for lower ones paralleling the already existing ones of the states. In later legislation there were established not only circuit courts of appeal, but district courts with original jurisdiction whenever federal laws were alleged to have been violated.[16] Repeated laws have provided for a growing number of district courts. Since the circuit courts hear appeals not only from the state systems but from the district systems as well, their expansion too has been considerable.

This dual system has necessitated a series of laws and decisions determining the jurisdiction of each. Generally speaking, it has been agreed that cases arising in state courts may be appealed to federal courts whenever it is alleged that a question affecting the Constitution is involved, but only after such a case has reached the highest court in a state.

The Supreme Court, at the distant end of a case that has passed through the state courts and been appealed to federal jurisdiction, has been allowed to choose whether it will consider the case. This, as has been pointed out, is often done because it gives the Court a chance to expound the Constitution—the main source, in fact, of contemporary constitutional law. But it is allowed only because of congressional fiat.

The arrangement is inherently impractical; there are duplications and frequent conflicts, and neither ought to have been allowed to develop, or, having developed, to be continued indefinitely. Other countries with later constitutions—India, Canada, Australia—have avoided these difficulties by having original jurisdiction concentrated in state courts with appeal to the national system. A reform accepting this arrangement would be appropriate in America, and would be especially desirable if the federal principle should be regarded as granting of powers to the states by all of the people through a constitution adopted by them. If that were the situation, inferior courts would take their place in a more logically devised system. And the rearrangement would be even more practical if the states were grouped to form larger administrative areas—also, of course, if the judicial system was really recognized to be a separate power, not subordinate to the legislature.

The present Constitution, providing a strictly limited grant of powers

16. The circuit courts were called that because of the act's requirement that Supreme Court justices should sit in various localities for the convenience of litigants. It proved so inconvenient for elderly justices to "ride circuit"—and "riding" was the only way to get around—that special courts of inferior jurisdiction were later established, and members of the Supreme Court were allowed to stay in the capital and hear only the fewer cases appealed from the circuits.

by the states to the federal government, has left their courts, as well as their other institutions, in being. But in the early days there was a Federalist majority in the Congress, considerably more nationalist than the majority of the framers had been, and it was they who included parallel district courts in the first Judiciary Act. The courts were to protect the Union against the encroachments of the separatists.

This was illogical, as so many government arrangements had to be when a compelling need for compromise existed. The courts were left to work out their jurisdictional problems just as were state and federal legislatures and executives. The result was as might have been expected: however careful judges were in observing what they called the "rule of comity,"[17] there remained conflicts never more than temporarily settled, as the meaning of Article III has not actually been settled. The resultant frictions tended to become more rather than less abrasive. Since the source of these was the Constitution, only its revision could eliminate the most troublesome ones. It is true that the rule did serve to meliorate somewhat the inherent differences in overlapping jurisdictions. Survival of the system would not have been possible if there had not been some agreement to compromise, but the residue of strain has always been visible in spite of the Rule of Self-restraint.

A coordinate system is inconvenient and expensive, but other objectionable features are more important. When the courts are intruding on the legislative process and, moreover, making constitutional law, state as well as lower federal courts are involved. Laws made in this way by inferior courts may or may not stand when they reach the Supreme Court after successive appeals. The Court may then announce a rule, but this way of making constitutional law can only be called absurd. That the clauses of the Constitution mean one thing to a lower court and another to a higher court, without their wording actually having been changed, is a substantial reason for concluding that the relevant constitutional clauses ought to be rewritten.

It has already been noted that even when interpretations are made by the Supreme Court, they do not have the finality and authority a constitution's clauses, if clear and unequivocal, would have. For one thing, a court cannot commit its successors. It is true that precedent is frequently cited, but this is done most often when it leads to the result favored for other reasons. Such reasons, it is quite apparent, are often to be found in the justices' views of contemporary issues. It has been noted that inter-

17. Sometimes defined as a "self-imposed rule of judicial morality whereby independent tribunals of concurrent jurisdiction exercise mutual restraint. . . ." But, of course, the rule had at least a distant relationship to the so-called comity clause (Article IV, section 1) providing that "full faith and credit shall be given in each State to the public acts, records, and judicial proceedings of every other State."

pretations of the commerce, due process, and equal protection clauses have on occasion been completely reversed, the latest decision being constitutional law for the time being. But what was yesterday permissible, today may not be; and this change will not have been preceded by amendment or even by the passing of a statute, only by the reasoning of a justice and agreed to by four of his colleagues.

It has to be noted, as well, that the progress of an issue from lower to higher courts—transfer, perhaps, from state to federal jurisdiction, taking years—may well have worn out the litigants or exhausted their resources, and what was once important may be so no longer. Of course if the issue is a serious constitutional one, something is in the end accomplished for the law if not for the litigants; but the law is not final, and a better result would be achieved if the Constitution should occasionally be reconsidered.

There would be a better situation, too, if court organization was simplified. The suggestion that states might group themselves for certain purposes, including the judicial system, thus reducing administrators to a more reasonable number, might be expected to improve the administration of justice—and especially if concurrent jurisdiction should be abandoned. Many more cases would originate in, and proceed through, the judicial systems of the aggregated states, coming to the federal courts only on appeal from the highest of the courts of the states. They would there be accepted by the specialized courts or, if the High Court of the Constitution so determined, be considered finally for their constitutionality. It is not contended that this reform, in itself, would much relieve uncertainty about the law. Cases would still reach their final determination in the highest court after considerable delay. There is no substitute for a clear and specific constitution. There would be certain cases arising under federal law, also, that it might be best to adjudicate originally in circuit courts. They ought, however, to be relatively few.

It can be seen that in judicial matters, if concurrent jurisdiction should be substantially reduced, a massive decentralization would follow. It is not proposed that this should take place, or should proceed, without due attention to the establishing of standards and such supervision as would guarantee their effective observation. But even though there would be difficulty, the gain in efficiency, if not in constitutional interpretation, might be worth making.

It may be anticipated as well that there will be differences and that supervision will be objected to. When such incidents arise, the higher jurisdiction would, of course, prevail. The autonomy of the lower jurisdiction, however, need not be unreasonably invaded.

To make sure of this, it is suggested that relief in courts of the states should be exhausted before appeal may be made to the high courts of the

Union. On the other hand, it is equally necessary in the general interest that the way to final judgment shall remain open.

Such a change, making for convenience and expedition, would not cure the prevalent judicial habit of legislating. It would not prevent, either, the remaking, from the benches, of constitutional law. That the courts may not legislate will have to be the result of a new rule that interpretations of statutes must go back to the legislature for clarification. That the courts may not rewrite the Constitution is a more difficult concern. They must make interpretations, but these may be narrowed if serious rewritings are referred to the amending process as statutes may be required to be referred to the legislative process—the one to the people, the other to the legislature.

Nevertheless, a court system with clear jurisdictional directives and without concurrent and potentially conflicting jurisdictions not only would assist in keeping the judiciary to its proper role but also would enable it to operate more expeditiously. Or so it is argued here.

What should be done about cases arising under specific national law—having to do, say, with customs, patents, forbidden combinations, or regulatory acts—is difficult to decide. Original jurisdiction for some—perhaps many—of these may not be left appropriately to the lower courts, but the rule might nevertheless be that all possible should be left to them. Certain of them might even be joint courts, a novelty, and perhaps impractical, but it might be tried.

Since justice under law is such a high endeavor, it ought to be under law made in the way indicated by the democratic profession Americans are committed to as a people. That is to say, it ought to be kept as close to the people as possible.

Administration of a Constitution

If statutes are for the governance of a people, the Constitution is for their governance too; and the administering agencies and their officials properly operate within its stated prescriptions. But most of the guiding rules for the judicial branch by the 1960s had been fixed not by the Constitution itself, or by amendments to it, but by the Judiciary Acts already spoken of.

Of these acts, that of 1925 still fixed most of the guiding rules. By 1945 they would be half a century old. Because appeals from lower federal courts and from state supreme courts would have grown to such a volume by that time, some way would have to be found either to enlarge capacity or reduce the number of causes to be judged. A previous act (that of 1916) had gone some way toward allowing discretion in choosing cases; but still, dockets were swollen and delays were defeating the purpose of appeal. The reform allowed the Supreme Court to select cases that seemed to it of public significance, allowing the others to be settled below. For this purpose the technique was to grant writs of certiorari when the case seemed to call for review. Also cases appealable from state courts were limited to those falling into one of two classes: (1) when a state statute was alleged to be inconsistent with the federal Constitution; (2) when the validity of a federal statute had been denied by a state court.

The choice having been made that the Supreme Court, instead of having its capacity enlarged, should have its work self-restricted, the nine justices could keep on as they had been, with the added duties involved in granting certiorari or not granting it. There would be a large number of these instances, but there would be many fewer cases to decide and those only ones having special significance. Rejection would not require the writing of opinions or even the giving of reasons.

This change was open to criticism because the selecting of a few cases to be heard from numerous appeals could hardly be done with the attention the procedure ought to have, and because the change was one that ought to have been made by amendment. Any case brought so far through the judicial system as to have reached the Supreme Court must have been costly to the litigants, and must also have left controversies unsettled for several years. Such cases deserved to have more careful study than was allowed by this method, and they ought to have been much more expeditious than in reality they could be. As this arrangement operated, the justices, in spite of some relief, remained properly busy, indeed overburdened, by work on the cases they chose to consider. It is obvious that the choosing among many cases for further hearing might be done by an adjunct court.

It could be seen later that the effort involved in the granting of certiorari was only one unfortunate result of the decision to limit the membership to nine and to concentrate in it all the highest judicial functions, with the chief justice sitting as one of the nine. Another was the hidden consequence of permission to accept or reject. To put it plainly, the Court was enabled to avoid any question it preferred not to consider; and this was sometimes done because whatever decision might be reached would be impolitic. Also, the Court's freedom of choice allowed it to disapprove, without saying why, a policy it preferred not to encourage. This behavior is not curable by any reorganization of the Court itself. The cause is the intergovernmental relations established by the Constitution, and particularly the necessity for the judicial branch to conciliate the Congress lest its jurisdiction be limited. None of the reorganization acts has affected this situation—and none could affect it.

It was, however, a gain to have accomplished a certain decentralization and to have given more responsibility to the inferior courts. The number of these, circuit and district, was necessarily enlarged. It would be better if the present work of the district courts should become the responsibility of the lower judiciary. The national circuit courts ought, however, to be retained for appeals from the highest courts of other jurisdictions, and remain a part of the national judiciary.[18]

This would be a further contribution to a general decentralization. Apart from reducing the pressure on the national system, however, it would have no considerable effect on the highest courts. These are long overdue for a relief only to be reached by having more of them, by having their memberships increased, and by relieving the justices of much grinding daily work.

To accomplish these ends more attention to organization is needed. To begin with, the chief justice must be thought of as the head of a system, not necessarily a member of one court. His duties, thus enlarged, would require judicial wisdom but not application to cases unless they merited his intervention as a statesman. If he appointed the judges of the courts within his province and made their assignments, both he and they could attend more expertly to their proper business. It is suggested that several federalized courts, if constituted, would have enough members and be sufficiently specialized to improve the judiciary's contribution to government. Certainly the reservation of a few—but distinctly constitutional—questions for the highest of them would allow their judges to study more carefully the public policies affected by their opinions.

There are several relief courts now. The oldest of these is the Court of Claims, dating back to 1853; but there are, besides, a Court of Customs and Patent Appeals, and a Tax Court.[19] Among these, it will be noticed, there is only one Court of Appeals.

It is known that the nine members of the present Supreme Court carry on the tradition of total involvement in every case accepted for judgment. None excuses himself except for reasons of prior connection as an advocate. Does no one of them tire? Is there no time when indisposition or weariness would keep an ordinary person away or require withdrawal for a time? Are there no issues deserving prolonged study? That it should not be so is incredible. Yet every case is supposed to have been considered by every justice unless he is actually incapacitated and absent.

18. There were, in 1972, ten circuits and one for the District of Columbia. Each had several judges (three to fifteen) and a total of ninety-seven.

The district courts, the trial courts of the federal system, had 333 judges in 90 districts with both civil and criminal business.

All decisions of the district courts might be reviewed by the circuit courts; appeals might also come from the Tax Court, the National Labor Relations Board, the Federal Communications Commission, and other federal agencies with judicial standing; but they might be considered without the presentation of new evidence.

19. The Tax Court reviews decisions of the Internal Revenue Service; formally, and curiously, it is a part of the executive branch.

Since a petition for certiorari is a request that a decision of a federal court of appeals or a state supreme court be directed to forward the record in the case for review, a rule about the granting of such requests has been devised. Four justices must vote to accept them. But they are to be granted "only when there are special and important reasons therefor." These reasons include conflicting decisions below, ones concerning issues not hitherto considered by the Court, or suspicion that the lower court has not done its work well. The Court, however, in seldom giving any reason for allowing the judgment of the lower court to stand, does defeat part of the purpose of certiorari, and this could be corrected.[20]

Certiorari was a much-needed device, but it was not enough. The axiom was not fully recognized that the one criterion more important than all others for decent government is that the administration of justice shall be, beyond question, fair and without delay. To meet this condition there would be required competent and impartial judges, efficient organization, and complete independence from interfering interest. The present system satisfies none of these criteria. Changes are suggested that it is believed would meet the requirements.[21] As to the first, judges are selected for partisan reasons, and often because of some claim recognized by the president, such as having been a compliant member of the Congress or having been otherwise useful in a presidential cause. These ought not to be reasons for choosing justices. Proper qualifications for judgeship are much more difficult to state, and, of course, competence has to be thought of in relation to the duty required. Some courts would obviously benefit from having judges with specialized knowledge—such as patents, customs, admiralty, or tax laws. Others would need members with broad learning, calm judgment, and concern for public policy; and this would certainly be true of those dealing with constitutional questions.

20. The so-called legislative courts are not considered here. These are tribunals established for a temporary or special purpose, and particularly for territories or for the District of Columbia. These may have duties not strictly judicial, such as revisions of administrative regulations. What is involved here is that the constitutional provision for life tenure and protection of salaries need not be observed. The District of Columbia courts, however, have been held to be both legislative and constitutional. This protects their tenure but allows them to have unusual powers.

21. Justice White in 1966 summarized the work of the Court in an address before the Bar Association's section, *Natural Resource Law, Natural Resources Lawyer* (1968), pp. 24–31, in the term beginning October 1966: "The total number of cases on the dockets was 3356 . . . this was 2½ times the total in 1951. Of these 2903 were disposed of. Four hundred and fifty-three cases were set for argument next term. Of the 2903 dispositions, 147 cases were argued orally and decided with written opinions. One hundred and thirty-one were summarily decided without argument, and 124 appeals were dismissed. Of 110 written opinions during last term, White said, deciding 147 cases, 53 dealt with constitutional issues. The 57 other cases mostly involved construction of federal statutes. Forty of 110 opinions dealt with criminal matters. The United States was party to between 40 and 50 percent of all cases heard and decided on the merits."

These are surely elementary considerations, yet it has been accepted for many years that regional and ethnic considerations are to be recognized first of all; there is a growing tradition that always one member must be a Catholic, one a black, and one a Jew; also, that there must be appointments from the West and South to balance those from the East, where the best-known lawyers are to be found servicing the large corporations. It has also become unlikely that judges from the lower benches will be advanced to higher ones; even the best of them will seldom be rewarded by promotion.[22] Mostly appointees have been heads of the government's legal establishment, former politicians, or persons known to have served the president well and to have supported causes he approved. This is true not only of lower courts but also of the Supreme Court and, perhaps especially, of the chief justice.

No formal inquiries would be useful in establishing qualifications; even past records would be interpreted as conforming or not conforming to the views of the appointing official. The likelihood that justices would see that causes are justly decided would be the best qualification; but if this is so, the president is the worst of all persons to make the choices. In the past, 90 percent of the appointments have gone to members of the president's party and, with few exceptions, to individuals having the president's views about public policy. A good many have been rewarded for services not to be counted as qualifications for membership on any court, much less the highest.

Bias in courts so constituted has been natural in the circumstances. The judges have become so important as legislators that no president can afford impartial appointments. And some presidents, frustrated by Supreme Court opposition and the life tenure of its justices, have tried to persuade the Congress to use its powers of control in ways that would suit their convenience. A vigorous attempt of this sort was made by Roosevelt in 1937. The opposition he encountered, even from his own partisans, showed how firmly the Court had anchored itself in the governmental system on its own terms. The resistance was strengthened, curiously enough, by Roosevelt's current prestige—something legislators naturally resented; he had just won a second term by a majority of unprecedented proportions, and legislators felt themselves degraded. But also opposition was aroused by the offensiveness of his proposal. The measures he presented would have added justices up to the number of fifteen to substitute for incumbents who passed the age of seventy, implying that beyond that age they could no longer understand the contemporary world. Since Justices Brandeis and Cardozo were the Court's most respected and most liberal justices, and both were over seventy, this argument was ridiculed—as it should have

22. In 1968 only two of the nine had had judicial experience.

been. Of course what Roosevelt wanted was a Court amenable to his policies—one that would find the various acts of his program constitutional. This seemed to a variety of concerned citizens an attack on the Constitution itself. The identification might be an irrational one, but there was no doubt of its prevalence. It served to defeat his scheme.

Like most lawyers, Roosevelt did not even consider undertaking the procedures of amendment. He preferred to have the Court do the amending, but he wanted it done in his way. Eventually he got the Court he wanted, but by replacements in normal course, not by the appointment of additional members. Also there was some reorganization, but not at the time he was pressing for it. The Roosevelt-Truman Court continued to have a liberal majority; indeed it lasted through succeeding administrations, to the annoyance of the Republican Eisenhower. The frustrated president not only had a hostile Congress but also a Court that continued to be liberal. He had added to his frustration by the mistaken guess that his choice for chief justice would be a conservative. This was Earl Warren, who should have been properly amenable; he had been a candidate for vice-president on the defeated Republican ticket in 1948. He was a disappointment; he turned out to be a free interpreter with liberal leanings, and his life tenure, once appointed, put him beyond the president's reach.

Presidents, as a matter of fact, very often cannot have supporting majorities on the Supreme Court. They seldom will have as long as appointments are made for life; but they will try as long as they have the appointive power or suitable influence with the Congress. It is suggested here that they should not have partisan ones. More, it is suggested that they would have no reason for wanting one if their own mission in the nation's service should be changed.

With all the counts against the Court and its procedures, its bulwarks against disturbances have grown stronger with time. If Roosevelt, with all his then public support, could not prevail, it is hard to see how other attritions may succeed. This, however, is not the only way. Roosevelt was operating within the accepted system. He merely proposed to weaken the Court in its ongoing contest with the other branches, and particularly with the presidency, and in so doing prevent its striking down the projects he thought it necessary to further. He might have been more successful if he had proposed a forthright amendment approving welfare principles. He was right in thinking it necessary to legitimize these, but he was wrong in thinking they could be made constitutional—and thus safe—without amendment.

There are other courts whose operations have constitutional importance —the inferior ones. But their situation has become strangely precarious. For them, the president actually has only ministerial powers of appointment. Names are presented to him by the politician of most consequence in the area where the judge is to sit. The fact is that judges on the lower benches have qualifications largely weighted by this sort of claim. They may be acceptable judges, but if they are, their competence is not likely to have determined their appointments.

It has been suggested that in any general reorganization of government the position of the courts would be reassessed according to other criteria and in a way to fit with other changes. There is need, as things are, for a legislative body separate from district representatives. There is need also for some restriction on the expansion of presidential powers. Neither is easily inferred from the present Constitution, but that is where these provisions ought to be located—rather than in extensions of judicial power. Such extensions are quite as foreign to the original American system as enlargement of the other branches without constitutional warrant.[23]

This is to speak only of the Courts in their legislative phase. If extensions cannot be eliminated entirely in a government of separated powers because the branches can never be so sharply defined as to eliminate differences, the conflicts can be so reduced as not to threaten confrontation; and such settlements can be arranged as will last until the next constitutional revision. If, as has been suggested, a revision were never more than a generation in the future, Court-made constitutional law would be properly recognized as having interim force. It would then soon need to be affirmed in the legitimate process of amendment.

Also, for constitutional interpretation, one of the most delicate of judicial duties, the highest court ought to be freed. It need not, as at the present, have to choose a few cases to be heard from hundreds asking for certiorari and, of those, another few having constitutional significance. It can have judges with fewer causes to decide and more opportunity for their study. Most important of all, its members can be chosen not because they are partisans holding views in accord with the president's, or because they owe a duty to some politician, but because they are known to have integrity, learning, and wisdom. It is, in fact, suggested that they be chosen by a chief justice. He might, indeed, be elected, but for a term at least twice that of any political officer, and by an electorate restricted to his professional peers. He might be ineligible for any other office; and it could be made certain that he is dedicated to the nation, not to any of its factions, its regions, its businesses, or its individuals.

The Rejection Syndrome

Others than members of the legal establishment strenuously object to amendment of the Constitution. Among those who comment about such things there appears to be surprisingly general gratitude that the framers made the Constitution so hard to change. In this professedly democratic

23. The present Senate is not a "higher" body; it is only a second popular one with a not too different constituency.

country it is evidently felt that the people cannot be trusted to decide on the content of their highest law. It even appears that the people themselves have been persuaded that they inherit unchangeable institutions and that any suggestion of revision is subversive.

Most members of the legal profession seem to be convinced that a majority will be misled by demagogues of the right or the left, that a radical or a reactionary "phase" or "mood" will prevail, and what would result would be impossible to live with for long. What is not said, but is obviously implied, is that voters are not sophisticated enough to understand what they might be asked to approve by those who would be entrusted with the drafting. This concern seems to spread easily among politicians—perhaps because so many of them are lawyers. But apparently citizens of varying views, even those who are annoyed in varying degrees by the Court's attitudes, recoil from the slightest suggestion that a new constitutional convention might be in order. They prefer merely to have the Court behave as they would like it to behave without any diminution of its powers.

This prevailing attitude naturally and inevitably makes the Court a center of controversy; and its justices are supported or condemned because of their political views, not because of their professional performances. Also it determines how justices will be selected. A president who expects them to support his program as long as he remains in office will make suitable appointments. An important by-product is that the proceedings of confirmation may be so partisan and inquisitorial that the Court may be seriously degraded.

It was to protect the Court that legal academicians invented the "living" theory during the liberal phase of emerging opinions. Others might, in ignorance, accept passively what they heard spoken of as the Court's presumption, but there existed an active band of loyalists. They might be motivated by strong approval of the Court's current expansion of the Bill of Rights, but it could be suspected that there was an underlying conviction that lawyers were superior shapers of public policy. That later majorities might have other preoccupations and make different interpretations was certainly ignored.

Concern was also expressed among the more learned during the 1960s about the campaign to be anticipated if consent to serious revisions should become a national issue. Ratification, they recalled, aroused serious controversy in the state conventions of 1788, and approval in most of them had narrow margins. It was concluded by those who knew about these contests that what would emerge from latter-day attempts at revision would be something much worse (in one way or another and from their point of view) than the present document.

Then there was the contrast in longevity between American institutions and those of other countries. It had to be admitted that unhappy things happened in those places where constitutions could be amended by simple legislative acts or by dictators' proclamations. Everywhere but in Britain easy changes had been disastrous. The people in such nations were really left with, at best, statutes and, at worst, decrees. Their constitutions were instruments of convenience for those temporarily in power, not a body of permanent principles shaped by search of the public conscience. Even in supposedly advanced nations—France, for example—new constitutions were adopted with every change in popular sentiment. Calling such documents constitutions screened political preference behind a respectable façade.

In the United States easy amendment has been regarded with something like horror by most students of law. This actually might originate in a fear that stricter regulation of business and increase of welfare expenditures might emerge. Or, at the other extreme of interest, there might be a kind of shuddering withdrawal at the thought of losing recent gains in civil liberties and a relaxing of controls favoring consumers. No one, it sometimes seemed, could be persuaded that there ought to be a modernized constitution.

It has been repeatedly pointed out here, however, that things are not as they seem, that the nation is by way of losing this much-admired law—not by honest constitutional revision, but by processes claimed to be valid but about as reputable, really, as those prevalent in countries held in low regard for their easy revisions. It has been so long since the Constitution was put together that the original has actually almost disappeared and would be largely vestigial except for the ministrations of the Court and for other modifying processes, all, of course, illegitimate. The professional protectors, it is suggested, are agitated by the wrong emotions. They might better resent revisions made in ways they could not approve if they were faced openly.

It has been admitted, and there is no desire here to deny, that practical inferences have advantages. There are, for instance, governmental activities not anticipated by the framers, and agencies established to carry them out. Since they are not forbidden, and since they are compelled to expand, they become numerous. This, however, affects mostly governmental enterprises not anticipated by the framers, although some were avoided by them because of the need for compromise.

An example of those not anticipated are the regulatory agencies not mentioned in the original Constitution or even in any amendment. An example of avoidance is the political system. It has grown up—began immediately to grow up after ratification—quite outside the formal institutional structure. For the most part it has never had a statutory framework. The framers, it has been pointed out, simply did not intend that politics should extend beyond the states to the nation. This was a futile hope, typical of the rather obtuse wellborn Federalists. Actually, within a short time, government without a political background could no longer be imagined. If the Constitution sets the pattern of institutions, why should political systems any longer be left out? They modify seriously those established in the document. But no mention of them is to be found there, and no amendment has instituted recognition of political activity.

Another method of altering the Constitution has been mentioned in other chapters. It is one to be regarded only with disparagement. This is the kind of habitual and recognized violation that gradually becomes accepted. Following their own inclinations, or those organizations they are concerned in, many people simply disregard inconvenient clauses, sometimes in flagrant ways. Such, for instance, was the resort to violence on the frontier; such have been frequent refusals to honor the pledges of the Bill of Rights; and there have been periods when taxes have been evaded and sumptuary laws disregarded. There have been others when the public services have been undermined by corruption or by favoring private interests.

Not only private persons have been so engaged. Governmental agencies have also disregarded the Bill of Rights; and to mention no other instances, each of the branches has expanded far beyond the understood limits fixed by the Constitution. In fact, out there among the branches, in no man's land, they have engaged in a fierce, if muted, struggle for powers not contemplated in the Constitution; and having won them have used them without apology and, finally, as a matter of course. The struggles have usually been finally compromised by recognition of the Rule of Self-restraint, so fundamental to the system, but often the compromises have come overlate.

Other violations have been widely known and have gone on for years—as did the segregation of blacks. It was this same sort of defiant injustice that workers suffered from in industry during several generations. Their claims to rights were savagely rejected whenever their demands conflicted with the interests of their employers.

Unless they are explicit and are enforced, constitutional laws are no more effective than any other kind. And lacking citizen demand they may simply go on being ignored. A case has to be brought; and if none is brought, if it stops somewhere in the succession of appeals, or if the Court refuses certiorari, the violation goes on indefinitely. This amounts to a tacit acceptance of amendment, but it is an uneasy one and may end at any time; also, it undermines the authority of the law. And law, especially that of the Constitution, ought not to have this kind of half-life. It allows problems to go on enlarging without solution. What a constitution is for is lost sight of when such violations or avoidances are accepted as "practical necessities," and when the processes of amendment are avoided.

It is usually felt that accommodations made by the Court are more legitimate than those resulting from neglect or violation. It is an unusual year when the Constitution is not construed to have some hitherto unsuspected meaning. Such interpretations are usually, of course, small and tentative, but some are more significant. In making them the justices are hindered only by their own discretion. Ready illustrations are to be found in the expansions of civil rights and liberties so characteristic of the Warren Court. But other majorities with other interests have been as free in construing clauses with other effects in equally strained ways.

It could be pointed out that the Bill of Rights is made up of amendments and that their acceptance could refute the arguments of those who speak so fearfully about that process. What happened so many years ago is, however, regarded as part of the original writing, amendment today, it is said, would be much more hazardous to long-accepted rules. This may well be true, but it hardly justifies avoidance. If amendments represent public conclusions they will be reaffirmed in any general reconsideration.

The original ratification in some states was conditioned on promises that the first ten amendments would be adopted forthwith. But there were also post-Civil War amendments. These made really substantive changes in civil rights, and it was with these that the Warren Court supported its expansions of the earlier ones. Perhaps these suggest that reconsideration can be had only in circumstances of crisis. But it was crisis that led Warren and his majority to the making of laws without the validity they might have had as amendments. And there was soon question whether such laws would stand. Many of them were obviously going to be reversed by the Burger Court.

The loudly voiced conservative objections to the Warren Court's opinions centered precisely on the overprotection of individuals by expansions of the Bill of Rights. One clause of the Bill (Article X), it might be noted, is a bulwark for the decaying principle of states' rights. It will be a severe shock to libertarians if some day a Court majority rediscovers it and decides on enforcement—or even on enlargement. There may be regrets, if that should happen, that amendment was not resorted to.

A typical expression of liberals' fear in 1968 was that of Theodore Sorensen, whose concern amounted almost to panic. He had the conviction that the country was in a period of reaction, and that if the way to amendment was opened recent progress would be reversed and its gains lost.[24] It was a curious contradiction, as are so many expressions of objection, that among the threatened liberties should be the one-man, one-vote principle. This was not to be found in the Constitution. It had been attached by the Court to the equal-protection clause of the Fourteenth Amendment. Sorensen was afraid of losing something that did not really exist.

24. *Saturday Review,* July 15, 1968, p. 17. There was, Sorensen said, a crisis, and what seemed likely to occur would be a "nightmare." He called his article "The Quick Campaign to Rewrite the Constitution."

Equal representation might be regarded as an essential of democracy, but it had never before been interpreted as synonymous with equal protection. Most state legislatures had not been redistricted as people had moved in large numbers from country to city, and there were complaints that rural legislators imposed their views on urban citizens and kept for their constituents an unequal share of the benefits financed by taxation. This was true enough, but there was a reasonable criticism that it was extreme to find justification for compulsory reapportionment in the equal protection clause intended to secure rights for ex-slaves (the Fourteenth Amendment was ratified in 1868). For a whole century no one had seen that equal protection of the law meant one man, one vote. To extend the meaning so far could fairly be said to be another substitution of judicial opinion for amendment. If the states had any autonomy left it must be that of determining their own methods of representation. Such methods were undoubtedly discriminatory; but if equal protection meant equal representation, an amendment, not a Court opinion, might have been expected to say so.

It is contended here that the Convention of 1787 was part of a valid process, available as a precedent. Able men, a majority of them devoted to the public interest, were delegated in the then accepted way to suggest a form for union and for its government. They understood that constitutions are materializations of the national will. That will might be diffuse, it might not be joined in by those who had prospered under colonial conditions and so were loyalists in another cause, but it was that of free men in a new nation who meant to have the kind of governance such men would find tolerable. They meant to make up their own minds.

It is true that there were those who had no intention of conceding their own or their political mentors' interests further than they felt forced to do, and were quite willing to protect them by sacrificing the interests of others. We have seen that some of these, when chosen to be delegates, would not attend; some went home early; some, at the end, would not approve. Among those not approving were such participants as Mason and Randolph. Patrick Henry, not attending, repeated his speeches about liberty and death, first made in 1775. The proposed government, he protested, would be as oppressive as colonial rule. But better counsel did in the end prevail. The ratifying conventions often turned into scenes of dissension; local-minded men, as Washington called them, did their best to prevent union from being established; but they lost.[25]

It is argued here that the same sort of history for another such effort

25. That some of these dissenters, Mason among them, refused to vote for ratification because the Convention had omitted a bill of rights is perhaps true. There is a suspicion, however, that what Henry, for instance, was concerned about was states' rights, not individual ones. Virginia had a bill of rights; that it was omitted from the Philadelphia draft was only another reason for suspecting that the states were endangered. But nothing in the federal draft threatened Virginia's bill.

might reasonably be expected. A beginning is needed, and even principles ought not to be beyond reconsideration. Patrick Henrys, or even Masons and Randolphs, are quite likely to appear again with anguished denunciations of tyranny. Congressional candidates and governors seeking higher office do still have, as a regular resource, cries of protest that Washington is a center of tyranny. They continue to picture the return of power to the states as a guarantee of justice. That this ignores the proved incapacity and, too often, the corruption of state governments is hopefully ignored. All those who react automatically to such terms as bureaucracy, centralization, irresponsible power, and the like can be counted on to fulminate. But it was so, too, in 1788.

Doubtless there has been too much centralization; it ought to be corrected; and a way of doing it believed to be credible is suggested here. The states might be encouraged to group themselves in such ways as would give them regional relevance. All areas would then be large enough to support effective administrations. Concordant constitutions would establish governments supplementary to that of the Union. Each state or grouping of states would, in fact, be larger in population and much larger in economic importance than the whole nation of 1787. Decentralization to such groupings would be more reasonable, certainly, than to, say, Rhode Island, Oregon, or Mississippi. Smallness beyond a certain limit, and in the usual conditions, can be more wasteful than gigantism.

The objections to amendment, it must be concluded, rest mostly on: (1) the difficulty of the process as established in the Constitution; (2) distrust of the people's judgment; and (3) satisfaction with the processes of change now in operation, mostly originating in the Court. It is argued that none of these is defensible. The first ought to be overcome, the second is unworthy, and the third is illegitimate.

If this is a fair assessment, a thorough reconsideration is rejected only for indefensible reasons.

The particular question for this chapter is: What position would be occupied by the judiciary if such a reconsideration should take place? This question, of course, is not separable from those about the other branches. What was decided about each would affect the others; but assuming, as we have, that changes would be made elsewhere, it is believed that those suggested for the judiciary would improve its situation in the whole system.

The courts of the states would be courts of first resort, and they would hear appeals until a constitutional issue made it necessary for the national courts to accept jurisdiction. It seems especially desirable to have the highest of these devoted wholly to what is now no more than a small fraction of their work. Constitutional interpretation will continue to be necessary. No matter how much oftener the process of amendment may be resorted to, how often entire revisions are undertaken, or how meticulous the drafting, there will be new conditions. These would occur if only because of the rapidity of modern change. And ambiguities are certain to show themselves in spite of meticulous effort to avoid them.

To reduce the need for unreasonably broad interpretations more careful legislative procedures must be provided. Advisory opinions are also suggested. And the emergency powers of government would be assigned to a Senate of different character. But differences would still arise, and the Court would have to do the settling.

About the desirability of advisory opinions there may be doubt. Strong tradition runs against them, beginning as far back as Jay's refusal to assist Washington with one. The argument then was carefully put by Jay: "There being three branches, in certain respects checks upon each other, and our being judges of a Court in the last resort, are considerations which afford strong arguments against the propriety of our extra-judicially deciding" the questions not presented in adversary cases.[26] Later refusals have rested on a different rule: that constitutional courts can render decisions only when an essential element is a final judgment binding on the parties; also, as Justice Jackson added, that no opinion ought to be "subject to later review or alteration by administrative action."

However useful the rejection of advisory duties may have been in former circumstances the contemplated changes would seem to make a difference. Objection rests on the assumption that adversary actions must be the only source of Court cases. This is, in fact, one of the severest limitations on interpretations of the Constitution, accounting, as it does, for delays until a relevant case happens to appear. The Court accepts only a few appeals for judgment, and those for reasons impossible to determine in advance; and this not only imposes hardships on litigants, but what is more important, the Constitution is kept in a constant state of ambiguity.

It is proposed, therefore, that advisory opinions be made available to the president and the legislature. By making clearer the meaning of the Constitution's provisions, they might avoid many costly and confusing controversies such as those about the division of powers, the regulation of business, civil liberties, and the like. Advisory opinions would also make unnecessary many of the private appeals made so difficult by the formalities of legal procedure.

Another desirable effect would be the centering of attention on needed changes in the Constitution. These then could be considered with reasonable promptness by a permanent commission on revisions. To have all essentially constitutional questions out in the open and freely discussed might not abate the fears of those who, like Sorensen, would prevent consideration

---

26. The questions asked by Washington had to do with construing treaties and laws in situations arising out of the French Revolution.

of them by anyone but the justices, much less any rewriting unless the mood of the people seemed favorable to particular views; but for those who believe that the Constitution, fully considered, is the people's to make, it would seem essential to a working democracy.

True, the Constitution must always be thought of as a restraint on people by themselves—or, to put it another way, an agreement to act in good conscience within rules for the whole community—but, with the proper processes of preparation, including delegation of preliminaries to those well qualified for the task (as were a majority of the framers), the electorate ought not to be carried away by the oratory of demagogues any more than were delegates to the Conventions of 1788.

It is proposed here that the first stages of the amending process be carried out in a way calculated to inspire trust because done by those who may clearly be expected to act in the general interest, and ratification would be preceded by thorough discussion. The voters would, as far as possible, be protected from latter-day Patrick Henrys as well as voters can ever be from specious appeals.

If done as is suggested, and if the people should still succumb to moods of malice or fear, that must be accepted as a penalty of democracy. It may not be so damaging either as warnings of the fearsome would have us believe.

Admittedly, there is in the proposal a quite different view of the Constitution than is now prevalent among lawyers and political scientists. It is not thought of as a final and perpetual rule of law, but rather, like all law, intended for particular use, subject to occasional review: except, of course, that this is the people's highest law, conceived as a solemn accommodation to duty, and adopted for such time as the duty it imposes remains relevant. But if, as is assumed here, it is theirs to make and to remake, it is strange that there should be such fretting about the exercise by the people of their most fundamental prerogative.

Inescapable Responsibilities

There are reasons for the Supreme Court's unique standing among Americans. The Congress, it is taken for granted, is obstreperous, obstructive, and given to serving the interests of its members' constituents, and it has never been held in high regard; the presidency is a fascinating center of power, sometimes approved, sometimes not, always subject to shifting opinion, and sometimes occupied by weak or headstrong incumbents. The Congress is a receiving and sorting body; the president is an initiator; but the Supreme Court holds the reputation of being austerely withdrawn from ordinary influences and devoted to keeping the nation true to its original intentions.

So far as there has been a national conscience, the Court has represented it. For this purpose the Supreme Court has guarded its behavior. Its members have given up all other concerns and devoted themselves singly and industriously to the orderly processes of the law. The justices do not leave the Court to take up other occupations with superior economic advantages. They do not interest themselves in affairs external to their duties. No other public officers are considered to have motives so pure and methods so respected.

This reputation is not quite deserved. The justices for long periods seemed to be mostly interested in the protection of business interests; again, there have been extended periods when the Bill of Rights has been reexamined and many of its provisions expanded. During both periods the Court has been attacked for its views and threatened in various ways. But the members have been known for detachment from their own concerns, for earnest devotion to justice, and for concentration on their proper affairs. The Court has been an exemplary institution in a sometimes disorderly democracy.

Even though the president occupies a position of eminence and is looked to for leadership, he can never be quite free of partisan responsibilities. The justices, however, hold themselves apart from such diversions and singly devoted to the high duty of constitutional interpretation. Even when they have a bias it is because they hold it to be best for the nation, and it appears in such recondite form that it is hardly recognizable for what it is.

This is a very general characterization, but the picture is not far from fair. It has been somewhat blurred a few times in extraordinary circumstances. Justices have been known to desire the presidency enough to give way at a party's insistence. Charles Evans Hughes did consent to be the Republican candidate in 1916, but it was generally felt that he had violated an unspoken rule that ought to be respected; it has not happened again.

Some justices have not been so admirably intelligent as could be wished. How could there have been a uniformly high level when most of them have been chosen for adventitious reasons? And whole classes have at times regarded the Court or particular justices as unfair—the workers at one period, business interests at another. Whether members are competent is, of course, a question separable from their biases. Biases may make them seem to have been impervious to reason when time has passed and circumstances have changed, but the fact would appear to be that some of the most intelligent have not understood their times and have bent the Constitution's clauses to their beliefs. Actual incompetence—meaning stupidity—has, however, been very rare.

The way appointments have been made ought not to have resulted in such virtues as the justices have been credited with. It has been noted that, with few exceptions, partisanship has been a controlling factor. That, after becoming a member, the justices should uniformly have taken on the strictly judicial habit is fortuitous. There may be some reason for believing that a doubtful method will always produce so acceptable a result, but one so dubious need not be depended on.

If one inevitable result of presidential choosing is that justices have allowed their social views to interfere with their judgments, those who have been predictably prejudiced have not been so in a partisan sense; and the few who have allowed presidents to use them, after appointment, for their own purposes have been very few and almost always have had the national interest as an excuse. When John Jay went to England at Washington's request he was acting in a nonjudicial capacity, but obviously as his country's most excellent representative. Justices Roberts and Warren presided over investigations of occurrences threatening to national unity (Pearl Harbor and the assassination of President Kennedy). And Justice Jackson was persuaded to preside over the trial of Nazi "war criminals" at Nuremberg. But all these were unusual deviations from the dedication to the Court's mission. Also, there was no hint in them of any but an interest transcending partisanship. Nevertheless, as each of these instances occurred there was a strong feeling, as there had been concerning the Hughes candidacy, that the justices ought not to come out, in this way, into the world. It was considered that they should hold themselves aloof, untouchable, singly devoted to detached consideration of the great issues brought to them on appeal, dispensers of justice and oracles of the highest law.

Curiously, because of their strict conception of judicial duties, the most serious departures from exclusive application to those duties occurred when Chief Justice Jay was a candidate for the New York governorship and when Chief Justice Marshall served also as secretary of state. These would have been unthinkable duplications at a later time, and judicial historians find them difficult to excuse except that they occurred before tradition was formed. They were, perhaps, examples that made such adventures unlikely for the future.

The standards so generally held to by the justices, and so respected by the profession they come from, are virtues precious to a democracy. The usual political approaches to public office are apt to show Americans at their worst. Speaking only of national elections, the contests among candidates have little relevance to competence for office. Appeals are specious, maneuvers are demeaning, and the trading that goes on in public privileges is disgraceful. It is proposed here to make changes in these processes; but a general electorate, it must be presumed, will go on making choices for reasons other than competence in prospective performance. Such is the presumption about the electorate. It is one that unaccountably has been regarded with tolerance since John Quincy Adams left office, ousted by unscrupulous Jacksonians. The few exceptions have only proved the rule.

To the extent that the strain of partisanship touches the judiciary it is proposed to try for its virtual elimination. Justices ought not to be chosen because they are remote from contemporary concerns, but they need not even be suspected of having any but a detached interest in them. For this purpose it might be better to have them chosen by the chief justice himself, who might be selected in a new way for a long, but limited, term and so be removed from party affairs. It is admittedly difficult to ensure both professionalism and concern with humanity among judges. Perhaps a choice has to be made as to which virtue will predominate. This, however, is not quite the same for the inferior courts as for the higher ones. It ought to be possible for the chief justice to secure both virtues in his national courts; a career in lower ones would separate the judges who are wise and good from those with narrow or biased interests. And selecting from them would be to choose from an already experienced list of eligibles.

To a remarkable extent, considering the way members have been chosen, and their former occupations, the Supreme Court has won and deserved a reputation for integrity; and it would be regarded as impious if proposed changes in the Constitution threatened any loss of credibility. True, there have been some irreverent critics of the Court's procedures. One, a distinguished jurist himself, said disparagingly that this "cult of the robe" hid a good deal of quite human weakness. Justices were after all subject to usual bafflements, even to confusions. They sometimes thought less of justice than of their irritation with provocative litigants, and it was not unusual to retain a tenderness for the interests of former clients.[27]

The exalted regard for the judiciary in general, and the Supreme Court in particular, may be exaggerated and may not be supported by close examination—"more myth than reality"—but there is no doubt that the judicial branch occupies a higher ethical level than the others.

There are discounts to be noted, of course, one being frequent disagreements. This is sometimes so active that it becomes unseemly and is known to outsiders. It is usually ideological too; Justices Jackson and Black had such differences for years. Other kinds of justices' annoyance with each other have had publicity. Frankfurter had a way of instructing his colleagues which they sometimes resented, and, like his mentor Brandeis and a few others before and since, was known to be a presidential consultant (asked or not asked) on matters not within his judicial warrant.

27. Judge Jerome Frank of the Second Circuit Court was an author as well as a judge. His *Law and the Modern Mind,* 2d ed., rev. (Garden City, N.Y.: Doubleday & Company, 1963) and *Courts on Trial: Myth and Reality in American Justice* (Princeton, N.J.: Princeton University Press, 1949) were written from behind the façade of judicial infallibility. He provided uncomfortable glimpses of judges in ordinary dress and with ordinary concerns.

The confines of the Court have seemed, fairly often, too restricted; when they have differed with their colleagues or with presidents about national policies, justices have found themselves unable to contain their certainty of being right. Such convictions, though, are quite apart from differences about the law, and it is these that tend to destroy the illusion of wisdom set in a matrix of hard logic. So many opinions are rendered by a majority of five, with four well-reasoned dissents, that the myth of infallibility would seem to be wholly unjustified; yet it has persisted, being fostered industriously, of course, by the profession.

Continuing respect is perhaps to be explained by a pluralistic democracy's desperate need for final judgments. Not only the integrity and operating utility of a people's government depends on such decisions, but free litigants as well cannot rest until there has been a concluding decree. The unique quality of a Supreme Court opinion is that there is no appeal from it; the case has been fought to an end, and adjustment has to be made to what has at last been determined. The loser may retire disgruntled, but he must retire. He does not, as in older times, refuse to accept the judgment and resort to some other open reprisal. He knows that if he does, the weight of disapproval will make his protest more costly than it can possibly be worth.

We have noted, however, that there is a flaw in this tacit agreement to accept judgments in adversary actions. The provision of the Constitution allowing the Congress to determine the Court's jurisdiction is sometimes invoked by annoyed legislators, and we have seen that resentment about invasion of legislative prerogatives may precipitate a reaction. The resort to revising the Court's allowance of latitude is always handy. It is curious that the framers did not, apparently, understand that they were preparing a confrontation capable of seriously damaging the web they had woven. The Congress might restrict the Court, but the Court might retort by rejecting the restriction. Then what would be the conclusion? This was not the only confrontation likely to occur under the terms of the Constitution, but it was potentially as damaging as any. There was, indeed, exaggerated trust in the Rule of Self-restraint.

Because Marshall allowed Jefferson a victory that hid a more devastating defeat, there was no move to reverse *Marbury* v. *Madison*—the victory was too acceptable to warrant protest over the defeat entangled with it—but other losers have been in better situations. Senator Dirksen and the southern conservative legislators, irked by the Warren Court, had a remainder of old resentments to count on in the sixties. They very nearly taught the Court a lesson in the need for caution when a superior power was being challenged with only the support of tradition.

Apart from the ambivalence of the Constitution, it is admittedly difficult to distinguish what ought to be the Court's realm of authority and what should belong to the legislature. This is a problem much discussed at times of serious difference. Remakers of the Constitution, or those who propose its remaking, always have to deal with this difficulty. The purpose is to restrict the ground where confrontations may occur. It is submitted that one certain improvement would be to abstract the fixing of judicial powers from the Congress and consign it to an amending process. For this to be practicable, amendment would need to be recognized as a regular and expected process. It would not be made more carelessly—not at all— but it would be going on all the time, and would thus become as familiar as statutemaking or presidential leadership. There would, for instance, be public discussion. Proposals and objections would follow one another. Finally, there would be acceptance or rejection. Citizens might be brought to regard their higher law in a new way—as something they were responsible for deciding about rather than something beyond human reach, an untouchable but antique rule guiding their common existence.

If the Constitution is peculiarly the property of the people and only they ought to make or change it, it is not something that ought to be kept beyond their reach, but something precious and intimate, belonging to themselves to remake if it should seem well to do so. It ought not to be consigned to any esoteric realm where lifetime acolytes expound its terms. The Court, as its guardian, has generally said that the Constitution was written for all time; but the Court has never meant what it said. The justices have adapted it, when circumstances required, to contemporary conditions, and as we have seen, they have done so quite often. Because of the justices' learning and their dedication, these adaptations have been found remarkably acceptable. The contradiction may have been overlooked, but it exists and is not to be disregarded.

The fierce repulsing of all suggestions for other methods of rewriting originates in this double recognition of the Constitution as sacred—and the Court as its sole adapter. Supporters who intensely dislike some decisions are reluctant to criticize. It is mostly the congressional critics, driven by the resentment of their constituents, who speak harshly of the justices; and even then it is not of the Constitution but of particular justices who, they say, have interpreted it improperly. Ordinary folk are inclined to accept this; it is only when the Constitution has lost its relevance that there is trouble, and then it is not often attributed to the real source. There is a diffused disillusion with democratic institutions, or there is such an individualized resentment as was represented during the sixties by the roadside signs in the South demanding the impeachment of Earl Warren.

The only formidable dissent to the sacred-document theory has come from the interpositionists, Calhoun being their spokesman of most note. His theory was repudiated by force in the Civil War, but it has appeared again from time to time when it would be most useful to politicians. It has, however, always met with the same stern rejection. It is suggested here that sacredness is a quality related to the people's deep intentions and that the Constitution ought always to be the materialization of these intentions. This quality ought to be preserved by continuous and careful updating and reconsideration.

Obsolescence, it is argued, is fatal to credibility and must somehow be avoided, at the same time keeping intact the respect so vital to democratic government and to the cause of justice. A procedure for this might lie in a permanent study of needed amendments by a judicial council advisory to the chief justice. It would be the council's duty to suggest such changes as would adapt the Constitution to contemporary circumstances and from time to time put forward specific amendments which, if the Senate agreed, might be submitted for approval at the next general election.

It is further suggested that such a council, supported by whatever expert assistance it might need, should prepare a complete revision after, say, twenty years—roughly, a generation—and that the existing one should be voided by its own amending clause after about twenty-five years. The theory governing this suggestion is that the processes of obsolescence will continue, perhaps accelerate, and will be ruinous to public confidence. Each generation is entitled to be freed from old conceptions and ought to be allowed at least its own governmental devices. The principles so often said to be timeless can as easily be perceived by one generation as another, and presumably, if they are still acceptable, can be carried over from one document to another.

The anticipated positive virtue of this suggestion is that it would provide relevant higher law, and that it would have been made by the people acting through processes they had themselves approved. The negative virtue is that it would relieve the Court of as much of its legislative duty as is owed to the need for modernizing outdated law, and return the Constitution to its proper position in government.

CHAPTER 12

REGULATION

Emerging Services

It seems necessary here—and it is done with due apology—to speak again of some issues already considered; these are, however, so critical that they ought to be kept in mind.

Stephen K. Bailey, director of the graduate program of the Woodrow Wilson School of Public and International Affairs at Princeton, has given it as his opinion that the ultimate objectives of public administration in a democratic society seem clear, and he has offered a definition:

> These objectives are to draw together the insights of the humanities and the validated propositions of the social and behavioral sciences and to apply these insights and propositions to the task of improving the processes of government aimed at achieving *politically legitimated goals by constitutionally mandated means.*[1]

Other discussants in the symposium in which Bailey participated wondered about the implication of this definition, but the words italicized above escaped entirely from consideration. Why? It seems a notable exclusion. The "politically legitimated goals" are certainly the ones most needing evaluation. That no one felt a need to examine them must be assumed to indicate consent. Evidently it was felt that since the goals had issued from a legislature, and had become statutes, administrators were prohibited from questioning them. This subservient acceptance of legislation

---

1. Bailey's quotation is an excerpt from the dialogue of a conference on "The Theory and Practice of Administration."

as a given in administrative discussion is traceable to custom; a law to bureaucrats is evidently assumed to be a legitimated extension of the Constitution.

It is even more notable that no one mentioned, in that exchange, the words "constitutional mandate." This is also remarkable, because it recognized another limitation as quite beyond any question, and this seemed even more restrictive. Practically nothing administrators do *is* constitutionally mandated. Why this neglect of the most crippling of all their abstentions? Why should concern about it be omitted from consideration among themselves?

The answer has to be speculative because search of the literature offers no answer. Perhaps, however, there is a sort of reply in the comment by Herbert Emmerich, formerly senior consultant in public administration at the United Nations, that the Supreme Court *could no longer be relied on to forbid extensions*. He said of the Court that it found justification in one of four constitutional grants of power: to provide for national defense, for the general welfare, for the regulation of commerce, and for fiscal management. Among these, he believed, there could be detected permission for government to do anything conceivable by the most imaginative administrator.

This is the justification accepted by professional administrators, but there is certainly more to be said. In the first place, it cannot be assumed that these are actually the "grants of power" Emmerich speaks of. They are, rather, enlargements of the assumed implications in constitutional clauses, phrases or words clearly intended to have other, and quite specific, meanings. The addition of new implications by way of reinterpretation is not "a grant of power." It is, rather, permission to go beyond a grant of power. To say that *anything not prohibited may be done* is to assume a peculiar—and quite unwarranted—view of the Constitution. It does, in fact, exactly reverse the intention of the framers and make their plain words sophistical. For instance, how can it be said that the central government has been awarded a boundless permission to act? The residual powers were given to states, *and they have not been taken away by amendment*. The corollary of this allocation is clearly that such powers do *not* belong to the federal government. None of the clauses mentioned modified this premise of the Constitution's structure. If they are interpreted as doing this they must be held to have this difference from the actual grant: they may be reinterpreted whenever five members of the Court agree to do so.

Federalism is somehow held to be an intact feature of the Constitution by the same people who see no limit to a national power that tends to nullify it. It is necessary only to look at the document and at the existing states to see that the original relationship is still a structural principle. Besides, the administrative profession is as busy improving the efficiency of state governments as that of the federal government.[2] They are therefore not ignorant of their operations.

In this curious illogic of our most respected administrators there can be seen something of the reason for the existing confusion. Overlaying the knowledge that the states are still there is the consciousness of their increasing difficulties. These are known to everyone, including the Court. The curious attitude of the justices that such weaknesses are fictional has to be accepted and gone on with as though it were final truth. If the appeals of states' righters have not been listened to lately by the justices, states' rights must have been discarded; and who are mere administrators to question what the High Court has concluded?

This is surely a temporary reliance. If such constrictions by interpretation are accepted as more than they are, everyone who is ever guided by them is being led into error that quite possibly may reveal itself in embarrassing circumstances. It is a fact that opinions are not amendments; only amendment can constitutionalize what is not in the original document. Tomorrow, or next year, the permissiveness spoken of by Emmerich may be withdrawn. The states may well emerge again, in an opinion, or a series of them, as they clearly appear in the Constitution. They are still sovereign bodies with all the original residual powers not granted to the central regime. They are there unchanged, in the Constitution.[3]

To say this again, and clearly, what emerges from the premise that anything not forbidden to the central government may be done is not only a reversal of the framers' intentions; it assumes that the Court will continue to be a constitutionmaking body, so powerful that it is able to alter the first structural premise of the Constitution. This is much higher legislation than the Congress can enact.

Of course the nations's administrators are not alone in this curious conclusion. It is one that is very generally accepted. If it gives no worry even to the fraternity of constitutional lawyers, who, on the contrary, accept it as final, it is easily seen why administrators should have no hesitation about reliance on it. To lawyers the Court is the nation's most elevated public body, and to suggest that its opinions are not embodied automatically in the Constitution is something they are not prepared to admit.

2. Through the Council of State Governments, for one thing; but much of the work of the Public Administration Service has been done for the states. And federal delegation has always been accompanied by insistence on minimums of efficiency resisted by state bureaucracies.

3. Except, of course, for such restrictions as appear in the supremacy clause (Article VI, section 2) and in the Thirteenth and Fourteenth Amendments, ratified in 1865 and 1868. But these, too, have been expanded by the same process of interpretation far beyond the intention of those who ratified them and, again, may be reinterpreted at any time.

In spite of this consensus, doubt refuses to be banished. It is still sometimes questioned whether Court opinion does really remake the Constitution. It is only logical to contend that nothing but amendment can change so sacred a document. And to go on, only an amendment can change a former amendment, a consideration of importance when it is recalled what happened, during the Warren regime, to the First, Fifth, Thirteenth—and even some others. It must occasionally be faced as a fact, even by administrators, that this is an insubstantial foundation for the organizational structure of government. It is, of course, beyond their control, but they ought not to ignore the footing they are counting on for their theory of deployment.

A student of our institutions who calls attention to the consequences of what was begun by Marshall,[4] and has been so expansively enlarged by some successor Courts, does not really get a reasoned argument in return.[5] What he does get from constitutional lawyers, especially academic ones, is simply the complacent statement that the Court is providing what is needed. This pragmatic reply would be more acceptable if "what is needed" did not in effect modify rather than interpret the Constitution, something several justices, although always in minority opinions, have from time to time expressed qualms about. Those who regard the Warren interpretations as gospel appear not to realize—or at least not to admit—that the same attitude toward the Bill of Rights as has been evident toward federalism might severely modify various provisions of the Bill as well. Faith that the justices will not go in that direction—a faith that proceeds from the way the justices went for thirty years during the Roosevelt-Warren Court regime—is not necessarily justified. That there would be a changed majority in the future was a thought so disagreeable that it seemed always to be ignored—but it did happen.

When it was required to interpret, say, the First or Fifth Amendment, it must be insisted that the Court did move—after 1935—in precisely the opposite direction from that of its opinions affecting the federal principle. The one was permissive, the other restrictive. Rights were enlarged, made more impregnable; but the federal principle very nearly disappeared. This stretching in both directions was accomplished by the same method of implication so effectively employed by Marshall. It is only realistic, however, to recall that it works, or may work, both ways.

It should be noted, also, that the justices confine permissiveness ex-

4. *Marbury* v. *Madison*, 1 Cr. 137 (1803). This, it will be recalled, was the decision asserting the Court's implied power to ignore the separation principle of the Constitution and establish itself in a position of supremacy.

5. Reference is made particularly to the so-called steel seizure case in 1952 (*Youngstown Sheet & Tube Co.* v. *Sawyer*, 343 U.S. 579), and the Powell case in 1967 (*Powell* v. *McCormack*, 266 F. Supp. 354). The one brought the presidency into the Court's purview, and the other asserted the Court's power to discipline the Congress. Judicial supremacy, in the latter case, reached an apparent absolute.

clusively to themselves. Prosecutors, for instance, cannot accumulate evidence as they like; police must restrain their treatment of suspects; obscenity and pornography become more and more difficult to check. If permissiveness has opposite effects in the two areas of reasoning—the extension of federal activities and the definition of liberties—there is the common reasoning, curiously enough, that both derive from a previous assumption. This is that the Court can come to any conclusion it likes, using the Constitution as a convenience and not as a literal set of directives.

It perhaps does not need to be repeated, but to avoid misunderstanding it will be said anyway, that these animadversions are not made to deplore the conclusions reached by this pragmatic method. It was necessary to enlarge federal activities and to reduce the powers of the states, and the Bill of Rights did need reinterpretation in contemporary circumstances. What is objected to is reaching right conclusions by means that are very likely to provide precedents for reaching wrong ones—and very wrong ones—in the future. There must be a lingering suspicion in most defensive minds that this procedure will have the consequences always latent in the use of doubtful means to gain desirable ends.

The most respectable of individuals, many of them lawyers trained in the strict rules of their profession, defend the Court heatedly and with indignation against any suggestion of impropriety. This is done purely in defense of the conclusions reached by the justices. A liberty needed affirmation, so the word "speech" is enlarged and becomes "expression"; it is even further stretched by a method called constructive or symbolic. "Equal" is divorced from "separate." These are illustrations of method. An even more surprising one is the belated use of the Thirteenth Amendment, ratified in 1865, to reach abuses not until 1968 recognized as in any way related to the prohibited "involuntary servitude."[6]

It must be said again that the significance of strained uses of the Constitution, or of its amendments, to enlarge the area of personal liberty, to protect persons rather than property, is the reversal these represent of the Court's attitude during the preceding period, a long one, lasting from the first significant expansion of industry until about 1935. Judges, generally, and the Supreme Court justices particularly, seemed during this period to be searching the Constitution for intimations that property rights were intended to be protected from the incursions of those who would diminish them.

When corporations were interpreted to be individuals and entitled to shelter from those who would reduce their powers over their workers and their customers, a very strong barrier was erected against reform. Indus-

6. Given an interesting preliminary analysis in "The New Thirteenth Amendment," *Harvard Law Review*, 82, 6 (April, 1969), 1294 ff.

trial properties were customarily protected from workers who were demanding better pay or improved working conditions. These were not regarded as rights and had no judicial recognition. What can almost be described as civil war went on sporadically for many years with the law consistently on the side of employers who were defending their property and their rights to establish wages and conditions of work. Public powers may as well have been in the employ of industrialists.

The conservative interest during this time found support in the due process clause of the Fourteenth Amendment, adopted just after the Civil War for the specific protection of blacks. It was ironic that the Court should have used it to protect corporations rather than the freed slaves. The developing rule was confirmed by Chief Justice Waite in 1886, speaking for a unanimous Court.[7]

It was not afterward questioned until Justice Black in 1938 flatly denied that the amendment could have been meant to protect corporations, and if it was not so meant he would not agree that it should be so used. From this time on there clearly existed a new trend toward the tightening of corporate regulation with judicial permission. In one case after another the Court held that businesses must conform to publicly set standards of working conditions, hours of work, and other protections for workers. Several notable jurists had already written stinging dissents to conservative opinions, and these gradually became majority rules. Brandeis, Holmes, Cardozo, and Stone were among the legal heroes of this transition period. But it should be noted that this was a reversal and that it shows how possible, even probable, reversals are.

Equally important were interpretations of the *equal protection* clause in the same Fourteenth Amendment. This again was intended to protect newly freed Negroes, but was for decades mostly used to prevent regulation of business.[8] But every phrase in section 1 was found of use to the conservative cause.

The slaughterhouse cases were indeterminate.[9] Justice Miller, for the majority, wrote that the law under attack, granting a butcher's monopoly objected to by others in the same occupation, could not be held to be a

---

7. In *Santa Clara County* v. *Southern Pacific Railroad Co.,* 118 U.S. 394 (1886). Cf. C. Herman Pritchett, *The American Constitution,* 2d ed., rev. (New York: McGraw-Hill, 1968), pp. 668 ff.

8. The clauses referred to here, it will be recalled, occur in section 1 of the amendment: "All persons born or naturalized in the United States, and subject to the jurisdiction thereof, are citizens of the United States and of the State wherein they reside. No State shall make or enforce any law which shall abridge the privileges or immunities of citizens of the United States; nor shall any State deprive any person of life, liberty, or property, without due process of law; nor deny to any person within its jurisdiction the equal protection of the laws."

9. 16 Wall. 36 (1873).

deprivation of property; a little later, however, an opinion allowing the regulation of grain warehouses was regarded as a victory for those who felt the control of business to be necessary.[10] It did not turn out to be the precedent advocates of regulation had hoped for, although exceptions were allowed for those affecting health and hours of work. Even in 1898 a statute in Utah fixing hours of work in mines and smelters was upheld on the ground that these were dangerous occupations.[11] And the first of Louis D. Brandeis's famous sociological briefs, so devastating to propertied interests, was accepted in 1908.[12] But these regulations, implementing the acknowledged power of government to intervene when health was to be protected, were not extended to economic matters.

It could be anticipated that there might be regulations to prevent the conduct of business in the old careless ways: that is, employing child labor, exploiting women in sweatshops, and forcing workers to accept excessive hours and indecent working conditions. But these matters were not so important to the concentrated economic interests as some others. The antitrust laws, so vigorously supported by the progressives of that time, threatened their very life. The first of these acts was passed in the 1880s in response to farmers' complaints about the monopolies with whom they had to deal, but they were strengthened again by the Clayton Act during the Wilson administration. Wilson was under the Brandeis influence, not himself being much learned in economic affairs, and the simplistic Brandeis dogma that bigness was badness was swallowed whole; it filled a gap in the president's policy. A crusade against big business appeared to be impending.

An antitrust division in the Department of Justice became more vigorous, and the trusts—excoriated by Theodore Roosevelt in the early 1900s —feared that now, some years later, they might find themselves forced to fractionalize. They staved off the threat, but in later administrations there were flare-ups of similar activity. Some concerns did have their expansion plans limited, and a few did have to divide themselves into smaller components. If, however, the intention was to ensure the effectiveness of competition the policy was a failure; and if it was to reduce the scale of enterprise, it was an even worse failure. Of the hundred or so automobile companies once started, by 1970 the number had been reducted to four, and of these two controlled 90 percent of the business. Much the same was true of the steel, aluminum, oil, electric, sugar, and meat-packing businesses. Corporations simply grew bigger as the nation grew bigger. So natural a development could not be regarded as malevolent even by doctrinaire Progressives.

It is hard to explain how a people as realistic and practical as the

10. *Munn* v. *Illinois,* 94 U.S. 113 (1877).
11. *Holden* v. *Hardy,* 169 U.S. 366 (1898).
12. *Muller* v. *Oregon,* 208 U.S. 412 (1908).

Americans are supposed to be could have allowed their government to persist in an endeavor as costly and unsuccessful as the breaking up of enterprise. Perhaps it was because the people are not so practical as is supposed. Having adopted the theory, they certainly refused to accept its refutation by facts. But there is, of course, an explanation. The policy was a necessary concomitant of free enterprise. By pursuing it the fiction could be maintained that competition still ruled the market. The alternative could not be faced. No monopoly, President Wilson had said, should be private. That sentence, from one of his speeches, was reiterated a whole generation later by F. D. Roosevelt. But the opposite of private is public, and that way led to government ownership. Should that be the policy?

Americans clearly meant to keep a pluralistic economy, and this involved making existence tolerable for competitive enterprise. This became difficult; freedom to compete became less a reality. But recurrent fear of monopoly by a few gigantic corporations was repeatedly stifled by the publicity accompanying flurries of antitrust activity. Suits were brought; a few concerns were disciplined; the public indignation was quieted.

It could not really be denied, nevertheless, that fewer and fewer enterprises held enormous assets and exercised the control over the economy that their assets warranted. The antitrust activities became irrelevant as expansion went on. And there was less public fear about bigness as such.

What blunted this concern about an incontrovertible situation was a new attitude on the part of the gigantic conglomerations of the later twentieth century. They now bargained collectively with their workers. They became so cozy with them, in fact, that they seemed to be in a conspiracy of good fellowship. The civil war in industry retreated into the past. Then, too, the old populist opposition simply disappeared with the phasing out of the family farm. The production of food and fiber was now conducted by businesses, not perhaps so big, but still similar to those engaged in producing industrial products. "Wall Street" and "the money barons" had been locutions capable of arousing political passion for a century; they were no longer heard.

The humanizing of business was perhaps, again, more seeming than real, but its support by massive advertising gave it a realistic glow. Television had not been available to the sugar or steel trusts in the early 1900s. Latter-day giants appeared to the public as sponsors for entertaining hours during consumers' evenings at home. What they were doing to the economy was not at once apparent; but if it had not been for the massive welfare programs begun by F. D. Roosevelt and expanded by President Johnson, it would have been widely understood that private monopoly did indeed exist, that it could not be extirpated by attacks from without, and that it thrived and grew because of its efficiency in exploitation as well as in management.

It was as true as ever that no monopoly ought to be private, but it was now known that the alternative was not necessarily public ownership or management. There were other possibilities—not yet much exploited, but still available. There were several varieties of mixed ownership and mixed management. These seemed to offer ways to begin new enterprises and to ensure that old ones did not use their power to exploit their fellow businessmen or the public. It also offered a way to get public work done more expeditiously than was possible when done by governmental bureaucracies with legislative affiliations.

Permissiveness in the legal system by now ran not only to the most surprising welfare schemes but also to adventurous combinations of government and private enterprise. No one could say, as he would have been able to say in a former generation, what the services to be performed by government would be. An observer would have noted then that the power to spend connoted the power to spend for almost any welfare program. He also would have noted, however, that no organization in government produced any goods or services for sale. The postal service was the exception to this rule until the Tennessee Valley Authority (TVA) was authorized as part of the early New Deal; however, eventually the post office was set free of many governmental restrictions.

From the precedent of TVA, itself resting originally for its legality on the government's power to control navigable streams, other schemes evolved. If power could be produced and sold, so might communication facilities such as the amazing satellites set in fixed orbits; and so Comsat was invented, a mixture of public and private ownership and management; and presently there was Amtrak, obviously the forerunner of other such enterprises.

It is more than likely, it is inevitable, that government in its modern phases will have the responsibility, of one or another kind, for organizations not before known. The Tennessee Valley Authority was not related to any department; it was responsible to the Congress. Aside from appointing its directors, the president had minimum power over it. True, F. D. Roosevelt did remove its first chairman because of "contumacy"; but nothing of the sort occurred afterward, even though President Eisenhower considered it to be a warning example of "creeping socialism" and appointed directors presumably hostile to public management.

A place evidently must be made for these new kinds of organizations. The present habit of consigning them to a mostly mythical executive office, or leaving them without any organizational affiliation at all, will not do. They must be brought into the scheme of government; their financing must not simply be left to their own contacts with private sources of funds; and if they affect or contribute to the national supply of power, of communication facilities, or even of raw materials, they must be related to other enterprises through a common policy.

For what must be done there is, however, no constitutional warrant. It can be had only by amendment. Court permissiveness is capricious even if it proceeds from elaborate rationalizations. The administrators must find a firmer footing. It is necessary that regulation be recognized as a constitutional necessity in a pluralistic economy. It clearly belongs to none of the traditional branches and should perhaps become a branch in itself. The governmental or semigovernmental enterprises are a way of getting things done, of providing services, not of regulating those who do them, and are therefore distinguished from the regulatory agencies whose mission is to establish good behavior among private enterprises—a quite different activity.

Affected with a Public Interest

It is sometimes said that the cost of regulation is the price paid for devotion to free enterprise, but this is paradoxical. Enterprise is certainly less free by the extent of regulation. The more regulation the higher the cost and, it would be thought, the more question whether the remaining freedom is worth the price to those regulated, as well as to those doing the regulating. This is a calculation Americans generally refuse to make, and there have been remarkably few alternative offerings—or even suggestions that alternatives are possible.

Free enterprise has seemed a permanent mythology, always assumed to be actual but never existing in reality.

It will be recalled that Eugene V. Debs was the candidate of a sizable party and a perennial presidential candidate, and that he was succeeded by Norman Thomas, who went on for many more years. Both offered "Socialist" alternatives to the business system. Neither persuaded many voters, and the number dwindled until support vanished altogether. What was offered was an import from other places and other times. It never took root in American soil. It was never really considered as the alternative to "capitalism."

Among the early Progressive, Populist, and Farmer-Labor movements, public ownership of the larger enterprises—and certainly public utilities— was a prominent demand, a policy verging on socialism but never admitting any relationship. A few local offices, and, in Minnesota and Wisconsin, governorships, were won by parties committed to public ownership. None, however, survived more than a few campaigns; and later Progressives dropped demands for the socialization of industry. On the contrary, they demanded more competition rather than less. They wanted the bigger enterprises either cut down in size by antitrust laws or rigorously regulated to give smaller competitors a chance. They were the parties of farmers and businessmen, not Socialists; the parties of small farmers and small business-men, not big ones.

There was some talk, occasionally, about the protection of consumers, especially those who used the services furnished by public utilities—transportation, communications, and power—but mostly these consumers turned out to be other businesses; and consumers never seemed to draw much political attention. The concern was that small competitors should not be ill-treated by large ones. Bigness in the view of Justice Brandeis's followers, for instance, was a code word for evil; and Brandeis dominated the policy thinking not only of organized Progressives but of the Democratic party from the time of Wilson (when the Clayton Act was passed and the Federal Reserve system established its twelve regional banks to break the Wall Street monopoly), through the regime of F. D. Roosevelt, and into that of Johnson, who was identifiably descended from the Populists of his home state.[13]

When regulation as a public policy is discussed, therefore, it is not to be understood as intended to protect individual consumers, although this is one of its defenders' minor professions; it mostly describes the prevention of monopoly and the outlawing of practices calculated to give large businesses advantages, real or potential, over smaller ones. It envisages an economy of many competing enterprises in every category of industry, including the facilitating ones of finance, insurance, and marketplaces, all policed, of course, by government to keep them within the boundaries prescribed by believers in competition.

But, more than this, it has represented a determination to avoid government ownership or operation of any enterprise, even those likely to be much more effectively conducted on a large scale than a small one. Nowhere else has there been an effort so concerted to keep government out of active economic operations. In other nations, utilities were normally considered to be of such a nature—"natural monopolies"—that public ownership and operation was a matter of course. It seems strange to visitors from other countries that telephones, power services, and railways should have their securities traded on the exchanges and should develop immense but private bureaucracies. It seems even stranger when they discover that there is a matching bureaucracy within government to protect small competitors' interests—and sometimes, but secondarily, the interest of citizens in the quality of service and the rates or prices to be charged.

The implementing of this policy had its origins far back in the economic and legal systems inherited from Britain. Centuries ago the regulation of common callings began in a small way. The category easily contained transportation and innkeeping; it was extended to other employments reasonably to be described as "affected with a public interest." This last

13. His father had been a Populist member of the Texas legislature, a supporter of the Fergusons. Cf. Eric Goldman, *The Tragedy of Lyndon Johnson* (New York: Alfred A. Knopf, 1969), pp. 44 ff.

phrase was carried over into American law when protection against monopolistic practices became important.[14]

Actually, as interpreted by American courts, the regulatory powers were more easily invoked under another rule—that of preventing or maintaining competition. The theory was that if businesses competed without large advantages—artificial, conspiratorial, or other—the interests of the public would be protected. Besides, this would make for a prosperous business society concurrent and consistent with family farms protected or subsidized with the same result in view. The incentive of profits to be made would stimulate initiative and would result in the best possible service to consumers; inefficient ones would not prosper; efficient ones would. But there was specific reliance on numbers. There had to be many businesses if a struggle for survival was to be operative—to reward the efficient and punish the inefficient. These, of course, were the principles of the dominant American economic theory—again, inherited from the British. Freedom of enterprise came as near to being universally accepted as any public policy in American history. It attached itself to democracy, and the two became inseparable in most people's minds.

These allied theories were generally agreed to be basic; however, they were only theories, often not translated into behavior. There was advantage for some in ignoring them, while others accepted their guidance. In a free situation it became apparent that the cleverest in evasion would prosper most. Competition did not protect either competitors or consumers unless it remained an inexorable condition. An enterpriser who gained an advantage of one or another sort prospered, expanded, and took business away from competitors. The advantage might be simply that of being a better manager, but it might also be one of having access to resources, of forcing preferential treatment from suppliers or from service industries (lower prices for large purchases, lower rates from railroads, and so on), or even of "cutthroat" treatment for competitors (temporary reduction of prices or rates to force them into bankruptcy, whereupon the offending larger enterprise recouped the costs of this campaign from consumers no longer protected by competition). Thus free competition tended to be its own destroyer.

American businesses and their lawyers proved to be extremely fertile in the invention of processes and devices to subvert the actual freedom presumed by the theory and enforced by public regulation. That freedom for some could be used to choke freedom for others was something not contemplated in the simplistic economics of the Progressives. It was this

14. In *Munn* v. *Illinois,* 94 U.S. 113 (1877), warehouses for the storage of grain were determined to be thus affected with a public interest, showing this to be an extensible category; but conservative courts stopped short of what might have been a long list of regulated enterprises. For instance, food processing and distribution were not to be regulated except as might be necessary for the protection of health.

anomaly that forced a decision in the confused and long-drawn-out political battles of the century following the Civil War when there was such a sudden and massive expansion of industry. The solution might have been the abandonment of a competition that inevitably resulted in the falling off of weak competitors; socialism or, at least, the part of it calling for the public ownership of those industries affected with a public interest might have been adopted. But this was not what happened. The determination, when worked out in hundreds of local campaigns, was to accept the promises of business. These offered not only the protection of consumers (including business users), but the open opportunity to join their ranks. Competition would see to it that if one seller did not offer a fair deal another would, and, to make all safe, anyone could start an enterprise and enter the competition. If he served well he would prosper. If he did not, he would suffer.

This policy appealed mightily to a nation of farmers and small businessmen, most of whom hoped to prosper and to grow larger. And it was agreed that those who did not abide by the rule that there should be no unfair advantage could and should be forced to conform. There were, after all, not many offenders; and they were highly visible. They could be "regulated."

The framers of the early antitrust acts approached the problem by the easiest method; they would break up the big enterprises and thus restore equal competition. But even then there was recognized to be a special class of "natural monopolies" whose breaking up would be inexpedient. But their behavior would have to be controlled. Thus there began a double effort to protect small businesses and consumers. Either the larger enterprises would be dissolved into smaller constituents or they would have to come under regulatory supervision. In any case the protection afforded by theoretical free competition would be attained.

The effort to break up the "trusts" was energetic at times but frequently —mostly during Republican regimes—was only nominal. If its effectiveness was measured by the continued expansion of big business, it was a failure. Critics pointed out that there was something lacking in the successive antitrust acts or else that prosecutions under them were strangely weak. Both criticisms were true, for both political and economic reasons. The businesses subject to prosecution were those that reduced competition by conspiracy, or those that combined to form a monopoly. Neither of these offenses could be proved easily, and prosecutions were seldom successful. They were long, complicated, and expensive. They required armies of lawyers. But the defendants had armies of lawyers too, more prestigious ones than the government could deploy, and their success in saving their clients from penalties was phenomenal.

Critics who judged the policy to be failing seemed to have remarkably weak voices. At least they did not prevail. Government went on its expensively futile way while businesses burgeoned. Finally, when the merger (or takeover) movement became a significant one, horizontal was added to vertical development; it seemed likely that the number of independent businesses would become minimal. If four hundred corporations dominated the economy in 1970, it would perhaps be two hundred in 1980, and these would be struggling among themselves for the control of further consolidations.

It must be said that statistics did not seem to support the generalizations of those who feared this was happening. The number of those entering business—and so competition—continued to grow, and the number of failures did not increase. The effect on the economy of the merger movement might be exaggerated. Yet it was certainly true that the larger enterprises did grow enormously larger still, and the growth was not altogether mere expansion; they continued to take over smaller enterprises, and if they did not abolish competion, they changed its nature.

The situation could already be described as something like *private socialism*. It was not government ownership, but it was public in the sense that shares were on the open market and could be bought by anyone. It was arrived at by devices allowable in spite of all the complicated rules. It must be set down as futile to hope that antitrust devices would check the extension of one management over larger and larger areas of business.[15]

There remained the protection of consumers by the regulatory agencies. If the breaking up of competition-choking combines did not create an array of small businesses actively in conflict, regulation might force them to behave with defined decency and fairness. The operative words in the regulatory formula were indeed *decency* and *fairness*. They were subject to interpretation, and any synonyms for them were as unclear as they themselves. What sellers consider adequate in these respects, buyers may very likely regard as swindles. The seller may, of course, resort to massive advertising expenditures to carry his point, but the buyer may not be cajoled, and sellers of services regulated by the central government have found supplementary supports necessary. Whenever possible, favorably inclined members have been maneuvered into positions on regulating commissions. This has seemed remarkably easy to do, although sometimes expensive. Campaign contributions placed where they will be most effective and lobbyists deployed to take advantage of politicians' gratitude have become a customary business activity. And a surprising array of favors can be exchanged between lobbyists and politicians.

This is more than condoned; it tends to be recognized. One of John-

15. The "conglomerates" are described and defended by Neil Jacoby in the *Center Magazine,* II, 4 (July, 1969). This defense is not questioned here; it may be pointed out, however, that their enlargement represents one more in a long list of failures to prevent the increase of size and the suppression of competition as an automatic protection of competitors and consumers.

son's first actions as president was to tell the heads of agencies that he expected them to help, not hinder, the businesses they regulated. Populists may be radical in one sense, but not in harassing business. Nixon, as president, made no such commitment; but his appointments spoke for him.

Bargains between businesses and governmental officials are, of course, secret; but the way politicians behave is evidence of alliance to anyone with even primitive information and a minimum of intelligence. It would seem elementary in the theory of regulation that such agreements ought to be suppressed. The difficulty is that this is quite impossible without altering many institutions, and the institutions that would have to be changed are regarded as untouchable. They are, indeed, freely identified as coterminous with liberty, individualism, freedom of enterprise—the whole list of traditional rights. That this is a mistaken view is as obvious as that the antitrust acts have failed, but the hackles of libertarians rise at the least suggestion of such reforms as would be required.

The truth is that regulation will never be effective unless legislators are chosen differently and their representative role is reconsidered, and this can be made possible only by some drastic revisions of governmental structure. At the least it will be necessary to provide for an expanded dialogue among voters so that choices may be made by others than political professionals.

The effect of such a change should be a more considered selection of policies and candidates, more concentration on public and less on private interests, and a long-delayed cleansing of the legislative apparatus. There will have to be reconsideration as well of the other governmental organs, and for the same purpose—to require of those who hold themselves out as public servants that they shall serve the public, not themselves or those they favor.

One Regulatory Device

It is assumed, as a fairly settled matter, that much economic enterprise will remain private or at least semiprivate. Even though elephantine private bureaucracies have all the undesirable characteristics so often attributed to governmental ones, they have other attractions which seem to outweigh their faults. If this is so it will be necessary to maintain for these businesses regulation of two sorts: the maintenance of fairness in interbusiness bargaining and the securing for consumers of decent goods and services at defensible prices or rates.

These require different approaches. It seems quite possible that the first—an interbusiness balance—might be gained by a series of such devices as were authorized in the National Recovery Act of 1934. These measures were so bungled in administration, and proved so offensive to Brandeis-minded Progressives, that they were abandoned when the Supreme Court found an excuse to overthrow the law. Nevertheless, the device will again be suggested as an alternative to suppression that manifestly does not work. First, however, it may be well to examine the National Recovery Act (NRA) experience to see whether its failure actually proves that cooperating authorities are undesirable.

The NRA originated among businessmen. A few leaders were rational enough to realize that they were not practicing what they preached. They professed to compete, but in practice they were always trying to avoid or suppress competition. Actually, they were aware that competitors did not exist as they were described in the books and that, to the extent that they did, they were the cause of waste and injustice—increasing costs and creating risks and uncertainties.

To escape from unwelcome pressures, and to reach agreed standards, businesses had for some time been feeling their way toward common codes of conduct intended to limit or stop such cost-cutting practices as child labor, adulteration, and false claims. In many industries fair practices had begun to be defined and information to be exchanged; many forms of cooperation were worked out, avoiding, of course—at least ostensibly—the allocation of markets and the fixing of prices. These had for a long time been illegal under the antitrust acts, and when they were resorted to it was in secrecy.

Herbert Hoover, as secretary of commerce, had begun in the early twenties to encourage the making of codes or agreements for fair practice. The organizing of trade associations for this purpose was carried out with government encouragement, and many were in existence before his presidency ended. It is interesting in this connection that F. D. Roosevelt, as a young practicing lawyer, had been involved in one of these associations. He had been engaged to organize a construction council, and had had some correspondence with Hoover about it. He was apparently not very clear about the purposes of the council or the limits of its operation, but the experience must at least have made him more friendly to the legitimization of trade associations when he became president in 1933.

It was suggested to him that the business disarray of the depression might well be tackled while the crisis was at its worst. Then, if ever, was a time for breaking out of old traditions and for trying new ventures. He did consent to the drafting of an act based on concentration, cooperation, and certain strategic controls to replace the simple suppression of attempts to cooperate.[16]

Those who collaborated in drafting the original NRA statute were rep-

16. Such a policy had been foreshadowed in an address made before his nomination. In what is known as "the Oglethorpe speech" (because it was made at that university in Atlanta) he said that bold experiment had become necessary because old policies had failed. And he spoke hopefully of planning and the establishment of new standards.

resentatives of business, such as General Hugh Johnson, who spoke for Bernard Baruch and others in New York, and economists who had hoped at last to begin the search for order to replace the chaos of competition. But at a certain stage others began to show interest. Frances Perkins, secretary of labor, saw in codes of fair practice the possibility of agreements that would prohibit child labor and would improve hours and conditions of work generally. John L. Lewis and other labor leaders saw in it a way to legitimize the collective bargaining they had been fighting for for so long. Representatives of consumers, hoping for better standards of quality and an end to false claims, saw the codes of fair practice as a more effective means of stopping the exploitation of consumers.

The act was much amended before passage. It was looked at with suspicion by orthodox Progressives who still believed in enforcing competition and had no faith in the ethical intentions of businessmen, organized or not. They were correct in complaining that the enforcement provisions were weak, and that chiselers would therefore not be stopped; the unscrupulous, they said, would take advantage of others' compliance with the codes. The act, as first drafted, had been vigorous; but the less scrupulous businessmen had been busy with congressional friends; and escape from discipline had been made all too easy. Another weakness, owed again to amendment, was that the implementation of "senior partnership for government," relied on by the original drafters, would not really have to be accepted in practice. Public members of code authorities were not left firmly in control, and businesses would be able to continue many of their old practices. The public interest was pretty well lost among the special claims, honored by the legislators, of business and labor. Altogether, the whole result was viewed with skepticism and agreed to with reluctance.

This opposition was so much an extension of an original dogmatic belief in the wickedness of big business that it had less force than it might otherwise have had. Justice Brandeis was shocked by the proposal and doubly shocked that Roosevelt should have sponsored it; he had supposed the new president to be an orthodox Progressive. Brandeis was now a justice of the Supreme Court and could not openly oppose, but the many new lawyers now coming to Washington—recruited by his disciples— were regularly entertained at his home and regularly lectured to. He felt that he ought to have been consulted. Wilson's New Freedom had relied on Brandeis's favorite aphorism, often heard by those who sat at his feet, that enterprises grown large must be bad. It was inevitable, he said, because bigness meant power and power would always be used, and when used, it must reduce the freedom of competitors.

It was sometimes pointed out to Brandeis that this was not the legal basis of the antitrust acts, which said nothing about bigness but relied on restraints of trade reached by collaboration. It was clear enough that such acts had not in fact prevented the development of larger and larger enterprises, and these had not necessarily conspired to suppress competitors. They may have had some initial advantages, may have been more efficient, or, for some similar reason, may have captured the market they held. Their bigness, however, was more often growth than the result of conspiracy or even of combining. Their competitors may have failed, but it was because of inability to attain comparable efficiency. There was no way to prevent growth except by saying outright that bigness was bad and outlawing it. This, even Brandeis, although he expounded such a view often enough, had not proposed as a statutory principle. The unrealities were obvious.

The fact was, as business leaders knew, that competition could not really be created. Competitors could not be furnished with equal initiative and competence. The most that could be done was to prevent the absorption of the small by the large, but often the small failed anyway and so could no longer compete. True, others were always beginning, but also the bigger businesses were always growing. Their proportion of the economy tended to increase as if by some natural law.

The issue had got to be an involved and indeterminate argument, going on and on in interested circles. As a young man F. D. Roosevelt had been an interested watcher as his predecessor, Theodore Roosevelt, had castigated the "malefactors of great wealth" in an earlier generation; but he had not missed the point that it was mostly talk and very little action. It was apparent from the first months of F. D. Roosevelt's presidency that his policy would distinguish, or try to, between goodness and badness in business practice, for he had promised during his campaign to do something about it. This came out strongly in his inaugural as he spoke of "money changers in the temple." The money changers, it was obvious, were the same malefactors the earlier Roosevelt had spoken of. There was no suggestion of abandoning the temple of commerce, but it had to be cleansed and made safe for those who would not defile it.

The behavior of financiers and of big business, generally, during the depression had lowered their prestige, a performance that gave Roosevelt the leverage he needed for a renewed attack.

If there were bad businessmen, there were also good ones or at least ones who would like to be good; and those who had conceived and argued for concentration and integration as a way of giving power to the well-intentioned had found him willing to listen. Since he saw readily enough that the integration had gone on in spite of antitrust laws and that mutual controls were a possible alternative to suppression, he would try to punish some and give others the means of governing themselves by more acceptable rules.

Industrialists dealt with each other; that is to say, steel manufacturers needed coal, textile manufacturers needed machinery, both needed communication and transportation facilities, and so on. There was a complex network of such relationships that might be organized to escape compulsions of the market. Codes of fair conduct might be imposed by decent competitors on those who were not so scrupulous. This was the possibility offered by the National Recovery Act.

In the trade agreements sponsored previously by the Commerce Department, there had been devices for requiring conformance from those who were unwilling to cooperate. They were to be persuaded not by public prosecution but by their fellow businessmen. The scheme had never really been legitimized, however, and this was what it was proposed to do now. A network of industrial boards, another of interindustry committees, having agreements concerning conduct, might achieve the advantages of large-scale industry without the exploitation that resulted from monopoly or near-monopoly. It would give the more ethical businessmen the support they needed to discipline their unscrupulous competitors. And it was part of the scheme that the committees should have a majority of public representatives.

The act was passed in the spring of 1933, seriously mutilated, but found acceptable by Roosevelt, who was sufficiently optimistic to hope that a way might have been found to reform the business system without systematic outside discipline. Within a year, however, NRA was an obvious failure. Even before the Court outlawed it the attempt at self-government had broken down.

Because this was the first and only alternative industrial policy with an operative device to substitute for suppression, it is worth asking why it failed. What succeeded was what had existed before—concentration without control; why was it that a way to control could not be found?

The reasons for NRA's abandonment were afterward popularly supposed to have been administrative. But it should be recalled that amendments to the original draft were numerous and crippling. Government representation on code authorities, depended on to support standards of conduct, was weakened by lobbyists' intervention; and other changes, such as lack of provision for planning mechanisms and for pooled investments to strengthen desirable enterprise, were either omitted or seriously fragmented. Others had strengthened private or group interests rather than those of the public. It was, in the end, not at all what the proponents of cooperation had hoped for. Then, too, the nature of the codes and their purpose had begun to change as the legislation advanced. From a device having as its intention integration and control, it was loaded heavily with directives having to do with reform. For instance, collective bargaining and the welfare of workers became prominent objectives, and these came to seem the main purpose of the legislation. These, it could be seen afterward, ought to have had separate legislation. The controversies they aroused obscured the original purpose of rationalizing the industrial system.

Before long the struggle over tangentials did usurp most of the effort and attention. Because of this, businessmen who had hoped to modify the acerbic relationships of the past felt that they had been unfairly treated. They began to bargain, and as the trading went on, codes that should have established fair competitive practices and eliminated the wastes of competition began to have price-fixing and market-limiting provisions, allowed by the administrator and the president as frank exchanges for collective bargaining, the abolition of child labor, and certain other welfare provisions. These had been the center of fierce struggles for many years; but the priceless exemption from antitrust restrictions, for many years an objective of big businessmen, was considered by them to be worth the price. They yielded reforms to gain freedom from governmental hostility; but the system of interindustry relationships was so weakened as to become farcical.

The codes were not supposed to allow price-fixing, and in the original conception they had no need to. Businessmen dealing fairly with each other in defined and supervised ways would still be competing. The most efficient would have the advantage of lower costs and might be expected to pass them on to consumers—whether the consumers were other businesses or ultimate individual ones. But the competition would go on within decent self-imposed limits. It would "fare."

To fix prices meant to prevent efficiency from having the effect it should have had. It was a protection for wasteful management. The more efficient would get in profits what should have gone to consumers; and these profits would be used as the directors of the concern might decide, not as the public interest would require.

When those who had wanted the NRA as a recognition of the potentialities in systematized competition saw what was occurring, they were aghast. But every effort they made to check the erosion failed. The National Recovery Adiminstration had been set up properly enough, with the usual governing board. On it were the heads of old departments—Labor, Interior, Agriculture, Justice, the Federal Trade Commission—and the secretary of commerce was chairman. An administrator was appointed by the president, but he was responsible to the board. Since the administrator was General Hugh Johnson, however, and since he was given ready access to the president, he first tolerated the board and then refused to report to it at all. When the board reviewed the industry codes worked out in the conferences he supervised, some of its members objected to provisions they felt ought not to be allowed, or suggested that safeguards ought to be added. The general refused to accept any suggested changes and appealed to the president. Roosevelt chose to uphold him. The board then simply stopped meeting and the general proceeded on his own, reporting only to the president.

A fairly desperate feeling began to develop inside the administration even before the NRA's operations had got well under way. There had been a certain euphoria abroad in the land just after Roosevelt's stirring inaugural, but that the new cheerfulness had no substantial basis insiders knew all too well. Unemployment had not been much relieved, and a desperate winter had to be faced. Roosevelt was in a mood to try anything that offered quick returns. Knowing this, Johnson urged a campaign, directed by himself, to have all enterprisers resume activity simultaneously. He called it a "reemployment agreement." He argued that since businesses bought from one another, and since their employees ultimately consumed the entire production, they might all start up at once and exchange their goods and services. If they did this, the economic paralysis would end and an upward movement would begin. The scheme had at least a simplistic attractiveness.

It is almost impossible for a later generation to relive with those who recall it the reemployment campaign of that summer and fall. An emblem was adopted—the Blue Eagle—to be awarded to those who cooperated. And those who did not earn an Eagle for display were to be labeled, most unpleasantly, as unpatriotic.

One result was that General Johnson pretty well abandoned any serious work on the industry codes—although he remained the NRA administrator. He campaigned up and down the land for the Blue Eagle scheme. He was an effective propagandist, specializing in epithets and vivid castigations. Before long he had the president making speeches too. The land resounded with hullabaloo.[17]

It all came to nothing, of course. Many enterprisers tried to comply; but when they called their workers back they could meet payrolls only if they could sell, and they could sell only if their customers could buy —and there were not enough of these. The commercial banks were still loaded with frozen loans and could advance only limited credits. Individuals who were deep in debt were obligated to pay them before they bought many goods. Payrolls did not really expand much, and the exchange of goods was not much increased. The initial booming start soon damped down to a dismal end.

By late fall, after only a few months of life, the symbolic Blue Eagle was dead. So was General Johnson in his public role. He had shouted himself into a frenzy and had perilously approached the ridiculous. Roose-

17. General Johnson made his defense of all this later on in a book called *The Blue Eagle from Egg to Earth* (Garden City, N.Y.: Doubleday & Company, 1935).

velt, in spite of the country's continued loyalty, was in danger of sharing the ridicule.

It was time for another resort—devaluation. Roosevelt tried raising prices by setting up a gold-buying device. The price the government would pay from day to day was fixed, and this was expected to affect directly the level of prices. He was now convinced that a rise to former levels—those at which most of the loans had been advanced—was necessary in order to decrease the vast burden of debt. Besides, he was being pressed, as he had been from the first by the many inflationists who believed that easy money was a sovereign remedy for depression.

The end of daily price fixing for gold was, however, not long delayed. Within a short time the Congress was asked to fix the relation of gold to the dollar. Manipulation had not worked as had been hoped. But the experiment had been tried, and the country generally was generous. It gave Roosevelt credit for trying.

During these months of diversion NRA codes were being processed in slovenly fashion and were being agreed to by the president without much study. They were more and more the product of old hands in the trade-association movement who knew what they wanted for their industries. This meant that they came closer and closer to price fixing and were less and less likely to have stabilizing provisions leading to integration. Also, provisions for supervision became weaker and weaker. It was obvious that the more powerful industrialists were writing them to suit their own requirements and not those of industry as a whole.

A good while before the Supreme Court found the NRA unconstitutional, Roosevelt found it an embarrassment. It had been discredited because flamboyant sideshows—John L. Lewis's furious struggle to legitimize collective bargaining, Frances Perkins's insistence on reformed working conditions, the blowing up and then the deflating of the Reemployment Agreements—distracted attention from the main business of code-making, and many unwise provisions crept into the codes against the objections of the Recovery Board before it was disbanded.

When the Court finally handed down its decree in the Schecter case,[18] Roosevelt professed an anger he could not really justify. The mistakes had been allowed to happen in emergent circumstances, and some were explainable. However, the presentation of the measure as a recovery act (rather than the stabilizing device it really was) in order to secure its acceptance and then the furious but futile attempt to use it as a stimulator were calculated to annoy even those who had sponsored it. These, added

18. *Schecter Poultry Corp.* v. *United States,* 295 U.S. 495 (1935). The NRA lawyers saw too late that they should have avoided this action, since it represented an attempt to enforce regulations in even the smallest businesses. It was called, even while being argued, "the sick chicken case."

to the reform features so surprising to the supporters of the stabilization idea, built up a formidable opposition.

Roosevelt did not try again, as he was to do with the Agricultural Adjustment Act when it, too, was struck down. That agency, overthrown by an incensed Court for another extraneous reason, was reworked and presented in a much-improved form. So NRA might have been. The welfare and labor standards could have been made the subject of separate legislation (as they later were in the Wagner Act), and the codes could have been reworked to rules that would have avoided any undue delegation of congressional powers.

But Roosevelt by this time was under new influences or, it might be said, in a new phase, usually called by historians the Second New Deal. He was no longer willing, or perhaps not able politically, to withstand the demands of those who were saying he should now return to the tradition of progressivism and to enforced competition as an economic policy.

So the opportunity was lost to accept the challenge of large management and learn how to use it in the inevitable rationalization of the economy. That still remained to be done. Any future revision of the Constitution, if it was expected to maintain a pluralistic society with privately operated businesses, would have to deal with the problems of management's behavior.

Self-regulation

This history of NRA has been outlined to substantiate the contention that the original Recovery Act was misnamed, was muddled in the beginning, was invaded by extraneous activities, and was discredited because it was confused with failures irrelevant to its purpose. But there was more than that. The doctrinaire "little business" types—who were identified with Brandeis—were infuriated by the attempt, delighted to see the discrediting, and overjoyed to be involved in its abandonment. And their disappoval always made Roosevelt uneasy. Throughout his political life he had considered himself a representative of progressivism, and of its commitment to small-scale enterprise, actively competing and protected by government from monopolists. He had a sense that this was an anachronistic policy, but evidently it was still alive in many minds, and he was reluctant to involve himself in the opposition of so many supporters.

By the subterranean communications system of those days Justice Brandeis sent word to the president that another NRA would be struck down if an attempt was made to revive it in any form. Roosevelt had rebelled briefly when the Schecter decision had come down; in an interview he had complained that the Court still lived in horse-and-buggy days. Modern business, he had said, required modern governmental controls. But he soon fell silent; he did not try again. He rested for the moment on gains in welfare and in collective bargaining. Moreover, the economy was reviving with exasperating slowness, and only because of government spending for relief with funds it did not possess. Renewed activity began to appear first in the farm states where the Agricultural Adjustment Administration was succeeding as NRA was failing. Farmers with larger incomes could resume buying factory goods. But real recovery had yet to be achieved. There were still, two years later, more than 10 million, probably 12 million, unemployed, a percentage of the labor force that would have been intolerable if it had not been at least a slight improvement over 1933.

Roosevelt's open reproof to Brandeis must have been a shock to the now venerable justice who had so long presided unchallenged over the Progressive cadres. But there was more to come. In 1936 Roosevelt had an unprecedentedly large vote for reelection, the highest percentage of the popular vote of any past president asking for a second term. This put him in a position, as he thought, to strike back at those who were keeping him chained to a theory he no longer believed in. He proposed early in 1937 to pack the Court as Lincoln had done when it had refused to approve his policies. In a message asking for legislation he insinuated that members over seventy were too old to understand the contemporary world, and among these members, of course, was Brandeis himself.[19]

Roosevelt obviously meant to have a Court amenable to industrial integration under government auspices. He had done a lot of thinking since the excursion into the never-never land of miracle-working reemployment agreements. Social Security had been accepted; and with a certain returning life in the economy, and with tremendous electoral backing, he would presently begin anew what had been abandoned. The Court must not be allowed to stand in the way.

Meanwhile rather vigorous antitrust attacks were resumed, as if to say to the businessmen who had refused support for NRA when he had expected it that they would see how they liked really enforced competition. They naturally disliked it very much and complained about its injustices. Perhaps Roosevelt thought they would agree to a new effort when the Court could be trusted to approve.

One trouble was that these businessmen, who ought to have been supporters in a renewed effort, had by now taken a determined anti-New

19. It will be recalled that the Constitution left the Court amazingly at the mercy of the Congress, both as to its makeup and as to its jurisdiction. Nothing was said about number of members; and about jurisdiction it was said (in Article III) that the Court, except in certain cases affecting foreign service officers and the states, should *have appellate jurisdiction, both as to law and to fact, with such exceptions and under such regulations as the Congress shall make.* The italicized passage has infuriated many a justice, but actually it has been used sparingly.

Deal stand. They especially opposed collective bargaining and immense expenditures for relief, as well as the subsidies for farmers. They could not bring themselves to approve anything Roosevelt proposed even when self-interest told them they should. They had been lavish supporters of an ultraconservative Liberty League during the last campaign and were depressed by the rebuff they had suffered. They had "taken a walk" in Al Smith's phrase, and were quite unable to find their way back. They were willing to accept their lawyers' views that Roosevelt's Court reform was an outrageous and unprincipled attempt to undermine the one stable institution of their traditional world. Anti-New Dealism had become a matter of principle. They made an unnatural coalition with the Progressives to oppose a revival of NRA.

Roosevelt never won them back. He had also permanently lost the Progressives, who, one by one, had left him because his was not the traditional policy they approved. Southern politicians had defected for other reasons—they disapproved of relief efforts benefiting blacks—and as soon as their patronage needs were met, they joined the Republican opposition; but they were still in complete charge as committee chairmen of the party's congressional command post. In fact, Roosevelt now had no dependable support except that of the voters, and it could be brought to bear only in election years.

After the impressive victory of 1936, the Congress never yielded anything not massively supported by the public. Congressmen went along with appropriations for relief but clearly were not willing to approve any innovations. The last legislative act of the New Deal was the Wages and Hours Bill; and it was passed only because Roosevelt's new allies, labor and the city machines, who had been enemies in 1932, organized an effective lobby. But they would not be allies in any attempt to revive self-government for industry.

Presently he was preoccupied with the attaining of a military posture that corresponded with the nation's latent power and was needed to counter the totalitarian threat across both bordering oceans. Much of the old New Deal was traded to the conservatives for military appropriations. And the rising emergency made any thought of permanent domestic change unthinkable. Besides, Roosevelt, along with the nation, now made a new discovery. When the original $3 billion spent for recovery was now multiplied by four, then five and more, the depression disappeared. No other treatment had much affected it, but massive distribution of purchasing power was a complete cure. Presently any thought of change in business arrangements was lost in the rush of activity. Everything was all right.

It was true that the old industrial disorder soon returned, and there was serious inflation. Preparations for war allowed certain controls that should have taught the same lessons as those of the First World War, but no one learned them.

Roosevelt was gone when peace returned, and his successor had no interest in measures looking to industrial self-government. Anyway, Truman had enough troubles with the peace and with a rapidly developing cold war. If anything, he was even worse off vis-à-vis the Congress than Roosevelt had been in his last terms. It was unusual for one of his recommendations to be given even a hearing. And none of any account ever became law.

The following Eisenhower years were—well, years of conservative control. The businessmen Eisenhower consulted had none of the statesmanlike qualities of Gerard Swope, Henry T. Harriman, and those others who had risen above their self-interest during the depression and had offered Roosevelt the NRA. Recognized integration was never even spoken of. The venture of the thirties had died; and it was felt that the need no longer existed, that countervailing forces were sufficient for industrial discipline. The merger movement was regarded as a means for achieving coordination. Of course this also exempted big business from government control, and there was still inflation, but it was a time to let things alone. So business became bigger and more profitable even though lurking problems were still potentially dangerous.

How well off was the economy in respect to fairness of exchange, and so of stability, in the undirected use of surpluses produced by vast profits? How well off were the consumers of goods and services? Were there likely to be more depressions? The answers to these questions were not clear.

If there was no need for integration because it had organized or was organizing itself, the problem could be forgotten. But if the existing system was one conducted by a few hundred giants in their own interest, with somewhat more regard, maybe, for the support they must have from consumers, it was not good enough; and it held a threat for the future.

There is no doubt that some significant changes had occurred. It was now more than a generation since the NRA effort. Growth had not stopped because institutions were frozen; it merely made the institutions more and more obsolete. There were corporations now as large, almost, as all of them had been in the 1930s. They had grown by expansion, by absorbing other corporations, and by merger. Antitrust lawyers had tried to prevent the reduction of competition by this process, but it had been reduced in spite of all their efforts. Some of the best-known corporate entities of the thirties had been erased; some new hybrids had appeared with such names as the Universal General Corporation, Dynamics Unlimited, United Investors, and so on. Into these had gone the enterprises of yesteryear to become divisions of enormous conglomerates related only through a conception called diversification—the idea being that if inefficiency, substitution, or other mischances affected one, the others would support it.

Diversification may or may not be a good thing, but there is no policy about it. It is not reached by laws intended to support competition. Plastics and food products do not compete. Neither do chemicals and machinery.[20]

This proliferation under cover of a blanket name would not have occurred if there had been the code control contemplated under NRA, in which there was to be organization on an industry plan. Big businesses are still watched and sometimes checked if they reduce competition by combination or by absorption; but it is still true that if they simply grow, and if competitors simply die, nothing can be done. No one was prosecuted when Studebaker stopped automobile production, for instance, and similar occurrences happen very often. This does not reduce competition, necessarily; but it is moved to a different level not really reached by public policy.

Some of the regulation ensuring fairer competition at least has been attempted by vastly enlarged regulatory agencies. These agencies have indeed had an amazing growth. Like industries, several of them are as large as all were in the thirties. They have enormous powers too. In some cases they may set rates, in some they may make rules for the conduct of operations, and in some they are empowered to issue licenses for doing business. These are life-and-death controls, and naturally they are the object of vast political interest.

It is said that although in their early days such agencies are active and effective, they later become lethargic. It is even charged that some are more adjuncts of industries than regulators of them. Even President Johnson, who was thought to have Populist leanings, said repeatedly that the regulatory agencies ought to help and not hinder business. His appointments to their membership seemed to indicate that he meant them to be subservient.

They were presumably meant originally to be above politics. They are, of course, quite outside the constitutional system—that is to say, they are not executive, legislative, or judicial; or, rather, they are all three but not attached to any of the branches. They were invented to meet a need and have grown because the need has grown. But there are important functions they do not and cannot perform—those are the integrative ones. The establishment of interindustry relations is quite beyond their assignment in the governmental system. They rather prevent any such development.

It has been suggested that all such agencies be incorporated into one "fourth branch." The locution was Senator Dirksen's, and, coming from him, it probably was meant to be an expression of irritation, just as Presi-

---

20. More is said about this in Neil H. Jacoby's paper "Corporate Concentration, Conglomeration and Competition" (presented at the Center for the Study of Democratic Institutions, July 8, 1969). Mr. Jacoby defends the merger movement as making competition more effective. The theory of countervailing powers was elaborated in the author's book *The Industrial Discipline and Governmental Powers* (New York: Columbia University Press, 1934).

dent Johnson's directive was. The fact is that innocuous as the agencies have often been, and cautious as they have always been, politicians do feel the pressure of protest from the businesses affected. It can be guessed that the move to bring them under one head is meant to reduce their independence and make them more amenable to the powerful legislators to whom they make known the favors they would like to have and are willing to pay for.

Those who conceived NRA did not have the present vast industrial conglomerates to think of, or the present enlarged regulatory bodies. They had a simpler organization in mind and simpler regulatory devices to study. It is worth asking, however, if they were not right to suggest self-policing to the extent of its probable effectiveness, together with the guidance of public partners serving as members of the control authorities. It is worth considering that industries doing much of the needed regulating themselves would then have more stable relationships, would develop standards, and would even police them more equably than has been done in the past. As long as politicians have close relations with the regulators there cannot be equal treatment for all. Even single-minded regulators will think first of the welfare of their agency, and its future may be jeopardized by offending those who make appropriations.

It is simply not credible that the antitrust suppressions help to serve the ends industry must be expected to serve. Those ends, however enlarged they may be, remain the same as they always were. They exist to produce and to distribute—that is to say, they are chartered by public authority for that purpose. Their aim may be to make profits—more and more profits— but this is an aim not always consistent with those of society, especially if it involves a competition that induces unscrupulous practices. The NRA was meant to bring these aims into a framework, making business objectives more consistent with social ones and reducing the number of offenders. Neither the antitrust efforts nor the regulatory ones have such an end in view. The one is suppressive; the other makes rules for conduct. There is little or no thought of relationship between them, of establishing each as part of a larger scheme with the public interest in view. The code authorities might have done this by developing research, circulating information, estimating markets, and making rules for fairness. At another level they would have set up formal relations with suppliers and consumers.

The business system is still hardly a system at all; that is to say, it is not formally integrated. It can be called a system mostly because producers meet in a market. And as its larger members have grown more powerful in comparison with its smaller ones, certain connections and communications beyond those of the market have been established. Partly, these are through financial facilities, and partly they are through the ordinary communications media. What one does, they all tend to do. Management devices spread through the salesman-buyer relationship of consulting specialists, computer manufacturers, and even insurance and banker facilities. There is system to this extent. There is even an estimate of the future in government and university forecasts, and in those narrower ones of the corporate economists. But there is an inbuilt tendency for the least scrupulous to set the standards for all—they can make more profits that way.

This is a somewhat more orderly situation than existed in the 1930s, the one that resulted in the Great Depression. And it has been made more orderly by the elimination of certain abuses of earlier days. Collective bargaining functions more effectively in large-scale than in small-scale industry. And it has almost been forgotten what the civil war between labor and capital was like in the days before collective bargaining was legalized. Then, too, there is now the Social Security system. The economic effect of access to a minimum income for nearly everyone has been to make permanently impossible the nearly complete disappearance, at intervals, of purchasing power. There are still periods of lessened activity, but in the former sense they cannot really be called depressions.

Then, too, there has been a gradual conversion to governmental responsibility for general economic conditions and a gradual acceptance of such devices as tax management, the easing and tightening of credit, the control of the money supply, and the expansion and contraction of spending. These devices, used with discretion under the guidance of fairly accurate analyses of current activity projected into the future, have increased the effectiveness of governmental influence. Some progress has been made, even if by indirection, toward what it was intended to achieve more directly by the NRA.

It may even have been a better way. Those who intended that the NRA become a stabilizing and integrating agency—something that would be uniquely suited to the American temperament and tradition—may have been too far ahead. There might come a time when acceptance of the necessary disciplines would be more likely. Persistent resistance will make almost any economic or social scheme impractical.

There was some semantic difficulty in those days about the word "planning." It did not belong to the Communists, and it did not forecast a corporative state, but it pleased those who preferred not to have their speculative activities curbed to pretend that it did. And they had some success in establishing that meaning for it. The term was a long time recovering its respectability. What the Roosevelt circle had been discussing in the spring of 1932, and what he suggested in his Oglethorpe speech in May, was planning in the sense of looking forward, making use of all abilities and resources to gain objectives, encouraging here and discouraging there; it was not the erection of a monolithic and rigid structure with fixed objectives, rigidly assigned duties, and perhaps governmental ownership.

The Rooseveltians were certainly more devoted to the tradition of pluralism, open arrangements, equal opportunity, and pragmatic management than they were pictured as being by those who castigated them as totalitarians of one or another variety. They were, however, convinced that the effective cause of the existing paralysis lay in the business system itself. It proceeded so much by hit and miss, its trials and errors were so extreme, its competition so wasteful, its exploitation of workers and consumers so ruthless, and, as a result of cutthroat competition, its speculators so pervasive, that it finally found its logical end in defeating itself and coming to an almost complete stop.

When Roosevelt suggested early in the spring of 1932 at Oglethorpe that there must be planning for the future and that experimentation with devices for stability must be carried on, the political branch of his organization was so disturbed and objected so strongly that during the following campaign he made no further mention of such means. He spoke only of ends. But he spoke of ends that could be reached only by such means. They might not be politically acceptable, but he thought he could make them so—when he had become president. But he avoided exposition of his intentions.

If the administration of the NRA was inept, it was largely because the need to find quick means for recovery was so insistent—and, after all, NRA was labeled a recovery measure. Also there was the opposition of those Roosevelt most wanted approval from. Those who worked in and around him after his first two years—during the "second New Deal"—were Brandeis disciples. They called him back to atomistic progressivism. He rejuvenated the antitrust division and listened when Brandeis sent word that although "integration and control" was out, there was nothing in the Constitution that limited spending. Deficits were already large; but lacking recovery, they ran on into the grossly enlarged budgets for the coming war. The long era of inflation had begun.

Roosevelt, then, never did conquer the depression. It was reduced by forces and devices that were one by one invented and experimented with through the postwar years, some of them fairly difficult ones, and most of them after he had died. A generation of orthodox Progressives had to be succeeded by a generation of pragmatists before cleavage to simple antitrust remedies could be abandoned. And even then the nostalgic longing for simpler times and simpler ways was strong enough to dominate the political dialogue of subsequent campaigns. Lyndon Johnson had the simplistic philosophy of progressivism still dominant and active in his mind, and later politicians found populism a popular appeal.

Goldwater in 1964 was the first businessman ever to be nominated for the presidency by a major party, but it was noticeable that the biggest businessmen were not his sponsors. They knew that the policies he advocated would be disastrous. This may prove to have been the last outbreak of outraged nostalgia. The disaster of its success would have been incalculable. It must be recognized, however, that there was something legitimate in the protest Goldwater represented. Its strength was not measured by the election returns. Many who did not vote for Goldwater had strong objections to current policies. They recognized that changes during the last few decades had curtailed the old liberties until they sometimes seemed to have disappeared. They did not like it; even if they consented to the new rules, they resented the proliferation of governmental controls; most of the rules were regarded as capricious and unnecessary; all were evaded when possible.

When Ernest Bevin, who had spent his life in union organization, was asked, when he had got to be foreign minister, how he would like the world arranged, he answered: so that he could go to Victoria Station and start for anywhere in the world without any questions being asked. Many others understood what he meant. Goldwater's promise of such a world was a dream; it was something to work for, not something to get by wanting, but it had the attraction of a return to better days when free commerce was a reality.

The old individualism nearly destroyed the nation once, and it would be more disastrous at a later time; but the desire to reconstitute it remained. The politicians were under notice about this, and their devices for stability and integration took some account of it.

Those who operate the devices, however, are never politicians. They are indifferent to the irrepressible demand for freedom. They always incline to proliferate annoyances, invent impediments, extend controls. The pragmatic devices used by government to preserve equilibrium and to ensure economic advance have a constant tendency to this sort of encroachment on freedoms. There are always those who, if they have the power, will tell others where and how they must live, travel, and conduct themselves. It is even worse to have this done by private bureaucrats. They have constantly to be kept in their places whether in or out of government.

On the other hand, supervision protects the food supply, works against the pollution of air and water, and operates as well against exploiters who would steal a good share of people's income if they were allowed. To draw lines is difficult. Limitations are resented, but many of them are necessary.

Actually, liberty is something most people want but have no title to. They are governed by the impulse to go on trying for it and getting some of it. And when the choices available at any former time are considered, they seem much more liberal than they are in later times; but consider what living was like—its hazards, its limitations, its ends. Consider the gains made in security, in opportunity, and the dignities of age and the reduction of poverty. The nation has at least made some progress, and the way is open—the same pragmatic way—to more. Our productivity tends to separate incomes from the need to labor for them; and a whole new era of opportunity and a whole new range of liberties will open as this goes on. But the institutions appropriate to stability and security are still to be found.

It is suggsted that self-regulation for industry under somewhat the same arrangements intended for the NRA is still appropriate. It is therefore not proposed that regulation in the interest of consumers be abandoned—not at all—but it is suggested that industries shall concert among themselves the relations and connections necessary to a planned and stable industrial system, and that this shall be done with government acting as "senior partner."

CHAPTER 13

THE EMERGENT SITUATION:
A SUMMARY

Emergence

To speak of an "emerging constitution" is a tacit recognition that what is being spoken of is not a rigid and unchangeable document; if it is emerging, it must be developing, probably enlarging, certainly changing. And if this is happening it must be materializing under influences of some sort. The important questions about it, then, would seem to be: What are these influences, and are they creating a system of governance adequate for existing circumstances?

It is quite evident that what is now this emergent constitution has become something its framers would not recognize if they could return to view it. Its clauses would appear to be much the same, the appended amendments would clear up a few ambiguities and remedy a few mistakes, but the structure would be altered so little that it would appear to be almost the same as it had been when adopted.

This, on closer study, would be discovered to be a mistaken conclusion. There would seem to be a sort of compendium whose items for one or another reason had been enlarged or diminished; and, strangest of all, there would be additions. The responsibility for allowing such departures to take place would have to be shared by every generation; but the recent generations, being the worst offenders, would have worked out the most elaborate rationalizations. However presented, these justifications would actually be defensive—explanations of accommodations to reality by processes other than those that were constitutional in nature. Something has been going on in what the framers would almost certainly have regarded as illegitimate ways. They themselves may not always have followed the exalted rule of disinterest and clung to the grand design of national integrity, but among them were those who knew the difference between constitutionmaking and legislation, administrative extrapolation, and judicial interpretation.

These last are processes of convenience, not doctrinal ones that issue from original sources and have their guiding objective in completion of the gestalt. Decisions related directly to ecology, on the other hand, are ones to be taken with the deepest devotion to responsibility. Man's position in the universe and on his earth, his dependence on his environment and his relations with other men—these are not matters safely left to the superficial determination of legislatures, the regulation of officials, or the opinions of judges. All of them are necessary, but all ought to be contained in a unified complex. If by now men have learned that they are not ordained to be permanent on this earth, then their constitution should reflect an effort to establish themselves more securely instead of contriving a system in complete disregard of nature's imperatives.

Americans, like others, have been careless about this. Even at their best times they have seemed to feel that the accumulative processes of law and the body of judicial precedent represent a sufficient wisdom. This is to confuse practical relations among quarreling individuals or maneuvering organizations with the conditions set for proceeding into the future. Genuine constitutional law does not take shape in these processes.

This difference, it can be inferred, was more apparent to the framers, or at least some of them, than it seems to have been to later generations. If those forefathers deviated in many respects from the course they should have followed, that was the more tragic because there would never—at least until now—be another meeting with similar terms of reference. That is to say, there has been no second constitutional convention. It is necessary to say also that there has been no considerable demand for one, and so no real consideration of the uniqueness of this kind of law. The self-satisfaction of Americans with pseudoconstitutional rule has proved impervious to all criticism and tolerant of all shortcomings. Many such shortcomings have, indeed, somehow been turned into virtues. Carelessness, controversy, and uneasy accommodation are defended as "evolutionary." They show that institutions "live."

This rationalization began with *The Federalist* for what were considered exigent reasons. Ratification was so imperative that such brilliant expositors as Madison, Hamilton, and Jay did not scruple to defend even the faults of the document as clever contrivances, necessary in the circumstances. John Marshall, by claiming for the Court, a little later, the power to interpret, relieved pressures that otherwise would have built up about many issues and would have made amendment, in spite of its inherent difficulty, inevitable; and other means have since been taken to evade the necessity. Nothing, or very little, done since has been, in the true sense, constitutional.

That first meeting in 1787 had the immediate responsibility for saving a people from the follies of localism, separatism, suspicion, and downright selfishness; a meeting that had to save and perpetuate a nation had often to deal with the maneuvering of politicians intent on getting or maintaining position in their own communities. Not all its members were seized with responsibility. But protecting their separate policies from inclusion in a whole, yielding only as much as was absolutely necessary for sheer physical protection, was not a way to create a union. All the thirty-nine (of the original fifty-five) who stayed to sign did not in the end agree; they had, in some crucial matters, not come to a conclusion. Instead of reaching clear rules they had substituted compromises. They had kept the obvious mental reservation that as time went on their views could be made to dominate the whole. But this the three writers of *The Federalist Papers* had no intention of disclosing. Deception was essential, and it did serve to damp down the fears of resisters; but this is no excuse for seeing in their essays the perfect rationale of constitutionmaking. They were not intended to be that. It may be guessed that no one knew better than the authors that many doubtful agreements had been made to gain the practical compromises necessary to ratification.

The most conspicuous of these doubtful agreements had to do with the central issue of the whole meeting—concession by the states of powers to a national government. When it was finished, it was still thought—or, at least, argued—that the states had retained their original sovereignty and had given up to the new central authority only the specific authority necessary to protection from foreign aggressors and from the divisive forces at work among themselves. This, at least, was the statement of what had been meant by those who for half a century made a political issue of strict construction. Others—the loose constructionists—found themselves in the difficult position of arguing that implied powers were inherent in the limited ones even when they were invisible.

The distribution arrived at in Philadelphia was not one that either side was enthusiastic about, but it did enable the meeting to be concluded with sufficient amity, and it served for a beginning. Actually it was an avoidance of the main issue; it furnished the material for controversy that again and again in subsequent years threatened to disrupt the nation. It has to be cited not as an illustration of consensus but of bargaining; what is so often praised is actually an example of the worst way to make a constitution. The framers did secure consent, but they did not discover and embody in their agreement the imperatives that would ensure the safety of the nation, and the penalties for this were not long delayed. Perhaps the issues were too dangerous to be adamant about; perhaps it was not a juncture in history when men could have discovered the imperatives they would be forced to recognize. Certainly civilization was arrested just then in a peculiarly sterile interlude. Every branch of science had taken a wrong turn. A system of politics founded on the physical and natural learning of that period must have been as impermanent as the foundation itself. It may be just as well that no such effort was found acceptable.

To say that the Constitution of 1787 was framed by learned men is to say that it was framed by men whose learning was soon to be discarded and overwhelmed by the century of discovery that was to follow. They cannot be blamed for not anticipating what was still totally hidden from them. This, however, does not excuse men of later generations who accepted their work as finished and failed to carry it forward.

There were those at Philadelphia who understood the proper technique of constitutionmaking. There were honest attempts to discover what the forces were that must be accepted as shaping policy. Madison, for instance, had been preparing his proposals for years. It was those who were there for another purpose who extracted concessions, and these still haunt American institutions.

Since the essential constitutional endeavor intended by the nationalists was impossible, it is hard to explain why it has never been undertaken in successor generations. For whatever reason, the document—produced at an unfortunate time, in exigent circumstances, and laced with compromise —was not taken as a beginning; it was enshrined. It can only be ventured as some sort of explanation that a constitution was badly needed and that one was created out of less solid materials than are recognizably adequate.

Practically, of course, the departures from the terms of the original have had to be drastic. And numerous ways of effecting them have been adopted. It is the result of all these departures that is meant when an "emerging" constitution is spoken of.

We have seen that the argument for having a constitution really comes down to the necessity for a sturdy and resistant framework of governmental institutions as well as a studied definition of citizens' rights and duties with appropriate powers to secure and enforce them. It does not follow that either the institutions or the rights/duties complex can be absolute; rights must not be allowed to become abuses or duties to become burdens; and governmental organization has to accord with circumstances. Reasonableness and accommodation must be paid attention to; governmental structures must occasionally be shored up, and sometimes even rebuilt. This is only to say that a constitution cannot be permanent; it must somehow be changed as circumstances require.

It should be said that shoring up is not necessarily a constitutional process; it may be legislative or judicial, and it can be provided for by the marking out of limits and standards. It is the rethinking and the rebuilding of structure that are essentially constitutional. Strengthening, making additions, and interpretation are necessary, but when they become so extensive that central intentions are no longer served, they no longer have the authenticity of constitutionalism.

It is interesting to speculate on the course political history might have taken if one provision had been more carefully considered in 1787. Once agreement was reached about controversial issues, it was still necessary to determine how amendment ought to be provided for; but not much thought seems to have been given to the problem. What dominated consideration when amendment was discussed was precaution against easy change; easiness would allow every majority, led by some demagogue, to impose its ideology on society and perhaps precipitate revolution. Amendment should not be too difficult either; if it were, obsolescence would set in at once, and in the course of years the charter would become little more than a surviving artifact from a former age. The framers did not acknowledge the importance of future accommodations at the end of their work. Perhaps they were tired; perhaps they left this one thing to the Committee on Style; perhaps the favoring of legislative over other processes carried over; or perhaps they did consider that they were infallible.

At any rate, amendment was made too difficult. Or, it may be better to say, it was entrusted to a procedure that would stifle any further genuinely constitutional consideration; actually, it was made practically impossible. Since it was left to the Congress to initiate, it was for the future mingled with the legislative process. It was ensured that such changes as might be made would come as the result of practical difficulties, not of reconsidering political architecture; and because of this insufficiency the changes that soon had to be made were inroads and additions approved by the Congress or inserted in tours de force by the Court; and then, with the Court's permission, by others, none of whom had any understanding of what was constitutional as contrasted with legislative, judicial, or merely customary. There was no further fitting to the imperatives of social change.

The problem of reconstruction is to find and embody in a new document the wisdom of more than the contemporary years and to provide a process of discovering and incorporating additional wisdom as time passes. Amendment has never been regarded as so serious a responsibility.

Amendment, it seems to have been agreed, ought to be difficult; a constitution ought not to be taken lightly; but beyond this, perception in Philadelphia was not very acute. It may be that the nationalists, giving way to the localists, felt that the Congress was sufficiently safeguarded by limited suffrage so that it could be allowed the several advantages it was given over the other branches. Not only was the right to originate amendment conferred on it but also the origination had to command two-thirds majorities. There was, it is true, an alternative way; on application of two-thirds of the state legislatures, the Congress could be prodded into calling a convention; but this can hardly have been expected to become operational. It never has.

The carelessness or mistake of the framers concerning future alterations would not have been so serious if the lower house had not been given an initial advantage in another article, seemingly innocent, but actually crucial —that of originating revenue bills, a provision gradually stretched by common consent to include the origination of appropriations as well.

In an indirect way that advantage was enormously enlarged by another, and somewhat later, occurrence: the first exercise of judicial review in 1803. This legalistic tour de force changed everything. It was a shift of power that appalled Jefferson, but its effect was somewhat modified by a practical consideration. Since the Congress had to be depended on for funds, the Court's newly assumed power would always have to be exercised with wariness about congressional consent; also, caution was made more necessary by another provision giving the Congress power to determine its jurisdiction. Opinions objected to by the Congress could be reversed by removing the subject from judicial reach. The effect of these hidden checks cannot be assessed. They would have to be measured by the unknowable restraint they may have had, but can only be inferred.

One result, however, is one we can be sure of: the only gateway to amendment, or to further constitutional (as contrasted with legislative or judicial) lawmaking, was effectively blocked. It would always stay blocked because any change of importance would almost certainly affect congressional prerogative; and that would never be allowed. The Congress has not only been immune to reform but has checked other initiatives that might affect indirectly its position among governmental institutions.

The framers were not usually so remiss. They were often very ingenious, as when, for instance, they attempted to balance a system of checks to establish substantial equality among the branches; their intention was to prevent the lodgment anywhere of supreme authority, an effort that would have succeeded if the congressional check had not been, by an almost undetectable permissiveness, made more effective than the others.

Along with an equality that was not quite perfect, there was created a tension that has been a continuing characteristic of relations among the branches ever since, worse at some times than others but occasionally rising to fierce conflict, especially in times of crisis when policy was in dispute. This may or may not have been anticipated; but it has been as troublesome, certainly, as any series of occurrences throughout the years.[1]

It has to be said that the scattered citizens of the late eighteenth century managed to find in the framers men of wisdom far beyond the average of capability; they were, of course, not *found*; they nominated themselves, or at least the leaders did. Their deliberations, represented by the Constitution, have to be credited with the protection of liberties and the definition of relationships during an early development that could not have occurred if this guidance had been lacking. It is not too much to say, as it often *is*

1. Cf. the author's *The Enlargement of the Presidency* (Garden City, N.Y.: Doubleday & Company, 1960).

said, that they gave the nation a new life. This ought not to be expanded beyond credibility; they were not infallible; it was a rescue operation. It succeeded in that, but it was not a new series of divine ordinances.

There still exists the formal organization agreed on: the Presidency, the Congress, and the Judiciary. Each of these, as was originally provided, owes its existence to a separate source of sovereignty: the Presidency and the Congress directly, by election; the Court indirectly, by appointment of the president—but for life. And these have interpenetrating or, as some commentators insist, interfering powers; and the situation of each, in relation to the other is less well established with every passing year. The undefined areas are more disputed than they would have been if left in a structure more carefully considered.

So much has survived even if much altered by processes other than amendment. The other notable structural characteristic is, of course, the state-federal relationship; and it too has survived in much the same condition of confusion. The states still have their own powers—in theory they possess all those not delegated to the central government—and even though the practice has notably weakened, the theory is still respected; the states remain prominent entities in the governmental scene.

None of these—States, Presidency, Congress, or Judiciary—is recognizably the original constitutional prescription; even the resemblance is clouded. What they are, what they do, and what they are becoming could not possibly be deduced from any reading of the document. There is, of course, nothing sinister about this; it would have to be true, since society, the economy, and people's demands have changed so much. This, however, only points up the fact that the divergencies have occurred without any changes in the prescription. Amendments, although there have been some, have none of them much affected the structural members of the edifice; and most amendments have resembled legislative rather than constitutional lawmaking. The blockage to amendment, whether or not intended, has been effective.

The amendments of some architectural significance are the Seventeenth and the Twenty-second. The one provides for the direct election of senators, and the other limits presidents to two terms. These are interesting changes, and the latter does affect one of the foundation timbers. But it does not affect the edifice nearly so much as other changes, not embodied in amendments, that have weakened or strengthened the traditional branches; or those additions attached to the old edifice by the thrust and parry of adversary actions. These have been quite outside the kind of consideration that characterizes genuine constitutionmaking. They have no legitimacy, not even, for the most part, any permanency.

It might be—and has been—argued that these changes are so necessary, and have come into existence so smoothly, that they need not be formally included in the Constitution. That this is, again, the same as arguing that there need not be a constitution is one of the blindnesses referred to above. There would seem to be ample evidence, for example, that the political system in all its parts is disorderly, subject to corruption, and inefficient for its purpose. The Republic would benefit, it would be thought, from its constitutionalization. But there is hardly a political scientist to be found who agrees; when asked, he begins a vague but enthusiastic discourse on the virtues of evolution. The inconsistencies, the favoritisms, the irregularities, and the lack of clear purpose that characterizes the regulatory agencies would seem to call for similar definition; but there is, again, no agreement that it ought to be undertaken.

The most earnest attempts to discover what much of the Constitution means today are unsatisfactory, a frustration accounted for by erosion, obsolescence, irrelevance, neglect, expansions, and interpretations; and this is as true of amendments as it is of the original document. It is quite realistic to say that it has become not much more than a compendium of references for departure.

The contribution of the Court to this chaotic situation has been considerable. In the course of years, as cases have been accepted by it for decision, it has provided elaborate extrapolations for some clauses, has narrowed others, and, with or without elaborate explanation, has reversed itself. For a hundred years no one has known what interstate commerce consists of, what "affected with the public interest" means, or whether there is a federal police power. These are illustrations of the condition created by interpretation.

None of these matters happens to be mentioned in the Constitution directly, but demanding interests have caused all of them—and many others—to be given some sort of recognition. There are many examples, also, of change in meanings, some owed to the Court, others to social change or to extension because of need. Of these last the political, planning, and regulatory systems are only the most massive. Almost as important have been the seizing of powers, desired but not granted in the original. All the branches have done this. Then there is the strange anomalous position now occupied by the states. The range of definition given to states' rights even now, after all the years of controversy, is almost as wide as it ever was, although there is a perceptible erosion of the states' powers.

For our purpose here it is important to recognize that the present situation is, in many respects, actually fluid, still in controversy, obviously in process of evolution. The nature of that process is frustratingly various and indefinite; no one can say how it is likely to be altered at any time by any agency, whether the alteration will be challenged, or whether it will not be reversed.

It is constantly necessary to recall that there are four species of law to be distinguished: judicial, legislative, administrative, and constitutional; and that constitutional law is, in its nature, vastly different from the others. It is properly reached by a different process, and its embodiment occupies a position of prestige and definition that can come only from deep and general commitment. It is by its nature unassailable except by the means that created it. If it is not that, it is not really constitutional.

Federalism

As has been suggested, the emergent constitution is nowhere more elusive than in the one area it might be thought would have been defined carefully in the Convention; after all, its main business was presumably to secure the Union. Yet the controversy about strict or loose construction of the clauses conferring power on the central government began at once and remained a source of contention for generations. Around it were formed the first political parties, and it was the cause of continued controversy.

Even after the ordeal of conflict the ambiguity remained, and even yet has not entirely disappeared. The trouble in 1865 was that the terms of peace were not, in some respects, any clearer about the issues presumably being fought about than they had been before the conflict. Only the simplest phase of what by then was a complex issue came to any kind of decision. It was settled that under no circumstances could any state leave the Union; but secession, as a doctrine, had arisen from a much more complicated controversy than was covered by this simple prohibition. The remaining unanswered questions have troubled our political, social, and economic life ever since.

The framers were sent to Philadelphia as delegates from the legislatures of the states; and since their terms of reference did include the directive to create "a more perfect union," the nationalists among the delegates considered that this implied a unitary government, one with a strong center and with the states clearly subordinated. Even those who would have preferred this interpretation, however, realized well enough that it would not prevail; and if they did not, they were soon instructed. The advocates of delegated authority, sharply defined, and clearly limited, with sovereignty remaining in the states, were obstreperously vocal; and if they had had their way, the new arrangement would have been but little different from the Confederation; this did not happen; but the ambiguity they created did remain.

The nationalists had to deal with these disunionists, and the result was sovereign states *and* a central government. Curiously enough, this was afterward regarded as one of the triumphs of the Convention; and federalism became an accepted principle. But there was an inherent and persistent strain in the ambiguous arrangement that has never disappeared, although the trend has been toward what the nationalists wanted in the first place. The growth of national power has been a painful progress, contested at every phase and, as any newspaper reader knows, far even today from being complete. States' righters are still unreconciled and still recurrently vocal. The futility of their resistance has long been apparent, but recognition of the inevitable, or even of the fact, is not to be taken for granted.

No student of our government would undertake to say at the present time in what sense the states are sovereign, as the theory of federalism requires. There is even question as to whether they have any remaining sovereignty at all. It seems to be the rule that the federal government may preempt areas of authority when the national interest requires it; and that the states must then give way; but the preemption is undertaken only in particular cases, cautiously and with reversions from time to time to earlier doctrine. Here, as in so many other places, the attitude of the Court's majorities is crucial. Cases defining the rights and powers of the states come to it only occasionally, and they are often concerned primarily with other issues. The powers of the states are thus reluctantly diminished. Moreover, it is still not granted by everyone that state powers may be defined at all in this way—such is still the contention not only of many political leaders in the old South but also of prestigious lawyers trying to shield corporate clients from the rigors of federal regulation; also there are vestiges of it in conservative resistance to the expansion of welfare measures.

The taking over by the federal government during the Roosevelt regime —the New Deal—of responsibility for distress caused by depression had the curious effect of seeming to resuscitate states' rights without actually doing so. The Rooseveltians saw no other way to carry out their responsibilities than by using the already tried method known as "state aid"— the allocating of federal funds to be administered by the states. Then, when Social Security was undertaken, and its administration was thus delegated, there was an enormous expansion of state bureaucracies. This seemed to be the only arrangement that would not be fought by the representatives in the Congress who still harbored strict constructionist views; but actually it was no more than a dispensing operation under federal directives.

State aid was not a new invention, of course; public improvements—as evidenced by the massive expenditures for highways when the automobile came in after the turn of the century—had followed this line; and even earlier there had been national roads and waterways. But there were subsidiary problems that once again seemed to raise the old issues. How free were grants to the states? What standards could be imposed by Washington? Since the beginning, local politicians had always contended that the federal government could not do more than make simple allocations. Furious quarrels had arisen about the use of the funds to sustain state highway departments that were manned by the party associates of reigning bosses. The elder Talmadge used this method with considerable success in Georgia, for instance; and when in 1934 the federal government asserted a duty to insist on clearing out his nest of incompetents, there was a furor all over the South. Wherever there were such interferences federal administrators won; but angry objections in the Congress made them extremely cautious about making any rules that might interfere with local politicians' prerogatives. It was necessary to invent a separate interstate highway system during later years to escape the confusions of planning that left the roads in the states with dead ends at their borders and devoid of any national purpose.

There really has been no agreement concerning the nature of federalism. Even today elaborate precautions are taken in matters having to do with allocations of funds. Local prerogatives are talked of tenderly even when they are not really honored. Many illustrations of this are available. For instance, when there was formed, in the forties, a national planning organization, the central offices were kept almost invisible; and elaborate headquarters, paid for with federal funds, were set up in all the state capitals. It was hoped by the modestly retiring National Planning Board that somehow the planners operating in forty-eight centers would coordinate themselves and produce a national plan. They never did; and presently when conservatives in the Congress were strong enough to trade with a president who needed their votes for defense appropriations, the planning organizations were abolished. Roosevelt expressed regret, but actually it was no loss. The hoped-for coordination had not materialized.

It has gone on this way. Both private and public organizations have supported states' rights for their own convenience. Businesses have often found it easier to influence legislatures in the states than the Congress in Washington, especially since the president, whose interests are national, is also involved in legislation. All sorts of interests often found it easier to have their way in state capitals than in Washington.

Support for this has not always come from strict constructionists or even from businesses. Justice Brandeis, in the twenties, and even earlier, gave the lead in a movement for state rather than federal regulation and was followed by a coterie of lawyers that expanded enormously when he became a justice. Brandeis did not originate the theory that bigness was inherently dangerous and ought always to be broken up, or that bigness was as evil in government as in business, but he was an eloquent and prestigious spokesman for it. He dominated President Wilson, who was weak in economic learning, and he had immense influence later on with F. D. Roosevelt and many of Roosevelt's associates.

There were antecedents reaching back to the frontier, but the particular antitrust syndrome originated in the resentment of farmers who felt themselves exploited by railroads and by creditors in the East. The post-Civil War migration to trans-Appalachia became a massive settlement movement on the Great Plains. The farmers there, being short of capital, borrowed freely; when droughts came, they were unable to pay. Besides, they resented the rates charged by the railroads for getting their products to market. They developed a bitter antibusiness sentiment that concentrated on railroads and processors. This first became populism, then progressivism. The demand for regulation turned into a demand for breaking up the rapidly forming concentrations of industry.

The immensely complicated and confused developments in this issue have never reached conclusion. At times the arguments have become almost incredibly absurd. One illustration of this is the picturing of the states (then forty-eight) as "laboratories" whose different approaches to regulation would lead to discovering the most effective public policy. Another with the opposite intention was furnished by some events in the early New Deal. The central idea of the National Recovery Administration was that if businesses in various industries were allowed to get together they would agree to eliminate unfair practices. It was expected that they would abandon, or at least reduce, the sort of competition that resulted in harm to workers as well as to themselves. When the National Recovery Act established a board to administer the NRA, it gave perceptive but sardonic observers pleasure to note that among those serving on that board there was a representative of the Antitrust Division of the Department of Justice, charged with keeping the businesses from doing what the board was instructed to see that they did.

As might have been expected, the board soon disappeared. It was not disbanded; it simply ceased to function. It found itself in need of defining what its functions were; and this would have committed Roosevelt to one or another of the theories he dared not become identified with—enforced competition or regulated integration. In this, he was no different from other statesmen. The NRA brought him to an intolerable contradiction, and he avoided choosing.

It is impossible to trace the history of this controversy here. The defenders of antitrust procedures did not rest altogether on states' rights, although its defenders usually enlisted supporters of the one in the cause of the other. There was, as well, the strong impulse of populism, the frontier revolt against urban capitalism. As populism became progressivism it was linked with economic laissez-faire. This was capitalism, too, but not on the Wall Street scale involving mergers, trusts, monopolies, and other such phenomena. The Progressive model was a small, independent, actively competing business. This was the Brandeis ideal, and it became orthodox. Not only the Congress but also state legislatures eventually passed antitrust laws, and there began another confused competition to see which would take precedence in harassing big business.

Businessmen naturally were confused. They had always favored free competition because that meant to be let alone, and that they yearned for. But if laissez-faire involved prosecutions whenever they combined to suppress practices they were heartily ashamed of (to say nothing of others they hoped to protect) and to gain efficiency from larger-scale operations, then they were in the same dilemma as the politicians. They did not know which to choose.

What they ended in doing was the same thing the politicians did; they retreated. If they ran into trouble they defended themselves as best they could, taking one or the other line as seemed at the moment most protective.

They usually escaped or, if they reached an impasse, tried another way of doing what they had wanted to do in the first place. Corporation lawyers were extremely skillful at skinning cats in alternate ways. But there were two particularly convenient resorts for businesses grown large enough to be endangered. They captured and used the Republican party; and they professed to be supporters of states' rights. The Republicans, without opposing regulation in theory, staffed the increasing number of federal regulatory agencies with friendly members; also, if there had to be regulation they preferred it to be done by the states, since legislatures and control commissions were more cheaply suborned. For fifty years the worst centers of corruption were the state capitals. They swarmed with lobbyists who bought the legislation they wanted or prevented legislation they did not want with amazing facility. The muckrakers who began with corruption in the cities soon found even more flourishing systems in the capitals.

None of this helped in positioning the states in the federal system; all of it in fact tended to confuse issues and especially to delay any sort of settlement. Even now the attempt to say what is the emergent situation cannot be definitive.

There is no escaping the fact of an original unwillingness to meet the issue that precipitated the Philadelphia meeting. Then the uncertainty was compounded by the peculiar history of the frontier and the Populist movement. The framers went some way, but still not very far, toward forming a "more perfect union"; really they left the issue unsettled.

The doctrine, subsequently accepted, that when the federal government preempts power the states may not resist is not conclusive, either; the ambiguities about it have allowed a mixed state-national administrative organization to grow up in absurd confusion, well illustrated by the situation of several cities whose charters must come from the states. They may be larger than the rest of the state and yet be forced to struggle continually for autonomy with an unfriendly rural legislature. And even though this disadvantage may have been modified by the reapportionment dictum of the Court, it is still likely that the cities will not share directly in state aids. For a long time they did not exist as far as the federal government was concerned. There has been some modification of this in recent years, but it would be impossible to define the situation with any precision.

Besides the confusions about the inability of the federal government to deal directly with New York or Chicago without the intervention of Albany or Springfield, whenever it was decided that the federal government must give assistance of some sort, there has been the important matter of collecting taxes to meet these obligations. Embarrassing situations still continue and are likely to become worse. In New York City, for instance, a citizen pays three income taxes—national, state, and city—to say nothing of levies on property and innumerable excises. The system has been thrown together in desperation by competing authorities requiring revenues regardless of the effect their collection may have on the economy—or on any other interest.

These situations result from the indeterminateness of power distribution in the federal system. A confusion that was originally the result of compromise has gone on degenerating until it now approaches the intolerable. If it can be said that state powers have declined, there are still those shrill voices from the South, echoed occasionally from northern capitals, whose officials find that states' rights speeches still appeal to their constituents. There are, moreover, enormous bureaucracies administering the ever-growing welfare measures. Their funds come from Washington, but very often this is not known by voters, who credit—or blame—their state officials for assistance—or the lack of it—that originates in Washington.

Federalism still exists, but it does not consist in specific powers delegated to a central government with the residual ones remaining in the states. Actually, the reverse is nearer the fact. But the distribution of power is not by a dependable rule. It changes; it progresses and then moves backward; it is this today and that tomorrow. No more can be said.

The Interdependent Powers

No invention of the framers has been regarded as more ingenious than the provisions for interdependence among the branches. Almost at once it began to be spoken of as "checks and balances." The preventing of lodgment anywhere or in any individual of unlimited authority was one that appealed alike to the "better people" and to the politicians who owed their places to the support from "the mob." This concept gained acceptance but created a problem. Where was leadership to come from and how could it be made effective?

The elite saw the checks partly as a deterrent to impulsive legislative majorities and partly as assurance that their own concurrence would be necessary in all decisions of any consequence. The Senate where they were dominant could not originate revenue measures, it was true, but it had to approve them before they were submitted to the president. Also the president was one of them; laws did not become operative until he had approved.

The president was to appoint judges to the Supreme Court (the Constitution did not call them "justices"). They had to be confirmed, but the popularly elected House was not admitted to the confirmation proceedings. The better people were in a fairly safe position. Taken together with an electorate limited to a very small number of reliable citizens, there was ample provision for stability and conservatism.

On the other hand, the sovereignty of the people was acknowledged. They were to elect the president and the Congress—the one nationally, the others by districts. Their representatives would control finances, and not the Senate alone but the Congress was given the power to pass measures over presidential vetoes. The Congress too could determine the jurisdiction of the Supreme Court (except controversies among the states or those affecting ambassadors) and could establish inferior courts. Most important of all, appropriations for all the branches, and even the salaries of president and judges, were to be determined by the Congress.

It was soon found in practice that the mutually limiting relations between the Congress and the president had been arranged in a way that resulted in maximum aggravation of each with the other. The president's subordinates, as departmental heads, were made subject to Senate approval; and not only the funds at their disposal for executing the laws but their salaries as well had to have congressional approval.

From the very first these arrangements caused ill feeling. Each branch was jealous of its powers and sought to extend them. For this extension there was ample room in the areas of constitutional silence, but often aggression extended beyond this area into the provinces claimed by other branches. A no man's land of perpetual controversy and tension was established; it was owed partly to brevity and partly to compromise, but it would become one of the conspicuous characteristics of the American system. It has always been the most difficult for outsiders to understand and one of the most difficult for apologists to explain satisfactorily.

Checks and balances have to be understood as having originated in the deliberate combination of separation and interdependence complicated by bargaining as the system was worked out. No branch could act, it was conceived, without the participation in some degree of another branch. This would make for caution, for consideration, and for deliberation. It may not have been expected that acrimony, blackmail, political compromise, and subterfuge would become chronic in such relationships; but that is what did result.

A president, to have his appointees confirmed, must dispense favors to senators. These favors are of indefinite range, depending on the senator's strategic position. On the other hand the senator who wants something for his state will need the president's assistance in getting it. The same is true in negotiations between the president and the House. The familiar pork barrel results from bargaining on the one side for the inclusion of projects to please localities and on the other for votes on measures the president sees as necessary. It is a complicated process involving by now a sizable presidential lobby and influential committee chairmen with numerous staffs. It is at best a wasteful way of arranging for legislative action, and at worst it results in periods when nothing seems to get done; neither party to the bargain will concede more than a minimum and then often will not deliver. Stalemate results.

This last is especially true when the president belongs to one party and the Congress, or one of its chambers, has a majority belonging to the other. This situation has existed with exasperating persistence through long periods of our history. After his first two years in office a president often finds that his party's majority in the Congress has disappeared; if he goes on for six years longer, as many do, they are likely to be ones of wrangling and frustrations with the national interest apparently the last thing being considered. It will be recalled that this happened to both Truman and Eisenhower with equally sterile results.

Rules are often emphasized by exceptions, and one occurred after President Johnson took office in 1963. There had been other exceptions less spectacular in the honeymoon period of Wilson and F. D. Roosevelt, but Johnson's experienced manipulation (he had for years been majority leader in the Senate) and an overwhelming majority of Democrats released a flood of long-contained measures. The dam had been breached by new representatives from urban areas. They disappeared in 1966, but in two extraordinary years of concurrence between the president and the Congress legislation was passed that had been overdue for a generation. The welfare state became a reality.

If this accomplishment seemed a miracle to Americans who were accustomed to congressional obstruction, it was because they had not expected it. They saw in this Eighty-ninth Congress the legislative institution of theory, one that met its responsibilities and responded to national needs. From cynical criticism public appraisal turned to pride. The Congress had found itself. The Constitution was vindicated.

Experience after the Sixty-third and Seventy-third Congresses should have shown that this was premature. Stalemate would return; it did return in the election of 1966. But the magnificent accomplishment of those two tremendous years did show what might happen if the Congress could be made permanently responsive to leadership.

If it seems strange that the framers should have built stalemate into the Constitution, it is at least partially explained as originating in the determined pluralism characteristic of American society from its beginning. This was consonant with laissez-faire in economics, the theory there being one of independent organizations bargaining for advantage. It became the theory too of progressivism in politics, and of its legal counterpart, the antitrust theory of *enforced* free competition.

These later developments seem not to have been anticipated by the framers. On the contrary it was thought that party politics (faction, they called it) had been avoided; they had no premonition of an economic system whose main urge would be the elimination of the very competition it regarded as fundamental.

Apologists for the separation principle have always had to dwell on its service to liberty and equally to avoid its hampering effect on progress. But this has grown too serious to ignore. Leadership in politics, so essential to a nation whose social and economic institutions, when left alone, developed powers quite equal, often, to those of government, was seriously hampered. Initiative could not come from a legislature with several hundred members. Even the most renowned senators have been more notable for resistance than for inventiveness; this was inevitable, since their source of power continually diminished in relation to the whole as the whole expanded. It had to come from the single national representative, the president; yet he lacked many of the requisites of leadership; and such as he did have were extraconstitutional. They emerged from a political system the framers had meant to avoid.

As the extraconstitutional party system developed, the president could run for office on a platform that committed his party; but members of the Congress, running in localities, often found themselves in disagreement with all or part of this commitment, and the president, asking for their support in order to fulfill party promises, might well find that it was not forthcoming. His leadership need not be recognized by legislators with different (and perhaps dissident) constituencies. The extended periods when there existed virtual paralysis in policymaking was the price of limited powers (checks). And short periods of release did really seem miraculous to a blasé public.

A remedy for this has never been found except in brief bursts of concurrent activity, such as happened in the Eighty-ninth, when the Congress recognized its pledges, gave way to the majority party's leader, and passed the measures he proposed.

Can the "honeymoon" be made permanent? Only, it would seem, by making the Congress as responsive to political directives as is the president. The choice may be between such a reform of the Congress or (as has often been advocated) making the president a subordinate of the Congress. This would be to adopt the parliamentary system.

At any rate, what has to be identified as the emergent situation is an intolerable one. There have been three spurts of accomplishment of two years each in a hundred-year period (more or less). The Congress has for the most part become an obstructive body, made so by the framers' structuring.

The Rights and Duties

It is one of the anomalies of the Constitution that there is a Bill of Rights but no Bill of Duties. This is not because the duties were prescribed in the body of the document and the rights added as amendments; there are none in the body either. Most commentators see nothing to criticize in this. For instance, when Justice Warren was governor of California, and was speaking to a legislative committee on constitutional revision (in 1947), he nominated bills of rights as "the heart of any constitution." It is by these, he said, that people are made secure in "liberty of conscience, of speech, of the press, of lawful assembly, the right to uniform application of the laws, and due process."

This was some ten years after the judicial crisis of 1937 when an extended period of interference in favor of property rights had ended and the Court had returned to intervention, as Professor Corwin put it, "on behalf of the helpless and the oppressed." What this involved at first was mere deference to the proper policymaking branches, but in a few years the justices returned to active policymaking again. The Warren Court was more "interfering" than the one it superseded, but, of course, in quite a different interest; the Burger Court, again, began at once to narrow its predecessors' interpretations concerning the "oppressed."

Shifts of this sort have become familiar. They seem to originate in an irrepressible impulse among justices to assert their views. Madison said (in No. 51 of *The Federalist*) that although the people themselves were no doubt the primary check on government, other checks were needed. They were federalism, the separation of powers, and judicial review. Since the first two of these are no longer as effective as Madison forecast, the justices seem unable to resist standing in the role of all three.

The attitudes and interests of the framers and of the legislators in the states who ratified their work have become, after an interlude, the continuing ones of the Court. As has been noted, there are those who maintain that the Convention was dominated by an elite who were intent on establishing a government favorable to themselves, and especially one that would protect property rights, ensure domestic tranquillity, and prevent disorderly majorities from becoming a recurrent nuisance. There had been disorders in New York, Philadelphia, and Boston—there were more of the unruly than there were of the elite. This posed a difficult problem, but the solution was found.

According to this view, the framers wanted a government both weak and strong: strong to keep order, but weak to prevent interference with their concerns; strong to bring in revenue, protect the frontiers, and present a coherent and prestigious face to the world, but weak in controlling the autonomous organizations of their society.

Those who incline to a conspiratorial view of human events will probably never be convinced that Madison, for instance, honestly thought essential liberties to have been made quite safe without the added specifications in the Bill of Rights.

There were more than the surviving ten of these amendments in the compendium of proposals brought together by Madison and presented to the House on June 8, 1789. At least four were eliminated in the subsequent dialogue; but the remaining ones, like so much else in the Constitution, represented specific limitations on the power of government to infringe the liberties of citizens. There is an emphasis in all constitutions on such limitations; but those in the American charter, with the addition of the amendments, do seem excessive.

The chief purpose of constitutionmakers for centuries was just this— the bringing of government within a containing, really a constricting, legal system. Whether it was a king or legislative majority, these late eighteenth-century Americans wanted it understood that government could not go beyond certain limits; no matter what desires were developed subsequently by officials, their powers were meant to stop at the barriers set by pre-emptory provisions.

This was made doubly sure by the amendment procedure that was prescribed. This may not have been the purpose, but it was certainly the result.[2]

After ratification and the promised adoption of the Bill of Rights, further change in any structural matter was nearly impossible. After the Eleventh Amendment, keeping the federal judiciary out of state affairs, and the Twelfth, correcting an obvious defect in election procedures, no amendment was adopted until after the Civil War. This was a period of ex-

2. The amending article (Article V) had a curious development in the Convention. Madison had said in explaining the Virginia Plan that "the assent of the National Legislature ought not to be required thereto." The Committee of Detail also saw it that way and produced a draft, adopted at the end of August, including only what later became the alternate plan for origination by the legislatures of two-thirds of the states. Hamilton objected. The states, he said, would never "apply for alterations but with a view to increase their own powers." He also insisted, seeing the point Mason had made earlier, that amendments would be needed, since what was done was sure to be defective. It would be better to provide for revisions, as Mason had said, "in an easy, regular, and constitutional way than to trust to chance and violence."

The plan of the Committee of Detail caused such dissatisfaction, and it was so late, that the amending provision was written on the floor with Madison drafting the form finally adopted. The curious last proviso, protecting the Senate from any future amendment, was added because of agitation by delegates from the small states. They were still suspicious, and still vigilant.

The early argument that amendment should be made easy and the still earlier one that the legislative branch ought not to be involved were somehow lost.

The protection of states' rights and not individual liberties was responsible for the kind of amending clause finally decided on.

pansion and change that should have generated corollary constitutional reconsiderations. The fact is that nothing of the sort happened. When in the late 1860s the Thirteenth, Fourteenth, and Fifteenth Amendments were ratified there had been none since 1804, and there would not be another until 1913. What happened in the social and economic life of the nation in those more than half-century stretches is well enough known. But it was not reflected in constitutional change; the whole period is a blank.

That it was Madison himself who offered the Bill of Rights for initiation by the Congress seems to argue that the original framers had no conspiratorial intention to omit such protections but may simply have thought the document they had adopted offered safeguards enough. After all, they had divided functions, separated the branches, and set them to check each other. Also—although this may have been more by accident than by intention—they had given the legislature, the direct representatives of people in the various localities, certain advantages, slight-seeming but actually important, over the other branches. Besides, the constitutions of the states had bills of rights, and it was more their business than that of the central government to protect liberties.

Madison, when he proposed the amendments in the First Congress, did understand that added duties were being conferred on the hitherto almost overlooked judiciary, and that this might be important. He spoke of "independent tribunals of justice" and said that they would form "an impenetrable bulwark against every assumption of power in the legislative or executive." This was, however, except for the expanded concept of judicial power, no more limiting than the restricting principles: federalism and interdependence. The one reserved vast powers to the states; and the other, making concentration of federal power impossible in the presidency or the Congress, left both states and individuals free of possible oppression.

Jefferson deeply resented Marshall's assertion of a judicial power to review legislative acts; but it was logical, and it has seldom been doubted that there will always be need for interpretation. This is not to say that there has not been stiff objection to the enlargement of this concept. It is still true that there are areas where only amendment can establish constitutional legitimacy.

It may be noted that there was another and perhaps more influential reason why the framers considered the Bill of Rights to be superfluous. This was the situation of citizens in that time. The enormous expanse of country to be occupied by pioneering farmers and shopkeepers made it seem absurd that their liberties might need to be guarded. Homesteads might be miles apart; villages were minuscule. What authority could reach them? And if liberties were circumscribed, where would the force come from to make it good? Early Americans were as independent as any people in the world's history and as varied in their interests; who could conceive that one group—or the small number of officials provided for governing—could become oppressive? This was a peculiar and temporary condition, presently to be changed by territorial expansion, industrial development, the growth of population, and urbanization; but none of this was foreseen.

Madison, seeming somewhat surprised that the omission needed defense, did speak of it in *The Federalist* after objection had been voiced:

> The smaller the society, the fewer probably will be the distinct parties and interests composing it . . . and . . . the more easily will they concert and execute their plans of oppression. Extend the sphere and you take in a greater variety of parties and interests; you make it less probable that a majority of the whole will have a common motive to invade the rights of other citizens.

This may have been the framers' view, but when the original draft went to the state legislatures for ratification, it was apparent that the suspicion of central power was still very strong, the same suspicion that had nearly caused the disappearance of any national government at all.

It was all very well for the politicians in the states to consent, as apparently they must, to a central authority with certain powers, but if it should be strong enough to invade individual liberties, they wanted it known from the outset what the limits were. They evidently considered that their positions as state politicians had been sufficiently protected by the compromises consented to by the nationalists. No objection was made about states' rights; it was their constituents who were suspicious; and the politicians were responsive.

Madison proposed, as seemed to him logical, that his compendium of amendments be inserted into the original document. Roger Sherman objected; he thought they ought to be appended, and he had his way. Late in August, 1789, the group of proposals went from the House to the Senate. There some changes were made. Two clauses were eliminated, one having to do with the excusing of conscientious objectors from military service, and one prohibiting any one of the three departments of the existing executive establishment from interfering with the other two.

This was not the end. Two other amendments accepted by the Senate were never ratified by the states. One would have specified the ratio between population and representatives and the other would have prevented any change in congressmen's pay until after a next election. The remaining ten, however, were readily ratified by the necessary eleven states (there were fourteen states by then) late in 1791.

The first group of these amendments offered protection for freedom of speech, press, assembly, and religion; the second made certain that soldiers should not be quartered in any unconsenting person's house and that citizens, organized as militia, should have the right to bear arms; the third specified that property could not be taken without compensation and that in criminal trials there should be no procedures favorable to the authorities.

This is the content of the Bill of Rights, and the reason it was added to the original Constitution. Whether or not it was necessary, it has been the center of an immense volume of litigation. It has been examined over and over by succeeding generations of judges and justices. Certain of the clauses may have fallen into disuse; but others have been made into declarations the framers could not have considered because the subjects of them did not yet exist. The volume of civil rights literature has never been so large as in recent years.

What is more interesting here is that because the rights have been applied to unanticipated situations, they have become what the judicial interpreters of succeeding generations have preferred them to become. Now, after so many years, with no textual change, it is quite impossible to say what most rights will be interpreted to mean in any adversary case. This is the emergent situation

As the society has grown more complex, rights have needed different kinds of protection. A need has even developed to protect unanticipated ones. An illustration of this is economic security, including all sorts of welfare safeguards. Only by extension amounting to invention can the original Constitution be said to cover them; past experience would indicate that such extensions will be made; but what judicial inventiveness will produce no one can say.

That no one can say what rights will be discovered to have been hidden in the meager fifty-five words of the First Amendment, or the somewhat more numerous ones of the Fourth, Fifth, and Sixth Amendments, may seem strange after 175 years of exposition in countless opinions. If agreed interpretations had been arrived at, the number of these cases would have tapered off. In fact they grow more numerous. Decisions, instead of making meanings clearer, have made them more indefinite. Appellants are consequently encouraged to see whether the Court cannot be persuaded to accept some interpretation convenient to them, and often it can. When this happens, cheers rise from some sources, groans from others; but at least it has been shown again that the Constitution lives. It lives a more and more precarious existence, obviously not even understood in arcane professional circles. But, obviously, those circles like it that way; at least they seldom mention the possibility of definition through amendment; or, to be extreme, the addition of a Bill of Duties, so much needed in ever more complicated urbanized environments.

The modern expansion of civil rights began, it is fairly accurate to say, with what has sometimes been spoken of as the "revolution" of 1937. It was at about this time that the generation of justices deeply concerned with property rights left the Court with foreboding farewells. McReynolds said that the Constitution was gone, and Butler and Sutherland agreed. Presently, Black, one of the new men, succeeded in bringing a liberalized First Amendment into applications of the Fourteenth. And thenceforth, the Court began to legislate again—this time in another interest, but with no more restraint.

The change here is sometimes said to have begun with the Carolene case, in a footnote to his opinion written by Justice Stone. This was preceded by intimations in other opinions, and especially in Cardozo's earlier statement that liberties were on "a different plane of social and moral values." But what Stone announced was the abandonment of interference in "legislative judgment" about commercial transactions. There might be, he said, "narrower scope for the operation of the presumption of constitutionality" when legislation, on its face, appeared to be within the specific prohibition of the first ten amendments.[3]

During the following twenty years the Court's lack of restraint frightened even some of the justices—among them Frankfurter, who spoke of "abandon." Following Black, however, the Court crossed into interference with state arrangements, and presently arrived at new restrictions on the treatment of defendants, of equality in education and representation (in state legislatures), and in other areas opened by the new freedom it had appropriated for itself.

It met some opposition. There were formidable attempts to persuade the Congress to limit the Court's jurisdiction—one attempt, especially, when it forbade prayer in public schools—and there were some suggestions of reversal by amendment. None succeeded. For the time being the Court obviously had a majority following among the electorate in its expansion of civil liberties. This was taken by liberals and, except for a few conservatives among them, by lawyers to be a happy development. The Court had at last become a "primary rather than an auxiliary check on government," something, as Professor Mason has protested, intended by neither the founding fathers nor Chief Justice Marshall.[4]

At least one justice, Harlan, energetically protested, insisting that the Constitution embodies no *political* theory. This was a point Holmes had made (as long ago as 1905) about *economic* theory. Harlan's outrage was caused by the tattered condition of the original Constitution after the Court's rough handling. He deplored the notion that the Bill of Rights was the principal guarantee of liberty. It was, he said, shallow not to recognize that the structure of our political system accounts no less for the free society we have.

3. *United States* v. *Carolene Products Co.*, 304 U.S. 144 (1938).

4. In "New Life for the Bill of Rights," University Press: *A Princeton Quarterly*, Fall, 1966, p. 31.

This echoes protests throughout American history concerning usurpation by the Court of both legislative and amending powers. Supporters of judicial expansion on the scale of recent decisions do have to explain, it would seem, why the Court is especially fitted for its expanded role. Is congressional lethargy to be considered an opportunity for judicial aggression? And is the admitted difficulty of amendment a sufficient reason for abandoning altogether the essentials of constitution-building?

It is argued, sadly, that the liberal concern for rights and liberties, and the momentary willingness of a Court majority to protect them in circumstances of an urbanized society, was used by the Warren Court for a dangerous expansion of its power. This was made easier, of course, by the developments that Justice Harlan deplored—the decline of federalism and the blurring of separation. It is not necessary, however, to reconstitute these in the inappropriate setting of the modern world to find ways for the redefinition of freedom. Rights and duties—these are properly constitutional; amendment could keep them that way. Do citizens really believe, it is asked, that the Supreme Court ought to be a constitutionmaker rather than, in no more than a restricted and carefully defined sense, its interpreter?

Nothing in the emergent constitution is more difficult to define than the limits of judicial power in the interpretation of civil rights.[5]

The Legislative Branch

It is quite obvious that the framers, in accepting the presidency—a real novelty—had General Washington in view. He was, indeed, highly visible; he was their presiding officer and, as well, the one authentic hero of national proportions in the company. More than any other among them— or in the whole country—he stood for what the delegates had come to Philadelphia to achieve: "a more perfect union."

Washington's was not a quick and brilliant mind; it was one that reached conclusions after long and careful consideration. It was all the more impressive, therefore, that he, who had served so well already, was convinced that a new start must be made, that the states must give way to a strong central government. He was convinced that it must be one drawing its resources from a national electorate and having sole responsibility in all matters of common concern.

For his purpose, Washington, along with the other nationalists, would have preferred a nearly complete disappearance of the states. As in other

5. An interesting theory of approach is suggested by Thomas I. Emerson in *Toward a General Theory of the First Amendment* (New York: Random House, 1966). That at such a distant remove from the original a quite new guide to the meaning of constitutional clauses can be suggested is in itself an indication of the expectation that the Court will continue to make constitutional law—at least about civil rights.

countries, they might become provinces, perhaps with an appointed governor; at least their situation in an integrated nation ought to be clearly subordinate.

It was apparent at once, however, that this could not be achieved; and much of the Convention's time and effort was devoted to finding an acceptable substitute. The states' righters represented local politicians or were themselves that, and they were much too strong to be ignored.

It seems not to have occurred to anyone that national legislators (congressmen) might be made to represent constituencies-at-large. Delegates from the reluctant states were not likely to accept a legislature representing the nation as such. This was not because there were not ones among them having the general good at heart; it was because so many felt forced to disregard this intention whenever it conflicted with that of their constituents.

From the first the most serious controversy concerned this issue. It precipitated a prolonged struggle that is often pictured as the small states against the large ones—Virginia against Connecticut. The large ones, having more voters, would dominate any legislative house that owed its existence to popular representation; the small ones would always be in the minority. Actually the issue was a larger one; it involved national as against local views. Madison's Virginia Plan was not especially favorable to Virginia; it was favorable to the whole as against its parts—the nation as against the states—and this the states' righters would not accept.

It was because of the intransigence of these delegates that the Senate was reluctantly agreed to by the nationalists. That in the second house the smaller states would have equal representation with the larger was outrageously undemocratic, but that was something the Convention did not worry about. The sovereignty of the people was, anyway, that of only a few people. If any of the Convention's compromises might have been expected to break down within a short time, it must certainly be this. Recognition of its nonpopular nature was so general that the power to originate revenue bills was withheld from it and kept for the House of Representatives alone. And when the Convention was closing and an amending clause was being appended its last provision precluded any future change that would affect the "equal representation" of the states.

The Senate was not, however, an unlikely invention. There were other arguments for it apart from its assuagement of the small staters' fears. For one thing it had a long history not only in other lands but in the colonies and the states of the confederation. The upper chamber usually was an elite body, often appointed rather than elected, and was regarded as a check on the more popular lower one. There was some talk in the Convention about "single-house legislative tyranny"; and even the nationalists found some attraction in the thought of a conservative second chamber. In the final draft, there were two provisions to ensure this. One was senatorial powers that lacked only that of initiating revenue bills to be equal to those of the House, and so were a deterrent to representative impulsiveness; but the other was the Senate's position as an advisory council to the executive.

The advisory function had been intended to be more important than appeared in the final draft. All that remained of it, after the nationalists had second thoughts about its limitations on the president, was confirmation of his appointees and the treaties he negotiated. Washington appears not to have understood the modifications. Early in his presidency he sought for *advice* as well as *consent* and was rudely turned away. He never tried again, but other presidents have from time to time. For instance, when treaties are in question it is usual to involve the Senate at an early stage of their negotiation to ensure consent. But generally speaking, the president has been kept at a distance.

The Senate, as it turned out, was a somewhat more nationally oriented body than the House. Since representatives came from districts, and since they were given only two-year terms, they immediately became active in the promotion or protection of local interests, thus appealing to those who could reelect them. To do something for New York would be of no advantage to a member from Delaware, something the Delaware member recognized at once; but he would trade, and there began at once a process of logrolling that would become a lasting custom. One result of this swapping soon became notorious—it acquired the inglorious name "pork barrel" —and was universally condemned; but it survived. It even survived the establishment, after prolonged agitation (in 1921), of a federal budget; but the trading, after the budget began to be shaped by an executive bureau and submitted as an integrated governmental program, continued to be about as flagrant and as irrelevant to the general good as it had always been.

The president's influence in favor of national interests, it had been hoped, would be improved by this device; but the hope was defeated by the same forces that had always made the lower house a local-interest body. The price of a congressman's vote for some general need was often a bridge, a post office, or an army post in his district.

Senators, on the other hand, turned out to be at least more willing to consider wider interests than those of the particular states they represented. These interests were, however, often private ones; and the senators found it easy to profit from alliances that ran against those of the public. Often, too, like the representatives, they bargained for projects wanted in their states; but their terms were longer, and this freed them from the continuous campaigning imposed by the two-year term of the representatives and the never-ending need to placate their constituents.

It would be possible to make too much of this difference, but there is another furnished by original provisions of the Constitution that force senators to take a wider view in some matters. The power to ratify or refuse to ratify treaties with foreign nations has not always turned out well. Foreign relations have not always been treated with the delicacy required by diplomacy. And secretaries of state have often felt badly used.[6]

The situation of the Senate became so notoriously antidemocratic that the single amendment affecting the legislative branch in all our history was adopted. It did not happen until 1913, but it made a significant change. It provided for popular election rather than election by state legislatures, and this considerably reduced the peculiar corruption developed in that body. This had really become insufferable. The careers of Webster and Clay, for instance, two of the senators held in greatest respect by their successors, were tainted with an unscrupulous willingness to use their positions to favor clients from whom they took pay. Direct election reduced this abuse; so, perhaps, has a general change in public expectation; but respected senators often still receive income from active firms they belonged to in private life, and obviously the connection is maintained because their public positions can be useful to private clients.

The Senate was, on the whole, an unhappy result of the compromising that so often characterized the Convention.[7]

These remarks about the legislative bodies cannot be left without some reference to their struggles with the president in the no man's land of constitutional ambiguity. It is often spoken of admiringly as providing a necessary "flexibility"; and certainly it is one source of that "living" quality spoken of by commentators. The difficulty with this is that it also permits unseemly struggles for advantage that clearer definition would have avoided. Alone, the silences of the Constitution would make a definitive description of the emergent situation impossible.

The most important legislative aggressions have usually had their support in bizarre interpretations of the framers' intentions. Many of these have been assertions of the right to control the executive establishment, clearly not contemplated in the Constitution, but not forbidden by it;

6. An illustration of this is the indignation of Secretary of State John Hay when a carefully negotiated treaty clearing the way for Panama Canal construction was rejected. He went so far as to resign, but was persuaded by President McKinley to continue. Hay spoke bitterly of "the power of one-third plus one of the senate to meet with a categorical veto any treaty negotiated by the President." There have been other distressing vetoes, for instance that of Wilson's Versailles Treaty, generally assessed by historians as resulting more from annoyance with the president than concern for the nation.

7. Further discussion of the origins of bicameralism and its history in the United States can be found in the useful paper of Dan Burhans, prepared for the Center for the Study of Democratic Institutions and discussed on March 23, 1966. It is entitled "A Critical Look at Bicameralism."

but there have also been extensions of investigative powers not contemplated in the Constitution either. Both have had disruptive effects.

Controls over the executive were asserted as an extension of the exclusive power to originate revenue measures. It was almost at once assumed that because that authority had been explicitly conferred, it carried with it the corollary right to originate appropriations; and this made the other branches subservient; it placed even the Senate in a secondary position. And the executive and the Court were compelled to plead for needed funds.

If the president was charged with the faithful execution of the laws and was made commander in chief of the armed forces, he still had to go to the Congress if he wished to make a change in his establishment, or if he wanted to reorganize the armed forces. He could do such things with perfect constitutional propriety, but actually he would not dare; funds would certainly be withheld.

Washington discovered this; and the first departments he thought appropriate were established not by executive order but, at his request, by an act of the Congress. This was a mistake; it confirmed his subordination and that of his successors in all matters having to do with the organization of means for executing the laws. And the Congress ever since has used that concession with complete ruthlessness in trading for patronage and other favors. Indeed one of the more serious complaints about the Congress is that it does interfere so frequently, and with so little regard for the national interest, in executive affairs. This is made worse by congressmen's lack of information and their habitual retirement into anonymity when executive actions are not generally approved.

There are careful studies that document these shortcomings. *Congressional Control of Administration* by Joseph P. Harris[8] deals in detail with the methods used by influential members for enforcing their wishes. These are amazingly ingenious and varied, the most important and ever-present element of coercion being the granting or withholding of funds felt to be essential by the executive. A bureau in a large department, having its request for funds examined in detail by a subcommittee, will find mysterious resistance until a hint is taken that an establishment had better be placed or maintained in a certain locality and even that a particular individual ought to be in charge—an individual, invariably, who is useful to the member. These suggestions, made over a long period of time by legislators from safe districts, and perforce followed, can, and often do, place them in practical control. The vice of this is irresponsibility; it has no relation to the general interest and not even to the carrying out of duties. It is solely for an extraneous purpose.

There are times when interferences are quite open. Every department

8. Washington, D.C.: The Brookings Institution, 1964.

recognizes some influences of this sort, and budget officers need no instruction in the arts of ingratiation. What the influential legislator wants is granted without pressure. It is a system, and it is immensely detrimental to administration. It never comes into the open. A project is undertaken, an appointment is made, a facility is maintained; if it is unnecessary, or if it should prove mistaken or useless, the real instigator cannot be identified. He can, of course, let it be known in his constituency that any credit from it is his and ought to be repaid in support, and in campaigns he may openly make such a claim; at the same time he will often denounce the executive for the extravagance and inefficiency involved.

A bureaucracy grown to several million, many or even most of whom are engaged in such projects and have been chosen in such ways, is bound to be inefficient; yet constant reforming efforts are stopped by the politicians before they get under way. The federal budget and the Civil Service were the result of many years of exposure and agitation; but congressmen have found ways to evade many of the limitations of both. Actually the trouble goes deeper than any reform has sought to correct. It goes to the representative arrangement itself, provided in the Constitution and accepted as necessary to popular sovereignty.[9]

Several developments, not anticipated by the framers, modified severely the original intention to have a legislative branch that would make laws with due consideration for the public interest. One of these was sheer expansion. The first House of Representatives had thirty-nine members; and the Senate at first numbered twenty-two (before long, twenty-eight). Aside from the number of constituents (each representative in the first House had 3,000), the gradual growth that resulted in a House of 400 (with constituencies of half a million) and a Senate of 100 made modifications of procedure essential if anything at all was to get done.

A committee system was devised to do much of the legislative work, the general body being limited to the briefest possible discussion. This finally resulted in voting for or against committee recommendations and not much else. Even further, the work of the standing committees was circumscribed by setting up one or two pilot committees to regulate the flow of legislative proposals for House action. Whether a vote should be taken at all was a decision inevitably concentrated in a speaker who made appointments, and in the chairmen of the steering committees.

Speakers were presently being, not inappropriately, called czars; and presidents with programs to effect had to deal with them as equals. But speakers tended to lose the ability to dictate as "safe constituencies" became the fiefs of chairmen. The imposition of seniority rules allowed a small number of these old hands to rule the House from their committee

9. This subject is discussed at some length in the author's *The Enlargement of the Presidency*.

rooms. Every chairman of a major committee was from one of these safe districts in the south when F. D. Roosevelt was proposing his New Deal. They defended the gateway for thirty years. That delay was the penalty for having a defective system. Finally the nation had an accumulation of problems that generations would be required for clearing up: a deficit of public facilities, cities grown ugly and dangerous, resources plundered, water and air polluted, a bureaucracy incapable of performing the duties required of it. The list could be indefinitely lengthened. Worst of all, the haste of the Johnson Congress to catch up provoked a reaction that again brought objectors into positions of such power that they could resume their blocking tactics, and his Great Society turned out to be confused and unworkable.

None of this was contemplated in the Constitution; it was, however, accepted, and must be said to have had the same effect as though it had been anticipated by the framers. This, of course, is to impute something very unfair to that gathering. Their mistakes were humanly inevitable. The real trouble was that they were never corrected in following generations

Since political parties, and representatives under party discipline, were not contemplated either, the loss of voices or influence by individual representatives in the House was unexpected. This was made much more significant by the virtual freezing of polarized opinion on important issues in many constituencies. Strict or loose construction is an example of this hard position holding. In many districts large majorities for one or another party continued to be returned over long periods—there was a "solid South," for instance, developed about the complex of "strict construction" and given emotional content by the South's defense of slavery. This resulted in extremely long periods of service for representatives from those constituencies. House membership became a lifelong occupation; and this, together with the rule of seniority, enabling experienced legislators to monopolize committee chairmanships, defeated the intent of the framers to have a legislature that discussed public issues and came to considered conclusions. The Congress soon became a completely different body than could be inferred from a reading of the Constitution itself. The Congress, in fact, has never been able to legislate as was contemplated.

Since the legislative branch, because of its expansion and peculiar organization, found itself unable to contemplate national needs or to debate matters of general interest, that duty was passed to the president; and the enlargement of this function made the president what he began to be called, after some fifty years: the "chief legislator."

True, the framers had said that the president might "from time to time give to the Congress information on the state of the Union," and might "recommend to their consideration such measures as he shall judge necessary," but it was certainly not intended that he should supplant it in formulating plans for the future or in establishing national policies.

The effect of this reversal was to make relations between the legislative and executive branches one of recurrent enmity and of continual acrimonious bargaining. The Congress, because of size and diversity, was inherently unable to concentrate on initiatives of its own; still it harbored a continual resentment directed at the president. He, elected by all the people, and committed to leadership, must try to get things done. For long periods the Congress became an obstructing rather than a legislating body, and sometimes its opposition was justified frankly as a mere desire to thwart a president.

This continual state of conflict made the Congress peculiarly receptive to the influence of the growing swarm of lobbyists for special interests that infested the Capitol. It was estimated that in the seventies there were at least a dozen lobbyists for every congressman. It was also estimated that of the bills introduced by congressmen, originating in other than presidential sources, about two-thirds were actually written by the interests they would favor. The congressional lobby was now spoken of quite casually by commentators as a "third house"—something that would have horrified the framers, but something, it must be said, that they made possible.[10]

Taken altogether, the evolution of the legislature from its original formation has resulted in characteristics so serious that it is no exaggeration to suggest a continuing crisis. There is a minimum of attention to national problems; there is a well-developed system of trading for local improvements; there is interference in matters members are not competent to handle; there is no possibility of creative leadership and an incessant resistance to that of the president. Worst of all, there is a sickeningly supine posture before the swarming lobbyists.

This is a dismal conclusion that Americans do not like to face. The truth is that the Congress has grown ineffective and more amenable to the influence of private interests. It has never been reorganized, largely because it controls the gateway to reorganization and because its reactionary elders have been able to maintain intact their control of the legislative majority to the initiation of amendment.

What is most needed is a return to the concept of considered legislation under constitutional directives: laws made by men of dedication who have in view the public good. They need not agree; they may even compromise their beliefs in order to get on with their duty. This is not serious for the

10. A horrifying accumulation of evidence of all that has been said here is by now available in books and articles by all sorts of investigators and commentators. One especially devastating account has been mentioned: Joseph Harris's *Congressional Control of Administration*, written under the auspices of The Brookings Institution.

legislative process. Laws, after all, are expected to serve a purpose and to be readily changed if they prove defective. The difficulty now is that neither the intent nor the giving way to practical considerations is a pure process. It is deeply corrupted.

The emergent constitution, as far as the legislative branch is concerned, has to be described in these unsatisfactory terms. It has lived all these years, but in many ways it has been a life no American can regard with pride.

The Executive Branch

Article II of the Constitution begins by saying that "the executive power shall be vested in a President. . . ." But even the most casual appraisal shows quite plainly that what a modern president most conspicuously does *not* do—himself—is to execute. He is very active in doing a good many things mentioned only tangentially; and he does many more not mentioned at all; but these require so much of his attention that he leaves administration to subordinates. He has at most only a sketchy knowledge of what goes on in the agencies nominally under his control, and except in the most general sense he does not direct their activities. He no longer has regular meetings—as earlier presidents did—with department heads. Most meetings are limited to a few with some knowledge of matters he regards as most pressing. There are no exchanges among a group of responsible officials about matters of policy. There is, in fact, no longer a cabinet as it was formerly meant.

Only when an administrative matter demands attention because a problem has developed is it considered by the president; and when a solution has been found or the crisis has passed, the subordinate in charge is left to carry on; the president then turns to another. There have been, in recent years, periods of months, sometimes many, when heads of important agencies, directly responsible to the president, have not been able to confer with him about their problems or policies. How could they when there are some two hundred of them?[11]

There have been proposals for remedying this—many of them. These have originated both in formidable inquiries such as those conducted by the Hoover Commissions and in continued studies of administration by

11. The count varies with the standard used. Some fifty are a direct administrative responsibility; another fifty are appointed by him and look to him for their policies although they are not by law required to do so; another fifty are nominally independent or semijudicial but maintain liaison with other agencies; still another fifty, more or less, are at work evaluating, investigating, conciliating, or bargaining under the direction of the presidential staff. One result is piles of paper that never grow smaller, and much of it never reached. Another is a constant waiting list of subordinates who need the president's personal direction but will never be able to see him.

governmental agencies for self-study. But the fact is that the situation has grown worse rather than better. That is, it has grown worse if the president is actually thought of as an administrator. Successive commissions and study groups never seem to consider that he has inevitably become something else and that sporadic attempts to restore his supervisory ministrations cannot succeed.

This persistent view of the president's duties originated in the clause vesting "executive power" in him, and, in a section devoted mostly to his relations with the Congress and the reception of ambassadors, of "taking care that the laws should be faithfully executed." The framers had to think of an establishment very different from the modern one. At the beginning it had two civilian departments, State and Treasury, each staffed with a few clerks; and not much more was contemplated. How the responsibilities of government have grown, everyone knows. The few clerks have grown to millions, the two departments to twelve with many other agencies added, and Washington's own staff of two or three to several thousand.

Attempts to translate the original constitutional phraseology into realizable administrative control have for some reason taken the line of assuming that presidents resemble the heads of business establishments. As the business grows, devices for delegation are simply multiplied. This mistaken conception has prevented any realistic appraisal of the office as such with its multiform responsibilities. Also it has left the immense governmental establishment without an effective directive system. The president is assumed to know all and do all. No more absurd assumption can be imagined. Yet there are no responsible suggestions for remedial reorganization.

While this expansion of the executive establishment has been going on and the faithful execution of the laws has become so obviously impossible for the president, even if he had no other duty, he has become the director of foreign relations, the chief legislator, the political leader, and, in an immensely extended sense, commander in chief. It will be noticed that one of these (the political leadership) is not mentioned in the Constitution, that another (legislative leadership) is referred to only indirectly (he is to inform the legislature . . .), and that the duty of commander in chief has become far more consequential than was contemplated by the framers. He now, in effect, declares war and directs its civilian as well as its military operations.

It can, of course, be said that all of this has been accommodation to circumstance; and this is true enough; but accommodation by amendment has not happened because of the original defect. There has been no genuine reappraisal of the presidential situation and consequently no reassignment of duties and powers.

Since the framers were familiar with small legislative bodies, they could be quite specific about what these assemblies might or might not do (without saying *how* it was to be done, since they assumed that traditional practices would continue). Presumably if the population had not grown, if the states had not become more numerous, if the economy had remained agricultural, and so on, the legislative prescription in the Constitution might have continued to serve well enough.

This familiarity, however, was not true of the presidency. The president was a new creation. In the framers' conception of him there are traces of Colonial governorships, but the recollections of revolution were too recent for these to have served as actual models. Those who would have liked a constitutional monarchy—Hamilton, for instance—spoke, but had little attention paid to what they said. The delegates agreed—after discussion—that union did require a strong central figure; this was all very well, but they were not together long enough, and not clear enough about his position in the government, to prescribe the responsibilities of the figure they had rather dimly conceived.

Prejudices were always warring with needs at the Convention, and the delegates' fear of conferring power very nearly matched their fear that unless the chief of state was free to act, the nation could not be saved. They could see that such a personage had to be created, but what he might do and might not do they really could not say, especially since they drew back from creating a magnified governor.

In a few matters they could be specific; they were agreed that he must be commander in chief. But when they accepted language about executive power, they were remiss. It should have been said that the president would be chief of state, and the prescription about faithful execution of the laws should not have been added. That they did not really mean him to be the executive, or that they had no intimation of the coming administrative expansion—probably the latter—is to be suspected from another passage giving the secretary of the treasury independent relations with the Congress, and in another giving the president the strange right of requiring in writing the opinion of the principal officer in each of the departments. It was as though they were never expected to confer. Also, when the creation of executive departments became necessary, it was assumed to be a congressional prerogative, not a presidential one. All this is the prescription for a remote supervisory relationship. It was nowhere said that he should be the chief executive in the sense of directing day-to-day operations. The modern extrapolation is a tortured one.

What seems to be difficult for present-day students to recall is that there was very little administering to do in Washington's time and that this cannot have seemed likely to be an important responsibility. Government, however, did expand rapidly, so rapidly that Jefferson was horrified. He

left his post as secretary of state in order to oppose from outside the outrageous expansions of responsibility that Washington, with Hamilton's advice, felt forced to assume.

Of course Jefferson discovered, when he assumed the presidency, that
an administrator was needed (the states could not do everything) and
that Hamilton had been right after all in his view of centralized powers. He
never made an acknowledgment of these discoveries, but as president he
was even more dictatorial than Washington had been. This was elaborately
concealed by democratic protestations; but that he ran the country no one
doubted during his terms, and indeed the same was true of two subsequent
ones when his pupils, Monroe and Madison, succeeded to the office. By that
time the president had become exactly what Jefferson had deplored—the
central executive who managed the federal establishment. There was no
one else to do what had to be done. The chief of state became the operational administrator for the whole government.

Jefferson was not one of the framers; he was abroad at the time of the
Convention, and he did not like what had been framed. He was infected
with French revolutionary and ruralistic ideas, and he thought the president
too kingly. He determined to change all this, if necessary by political means.
If what happened when he succeeded and himself became president was
just the reverse of his expressed intentions, this could happen because the
document was ambiguous about the presidency and because by becoming
a political leader he could be nearly as royal as any president in the whole
line and at the same time do nothing that could be said to be unconstitutional.

Noting that the framers had not visualized the presidency in anything
like the detail of the legislative branch, it has been suggested above that this
was indeed because they had every day to sit under Washington as he
presided over their sessions. His tremendous prestige and his serenity
throughout the sometimes acrimonious discussions gave them a sense of
security. If he was to take charge of the nation there was no need for
specification. How much truth there is in this supposition no one can be
certain; probably a good deal.

However it happened, the developments of the next hundred years
demonstrated that deficient specification about the office was an omission
with serious consequences. The president could be chief of state, but in an
expanded government he could not be chief administrator too. After watching constitutional monarchy at work so long in Britain's vast empire, the
framers ought to have known that the combination was unworkable. At any
rate the conflict between the two has left the nation at this considerable
distance without an effective administrator when there is a most demanding
need for one.

It is clear enough now that a chief of state is the first need; and it may be that a commander in chief who is a civilian is next; but this ought not to prevent the nation, as it does, from having responsible direction for its domestic affairs.

The accumulating difficulties of administering an organization of the size and scope reached by the presidential establishment under the conditions developed in the United States began to cause critical reappraisals as soon as expansion began, and there have been many since. The federal government was not long in becoming the largest operating organization in any but the Communist nations. Some modifications resulted from the setting up of the Civil Service Commission in 1883, and later from the institution of the Budget Bureau in 1921. Much was hoped from both these innovations by students of government; but although the beginnings of a professional service were discernible, and the estimates of expenditure submitted annually by the president became more orderly, both were frustrated because of the hostility of the Congress. Both innovations had been resented by the legislature; and, of course, neither had any constitutional identity, so both could be largely ignored.

In F. D. Roosevelt's administration, the need for a comprehensive study of the presidential establishment had become urgent. He had already asked for and got, in the circumstances of depression, a certain freedom in reorganizing and adding to executive agencies; later, also, the formidable studies made first by the Public Administration Center and then by the Hoover Commissions resulted in reducing the number of agency heads reporting directly to the president, giving him more assistants, and devising a somewhat more logical organization.

Nevertheless, until the Eisenhower presidency, the establishment remained in an acutely unsatisfactory state. It continued to grow, the number of agencies proliferated as more duties were assumed, and the inability of the president to exercise effective control grew more and more notorious.

The difficulty with the earlier studies seemed to be that they insisted on regarding the president as a sort of tycoon, and the pattern for his functioning was clearly borrowed from big business. The conception was that he gave orders and they were carried out by a staff and by agency heads responsible to him for their employment. It was generally overlooked that he was a political leader, and was also, by default, chief legislator, responsibilities business executives do not have. Also that his associates were politicians too with commitments of their own, not necessarily the same as his.

Eisenhower was able to do a good deal better. His army training had given him experience in using a staff, and this he brought to the presidency. It gave his administration more control and much more cohesion than it had ever had before. It was notorious, however, that Eisenhower had a deficient conception of political leadership; personally he had no need to hold attention by popular appeals—he was a hero, and so invulnerable. This, also, had its effect on his other duty of originating legislation. He was the feeblest in this respect of any modern president. There was not much that he would have liked to see done, and even that did not seem to him essential.

It will be noticed that the growth in scope and responsibility of the presidential office was altogether extraconstitutional, a development not anticipated by the framers, and so not provided for. Also throughout its history no amendment had affected the office, except an unfortunate one limiting the president to two terms and thus reducing his second-term political influence. There had been no expression of intention by the electorate to modernize the presidency. There was only the approval of candidates in national elections. It could perhaps be said that the expansion of the presidency had become constitutional by the obvious favoring of the more active and bolder among candidates, and this did help to strengthen the president in his repeated conflicts with the Congress, but such accretions have no permanency, and they are under recurrent attack from both the other branches.

What has to be said is that the modern presidency is not at all like that of Washington, and that its enlargements are not legitimized. Consequently, vast areas of presidential activity are in constant controversy, and there are vast areas that he must neglect simply because he is one man and can do no more than one man can do. It is often argued that this, like other vague areas of constitutional direction, has allowed development to proceed without the constriction of rigid definition. But what can happen in such a situation is easily illustrated from historical incidents, sometimes very costly indeed and with sinister implications for the future.

From the president's side it has permitted the development of that undefined residual power that has come finally to be spoken of as the Doctrine of Necessity; and from the side of the other branches, it has at one time resulted in such congressional attacks as the Tenure of Office Act and at another by such a Supreme Court pronouncement as occurred in Truman's presidency in the steel cases.[12] Surely such disorienting struggles as these cannot be regarded with indifference. They involve issues too important to remain in their present state. The temporary dominance of one or another branch of government without any certainty that attack will not happen at any moment is intolerable in a civilized society.

If there is need for a Doctrine of Necessity, if there will recurrently be situations calling for the urgent use of residual powers, the conditions of their use ought not to be entirely at the mercy of conflicting agencies or be defined by one of the branches in its own interest.

12. *Youngstown Sheet & Tube Co.* v. *Sawyer,* 343 U.S. 579 (1952). The Doctrine of Necessity was discussed in Chapter 5 of this volume.

This is a dismal assessment of the emergent presidency. The interpretations of the original Constitution have been so unrestrained that the contemplated figure is no longer recognizable except as chief of state. That remains. But the political leadership assumed by the president has done infinite harm by subjecting the nation's symbol of unity to the exigencies of electoral conflicts. A president who emerges the victor from campaigning is smeared with all the defamations his opponents have been able to invent. He is no longer the remote and serene Washington figure.

The sudden transformation expected after election is not often successfully made. The president is still the political leader. Americans can take little satisfaction in a look backward at the indignities suffered by their chiefs of state because of this extraconstitutional responsibility.[13]

The Saint Gaudens figure seated in the Lincoln memorial is hard to reconcile with the simian beast of the 1864 campaign. Even Washington, before he retired to Mount Vernon, was splattered with political mud. And later presidents have suffered indignities of incredible extremity.

The president, however, *is* this figure compounded of detractory lies, of immense but indefinite responsibilities he cannot possibly meet; he is the symbolic chief of state; he is the neglectful administrator; he is chief legislator. The emergent constitution has made it so.

The Judicial Branch

If the framers specified very sketchily the powers and duties of the president, those for the judiciary were even more scantily treated. This, however, was probably for quite a different reason; the presidency was not at all clearly visualized, and courts were familiar—even more familiar than legislatures. Many at the meeting were lawyers, and what lawyers did when they became judges was well known: they decided who was right and who was wrong when cases brought by complainants came before them, and they were guided by constitutions or enabling acts as well as by common law.

What was said, after a clause vesting the judicial power in "one Supreme Court, [and] in such inferior courts as the Congress shall . . . ordain . . ." was that jurisdiction should "extend to all cases, in law and equity, arising under this Constitution, the laws of the United States and treaties. . . ."

Problems concerning the judiciary arise out of the extrapolations—made by the courts themselves—from this sentence. The questions of most consequence turn on the meaning of "under this Constitution." Did that mean simply that cases between claimants for decision in the system

13. Recounted in nauseous and elaborate detail in B. R. Felknor, *Dirty Politics* (New York: W. W. Norton & Company, 1966).

of arrangements established in the new government should have recourse to the Court; or did it mean that the Court could decide questions *about the Constitution*? The first would be a far more limited and simple interpretation. The second would allow the Court to determine that laws were or were not in accord with the Constitution and what other branches and officers of government might and might not do. In a document so brief and general, this reading would give the Court added authority because of its control over the other branches.

Chief Justice Marshall, who was a Federalist, saw the Court as an instrument of an evolving nationalism, able to direct and discipline other officers of government, who, if left alone, might behave as *they* believed the Constitution to intend. Jeffersonianism was ascendant, and if under Jefferson's devious leadership the Congress should decide to reduce federal power in favor of that of the states, the Supreme Court, defending the Federalist conception, would prevent it; the opportunity to do this was presented in the case of *Marbury* v. *Madison*.[14]

When the Marbury opinion was written, it was done in a way that prevented Jefferson from making the reply he would have liked to have made. The opinion held that a law was not in accord with the Constitution; but it was not the law that was in controversy; it was Marbury's claim to an office. The significant finding was hidden behind Marbury's problem. So nothing was done or even said, and the precedent was allowed to stand.

It was a very slow and gradual, but quite logical, advance from this original assertion that finally resulted in the seizing by the Court of the power presidents had assumed from time to time under what came to be called the Doctrine of Necessity.

As the life of the nation unfolded there came times when something not provided for in any recognizable grant of power simply had to be done. There was no provision for emergency, but there was no possibility that emergencies could be met by anyone but the executive. He had the resources; he could move quickly. Disaster could thus be avoided or essential advantage could be gained.

The residual or unmentioned powers used in such instances by presidents were defined by Attorney General Jackson as "aggregate"; they were, he said, justifiably used whenever a crisis called for action without delay. The Court as it was then constituted (or a majority of its justices) was not satisfied with this; and we have seen that when President Truman, during the Korean War, issued an order seizing the nation's steel mills to prevent the stoppage of production when the workers struck, the Court held that he had exceeded his grant of power. If, however, he was not to

14. 1 Cr. 137 (1803).

decide whether an emergency existed and what would have to be done because of it, some other provision would have to be made for meeting it. The crisis would not simply go away; and if it should not be met, any degree of damage to the national interest might result.

What, in effect, was said by the majority opinion (or opinions, for there were several) was that the Court itself would decide when an emergency existed and what the president could, or could not, do to meet it. This action in emergency, resorted to many times in the past, was thus deleted from the presidential powers—that is, if the Court actually succeeded in having the last say in the matter.

Chief Justice Vinson did not agree with the majority of his Court. He cited, in his dissent, a total of twenty-five instances when such powers had been used by presidents in the past, and called attention to the Court's tacit consent to most of them; he also made a few acid remarks about its impotence if it did not consent. What, he asked, could it do if the president did not agree?

Practical considerations center, of course, on the president's control of the administrative agencies, and in his ability to act at once and with a variety of instruments when the national interest is threatened in any way. The Court, it was pointed out by Vinson, is essentially a passive body, unable actually to take action, in recess for months at a time, and unable to make decisions unless and until a case comes to it from an adversary appeal, after trial in lower courts. The months or weeks of delay involved in its procedures make the Court's claim one that, if taken as absolute, might allow the nation to be seriously jeopardized while delays were prolonged in some future emergency. The Court might just not be there; if there, it might not have the matter before it; and if there, and permitted to decide, it could *say* but it could not *do*. It had no administrative arm.

This decision illustrates the position reached by the judiciary from extrapolation of simple words in the Constitution. The Court claims to be able to say to the other branches that they have exceeded their powers or have not fulfilled their duties. This, its critics say, denies all other branches the independence intended by the framers and destroys the balance of powers.

It is to be noted that, in the Court's view, there is no authority able to say that the Court itself has exceeded its powers or has not met its duties. That this was inherent in Marshall's view had never been really made plain until the opinion in the steel case. With all its weaknesses as the determinant in balance-of-power issues, its lack of popular mandate, its dependence on the vagaries of adversary reference, and its lack of ability to enforce its edicts, it stands finally in the position of asserting a power it can use only if others recognize its authority.

This separation-and-balance principle had been very much in the delegates' minds at the Convention. It is often attributed to their reading of Montesquieu, but this probably served only for support. They had a double problem that the principle seemed to solve; their experience with George III and with Colonial governors warned them against executives with unchecked power; at the same time legislatures were often responsive to popular clamor for easy but unwise actions. They had especially in mind the legitimizing of paper money whenever large numbers of voters had debts to pay.

The separation principle, then, must be understood in the same way as federalism. It was a compromise, intended to pacify disagreeing delegates —those who wanted the legislature to be supreme, and those who favored a strong executive. The Congress elected frequently from localities, under state rules, would check the president. The president, whose constituency was national, would veto unwise legislation.

Whether the third branch, the judiciary, was regarded as part of this compromise is not clear. The instability of the arrangement certainly gave the Court its opportunity to intervene. But the question of original intention was still being argued after nearly two hundred years.

There is, of course, the excuse that the framers produced a document that had to be interpreted by *some* authority. There are so many silences, so many ambiguities, and so many potential conflicts that there has often to be some resolution of contentions. Who is to do this? It is sometimes argued that conflict itself is the best resolver and can usually be depended on. This was the view of Justice Brandeis. He maintained that the tensions generated by the Constitution were deliberately intended by the framers. They were the active principle in separation, meant to prevent permanent lodgment of arbitrary power anywhere in the structure.

Walter Lippmann, having a similar view, and commentating on an assertion by President Johnson that he "had been elected by the American people to decide" his course in Vietnam, was moved to eloquent outrage. In reproving the president, he spoke of "the quintessential principle that nowhere in American society shall anyone exercise arbitrary power." He went on:

> The Founding Fathers took measures to prevent the exercise of arbitrary power by the Congress, by the courts, by the executive, and by the people themselves. This is the prevailing principle in the whole constitutional system. This is the ruling principle of Americanism, and the defiant words of the Omaha speech, when they are read in the light of what has been done since February 1965, offend the sovereign principle of the American commonwealth.[15]

This is so representative an instance of the difficulties involved in defining powers that it may be pursued somewhat further. The question

15. *Newsweek,* July 18, 1966, p. 17.

was whether the nation should remain at peace or should go to war. The words of the Constitution about this are plain, even if they have an antique flavor. It is said that the Congress shall have the power "to declare war, grant letters of marque and reprisal, and make rules concerning captures on land and sea." But modern conflicts are more likely to have instant outbursts than to result from failures of prolonged negotiation; and to wait for the Congress to make a declaration of war, to say nothing of waiting for the Court to say whether the Congress can do so in the particular circumstances, might well be to allow the nation and all its people to be destroyed.

Lippmann himself arrived at his indignant denunciation, and his eloquent statement of American "principle," after rather more thoughtful appraisal of the difficulty presented by the modern sort of emergency:

There is no denying, of course, that the President has very large powers, that the role of the Congress in declaring war is insubstantial. For my own part I think this is a good thing: better that the President should prevail than that there should be a stalemate when there is a vital national interest at stake.[16]

Still, his outrage boiling up again, he went on:

What seems to be wholly unacceptable in the Omaha doctrine of the Presidency is that it is like a claim to arbitrary power, a claim that in making these momentous decisions, the President, once he is elected, is bound only by his personal views, not by any kind of mandate or covenant with the people who elected him.[17]

If this sounds somewhat as though the indignation arose because the president was behaving in a manner not approved by Lippmann, it does call attention to a principle that underlies the constitutional conception of the framers. But this principle was ambiguously stated; it allowed interpretations that differed, and in their way encouraged the existence of conflicting views over long periods with no possibility of resolution.

It is in view of this ambiguity—now become in many instances dangerous—that it is so important to realize the need in any constitutional system for clearly defined residual powers. The world is not what it was; the dangers are not merely those of sudden conflict—they are those of destruction—but these residual powers do not now have the lodgment claimed by the Court; actually they are precisely where they have always been—in the presidency. Emergencies belong to him; they are his to meet.

It is all too evident that the framers did not draw up a completely self-explanatory document; but it is evident too, after much experience, that one could never in any circumstances be drawn up that would be

16. *Ibid.*
17. *Ibid.*

applicable in every exigency. This is not because of any lack of skill or wisdom but because the world changes, and men's situation in it changes; and because this happens, often, with unpredictable force and rapidity.

This does not imply that some effort could not have been made by the framers to anticipate emergencies; but the fact is that they did not. The allocation of a residual power to be used only in the most urgent circumstances, generally defined, would have been the minimum precaution against the dangers visible even then. The omission was the more serious because these were not only dangers likely to develop from disaster, but the danger that emergency might be an excuse for the seizure of powers that would nullify the clauses intended to prevent the permanent lodgment anywhere of arbitrary authority. No precaution is to be found in the Constitution. Emergencies, once declared, are slow to terminate if no rule is applicable.

In recent years a good deal of scholarly effort has been expended in trying to demonstrate that Madison expected the Court to play the institutional role indicated for it by Marshall. There is, however, a curious contradiction in this. It often begins with a criticism of the historian Charles A. Beard, who, it is said, meant to discredit judicial supremacy by showing that it was no more than an attempt to protect the framers' "interests."[18] If this was what Beard intended, and if he misinterpreted Madison (in *The Federalist*), then Madison, freed of this charge, can be said to have been expounding and, in his constitutional draft, trying to institutionalize eighteenth-century political theory. This theory did give the judiciary a position of importance, if not of supremacy; and this seemed to come into the Constitution.

The antagonism among American historians seems to be fairly polarized between those who are "progressive"—those who want the Constitution to permit the development of a welfare state—and those who are "conservative"—who want the Constitution interpreted as a defense against this sort of thing. This is, perhaps, a simplified description, but it is roughly true.

It seems not to be considered that the original document may be taken literally, or that the position of the judiciary among democratic institutions ought, from time to time, to be reconsidered by other than those who are arguing for or against the position it has defined for itself.

The controversy is really irrelevant. The emergent situation is this: the Court assumes to have wide powers not only in cases arising *under* the Constitution, but in ones *about* the Constitution. By interpretation this is taken to extend into the region of separation; the areas of silence belong to the Court.

18. Charles A. Beard, *An Economic Interpretation of the Constitution* (New York: The Macmillan Company, 1913).

Ever since this doctrine was made explicit by Marshall (whether or not it can be traced to Madison) it has been in dispute. Especially presidents, nearly every one of them, have in one or another way asserted an original power, coming to them from the national electorate. This, they contend, is beyond the competence of the Court just as it is beyond the reach of the Congress.

This is true, as well, of the Congress, although by reason of difference in position; it has been less assertive in contests with the Court than have presidents. It is making laws; the president is acting. It may stop to question the constitutionality of measures before it; but the president often may not hesitate.

No president in American history bent to Court decree until Truman allowed himself to be reprimanded, and the end of that may be the Vinson minority view rather than that of the then majority. But the Court does have an extraordinary prestige, and this supports its own interpretation. Still the central doctrine of the Constitution is certainly that of separate and independent branches, and this is inconsistent with the ability of any one of them to define for the others the area of its authority.

The Courts may more easily be challenged by the Congress than by the president, especially since the challenge may never mention the supremacy doctrine. A simple congressional majority may restrict jurisdiction. The president is in a more difficult position. He cannot so easily influence judicial attitudes, even though he does often have public opinion on his side. He does, however, have a certain resisting power. The Court cannot force him to do or not to do anything if he decides differently. Such bold directives as were used in the steel case would not be respected by a determined president. The Court could do no more about it than it could when Jackson refused to enforce one of its decrees. It is important that the Court is further from the president's reach than from that of Congress. Lincoln prevailed in a "packing" attempt (with congressional concern), but Roosevelt, when he tried the same maneuver, was condignly defeated. This was a signal victory for the justices; but it was a battle that was won, not a war. It settled none of the issues about separation.

In later years the justices have been brash. They were formerly most discreet in recognizing their own limitations. For some time they recognized a "political" field they must not invade. Brandeis, recognizing the shaky ground occupied in the assertion of supremacy, always tried to avoid the questions affecting the powers of other branches; these were the ones regarded as "political"; and he was followed by Frankfurter and by Harlan.

It is another curiosity of the present situation, recalling the half-century and more of attacks on the Court by the Progressives, who denounced it as the protector of property rights, that later criticisms from the same Progressives were precisely the reverse. The Court has been said, again and again, not only by outsiders but by such dissenting justices as Black, to have "abdicated" its proper function because of timidity in rebuking both president and the Congress in matters having to do with civil rights.

Even justices who have understood the practical difficulties of asserting themselves have not admitted that supremacy is doubtful doctrine. They have held back because self-restraint, in their view, was indicated— on practical, but not on doctrinal, grounds. Justice Jackson was an expositor of this view. There are decisions, he said, that "are wholly confided by our constitution to the political departments of the government. They are delicate, complex, and involve large elements of prophecy. They are and should be undertaken only by those directly responsible to the people. . . . They are decisions of a kind for which the Judiciary has neither aptitude, facilities, nor responsibility and have long been held to belong in the domain of political power not subject to judicial intrusion or inquiry."[19]

Thus Justice Jackson, who had once been attorney general and, a number of times, had defended the president in the necessary but doubtful extension of his powers. But four years later Jackson concurred with the majority in the steel case. What he had meant to say, earlier, was that if "political" matters had long been held to belong in a domain not subject to judicial intrusion, it was because the Court held this to be true, not because it was constitutional doctrine, evident on its face. Actually he gave away much less than he seemed to in saying that certain "decisions are confided by our constitution . . . to political departments." They are if the Court defines them as "political"; and only if it does, or so the Court holds.

The difference in interpretation, the recurrent controversy, it has to be admitted, is inherent in the ambiguity of the original Constitution. No matter what one of the branches contends, the powers of the others are, if not clearly defined, inherent and untouchable. What the Congress or the president claims will be possessed if the situation is favorable.

The position of the Court in the emergent constitution is, in its own view, central rather than peripheral. It assumes to have a wide discretion in allocating authority, and this assumption is defined by the profession judges are drawn from. It presumes to be the repository of residual powers; it determines whether laws and actions are permissible; it is an issuer of directives for the executive; and it defines its own authority.

It must be said that the longer the nation goes on without reworking its Constitution in a proper process, the more disposition there is generally to accept the Court at its own valuation.

It should be recalled that no amendment has touched the Court since the Eleventh, ratified in 1798 (affecting its jurisdiction). The Court's solid

19. *Chicago & Southern Air Lines* v. *Waterman Steamship Co.*, 333 U.S. 103 (1948).

constitutional powers are those conferred in the late eighteenth century, and it has no others of this legitimate sort. This is not a realistic appraisal, of course, but any more realistic one rests on supports quite as weak as those of the other branches. It must rest on custom and general acceptance.

Missing Branches: Political, Planning, Regulatory

Attention has been called here to important areas of public responsibility that had no original constitutional recognition and have had none since that time. They indisputably belong to the emergent constitution, but no amendment has given them legitimacy, and for some (or, at least, one) there is not even any systematic legislative recognition.

Of the numerous functions not anticipated by the framers, at least some have quite logically been added to or incorporated in the existing branches. It is a matter of judgment, very often, whether this has been satisfactory. There are those who would say that education, welfare, and information are scandalously subordinated within the executive branch. There are others who suggest changes in the executive office to make it more consonant with presidential duties. It would, perhaps, no longer be an administrative office in the original sense, since the duties of chief of state, political leader, maker of foreign policy, and chief legislator have overwhelmed the president and made it impossible for him personally to see that the laws are faithfully executed.

If there were a real administrator, however, education, welfare, and similar areas of interest would seem to fall within his sphere. They are duties; and they do not, more than others, extend themselves into legislative or judicial realms.

This may be an unacceptable way of classifying; however, there seem to be three areas (at least) that require lifting to the level of the original branches. They are as important now as those others, and giving them status would be more a matter of recognition than of invention. At the same time such elevation would confer a legitimacy they now lack—and badly need. These are political, planning, and regulatory functions.

The political function is one of the strangest of all lacunae in the Constitution. It is the source of power; it is the directive for government; it affects significantly every individual and every organization of society. Yet it exists in a legal vacuum. Its only recognition consists of provisions for election, and even these are mostly passed to the states.

Because of lack of recognition, political processes have settled into indefensible patterns and have spawned strange and inappropriate institutions. If any part of American political life needs reform, discipline, and orderly development, it is certainly this one. It exists, it is an emergent, but it has no formal recognition.

The regulatory function, borrowing from all the branches, violating everywhere the principle of separation, and proliferating until its bureaucracy is more than half the whole, is similarly maverick. Its agencies are, indeed, established by law; but the Congress had no authorization to establish them. Their personnel are appointed, not elected, and regulatory agencies perform functions of all categories.

This is obviously the unacknowledged result of a generally accepted economic theory—that free competition can be enforced—but since that has intolerable results, it must be made "fair" by regulation.

If this is what Americans believe, it should be acknowledged. But there is an uneasy suspicion that industrial civilization has outgrown the theory of laissez-faire and that regulation should be based rather on the principle of pluralism—understood not as having its source in competition but in useful diversity, constituting a loose system. That the looseness is tightening is generally recognized. Industrial organization is in a transitional phase; but as long as it is not reexamined and brought into concordance with some accepted theory, its agencies will behave in the inconsistent and chaotic fashion characteristic of their present existence. They do exist, however; they have emerged; and obviously they belong, however uncertainly, to the emergent constitution.

The same can be said of the planning function. It exists in separated pockets, uncoordinated, a travesty. No one doubts that looking ahead is necessary, and it has to be done in every agency unless it is to proceed blindly. But the directives for it are missing. They simply do not exist. It was not contemplated in the original, and nothing touching it has ever been added.

Let us, then, speak again of these three functions.

Missing Branch: (1) Political.   The mythical man from Mars visiting earth and coming to the United States, with no more knowledge than he had found in a close reading of the Constitution, would be confounded by what goes on in a presidential election. In the original document he would have read a passage concerning the choosing of a president: "Each state shall appoint, in such manner as the legislature thereof may direct, a number of *electors*, equal to the whole number of Senators and Representatives to which the state may be entitled."

The passage goes on to say that these electors are to meet in their respective states, and vote by ballot for two persons; and that finally the result is to be reported. The person having the greatest number of votes will become president; and the person having the next greatest number of votes will become the vice-president.

It would be further explained to him that the intent was to have the "best people" in each state perform this duty, they being fairly certain to choose one of themselves to be president and another (from another state) to be vice-president.

It would be necessary, however, to inform the visitor that there had been a rather involved amendment (numbered XII) to this section, making a change in the procedures, it having been found at once that the designation as vice-president of the person receiving the second number of votes resulted in some undesirable consequences. It was judged that separate voting for president and vice-president would be better. There is still, he would be told, an electoral college; its members are still voted for; and electors, although they seem to be free to vote for the mythical best man of their choosing, actually are not free, or are not supposed to be. They themselves have been chosen on a party ticket, and when they meet they are expected to vote for a candidate designated in another process as the choice of the party.

"Party?" it would be asked. There is nothing said about a party, or about any pledge by electors to follow any judgment but their own. At this point the instructor would have to explain the elaborate process extrapolated from the simple terms of the Constitution. It would, indeed, have to be explained that although the electoral college still exists, the actual (and extraconstitutional) process of choosing it is a way of escaping the original intention of the framers to protect the voters from themselves. They are now able to choose, he would be told, even if indirectly, by having made the electoral college captive in a more democratic procedure.

This procedure, it would be explained, has grown up without any sort of legal existence. It consists of gatherings called conventions, met to choose candidates representing like-thinking voters from all over the country. These conventions are meetings of "delegates," the number determined by legislation of the parties themselves and not identical in all of them, or even in the two dominant ones, and with the manner of choosing similarly determined.

It would have to be said that parties had been found useful as a way of putting forward candidates, not only for the presidency but also for all elective offices; and that they had become permanent or semipermanent organizations. This was in part to further the ideas they sponsored; but soon they had become the instruments of ambitious leaders who used them to get into office and to stay there. They were a rich source of favors and patronage. There were legislative and administrative returns available for those who gave them support. Their tentacles reached out into social and economic institutions, gradually becoming inextricably entwined with every activity of national life.

No doubt the man from Mars would still be confused, and it has to be said that many Americans living with the political system are confused also. The political process sometimes seems to go on quite outside the area of the ordinary individual's interest. Many become aware of the process only when solicitation for the election of one or another candidate begins. The average individual does not participate in choosing those candidates, and he may feel that neither is the sort he would like to vote for. This, indeed, is all too often the dilemma he is caught in.

It is impossible to trace here, even briefly, the developments that resulted in this deplorable situation. After Washington's time, Jefferson, having had lessons in France, showed Americans the possibilities in the party system. Presently the frontier produced another leader who was as much convinced as Jefferson that democracy demanded the apparatus of political organization. It was Jackson and his satellite, Van Buren, who adapted the Convention, invented by their enemies, the Whigs, to the uses of party control. It too developed rich possibilities of profit for politicians.

The early conventions were irregular and undisciplined gatherings of uncertain size. The legitimacy of delegates was questionable, so questionable that soon the conventions began making rules apportioning delegates to states and congressional districts. Usually they did not say how delegates were to be chosen. The size of the meetings and their procedures gradually became regularized; but to this day delegates are chosen in a variety of ways, some by primaries, some by state conventions, and these bodies, having other partisan duties, are governed by rules of their own making.

As a result, the president and vice-president are elected by voters who have only the choice offered them as the result of party meetings not anticipated in the Constitution. They can choose one of two or three who have been selected in a process they probably did not participate in. They do not have even that choice with absolute certainty. There is still the electoral college. It is customary for the electors, meeting in each state, to choose the candidate of the party they belong to; but they need not do so; and there have been instances when they have refused. None of these refusals has actually made a difference in the presidential choice, but it is not a situation to be relied on for producing a legitimate president. The whole process becomes so remote and unsatisfactory that when, on election day, voters are supposed to go to the polls, a very large percentage of them simply do not go. They become, in effect, nonparticipants.

Another partisan situation arising out of the Constitution causes some uneasiness. In federal voting the conditions for eligibility are not set by federal legislation but are fixed by state law. This is because of a clause in the Constitution saying "electors [that is, voters] in each state shall have the qualifications requisite for electors of the most numerous branch of the state legislature." This applied only to representatives; but representatives and presidents alike are voted for by electors who have been registered under state laws; and states have often imposed conditions intended to prevent some citizens from voting at all. Much of the struggle for black civil rights has centered in this state control of eligibility for federal voting; and there is not even now any general rule about voting even for federal officials, much less for officials of local government.

The Fifteenth Amendment, adopted to continue the principles established by the Union victory in the Civil War, said that the right to vote should "not be denied or abridged by the United States *or by any State* on account of race, color, or previous condition of servitude." This proved to be so easily evaded that most blacks continued to be excluded from registration in many states; they may as well have been slaves still. The amending process has never been used forthrightly to cure this weakness; rather, piecemeal and ineffective attempts have been made to gain the same end without really transferring the determination of qualification for voting to federal jurisdiction. Finally one such amendment (Article XXIV) outlawed the poll tax method of excluding blacks, a device already abandoned practically everywhere for more effective and subtler ones—such as the easily manipulated literacy tests. When the amendment became effective it changed matters in only one recalcitrant state—Virginia. The rest of the South had been more agile.

The whole history of partisanship is one of irresponsibility, of confused standards or rules, of manipulation by special interests, often becoming outright corruption. Lacking any constitutional recognition, it is as obvious as anything can very well be that this sort of thing will go on and on. That the very springs of democracy are muddied has not so far been enough to force the kind of remedial action needed. What has emerged is something no American can accept with satisfaction.

Missing Branch: (2) Planning.   One after another, agencies of government have been forced to invent means for anticipating the future. What is spoken of technically as lead time has tended to extend. The simple provision of a building facility for a post office may well require six or seven years, and larger ones considerably longer. The budget, however, is made and approved annually, and attempts to revise this custom have always been rejected by the Congress. Nevertheless, as far as the operations of government are concerned, what is approved is a commitment to the future. That future must have been planned.

The difficulty with agency planning is that it is done without any studied relationship to a whole. The result is that no function is linked to others, and all of them are not directed to a desirable end that is at the same time possible. This could be done only if there existed a central planning agency.

It is not difficult to understand why such an agency has not been set up. There are a number of reasons, the first being that planning seems inconsistent with the pluralism of American society. To plan, it is feared, means to fix ends; and to fix ends means to direct activity toward these ends. Such direction would interfere with economic and social undertakings. This seems intolerable.

There is no objection to certain sorts of physical planning. Every corporation does it. Governmental agencies do it. It is the thought of government doing it for corporations that is so offensive. It would limit initiative, would make speculative ventures more difficult, and would certainly be inimical to the elaborate and costly apparatus of persuasion now become so powerful.

There is still another objection. The marking out of desirable objectives and directing activity toward them is inconsistent with free enterprise. The rationale of that system requires small competing units operating in an unregulated market. The objective is to make a profit, and a profit may result from furnishing a needed good or service, or it may result from furnishing one that is not needed but that consumers can be persuaded to take anyway. There are, of course, rules about this. Consumers are to an extent protected from fraud, and the theory is that the furnisher of the best good or service will get the business.

If the theory ever described reality, it does so no longer. Competition on the classic model has all but disappeared. In its place there are large aggregations whose plans have been projected a long way ahead. To these the consumer must conform. His choices are reduced to a range carefully limited so that producing facilities can be scheduled.

In this respect the change that has come over the whole of society has had some recognition in governmental practice; if for no other than technological reasons it has had to. Every government agency plans. Agriculture knows how much food and fiber will be needed and does something to arrange for its production. The Post Office knows what the demands on it will be and prepares to meet them. And this is true of all operating organizations.

The emergence of planning has, however, been consistently discouraged beyond the facility stage. There is no central agency for anticipating social needs and estimating the resources available for meeting them. The emergent constitution has yet to recognize planning as a necessary function of a society.

Missing Branch: (3) Regulatory.   Looked at with the hindsight furnished by our position late in the twentieth century, about the most glaring omission from the Constitution is any recognition of economic life—at least of the kind we know now. That this is easily enough explained does not repair the omission. There were in the 1780s no countrywide economic empires; there were only small local businesses, shops mostly, where the simple tools of production and even most of the consumers' goods needed by a self-sufficient rural population were made. When goods did go into commerce they did not go far. There were tanneries, there was furnituremaking, and there were harness shops in nearly every locality; and many things were made in the home, even cloth and clothing.

In view of this, it is curious that the Philadelphia meeting should have originated in the concern of a few citizens with estate or trading interests who objected to interferences with interstate commerce. These must have seemed only minor to most citizens; but not, for instance, to Washington, whose seat on the Potomac involved him in a waterborne commerce with several states and with foreign nations.

Section 10, Article I, of the Constitution was a sort of Bill of Rights for merchants and landed enterprisers. It excluded the states from all foreign dealings, prohibited them from laying imposts on commerce, and made sure that they would not be authorized to possess the means for interfering—no army or navy, and no bilateral arrangements. What the states could not do in these respects was reinforced by Article I, section 9; there it was said flatly that:

No tax or duty shall be laid on articles exported from any state.
No preference shall be given by any regulation of commerce or revenue to the ports of one state over those of another; nor shall vessels bound to, or from, one state be obliged to enter, clear, or pay duties in another.

This seemingly comprehensive prohibition did not, however, prevent a long and acrimonious controversy in the next century concerning interstate commerce. The debate arose because the framers failed to define that commerce. This was natural enough; everyone knew what interstate commerce was and what it was not in 1787; but in the middle of the next century it began to be something quite different. When this happened the implied constitutional definitions became a matter that interested parties could and did dispute about. Like so much else, the emerging rule, after the Court had mauled the subject for decades, and had reversed itself more than once, erected a prohibition much more far-reaching and comprehensive than the simple one in the Constitution.

It was clear once that a tanner, an axmaker or harnessmaker, or a furniture manufacturer was not engaged in interstate commerce. He was therefore, beyond the reach of federal regulation. It is quite as clear that their modern equivalents *are* engaged in interstate commerce and that consequently the federal government may, according to the original definition, assert the power to regulate them if the courts determine it to be necessary. For many industries and commercial enterprises regulation was so determined in the course of time.

Regulation, however, is a word not to be found in the Constitution. In 1787 prohibitions were enough, since they had to do with simple activities. When, however, weaving moved into mills, buttermaking into creameries, and furniture shops became factories, their products began to merge with a nationwide commerce whose strands could be untangled only by the most sophisticated analyses. Then the problem became one that escaped the constitutional reach altogether because no such development had been anticipated and no amendments were made.

If it had been decided, along about 1850, that the nation was to have a socialist economy, that is to say, that the facilities for production were to be publicly owned, a regulatory system would not have been demanded for public protection. But that did not happen. Economic activities expanded in complete freedom for a long time. There was a theory about this: it was that competition among enterprisers would cause them to regulate each other. It soon became apparent, however, that as a public policy this was a mistake. Competitors, in order to reduce costs, abused their workers and, in order to make profits, exploited the consumers of their products. Railroads and other utilities, being monopolies, charged what they liked for their services; other businesses, getting together, decided not to compete but to make arrangements among themselves about the prices they would charge. This eventually created a situation so chaotic that protection against the worst abuses became a condition of peaceful existence. There were other situations, not perhaps to be defined as the worst, but still not to be tolerated by a people free to protest and to vote; and these became the subject of endless controversy. Should they or should they not be regulated? And, if so, what should be the standard? Only the Court could say, and it had no clear directive. A "rule of reason" was invented for such difficult areas. But no one could say it was really allowable.

Regulation began with transportation—canals, then railroads—and spread to other public utilities and certain employments or occupations "affected with a public interest." By the end of the century it was a movement; in another half-century it had become an accepted system. It was the other half of the "American Way." No one contended any more that free enterprise would be possible without regulation. The question had become technical; how much was necessary, how could it best be done, what government—state or federal—should do it, and so on.

On the way, the protest of the prairie-state Populists in the eighties had become progressivism as it moved eastward and had settled into the left wings of both great political parties. There was philosophy about it. The Progressives, far from being socialistic, were perhaps more ardent free-enterprisers than those they described as "monopolists," money barons, or some other sort of antisocial being. As far as free enterprise was concerned, the trouble was that it was no longer free.

It was for the Supreme Court to invent a rule about regulation, or at least to say what of it could be approved. For a guide, the Court first reached back to English common law; and in *Munn v. Illinois*[20] it used the phrase "affected with a public interest" to describe the callings that might come under the states' police powers. This particular case was allied with agitation over railroad rates; it had to do with the charges for warehousing grain.

Storage was nominated as a public utility, and the principle was presently extended to other "common callings." The courts in time seemed to regret the use made of the public interest doctrine. A long line of justices was more interested in the protection of business interests than in farmers' cries for justice; and when corporation lawyers argued that regulation might easily be a taking of property "without due process," thus invoking the Fourteenth Amendment, courts were inclined to agree. This amendment, intended to consolidate the civil rights advances made by the Civil War, was not easily adapted to this use; but the justices, by accepting the fiction that corporations were "persons," found it possible.

The extension of regulation to further businesses was much more difficult. A huge volume of literature arose defining what was "reasonable" and *therefore not* a taking of property without due process. Out of this arose conflicting theories about the fixing of public utility rates. It was clear that they could be regulated, because if they were not common callings, nothing was; but the Court undertook to be the arbiter about extension of such regulations. Lawyers for the utilities wanted a rule that would allow their clients to "reproduce" their properties; lawyers for the public invented a "prudent investment" theory and argued that this should be used in calculating allowable rates.

At times, depending on the movement of prices, there were reversals of argument. Reproduction cost was more attractive to businesses if prices were going up, less attractive if they were going down. The justices of those years, it must be said, were often inclined to the protection of property rights in any case; and so were inclined to accept the arguments of the corporation lawyers. After all, they themselves—many of them—had recently had similar clients.

Another complication in the long struggle for regulation was the question whether the federal or state governments had jurisdiction. This was an important matter. The corporate interests, finding it easier to influence state legislatures and state regulatory bodies than federal ones, wanted it held that "interstate commerce" was a narrow concept. They argued that there had to be a massive indication of activity in more than one state, and that a business whose operations were within one state might move its goods where it liked without actually engaging in commerce that was interstate in the constitutional sense.

20. 94 U.S. 113 (1877).

The opposing argument was that the concept was so broad a one that almost any business had interstate connections, and that the federal government could take jurisdiction on the mere showing that goods were marketed across a border or that materials for manufacture came from another state.

The courts, trying to please their more prestigious pleaders, fell finally into the position of saying that some businesses could not be reached under either state or federal law for regulatory purposes. This immunity still remains a glaring example of what may happen when bodies constituted as the federal courts are have full authority to create constitutional doctrine. In this case the Supreme Court found corporations to be persons, accepted the duty of determining a rule of reason, and defined interstate commerce to suit its prejudice—one way at one time, and another way at another time.

There is another matter concerning regulation that must be mentioned: the kind of agencies assigned to watchkeeping under various regulatory acts, and the sort of rules they have adopted under the monitory eye of judges. It is perhaps not necessary to say that this came out at a minimum of bother for business. The regulatory bodies would usually rather be underzealous than overzealous. Few have been rebuked for not protecting the public; many have been sternly reprimanded for protecting it "unreasonably."

Besides, as would be obvious, much depended on the manning of the agencies set to watch and regulate businesses. In Republican times, the agencies had a way of turning out to be friendly, sometimes indistinguishable in their behavior from corporate lawyers; at other times, usually in reformist periods, they tried harder to distinguish the public interest and to act in accord with it. These periods never lasted long, or had much effect. Regulatory bodies in general showed a distinct tendency to soften, to become so identified with the industries they represented that sooner or later they took on the aspect of adjuncts rather than antagonists. Since the president could appoint but could not discharge the regulators, as F. D. Roosevelt was told in the Humphrey case,[21] they were usually staffed with longtime members whose enthusiasm for trouble was notably weak even when they had not actually emerged from the service of the subject corporations—as many did—on the theory that only persons of experience could really understand the business they were to supervise.

This leads to consideration of the other tack taken by those who would keep free enterprise in the production and distribution of both goods and services. This was represented by the formidable line of antimonopoly measures beginning in the late 1880s.

21. *Humphrey's Executor* v. *United States,* 295 U.S. 602 (1935).

It might be predicted from the known facts that in another generation or two the persistent effort represented by the successive measures generally known as the antitrust acts, beginning with the Sherman Act in 1890, would have become a source of wonder that so farcical a charade could have been taken so seriously and accepted so confidently as an economic policy in the period when industry was taking on the modern characteristics of large-scale and nationwide marketing areas.

Anyone who made that prediction, however, would have to explain its persistence, the rejection of all alternatives, and the recurrent convulsions of rejuvenation. The explanation, of course, is to be found in the dilemma presented by the economies of concentration and enlarged operation developing in an environment of *laissez-aller*.

The small business in our cultural history calls up much the same emotions as the family farm. The family farm was supposed to foster the virtues of independence, solidity, initiative, and attachment to the liberties of the pioneers. The small business was supposed to foster independence, initiative, and the freedoms of the rural village. These were regarded as sufficiently precious to be worth preserving at any cost. And it was an unquestioned assumption that the virtues were the result of the circumstances. A sturdy peasantry did in fact continue to be talked of long after it had disappeared. So also did "free" enterprise.

That initiative could be expressed in the financing and management of large enterprises as well as small ones was demonstrated by the very phenomena the antitrust acts were meant to suppress. These were the combinations and trusts that by the 1880s had come into control of such industries as sugar, meat packing, minerals, transportation, communications, and other public utilities. There was initiative enough, but it did lack restraint; and what may have been arranged with the purpose of effecting economies in production or marketing was all too easily adapted to the control of prices. And this was true both of prices paid to producers of raw products—particularly farmers—and of those asked of the consumers. "Middleman" became an opprobrious term. The financiers who put together combinations and extracted the prospective profits by "watering" the resulting securities, thus making it impossible for producers or consumers to benefit, were so obviously public enemies that their freedom could hardly be expected to last. They really had asked for what they got. They were, said the politicians, in response to widespread protest, in "restraint of trade." They had conspired. They should be punished, and the situation they had disrupted should be restored.

Small businessmen and farmers conceived that they had done well enough when they had traded with each other in a largely face-to-face arrangement. One had no considerable advantage over another. This was so much in the American grain that the impulse to preserve it was irresistible. It would be done, if necessary, by force. The antitrust method was first tried in various of the states; but this was soon recognized to be useless; all such industries were larger than any one state; and there was immediate danger of competition among state legislatures to shelter interests when they could expect some return of favor. The United States Senate was reachable by those same interests. The senators were elected by the same legislatures and were easily suborned by legal fees or campaign contributions. It took a really overwhelming indignation among their constituents to move them.

That indignation was forthcoming; and as all politicians must, legislators were forced to recognize that there were many more farmers and small businessmen than there were monopolists; and all of them could vote. So the Sherman Act was passed. It provided that "Every contract, combination in the form of trust or otherwise, or conspiracy, in restraint of trade or commerce among the several states, or with foreign nations . . ." was illegal; and the federal government was authorized to proceed against such "trusts." They were to be dissolved, and "dissolved" meant returned to the status quo ante. They were to be as if they had never been.

It was not effective. Corporation lawyers soon found a profitable practice in pointing out that such terms as "trust," "combination," and "restraint" were ambiguous; and that "conspiracy" was not only hard to define but almost impossible to prove. The case of *In re Debs*[22] made the whole effort absurd by applying it to labor organizations. Between 1890 and 1900 only fourteen suits were instituted under the law, and four of these were against unions. Trusts continued, if not to flourish, at least to exist and expand under other names and with other legal devices.

Matters went on this way through the Republican years that lasted until 1912, when Wilson, profiting from Progressive attritions on the Republican party, attained the White House as a Democrat. He was distinctly a minority president, but he was in power, and he needed a policy. He had been the kind of university president who thought it his duty to instruct the public, and he had done it on the lecture circuit—so popular in preradio and premovie days. He had talked in a confident, tutorial way to innumerable audiences of middle-class people, defining for them the morals and standards proper to staid, Christian folk. It was nothing very different from what they heard from their own ministers; but coming from the president of Princeton, it seemed more authoritative. Sometimes he went further; for instance, as labor unions became obstreperous, he denounced them; and populism, he explained, was inadmissible, a radical threat to democracy. So was its prophet, Bryan. Wilson always came down, in these discourses, on the side of order and tradition.

22. 158 U.S. 564 (1895).

in opposition to growth and continued to insist on proliferation. If, during this time of rapid expansion, there had been a policy of understanding and containing it, the subsequent difficulties might have been avoided, or at least they might not have been so serious. For the course taken allowed the uncontrolled boom of the twenties to escape all boundaries and end in the crash that was the inevitable result of chaos.

During this time there had been some thoughtful big businessmen, and a few economists, who had seen that some sort of order must be imposed on the economic system. Businesses, grown large, and each following its own course, fell into competition to exploit their workers, the consumers of their products, and, whenever it was possible, one another. When President Hoover had been secretary of commence he had had some intimations of the necessity for change; and he had fostered trade associations whose purpose was to foster cooperation among businesses to increase efficiency and to escape the worst kinds of competition.

It will be recalled that Franklin D. Roosevelt, so soon to succeed Hoover, was involved in the establishing of one of these—the Construction Council. So when he became president after the Great Depression had lasted two and a half years, getting worse all the time, he recalled the promise of this cooperative movement and sponsored the National Industrial Recovery Act. It was passed in 1933, with the intention of making a system of planning and cooperation, but instituting public controls to make certain that the abuses of the past did not recur.

The NRA did not last. It fell into disrepute for trying to do too much too quickly and was disliked by those business concerns whose competitive practices were curtailed in the interest of decency. But it might have survived the sabotage and displeasure of the chiselers if the opposition of the Brandeis followers had not been so virulent. With Brandeis on the Court, fuming at the reversal of the policies he had persuaded Wilson to adopt, the first opportunity was taken to declare the act unconstitutional.

Roosevelt had always been deferential to Brandeis; and Brandeis supporters had, by 1934, infiltrated the New Deal agencies; the attempt to reconstruct NRA to satisfy the Court's objection was aggressively talked about by Roosevelt for some time, but in the end he let the matter rest. He moved to rejuvenate the Antitrust Division in the Department of Justice, made Thurman Arnold its director, and started on a determined attempt at enforcement. Everything big was to be made little again.

There is reason to believe that Roosevelt expected this effort to fail, and in fact, it did no more than harass certain of the businessmen who had been careless in planning their mergers. But it had only the slightest effect in preventing growth, and the country entered on a period of business expansion that made everything in the past seem minuscule.

When Roosevelt finished with his defiance of Brandeis, he asked what there was to take the place of the NRA attempt to civilize competition. Word came back from the Justice that if Roosevelt would study the Constitution he would discover that there was absolutely no limit to the power of the Congress to tax, and equally no limit to its spending power. This might seem like the repair of ravages that ought to have been prevented from happening, but it was something. Social Security was instituted, rather modestly at first, but with the implication that eventually it might mean income for everyone quite divorced from wages. Since the most distressing result of industrial chaos was the unemployment resulting from unplanned production, the promise of relief without work seemed to Roosevelt a tolerable substitute for the NRA that he now judged had been begun a generation too soon.

Before and after the Roosevelt/Truman years there were Republican regimes when the regulatory agencies functioned so lackadaisically that they may as well not have existed. But they were not abandoned, and occasionally they showed signs of life. It was clear that they were by now an accepted part of government and in that sense had become legitimized. There was no attempt to coordinate their work; the attempt to do this after a report from James M. Landis, a Brandeis follower who had had experience as a regulator, simply died; nothing was done.

Regulation then, without having the directive of constitutional recognition, and so having only the methods and standards imposed by legislation or by the courts, exists as a governmental appendage, recognized but not legitimized. It has been embodied in numerous agencies, from the rather small Pure Seed law, hidden in the Department of Agriculture, to the gigantic bureaucracies of the Interstate Commerce Commission and the Securities and Exchange Commission. By the sixties many of these had no attachment to an executive department and were usually spoken of as semijudicial (whatever that meant), but there were many others within the departments and presumably related to the purposes of those organizations.

The subsequent situation would seem to be this: as long as economic facilities are privately owned and managed, the necessity for imposing fair practices on them will remain. The tendency they display to escape whenever possible from the confines of regulation is owed to their nature. There is a clear choice between public ownership and/or management, and the imposition of public rule. The difficulty with this last is that profit-making is a powerful urge and historically has overcome all attempts to contain it and impose fair practices. Nevertheless such attempts are made and tend to become more elaborate. Agencies for the purpose are an accepted accompaniment of pluralistic economic organization; however, they exist in the emergent—but illegitimate—area of constitutionalism where definition of their status and powers is indeterminate.

Finally, it has been argued here that a constitution is necessary. The deficiencies of a "living" constitution—that is, one made up of variations on a theme set by an original unchanging document—have been outlined, and general criteria for a revised charter have been put forward.

If a constitution is needed, and if the existing one is inadequate, the revisions to be made ought to be guided by the great purposes of the nation in the present. These are partly those understood by the framers in 1787 and traditional in the American culture, and partly those of a society and an economy very different from that known to the framers, one that is moving into a highly technological future with enormously expanded economic potentialities to support a cultural development beyond any present imagining.

The year of 1787 was peculiarly a year of transition. The original compact among the states had failed to maintain a general government, and the life of the nation was in jeopardy. The elevated sentiments of the war years had died away. The states were interfering with one another's commerce, and were refusing to meet the obligations of union. The respect of other powers was declining, and Spain in the southern states, and Britain and France in the North and the West, threatened reconquest.

The delegates to the Convention were charged to resuscitate the Union and for this purpose to revise the Articles of Confederation. It was clear to the ablest and wisest among them, however, that something more drastic was needed; in nearly four months of a hot Philadelphia summer thirty-nine delegates of the actual seventy-four who had originally been designated (fifty-five had actually attended) agreed on a new government suited to the circumstances of the time. It was satisfactory to none, but it was acknowledged to be at least a workable compromise.

Unfortunately the technological and cultural changes so shortly to take place were not yet within sight. The forests were just being cleared for farming; coal had not yet come into use; Eli Whitney was still three years from the first operation of his cotton gin. The delegates in Philadelphia could not know what these developments would come to imply. The economy of the South rested on slavery; commerce was carried in sailing vessels; there were few roads, and those were hardly more than paths through the forests, so that travel was largely on horseback. The industrialization based on power from fossil fuels, improved transportation and communications, as well as the use of machinery, was beyond the horizon. The Constitution of 1787 was, as a consequence, the product of a handicraft culture. True, Philadelphia was a city of 40,000, New York somewhat smaller, and Boston and Baltimore half that size; but 95 percent of the people were working farmers. And it was expected that this would continue to be so.

There were some principles, of course, as precious to later citizens as to the framers. The people were to be sovereign and were to choose their representatives. This indicated a government whose limitations were to be strictly marked. The tripartite structure reflected these ideas, its branches opposed to one another so that none would accumulate oppressive powers.

Concern for protection from arbitrary authority was much stronger than the desire for governmental services. Then too there was a pervasive worry about people's impulsiveness. In the wake of revolution there had been outbreaks of violence in the cities and refusals by farmers to pay their debts. Property was endangered from all sides. So it was agreed that only one house of the legislature was to be directly elected, and that by voters who possessed substantial properties.

There was another overriding concern: many delegates wanted to preserve states' rights, and even those who did not feared that inroads on those rights would make ratification less likely. All recognized the necessity for conciliating the politicians who controlled the governments of the states and who were jealous of their prerogatives; it was this that resulted in a Senate with equal representation from all the states, thus making the smaller equal to the larger.

The resulting government was thus in many respects made up of compromise institutions. The delegates failed to reach real agreement about a division of state and national powers, and there were unresolved quarrels about slavery, a national army, and several other issues.

A revised constitution would certainly add more branches. It would more carefully work out their relations. It would relieve the president of many responsibilities. It would reform the legislature in the direction of national rather than local responsibilities. Especially, it would reflect modern concerns for duties of citizens to one another. The new government resulting would be one with institutions for looking ahead and making the best possible use of resources. It would reflect the national consensus on important issues and anchor them in legitimacy.

If the Constitution's deficiencies for these later days is accepted as substantially accurate, several characteristics are conspicuous.

One of these is the blurring of borders on every side, of an amorphous mass, with consequent inability to say with authority what any clause means. This results from many tentative testings. All three branches have invaded the no man's land between them and have sometimes found themselves in conflict with the other branches. And all three have assumed powers regarded as necessary to their responsibilities but not mentioned in the original charter.

There would seem to be a choice, now that this indeterminateness has become so prominent a characteristic, between accepting it as a satisfactory method of constitutional change or of rejecting it in favor of a renewed effort, similar to that of 1787, to assign powers and responsibilities within government and the rights and duties of the citizen.

If no such effort is made, the processes of change will go on as they have until now. That course is one that is often argued for by those who say that it provides for a necessary accommodation to circumstances. The inability of those governed by it to determine for themselves (or have determined for them by their lawyers) what is permitted and what is not is regarded as a small price to pay for the chance that they may be allowed the interpretation they prefer. It will be allowed, of course, unless there should be a challenge, and even then there will be a generous stretch of time before their claim is rejected or modified.

Opposed to this view are those who think another process of constitutional change preferable. They insist that amendment is the only truly legitimate way of making constitutional law. The alternate process, they say, never settles any issue; it may seem to be decided, but it may turn out not to be. This is because, in fact, one view is as good as another except when one has constitutional authority.

Those who hold this view insist that constitutional law is different from other law, since it is a statement of considered principle rather than a directive to the executive. It is admitted that principles will always need adaptation to new situations, but they argue that the situations ought not to be a hundred or more years removed from the statement of principle and thus quite alien to a document framed before the situations were visualized. Constitutional restatement, and the return of legitimacy, is entirely possible and quite practical. It is even argued that only what Judge Jerome Frank called "the cult of the robe" stands in the way. But there is another obstacle. This is the closed gateway in the original amending clause. This would have to be opened in a most difficult operation if any general recasting is to be undertaken.

Meanwhile it can do no harm to consider what a rejuvenated Constitution would be like; such an exercise may even constitute a demonstration of the distance we have come from the venerated original and how its provisions are being tortured in the constant conflict over its archaic meanings. The intention of this book has been to demonstrate that such restructuring is, indeed, necessary.

CHAPTER 14

A PROPOSED CONSTITUTIONAL MODEL
FOR THE NEWSTATES OF AMERICA

The arrangements argued for in this book would naturally lead to the formulation of a model. Models are, after all, ways of considering the consequences of what has been argued for; and one after another has been elaborated and discussed at the Center for the Study of Democratic Institutions.

On examination each succeeding version has been found faulty in one or another respect. Attempts have been made to correct these. To do this and yet to respect the integrity of a system required repeated efforts.

No such model can ever be regarded as finished. It can only be said that it is what has seemed best at the time. Changes will still be made in the future. They cannot be prevented, but they can be provided for. Perhaps the worst mistake made by the framers in 1787 was that amendment was given over to the Congress and the state legislatures (with one alternative so awkward it has never been used). In consequence, there have been no substantive amendments in two centuries of rapid national development.

From a system of states each having original sovereignty, we have become a close-coupled nation with central responsibilities not anticipated by the framers. The stresses and strains of an outmoded system expected to do what only a modernized one could possibly accomplish are apparent everywhere, but nowhere so clearly, perhaps, as in the legislative branch, where amendment was expected to originate but has, in reality, been effectively blocked.

It will be found, in consequence, that the most drastic changes in the proposal submitted here are in the legislative branch. Not only is the House of Representatives given a percentage of at-large members (thus turning the attention of the House to national rather than local affairs), but the Senate has been made an appointive body with life terms for the same purpose.

The reformed Senate would also correct the worst malapportionment remaining in the American system.

The other considerable change is the consolidation of states into fewer and, it is hoped, more effective regional groupings, thus at last recognizing the nation as one system rather than a confused fifty.

There are other changes, some in the Presidency, some in the Judiciary, but none of them is drastic. There have been complaints about both. As to the Presidency it has been concluded that its faults are mostly to be found in the Congress. As to the Judiciary, its faults lie mostly in its sheer inefficiency and so its incapacity to reach the criterion of equal justice under law.

It will be noticed that the general emphasis on the protection of individuals from the exercise of governmental powers has been supplemented with a list of responsibilities. The original Constitution was drafted in the aftermath of rebellion against arbitrary authority exercised from abroad and in a time when wide spaces and sparse populations made it less necessary to find ways for accommodation to one another of far more crowded and interrelated groupings.

Another generalization adhered to has been that a plural economy is still possible in a world whose recent revolutions have developed in their wake various kinds of authoritarian regimes, some communist, some dictatorial, but all consigning production and distribution to state bureaucracies. For this purpose systems of planning and self-management within social criteria have been worked out. The problem of preserving initiative and decentralization within rules calculated to guard the interests of the whole has been dealt with in ways it is hoped may meet with approval.

It remains to say that the Center fellows are convinced that the time has come for a reassessment of our basic law. They are not convinced that the right answers have been found. The model here is to be taken as a beginning, not an end.

P R E A M B L E

So that we may join in common endeavors, welcome the future in good order, and create an adequate and self-repairing government—we, the people, do establish the Newstates of America, herein provided to be ours, and do ordain this Constitution whose supreme law it shall be until the time prescribed for it shall have run.

ARTICLE I

Rights and Responsibilities

A. Rights

SECTION 1.   Freedom of expression, of communication, of movement, of assembly, or of petition shall not be abridged except in declared emergency.

SECTION 2.   Access to information possessed by governmental agencies shall not be denied except in the interest of national security; but communications among officials necessary to decisionmaking shall be privileged.

SECTION 3.   Public communicators may decline to reveal sources of information, but shall be responsible for hurtful disclosures.

SECTION 4.   The privacy of individuals shall be respected; searches and seizures shall be made only on judicial warrant; persons shall be pursued or questioned only for the prevention of crime or the apprehension of suspected criminals, and only according to rules established under law.

SECTION 5.   There shall be no discrimination because of race, creed, color, origin, or sex. The Court of Rights and Responsibilities may determine whether selection for various occupations has been discriminatory.

SECTION 6.   All persons shall have equal protection of the laws, and in all electoral procedures the vote of every eligible citizen shall count equally with others.

SECTION 7.   It shall be public policy to promote discussion of public issues and to encourage peaceful public gatherings for this purpose. Permission to hold such gatherings shall not be denied, nor shall they be interrupted, except in declared emergency or on a showing of imminent danger to public order and on judicial warrant.

SECTION 8.   The practice of religion shall be privileged; but no religion shall be imposed by some on others, and none shall have public support.

SECTION 9.   Any citizen may purchase, sell, lease, hold, convey, and inherit real and personal property, and shall benefit equally from all laws for security in such transactions.

SECTION 10.   Those who cannot contribute to productivity shall be entitled to a share of the national product; but distribution shall be fair and the total may not exceed the amount for this purpose held in the National Sharing Fund.

SECTION 11.   Education shall be provided at public expense for those who meet appropriate tests of eligibility.

SECTION 12.   No person shall be deprived of life, liberty, or property without due process of law. No property shall be taken without compensation.

SECTION 13.   Legislatures shall define crimes and conditions requiring restraint, but confinement shall not be for punishment; and, when possible, there shall be preparation for return to freedom.

SECTION 14.   No person shall be placed twice in jeopardy for the same offense.

SECTION 15.   Writs of habeas corpus shall not be suspended except in declared emergency.

SECTION 16.   Accused persons shall be informed of charges against them, shall have a speedy trial, shall have reasonable bail, shall be allowed to confront witnesses or to call others, and shall not be compelled to testify against themselves; at the time of arrest they shall be informed of their right to be silent and to have counsel, provided, if necessary, at public expense; and courts shall consider the contention that prosecution may be under an invalid or unjust statute.

B. Responsibilities

SECTION 1.   Each freedom of the citizen shall prescribe a corresponding responsibility not to diminish that of others: of speech, communication, assembly, and petition, to grant the same freedom to others; of religion, to respect that of others; of privacy, not to invade that of others; of the holding and disposal of property, the obligation to extend the same privilege to others.

SECTION 2.   Individuals and enterprises holding themselves out to serve the public shall serve all equally and without intention to misrepresent, conforming to such standards as may improve health and welfare.

SECTION 3.   Protection of the law shall be repaid by assistance in its enforcement; this shall include respect for the procedures of justice, apprehension of lawbreakers, and testimony at trial.

SECTION 4.   Each citizen shall participate in the processes of democracy, assisting in the selection of officials and in the monitoring of their conduct in office.

SECTION 5.   Each shall render such services to the nation as may be uniformly required by law, objection by reason of conscience being adjudicated as hereinafter provided; and none shall expect or may receive special privileges unless they be for a public purpose defined by law.

SECTION 6.   Each shall pay whatever share of governmental costs is consistent with fairness to all.

SECTION 7.   Each shall refuse awards or titles from other nations or their representatives except as they be authorized by law.

SECTION 8.   There shall be a responsibility to avoid violence and to keep the peace; for this reason the bearing of arms or the possession of lethal weapons shall be confined to the police, members of the armed forces, and those licensed under law.

SECTION 9.   Each shall assist in preserving the endowments of nature and enlarging the inheritance of future generations.

SECTION 10.   Those granted the use of public lands, the air, or waters shall have a responsibility for using these resources so that, if irreplaceable, they are conserved and, if replaceable, they are put back as they were.

SECTION 11.   Retired officers of the armed forces, of the senior civil service, and of the Senate shall regard their service as a permanent obligation and shall not engage in enterprise seeking profit from the government.

SECTION 12.   The devising or controlling of devices for management or technology shall establish responsibility for resulting costs.

SECTION 13.   All rights and responsibilities defined herein shall extend to such associations of citizens as may be authorized by law.

ARTICLE II

The Newstates

SECTION 1.   There shall be Newstates, each comprising no less than 5 percent of the whole population. Existing states may continue and may have the status of Newstates if the Boundary Commission, hereinafter provided, shall so decide. The Commission shall be guided in its recommendations by the probability of accommodation to the conditions for effective government. States electing by referendum to continue if the Commission recommend otherwise shall nevertheless accept all Newstate obligations.

SECTION 2.   The Newstates shall have constitutions formulated and adopted by processes hereinafter prescribed.

SECTION 3.   They shall have Governors, legislatures, and planning, administrative, and judicial systems.

SECTION 4.   Their political procedures shall be organized and supervised by electoral Overseers; but their elections shall not be in years of presidential election.

SECTION 5.   The electoral apparatus of the Newstates of America shall be available to them, and they may be allotted funds under rules agreed to by the national Overseer; but expenditures may not be made by or for any candidate except they be approved by the Overseer; and requirements of residence in a voting district shall be no longer than thirty days.

SECTION 6.   They may charter subsidiary governments, urban or rural, and may delegate to them powers appropriate to their responsibilities.

SECTION 7.   They may lay, or may delegate the laying of, taxes; but these shall conform to the restraints stated hereinafter for the Newstates or America.

SECTION 8.   They may not tax exports, may not tax with intent to prevent imports, and may not impose any tax forbidden by laws of the Newstates of America; but the objects appropriate for taxation shall be clearly designated.

SECTION 9.   Taxes on land may be at higher rates than those on its improvements.

SECTION 10.   They shall be responsible for the administration of public services not reserved to the government of the Newstates of America, such activities being concerted with those of corresponding national agencies, where these exist, under arrangements common to all.

SECTION 11.   The rights and responsibilities prescribed in this Constitution shall be effective in the Newstates and shall be suspended only in emergency when declared by Governors and not disapproved by the Senate of the Newstates of America.

SECTION 12.   Police powers of the Newstates shall extend to all matters not reserved to the Newstates of America; but preempted powers shall not be impaired.

SECTION 13.   Newstates may not enter into any treaty, alliance, confederation, or agreement unless approved by the Boundary Commission hereinafter provided.

They may not coin money, provide for the payment of debts in any but legal tender, or make any charge for inter-Newstate services. They may not enact ex post facto laws or ones impairing the obligation of contracts.

SECTION 14.   Newstates may not impose barriers to imports from other jurisdictions or impose any hindrance to citizens' freedom of movement.

SECTION 15.   If governments of the Newstates fail to carry out fully their constitutional duties, their officials shall be warned and may be required by the Senate, on the recommendation of the Watchkeeper, to forfeit revenues from the Newstates of America.

ARTICLE III

The Electoral Branch

SECTION 1.   To arrange for participation by the electorate in the determination of policies and the selection of officials, there shall be an Electoral Branch.

SECTION 2.   An Overseer of electoral procedures shall be chosen by majority of the Senate and may be removed by a two-thirds vote. It shall be the Overseer's duty to supervise the organization of national and district parties, arrange for discussion among them, and provide for the nomination and election of candidates for public office. While in office the Overseer shall belong to no political organization; and after each presidential election shall offer to resign.

SECTION 3.   A national party shall be one having had at least a 5 percent affiliation in the latest general election; but a new party shall be recognized when valid petitions have been signed by at least 2 percent of the voters in each of 30 percent of the districts drawn for the House of Representatives. Recognition shall be suspended upon failure to gain 5 percent of the votes at a second election, 10 percent at a third, or 15 percent at further elections.

District parties shall be recognized when at least 2 percent of the voters shall have signed petitions of affiliation; but recognition shall be withdrawn upon failure to attract the same percentages as are necessary for the continuance of national parties.

SECTION 4.   Recognition by the Overseer shall bring parties within established regulations and entitle them to common privileges.

SECTION 5.   The Overseer shall promulgate rules for party conduct and shall see that fair practices are maintained, and for this purpose shall appoint deputies in each district and shall supervise the choice, in district and national conventions, of party administrators. Regulations and appointments may be objected to by the Senate.

SECTION 6.   The Overseer, with the administrators and other officials, shall:

a. Provide the means for discussion, in each party, of public issues, and, for this purpose, ensure that members have adequate facilities for participation.

b. Arrange for discussion, in annual district meetings, of the President's views, of the findings of the Planning Branch, and such other information as may be pertinent for enlightened political discussion.

c. Arrange, on the first Saturday in each month, for enrollment, valid for one year, of voters at convenient places.

SECTION 7.   The Overseer shall also:

a. Assist the parties in *nominating* candidates for district members of the House of Representatives each three years; and for this purpose designate one hundred districts, each with a similar number of eligible voters, redrawing districts after each election. In these there shall be party conventions having no more than three hundred delegates, so distributed that representation of voters be approximately equal.

Candidates for delegate may become eligible by presenting petitions signed by two hundred registered voters. They shall be elected by party members on the first Tuesday in March, those having the largest number of votes being chosen until the three hundred be complete. Ten alternates shall also be chosen by the same process.

District conventions shall be held on the first Tuesday in April. Delegates shall choose three candidates for membership in the House of Representatives, the three having the most votes becoming candidates.

b. Arrange for the *election* each three years of three members of the House of Representatives in each district from among the candidates chosen in party conventions, the three having the most votes to be elected.

SECTION 8.   The Overseer shall also:

a. Arrange for national conventions to meet nine years after previous presidential elections, with an equal number of delegates from each district, the whole number not to exceed one thousand.

Candidates for delegates shall be eligible when petitions signed by five hundred registered voters have been filed. Those with the most votes, together with two alternates, being those next in number of votes, shall be chosen in each district.

b. Approve procedures in these conventions for choosing one hundred candidates to be members-at-large of the House of Representatives, whose terms shall be coterminous with that of the President. For this purpose delegates shall file one choice with convention officials. Voting on submissions shall proceed until one hundred achieve 10 percent, but not more than three candidates may be resident in any one district; if any district have more than three, those with the fewest votes shall be eliminated, others being added from the districts having less than three, until equality be reached. Of those added, those having the most votes shall be chosen first.

c. Arrange procedures for the consideration and approval of party objectives by the convention.

d. Formulate rules for the *nomination* in these conventions of candidates for President and Vice-Presidents when the offices are to fall vacant, candidates for nomination to be recognized when petitions shall have been presented by one hundred or more delegates, pledged to continue support until candidates can no longer win or until they consent to withdraw. Presidents and Vice-Presidents, together with Representatives-at-large, shall submit to referendum after serving for three years, and if they are rejected, new conventions shall be held within one month and candidates shall be chosen as for vacant offices.

Candidates for President and Vice-Presidents shall be nominated on attaining a majority.

e. Arrange for the *election* on the first Tuesday in June, in appropriate years, of new candidates for President and Vice-Presidents, and members-at-large of the House of Representatives, all being presented to the nation's voters as a ticket; if no ticket achieve a majority, the Overseer shall arrange another election, on the third Tuesday in June, between the two persons having the most votes; and if referendum so determine he shall provide similar arrangements for the nomination and election of candidates.

In this election, the one having the most votes shall prevail.

SECTION 9. The Overseer shall also:

a. Arrange for the convening of the national legislative houses on the fourth Tuesday of July.

b. Arrange for inauguration of the President and Vice-Presidents on the second Tuesday of August.

SECTION 10. All costs of electoral procedures shall be paid from public funds, and there shall be no private contributions to parties or candidates; no contributions or expenditures for meetings, conventions, or campaigns shall be made; and no candidate for office may make any personal expenditures unless authorized by a uniform rule of the Overseer; and persons or groups making expenditures, directly or indirectly, in support of prospective candidates shall report to the Overseer and shall conform to his regulations.

SECTION 11. Expenses of the Electoral Branch shall be met by the addition of one percent to the net annual taxable income returns of taxpayers, this sum to be held by the Chancellor of Financial Affairs for disposition by the Overseer.

Funds shall be distributed to parties in proportion to the respective number of votes cast for the President and Governors at the last election, except that new parties, on being recognized, shall share in proportion to their number. Party administrators shall make allocations to legislative candidates in amounts proportional to the party vote at the last election.

Expenditures shall be audited by the Watchkeeper; and sums not expended within four years shall be returned to the Treasury.

It shall be a condition of every communications franchise that reasonable facilities shall be available for allocations by the Overseer.

ARTICLE IV

The Planning Branch

SECTION 1.   There shall be a Planning Branch to formulate and administer plans and to prepare budgets for the uses of expected income in pursuit of policies formulated by the processes provided herein.

SECTION 2.   There shall be a National Planning Board of fifteen members appointed by the President; the first members shall have terms designated by the President of one to fifteen years, thereafter one shall be appointed each year; the President shall appoint a Chairman who shall serve for fifteen years unless removed by him.

SECTION 3.   The Chairman shall appoint, and shall supervise, a planning administrator, together with such deputies as may be agreed to by the Board.

SECTION 4.   The Chairman shall present to the Board six- and twelve-year development plans prepared by the planning staff. They shall be revised each year after public hearings, and finally in the year before they are to take effect. They shall be submitted to the President on the fourth Tuesday in July for transmission to the Senate on September 1 with his comments.

If members of the Board fail to approve the budget proposals by the forwarding date, the Chairman shall nevertheless make submission to the President with notations of reservation by such members. The President shall transmit this proposal, with his comments, to the House of Representatives on September 1.

SECTION 5.   It shall be recognized that the six- and twelve-year development plans represent national intentions tempered by the appraisal of possibilities. The twelve-year plan shall be a general estimate of probable progress, both governmental and private; the six-year plan shall be more specific as to estimated income and expenditure and shall take account of necessary revisions.

The purpose shall be to advance, through every agency of government, the excellence of national life. It shall be the further purpose to anticipate innovations, to estimate their impact, to assimilate them into existing institutions, and to moderate deleterious effects on the environment and on society.

The six- and twelve-year plans shall be disseminated for discussion and the opinions expressed shall be considered in the formulation of plans for each succeeding year with special attention to detail in proposing the budget.

SECTION 6.   For both plans an extension of one year into the future shall be made each year and the estimates for all other years shall be revised accordingly. For nongovernmental activities the estimate of developments shall be calculated to indicate the need for enlargement or restriction.

SECTION 7.   If there be objection by the President or the Senate to the six- or twelve-year plans, they shall be returned for restudy and resubmission. If there still be differences, and if the President and the Senate agree, they shall prevail. If they do not agree, the Senate shall prevail and the plan shall be revised accordingly.

SECTION 8.   The Newstates, on June 1, shall submit proposals for development to be considered for inclusion in those for the Newstates of America. Researches and administration shall be delegated, when convenient, to planning agencies of the Newstates.

SECTION 9.   There shall be submissions from private individuals or from organized associations affected with a public interest, as defined by the Board. They shall report intentions to expand or contract, estimates of production and demand, probable uses of resources, numbers expected to be employed, and other essential information.

SECTION 10.   The Planning Branch shall make and have custody of official maps, and these shall be documents of reference for future developments both public and private; on them the location of facilities, with extension indicated, and the intended use of all areas shall be marked out.

Official maps shall also be maintained by the planning agencies of the Newstates, and in matters not exclusively national the National Planning Board may rely on these.

Undertakings in violation of official designation shall be at the risk of the venturer, and there shall be no recourse; but losses from designations after acquisition shall be recoverable in actions before the Court of Claims.

SECTION 11.   The Planning Branch shall have available to it funds equal to one-half of one percent of the approved national budget (not including debt services or payments from trust funds). They shall be held by the Chancellor of Financial Affairs and expended according to rules approved by the Board; but funds not expended within six years shall be available for other uses.

SECTION 12.   Allocations may be made for the planning agencies of the Newstates; but only the maps and plans of the national Board, or those approved by them, shall have status at law.

SECTION 13.   In making plans, there shall be due regard to the interests of other nations and such cooperation with their intentions as may be approved by the Board.

SECTION 14.   There may also be cooperation with international agencies and such contributions to their work as are not disapproved by the President.

ARTICLE V

The Presidency

SECTION 1. The President of the Newstates of America shall be the head of government, shaper of its commitments, expositor of its policies, and supreme commander of its protective forces; shall have one term of nine years, unless rejected by 60 percent of the electorate after three years; shall take care that the nation's resources are estimated and are apportioned to its more exigent needs; shall recommend such plans, legislation, and action as may be necessary; and shall address the legislators each year on the state of the nation, calling upon them to do their part for the general good.

SECTION 2. There shall be two Vice-Presidents elected with the President; at the time of taking office the President shall designate one Vice-President to supervise internal affairs; and one to be deputy for general affairs. The deputy for general affairs shall succeed if the presidency be vacated; the Vice-President for internal affairs shall be second in succession. If either Vice-President shall die or be incapacitated, the President, with the consent of the Senate, shall appoint a successor. Vice-Presidents shall serve during an extended term with such assignments as the President may make.

If the presidency fall vacant through the disability of both Vice-Presidents, the Senate shall elect successors from among its members to serve until the next general election.

With the Vice-Presidents and other officials the President shall see to it that the laws are faithfully executed and shall pay attention to the findings and recommendations of the Planning Board, the National Regulatory Board, and the Watchkeeper in formulating national policies.

SECTION 3. Responsible to the Vice-President for General Affairs there shall be Chancellors of External, Financial, Legal, and Military Affairs.

The Chancellor of External Affairs shall assist in conducting relations with other nations.

The Chancellor of Financial Affairs shall supervise the nation's financial and monetary systems, regulating its capital markets and credit-issuing institutions as they may be established by law; and this shall include lending institutions for operations in other nations or in cooperation with them, except that treaties may determine their purposes and standards.

The Chancellor of Legal Affairs shall advise governmental agencies and represent them before the courts.

The Chancellor of Military Affairs shall act for the presidency in disposing all armed forces except militia commanded by governors; but these shall be available for national service at the President's convenience.

Except in declared emergency, the deployment of forces in far waters or in other nations without their consent shall be notified in advance to a national security committee of the Senate hereinafter provided.

SECTION 4.   Responsible to the Vice-President for Internal Affairs there shall be chancellors of such departments as the President may find necessary for performing the services of government and are not rejected by a two-thirds vote when the succeeding budget is considered.

SECTION 5.   Candidates for the presidency and the vice-presidencies shall be natural-born citizens. Their suitability may be questioned by the Senate within ten days of their nomination, and if two-thirds of the whole agree, they shall be ineligible and a nominating convention shall be reconvened. At the time of his nomination no candidate shall be a member of the Senate and none shall be on active service in the armed forces or a senior civil servant.

SECTION 6.   The President may take leave because of illness or for an interval of relief, and the Vice-President in charge of General Affairs shall act. The President may resign if the Senate agree; and, if the term shall have more than two years to run, the Overseer shall arrange for a special election for President and Vice-President.

SECTION 7.   The Vice-Presidents may be directed to perform such ministerial duties as the President may find convenient; but their instructions shall be of record, and their actions shall be taken as his deputy.

SECTION 8.   Incapacitation may be established without concurrence of the President by a three-quarters vote of the Senate, whereupon a successor shall become Acting President until the disability be declared, by a similar vote, to be ended or to have become permanent. Similarly the other Vice-President shall succeed if a predecessor die or be disabled. Special elections, in these contingencies, may be required by the Senate.

Acting Presidents may appoint deputies, unless the Senate object, to assume their duties until the next election.

SECTION 9.   The Vice-Presidents, together with such other officials as the President may designate from time to time, may constitute a cabinet or council; but this shall not include officials of other branches.

SECTION 10.   Treaties or agreements with other nations, negotiated under the President's authority, shall be in effect unless objected to by a majority of the Senate within ninety days. If they are objected to, the President may resubmit and the Senate reconsider. If a majority still object, the Senate shall prevail.

SECTION 11.   All officers, except those of other branches, shall be appointed and may be removed by the President. A majority of the Senate may object to appointments within sixty days, and alternative candidates shall be offered until it agrees.

SECTION 12.   The President shall notify the Planning Board and the House of Representatives, on the fourth Tuesday in June, what the maximum allowable expenditures for the ensuing fiscal year shall be.

The President may determine to make expenditures less than provided in appropriations; but, except in declared emergency, none shall be made in excess of appropriations. Reduction shall be because of changes in requirements and shall not be such as to impair the integrity of budgetary procedures.

SECTION 13.   There shall be a Public Custodian, appointed by the President and removable by him, who shall have charge of properties belonging to the government, but not allocated to specific agencies, who shall administer common public services, shall have charge of building construction and rentals, and shall have such other duties as may be designated by the President or the designated Vice-Presidents.

SECTION 14.   There shall be an Intendant responsible to the President who shall supervise Offices for Intelligence and Investigation; also an Office of Emergency Organization with the duty of providing plans and procedures for such contingencies as can be anticipated.

The Intendant shall also charter nonprofit corporations (or foundations), unless the President shall object, determined by him to be for useful public purposes. Such corporations shall be exempt from taxation but shall conduct no profitmaking enterprises.

SECTION 15.   The Intendant shall also be a counselor for the coordination of scientific and cultural experiments, and for studies within the government and elsewhere, and for this purpose shall employ such assistance as may be found necessary.

SECTION 16.   Offices for other purposes may be established and may be discontinued by presidential order within the funds allocated in the procedures of appropriation.

ARTICLE VI

The Legislative Branch

(The Senate and the House of Representatives)

A. The Senate

SECTION 1.   There shall be a Senate with membership as follows: If they so desire, former Presidents, Vice-Presidents, Principal Justices, Overseers, Chairmen of the Planning and Regulatory Boards, Governors having had more than seven years' service, and unsuccessful candidates for the presidency and vice-presidency who have received at least 30 percent of the vote. To be appointed by the President, three persons who have been

Chancellors, two officials from the civil services, two officials from the diplomatic services, two senior military officers, also one person from a panel of three, elected in a process approved by the Overseer, by each of twelve such groups or associations as the President may recognize from time to time to be nationally representative, but none shall be a political or religious group, no individual selected shall have been paid by any private interest to influence government, and any association objected to by the Senate shall not be recognized. Similarly, to be appointed by the Principal Justice, two persons distinguished in public law and two former members of the High Courts or the Judicial Council. Also, to be elected by the House of Representatives, three members who have served six or more years.

Vacancies shall be filled as they occur.

SECTION 2.   Membership shall continue for life, except that absences not provided for by rule shall constitute retirement, and that Senators may retire voluntarily.

SECTION 3.   The Senate shall elect as presiding officer a Convener who shall serve for two years, when his further service may be discontinued by a majority vote. Other officers, including a Deputy, shall be appointed by the Convener unless the Senate shall object.

SECTION 4.   The Senate shall meet each year on the second Tuesday in July and shall be in continuous session, but may adjourn to the call of the Convener. A quorum shall be more than three-fifths of the whole membership.

SECTION 5.   The Senate shall consider, and return within thirty days, all measures approved by the House of Representatives (except the annual budget). Approval or disapproval shall be by a majority vote of those present. Objection shall stand unless the House of Representatives shall overcome it by a majority vote plus one; if no return be made, approval by the House of Representatives shall be final.

For consideration of laws passed by the House of Representatives or for other purposes, the Convener may appoint appropriate committees.

SECTION 6.   The Senate may ask advice from the Principal Justice concerning the constitutionality of measures before it; and if this be done, the time for return to the House of Representatives may extend to ninety days.

SECTION 7.   If requested, the Senate may advise the President on matters of public interest; or, if not requested, by resolution approved by two-thirds of those present. There shall be a special duty to note expressions of concern during party conventions and commitments made during campaigns; and if these be neglected, to remind the President and the House of Representatives that these undertakings are to be considered.

SECTION 8.   In time of present or prospective danger caused by cataclysm, by attack, or by insurrection, the Senate may declare a national emergency and may authorize the President to take appropriate action. If the Senate be dispersed, and no quorum available, the President may proclaim the emergency, and may terminate it unless the Senate shall have acted. If the President be not available, and the circumstances extreme, the senior serving member of the presidential succession may act until a quorum assembles.

SECTION 9.   The Senate may also define and declare a limited emergency in time of prospective danger, or of local or regional disaster, or if an extraordinary advantage be anticipated. It shall be considered by the House of Representatives within three days and, unless disapproved, may extend for a designated period and for a limited area before renewal.

Extraordinary expenditures during emergency may be approved, without regard to usual budget procedures, by the House of Representatives with the concurrence of the President.

SECTION 10.   The Senate, at the beginning of each session, shall select three of its members to constitute a National Security Committee to be consulted by the President in emergencies requiring the deployment of the armed forces abroad. If the Committee dissent from the President's proposal, it shall report to the Senate, whose decision shall be final.

SECTION 11.   The Senate shall elect, or may remove, a National Watchkeeper, and shall oversee, through a standing committee, a Watchkeeping Service conducted according to rules formulated for their approval.

With the assistance of an appropriate staff the Watchkeeper shall gather and organize information concerning the adequacy, competence, and integrity of governmental agencies and their personnel, as well as their continued usefulness; and shall also suggest the need for new or expanded services, making report concerning any agency of the deleterious effect of its activities on citizens or on the environment.

The Watchkeeper shall entertain petitions for the redress of grievances and shall advise the appropriate agencies if there be need for action.

For all these purposes, personnel may be appointed, investigations made, witnesses examined, postaudits made, and information required.

The Convener shall present the Watchkeeper's findings to the Senate, and if it be judged to be in the public interest, they shall be made public or, without being made public, be sent to the appropriate agency for its guidance and such action as may be needed. On recommendation of the Watchkeeper the Senate may initiate corrective measures to be voted on by the House of Representatives within thirty days. When approved by a majority and not vetoed by the President, they shall become law.

For the Watchkeeping Service one-quarter of one percent of individual net taxable incomes shall be held by the Chancellor of Financial Affairs; but amounts not expended in any fiscal year shall be available for general use.

B. The House of Representatives

SECTION 1. The House of Representatives shall be the original law-making body of the Newstates of America.

SECTION 2. It shall convene each year on the second Tuesday in July and shall remain in continuous session except that it may adjourn to the call of a Speaker, elected by majority vote from among the Representatives-at-large, who shall be its presiding officer.

SECTION 3. It shall be a duty to implement the provisions of this constitution and, in legislating, to be guided by them.

SECTION 4. Party leaders and their deputies shall be chosen by caucus at the beginning of each session.

SECTION 5. Standing and temporary committees shall be selected as follows:

Committees dealing with the calendaring and management of bills shall have a majority of members nominated to party caucuses by the Speaker; other members shall be nominated by minority leaders. Membership shall correspond to the parties' proportions at the last election. If nominations be not approved by a majority of the caucus, the Speaker or the minority leaders shall nominate others until a majority shall approve.

Members of other committees shall be chosen by party caucus in proportion to the results of the last election. Chairmen shall be elected annually from among at-large members.

Bills referred to committees shall be returned to the house with recommendations within sixty days unless extension be voted by the House.

In all committee actions names of those voting for and against shall be recorded.

No committee chairman may serve longer than six years.

SECTION 6. Approved legislation, not objected to by the Senate within the allotted time, shall be presented to the President for his approval or disapproval. If the President disapprove, and three-quarters of the House membership still approve, it shall become law. The names of those voting for and against shall be recorded. Bills not returned within eleven days shall become law.

SECTION 7. The President may have thirty days to consider measures approved by the House unless they shall have been submitted twelve days previous to adjournment.

SECTION 8. The House shall consider promptly the annual budget; if there be objection, it shall be notified to the Planning Board; the Board shall then resubmit through the President; and, with his comments, it shall be returned to the House. If there still be objection by a two-thirds majority, the House shall prevail. Objection must be by whole title; titles not objected to when voted on shall constitute appropriation.

The budget for the fiscal year shall be in effect on January 1. Titles not yet acted on shall be as in the former budget until action be completed.

SECTION 9.   It shall be the duty of the House to make laws concerning taxes.

1. For their laying and collection:
   a. They shall be uniform, and shall not be retroactive.
   b. Except such as may be authorized by law to be laid by Authorities, or by the Newstates, all collections shall be made by a national revenue agency. This shall include collections for trust funds hereinafter authorized.
   c. Except for corporate levies to be held in the National Sharing Fund, hereinafter authorized, taxes may be collected only from individuals and only from incomes; but there may be withholding from current incomes.
   d. To assist in the maintenance of economic stability, the President may be authorized to alter rates by executive order.
   e. They shall be imposed on profitmaking enterprises owned or conducted by religious establishments or other nonprofit organizations.
   f. There shall be none on food, medicines, residential rentals, or commodities or services designated by law as necessities; and there shall be no double taxation.
   g. None shall be levied for registering ownership or transfer of property.
2. For expenditure from revenues:
   a. For the purposes detailed in the annual budget unless objection be made by the procedure prescribed herein.
   b. For such other purposes as the House may indicate and require the Planning Branch to include in revisions of the budget; but, except in declared emergency, the total may not exceed the President's estimate of available funds.
3. For fixing the percentage of net corporate taxable incomes to be paid into a National Sharing Fund to be held in the custody of the Chancellor of Financial Affairs and made available for such welfare and environmental purposes as are authorized by law.
4. To provide for the regulation of commerce with other nations and among the Newstates, Possessions, Territories; or, as shall be mutually agreed, with other organized governments; but exports shall not be taxed; and imports shall not be taxed except on recommendation of the President at rates whose allowable variation shall have been fixed by law. There shall be no quotas, and no nations favored by special rates, unless by special acts requiring two-thirds majorities.
5. To establish, or provide for the establishment of, institutions for

the safekeeping of savings, for the gathering and distribution of capital, for the issuance of credit, for regulating the coinage of money, for controlling the media of exchange, and for stabilizing prices; but such institutions, when not public or semipublic, shall be regarded as affected with the public interest and shall be supervised by the Chancellor of Financial Affairs.

6. To establish institutions for insurance against risks and liabilities, or to provide suitable agencies for the regulation of such as are not public.

7. To ensure the maintenance, by ownership or regulation, of facilities for communication, transportation, and others commonly used and necessary for public convenience.

8. To assist in the maintenance of world order, and, for this purpose, when the President shall recommend, to vest jurisdiction in international legislative, judicial, or administrative agencies.

9. To develop with other peoples, and for the benefit of all, the resources of space, of other bodies in the universe, and of the seas beyond twelve miles from low-water shores unless treaties shall provide other limits.

10. To assist other peoples who have not attained satisfactory levels of well-being; to delegate the administration of funds for assistance, whenever possible, to international agencies; and to invest in or contribute to the furthering of development in other parts of the world.

11. To assure, or to assist in assuring, adequate and equal facilities for education; for training in occupations citizens may be fitted to pursue; and to reeducate or retrain those whose occupations may become obsolete.

12. To establish or to assist institutions devoted to higher education, to research, or to technical training.

13. To establish and maintain, or assist in maintaining, libraries, archives, monuments, and other places of historic interest.

14. To assist in the advancement of sciences and technologies; and to encourage cultural activities.

15. To conserve natural resources by purchase, by withdrawal from use, or by regulation; to provide, or to assist in providing, facilities for recreation; to establish and maintain parks, forests, wilderness areas, wetlands, and prairies; to improve streams and other waters; to ensure the purity of air and water; to control the erosion of soils; and to provide for all else necessary for the protection and common use of the national heritage.

16. To acquire property and improvements for public use at costs to be fixed, if necessary, by the Court of Claims.

17. To prevent the stoppage or hindrance of governmental procedures,

or of other activities affected with a public interest as defined by law, by reason of disputes between employers and employees, or for other reasons, and for this purpose to provide for conclusive arbitration if adequate provision for collective bargaining fail. From such findings there may be appeal to the Court of Arbitration Review; but such proceedings may not stay the acceptance of findings.

18. To support an adequate civil service for the performance of such duties as may be designated by administrators; and for this purpose to refrain from interference with the processes of appointment or placement, asking advice or testimony before committees only with the consent of appropriate superiors.

19. To provide for the maintenance of armed forces.

20. To enact such measures as will assist families in making adjustment to future conditions, using estimates concerning population and resources made by the Planning Board.

21. To vote within ninety days on such measures as the President may designate as urgent.

ARTICLE VII

The Regulatory Branch

SECTION 1.   There shall be a Regulatory Branch, and there shall be a National Regulator chosen by majority vote of the Senate and removable by a two-thirds vote of that body. His term shall be seven years, and he shall preside over a National Regulatory Board. Together they shall make and administer rules for the conduct of all economic enterprises.

The Regulatory Branch shall have such agencies as the Board may find necessary and are not disapproved by law.

SECTION 2.   The Regulatory Board shall consist of seventeen members recommended to the Senate by the Regulator. Unless rejected by majority vote they shall act with the Regulator as a lawmaking body for industry.

They shall initially have terms of one to seventeen years, one being replaced each year and serving for seventeen years. They shall be compensated and shall have no other occupation.

SECTION 3.   Under procedures approved by the Board, the Regulator shall charter all corporations or enterprises except those exempted because of size or other characteristics, or those supervised by the Chancellor of Financial Affairs, or by the Intendant, or those whose activities are confined to one Newstate.

Charters shall describe proposed activities, and departure from these shall require amendment on penalty of revocation. For this purpose there shall be investigation and enforcement services under the direction of the Regulator.

SECTION 4. Chartered enterprises in similar industries or occupations may organize joint Authorities. These may formulate among themselves codes to ensure fair competition, meet external costs, set standards for quality and service, expand trade, increase production, eliminate waste, and assist in standardization. Authorities may maintain for common use services for research and communication; but membership shall be open to all eligible enterprises. Nonmembers shall be required to maintain the same standards as those prescribed for members.

SECTION 5. Authorities shall have governing committees of five, two being appointed by the Regulator to represent the public. They shall serve as he may determine; they shall be compensated; and he shall take care that there be no conflicts of interest. The Board may approve or prescribe rules for the distribution of profits to stockholders, allowable amounts of working capital, and reserves. Costing and all other practices affecting the public interest shall be monitored.

All codes shall be subject to review by the Regulator with his Board.

SECTION 6. Member enterprises of an Authority shall be exempt from other regulation.

SECTION 7. The Regulator, with his Board, shall fix standards and procedures for mergers of enterprises or the acquisition of some by others; and these shall be in effect unless rejected by the Court of Administrative Settlements. The purpose shall be to encourage adaptation to change and to further approved intentions for the nation.

SECTION 8. The charters of enterprises may be revoked and Authorities may be dissolved by the Regulator, with the concurrence of the Board, if they restrict the production of goods and services, or controls of their prices; also if external costs are not assessed to their originators or if the ecological impacts of their operations are deleterious.

SECTION 9. Operations extending abroad shall conform to policies notified to the Regulator by the President; and he shall restrict or control such activities as appear to injure the national interest.

SECTION 10. The Regulator shall make rules for and shall supervise marketplaces for goods and services; but this shall not include security exchanges regulated by the Chancellor of Financial Affairs.

SECTION 11. Designation of enterprises affected with a public interest, rules for conduct of enterprises and of their Authorities, and other actions of the Regulator or of the Boards may be appealed to the Court of Administrative Settlements, whose judgments shall be informed by the intention to establish fairness to consumers and competitors and stability in economic affairs.

SECTION 12. Responsible also to the Regulator, there shall be an

Operations Commission appointed by the Regulator, unless the Senate object, for the supervision of enterprises owned in whole or in part by government. The commission shall choose its chairman, and he shall be the executive head of a supervisory staff. He may require reports, conduct investigations, and make rules and recommendations concerning surpluses or deficits, the absorption of external costs, standards of service, and rates or prices charged for services or goods.

Each enterprise shall have a director, chosen by and removable by the Commission; and he shall conduct its affairs in accordance with standards fixed by the Commission.

ARTICLE VIII

The Judicial Branch

SECTION 1.   There shall be a Principal Justice of the Newstates of America; a Judicial Council; and a Judicial Assembly. There shall also be a Supreme Court and a High Court of Appeals; also Courts of Claims, Rights and Duties, Administrative Review, Arbitration Settlements, Tax Appeals, and Appeals from Watchkeeper's Findings. There shall be Circuit Courts to be of first resort in suits brought under national law; and they shall hear appeals from courts of the Newstates.

Other courts may be established by law on recommendation of the Principal Justice with the Judicial Council.

SECTION 2.   The Principal Justice shall preside over the judicial system, shall appoint the members of all national courts, and, unless the Judicial Council object, shall make its rules; also, through an Administrator, supervise its operations.

SECTION 3.   The Judicial Assembly shall consist of Circuit Court Judges, together with those of the High Courts of the Newstates of America and those of the highest courts of the Newstates. It shall meet annually, or at the call of the Principal Justice, to consider the state of the Judiciary and such other matters as may be laid before it.

It shall also meet at the call of the Convener to nominate three candidates for the Principal Justiceship whenever a vacancy shall occur. From these nominees the Senate shall choose the one having the most votes.

SECTION 4.   The Principal Justice, unless the Senate object to any, shall appoint a Judicial Council of five members to serve during his incumbency. He shall designate a senior member who shall preside in his absence.

It shall be the duty of the Council, under the direction of the Principal Justice, to study the courts in operation, to prepare codes of ethics to be observed by members, and to suggest changes in procedure. The Council may ask the advice of the Judicial Assembly.

It shall also be a duty of the Council, as hereinafter provided, to suggest constitutional amendments when they appear to be necessary; and it shall also draft revisions if they shall be required. Further, it shall examine, and from time to time cause to be revised, civil and criminal codes; these, when approved by the Judicial Assembly, shall be in effect throughout the nation.

SECTION 5.   The Principal Justice shall have a term of eleven years; but if at any time the incumbent resign or be disabled from continuing in office, as may be determined by the Senate, replacement shall be by the senior member of the Judicial Council until a new selection be made. After six years the Assembly may provide, by a two-thirds vote, for discontinuance in office, and a successor shall then be chosen.

SECTION 6.   The Principal Justice may suspend members of any court for incapacity or violation of rules; and the separation shall be final if a majority of the Council agree.

For each court the Principal Justice shall, from time to time, appoint a member who shall preside.

SECTION 7.   A presiding judge may decide, with the concurrence of the senior judge, that there may be pretrial proceedings, that criminal trials shall be conducted by either investigatory or adversary proceedings, and whether there shall be a jury and what the number of jurors shall be; but investigatory proceedings shall require a bench of three.

SECTION 8.   In deciding on the concordance of statutes with the Constitution, the Supreme Court shall return to the House of Representatives such as it cannot construe. If the House fail to make return within ninety days the Court may interpret.

SECTION 9.   The Principal Justice, or the President, may grant pardons or reprieves.

SECTION 10.   The High Courts shall have thirteen members; but nine members, chosen by their senior justices from time to time, shall constitute a court. The justices on leave shall be subject to recall.

Other courts shall have nine members; but seven, chosen by their senior, shall constitute a court.

All shall be in continuous session except for recesses approved by the Principal Justice.

SECTION 11.   The Principal Justice, with the Council, may advise the Senate, when requested, concerning the appropriateness of measures approved by the House of Representatives; and may also advise the President, when requested, on matters he may refer for consultation.

SECTION 12.   It shall be for other branches to accept and to enforce judicial decrees.

SECTION 13.   The High Court of Appeals may select applications for further consideration by the Supreme Court, of decisions reached by other courts, including those of the Newstates. If it agree that there be a constitutional issue it may make preliminary judgment to be reviewed without hearing, and finally, by the Supreme Court.

SECTION 14.   The Supreme Court may decide:

a. Whether, in litigation coming to it on appeal, constitutional provisions have been violated or standards have not been met.

b. On the application of constitutional provisions to suits involving the Newstates.

c. Whether international law, as recognized in treaties, United Nations agreements, or arrangements with other nations, has been ignored or violated.

d. Other causes involving the interpretation of constitutional provisions; except that in holding any branch to have exceeded its powers the decision shall be suspended until the Judicial Council shall have determined whether, in order to avoid confrontation, procedures·for amendment of the Constitution are appropriate.

If amendatory proceedings are instituted, decision shall await the outcome.

SECTION 15.   The Courts of the Newstates shall have initial jurisdiction in cases arising under their laws except those involving the Newstate itself or those reserved for national courts by a rule of the Principal Justice with the Judicial Council.

ARTICLE IX

General Provisions

SECTION 1.   Qualifications for participation in democratic procedures as a citizen, and eligibility for office, shall be subject to repeated study and redefinition; but any change in qualification or eligibility shall become effective only if not disapproved by the Congress.

For this purpose a permanent Citizenship and Qualifications Commission shall be constituted, four members to be appointed by the President, three by the Convener of the Senate, three by the Speaker of the House, and three by the Principal Justice. Vacancies shall be filled as they occur. The members shall choose a chairman; they shall have suitable assistants and accommodations; and they may have other occupations. Recommendations of the commission shall be presented to the President and shall be transmitted to the House of Representatives with comments. They shall have a preferred place on the calendar and, if approved, shall be in effect.

SECTION 2.   Areas necessary for the uses of government may be acquired at its valuation and may be maintained as the public interest may require. Such areas shall have self-government in matters of local concern.

SECTION 3.   The President may negotiate for the acquisition of areas outside the Newstates of America, and, if the Senate approve, may provide for their organization as Possessions or Territories.

SECTION 4.   The President may make agreements with other organized peoples for a relation other than full membership in the Newstates of America. They may become citizens and may participate in the selection of officials. They may receive assistance for their development or from the National Sharing Fund if they conform to its requirements; and they may serve in civilian or military services, but only as volunteers. They shall be represented in the House of Representatives by members elected at large, their number proportional to their constituencies; but each shall have at least one; and each shall in the same way choose one permanent member of the Senate.

SECTION 5.   The President, the Vice-Presidents, and members of the legislative houses shall in all cases except treason, felony, and breach of the peace be exempt from penalty for anything they may say while pursuing public duties; but the Judicial Council may make restraining rules.

SECTION 6.   Except as otherwise provided by this Constitution, each legislative house shall establish its requirements for membership and may make rules for the conduct of members, including conflicts of interest, providing its own disciplines for their infraction.

SECTION 7.   No Newstate shall interfere with officials of the Newstates of America in the performance of their duties, and all shall give full faith and credit to the Acts of other Newstates and of the Newstates of America.

SECTION 8.   Public funds shall be expended only as authorized in this Constitution.

ARTICLE X

Governmental Arrangements

SECTION 1.   Officers of the Newstates of America shall be those named in this Constitution, including those of the legislative houses and others authorized by law to be appointed; they shall be compensated, and none may have other paid occupation unless they be excepted by law; none shall occupy more than one position in government; and no gift or favor shall be accepted if in any way related to official duty.

No income from former employments or associations shall continue for their benefits; but their properties may be put in trust and managed without their intervention during continuance in office. Hardships under this rule may be considered by the Court of Rights and Duties, and exceptions may be made with due regard to the general intention.

SECTION 2.   The President, the Vice-Presidents, and the Principal Justice shall have households appropriate to their duties. The President, the Vice-Presidents, the Principal Justice, the Chairman of the Planning Board, the Regulator, the Watchkeeper, and the Overseer shall have salaries fixed by law and continued for life; but if they become members of the Senate, they shall have senatorial compensation and shall conform to senatorial requirements.

Justices of the High Courts shall have no term; and their salaries shall be two-thirds that of the Principal Justice; they, and members of the Judicial Council, unless they shall have become Senators, shall be permanent members of the Judiciary and shall be available for assignment by the Principal Justice.

Salaries for members of the Senate shall be the same as for Justices of the High Court of Appeals.

SECTION 3.   Unless otherwise provided herein, officials designated by the head of a branch as sharers in policymaking may be appointed by him with the President's concurrence and unless the Senate shall object.

SECTION 4.   There shall be administrators:

a. for executive offices and official households, appointed by authority of the President;

b. for the national courts, appointed by the Principal Justice;

c. for the Legislative Branch, selected by a committee of members from each house (chosen by the Convener and the Speaker), three from the House of Representatives and four from the Senate.

Appropriations shall be made to them; but those for the Presidency shall not be reduced during his term unless with his consent; and those for the Judicial Branch shall not be reduced during five years succeeding their determination, unless with the consent of the Principal Justice.

SECTION 5.   The fiscal year shall be the same as the calendar year, with new appropriations available at its beginning.

SECTION 6.   There shall be an Officials' Protective Service to guard the President, the Vice-Presidents, the Principal Justice, and other officials whose safety may be at hazard; and there shall be a Protector appointed by and responsible to a standing committee of the Senate. Protected officials shall be guided by procedures approved by the committee.

The service, at the request of the Political Overseer, may extend its protection to candidates for office; or to other officials, if the committee so decide.

SECTION 7.   A suitable contingency fund shall be made available to the President for purposes defined by law.

SECTION 8.   The Senate shall try officers of government other than legislators when such officers are impeached by a two-thirds vote of the House of Representatives for conduct prejudicial to the public interest. If Presidents or Vice-Presidents are to be tried, the Senate, as constituted, shall conduct the trial. Judgments shall not extend beyond removal from office and disqualification for holding further office; but the convicted official shall be liable to further prosecution.

SECTION 9.   Members of legislative houses may be impeached by the Judicial Council; but for trials it shall be enlarged to seventeen by Justices of the High Courts appointed by the Principal Justice. If convicted, members shall be expelled and be ineligible for future public office; and they shall also be liable for trial as citizens.

ARTICLE XI

Amendment

SECTION 1.   It being the special duty of the Judicial Council to formulate and suggest amendments to this Constitution, it shall, from time to time, make proposals, through the Principal Justice, to the Senate. The Senate, if it approve, and if the President agree, shall instruct the Overseer to arrange at the next national election for submission of the amendment to the electorate. If not disapproved by a majority, it shall become part of this Constitution. If rejected, it may be restudied and a new proposal submitted.

It shall be the purpose of the amending procedure to correct deficiencies in the Constitution, to extend it when new responsibilities require, and to make government responsible to needs of the people, making use of advances in managerial competence and establishing security and stability; also to preclude changes in the Constitution resulting from interpretation.

SECTION 2.   When this Constitution shall have been in effect for twenty-five years the Overseer shall ask, by referendum, whether a new Constitution shall be prepared. If a majority so decide, the Council, making use of such advice as may be available, and consulting those who have made complaint, shall prepare a new draft for submission at the next election. If not disapproved by a majority it shall be in effect. If disapproved it shall be redrafted and resubmitted with such changes as may be then appropriate to the circumstances, and it shall be submitted to the voters at the following election.

If not disapproved by a majority it shall be in effect. If disapproved it shall be restudied and resubmitted.

Article XII

Transition

Section 1.   The President is authorized to assume such powers, make such appointments, and use such funds as are necessary to make this Constitution effective as soon as possible after acceptance by a referendum he may initiate.

Section 2.   Such members of the Senate as may be at once available shall convene and, if at least half, shall constitute sufficient membership while others are being added. They shall appoint an Overseer to arrange for electoral organization and elections for the offices of government; but the President and Vice-Presidents shall serve out their terms and then become members of the Senate. At that time the presidency shall be constituted as provided in this Constitution.

Section 3.   Until each indicated change in the government shall have been completed the provisions of the existing Constitution and the organs of government shall be in effect.

Section 4.   All operations of the national government shall cease as they are replaced by those authorized under this Constitution.

The President shall determine when replacement is complete.

The President shall cause to be constituted an appropriate commission to designate existing laws inconsistent with this Constitution, and they shall be void; also the commission shall assist the President and the legislative houses in the formulating of such laws as may be consistent with the Constitution and necessary to its implementation.

Section 5.   For establishing Newstates' boundaries a commission of thirteen, appointed by the President, shall make recommendations within one year. For this purpose the members may take advice and commission studies concerning resources, population, transportation, communication, economic and social arrangements, and such other conditions as may be significant. The President shall transmit the commission's report to the Senate. After entertaining, if convenient, petitions for revision, the Senate shall report whether the recommendations are satisfactory but the President shall decide whether they shall be accepted or shall be returned for revision.

Existing states shall not be divided unless metropolitan areas extending over more than one state are to be included in one Newstate, or unless other compelling circumstances exist; and each Newstate shall possess harmonious regional characteristics.

The Commission shall continue while the Newstates make adjustments among themselves and shall have jurisdiction in disputes arising among them.

SECTION 6.   Constitutions of the Newstates shall be established as arranged by the Judicial Council and the Principal Justice.

These procedures shall be as follows: Constitutions shall be drafted by the highest courts of the Newstates. There shall then be a convention of one hundred delegates chosen in special elections in a procedure approved by the Overseer. If the Constitution be not rejected it shall be in effect and the government shall be constituted. If it be rejected, the Principal Justice, advised by the Judicial Council, shall promulgate a Constitution and initiate revisions to be submitted for approval at a time he shall appoint. If it again be rejected he shall promulgate another, taking account of objections, and it shall be in effect. A Constitution, once in effect, shall be valid for twenty-five years as herein provided.

SECTION 7.   Until Governors and legislatures of the Newstates are seated, their governments shall continue, except that the President may appoint temporary Governors to act as executives until succeeded by those regularly elected. These Governors shall succeed to the executive functions of the states as they become one of the Newstates of America.

SECTION 8.   The indicated appointments, elections, and other arrangements shall be made with all deliberate speed.

SECTION 9.   The first Judicial Assembly for selecting a register of candidates for the Principal Justiceship of the Newstates of America shall be called by the incumbent Chief Justice immediately upon ratification.

SECTION 10.   Newstates electing by referendum not to comply with recommendations of the Boundary Commission, as approved by the Senate, shall have deducted from taxes collected by the Newstates of America for transmission to them a percentage equal to the loss in efficiency from failure to comply.

Estimates shall be made by the Chancellor of Financial Affairs and approved by the President; but the deduction shall not be less than 7 percent.

SECTION 11.   When this Constitution has been implemented the President may delete by proclamation appropriate parts of this article.

INDEX

INDEX

74 75 76 77 10 9 8 7 6 5 4 3 2 1